THE COMPLETE BOOK OF

GOLF

THE NEW YORK TIMES SCRAPBOOK
ENCYCLOPEDIA OF SPORTS HISTORY

FOOTBALL
BASEBALL
BASKETBALL
TRACK AND FIELD
GOLF
TENNIS
BOXING
SOCCER/PROFESSIONAL HOCKEY
WINTER SPORTS
OUTDOOR SPORTS
INDOOR SPORTS
WATER SPORTS
HORSE RACING/AUTO RACING

THE COMPLETE BOOK OF
GOLF

EDITED BY
GENE BROWN

INTRODUCTION BY
FRANK LITSKY

ARNO PRESS
A NEW YORK TIMES COMPANY
NEW YORK/1980

THE BOBBS-MERRILL COMPANY, INC.
INDIANAPOLIS · NEW YORK

Library of Congress Cataloging in Publication Data

Main entry under title:

The Complete book of golf.

    (The New York times scrapbook encyclopedia of sports history.)

    Issued also under the title: Golf.
    Collection of articles reprinted from the New York times.

    Bibliography: p.

    Includes index.

    SUMMARY: Traces the history of golf as presented in articles in
the "New York Times."
    1. Golf. 2. Golf—History. [1. Golf] I. Brown, Gene. II. New
York Times. III. Series.

GV936.G6 1979   796.352   79-92319
ISBN 0-405-12689-1 (Arno)
ISBN 0-672-52636-0 (Bobbs Merrill)

Manufactured in the United States of America

Appendix © 1979, *The Encyclopedia Americana.*

The editors express special thanks to The Associated Press, United
Press International, and Reuters for permission to include a number of
dispatches originally distributed by those news services.

Project Editors: Arleen Keylin and Christine Bent
Editorial Assistant: Jonathan Cohen

Photographs courtesy UPI on pages: X, 3, 12, 20, 62, 66, 69,
102, 112, 123, 128, 141, 159, 186, front and back cover.

CONTENTS

INTRODUCTION

No sport appears easier to understand or easier to play than golf. A small ball is struck by a club until the ball goes into a hole. The winner is the player who requires the fewest shots to put his ball into a series of holes over a course.

That is an oversimplification because golf is incredibly complex. It is a frustrating, humbling game that challenges players on every level.

It is played on a nine-hole or 18-hole course that incorporates the natural terrain, such as hills, ravines, streams, trees, bushes, other heavy growth and natural hazards. There are also man-made hazards, notably sand traps that guard the long area leading to the cut (the fairway) and the smoothly trimmed area surrounding the cup (the putting green).

The first shot on a hole is hit from an area known as the tee. A typical hole measures 100 to 500 yards from tee to green. Each hole has a par, the number of strokes a good golfer should need to complete the hole without error. Par generally runs from three strokes for a short hole to four and five for longer ones. A typical 18-hole championship course encompassing 6,000 to 7,200 yards in hole length, will have a total par of 72.

For most of its existence, golf has been a plaything of rich amateurs. Professional tournaments became significant in the 1920's. Most golf today is played by amateurs at local clubs, but the best-known golfers, male and female, are the few hundred who play on the professional tours for ever-increasing prize money.

Golf probably began in the 15th century, despite vague references to it at least three centuries earlier. It was played in Scotland in the 1440's and 1450's, but it took so much time from the practice of archery (the bow and arrow were the chief weapons of warfare then) that it was banned in 1457 and again in 1491.

Nevertheless, King James IV played the game avidly in 1503. His granddaughter, Mary, was a golfer, and about 1552, during her reign as Mary, Queen of Scots,

the St. Andrews course in Scotland was founded. It is now the most famous course in the world. The first golf club, Royal Blackheath, was formed in 1608.

For more than two centuries, the game was played socially in Scotland and England. The first tournament was played in 1860 in Prestwick, Scotland, and was held annually. In 1865, it was declared "open to anyone," which meant players from any club or any nation could play. It thus became known as the British Open championship. In modern times, the designation of "open" means that a tournament is open to professionals and amateurs alike. In the early years, there were no professionals.

Golf came to North America via ship officers from Scotland or England. In the 1850's or 1860's, they built one three-hole course in Montreal and another in Quebec. In 1873, the Royal Montreal Golf Club was founded, the first club in North America known to have provided facilities for golf.

Literature from the 1790's shows that "golf clubs" and "golf greens" existed in the United States, but there was no record of golf being played. These clubs apparently were strictly social.

People in White Sulphur Springs, a resort area in West Virginia, contend that golf was played there in 1882. However, most historians agree that the game was brought to the United States in 1885 by Joseph Fox of Philadelphia. Fox had seen golf in Scotland in 1884, and he introduced it to friends at his summer home in Foxburg, Pa. In 1887, the Foxburg Golf Club was founded, the first of its kind in the United States.

John G. Reid, a Scotsman who lived in Yonkers, N.Y., had a friend bring golf balls and clubs from Scotland. In 1888, Reid led friends to a cow pasture and showed them the game. Because space was insufficient, he took over 30 acres and laid out a six-hole course, also in a pasture. Later that year, he formed the St. Andrew's Golf Club of Yonkers, named for the mother club in Scotland but adding an apostrophe to the spelling.

Yonkers is a suburb of New York City, and golf quickly spread to other suburbs in New York State, New Jersey and Connecticut. It was also introduced to Middlesborough, Ky. All of these sites built nine-hole courses. The first 18-hole course in the United States was built in 1893 in Wheaton, Ill. Championship courses now are always 18 holes.

In 1894, St. Andrew's decided to stage a tournament "open" to the world," and it became known as the United States Open Championship. It was held at match play, and Willie Dunn won.

Tournaments then were generally conducted at match play, in which the winner was the player who won (by shooting a lower score) the most holes. It was a direct-elimination competition, and favorites often were eliminated in early rounds.

Match play is seldom used now in important competition, though it is popular in friendly play and in tournaments among members of one club. Major tournaments now favor medal play, in which the winner is the golfer who shoots the lowest score for a given number of holes (often 72 holes over four days).

Golf leaders realized in 1894 that they needed an organization to adopt rules of play and run the sport. Five clubs—two in New York and one each in Massachusetts, Rhode Island and Illinois—formed the organization that became the United States Golf Association. It still is the governing body of American golf.

The new organization quickly established championship tournaments. In 1895, it staged the first United States Amateur Championship, a United States Open the next day and a United States Women's Championship later in the year.

The golf balls and clubs of that era, though not primitive, were hardly as sophisticated as the equipment of the late 20th century.

The first golf balls were made of feathers stuffed tightly into thin leather bags, which were then sewed closed. A major improvement came in 1848 with the introduction of gutta percha (or "gutty") ball. This ball was made from the juice of trees in the Malay Peninsula, with a hardening process similar to that used to make crude rubber. A good player could drive a ball made of feathers 175 yards, a gutta percha ball 225 yards.

In 1899, the rubber ball now in use was invented in the United States. It is small and hard, with a dimpled skin covering tightly wrapped rubber and often a liquid core. The American ball has a maximum weight of 1.62 ounces and a minimum diameter of 1.68 inches. The British ball has the same weight but is slightly smaller, with a maximum diameter of 1.62 inches.

Early golf clubs were crafted by hand. They had shafts of ash or hickory and heads (striking areas) of wood or iron. The heads are still made of wood and iron, but steel shafts were introduced in 1929.

Modern clubs are made by machine, and they can be purchased in sets in which one club varies from the others only in the degree of loft on the head. The more angled the loft, the higher the ball will be hit, and a higher flight means less distance.

That means that the golfer should almost always have available a club that meets his immediate need. Accordingly, he can choose among four or five woods (wooden-headed clubs used for hitting long distances), nine or ten irons (iron-headed clubs used for hitting shorter distances) and a putter, a club with a flat metal blade used on putting greeens.

The clubs are carried in a cylindrical golf bag. Players are allowed to carry only 14 clubs, although the average club amateur gets by very well with only seven or eight.

Until 1913, golf in the United States interested only the rich people who belonged to clubs. They were amateurs, and the relatively few professionals in America taught golf at these clubs.

One tournament reversed all that. The 1913 United States Open Championship was played in Brookline, Mass., at a club that grandly called itself The Country Club.

The tournament favorites were Harry Vardon and Ted Ray, English professionals in the United States just for this tournament. Perhaps the most obscure player was Francis Ouimet, a 20-year-old amateur and the son of a gardener. Ouimet lived across the street from the club, and he had caddied there for 10 cents an hour plus tips.

Incredibly, after the 72 holes of the tournament, Vardon, Ray and Ouimet were tied for first place at 304. In a 18-hole playoff the next day, Ouimet shot 72, Vardon 77 and Ray 78.

Francis Ouimet (wee-met) had become the first amateur to win the United States Open Championship. *The New York Times* ran the story atop page 1. The American public had been awakened to golf, and the popularity of the game soared.

Foreign professionals, mostly British, emigrated to the United States, and American amateurs turned professional to teach. In 1916, the Professional Golfers' Association of America (PGA) was formed, and it held its first tournament that year.

In that era, the professional golfer was a teacher, a working man who used the servants' entrance to the club but never the dining room or the bar. Only the best earned as much as $50 a week.

The man who changed that was Walter Hagen, a flamboyant American professional who drank, partied and tipped like a potentate. He thought nothing of throwing his arm around the Prince of Wales while telling him a story. His social and professional lives were so intertwined he once showed up at the first tee in evening dress from the previous night.

It helped that he was a great golfer. He won more than 75 tournaments, including five PGA championships, four British Opens and two United States Opens. So when Hagen walked into a club dining room or bar, he was accepted, and in time so were his fellow pros. At a 1967 testimonial dinner, Arnold Palmer, the hero of a later generation, told Hagen, "If it were not for you, this dinner would be downstairs in the pro shop and not in the ballroom.''

Hagen's major rival in the 1920's, an era of great heroes in many sports, was Bobby Jones, an amateur from Atlanta. From 1923 to 1930, Jones won five United States Amateurs, four United States Opens, three British Opens and one British Amateur. In 1930, he became the only man in history to win those four tournaments in one year, a feat that became known as the ''Grand Slam.''

Jones, though only 28 years old, immediately retired from tournament golf, a victim of the pressure and intensity of the ambition.

''Sometimes I'd pass my mother and dad on the course, look at them and not even see them because I was so concentrated on the game,'' he said. ''Afterward, it made a fellow feel a little silly.''

Jones was the last amateur golfer to captivate the public. He was later a founder of the Augusta National Golf Club in Georgia and its celebrated tournament, the Masters. The modern Grand Slam, never yet achieved in one year, embraces the Masters, United States Open, British Open and PGA championship.

The best-known players in later years have included Byron Nelson, Ben Hogan, Sam Snead, Arnold Palmer and Jack Nicklaus. They have been stars of the PGA Tour, a series of weekly tournaments that now runs almost year round.

Nelson's most successful year was 1945, when he won 19 of the 31 tournaments, including 11 consecutive over five months. Hogan, a small, intense man, almost died in a 1949 highway automobile accident, but he played in a tournament 11 months later and won the United States Open four months after that. Snead, Hogan's contemporary, won every major title except the United States Open.

Public acceptance of tournament golf increased dramatically in the 1960's because of Palmer and his flair for the storybook finish. In the 1960 United States Open at Denver, trailing by seven strokes entering the final 18 holes, he shot a 65 and won. On the last two holes, where Hogan, winner of four United States Opens, took 6 and 7, Palmer shot 4 and 4. The public loved Palmer's attacking style, and the huge crowds that followed his every round became known as Arnie's Army.

In all, Palmer won 61 major tournaments in the United States and many more overseas. He won the Masters four times, the British Open twice and the United States Open once.

When Palmer won the 1960 United States Open, the runner-up was a 20-year-old amateur named Jack Nicklaus. In time, Nicklaus succeeded Palmer as the most successful tournament player, though for many years he enjoyed little public popularity. The reason, wrote Red Smith, was that Nicklaus ''was an upstart and an interloper, the crasher who had dared to expose Arnold Palmer as merely human.''

Nicklaus has been remarkably consistent. In his first 17 years (1962 to 1978) as a professional, he was first in tour earnings eight times, second five times, third twice and fourth twice. In that span, he set the record of 17 victories in so-called major tournaments—five Masters, four PGA, three United States Opens, three British Opens and two United States Amateurs. In the late 1970's, he cut down on the number of tournaments to spend more time with his family and many businesses.

In 1935, the tour's 34 tournaments offered $135,000 in prize money, with the highest total purse $9,500. In 1979, those figures were 45 tournaments, $12.6 million in purses and a purse of $440,000 for the Tournament Players Championship. In 1958, Palmer was the tour's leading money-winner with $42,607. In 1978, Tom Watson led with $362,429.

The women's tournament circuit had its beginnings after World War II with the formation of the Women's PGA. In 1950, 12 women professionals formed the Ladies Professional Golf Association, the organization that still conducts the women's tour.

One of the 12 founders was Babe Didrikson Zaharias, probably the best woman athlete and the best woman golfer ever. In her first round of golf, never having taken a lesson, she shot 95 for 18 holes. After three lessons, she shot 83. She won 17 amateur tournaments in a row, and she won 55 amateur and professional tournaments in 15 years.

Though purses for women's tournaments have always been far less than those for men, the gap closed in the late 1970's. Total purse money grew from $140,000 in 1956 to $1,471,000 in 1973 to $4.4 million for 38 tournaments in 1979.

Mickey Wright of San Diego, Calif., holds the all-time record of 82 tournament victories, mostly in the 1960's. Kathy Whitworth was the leading money winner in eight years between 1965 and 1973. Nancy Lopez, a 21-year-old rookie, won nine of the 38 tournaments in 1978, and in her first 12 months on tour (July 1977 to July 1978) she won $189,813, more than any other golf rookie, male or female.

—Frank Litsky

CHAPTER 1

THE GOLDEN AGE OF GOLF

What Babe Ruth was to baseball, Bobby Jones
was to golf. Jones dominated the sport in the
1920's and his "grand slam" in 1930 was one of
the game's great landmarks.

GOLFERS GETTING READY

Links Improved and Members Practising for Tournaments.

PARK, A SCOTCH CHAMPION, HERE.

Will Play a Match with Dunn on the St. Andrew's Links Tournament to Be Played at Yonkers.

The golfing season is rapidly approaching and within the next month the game will be fairly under way in a score or more of enterprising clubs. Although a little early in the season, the links of many of the leading clubs have been put in first-class condition, and the more energetic devotees of the game have been busily engaged in getting back in their old-time playing trim again.

Among those who pursue golf, not so much for the social features which have been mingled with it, but from the standpoint of genuine science and solid playing, the game may be raised to a higher tone and dignity this season than it has ever before enjoyed in America. This is due to the successful organization of the United States Golf Association, which includes in its membership most of the prominent clubs in the country. This association will exercise a general supervision over the game throughout the country, its laws being accepted as the authority on the game in America, and it will take general charge of the championship matches. Thus the game is brought within the limts of definite organization, and as the leading clubs are represented on its Governing Board, all will have an interest in its success and in upholding its regulations. Theodore A. Havemeyer, who is an enthusiast on golfing and a member of the Newport Golf Club, is President of the association. Samuel J. Parrish and C. B. Macdonald of Chicago are Vice Presidents, and H. O. Talmage is Secretary.

April 28, 1895

SOME FAMOUS GOLFERS

Men Who Have Made Their Mark in Playing the Historical Game.

REMARKABLE JUMP TO POPULARITY

No Sport Has Advanced So Rapidly in This Country—Played for 400 Years in Great Britain.

In the history of American field sports there can be found no outdoor pastime that developed and attained such popularity in a comparatively short period of time as the game of golf. That it has all the requisites that go to the make-up of a general amusement there is no doubt. The members of both sexes—young, old, and middle-aged—can take part in it without being in constant dread of and of the mishaps that characterise the other sterner sports of the present day.

The history of golf shows that the game has been played for at least 400 years, but even if any records survived of doughty champions of the Middle Ages—and, so far as we know, they do not—their performances would probably be regarded with less interest than those of latter-day players in America and England, who are known either personally or by reputation to the present generation.

In looking back sixty years or so, the foremost figure that strikes the eye is undoubtedly the celebrated Allan Robertson. While Allan was a most formidable player, he does not seem to incur any danger of having his merits underestimated; rather, indeed, the contrary; and he is sometimes spoken of as having never been beaten. His style of play was an easy and graceful one; he played with long and light clubs, of each and every one of which he was a complete master. Time after time he could be trusted to land a full play-club or spoon shot as close to the hole as he would have done had he pitched it with an iron thirty or forty yards. His most brilliant performance was on Sept. 15, 1858, on the St. Andrew links (England) in a match with a Mr. Bethune, when he holed the links in 79, a performance that has not since been equaled nor is it likely to be for generations to come. In 1859 Allan developed an attack of jaundice, from which he never recovered, and in September of that year he breathed his last.

With Robertson were the brothers Pirie, Tom Geddes, and James Dunn, all residing in the neighborhood of the St. Andrew links. Tom Morris was the only one who could at all approach Allan. Every fine day, even now, he hobbles out to the St. Andrew links. Less than a month ago the regular patrons of St. Andrew's presented the octogenarian with a purse of $2,500.

As baseball and horseracing run in families, so does golf, in perhaps a greater degree; and to mention the name of Park is to call up a host of brilliant reminiscences, records of championships won by one or other of the representatives of that name, and generally such deeds of derring-do as every golfer would fain aspire to. The first of the family who made himself famous was Willie Park, senior, who has altogether given up play. He began to make fame for himself about 1853, and so strong a player had he then become, that money in abundance was forthcoming to back him against Allan Robertson, but the latter could not be induced to play a match. However, though he declined, a foeman worthy of Park's steel was found in Tom Morris, who took up the gauntlet, nothing loath. But the backers of Morris knew very well what they were about, and the result of the first match, and, indeed, of the second also, each of them over four greens for $500 a side, was the infliction of a thorough and decisive drubbing by Morris.

But unbroken success at golf is seldom or never attained, and Park, nothing daunted by his previous unpleasant experiences of the Tartar, Morris, with commendable assurance, issued a challenge in his turn, this time completely turning the tables on his rival and emerging a triumphant victor. In 1860 the first competition for the championship belt was begun. Thirty-six holes over Prestwick were played, and the issue decided by strokes. Parks was successful, and carried off first honors with a score of 174. On two subsequent occasions he repeated his triumph, in 1863 and 1866, with scores of 168 and 169, respectively, and was again successful in 1875, with a score of 166. His last appearance was at the championships of 1886, when, though a mere shadow of his former self, he managed to play one very good round out of the four. His style was most graceful; his swing was easy, with a pause at the end of it, and the balls traveled well; and, his putting was most excellent.

David Park, brother of Willie, was a very fine player, but though he several times ran well up in competitions, he could never achieve championship honors.

A third brother, Mungo Park, was successful in winning the championship in 1874, with a score of 159.

The abundant honors reaped by the family are in no immediate danger of being forgotten; on the contrary, there appears to be every prospect of a considerable accretion to the pile, for the exploits of Willie Park, Sr., are likely to be reproduced, if not excelled, by his son, who is already entitled to write "ex-champion" after his name. Born in 1864, and brought up in all the traditions of the game, he early evinced an aptitude for it which gave promise of great things to come in the future. At the age of sixteen he was engaged as greenkeeper by the Ryton Golf Club, where he staid four years, at the end of which time he started in business as a club and ball maker. His first public performance of note was a success at Alnmouth, at the age of seven-

teen, when he carried off first honors in a field representative of the best modern talent.

In 1886 he was again to the front at Troon. Here all the leading talent of the day was assembled, and young Willie, one of the last to come in, produced an admirable card of 148. In 1887 he entered for the open championship and won it in 161. Of all modern players Park is the most imperturbable. He appears encased in a triple armor of philosophical composure.

His style of play is deliberate in the extreme. He drives a beautiful long carry; his iron play is powerful and accurate, and his putting good; nor is he apparently converted to the modern style of putting entirely without a cleek. There is one shot, however, which has always caused him considerable trouble, and that is to make a ball loft and lie off an iron. So to weather his rock he has set his wits to work and evolved an implement which appears to give him every satisfaction. Without being either a lofting iron or mashie, it partakes of the characteristics of both; its shape brings the upper part of the blade, which is very concave, nearer to the ball, and so, while less turf is taken, a very considerable back spin is put on the ball, which is sent very high in the air, and falls almost without any roll.

Others of less note, but great men, are Willie Campbell, Tom Morris, Jr., and Willie Fernie. Two other names that deserve especial mention are Sir Robert Hay and Mr. George Glennie. Mr. Glennie began the game while young, and very soon made his mark. In a competition among students they decided to handicap him by allowing him only one club to play with, and he was to have no voice in its selection. A very battered and disreputable-looking middle spoon, which had seen better days, was given him, but this unpromising implement proved effective in his hands, and he was too good for his field.

One day his partner was a very eminent golfer, and, as luck would have it, Mr. Glennie put the ball into the Swilcan Burn, and when the party arrived the sphere was found to be a "floater," and was gayly pursuing its career seaward on the "drumlie" current. The artist remarked that he thought he could manage to play it, so he went into the burn at a spot where he could intercept the ball, and, so to speak, take it on the wing.

The daring idea was crowned with success. Splash went the niblick, away went the ball, and finished dead at the hole, which was by this stroke placed to his credit.

The most notable feature in the American golf world is the growth of golf clubs, each one of which has brought out a number of new players. Prominent among these are Charles B. MacDonald of Chicago, L. B. Stoddart, W. H. Sands, A. L. Livermore, James Park, George E. Armstrong of the St. Andrew's, Dr. Charles Claxton of Philadelphia, Dr. E. C. Rushmore, E. C. Kent, and Alfred Setton, Jr., of Tuxedo, William Shippen, Henry P. Phipps, and James A. Tyng of Morristown. These, with many others, have given evidence of much improvement, and their work of the last season ranks them as players not very easy to defeat.

In summing the season's work in brief, the highest honor belongs to George S. MacDonald of Chicago, who is now the amateur champion of America. In the championship contest held under the auspices of the United States Golf Association on the links of the Newport Golf Club in October he won the thousand-dollar cup presented by Theodore Havemeyer, President of the association. Second honors in that tournament went to Charles E. Sands of the St. Andrew's Club, a player of this year's standing. Dr. Charles Claxton brought the golfing qualities of the Philadelphia Country Club prominently to the front by winning third place. The fourth title fell to J. Armory of the Brookline Country Club of Boston.

December 27, 1895

BRITISH GOLF CHAMPIONSHIP.

Harry Vardon Wins the Honor in Scotland the Second Time.

The recent victory by Harry Vardon of the open championship of Great Britain is the second he has had for that honor. Willie Park, who led up to the final round, is probably better known in this country than any of the other prominent foreign professionals. He was Great Britain's open golf champion for 1887 and 1889. He has made two visits to this country, the first time being about three years ago, when he played over most of our links. A series of three contests for $600 was arranged between him and Willie Dunn, the games being played at Shinnecock, Morristown, and St. Andrew's, and Park won. His brother, Mungo Park, is the professional at the Dyker Meadow Golf Club, Brooklyn, and

Harry Vardon was, according to some experts, the greatest golfer of all time. He was a record six-time British Open champion and in the U.S. Open he won in 1900, tied for first but lost in a playoff in 1913, and at the age of 50, tied for second in 1920.

has just gone to Boston to play in the open championship of America next week at the Myopia Hunt Club.

Champion Vardon is one of the two foreign professionals, the second being James Braid, whom the St. Andrew's Golf Club desired to bring over to America in the Fall. The idea failed to arouse the expected enthusiasm for professional golf, and the scheme had to be dropped. Now that Vardon has won the championship of Scotland and England, it is possible that the St. Andrew's and other golf clubs may take up the idea with more success.

June 10, 1898

AMATEUR GOLFERS DEFINED

Several Important Changes Made by the New Regulations.

Golfers in general heartily commend the new rules defining the status of an amateur golfer which went into operation last week by act of the Executive Committee of the United States Golf Association. The rules are practically amendments of the amateur regulations which went into effect Jan. 1, 1897. Although made at that time as strict as it was thought necessary to preserve the highest amateur standing of the game, two or three weaknesses have appeared from time to time, and other features have arisen which it seemed advisable to embody in the rules.

Among these was the gradually growing practice of assumed names, and the clear understanding that a professional in golf is not only one who has used golf for financial gain in any way, but who is considered a professional in any other sport. The new rules have been compiled with the aid of advice from several able lawyers who are well-known as golfers, and they draw the amateur line as clearly and strictly as it is, probably, possible to be done. They are in full:

Section 9. No person shall be considered an amateur golfer who has played for a money prize in a match or in an open competition, or who has received money for giving lessons or exhibitions of his skill in the game of golf; or laid out or taken charge of golf links for hire; or who has ever carried clubs for hire after attaining the age of fifteen years; or who has ever personally made for sale golf clubs, balls, or any other articles connected with the game of golf, or who, after the adoption of this section as amended, shall be classed as a professional in any athletic sport.

Section 10. No person shall be eligible to compete for the amateur championship of this association who does not conform to the conditions of Section 9, or who after Jan. 1, 1897, has received compensation for services performed in any athletic organization, or who plays the game or frequents golf courses, for the purpose of exploiting his business; nor shall any one be eligible to compete who hereafter shall enter any golfing competition under an assumed name. Any person having become ineligible by a violation of any of the provisions of this section may be duly reinstated upon his giving satisfactory evidence of meriting it. Only members of clubs belonging to this association, and those entitled under the rules of an associate or allied club to the use of the links, in whole or in part, for a period not less than the entire current season, may compete for the amateur and women's championships. Competitors must enter for the championships through the secretaries of their respective clubs, who, in sending in their names, shall be held to certify that the players are qualified amateur golfers in accordance with the terms of Sections 9 and 10.

Any case not covered by the foregoing sections will be decided by the Executive Committee on its individual merits.

SEVERAL IMPORTANT CHANGES.

An important change in Section 10 clearly defines just what business shall be considered subject to golf professionalism. That is, any one shall be classed as a professional who "plays the game or frequents golf courses for the purpose of exploiting his business." Under the old rule it was somewhat ambiguous as to whether a manager or member of a firm whose goods were used in golf in any capacity should be classed as a professional. Under the former rule, this question arose several times, but it seemed an injustice to place a man in the professional class whose goods were used in golf. But, on the other hand, a salesman of such a business who visits golf clubs for the purpose of securing orders from members, or introducing his wares, has, ever since 1897, been considered as a professional, and his status remains unchanged by the amendments.

It has further been pointed out that the rule might be so stretched as to include writers on golf subjects. Could it be claimed that they "frequent the links for the purpose of exploiting their business"? It might be so claimed in that it is surely necessary to see golf contests in order to become properly qualified to write upon the subject. If the rule should be so construed, which, by the way, seems unlikely, it would make Horace Hutchinson, the popular writer on the game in England, a professional in America, as well as Whigham, Findlay Douglas, W. G. Van T. Sutphen, and a score of others who do more or less writing on golf. With the exception of this possible ambiguity, the rules are firmly and clearly defined.

The prohibition of assumed names evidently came as a surprise to many golfers, but it was not entirely unexpected. While the use of fictitious names has not been very serious, it nevertheless contained the germs of possible difficulties, as a man's name might become known by reputation in other clubs, where personally he was unknown, and should he enter their tournaments under his own name he might thus secure a higher handicap, if he wished to deceive, than would be given under the assumed name. Many of the golfers in this city who were spoken to last week on this subject approved the rule thoroughly.

"The assumed name has no place in amateur golf," remarked one. "The game wants to be kept above the least suspicion. I believe its amateur basis is the highest and best of any sport to-day, and it must be kept free from the slightest professional taint. The United States Golf Association has done well for golf in America. Possibly it made a mistake in giving the championship to Chicago this year, but, on the whole, golfers should stand by the association, for it has committed no palpable errors, and has done a great deal that is worthy of the highest commendation."

Among the Boston and Philadelphia golfers the rules have been received with many expressions of favor. One of the few objections is pointed out by The Boston Herald regarding the old rule that no person shall be considered an amateur golfer who had ever played a match game against a professional for a money bet or stake. The Boston Herald comments as follows:

"This is omitted in the new rules, for the reason that the committee thought it could not be enforced, or, if enforced, it would thin the ranks of amateurs very materially; and, furthermore, that it was a private matter with which they were not called upon to deal. While it may be charged by some that the committee did not take high ground in this matter, its members maintain that their course was reasonable and fair to all. Still, the new rules draw the line on the word amateur more closely by making it exclude all who are considered professionals in any athletic sport. It is determined to do everything possible to keep the two classes distinct."

May 28, 1899

VARDON THE GOLF HERO

His Admirers Will Have a Chance to See Him Play To-morrow.

ON LAURENCE HARBOR LINKS

The English Champion Talks of His Methods of Play—Praises the Garden City Golf Course.

Golfers may readily be excused for their enthusiasm over the arrival of Great Britain's open champion, Harry Vardon, if, indeed, any one is disposed to cavil at them on that score, for Vardon is unmistakably the most brilliant golfer that has ever set foot upon American soil. The golfers are no more excited over the exponent of their game than have the followers of other sports been at various times over foreign visitors who have attained fame in their respective lines.

This is, moreover, the first time that an English championship holder has ever visited our shores. When Willie Park first came over about three years ago he was a former champion. For two years Vardon held the open championship of the United Kingdom, but by his victory last year he added a third championship triumph to his list of golf trophies, and it will be long before another golfer can come to America with a better or worthier record than Vardon possesses.

***

Those who remember Willie Park's coming and the ovation he received at every course he visited cannot be anything else than joyous at the prospect of seeing the ablest foreign golfer that has come here since that time. So far as outward appearances go, Vardon's arrival has been quieter than was Park's, but the enthusiasm is no less, and when milder weather causes the warm blood of golfing ardor to flow more freely in the metropolitan district matches may be arranged with even more rapidity than they were for Park. There may be this difference, however. Park came here to establish a golf club business, which has since been abandoned, and, while professional matches were arranged for him—notably the famous three-cornered one with Willie Dunn—Park gave exhibitions at several clubs freely. Vardon, on the other hand, is out for business as well as pleasure.

While one or two of our professionals might be bold enough to meet Vardon for a money purse, it is doubtful if many matches of that sort could be arranged. It is not at all likely that any professional would back himself very heavily, nor is it more certain that a professional would care to meet Vardon, knowing that the second ma. could not even see the color of the money.

Vardon is willing to play any one who wishes to meet him, professional or amateur, or give any golfing exhibition that may be asked, but for these he is to be paid as any other performer would be. On the free basis Vardon would surely be overwhelmed with invitations, but even on the "pay-up" policy there will probably be enough clubs ready to keep Vardon tolerably busy until he returns to England.

***

"It looks to me," remarked a Stock Exchange golfer, "as though the clubs that Vardon first visits would make money out of it. His fame has traveled so well ahead of him that every eager golfer is anxious to see him right off. When these men go to the club that has Vardon for the star attraction, they must all eat, surely smoke, and most all drink. They have to buy these things at the club. The club will have a first-class time, there will be plenty of sport and goodfellowship; it will give the club a few more inches of reputation, and I don't think its purse will be very empty toward the close of the day, even if $100 or $200 has been transferred to Vardon's pocket."

***

There is surely a good deal of truth in this statement, and it is even possible that an idea was gaining headway that non-members would be charged an admission fee, for the Secretary of the Laurence Harbor Country Club has publicly announced that no such fee will be charged. Vardon will make his début on American links at that club, near Red Bank, N. J., to-morrow, playing the best ball of two amateurs, Mortimer M. Singer, and Findlay Douglas, or John M. Ward for the other. Eighteen holes will be played in the morning, beginning about 10:30 o'clock, and eighteen in the afternoon. The grounds will be open to all who wish to see Vardon play, and the Secretary states that ample tents will be set up, wherein refreshments may be obtained at all hours of the day. With fine weather the club is likely to be overrun with golfers, for Vardon will not be seen in this locality again until almost two months later. Our local links are really not in condition for good golf at this time.

On Tuesday morning Vardon will start for Florida, and four matches have already been arranged for him, the first to be held on Saturday at St. Augustine, and the others during the following week at Ormond, Palm Beach, and Miami. There is just now the finest galaxy of professionals in Florida that has ever been seen there, including America's open champion, Will Smith, Alexander H. Findlay, George Low, Harry Rawlins, Launcelot Sewos, and Arthur H. Fenn. The latter is the only native American golfer, he having learned the game hereabouts five or six years ago, and for the first two years he acquired a wide fame as an amateur. All of these professionals and several others will play with Vardon, and the amateurs who are there have a treat of grand golf before them.

***

Vardon returned to the city yesterday from a business trip to Chicopee Falls, Mass. The only golf course in the vicinity of New York he has yet seen is the one at Garden City. Josiah Newman, editor of Golf, took him there early in the week, and it will be pleasing to know that the high praise bestowed upon that course by our own players has been amply justified by the great champion himself. Vardon played over a part of the course. Near one of the admirable bunkers he said:

"Why, this is grand; this is like Sandwich. Really, although I had heard a great deal of your courses, I did not think you had anything quite as fine as this. It's well suited for any championship tournament."

••

"What kind of a fellow is Vardon?" "How does he look?" have been the questions almost universally asked of those who have been among the first to meet the champion. The personal appearance of any hero is always interesting. It may be stated at once that Vardon carries none of the marks of his three championships on the exterior. Many a one-year amateur is far more pompous in his golfing talk and regalia than is Vardon. No one could be more modest than he. His frank, clear-cut face lights up easily with a cheerful smile, and, although his reputation as a talker is not great, he replies readily and to the point to all questions. Indeed, he submitted most gracefully to the volley of questions literally fired at him during the two days after his arrival.

Alexander H. Findlay, the head professional in Florida, and who has charge of many courses around Boston, has a deep admiration for the personal and golfing qualities of Vardon, whom he had the pleasure of playing in a friendly match of fifty-four holes last Fall in England. Findlay has written the following excellent account of Vardon, which, coming from a brother golfer, can hardly be improved upon:

"Let me in a few words give you an idea of what Harry is like. In the first place, he differs from me very much, as he is quite nice looking, and is greatly admired by the ladies. I weigh 155 pounds; so does Vardon to an ounce. I stand 5 feet 11 inches; so does Vardon exactly; he drives a fairly good ball; he drives a better. (I don't mean quality, I mean distance.) Vardon is exceptionally quiet and unassuming, free from the wickedness and vices that often beset young golf professionals. He smokes a briar pipe all the while during a friendly match, is seldom on the aggressive regarding conversation, &c., speaks when he is spoken to, and that very politely. He is passionately fond of golf and association football. The latter is the great Winter pastime there, and Vardon will go a long distance to witness a game, providing it doesn't clash with his golf appointments."

••

A good deal has been said about Vardon's style in playing. It is true that he is not a representative of the orthodox system of golf. His style of play will not be found in any of the numerous books on "How to Play Golf." Vardon does not go by rules,

but by what comes naturally and easily to him, and his rules are those of experience and observation from long practice on the links. J. H. Taylor, the former English champion, has a great deal of Vardon's style.

"I know that neither Taylor nor myself go by the books," said Vardon last week, "yet between us we have won five out of the last six open championships. We were the pioneers in gripping the club with overlapping fingers; and also the first to use short shafts for the wooden head clubs. The short clubs have now been very generally adopted by amateurs and professionals throughout England. The shorter handles give me a better command of the club, for there are no protruding ends to get in the way. Although shorter in length, my grip on the shaft is as far in inches from the club head as in the grip of those who use the longer shafts, for when I take a full shot my left hand is flush with the leather top, while the others let the shaft stick out for two or three inches at that end. Both my hands are practically united by the overlapping of the little finger of the right hand on the index finger of the left hand, with the left thumb straight down the shaft, under the right palm, and the right thumb nearly as straight. This gives me a perfectly firm grip, every finger and thumb helping in the firmness, and also gives me accuracy. I believe the looser method tends to wildness in direction, leading to sliced and pulled balls."

••

Vardon brought over thirteen clubs with him. "They are all beauties, too," he said, "the pick of nearly four hundred that I have used at different times."

This set consists of two drivers, one brassey, two driving mashies, two cleeks, two putters, a niblick, two lofters, and a special club of his own make, having a deep face resembling the driving mashie. One of the putters is known as a goose-neck putter, from the shape of the iron above the head. That putter Vardon would not part with for many times its original cost, for he has had it three years, and used it in two of his open championship victories. He generally uses a cleek for a long put and the goose-neck for putter on the green. Unlike many foreign players, Vardon does not use a wooden putter.

Vardon will remain in the United States until about the middle of May, when he will return to England to defend his title to the open championship in the annual tournament which will be played in June on the old St. Andrews links, Scotland.

February 11, 1900

©VOLK

Woman's Game of Golf.

Written for THE NEW YORK TIMES

By LILIAN BROOKS,

Author of "Drives and Putts," in collaboration with Walter Camp.

THE organization of the Women's Metropolitan Golf League would seem to indicate the approach of some solid foundation for the game in our country as a woman's sport, and this first attempt at organization brings into prominence one or two problems, upon the proper solution of which much depends. What are the possibilities and what are the limitations of the game for women as a whole? The variance of the scores of even our best players from year to year suggests to many the thought that we have no stability whatever, and the further fact that so few women, among the large number who play, have succeeded in scoring under a hundred, raises the doubt as to whether the actual scientific game is within our reach at all. Among men golf is constantly progressing; new stars overthrowing old favorites has become a part of the history of every great tournament. Can women say the same of their game and of themselves, and how do they stand in comparison with men?

It is a "sign of the times," a significant indication of the steady march of progress, that men and women are constantly drawing comparisons between each other. We have grown accustomed to this, and it is only when we approach a comparison in the subject of athletics in any form that we realize that the emancipation of women has been almost entirely intellectual, not physical. Forced forward by necessity, conviction, or ambition, we have thrown our brain power into competition with men, and have gained for ourselves an honorable place among artists, workers, and breadwinners. But physically where are we? A thousand times better off than we used to be, but far, how very far, from what we some day hope to be.

That we should be physically inferior is only the logical effect of an easily discovered cause. Born with less strength to begin with, we have had no systematic training in physical development, and what nature tried to do for us herself, fashion and conventionality speedily destroyed. While our brothers were playing baseball or climbing cherry trees, we were sitting with our feet dangling from a high piano stool, thrumming finger exercises, melancholy and submission stamped on the droop of our two little pig-tails. When the boys went to college and tried for the 'Varsity, we in our turn went to school and developed along with them our brains, our accomplishments, and our perceptions of people and things, but there we stopped. Latterly the bicycle has done more to emancipate us from the tyranny of clothes and conventionality than anything that has ever been given us. Oh! those first days, when in short skirt, easy shirtwaist, and a hat that would actually stay on, we flew along the winding, blossoming country roads free as the air we breathed. There

has been no sensation since quite like it, yet we seem to be unfaithful to our first love. It is because still another sport has been given us, which needs less violent exertion than bicycling, yet requires nerve, skill, strength, endurance, and self-mastery. People say bicycling has gone out, riding has gone out, that golf will go out. This is not true. Each sport will find its proper place and sphere of usefulness. The first two have only ceased to be a fashionable fad. Golf is rapidly losing that character. We can now look about us and see exactly where we stand.

Bicycling is not and cannot be a game. Golf is distinctly a contest. When women took up golf they not only had to learn to play that game, but a game. Tennis among women seemed to have been confined to comparatively few. Men have played games all their lives—they and their fathers before them. They have competed all their lives, and will go on competing to the end. Life is the same old question of the "survival of the fittest." Primitive man fought for his daily bread with a pointed stick or a jagged stone. Modern man sits in his office and fights with his brains. It is the same object, only the method of attaining it has changed. In consequence, in golf, as in every contest, men have the advantage over women of familiarity with competitive play. That it is hard for us to get accustomed to competition is proved by the results of the first matches three or four years ago. Our practice scores were good for beginners, but our competitive medal scores were simply heartbreaking. It is largely so still; the nervous element and the strain of competing against the whole field accounts for the difference of many a point between practice and competitive play. In match play there is the keenest kind of competition, but it is narrowed down to one individual, who is before your eyes, who plays along with you stroke for stroke, who stumbles and falls, and recovers just as you do, taking your mind completely off that worst of all hobgoblins, a good score. Woman's greatest difficulty seems to be in the long game. Some people consider it almost insurmountable. To my mind, however, it can be overcome. In low scoring, aside from a general accuracy, careful study leads to the conclusion that the second shot is the most important. A long drive by a man or a woman is a poor affair if the second shot is foozled, yet a poor drive has sometimes been retrieved by a brilliant brassey. Herein lies our first best chance, as a brassey for some unknown reason is a woman's best club. Realizing this, she uses and abuses it, often taking it for a comparatively short approach, because the lie is tempting, or more especially because she is absolutely at sea and helpless regarding distances varying from thirty-five yards to seventy-five. What she gains by a good drive and a good brassey she throws away by her wretched long approach. It has become something of a cant phrase to say that women approach and putt well. They do putt beautifully and approach well, twenty yards away from the green, but about the real approach, which is usually the third shot, varying from thirty-five yards to seventy-five, women as yet know nothing. This means that we are weak on our long irons, and every woman who really wishes to round out her game and lower her score permanently should concentrate her attention on first her second shot, and second, her cleek and her mid-iron. The two latter she should practice every day of her life. She is sure to work at her drive and brassey, the reward is so great, but the long irons are uninteresting in comparison, and in consequence, women have failed to recognize their importance.

In the matter of regular practice we are also somewhat hampered. A man after he has been a few years out of college generally settles down to two things, his business and his exercise, which is usually his pleasure. He makes an appointment to play golf, and he keeps it with the same precision that he keeps a business appointment. If he does not, the other man is usually anxious to know the reason why. A woman, whether married or single, never gives up her social life, and although it is a general impression among some men that she has really nothing to do, her hours, and minutes even, are filled with a thousand and one things—business and pleasure running into each other at all seasons and all hours. She makes an engagement to play golf, and a dozen household or charitable, or social, or educational duties pull the other way, and in despair golf goes to the wall. In Midsummer a woman has more time for regular practice, and it is for this reason that in May her scores are high, and in October low, after the freedom and healthful open air life and opportunities for hard work. This leads us to the belief that practice and intelligent study will bring a really scientific game within the reach of any woman who has actual golfing ability. The rising generation should produce some fine players, equal to Beatrix Hoyt or Lady Margaret Scott. Both of these women had the exceptional advantages of beginning when very young. Beatrix Hoyt was only fifteen when she won her first championship at Morristown, and Lady Margaret Scott handled the clubs as a child and learned the game playing with her father and brothers. There is a certain ease which comes from beginning early, which is not usually attainable when the game is taken up later. Lady Margaret Scott has a very long and powerful swing, acquired of course from playing constantly with men. She did what she saw others do. A woman can do nothing that will improve her game as much in practice as to play a man's course with some of her friends. The fact that she must work, must carry the obstacles, gives her just the stimulus she needs. Nothing is so great a help to progress as to

be obliged to do something that you yourself think, but particularly some one else thinks, is just a little beyond you, and for this reason the idea of women withdrawing altogether and having clubs or courses of their own is not a good one. It is true that at Morristown and Philadelphia, where such clubs first flourished, women have attained the highest golfing standard so far. Women do not run these clubs entirely by themselves. With all our new independence and liberty and power, men still watch over us with the old chivalry, plan for us, and push us forward to still greater freedom. The country clubs are now looking after our golf and are doing more to further our interests than we could hope to do by ourselves. Of course, there is some dear old gentleman, to whom the sight of a petticoat on the golf links is like a red rag to a bull, but he is generally forgiven, as we know his wife has spoiled him, and his daughter neglected his education. When a young man is bothered by a fluttering skirt in the distance it is usually because he has no other serious occupation.

The question of a proper course is something of a problem. There are two kinds. In one the difficulty is all distance, and there are few hazards. St. Andrews, Scotland, is a course of this description. Then there is the course where the difficulty is in the long carry, as at Sandwich, England. St. Andrews, in spite of its distance, might be possible for a woman, as the turf is not heavy but very fast, giving a long roll, and the greens perfection. Sandwich would be impossible, for no American woman can carry from 110 to 120 yards. Our courses are not nearly so difficult as those abroad, so perhaps the little school girl of to-day will in three or four years play them in competition as they stand.

The team matches arranged by the Metropolitan League are sure to be beneficial and stimulating, provided a few enthusiasts are not required to do too much. The number of matches arranged for each club

seems to be rather too many. Had the teams been limited to four instead of six, it would have made the schedule much more possible. Aside from that, however, golf has brought about the first actual approach toward organization in athletics that women have ever attempted, and it is a long step forward in the right direction. It should encourage struggling players, for in every club there are always one or two who are far above the rest, and to whom every scratch competition is accorded as a foregone conclusion. Handicaps are at best unsatisfactory to both contestants and the Handicap Committees. In a team match the chances are that the pairs will be evenly matched, and no one grudges the best players their prominent places. Team play should develop also an esprit de corps, should teach the sinking of individualism for the good of the combination. At college men get years of training in these principles, and it does not seem too much to say that in that very training lie the germs of high character, patriotism, and heroism. A little patience, much courage, belief in ourselves, and the same generous help and encouragement from men, and women's golf as a true sport will be on a firm foundation. The best result as a whole that she can hope to attain is, after all, to play as good a comparative game of golf as a man, simply because nature, for her own inscrutable ends, designed us the weaker vessel, but a woman can make her golf a truly great boon; she can bring to it every bit of mind and nerve and skill and endurance and sportsmanship that she has in her whole body; she can learn to win without vain boasting, and lose with a good grace, and in so doing take upon herself the complexion of those who play the game, not for silver cups or newspaper notoriety, but for the actual enduring love of it.　　LILIAN BROOKS.

June 10, 1900

VARDON GOLF CHAMPION

J. H. Taylor, Great Britain's Premier Golfer, Was Second.

WINNER LED BY TWO STROKES

Former American Champion "Willie" Smith Was Fifth—Dyker Meadow's Professional Well Up.

CHICAGO, Oct. 5.—Before the largest gallery that ever witnessed a golf championship in America, Harry Vardon, former champion of Great Britain, won the United States Golf Association open championship from Great Britain's premier golfer, J. H. Taylor, by the narrow margin of two strokes, on the Chicago Golf Club links, at Wheaton, this afternoon. For two days these wonderful golfers from English links had battled, far in the lead of the representative field of English, Scotch, Irish, German, and American players, for the title of Champion of the United States. With them, although not so close up as he might have been, was the holder of the emblem, Willie Smith.

David Bell of Carnoustie, the professional at Midlothian with former champion Willie Smith, gained third place in the championship, with a total of 323 strokes. Bell won the $150 in cash and the gold medal presented by a big golf supply house for the American engaged golfer who finished next to Vardon and Taylor.

Laurence Auchterlonie of Glenview, formerly one of the best amateurs at St. Andrew's, Scotland, was fourth, with 327 strokes. Fifth place fell to Willie Smith, whose total was 329.

George Low of Dyker Meadow, who recently, with Tom Hutchison as a partner, defeated Vardon in a "best ball" match 11 up 10 to play, was sixth, with a total of 331. Tom Hutchison of Shinnecock Hills was seventh, with a total of 333, and Harry Turpie of Edgewater was the eighth man—last prize winner—with a score of 334.

Several amateurs started, but only a few concluded the 72 holes of play. Charles B. MacDonald, formerly amateur champion of the United States, played through to the end, and captured the United States Golf Association trophy, with a score of 352.

Weather conditions for the two days of the open championship could not have been improved upon at this season of the year. A strong southerly wind blew across the links each day, and this made golf difficult during the last round, to even Taylor and Vardon. Vardon seems to have played a bit more consistently than his rival. All the interest in the first round of play centred in the two foreigners. When Taylor turned in a 76 to Vardon's 79, the critics predicted that Vardon would let himself out. This he did in the second round, and made 78 to Taylor's 82, and having one stroke the advantage. Vardon's concluding rounds in 76 and 80, to Taylor's 79 and 78, showed the closeness of the race. It was not until the last hole had been played by Vardon—and he putted so indifferently on the eighteenth green that some feared a tie would result—that the gallery dared cheer the Isle of Jersey man as the victor. The medal scores of the three winners for the tourney follow:

Harry Vardon, Ganton, England—

Out	5	4	4	4	5	5	5	4	4—40		
In	4	4	4	6	5	4	4	4	4—39—79		
Out	4	5	4	5	4	5	4	4	3—38		
In	4	5	5	5	4	4	4	6	4—40—78		
Out	5	3	5	5	4	6	4	4	3—39		
In	3	3	5	6	4	4	4	4	4—37—76		
Out	5	5	5	5	5	5	3	3	4—40		
In	3	4	5	5	4	5	4	5	5—40—80—313		

J. H. Taylor, Great Britain—

Out	5	5	5	5	4	5	4	4	4—41		
In	4	4	5	4	4	3	4	4	4—35—76		
Out	5	5	5	4	6	4	4	4	4—41		
In	3	4	5	6	4	4	6	4	5—41—82		
Out	5	5	5	5	4	5	4	4	3—40		
In	4	4	5	5	3	4	4	5	5—39—79		
Out	3	5	5	6	5	5	4	4	3—42		
In	3	4	4	5	3	4	4	4	5—36—78—315		

David Bell, Midlothian—

Out	5	5	4	5	4	7	4	3	3—40
In	4	4	5	4	4	4	3	5	—38—78
Out	4	6	6	4	5	6	4	5	3—43
In	3	4	6	6	4	4	4	4	6—41—84
Out	6	4	5	5	5	6	4	5	4—44
In	3	6	4	5	4	4	4	5	—39—83
Out	5	5	5	4	5	6	4	4	3—41
In	3	4	5	4	4	5	5	—37—78—323

The summary of the tournament follows with best scores other than above.

William Smith, Midlothian, 329; David Bell, Midlothian, 323; Alex Campbell, Brookline, 335; Stuart Gardiner, Lenox, 336; George Low, Dyker Meadow, 331; L. Auchterlonie, Glenview, 337; Val Fitzjohn, Sadaquada, 338; Tom Hutchison, Shinnecock, 333; Robert Simpson, St. Louis, 343; Willie Anderson, Coconamoc, 339; Harry Turpie, Edgewater, 334; W. H. Way, Detroit, 344; James Foulis, Chicago, 343; Fred Herd, Washington Park, 344; Alex Smith, Washington Park, 340; William Norton, Lakewood, 345; A. Smith, Edgewood, 344; W. B. Schooman, Detroit, 350.

Amateurs: C. B. McDonald, Chicago, 352; William Holabird, Jr., Glenview, 361; H. R. Johnstone, Chicago, 356; W. E. Egan, Onwentsia, 379.

C. B. MacDonald, who is the man who introduced golf in the West and laid out the Chicago Golf Club links, and who is President of this club, which acted as host for the professionals who attended the opening tournament, said he was happy over winning the amateur trophy, but not proud of his score or the fact that he beat a slim field.

October 6, 1900

TRAVIS EXPLAINS NEW GOLFING CODE

Says That Changes in Rules Imply a Decided Improvement in the Game.

HAZARDS MUST BE DEFINED

Compulsory Playing of Stymies Favored as Calling for Highest Degree of Skill.

In golfing circles it is but natural that the new code of rules which will go into effect with the new year has attracted widespread attention, for while there are no radical changes, a number of important amendments have been made to the old formula with which it will be absolutely necessary for golfers to be familiar. Some criticisms have been made to certain of the changes abroad, but the general consensus of opinion is that what changes have been authorised will make for the better conduct and appreciation of the game. The United States Golf Association, which sent a carefully prepared draft of recommendations last Spring to the Rules Committee of the Royal and Ancient Club of St. Andrews, Scotland, will formally adopt the new code at its annual meeting early in January, and there is not the slightest indication that a single objection will be made to any portion of the accepted code.

Walter J. Travis, who has made as close a study of the technicalities of golf as any one in this country, has issued a unqualified indorsement of the new code, and as editor of The American Golfer, he says, in the current number:

"The new rules, as a whole, will be hailed with delight and universal approval by all loyal supporters and true lovers of the royal and ancient game, and their thanks will go forth not only to the Rules of Golf Committee of St. Andrews, but also to the present officials of the United States Golf Association, which organization for the first time in its history has

been officially recognized and represented in the councils of the governing body. No one, in going carefully over the new rules, can fail to be profoundly impressed with the prodigious amount of thoughtful care bestowed on their compilation."

In dealing with some of the changes in detail, Mr. Travis says that they must be frankly admitted as distinctly in the line of improvements over the former code. Railways and fences will no longer be regarded as hazards, but permanent grass within a hazard is to be considered part of the hazard. This omission in the old rules, says Mr. Travis, read in conjunction with the new rule simply means that at present when a ball is in a hazard, whether it be on grass or not, the club shall not be so led under penalty of the loss of the hole, implying that now all hazards must be carefully defined.

Mr. Travis approves heartily of the change which prevents a golfer from using the back of his hand to smooth down the line of his put. Commenting on this, he says:

"Loose impediments may be lifted from the putting green and dung. Worm casts, snow, and ice may be lightly scraped aside with a club, but otherwise the line of put must not be touched. Brushing with the hand means the loss of the hole. A very important change, and a most excellent one."

"It is gratifying to note," adds Mr. Travis, "the reinstatement of the rules of etiquette in the regular code and also the addition of several desirable features, including the duties of players looking for a lost ball. In this connection it will be observed that the section has been amplified which stipulates that players looking for a lost ball should allow other matches coming up to pass them; they should signal to the players following them to pass, and having given such signal they should not continue their play until these players have passed and are out of reach."

Other important alterations are: No one shall stand to mark the line of play through the green or from a hazard. Penalty, loss of the hole.

It is no longer necessary to drop a ball from the head. Face the hole, stand erect, and drop behind, over the shoulder.

Under no circumstances shall a practice swing be taken anywhere, except on the tee, when the ball is not in play, under penalty of loss of the hole.

Casual water on a putting green is now practically non-existent. When a ball is on a green a clear put to the hole is permissible, free from intervening water.

On the much-mooted question as to whether stymies shall be played or not, Mr. Travis says:

"Stymies form an integral part of the code, and, therefore, should be played. They are defensible on the ground that they are capable of being negotiated by the exercise of the highest degree of skill. In match play competition, it is absolutely essential that all contestants should be compelled to play stymies, otherwise great injustice may be worked. The new rules make their playing compulsory under penalty of disqualification."

December 6, 1908

GOLF BOOMED BY TAFT.

Public Links Overcrowded by Recent Big Increase of Players.

The fact that President Taft has chosen golf as the best out-of-door sport to keep him in good physical condition is responsible for an unprecedented congestion of players on the city's golf courses, according to the men who have charge of the various links.

The number of players, it is said, on the Van Cortlandt and the Forrest Park links have more than doubled since Taft's election and the publicity which has attended the President's almost daily play. In a way, it is pointed out, the fact is indicative that Americans are imitative in their patriotism, and diligently follow the examples set by the head of the Nation.

Within the last few weeks many new lockers have been added to the clubhouse at Van Cortlandt, and there is a waiting list of applicants for more than double the number of lockers now in use. At the Forest Park clubhouse the congestion is even worse.

"The fact that golf is President Taft's favorite game is undoubtedly responsible for the great increase in the number of players this year," said Tom White, the

keeper of the Van Cortlandt Club house. "Last year it used to be tennis, because that was President Roosevelt's hobby. Now the tennis courts are almost deserted, except for the habitual players.

"Many of this year's golf players are of an entirely different calibre from those of former years and they show in many ways that the President's partiality for the game has influenced them largely in taking up the sport. These admirers are easily singled out. They constantly discuss the fine points of the President's game as they read about it in the papers and have long discussions as to the kinds of clubs the President uses.

"This idea is now so widespread that an enterprising firm has put out the 'Taft putter,' of which numbers are being used. It is just an indication of the way people allow those in high places to set the fashion for them, in other things besides dress.

"I expect the craze to increase from now on until the end of the President's term, and, certainly, if it keeps up at the present rate the city will have to establish new golf links to take care of the players. Even now it is almost impossible to play on the public courses on Saturdays, Sundays, and holidays, the congestion is so great."

Reports of greatly increased attendance at private golf clubs all over the country show that the interest in the game is not confined to any one locality, but has spread generally.

August 9, 1909

BRAID GOLF VICTOR AGAIN.

Title Holder Wins Championship Fifth Time in Open Tournament.

SAINT ANDREWS, Scotland, June 24.—The open golf championship tournament was concluded to-day with a victory for James Braid, title holder of 1901, 1905, 1906, and 1908. Braid's aggregate score in the four rounds for the championship was 299. Aleck Herd was second, with a score of 303, and G. Duncan third, with 304.

D. J. Ross of Massachusetts and Willie Smith of Mexico were the only transatlantic competitors. Both were well up at the finish, Ross having a score of 309. Smith, who was the American open champion of 1899, broke the record of the links in the second round yesterday, scoring 71. Smith's aggregate score was 308. This feat was duplicated by Duncan in the third round to-day. The half dozen amateurs competing were never prominent in the play.

June 25, 1910

GOLF IN AMERICA HAS MADE BIG GAINS

Players Increasing in Number, Links Are Numerous, and Game Gives Many Employment.

Although golf in America is still in its swaddling clothes as compared with the game on the other side of the Atlantic, it has much to be proud of, for unquestionably the royal sport has worked wonders in a comparatively short time. It is doubtful if even the most optimistic devotees of driver and iron ten years ago would have dared to predict that in 1910 golf would give employment to thousands, and add to the attractions of hundreds of towns and villages. Had he ventured such a prediction he probably would have been placed in the same category as the man who prophesied that a heavier-than-air machine could fly from New York to Philadelphia.

Time has shown that golf is not a pastime to be taken lightly, but, rather, seriously. Practically every other game has its limitations as to season. Not so with golf, for, only a foot or more of snow will prevent the golfer from making his rounds of the links, and weather is never too hot to prevent it, either.

No longer does the man in the street gaze at the golfer with his set of clubs as a curiosity. Nor is the "hockey player" remark so frequently heard. One might hear a man of the navy type inform his friend that golf is a "rotten game," but even this is a sign of progress, for he knows it is golf and not hockey.

The huge strides golf is making, and has made, is conclusive proof of its fascination. Ten years ago the golfer had to travel much longer to reach a golf course than he does at present. Every town of any size at all has its golf course. No seaside resort is a complete success unless it has its own links, and it is the knowledge that golf is to be had that frequently brings the visitor and his family. This is also true of many inland resorts.

This means business for the resort or the village in or near which the course is located. Even in ten years Garden City has made big strides in the way of improvement and much of it is due to the golf course there. Incidentally, Garden City now has two courses, the second being the Salisbury links, over which the recent tournament of the Eastern Professional Golfers' Association was played. This is by no means an exceptional case, for there are a great many other cities and towns where similar instances might be cited. Landowners are quick to realize the fact that the ground they have hitherto looked upon as being scarcely worthy of consideration is valuable from a golfing point of view, and he charges more per acre for it than he does for his best agricultural land.

With regard to the employment that the game provides it is difficult to estimate it. Professionals and their assistants, ground-keepers, caretakers, iron head-makers, golf ball makers, &c., are dependent upon the game, while there are thousands of boys, and even men, who make their living as caddies. The list could be considerably increased, even to those who earn their livelihood by making mixtures for the extermination of worms and other ground pests.

It seems a pity that the expenses of golf are such as to debar those who have scarcely more than a comfortable income from participating in the pleasures of the game, but even this may soon be relieved, for at present there are public links which are very well patronized by persons in ordinary walks of life. It is quite possible, however, that in a few years various municipalities will take more of an interest in the sport than at present, for, rapid as the growth of the game has been it is still in its infancy.

From the health point of view golf is a well-known preserver of youth, not only being prescribed by physicians as a health restorer, but being played by physicians themselves who practice what they preach.

August 7, 1910

AMATEUR AND 'PRO' STYLES IN GOLF PLAY

There Is a Distinct Difference, but It Is Difficult to Analyze.

In the course of innumerable discussions at the "nineteenth hole," where more golf is played than on the links, it is frequently remarked, in speaking of one person or another, that it could be seen he was a professional by his style, or that he had the "regular professional style." Such remarks as these would seem to indicate that there is a general opinion that in golf there is rather a marked difference between the styles of professional and amateur players.

Naturally, the professional plays better than the amateur, but it is to be inferred from the foregoing questions that there is something about the methods of the professional that is peculiar to this class. It seems to be a distinction peculiar to golf, or, at any rate, it is one which would be quite difficult to establish in another branch of sport. Apart from mannerisms common to individuals, there are few characteristic features of style in other sports which can be regarded as typical either of the amateur or of the professional player. In golf, however, there is something about the style of the professional which the amateur seldom or never acquires. The distinction is rather difficult to analyze, but it seems to consist in a bolder and more confident aspect in the address and greater snap in execution on the part of the professional. The amateur seems more diffident in his attitude and slower in play.

Several interesting points of speculation are opened by the question of how far these differences in style reflect the mental attitude of the two classes with regard to the game. It is commonly supposed that the reason of the superiority of the professional golfer over the amateur is that he knows he has a living to make by the very manner in which he plays. On how well he can play depends his reputation, and it is reputation that brings in dollars. The professional cannot afford, therefore, to play badly in the generally accepted sense of the term, consequently he is continually trying to do his best. He is always playing up to concert pitch.

The amateur, on the other hand, it is contended, has not this constant spur to force him to put forward his best foot, as it were. He does not take it very seriously if he does not play in a particularly brilliant fashion, and if he does he is prone to embark on theories and experiments with more or less disastrous results. In this way he is likely to lose confidence in himself, and his style no less than his execution reflects his weakness.

Undoubtedly there is a great deal in these arguments, but others are inclined to believe that the professional style and methods are really a separate cult. The caddie, or embryo professional, models himself after the leading professionals almost entirely and in a purely imitative manner. The amateur, on the other hand, if he does imitate the professional, does so with certain reservations born of the fact that he is an amateur and cannot hope to emulate the skill of those who devote their lives to the game with anything but an ordinary degree of success. He is rather more likely to model himself after some champion amateur, which may account for the perceptible difference that there is between the styles of the professional and amateur players.

Considering the wide diversity in styles that there is among golfers, it is remarkable that there should be this general distinction between the two classes of players. There are, of course, amateurs who use a style similar to that of a professional, chiefly through the fact that they have been taught the rudiments of the game by the man to whom they are similar.

February 23, 1913

DEGRADING GOLF.

The managers of the famous Country Club at Brookline, Mass., will do themselves and their club injustice if they fail to take action of some sort in regard to the rowdyism which has lately disgraced the ancient and honorable game of golf on their course. The circumstances thus far, of course, reflect no sort of discredit on the Brookline club, for everybody knows that no member of that organization of well-bred men would demean himself by a show of favoritism while following a golf match. Cheers and cries of encouragement or the reverse are wholly out of place in the game of golf. As a matter of fact that game does not lend itself easily to exhibition purposes. However, when spectators are permitted to follow a match they should be held strictly to the rules. Not a word should be spoken during the play, and no expression of approval or disapproval should be permitted at any time.

Mr. JEROME TRAVERS was insulted at Brookline Friday, as VARDON and RAY, the two English professionals, had previously been insulted by the crowd of irresponsible sightseers permitted to walk over the course. Certainly a golfer like Mr. OUIMET should be among the first to discountenance a manifestation of this sort in his favor, though Mr. TRAVERS, like VARDON and RAY, may regard it as beneath notice. Golf is peculiarly a nervous game; many players who do very well in club matches under ordinary conditions "go to pieces" when spectators follow them. In the history of golf in Great Britain there have been no manifestations of gross ill-breeding comparable with those recently seen at Brookline. The fault is not with that club, as we have said, but an expression of disapproval of the ill-bred cheering from the Brookline Governors would be appropriate and would go far to prevent such vulgar exhibitions in the future.

September 28, 1913

BRITISH GOLF CHAMPION.

J. H. Taylor Wins Open Title the Fifth Time—Ray Second.

HOYLAKE, England, June 24.—The British open golf championship was won here to-day by the veteran English player, J. H. Taylor, with the fine aggregate of 304 strokes for the four rounds of 18 holes each, his score for the rounds in order being 73, 75, 77, and 79. This is his fifth open championship. Last year's champion, Edward Ray, was second, with 312 strokes, his score by rounds being 73, 74, 81, and 84.

Harry Vardon, who has won the open championship five times, tied with Michael Moran, the Irish champion, for third and fourth places, with 313 each. Vardon's score by rounds was 79, 75, 79, and 80.

John J. McDermott of Atlantic City, open golf champion of the United States, tied for fifth and sixth places with T. G. Renouf, their grand aggregates being 315 each. McDermott's score by rounds was 75, 80, 77, and 83. Tom L. McNamara of Wollaston, Mass., took 85 strokes to make the third round. His aggregate for the three rounds was 248, as his scores for the first and second rounds were 80 and 78. He was placed twenty-fourth, with an aggregate of 325 strokes for the four rounds, his score by rounds being 80, 78, 85, and 82.

Among the intervening scores were those of Arnaud Massy, former French champion, 317; Alex Herd and Graham, Jr., 318 each, and James Braid, 321.

June 25, 1913

TRAVERS AGAIN WINS GOLF CHAMPIONSHIP

John G. Anderson of Boston Defeated for Amateur Title at Garden City, 5 and 4.

ALL EVEN IN FIRST ROUND

Champion Draws Away from Opponent in Afternoon, Massachusetts Player's Putting Becoming Erratic.

Jerome D. Travers of Upper Montclair for the fourth time in his career won the amateur golf championship of the United States yesterday at Garden City by defeating John G. Anderson of Brae Burn in the thirty-six-hole decisive match by 5 up and 4 to play.

It was a great match, and "Jerry" found himself opposed to a man from Massachusetts who was the only representative of that State in the final round in seventeen years. Moreover, he found Anderson no mean opponent, as shown by the fact that the match at the end of the early round was all square. Anderson is Professor of English in the Fessenden School at West Newton, Mass., and was the teacher of Philip Carter, the junior metropolitan champion, in both English and golf. Anderson won the Massachusetts championship in 1907, and again in 1911. Three years ago he went to France to compete in the French championship in the course of a tour of Europe, and played Charles Evans, Jr., in the final round, Evans winning after two extra holes. It has been a long time since Massachusetts has had a place among the factors in American golf. Francis Ouimet, on whom so much reliance was placed, fell at the hands of Travers earlier in the tournament, and it was left for Anderson to uphold the golf of the Bay State. His defeat of Evans has been fully chronicled, but it was a different proposition for him to face when he got up against the redoubtable "Jerry." It didn't save the fighting professor the least, for he has been an athlete and golfer for years. He cared nothing about anything but holding his man, and this he did successfully all the

morning. For instance, it was Anderson who drew into the lead at the start by winning the first hole in 4 to 5. Then Travers came in for a win at the second, and again at the third, when Anderson pulled his drive into the adjoining fairway.

Travers became two up at the fourth. Then followed two halved holes. Anderson getting a chance to overcome some of his opponent's lead at the long seventh, when Travers got into trouble. By means of sterling golf, Anderson captured the next two holes, and actually was 1 up on the champion by the time the turn was reached. Neither man had done well thus far, but, realizing that something better must be forthcoming, they started out to play real golf, and their figures of 37 coming in attest to that fact. These figures are only one over par.

Three halved holes marked the start of the inward nine, then Anderson became two up at the thirteenth by means of a long putt for a four, one under par. Travers drew up at the next and squared the match on the sixteenth. A superb four at the long seventeenth won that for Travers, but he lost his lead at the eighteenth hole over the pond when he used his mashie from the tee, the mashie of which he has lately been fearful, and pulled to a trap, requiring four for the hole, a short one. Thus the morning round was level.

Anderson with wholesome fear of being short of the first green in the afternoon, played his second too strongly and it went over the green, so that he lost the hole. The second, too, went into Travers's bag when Anderson failed on a putt. It was by means of remarkable recoveries from trouble that won the long fourth hole for Travers. He sliced his drive into a pit, then proceeded to get his ball into the fairway of the fifth, from which he got to the green. He was too long for Anderson on his irons here, and with a stroke advantage to the green won the hole. The winning of the fourth placed Travers three up, and from this point to the turn they simply were content to halve all the holes. Neither man could do anything the other was not able to equal. Their driving was practically of the same length, and wonderful approaches at times on Anderson's part were promptly equalled by the champion. Thus the struggle reached the turn with Travers still three up, the champion playing out in 39, much better than the morning, and Anderson going out in 42.

Travers drew further away at the tenth and

eleventh holes through poor putting on the part of the Massachusetts representative. A fine halve at the twelfth followed, when Anderson made a remarkable recovery over a mound and got down a good put. Two halves left Travers the winner on the fourteenth green by 5 up and 4 to play.

When they shook hands Anderson smiled as if he really meant it, and as if it was a real pleasure to lose a match replete with remarkable incidents. The crowd was estimated at 6,000 persons. The card:

Travers, out...5	3	4	5	4	5	7	5—43		
Anderson, out.4	4	5	6	4	5	5	4—41		
Travers, in...4	4	3	5	4	4	4	5—37—80		
Anderson, in...4	4	3	4	5	4	5	3—37—78		
Travers, out..5	3	4	5	4	5	4	4—39		
Anderson, out..6	4	4	6	4	4	5	4—42		
Travers, in...4	4	3	5						
Anderson, in...5	5	3	5	4					

There were several English writers in the gallery, one of whom declared that the crowds at Garden City were as large as almost any at the world-famous matches in Europe. There was no holding the crowd toward the close of the match. It ran over sand traps and failed to observe the admonition of the officials to "Keep back." Many well-known golfers were seen there, including the former champions Findlay S. Douglas and Walter J. Travis, Hamilton K. Kerr, George H. Barnes, Gardiner W. White, Dr. A. T. Haight, Miss Marion Hollins, the women's metropolitan champion; Earle H. Eaton, and Roy Webb. Fred Herreshoff caddied for Travers.

September 7, 1913

JEROME TRAVERS

OUIMET WORLD'S GOLF CHAMPION

Twenty-Year-Old Amateur Defeats Famous British Professionals for Open Title.

REMARKABLE GOLF FEAT

Covers the 18-Hole Course at Brookline in 72 Strokes— Vardon 77, Ray 78.

SPLENDID DISPLAY OF NERVE

First Amateur to Win American Open Championship—Big Gallery Makes Demonstration at Finish.

Cards of the Players.		
OUIMET.		
Out ...5 4 4 4 5 4 4 3 5—38		
In .....3 4 4 4 5 4 3 3 6—34—72		
VARDON.		
Out ...5 4 4 4 5 3 4 4 5—38		
In .....4 4 5 3 5 4 3 5 6—39—77		
RAY.		
Out ...5 4 5 4 5 4 3 3 5—38		
In .....4 4 5 4 5 6 4 5 3—40—78		

BROOKLINE, Mass., Sept. 20.—Another name was added to America's list of victors in international sport here to-day when Francis Ouimet, which for the benefit of the uninitiated is pronounced we-met, a youthful local amateur,, won the nineteenth open championship of the United States Golf Association.

The winning of this national title was lifted to an international plane, due to the sensational circumstances of the play and to the calibre of the entrants whom Ouimet defeated during his march to victory. Safely berthed in his qualifying round, the boy trailed the leaders in the first half of the championship round; tied with Harry Vardon and Edward Ray, the famous English professionals, for the first place in the final round, then completely outplayed them to-day in the eighteen-hole extra round which was necessary to decide the 1913 championship.

Ouimet won with the score of 72 strokes, two under par for one of the hardest courses in the country. Vardon finished five strokes behind Ouimet with 77; Ray took third place with 78.

Ouimet's Rank in Sport.

It was not the actual defeat of this famous pair of golfers so much as the manner of that defeat that entitles Ouimet's name to rank with that of Maurice E. McLoughlin, champion in tennis; Harry Payne Whitney, leader in polo, and James Thorpe, victor in athletics. Ouimet, a tall, slender youth, just past his teens, outplayed and outnerved not only Vardon and Ray in the play-off, a wonderful fact in itself, but succeeded in battling his way through the largest and most remarkable field of entrants that ever played for an American title. When the qualifying rounds began last Tuesday the lists contained 170 names, including in addition to Vardon and Ray, those of Wilfred Reid, another well-known English player; Louis Tellier, a French professional of note; a few high class ama-

FRANCIS OUIMET.

VARDON
© AMERICAN PRESS

RAY © AMERICAN PRESS

teurs, and a host of American and foreign professionals playing for United States and Canadian clubs.

When Ouimet holed his final stroke on the home green of the Country Club this afternoon the 8,000 persons who had tramped through the heavy mist and dripping grass behind the trio of players for almost three hours realized what the victory meant to American golf, and the scenes of elation which followed were pardonable under the circumstances.

The Winner's Perfect Form.

The pride in the young American's victory was all the more justified because of the fact that he had won without fluke or flaw in his play, responding in perfect form to a test of nerve, stamina and knowledge of golf never before required of a player in a national tournament. All through the crucial journey around the 18-hole course Ouimet never faltered. In fact his play might be termed mechanical, so perfect was it under the trying weather and course conditions. He appeared absolutely without nerve, playing from tee to fairway, from fairway to green and finishing each hole with a splendid exhibition of putting. His veteran opponents, tried players of many a hard-won match in various parts of the world, broke under the strain, leaving Ouimet to finish as coolly as he had started.

The very fact that Vardon and Ray could not hold up under the stress of the struggle shows the titanic form and strain of the final round of the championship. Vardon has five times won the English open championship, and in 1900 won the American open at Wheaton, Ill., defeating J. H. Taylor, England's greatest golfer and present champion.

Before the tournament began Ray, Vardon, and Reid were 2 to 1 favorites to win over the remainder of the field. Even after Ouimet had tied with his two opponents of to-day, wagers were laid at 5 to 4 that one of the two Englishmen would defeat him and even money on Ray or Vardon against Ouimet alone.

The scenes of jubilation on the home green after the match had been won.

were, therefore, but natural expressions of pride and pleasure at Ouimet's success in retaining a championship for America which was considered earlier in the week destined to cross the Atlantic.

Ray and Vardon Cheered.

Thousands of dripping rubber-coated spectators massed about Ouimet, who was hoisted to the shoulders of those nearest to him, while cheer after cheer rang out in his honor. Excited women tore bunches of flowers from their bodices and hurled them at the youthful winner; hundreds of men strove to reach him in order to pat him on the back or shake his hand.

Ray and Vardon, whose fight for the open championship brought out the possibilities of Ouimet as a golfer, were not forgotten in the celebration of victory. Each Englishman got a three times three before the parade started for the dressing quarters, where the recent competitors changed to dry clothing for the presentation of the medals and other prizes.

During this ceremony, in which Secretary John Reid, Jr., acted as master of ceremonies, both Ray and Vardon took the opportunity to praise Ouimet as a sportsman and golfer. Ray said that Ouimet had played the best golf during the four-day struggle that he had ever seen in America and that it had been an honor to play with him and no dishonor to lose to him. Vardon brought cheers from the gallery when he frankly stated that they had never had a chance to win with Ouimet, during the play-off, because the lad played better golf and never gave them an opening at one of the eighteen holes. He congratulated Ouimet and America on the victory and proved a popular speechmaker as well as golfer. Secretary Reid, in awarding the championship medal to Ouimet, the trophy to the Woodland Club of Auburndale, Mass., which he represented, and cash prizes to Vardon and Ray, took occasion to apologize "in a slight way" as he put it, for the outbursts of cheering at inopportune times.

This was a delicate reference to a feature of to-day's play which is quite likely to be a subject of international comment by the golfing contingents of England and the United States. The management of the tournament has been the subject of much praise, but to-day the gallery several times violated the keen ethics of the sport, by cheering wildly whenever Ouimet gained a point. The same outbursts occurred yesterday, but Ouimet was then playing with George Sargent, who had no chance for first place in the final half of his round. To-day it was different, for both Ray and Vardon were playing shots either just before or after Ouimet and it was plainly evident that these outbreaks annoyed them. Approaching the seventeenth hole, Ray deliberately stopped in the midst of a swing and refused to play until the cheering ceased. This action of the gallery had little or no effect on the result of the match, but a number of golfers publicly voiced their regret that cheering like that at boat races or football games should have occurred, although they realized and stated that it was impossible to check these national outbursts of enthusiasm when Ouimet made particularly good plays.

How the Strokes Were Made.

It was exactly 10 o'clock when the trio of players teed up in the drizzle for the start. The fairways and greens were watersoaked and in many places churned to the consistency of muddy paste by the trampling of hundreds of feet during the last three days of rain. Overhead low-hanging gray clouds appeared to be part of the mist which would have made the most ardent Scotch golfer feel perfectly at home. The first and second holes were recorded in fives and fours for all three players.

Both Ray and Vardon outdrove Ouimet from the tees, but both sliced and pulled slightly, while the ultimate winner held true to the course.

The first break came at the third hole, where Ray took a five, while the other two players holed in four. There was no advantage either way on the fourth and fifth, but Vardon took the lead in the sixth with a three, while Ray and Ouimet required four. Ray drove furthest, but Vardon's approach was right on the green and he holed a comparatively easy putt, while Ray and Ouimet needed two.

Vardon and Ouimet took four for the short seventh, approaching indifferently, while Ray was on the green in two and holed a brilliant put for three, drawing up even with Ouimet. Vardon lost his lead in the eighth, when, after getting on the green in two, he putted badly, requiring two to hole. Ouimet's second was within a foot of the pin, and he scored an easy three. Ray arose to the occasion with a beautiful 25-foot put for a three also. All took fives on the ninth, the longest and hardest hole of the course, being 520 yards of hill and dale, known as the Himalayas.

It therefore came about that the two Englishmen and the American youth played the greatest match in the history of golf on this continent, turning for home all square at 38.

Ouimet immediately jumped to the fore with a three on the short tenth. All were on the green in one, but Ray and Vardon each needed three putts to hole, while Ouimet, from his more favorable lie, scored with two. This gave him a lead of a stroke and marked the beginning of the end.

The eleventh was halved in four, but Ouimet picked up another stroke on the twelfth. He outdrove both opponents from the tee and his approach was within eight feet of the hole, but he took two putts for a four. Ray and Vardon both had trouble in getting to the edge of the green in twos, and, putting poorly, halved in five. All landed on the thirteenth green with their second shots, but Vardon's perfect putt gave him a three, while Ouimet and Ray took two for fours.

The fourteenth was halved in five, and with but four holes to play Ouimet was leading by the narrow margin of one stroke. Vardon stayed with him on the fifteenth, each getting a four, but Ray, after hitting a spectator with his sliced drive, reached the sand trap on the mashie shot. He required two to get on the green and two putts for a six. He was now four strokes behind Ouimet and three behind Vardon, and his experience appeared to break his playing nerve.

On the sixteenth, the shortest hole of the course, all played the 125-yard iron shot to the green. Vardon and Ouimet made par threes, but Ray required three putts for a four, so off was he on his game.

Ouimet won the match and title on the seventeenth, when he got a three for his opponents' fives. The youngster drove far down the fairway, was on the green in two, and holed a short putt, one stroke below par. Vardon, who had been showing signs of the strain, hooked his drive into a trap, took three to the green, and two putts to hole. Ray was in deep grass, and, playing as though he had given up hope, halved the hole with his countryman. He rallied and scored a three on the home hole with a long putt, while Ouimet, playing safe, had a par four. Vardon's second shot was short, landing in the mud of the race course, and when he finally holed for the last time of the match his card showed a six.

A resume of the play shows that while Ouimet was frequently outdriven with iron and wood, his game was far steadier and more consistent than that of either Ray or Vardon. The two Englishmen showed a tendency to slice and pull their first and second shots, which got them into trouble frequently. While Ouimet did not get the distance of his competitors, he played line shots all during the match, his direction being little short of remarkable, considering the soft, muddy condition of the turf. In putting, too, he was steadier and more accurate than either Ray or Vardon.

September 21, 1913

MISS DODD CHAMPION.

English Title Holder Wins Canadian Golf Honors, Too.

MONTREAL, Oct. 4.—Miss Muriel Dodd, champion lady golfer of England, to-day won the ladies' golf championship of Canada by defeating Miss Florence Harvey of Hamilton, Ont., her opponent in the final of the Canadian women's golf championship, by 7 up and 6 to play.

October 5, 1913

"GUTTY" LOSES IN TEST.

Rubber-Cored Golf Ball Best for the Ordinary Player.

Special Cable to THE NEW YORK TIMES.

LONDON, April 2.—Great interest was attached to a golf match over the Sandy Lodge course to-day, in consequence of a heated discussion of the respective merits of the old solid india-rubber ball known as the "gutty" and the modern rubber-cored ball, first introduced from America. Taylor and Braid opposed Vardon and Duncan in a four-ball match over thirty-six holes.

One couple played with "gutties" and the other couple with "rubber cores" for the first eighteen holes, each side changing balls for the second eighteen holes. The result, as was expected, ended in a victory for the "rubber cores."

Vardon and Duncan, using the modern ball, were 5 up on their opponents at the end of the first round. Changing to "gutties" in the afternoon, Vardon and Duncan lost four of these five holes, gaining the victory on two rounds by 1 up. The net victory for the "rubber cores" thus was nine holes in thirty-six.

During the afternoon a driving competition was held. Braid driving a rubber-cored ball 278 yards and Duncan sending a "gutty" 240. The test clearly showed the advantage of the rubber-cored ball, certainly in distance of "run" after the ball's first bounce, and proved conclusively that it made golf easier for the ordinary player, although the difference it made to champions was not so great as might be expected. The best round with the "gutty" was Braid's 70, and the best round with a rubber core was Vardon's 67.

April 3, 1914

VARDON GOLF CHAMPION.

Ouimet Not Among First Fifty in British Open Tournament.

LONDON, June 19.—At Prestwick today Harry Vardon won his sixth British open golf championship, after a dingdong struggle with G.H. Taylor, who was the holder of the championship. At the end of the third round this morning Taylor was leading Vardon by 2 strokes, but he could do no better than 83 for his fourth round in the afternoon, Vardon winning with an aggregate score of 306, against Taylor's 309. The scores for the four rounds were: Vardon, 73, 77, 78, 78; Taylor, 74, 78, 74, 83.

Francis Ouimet, the American open champion, failed to show any improvement today, his two rounds today of 85 and 82 giving him a total of 332. Ouimet did not finish among the fifty players.

June 20, 1914

AMERICA'S PIONEER GOLF COURSE AT WHITE SULPHUR SPRINGS

Laid Out 32 Years Ago by Half a Dozen Men Who Were Ridiculed for "Following a Big Marble Over the Hills."

Special to The New York Times.

White Sulphur Springs, W. Va., June 27.

IF local wiseacres are right in their claims, the original golf links in the United States were laid out here in 1882 at Oakhurst, the estate of Mr. Russell Montague of Boston, thus antedating by four years the course laid out by the St. Andrews Club in Yonkers, generally conceded to be the oldest in this country. The Oakhurst links are still in existence.

A peculiar chain of circumstances led to the founding of the original golf club and the laying out of the links.

It was in the days when coaching was at its zenith, and "morning germans" that started before noon and waned only with the dawning of another day brought the White Sulphur Springs to the topmost rung of fame as a resort. Saratoga Springs was at that time its only acknowledged rival, Newport still being in its infancy.

Back in the Alleghany Mountains, a couple of miles from the hotel and cottage colony, nearly 3,000 feet above sea level, there nestles between two commanding ranges a valley that is very Scotch in the characteristics of its scenery. Here—at Oakhurst—the Summer home of Mr. and Mrs. Russell W. Montague of Boston, were the first golf organization and course in the country. The club was informal and there were only half a dozen members, but regular medal plays were a feature, and for six successive Christmas Days the players met in what might be termed the first series of annual tournaments in the United States. The players were handicapped and scores were kept from year to year for classification and record.

Greenbrier County was originally settled principally by Scotch and Scotch-Irish. Later in the sixties and seventies a small coterie of Scotchmen and Englishmen with varied interests on this side of the water formed a little colony of their own near the White Sulphur Springs.

Mr. and Mrs. Montague placed their estate at the disposal of George Grant and a number of their English and Scotch neighbors when the latter told them that the Oakhurst acres would make an ideal course. Mr. Grant, who came from London to take the baths at the Springs for rheumatism, had the adjoining place, Greycliffe. He and his nephew, Lionel Torrin, an English tea planter who had played golf in East India, Scotland, and England, mapped out the course.

A couple of years passed before it was in perfect condition, but neither time nor expense was spared, and today the Oakhurst links stand as a monument to Grant and Torrin. They had the benefit of advice from Alexander and Roderick McIntosh McLeod of Dalvey, Scotland, whose place was a mile away in the same valley. Mr. Montague, a Harvard '74 man, who had played at St. Andrews and a number of the other Scotch clubs, also assisted and with George M. Donaldson, also from Scotland, made up

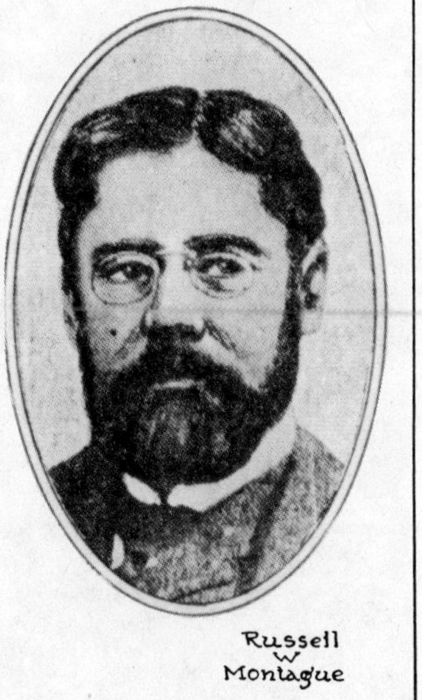

Russell W Montague

An ex-caddie and the son of a gardener, Francis Ouimet stole the British Open from the greatest golfers of his day and became an instant hero.

Bobby Jones, golf giant of the '20's, is seen here at the Essex County Club in New Jersey.

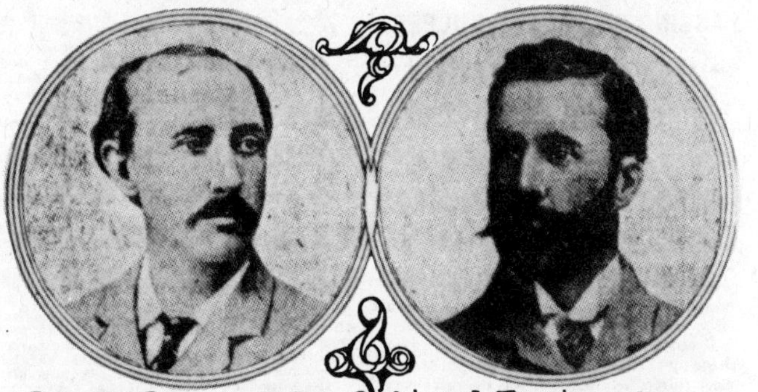

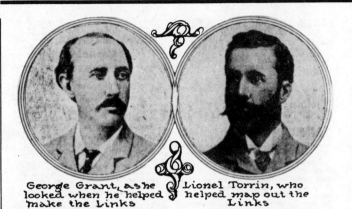

George Grant, as he looked when he helped make the Links — Lionel Torrin, who helped map out the Links

the membership of the original golf club. He was the only American membership of the original golf club. He was the only American member.

The Montague estate was admirable for golf links. There were nine holes and over 2,700 yards were covered. The driving tees were grass and the putting greens, though they have not received attention since the links were abandoned five years ago, when the White Sulphur Springs course was laid out, may still be noticed by the most casual.

Conditions for golf were entirely different in 1882, when five Britishers and one American represented the total number of golfers, from what they are today, when the number of players runs into the thousands.

The cups still in the ground at Oakhurst are cumbersome; they are thicker and heavier than those used today. Clubs, too, have changed somewhat, as may be seen when the latest are compared with those first used at Oakhurst, and still in Mr. Montague's possession.

Solid brass was used in the construction of all the heads in the iron clubs, and the wooden heads of the drivers and brassies were longer and narrower.

The balls brought over from Edinburgh were larger and much heavier than ours and always sank in water. They had little or none of the bounce and carry of the present-day ball. However, the Oakhurst players always insisted that they have never had as keen enjoyment out of the game at any of the clubs where they have played as at their own links, with their old golf clubs and balls.

There were no golf supplies to be had in this country in the early eighties, so the Messrs. McLeod, Grant, Donaldson and Torrin had them shipped over from their home clubs, and Mr. Montague was supplied by them.

Mr. Donaldson had a funny experience once when he arrived at the New York Custom House following a visit to his home in Scotland. It was in the late eighties, and he had brought over an unusually large supply of clubs and balls for himself and his friends. The Customs Inspectors at New York were dubious, and, following an hour's conference, insisted upon retaining the supplies until they had an official ruling from the Treasury Department at Washington before Mr. Donaldson could take possession of the clubs.

One of the Inspectors insisted that no one ever played a game with such "implements of murder." Mr. Donaldson was irate and stormed, but nevertheless he had to leave New York minus the clubs and wait a weary six weeks before the customs officials decided that the sticks were harmless enough to enter the country.

The players who "followed a big marble over the hills" were the butt of much scorn and ridicule from visitors at the Springs, who frequently drove over in coaches to see "those funny Scotchmen and Montague play marbles with sticks."

From time to time visitors tried the game, but when they found great difficulty in even hitting the balls they proclaimed it "silly" and went back to their dancing, croquet, and tennis. It is a tribute to Mr. Montague that, thought he failed to interest his friends for twenty years in the game, his prediction that it would rival the most popular sports when once it took hold, has been more than fulfilled.

Mr. and Mrs. Montague are spending this season at Oakhurst and the original American golfer in the States is the only member of the original Oakhurst golf club left at the White Sulphur Springs. Mr. Grant lives in London, and Greycliffe is now occupied by Mr. and Mrs. Thomas Tuke of England. The McLeods are at their ancestral home, Dalvey, in Scotland. Mr. Torrin lives in London. Mr. Donaldson was the only one of the golfers to marry an American girl. His wife was Miss Sallie Ould, daughter of Judge Ould and half-sister of Mrs. James Brown Potter, formerly Miss May Handy of Richmond. Mr. Donaldson lives in an adjoining county where he has big lumber interests.

Mr. Donaldson and Mr. Montague occasionally meet for a game, but when they do, they turn their backs on their own links and wend their way to the Greenbrier Golf Club where they play over a splendid course laid out by Charles Blair MacDonald, "The Father of American Golf," who is shortly to be entertained both at the Greenbrier and at the original links.

June 28, 1914

GOLF CONTROVERSY RAGING.

Which Had First Links, White Sulphur Springs or Yonkers?

Special to The New York Times.

WHITE SULPHUR SPRINGS, W. Va., Aug. 1.—A tempest in a teapot has been raging here for over a year, and now it threatens to boil over. It started when White Sulphur came forward with the claim that the original golf links in the States were laid out here at Oakhurst, the estate of Russell W. Montague, and that the links here antedated by several years the supposed original links at the St. Andrew's Club in Yonkers.

As the course here was used as early as 1882, White Sulphur Springs so far has the best of the argument, but the discussion still goes on. Most golfers in the country with a knowledge of the history of the game in America have for years supposed that the links just above New York City were the original ones until the publication of a detailed account of the Oakhurst links and players, some of whom are here at present.

The original clubs still in Mr. Montague's possession are to be put in a glass cabinet in the Golf Clubhouse this week.

The August season, which is the gayest at this all-the-year-round resort, was most auspiciously ushered in tonight with numerous informal suppers.

Invitations are being issued for the usual private affairs that are the big features of the Summer season here. They will include a bal poudre, two subscription and numerous private Germans and cotillions, thes dansants, supper dansants, and a garden fete.

The season never is really dedicated until the dancing of the "White Sulphur Riley," a stately minuet, which for seventy-odd years has been danced at least once each season. It is danced by women only, and this week it preceded a ball, followed by a supper dansant. Those dancing it included Miss Hilah C. French of New York, Mrs. Sydney Wynne Ffoulkes, Mrs. J. Kellogg Bradley, the Misses Bertha and Frances Clark of Philadelphia. Miss Doris Haywood of Washington, Mrs. John D. Potts, and Miss Nell Potts of Richmond.

August 2, 1914

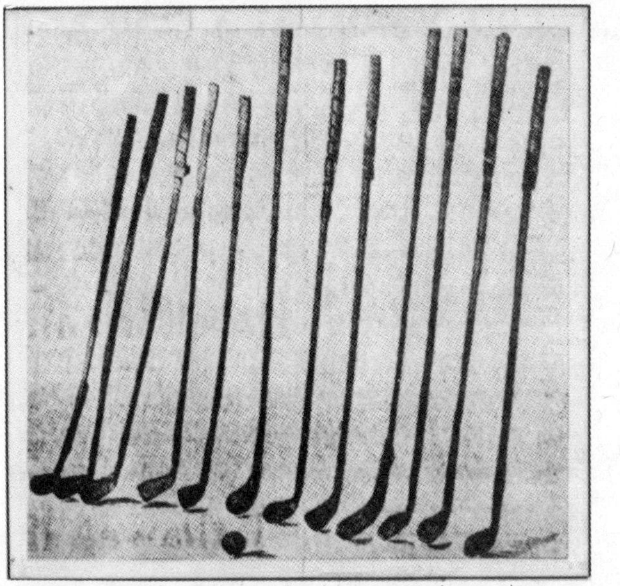

First Golf Clubs used in the United States

WALTER HAGEN WINS OPEN GOLF TITLE

Rochester "Pro" Makes 72 Holes in 290, with "Chick" Evans One Stroke Behind.

CHICAGO, Aug. 21.—Walter C. Hagen, 22 years old, native professional of Rochester, N. Y., today displaced Francis Ouimet as open golf champion of America, by winning the tournament at Midlothian with a medal score of 290 for the seventy-two holes.

Ouimet fell off in his play, taking 298 for his total, and it fell to the lot of Charles Evans, Jr., Western amateur champion, hampered by a wrenched right ankle, to furnish Hagen's chief opposition. Outplaying the whole field in a spectacular finish that electrified the long gallery, Evans made two rounds of 71 and 70 and finished with 291, just one stroke behind Hagen.

Evans's score of 141 for today was the best double round of the tournament, and was accomplished despite several missed putts. His ankle seemed to bother his putting more than his long work and iron shots. His tee shots spanned some 300 yards of the fairway nearly every time. His irons were nearly all perfect, but, in the last nine holes, he missed three short putts and had no luck with long ones. He finally drove the edge of the eighteenth green, 277 yards, and had left one putt for a half with Hagen.

The spectators stood on tiptoe while the Chicagoan tried the thirty-foot putt. He missed by twelve inches and the championship went to Hagen.

Ouimet lost the title with graceful equanimity. He had no fault to find, he said, having fallen off his game, as others had done before. He won the title last year at Brookline, tying with Harry Vardon and Edward Ray, British professionals, at 304. In the play off, Ouimet made 72 to Varden's 77 and Ray's 78.

Hagen's victory was accomplished by steady playing. Yesterday he made a record of 68 for the course by good work, aided by spectacular putting. He took 74 in the afternoon, leading the field at the end of the first day with 142. Today he fell off a trifle, taking 75 for the first round and 73 for the second. The best of his game came on the last nine holes, where, holing putt after putt, he made 35, two under par.

The new champion was born in Rochester, learned golf there and had not made any record outside his native city until the present tournament. He is slight in build, but follows Vardon's system of shooting straight for the flag all the time.

Tom McNamara of Boston, who had played the most consistent golf of the meet, scoring 72, 71, and 76 for the first three rounds, besides 145 in the elimination, fell off badly this afternoon, taking 83 for the last round, and finishing out of the money with 302.

George Sargent of Chevy Chase, champion in 1909, when he scored 290 at Englewood, tied with Fred McLeod of Washington, D. C., for third place.

M. J. Brady of Wollaston and James Donaldson of Glenview Club, Chicago, tied with Ouimet for fourth prize. Louis Tellier of Canoe Brook Club, Summit, N. J., formerly open champion of France, was fifth best, with 299, while J. J. McDermott of Atlantic City, twice champion, and Arthur Smith of Columbus, Ohio, closed the list of prize winners with 300 each.

A new amateur expert, William Rautenbusch of Chicago, attracted attention by scoring 301, just outside the ten prize winners. He learned his golf on a nine-hole public links that has no bunkers, plays infrequently, and had never seen the Midlothian course until he started in the present tournament. His rounds were 76, 75, 75, 75. The next best amateur was Warrren K. Wood, formerly Western champion, who scored 305. The final scores:

Player.	Today.	Total.
W. C. Hagen, Rochester	148	290
*Charles Evans, Edgewater	141	291
George Sargent, Chevy Chase	146	297
*Francis Ouimet, Woodland	153	298
M. J. Brady, Wollaston	148	298
James Donaldson, Glenview	147	298
Louis Tellier, Canoe Brook	152	299
J. J. McDermott, Atlantic City	149	300
Arthur Smith, Columbus, Ohio	148	300
*William Rautenbusch, Chicago	150	301

James Simpson, Milwaukee, 154, 301; J. J. O'Brien, Mansfield, Ohio, 156, 302; Joe Mitchell, Upper Montclair, 156, 302; Bob Peebles, Topeka, 149, 302; James Barnes, Philadelphia, 153, 302; Tom McNamara, Boston, 159, 302; George Simpson, Omaha, 153, 302; C. H. Hoffner, Atlantic City, 149, 302; Dan Kenny, Olean, N. Y., 152, 303; Tom Kerrigan, Dedham, 154, 303; *Warren Wood, Homewood, 155, 305; Alex Ross, Braeburn, 158, 305; Walter Fovargue, Skokie, 154, 306; Jack Monro, Chicago, 150, 307; R. M. Thompson, Glenridge, N. J., 153, 307; Otto Hackbarth, Hinsdale, 152, 309; C. Nelson, Oklahoma City, 152, 310; Jack Burke, Port Arthur, Canada, 158, 310; Fred Brand, Mount Lebanon, 158, 310; Tom Vardon, Ontwentsia, 159, 311; W. J. Bell, Toronto, 153, 312; K. P. Edwards, Midlothian, 159, 312; H. Lagerblade, Youngstown, 159, 312; Alex Taylor, Ravisloe, 156, 313; William Kidd, Algonquin, 156, 313; C. W. Hall, Birmingham, 162, 315; Jack Jolly, Newark, N. J., 157, 315; *Jack Neville, San Francisco, 161, 316; George Cummings, Toronto, 158, 316; Dave McKay, Bellevue, 158, 317; John Gatherum, Ridgemore, 162, 317; Andrew Campbell, Philadelphia, 155, 318; J. C. Hackbarth, Midlothian, 162, 319; Jack Croke, Calumet, 160, 320; Willie Maguire, Houston, 163, 320; A. G. Herr, Lincoln, Neb., 162, 320; J. C. Green, Hot Springs, Va., 161, 322; J. R. Thompson, Philadelphia, 167, 325; Frank Adams, French Lick, 164, 325.

*Amateurs.

August 22, 1914

GOLF HISTORY AT A GLANCE.

Landmarks in the Progress of the Game from the Year 1457.

1457—Parliament ordains that golf be "utterly cryit doune, and nocht usit."
1491—Another law to the same effect.
1503—King playing golf extensively.
1552—Earliest reference to golf being played at St. Andrews.
1608—Present Royal Blackheath Golf Club founded.
1735—Present Edinburgh Burgess Golfing Society founded.
1744—Present Honorable Company of Edinburgh Golfers founded.
1754—Present Royal and Ancient Golf Club founded.
First Royal and Ancient Golf Club Competition.
1787—Glasgow Golf Club founded.
1818—Manchester Golf Club founded.
1829—Calcutta Golf Club founded.
1834—Royal and Ancient Club given that title.
1837—Royal and Ancient King William IV. medal first competed for.
1848—Gutty ball came in. ("Featheries" previously.)
1849—Famous foursome, Allan Robertson and Tom Morris vs. Brothers Dunn. Former couple won.
1853—Willie Park, Sr., played Tom Morris twice for £100 stake each time. Park won both.
1854—Royal and Ancient Club's clubhouse completed.
1859—Allan Robertson died.
1860—Open championship established. (Willie Park, Sr., winner.)
1863—King Edward VII., (then Prince of Wales) Captain of the Royal and Ancient Club.
1864—Present Royal North Devon Golf Club founded.
1865—London Scottish Golf Club founded.
1867—Tom Morris, Sr., won open championship for the fourth time.
1869—Present Royal Liverpool Golf Club founded.
1870—Tom Morris, Jr., won open championship for third time in succession and became owner of the belt.
1871—No championship.
1872—Tom Morris, Jr., won open championship for fourth time.
1873—Open championship first played for at St. Andrews.
1874—Open championship first played for at Musselburgh.
1875—Tom Morris, Jr., died.
Willie Park, Sr., won open championship for fourth time.
1878—Oxford and Cambridge University match first played.
1879—Jamie Anderson won open championship for third time in succession.
1882—Bob Ferguson won open championship for third time in succession.
1886—Amateur championship established. (H. G. Hutchinson winner.)
1887—Royal St. George's Golf Club founded.
1888—John Ball won amateur championship for the first time.
1889—Open championship last played for at Musselburgh.
1890—John Ball won both open and amateur championships.
1891—Parliamentary Handicap established.
1892—Championship of India established.
Open championship first played for at Muirfield. (H. H. Hilton winner.)
Edward Blackwell drove 366 yards from seventeenth tee at St. Andrews.
Amateur championship first played for at Sandwich.
1893—Ladies' championship established.
1894—J. H. Taylor won his first open championship.
Open championship first played for at Sandwich.
Right Hon. A. J. Balfour Captain of the Royal and Ancient Club.
Organization of the United States Golf Association.
1895—American open and amateur championships established.
1896—Harry Vardon won his first open championship.
F. G. Tait won his first amateur championship.
1897—Open championship first played for at Hoylake. (H. H. Hilton winner.)
1898—Coburn Haskell first experimented with Haskell rubber-cored ball in America.
1899—H. Vardon defeated Willie Park in a seventy-two-hole match.
Western Golf Association founded, Chicago, Ill.
1900—F. G. Tait killed in South Africa.
J. H. Taylor won his third open championship.
1901—H. H. Hilton won amateur championship for the second time.
James Braid won the first open championship.
1902—Rubber-cored ball introduced into Great Britain.
Amateur international match first played.
1903—Harry Vardon won his fourth open championship.
News of the world tournament established.
Professional international match first played.
W. J. Travis, (America,) won amateur championship.
1906—James Braid won his third open championship. International foursome over four courses—St. Andrews, Troon, St. Annes, and Deal—for £400, J. H. Taylor and H. Vardon vs. James Braid and A. Herd. Taylor and Vardon won by 13 and 12.
1907—John Ball won his sixth amateur championship.
A. Massay, (France,) won the open championship.
Deal added to list of open championship courses.
Appeal for patent in rubber-cored ball rejected by House of Lords.
1908—Tom Morris, Sr., died.
James Braid won his fourth open championship in the record score of 291.
New code of rules adopted.
1909—J. H. Taylor won his fourth open championship.
1910—John Ball won his seventh amateur championship.
Jubilee of open championship, James Braid winning for the fifth time.
New rules passed, excluding centre-shafted clubs.
1911—H. H. Hilton won the British and American amateur championships.
Harry Vardon won his fifth open championship of Great Britain.
1912—Jerome D. Travers won the American amateur championship a third time.
Harry Vardon won the News of the World championship.
1913—Francis Ouimet, a Boston Amateur, 20 years of age, defeated the professional golfing world of America, including Vardon, Ray, Tellier, and Reid, from Great Britain and France, in the open championship of the United States, at Brookline.
Miss Ravenscroft of England won the women's championship of America.
"Jerry" Travers won amateur championship of America for the fourth time.
1914—Harry Vardon won sixth open championship of Great Britain.
Oswald Kirkby won metropolitan open and New Jersey championships.
Walter Hagen, an American home-bred, 22 years old, won the open championship of United States with a score never made before over a championship course in an American national championship, namely, 290 strokes for 72 holes.

—From Spalding's Official Golf Guide.

August 30, 1914

GOLF RULE FOR "PROS."

They Will Get All of Money Prizes in Open Tournaments.

In future the entire amount of money prizes given in the national open championship under the auspices of the United States Golf Association will be divided among professionals, and in determining the award scores made by amateurs will be eliminated.

Such was the word received last night from U.S.G.A. headquarters. In the past it has been customary to allow an amateur to share the honors with the "pro", provided the score of the first named was good enough to get him into the prize list. Of course, he received no money. With regard to that, the Executive Committee has unanimously voted to amend Section 20 of the bylaws as follows:

"Strike out 'In the event of an amateur winning any of the above prizes he shall be given an equivalent in plate,' and substitute therefor:

" 'If the score, made by an amateur should entitle him to any of the above prizes he shall be given a suitable trophy in plate.' "

Concerning "Etiquette of Golf" the following new section has been drafted:

"Players who do not continue in the match play rounds of a tournament shall be considered to have forfeited any prize they may have won in the qualifying round."

This is to discourage the practice of dropping out of a tournament after taking part in a qualifying round and being drawn for match play. When a golfer fails to keep his match play appointment it often works to the detriment of the tournament.

April 23, 1915

PASSING OF "HOBO" GOLFER.

Players Now Wear Special Clothes on Links, and Not "Castoffs."

The day when the golfer thought it was necessary to look like a tramp to play good golf is passed, according to The Washington Post. Golf clothing is now as formal as the dress suit. At one time, any sort of "duds" was worn, and it was a common thing to see the most heterogeneous collection of clothing on the course. This never applied to women players, for they have always presented a neat appearance, for no woman likes to look unattractive, particularly to other women.

It was not an unusual sight to see a big car drive up to the clubhouse and unload a lot of men golfers whose dress was the last thing in the sartorial line. Ten minutes later the same crowd would make their appearance at the first tee in the worst lot of clothing imaginable.

Most of the golfers would wear the oldest sort of sweaters, soiled shirts, without collar or tie, and trousers smeared with dirt they had rubbed from their hands after teeing. Some would wear coats and some were without the one thing that is absolutely necessary to the English golfer. It was never possible to tell the station of the golfer from his golfing costumes. Even men who wear evening clothes nearly every evening in the week were not guiltless.

Then all of a sudden things changed. Golfers came to realize that it was possible to be comfortable in well-fitting clothes, that it was possible to wear both collar and tie without interfering with the golf; that soiled shirts and trousers were no longer de rigueur. Tailors began to make a specialty of golf clothing and the knickerbockers of our youth began to make their appearance on the links in great number. As a result, the sloppily clad player is the exception now. Men as well as women are as well dressed on the links as off.

It took some golfers years to realize that it is possible to play golf in a coat. Men would wear sweaters, for these gave them plenty of freedom, but any tailor can build a coat that has the same advantages as the sweater. Naturally, as the weather becomes warmer, the coat is laid aside.

Over in Great Britain, not to wear a coat on the links is as bad as driving a ball off a putting green. It is a custom that has been handed down for a century or more. In tennis and in other sports over there it is not necessary to don the coat, but it is just as essential a part of the golfer's clothing as are shoes. And this custom is the one that proved so much of a handicap for the American players.

With the exception of Walter J. Travis—who is an Australian—none of the big American players wears a coat in midsummer. Being forced to wear them in the British amateur championship was quite a hardship.

British professionals who play here soon get used to American habits, and you will find them playing well without coats.

August 17, 1915

3,500,000 GOLF PLAYERS.

Nearly That Number in Country, with Interest in Game Spreading.

The total number of men and women who play golf is greater than the total number of men and women who watch and play baseball, according to The Cleveland Plain Dealer. Golf is becoming a national game, because both men and women can play the game. Baseball has its devotees only in the masculine ranks. Women can watch the game, but few can either understand or play it.

Baseball is too strenuous for the person who does not play regularly. Many play until they reach 21. After that they quit the game as a regular form of exercise and pleasure, unless they go into the professional ranks. But golf is a game for all ages. The old as well as the young can play. It gives one as much fresh air as does baseball, and it keeps one healthy without straining the muscles

Those who could afford to play baseball can afford to play golf. It is not much more expensive. A set of golfing clubs, balls and other equipment does not cost much more than a baseball uniform, a half dozen bats, spiked shoes and other baseball paraphernalia.

There are in America today something like 600 golfing clubs allied with the United States Golf Association. That represents a golf population of at least 500,000. That is only a small part of the army of golfers. In every city where there are public links there are many golfers not associated with golfing clubs. They play either on the public links or on the private links at the invitation of some friend who happens to be a member of a club.

There are between 2,500,000 and 3,500,000 golfers in America today. When the big cities have completed their proposed public links the golfing army will be perhaps increased 2,000,000. It is estimated that there are about 200,000 golfers in New York City and vicinity, while there are about 800,000 in the State. Pennsylvania has about 400,000 putters.

Even for the spectator golf has more beneficial results. At a baseball game the spectator watches the play from the grandstand. At a golf match the spectators must do as much "leg work" as the players. He has to walk over the entire course if he wants to see all the play. Thus the golf spectators gets almost as much beneficial exercise as the golfer, while the only thing a baseball fan gets is cramped limbs and fresh air. In chilly weather the golf spectator can walk around and keep warm. The fan must sit in the stand and suffer chills.

"What is there about this game of golf that has increased its players from the 5,000 of ten years ago to the 2,500,000 or 3,500,000 of today?" is the question. And the answer is: "Try the game once."

September 19, 1915

ASSOCIATION FOR GOLF PROFESSIONALS

Want Voice in Conduct of Championships—To Uplift Its Members.

At a luncheon at the Taplow Club yesterday given by Rodman Wanamaker, which was attended by many prominent amateur and professional golfers, a movement was started to form an association of professional golfers of national scope. Up to this time all the professional golf associations in this country have been sectional in character, and they have never been able to cope with the questions of national importance in the golfing world. The men behind the present movement are those who are past and present champions, and leaders in the game of golf, including Francis Ouimet, A. W. Tillinghast, John G. Anderson, Gilbert Nicholls, Alec Smith, George Low, and many others.

According to Gilbert Nicholls, metropolitan open champion, who is one of the prime movers in the proposed organization, the association will benefit the whole golf world, both amateur and professional. At present the professional is laboring under many handicaps. He has no voice in the selection of the course or the conducting of the tournament for the national open championship, the Metropolitan open championship, or any other championship for which professionals are eligible. The task of bringing together the professionals who are out of work and the golf clubs that are in need of professionals is another phase of the work which this organization will take up.

For the benefit of the amateur organizations it is proposed that the professionals appoint a committee to investigate the character and the qualifications of all applicants for membership in the association, and that the organization stand responsible for the conduct of its members. The other side of this matter was also taken up, where the professional suffers at the hands of the club members who are lax in the payment of the professional for his services and supplies. With a powerful organization behind the professional it is felt that this evil would be curtailed.

The professionals feel that such an organization as they contemplate cannot be a success without the co-operation of amateurs, and for that reason a few prominent amateurs have been asked to accept positions on the controlling board which will direct the affairs and the policies of the association.

A committee of seven professionals was appointed to draw up tentative by-laws for the proposed association and to choose a permanent committee of a wider character to carry out the same work. The members of this committee are James Maiden, Nassau Country Club; James Hepburn, National Golf Links of America; Gilbert Nicholls, Great Neck Golf Club; Herbert Strong, Inwood Country Club; John Mackay, Dunwoodie Country Club; John Hobens, Englewood Country Club, and Robert White. About fifty professionals who were present enrolled as charter members of the organization.

It was also announced that Mr. Wanamaker, who is an enthusiastic golfer, will donate a cup and prizes for a world-wide tournament to be conducted along the plan of the News of the World tournament abroad, where the players qualify in districts and the survivors meet at some appointed course to finish the tournament at match play. This tournament will be open to both amateurs and professionals, native and foreign.

Another matter touched upon by the speakers was the necessity for educating the average professional and greens committeemen in golf course architecture.

Among the prominent amateurs and professionals present were A.W. Tillinghast, W.W. Harris, John G. Anderson, Francis Ouimet, John Sullivan, Gardiner White, J.G. Hollander, Walter Hagen, Thomas L. McNamara, Joseph Mitchell, W.G. Green, John Williams, Harry Vinal, John Hagen, H. Singleton, William Collins, and T. Fotheringham. There were about seventy-five guests present.

January 18, 1916

Sports

A Great American Golfer.

The national open championship of 1916 is a thing of the past, and on the pinnacle of golf in this country stands a figure that is attracting the admiring wonder of golf enthusiasts for at least four good reasons. Chick Evans is young, and that in itself is attractive; he earned the title by the skill of his hands and the courage of his heart, and that makes it a matter of justice; he is an amateur, and by this token he is the idol of thousands of those who love the game for what there is in it, not for what they can get out of it; he is an American, and throughout the country has swept a feeling of pride that a homebred youngster has been able to defeat those who, only a few short years ago, came to these shores to teach us how to play the game—the Englishmen whose golf is their lifework, the Scotchmen whose golf is their religion!

This is no sudden leap to fame for Evans. The wonder of it is, not that he has won a national championship, but that he never won such a title until now. The highest honors in golf evaded him so successfully year after year that it almost seemed as if the finest amateur golfer in this country, according to those who not only should know but do know, was never formally to mount the throne which is reserved for just such an accomplished personage. On five occasions he won the medal in the qualifying round of the national amateur championship, and on the same five occasions he was eliminated in the succeeding rounds of match play. Any golfer who can make such a record in the qualifying rounds must be of the highest order, and any golfer who does this and is then eliminated by players of avowedly lower calibre must have a weak link in an otherwise flawless chain of shots.

The weak link with Evans is putting. Unfortunately he knows it. Being young, he reflects upon it too much, with the result that matters grow worse instead of better. When Chick Evans is putting, he can defeat any golfer in the country. Almost single-handed he did what required the combined skill of Alec and MacDonald Smith—he defeated Vardon and Ray when they toured this country in 1914. At Minikahda last week the putts from the face of his club ran straight and true to the cup, with the result that he won the national open championship with the lowest score ever made in such a tournament. With the confidence that this victory has given him, his weakest link should strengthen until its weakness is no longer perceptible to his opponents, or, most of all, to himself.

Long off the tee, straight through the green, graceful and natural in every shot, Evans needs only to make his good putting permanent in order to insure the permanency of his position at the top of American golf.

July 3, 1916

Golf Clubs Make It Hard for Women to Play

Restrictions on Saturdays, Sundays, and Holidays Are the Rule at Most of the Organizations Round About New York

At Sleepy Hollow Women May Play on Saturdays, Sundays and Holidays Before 8:30 or After 11 o'Clock   (By Photo News Service.)

Although golf has been called a royal game, its privileges, in this country at any rate, do not appear to descend in the female line. The Salic law is applied to this ancient and honorable sport. In spite of the fact, or perhaps because of the fact, that thousands of women play golf at scores of clubs within a fifty-mile radius of Times Square, certain restrictions have had to be thrown about their use of the courses. This may be one of the next points of attack for the ardent feminists, some of whom would doubtless insist that they and their sisters had quite as much right at all times on the links as the mere men. However, whatever suffrage the women members of the many clubs may have, it does not appear to have been exercised to extend to them the unlimited usage of the course.

Saturdays, Sundays, and holidays are the days when many of the clubs put a complete or partial ban upon the fair sex in relation to the fair green. They may come to watch but not remain to play, to paraphrase the old adage. The reason behind this prohibition is not far to seek. These are the days on which the tired business man feels it—and not unjustly—his peculiar prerogative to rest and recreate. Obviously, if he is a golf player and therefore lost to other forms of outdoor sport, he wants the links to himself and his male friends, at least for a part of the day. The result is a host of varied limitations upon woman's freedom of the links.

There are some clubs, indeed rather a large number, in which no attempt is made to limit the play. In some cases this is due to the fact that there are few women members and they do not serve to crowd the course unduly on the days when it is most in use. In other cases the lack of restriction appears to be due to the recognition of self-imposed rules on the part of the women members, and their habit of allowing the men to get ahead or play through without interference. Several clubs set aside special days in each month for the use of their feminine members or for visiting women. The variations in the treatment of the subject are of the widest, but they are not the less interesting on that account.

It would not be entirely correct to say that the strictness of the limitations upon woman golfers varies directly with the skill—average skill—of the men in the club, but it is true that some of the most severe rules are to be found in clubs many of whose members are in the expert class. For example, the Garden City Golf Club, which numbers in its membership such redoubtable players as W.J. Travis, George T. Brokaw, J.M. Ward, and W.B. Rhett, to mention but a few, allows women to play on Monday and Friday mornings only and limits this privilege still further by requiring them to start before 11 o'clock. Such a thing as women on the course on a Saturday or Sunday is unheard of. In this most monastic of golf clubs women are not even welcomed within the doors of the club house, although they may make themselves at home on the veranda.

There is nothing about these restrictions at Garden City which is meant to be unchivalrous or ungallant. They arise from the fact that it is strictly a golf club—not a general country club—in the first place, and, secondly, from the general character of the membership, which is made up of men who wish to play golf undisturbed by any interfering element.

Another of the Long Island courses, that of the beautiful Piping Rock Club at Locust Valley, is also rather strict about its links. Women may not play on week days before 11:30 in the morning or after 3 in the afternoon. Nor may they play at all on Saturdays or Sundays unless they are accompanied by a member. This does not leave a very large part of the week open to the feminine swingers of clubs, but it has the effect of giving them the course very much to themselves on the week days, and is likely therefore to be appreciated by the more enthasiastic.

At the Great Neck Golf Club, at Great Neck, L.I. there are no set rules. The men have the right of way, however, and the women make no difficulty about letting them go through on the crowded days. In fact, the women at this club have a little organization of their own which makes it its business to police the course and see that the men are able to play through when the fairway is congested. By so doing they have probably earned sufficient gratitude from the members of the sterner sex to protect them for all time from any adverse legislation. This club has about fifty women members.

Just to show that the clubs known for their keen golf are not always to be found in the column of restrictions against the women, the Baltusrol Golf Club, at Baltusrol, N.J., may be cited. There are no restrictions, although among the low handicap men who make it their home club may be mentioned Max Behr, L.H. Conklin, E.P. Rogers, and C.E. Van Vleck, Jr. This lack of prohibitive rule may be partly explained by the fact that the course is a long, hard, and much-trapped one, and not at all the kind that usually appeals to the woman golfer of any but first rank.

At the Ardsley Club at Ardsley-on-Hudson there are no restrictions of a formal character, although there used to be some on the books. It has been found that women who wish to play on Saturdays and Sundays have good judgment and exercise the courtesy of the green, which permits the faster-playing men to go through, and if there is any tendency to obstruct the play or the course is unusually crowded the caddie master requests the women players to hold back—say between 12:30 and 3 o'clock—so that the men may have a start.

Not far away from Ardsley to the eastward, at the Apawamis Club, at Rye, the rules are of the definite rather than of the unwritten character. There no women may play on Saturday between the hours of 12 and 3 or on Sundays or holidays until after 3 o'clock. Here again the nature of the course undoubtedly has a good deal to do with the framing of the regulations, for Apawamis is of a sort to appeal to the woman player—which is not to say, by any means, that it loses anything of its allurement for the men. But it is not a course in which one must be eternally "slugging," to lapse into the jargon, and probably requires less of muscular effort than many other courses in this vicinity.

When one switches westward again to the Hudson River Valley, one finds another club with definite restrictions and a proviso to boot. This is the Sleepy Hollow Country Club at Scarborough-on-Hudson, where, by the way, the interesting "father and son" tournaments have been held with so much success. Parenthetically, this club was the scene not long ago of one of those lucky shots where a man puts his mashie or his mid-iron down in one. The difference about this particular shot was the way in which it was reported. A tyro golf writer interviewed the lucky player and announced in his story naively: "Mr. Blank said he had never made the hole in one before."

But to get back to the women who play golf at Sleepy Hollow they may play on Saturdays, Sundays, and holidays only if they start before 8:30 or after ll o'clock in the morning, and only—and here is the proviso aforementioned—if they do not obstruct the men.

The Upper Montclair Country Club, at Upper Montclair, N.J., which proudly boasts of the redoubtable Jerome D. ("Jerry") Travers as its star member, has about two score women members.

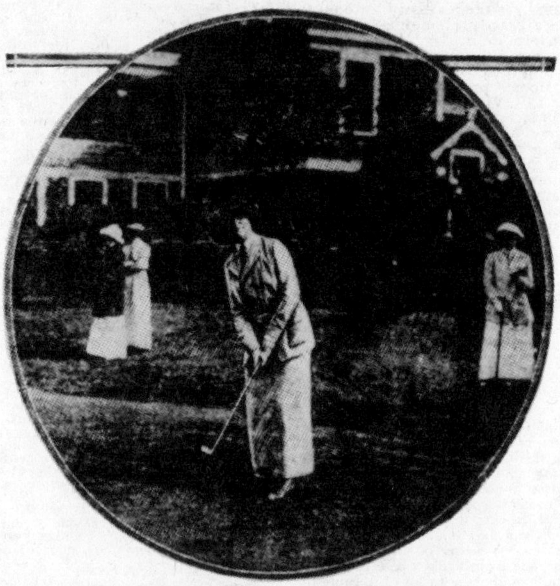

The Englewood Club Imposes No Restrictions on Women

But they must walk circumspectly on the days when their helpmates, brothers, and favorite young men can get away from business and devote themselves to what for the moment becomes the business of life. On holidays they are not permitted to use the course at all. On Saturdays they can play in the morning, and on Sundays after 3 o'clock in the afternoon. Here again it may be that the character of the course has an influence on shaping the rules, for, in spite of its hilliness, Upper Montclair has fairway and greens that should have a strong appeal to women players.

Wheatly Hills Golf Club at East Williston, that delightfully scenic part of Long Island, is one which has no restrictions as to its women members, but guests of the fair sex must be accompanied by members in order to play on the days of comparative congestion. Another of the unrestricted links is that of the Nassau Country Club at Glen Cove, L. I. At the Oakland Golf Club, at Bayside, L. I., women play from time to time, but they are not to be found in great numbers at any time, and not at all on the holidays. It is essentially a man's golf club. At the South Shore Country Club, at Bay Shore, L. I., there are no restrictions, and not a few women are to be found on the course on Sundays.

Wykagyl Country Club at New Rochelle appoints a special woman's day. The first Tuesday in each month is set aside for this purpose. Only those women who are associate members are permitted to play before 3 o'clock in the afternoon on holidays, Saturdays, and Sundays, and as there are but fifteen or twenty of these members, they do not have a tendency to clog the course. Just the opposite is the case at Dyker Meadow Golf Club, which has its course within the limits of Brooklyn. There is great practical difficulty in the way of allowing the women to play on Saturday or Sunday since the nine-hole course is overcrowded by its men members alone. For this reason the fair Dyker Meadowians must be content with the golf they can get on week days.

At the Saegkill Golf Club at Yonkers there are no rules in force which exclude women from the course at any time save when special competitions or the club handicaps are in progress. But this lenity is not to be found at the Siwanoy Country Club at Mount Vernon, where women are permitted to play on the week days at will, but must limit their Saturday use of the links to the morning hours, and may not play at all on Sundays or holidays. The Richmond County Country Club at Staten Island, on the other hand, has no restrictions governing its women members.

There is a large woman membership at the Hackensack Golf Club at Hackensack, N. J. In fact, about 275 women belong to this club, although by no means are all of them active golf players. In spite of this large feminine representation the men members have been audacious enough to enact strict rules which forbid the use of the course by women on Saturdays, holidays, or Sunday mornings.

At the Haworth Club, at Haworth, N. J., the men are very gallant. Not only have they no rules which keep women from playing on the days when the men are home from business, but it has come to be a rather general custom for those men who have golf-playing wives to play a round or two early in the day on Sunday with their male rivals and then go round later in the day wtih their better halves. This arrangement is said to cause general satisfaction and keep the club in a harmonious state. However that may be, it is an interesting variation of the restriction question.

Some of the other New Jersey courses are not so liberal in the matter of golf for women. At the Morristown Field Club, for instance, women may not play on Sundays. At the Canoe Brook Country Club at Summit they are permitted to play on Saturdays, Sundays, and holidays, but not before 10 in the morning or after 2:30 in the afternoon, while at the Country Club of Glen Ridge, which has about forty women members, the general custom is for them to let the men play ahead on the crowded days, although there are no fixed rules. At the Essex County Country Club, at West Orange, on the other hand, there are no restrictions of any kind against members or the wives of members. There are a number of women in the club who hold the golf privilege independently.

Although it has one of the most popular and, therefore, crowded courses in the Metropolitan district, the Englewood Country Club imposes no restrictions on its 125 associate women members. In addition to this membership it has some thirty or forty "house" members, who may play on week days only on payment of the course fee of $1. In spite of its lack of restriction it may be assumed that the sprinkling of women is rather slight at Englewood on those many Saturdays and Sundays in the season when players, in order to get a round, are sent off in pairs every five minutes, beginning surprisingly early in the morning.

At the Deal Golf Club, at Deal, N. J., women are especially asked not to "take a time" at the start. Any member may bring a woman guest on Saturday or Sunday, and any associate woman member may play, but in either case they are requested not to specify a particular hour or minute for starting, but just to come along and take their turn as they may find it.

The Arcola Country Club at Arcola, N. J., is among the most hospitable in the vicinity to the ladies. Not only does it not legislate against them if they are members at the week-ends or on holidays, but it sets aside Friday of each week as a day on which any women in the Metropolitan district may play over the course without charge. This applies, of course, to non-members, and is a rather unusual provision, especially when it holds good so many times a year.

The Morris County Golf Club at Convent, N. J., has had the misfortune to lose its clubhouse by fire, and this causes a practical difficulty which prevents it from taking care of women players for the most part. Before its loss, however, it had a rule which permitted visiting women to play on the third Tuesday of each month, and it never imposed restrictions as to play on its women members.

The Plainfield Country Club at Plainfield, N. J., extends its prohibitions to include junior members of both sexes. The juniors may not play after noon on Saturdays, nor at all on Sundays. Adult women may play on these days provided they are full members, otherwise they can play only if accompanied by a full member or a man. At the Scarsdale Golf and Country Club at Hartsdale in Westchester there are no restrictions on the play of women, but across the Connecticut line at the Wee Burn Golf Club at Noroton women are not permitted to play on Saturdays between the hours of 12 and 3 or on holidays until after 3:30 o'clock.

And so it goes all through the long list of clubs which demonstrate the popularity of golf hereabouts.

A bit of mathematics could easily show that there are more than a hundred women in the metropolitan district alone who could make the leaders of a decade ago look to their laurels, while the recent championships, with their starters close to a hundred in number, show the true enthusiasm for golf which the women of this country are exhibiting. This is indicated even more strongly, however, by the multitude of women not of championship or near championship calibre who are seen regularly on the links. They are getting a lot out of their golf in enjoyment and wholesome exercise, and even the Chairmen of the greens committees who feel called upon to rule them off the course on the busy days would hardly deny that they are contributing a lot to the game as well.

At any rate they are quite undaunted by Saturday and Sunday rules, these women golfers. And by accepting the situation resulting from congested courses and the habit American men have of crowding all their sport into the week-ends, they are manifesting a sportsmanship which makes it quite obvious why the clubs—even the crowded ones—do all they can to make them as welcome and as comfortable as the circumstances will permit.

July 30, 1916

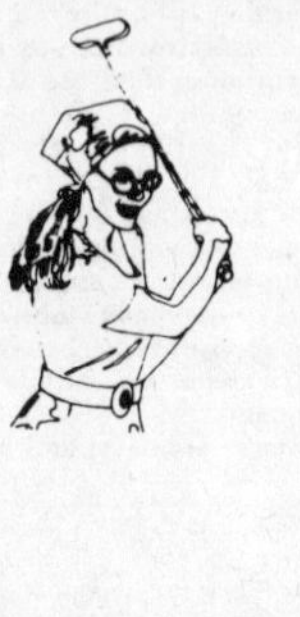

GEORGIA HAS GOLF MARVEL.

Thirteen-Year-Old Boy Lowers East Lake Club's Par by Five Strokes.

According to reports from Georgia there is a 13-year-old golfer in that part of the country who will soon give Chick Evans and Jerry Travers cause to look to their laurels. The boy is Bob Jones of the East Lake Country Club at Atlanta. Thomas B. Paine, Chairman of the House Committee of the club, is sponsor for a card of 68 that the youngster turned in for the 6,464-yard links of the home club. This ties the professional record for the course made by Stewart Maiden, a brother of Jimmie Maiden of Nassau, who is the professional in charge of the links.

Par for the long course is 73, and as he exceeded par by a stroke on two holes, he was required to beat par by a stroke on seven other holes. On the journey to the turn he got the 320-yard par 4 third hole in 3, the 440-yard par 5 fourth hole in 4, and the 230-yard par 4 eighth hole in 3, completing his outward journey in 34 strokes, three under par. He lost a stroke on the first hole coming in, but a 3 on the 380-yard par 4 twelfth hole brought him even again. On the 400-yard thirteenth he took another 3, but lost this advantage by getting a 6 on the 450-yard fourteenth. A 4 on the 480-yard fifteenth and a 2 on the 190-yard home hole gave him 34 strokes for his inward journey and a 68 for the entire round. His card follows:

Out 4 3 3 4 5 3 4 3 5–34
In 5 3 3 3 6 4 4 4 2–34–68

Last year when only 12 years old the boy won the championship of the Roebuck Springs Golf Club, an invitation tournament at Birmingham, Ala., the championship of the East Lake Country Club at Atlanta, the championship of the Druid Hills Country Club, and set new amateur records for the two last-named links.

July 6, 1916

VAST IMPROVEMENT IN WOMEN GOLFERS

Season's Advance Shown by Play of Miss Stirling, Miss Caverly, and Others.

When Howard F. Whitney, Secretary of the U.S.G.A., announced recently that the women golferswould be allowed to select their own course and dates for the 1917 championship, it was not taken as an indication of the "feministic" trend of modern times, nor even as a tribute to the superwoman, who, now that she has become acclimated, will doubtless appear on the links next season, but it was the fitting official recognition that the 1916 season saw greater improvement in women's golf than in any other department of the game in this country.

It has long been the wail of many golf experts that America had few women golfers, or perhaps none at all, who could safely and sanely be placed in the same category with the fair golfers of Great Britain and Ireland. When Miss Muriel Dodd and the former Miss Gladys Ravenscroft appeared at the women's national championship at Wilmington in 1913, they seemed so much superior to the native American golfers that pessimistic prophets agreed unanimously on the dismal outlook in women's golf for a decade to come.

The play of the youthful women's national champion of 1916, Miss Alexa Stirling of Atlanta is alone enough evidence to overturn these prophecies, but the outlook becomes even brighter after a scrutiny of the season's records of some of the other women golfers in the season which has just drawn to a close. Not to speak of the acquisition of Mrs. W.A. Gavin, who played from an American club in the national championship tournament this year, this tournament was marked by the fine play of four American women golfers, Miss Stirling, the ultimate winner; Miss Mildred Caverly, runner-up, and the two semi-finalists, Mrs. Thomas Hucknall and Mrs. C.C. Auchincloss, both metropolitan golfers. In addition to the individual play of these women, the successful team competition that the Women's Metropolitan Golf Association carried through its busiest season has given an impetus to women's golf that will carry it far in the coming year.

Of the work of Miss Stirling through the season nothing need be said except that she won everything in sight. Starting with the Southern championship at Chattanooga, where she won medal, title, driving, approaching, and putting contests, she continued her victorious march through the Huntingdon Valley tournament for the Berthellyn trophy, defeating the then national champion, Mrs. C.H. Vanderbeck of the Philadelphia Cricket Club by a decisive margin, and she fittingly closed the season by winning the national championship at Belmont Spring in early October.

It is not so much what she won, but the manner in which she did it that brings so much glory to this nineteen-year-old Southern girl, and so much pride to the women's golfing contingent in general. After watching her through tournament after tournament, John G. Anderson and other capable critics have pronounced her not a "fine woman golfer," but just a "fine golfer," with all that goes to make up a first-class individual of this rare species. Taught from her early childhood by the keen eye and the astute brain of Steward Maiden, the Atlanta professional, Miss Stirling plays every shot in the very mode and method of her instructor. Only one other amateur golfer plays with the entrancing style of the women's national champion and that is Bobbie Jones, Georgia State amateur champion, another pupil of Steward Maiden, who considerably enlivened things for Bob Gardner and other prominent golfers in the national amateur championship at Merion.

The runner-up to Miss Stirling in the national championship at Belmont Spring, Miss Mildred Caverly of the Philadelphia Cricket Club, is another of the younger set who has come forward rapidly in the last season. She is now the possessor of the Philadelphia title, and in her quest for the Berthellyn trophy and the national championship, it required the full powers of Miss Stirling to turn her from her goal.

A fine free player, especially from the tee, the young Philadelphian has a brilliant future in golf before her if she continues her progress. At Belmont Spring she profited by the help of two very capable instructors who were aiding her to perfect that ever-inefficient department known as the short game. One was Stewart Maiden, the Atlanta professional; the other was Miss Alexa Stirling, her conqueror in the final match for the title. On the afternoon before the final contest the ultimate winner spent the better part of an hour instructing her prospective opponent in the mysteries of the chip shot.

The play of Miss Stirling and Miss Caverly was no surprise, however, but what did cause astonishment was the appearance of two metropolitan players, Mrs. C.C. Auchincloss of Piping Rock and Mrs. Thomas Hucknall of Forest Hill, in the semi-final round. Certainly metropolitan golfers had a right to high position, but these were not the particular New York representatives that were looked upon for such brilliant performances. Mrs. Hucknall had taken up the game at a comparatively recent date, and Mrs. Auchincloss was playing in her first national tournament.

Mrs. Hucknall expected nothing but summary elimination when she faced the former national and international champion, Mrs. J.V. Hurd of Pittsburgh, in the first round. She won this match, however, and then defeated Miss Ethel Campbell of Philadelphia and Miss Laurie Kaiser, runner-up in the Western championship, before she succumbed to Miss Caverly in the semi-final round. Mrs. Auchincloss had two sensational battles on the Belmont links. To the utter astonishment of herself and the assembled multitude, she defeated Mrs. William A. Gavin, women's Eastern champion, and one of the favorites for the title, in the third round of match play. As if this were not enough distinction for a tournament tyro, she played against Miss Stirling on the following day and was the only player in the tournament who carried the women's national champion to the home green, where the last putt by the Atlanta girl decided the match.

With the sterling work of these golfers in the national championship, and with such players as Mrs. Vanderbeck and Mrs. Q.F. Feltner, five times the metropolitan champion, held in reserve for the coming season, the outlook for women's golf in America is more than hopeful—it is bright.

November 26, 1916

Current Events

Standardizing Golf Balls.

Coincident with the rumor that a new golf ball with a wonderful flight or carry is to appear this Spring comes the suggestion that golf balls be standardized as baseballs are. The objection raised against the new ball is as follows: Why keep on increasing the length of the links, setting traps at certain distances from the tees, regulating water hazards, and speculating upon natural difficulties when some man can invent a process of making a ball with an extra flight of twenty yards or so that will completely upset the whole scheme of the golf world as exemplified in the courses themselves?

Yard after yard has been added to course after course, until the average high-class links is 6,400 or more yards in length. Is this the limit, or will the supercourse on which the superman will play in the next decade or so extend over 7,000 yards? Many of the wiser critics of the game are shaking their heads in a warning manner over the alarming situation. Will the golfer of the future need the endurance of a camel and the walking qualifications of an Edward Payson Weston? On a purely mathematical basis, if the length of golf courses increases in the next fifteen years in the same proportion as that in which it has increased since 1902 the lot of the golfer will be hard indeed.

However, it is highly improbable that this will be the case. As the old gutty ball passed into disuse and the lively ball was brought into play the links were necessarily lengthened as progress was made by the manufacturers in the improvement of the new balls. Now the process of making golf balls has risen to such a state of perfection that improvements do not tend toward greater distance, but to better control. Undoubtedly a ball with a greater flight than any of the varieties used in the championships can be made by many of the leading manufacturers, but they do not make them, nor is it probable that they will make them. The loss of control would not be balanced by the gain in distance. The links are safe for the nonce.

March 26, 1917

NEW GOLF CLUB INVENTED.

Since distance has become the bugbear of the golf links and as architects have universally accepted the course of 6,000 yards and more, makers of drivers, spoons, and brassies are vying with the manufacturers of golf balls for something which will help the expert, as well as the duffer, to get over the ground easier. In the last few years many improvements have been made in golf balls but it remained for Peter Robertson, professional at the Yahmundasis Golf Club, to discover a new club, one which he guarantees will send the elusive ball flying over all of the rough and much of the fairway of any course.

Robertson's innovation is not in the build of the wooden clubs, but rather in the finish. He has weighted the club from the bottom, putting the weight under the ball instead of directly behind the centre of the ball, which has been customary in most drivers and brassies.

Robertson has built a brass plate which covers the bottom of the club head and dips up the back of the club head of a point just below where the centre of the ball would fit. He contends that a ball, to get the greatest distance, should be hit so that the greatest weight of the club is below the middle of the ball. Furthermore there is claimed for this most recent invention in golf the fact that there is stability of club weighted with lead, the Robertson plate being screwed to the bottom of the face of driver or brassie as the case may be. The principle has also been applied to putters.

At the Yahmundasis Club more than three-fourths of the wooden clubs are of the Robertson type, and the principle has been taken up as well by a number of prominent golfers of other courses. Gillman Tiffany, after his return from a match at Elmira for the benefit of the Red Cross a few days ago, remarked that he considered the Robertson type of club one of the most valuable he had ever used.

July 28, 1918

EVANS SHORN OF LAST GOLF TITLE

Since Defeat by Ouimet Holder of Many Crowns Has Nothing to Adorn Brow.

When Francis Ouimet holed his winning putt on the home green against Chick Evans in the second round of the national amateur championship at Oakmont last week he robbed the Chicagoan of his last title, national amateur champion. Ever since that July day in 1909 when the brilliant youngster from the Edgewater Club first sprang into prominence by capturing the Western amateur championship he has been a peril to all opponents through the green, and has garnered many and important titles in his ten years of tournament play. At Flossmoor, in 1909, the practically unknown youngster had to defeat Albert Seckel, then intercollegiate champion, in the final round for the Western title, which he did by the narrow margin of 1 up.

He lost this title in the following year in the final round against Mason Phelps, but he since won it three separate times in 1912 at Denver, in 1914 at the Kent Country Club, Grand Rapids, Mich., and in 1915 at Mayfield. He was also medalist in several of these tournaments, where he eventually captured the title. Francis Ouimet slipped out West in 1916 and snared the championship, and upon the resumption of play this year Harry Legg of Minnikahda fell heir to the honor.

Evans not only won the Western amateur championship on four occasions, but he invaded the professionals' territory at the Beverly Country Club links in Chicago and defeated George Simpson for the Western open title. A peculiar thing about this open championship was that it was held at match play instead of the usual medal play style which the pros prefer. However, Chick showed he was an adept at both styles by taking not only the title, but the medal in the qualifying round with a score of 71.

Makes American Record.

Not satisfied with Western and sectional titles, Evans bent all his efforts toward annexing the national championships, but he was doomed to a long hard journey before he finally obtained the desire of his heart at Merion in 1916, where he defeated Bob Gardner, defending champion, in the final round for the national amateur championship. It took him all the seven biblical years of labor to accomplish this, but when it was done it was worth all the trouble, for he had fought his way to a double throne, national amateur and national open championship, in a single year. Before he captured the amateur title at Merion in September he had already brought home the national open title at Minnikahda in June, where he tore the prize from the outstretched hands of the best home-bred and foreign-born pros that America could muster.

His victories in 1916 set a high-water mark in American golf, for it was the first time in the history of the royal and ancient game in this country that any one had ever captured the amateur and open titles in a single year. This feat had been accomplished only once before in the history of the game, when the great English amateur, John Ball, in 1890 won the British amateur championship at Hoylake and the British open championship at Prestwick.

Due to the suspension of competition during the war Evans held this high seat of honor until this season. He defended his open title at Braeburn, but Walter Hagen and Mike Brady left him struggling back in the field, with Hagen eventually winning from the Boston pro and capturing the title for the second time. Chick came to Oakmont with but one title to defend of all those that had formerly adorned his brow.

Just Plain Charles Evans.

When he encountered Francis Ouimet he knew that it was "do or die" for him, and if he had successfully passed the Bostonian in all probability he would have retained his title. But Francis had been saving for this match for all of four years. He had but one ambition at Oakmont—to meet and defeat Chick

Evans and settle the question of superiority which adherents of both players had so long and bitterly debated. Ouimet won, and though he was defeated the next day by "Woody" Platt of North Hills, he retired content from the tourney.

Ouimet still holds a title, being the present Massachusetts amateur champion, but Charles Evans, Jr., of Edgewater, former Western amateur champion, former Western open champion, former national open champion, and former national amateur champion, took his sorrowful way back to Chicago as Charles Evans, Jr., Esq., from the Edgewater Club. But Chick has lost none of his skill, as his great match with Ouimet testified, and it will not be long before he once again will surround himself with medals and titles that are due to a golfer of his ability.

S. Davidson Herron of Oakmont, or "Davie" as he is better known in the Pittsburgh area, is a hitter of terrific might from the tee. To the casual observer, he appears to be too much of a mountain of flesh to get many results, but if the casual observer follows "Davie" in a breathless hike over Oakmont's hills and dales, he is more than likely to offer profuse apologies to the new national amateur champion, for he is quick on his feet, quick with his hands and still quicker with his brains. His swing is not the long graceful whirl of Max Marston, nor has it the natural beauty of the form of Bob Jones, but it is fast and symmetrical, and gets results that awe those who see him play for the first time. Four hundred and sixty yards uphill is as good as 500 yards on the level any time, and Herron was regularly home in two shots to the 462 yard ninth green. Not two wooden club shots at that, for in the final round against Jones he was hole high twice with a drive and a midiron. Jesse Guilford, Bob Gardner, and other long hitters had best look to their laurels in this field, for "Davie" looks to be treading right on their heels, and crowding them fast.

August 26, 1919

BARNES KEEPS TITLE BY BEATING M'LEOD

Champion of the Professional Golfers Wins Final Match by 6 and 5.

PUTTING DECIDING FACTOR

Long Jim Gives a Wonderful Display on the Greens — $500 Purse Goes with Title.

Jim Barnes, the long, lanky Britisher who is now attached to the Sunset Hill Club of St. Louis, retained his title of golfing champion among professionals by winning the final round at Roslyn yesterday from Freddy McLeod of the Columbia Club, Washington, D. C. The 1919 tournament ended on the thirty-first hole with Barnes 6 up and 5 to play.

Yesterday's victory gave Jim Barnes his fourth championship on American links this season. Previously he had won the Western and Southern open titles and the North and South open. In the eyes of many he stands today as the greatest professional golfer in the United States, although there will always exist the disappointing feature of this year's pro tournament that Walter Hagen, national and metropolitan open champion, did not compete. Hagen had his opportunity to qualify, in common with every other golf instructor, and he declined to be a participant. But the followers of professional golfing will concede to Jim Barnes one certain honor. In match play there is probably no other adopted foreigner or home-bred who can compare to this tall Cornishman.

In defeating Fred McLeod yesterday, Barnes succeeded to his title as peer of the pros, which he won in 1916 at Siwanoy and which had not since been put up for competition. McLeod gained the final round by triumphing decisively over such stars of the links as J. Douglas Edgar of Atlanta, the Canadian open champion, and George McLean, who beat Mike Brady, the runner-up this year to Hagen. And Barnes himself put out of the running such recognized leaders as Bob Macdonald and Emmet French there was no mistake, no fluke victories at Roslyn over the Engineers' Club course last week.

A Match of Golfing Gems.

Every possibility of golf was included in the rare treat offered yesterday to six or seven hundred bred-in-the-bone fans who comprised the gallery. There was an abundance of putts from twenty to thirty feet long. There were chip shots dead to the pin which evoked gasps of wonder. And as a finale to the tournament there was an approach shot in the afternoon round made from a point eighty yards from the hole which ran in. Such performances are not every day occurrences even on the easy courses. It takes not merely professionals but top-notch professional linksmen to play such golf.

It would have been hard to find a more interesting pair for a final round of championship play than Barnes and McLeod. The former, long, lanky, deliberate, is every inch the golf marvel of story books. The latter, small, slender, quick, is a typical challenger and opponent. And between them, they exhibited match playing yesterday the equal of which doesn't exist.

There was nothing about yesterday's round which indicated McLeod was hopelessly outclassed. This 1908 national open champion actually led the great Barnes during a good part of the morning round, and he never stopped trying until the final putt had been cupped in the afternoon. McLeod began work yesterday by winning the first hole. At the turn he was ahead and after ten holes he led by 2 up. Right then and there some magnificent golf began which amply repaid the several hundred New Yorkers who made the long trip to Roslyn. Barnes came up from behind because he had to, and he continued to play winning golf because he had to play superior golf to shake off an opponent of McLeod's breed.

Barnes's Game Is a Study.

Golfers who give up easily, golfers who quit without half trying, should study Jim Barnes's game. Those who play well enough when winning but who fall down hopelessly once they drop behind would do well to profit by his methods.

Barnes gave two shining examples last week of pulling up in the pinches. On Wednesday, after Otto Hockbarth had him 3 down at the eighteenth, Barnes jammed his toe on the accelerator and speeded up to a brand of golf that was unbeatable. Again yesterday he was faced with the same conditions, but instead of simply holding his own, he uncorked a system of golf which rapidly as well as surely took him into the lead. Jim Barnes, when playing the match game, has nothing if not a reserve of winning golf. He appears to stroke his game always just a little better than his opponent. He doesn't try to win by wide margins when narrow advantages are sufficient. He tries out a rival's nerve and mettle and fits his own game accordingly. When up against a dangerous adversary he turns loose the best playing he has; against a weak opponent he merely plays well enough to win and does not exert himself. That constitutes top-notch golf. That is the secret of Barnes's phenomenal game.

Yesterday morning Long Jim put Freddy McLeod to the test. He played along at an average ability for a time until he found himself 2 down. Only then did the real, successful, victorious Barnes begin to come into display.

Barnes Loses First Hole.

Barnes lost the first hole by somewhat careless golf. His second shot lodged in a sand trap and his third was wasted trying to get out. He was on the green in 4 and in the cup in 6, to McLeod's 4. Each furnished a surprise at the second. Here is a par 4 hole, which both men halved in birdie 3s, Barnes as a result of a 12-foot putt, and Freddy with one eight feet long. Long Jim took another birdie 3 on the third, squaring the match when McLeod did a 4. The champion's approach was one of those strokes which cause golfers to brag long and vociferously. It was a pitch shot dead to the pin.

The fourth should have been McLeod's. Barnes drove to the rough, approached short, but he clipped up well and sank a 15-foot putt for a halve. Then they divided on the next two, still keeping the match all square. McLeod topped his drive and directed his brassie poorly on the fifth, losing the hole, but his rolling putt of 12 feet for a 3 on the next beat Barnes. They halved the seventh.

The Scot won the short eighth when Barnes played like a Van Cortlandt dub. He pulled his drive into the trees, as he did all the week almost without exception at this tricky hole. Stymed behind a tree, he had to wrap one leg around the trunk in snakelike fashion. With this handicap he pitched far across the green to a sand trap and picked up, conceding the hole. They halved the 565-yard dog-legged ninth hole after both had wasted shots trying to gain the green, and McLeod stood 1 up at the turn.

McLeod Reaches 2 Up.

Barnes got trapped on the tenth, flubbed one more, and then pitched fifty yards too far with his nibblick and again conceded a hole to the Washingtonian, making the latter 2 up.

Right here enters the steady, sure, victorious Barnes. He was 2 down and in a dangerously bad position. But Barnes can win when he has to, and how he began. In the remaining eight holes of the first round, Barnes actually won seven, and halved one changing his standing from 2 down to 5 up by the end of the morning round.

In baseball they would call this a rally; in golf it is a Barnesism.

On those eight holes, Barnes stroked for a total of one under par, two being made in birdies, one in a single stroke over par and five were halved with the regulation figures.

Although McLeod was outdriven on practically every tee, his downfall was due directly to his wretched putting. On the eleventh green he only rimmed the cup when he should have sunk his ball. On the twelfth and seventeenth he missed halves by failing to putt down from ten to twenty inches away.

Barnes Putts Carefully.

Barnes never attempted to use his putter without first sizing up his line of direction and the surface of the green. Above all he was slow and careful. McLeod putted hurriedly and, it would seem, without sufficient aim.

The morning cards:

Out—										
Barnes	6	3	3	4	4	4	4	6	6—40	
McLeod	4	3	4	4	5	3	4	3	6—36	
In—										
Barnes	6	4	4	4	2	4	5	4	4—37	—77
McLeod	4	5	5	5	3	5	5	5	5—42	—78

In the afternoon, starting the second round, McLeod promptly won the first, and the match stood 4 up for Barnes. Then followed some playing which was more good and bad luck than high-class golf. Barnes won the second, after Freddy had thrown it away by two short approaches. The third went halved.

McLeod pitched over into a trap on the fourth, then used his niblick with such force that his third sailed across the green and into a field high with grain. Freddy called it a lost ball and cut short the search. Again McLeod failed to hole a short putt, and the fifth went to Barnes. They halved the next, and on the seventh McLeod drew a hearty round of applause by winning after an approach dead to the pin.

McLeod Holes 80-Yard Approach.

The eighth provided one of those rarities of golf which always go down in history. McLeod drove to a mean hanging lie in a sand trap, and made matters worse by pitching across the green to tall grass. But from a seemingly impossible lie atop a pile of dry weeds and debris, 80 yards from the cup, Freddy niblicked to the green and the ball rolled in for a 3. The shot would not be duplicated in a hundred years.

McLeod continued to win his third straight by taking the ninth after Barnes had twice played short. That put the champion only 4 up at the turn.

Again it was McLeod's putting which kept him underneath. He lost the tenth by missing a roll four feet long after Barnes had holed one from fully twenty feet from the pin. Long Jim made it 6 up on the eleventh by taking advantage of McLeod's waste of opportunity in the rough off the course. Freddy took the twelfth, however, after Barnes's approach shot had been played too strong.

Long Jim Makes 30-foot Putt.

Barnes showed perhaps the greatest example of his wonderful ability on the thirteenth, which proved to be the last. This hole is 413 yards long for a par 4. Even after slicing, Barnes played his approach shot with such accuracy that he reached the green handily. He was thirty feet from the hole and most golfers would have played this safe, with two putts. Not Jim Barnes. He played for a win and got it by rolling down the putt. This finished the match, 6 and 5.

The afternoon cards:

Out—									
Barnes	5	5	4	4	4	4	5	4	6—41
McLeod	4	6	4	*	5	4	4	3	5
In—									
Barnes	3	4	5	3					
McLeod	4	5	4	4					

Handsome prizes accompanied the victory yesterday. Barnes received the purse of $500 and a diamond medal as well; and his club becomes the holder of a silver trophy for one year. McLeod's share as runner-up is a purse of $250 and a gold medal. These awards are donated annually for the pros' tournament by Rodman Wanamaker.

September 21, 1919

GOLFERS NOT HELD TO STANDARD BALL

It Applies Chiefly to Championships, but Is Expected to Become Generally Popular.

Although the date on which the rule on the new standard ball will go into effect is May 1 of this year, still more than three months distant, speculation is rather strong among golfers as to just what it is going to mean. It is understood, of course, that the new standard will be 1.62 inches in diameter and 1.62 ounces (avoirdupois) in weight. This ball will be played in all championship tournaments. But what appears to puzzle the golfing public is whether that will be the only ball turned out by manufacturers or will they continue to make them of other specifications and the like.

Briefly it may be stated that there will continue to be an output of balls of other specifications. Mainly because there is a very persistent demand for them and also because the new rule does not prohibit their manufacture or use even in championship tournaments, for that matter. What the rule really prescribes is that for a ball weighing as much as 1.62 ounces, the minimum diameter must not be less than 1.62 inches.

This does not prevent the use of a ball of that diameter that weighs less. Neither does it prevent the use of a heavier ball, provided the diameter is larger. The real purpose of the rule is to prevent the use of the small, heavy ball, since its small mass with extra weight tends to extra momentum, when driven by a strong force, and was deemed to be throwing out of proportion thousands of golf holes in the country, thereby necessitating the additional expenditure of hundreds of thousands of dollars in alterations to keep pace with the development of balls.

Favored by Strong Players.

As a matter of fact, the use of the small, heavy ball was confined practically to the low handicap player, or at any rate to the husky, robust walloper, who could also scoop the small spheroid up from a close lie. On the other hand, thousands of players throughout the country prefer a larger, lighter ball, and will continue to play it undisturbed by the new ruling.

The attitude of ball manufacturers generally has not been announced to the golfing public. However, it is known that one of the largest manufacturers in the country will go in strongly for the production of the new standard article. This firm, by the way, makes one of the most popular, if indeed, not the most popular ball used in the United States, and its efforts will be directed largely toward retaining the patronage of the low handicap men with a ball meeting the new requirements.

There may be a ray of sunshine for the golfer in the situation which has developed from the enactment of the standard regulation. This has to do with a reduction in the price of balls already made up and in stock, which do not come within the new requirements. One prominent manufacturing company, stocked up with the small, heavy balls, expects to announce before many more weeks a reduction in price on these.

This reduction should meet with a hearty welcome from golfers. In these days of frenzied finance the cost of golf is ridiculously high, and anything that tends toward trimming the expense involved ought to prove popular. There is little reason to believe that the above stock will not find ready purchasers. Of course they cannot legally be used in tournament play, at least championship tournaments. But such play constitutes but a small percentage of the total of golf played in the country. For every round of tournament play, there is, roughly speaking, at least twenty in friendly matches, and the saving represented in a reduced price on balls in such matches will be very considerable.

Experts Test New Ball.

Incidental to the new ball, a few experiments abroad of a somewhat interesting nature have been made. George Duncan, British open champion, and Abe Mitchell did a bit of experimenting with the standard ball a short time since. They tried several of the standard article along with others with which they had been accustomed to playing, and announced afterward that they got better distance with the new ball than they did with their old favorites.

Experts over here have yet to make any comparison, at least none have been reported. However, several well known professionals have expressed doubt as to whether or not introduction of the standard ball is going to make any appreciable difference in the game. They scout the idea that a player can make any adequate test, since it is next to a physical impossibility for a man to play ten or twenty shots and put the same amount of force and timing into any three or four of them. Until results are authentically settled by means of some mechanical device, the prevailing opinion here is that no appreciable difference between the new standard ball and the old one in most popular use will be observed.

January 23, 1921

HUTCHISON CAPTURES BRITISH GOLF TITLE

Chicago Player Becomes First American to Win Coveted Open Championship.

HAS NINE-STROKE MARGIN

Leads Roger Wethered by 150 to 159 at End of 36-Hole Playoff at St. Andrews.

FIRST ROUND HARD FOUGHT

American Three Strokes Ahead at the Turn After Brilliant Struggle, but Gains Rapidly.

Copyright, 1921, by The New York Times Company.
Special Cable to THE NEW YORK TIMES.

ST. ANDREWS, June 25.—Jock Hutchison of Chicago won the British open golf championship today for America, beating Roger Wethered, the young Oxford amateur, by 150 to 159. At the end of the first round Wethered, with 77, was only 3 down, but after that experience began to tell in decisive fashion.

Hutchison played magnificently in the final round, while Wethered seemed to suffer from nerves. He had a chance to get up at the second hole, but threw it away by poor putting, and then Hutchison made the fifth and longest hole in a splendid 3. His play from then on aroused the greatest enthusiasm among his old friends at St. Andrews. He was a caddie there before he

went to America, and it was generally admitted that never had a finer performance been seen on the historic links than his last round. He was actually twelve strokes ahead at the fourteenth hole, but Wethered cut his lead down by three at the end.

It was the first time that an American player has won the British open, and the feat was accomplished only after an exhibition of great brilliancy and a struggle that was hard fought to the extreme in the earlier stages. Rarely has a more thrilling exhibition been seen on the famous Old course.

Hutchison was a 5 to 1 favorite when the replay for the open championship began at St. Andrews this morning, but he had to produce his very best game to lead at the end of the morning round by three strokes, 74 to 77. Wethered, after being four strokes behind at the tenth hole, rallied wonderfully. Against any one less skilled than Hutchison in playing the low-running approach, which St. Andrews rewards so handsomely, or the high-pitched approach when the occasion made it appropriate, the young English amateur would have held his own.

The only marked difference between the men was that, whereas Hutchinson showed he could play either kind of approach, Wethered always got up to the hole with a high pitch. That he dropped behind at one stage was due to the fact that he could not always prevent these shots from running over the green.

Heat Favors American.

It was a day of glorious sunshine, although the heat was likened to that of Chicago in midsummer, and people thought that Hutchison would feel at home, in the double sense that he was playing on the course where he learned the game and in temperature to which he has become accustomed since making his home in America nineteen years ago.

The players shook hands heartily before starting, and it was a fine sporting game, with Hutchison's efforts making the hearts of his former fellow-townsmen palpitate. The American gained a lead of two strokes at the third hole with a great 3. A beautiful shot with the ribbed mashie niblick, which he used very effectively all day, and a 4-yard putt put Wethered level at the fourth, 427 yards, with an equally brilliant 4. Hutchison took a 6 here through missing his drive and finding the bunker with his third.

A remarkable hole was the seventh. Wethered after a bad drive bunkered his second and made a recovery shot that rolled down the slope. He holed out from fifteen yards for a 4; then Hutchison holed a 9-yard putt for the same score. This began a sequence of 3's. The American did the short eight in that figure and also the ninth, where he got down a 3-yard putt. At the tenth he raised a great cheer by laying an approach of ninety yards to within two feet of the pin.

Wethered in Rally.

Wethered was now four strokes behind, but he began to recover them at the thirteenth with some brilliant shots. At the next two holes he reduced his deficit to one. Going to the seventeenth he pulled his drive and, using his spoon for the second shot from a bad lie, he missed it and had to struggle for a 5 while Hutchison had a beautiful 4. Going to the last hole after a long delay in marshalling the crowd, Wethered hit a roll-mashie niblick shot which finished rolling on the grassy slope beyond the green and he took a 5. Hutchison played a correct St. Andrews shot, running his approach to within three yards of the pin, but just missed the putt. "Oh, Jock!" one of his old St. Andrews friends wailed in anguish, but Hutchinson had made few such slips as this.

The scores were:

Hutchison—
Out .... 4 5 3 6 5 4 3 3 —
In .... 3 4 4 5 5 4 5 4 —

Wethered—
Out .... 4 5 5 4 6 4 4 4 —
In .... 4 7 4 7 4 4 5 4 —

There was a quick and dramatic turn in the afternoon. For two holes Wethered seemed to be continuing his great fight, and he had a fine chance of reducing his deficit

to two strokes at the second hole. There Hutchison was bunkered from the drive, and only just got out with his next. Wethered was on the knoll at the corner of the green in the same number of strokes, but instead of playing his long putt dead he ran two yards past, and missed the return putt, each man taking 5. If Wethered could have regained his stroke here he would have been dangerously close to Hutchison, and that in itself would have given him heart. But Hutchison having had a narrow escape saw to it that his rival had no further opportunity.

Reaches Turn in 33.

From this point on his golf was simply magnificent. None better has been seen in any championship. He reached the turn in 33, which has been done by only two men in the whole week—Tom Kerrigan and Arnaud Massey.

Hutchison began to forge well ahead in the second round. At the fourth hole he had a 4 against Wethered's 6. The latter paid too much heed to the cross wind here. He played his mashie approach into a wind blowing from left instead of going straight for the pin. But the ball did not come around, it dropped into a bunker to the left of the green. Then Hutchison applied what was almost the finishing touch at the fifth, the longest hole on the course, measuring 530 yards. He got down for a 3, while Wethered had only an ordinary 5, and so lost another two strokes, which made him altogether 7 behind.

Hutchison now was playing like a machine. He followed up a perfect approach to the sixth by holing a four-yard putt for a 3 against Wethered's 4 and holed a two-yard putt for a 4 at the seventh. Here Wethered, his confidence shaken, frittered away an opportunity by taking three putts in four yards and a 5 for the hole. The amateur was letting himself go at his hardest from the tee and was outdriving Hutchison by thirty yards. Now Wethered drove to the ninth and tenth greens, 306 and 323 yards, respectively, but could not putt, and Hutchison, playing with his head, held his own.

The American led by 9 strokes at the turn. He took two shots in the formidable bunker to the left of the eleventh green, a short hole which has been the grave of many hopes, but he secured a 5 against a 4. Wethered then had many misadventures, having to play back into a bunker at the fourteenth. He was twelve strokes down then, but recovered three in the last three holes, which was all he could save from the ruins.

The cards:

Hutchison—
Out .... 4 5 4 4 3 4 4 3 3—33
In .... 4 5 5 4 5 4 5 6 5—13

Wethered—
Out .... 4 5 4 6 5 4 5 3 3—39
In .... 4 7 4 7 4 4 6 4—43

Hutchison was greeted with a great round of applause by the 5,000 onlookers when he holed the last putt. He was presented at once with the championship cup and was carried shoulder high from the green, waving the cup aloft and calling for three cheers for the British players. He sails with the cup next Saturday, accompanied by Duncan and Mitchell, who are going to try to bring back the United States cup.

Hutchison's Victory Hailed.

Golfers in the metropolitan district were elated yesterday when word was received that Jock Hutchison, the genial Scotchman who holds forth as professional at the Glen View Golf Club, just outside of Chicago, had won the British open golf championship. And there were reasons. In the first place, it was the first time that any American had ever succeeded in capturing the greatest honor that can come to any golfer; in the second place, the winner is perhaps the most popular member of the professional golf fraternity; and in the third place, his victory was especially welcome after the dismal failure attending the invasion of the two other American forces, the amateurs at Hoylake and the women at Turnberry.

Hutchison's victory is, perhaps, as popular on the other side of the water as on this, for his home is but a short distance from the course on which he yesterday won his honors, and it is the course on which he gained his experience.

It was over this same course, upon the occasion of a visit to his old home during the Winter months, that Hutchison gave an inkling of his achievement yesterday by breaking the course record. Upon his return to this country he immediately joined the other golfers in the South, where he succeeded in capturing most of the honors that were in sight, ending with the winning of the North and South championship at Pinehurst.

At that time he ventured the opinion that, if the plan to send a team of

American pros to the British open championship materialized, the title would come to America, and he proved himself to be a good prognosticator. Even shortly before he sailed, Hutchison playing in exhibition foursome along with Jim Barnes and George McLean at St. Albans, in a playful moment predicted that he would capture the title. It was not a boastful declaration but merely indicated the Scotsman's supreme confidence.

Hutchison came to American shores seventeen years ago, attracting the attention of William Carnegie, a nephew of the late financier, who placed him on a course at Cumberland Island. He went to the Allegheny Country Club, Pittsburgh, and, after winning the Western Pennsylvania open title five times and the Western open once, was engaged as professional at the Glen View Golf Club, Chicago.

His first real achievement in the golf world came when he tied for second place in the Western open in 1916 and the same year he was second to Chick Evans in the national open, taking 288 strokes as against 286 for Evans.

He did not get close to the top again until 1920 when he won the Western open and the P. G. A. title and also tied with Leo Diegel. Jack Burke and Harry Vardon for runner-up, one stroke behind the winner, Ted Ray.

Beginning last Winter, he seemed to come into his own, for after his performance at St. Andrews, where he set a new record for the course, he returned and rushed to the South, where he won the majority of tournaments in which he started.

June 26, 1921

Bobby Jones, Using Only One Hand, Has 42 for Nine Holes

ATLANTA, Sept. 6.—Bobby Jones, Atlanta's youthful golfer, has added new laurels to his record of achievements in the golfing world. Playing only with his right hand yesterday, he shot a 42 on the first nine holes of the East Lake course, a distance of 3,320 yards. He made a 6 on the 610-yard fifth hole and a 4 on the 525-yard ninth. Jones suffered burns to his left hand last week which rendered that member useless for golfing purposes for a while, but he expects to play in the national amateur championship tournament at St. Louis.

September 7, 1921

Walter Hagen ("The Haig") was the preeminent professional golfer of the 1920's.

Gene Sarazen was one of the early greats of golf. He won seven major titles, including three PGA's and the first Masters.

HAGEN WINS GOLF HONORS OF P. G. A.

Defeats Barnes, 3 and 2, in Championship Round of Pro Tourney at Inwood Club.

TRIUMPH DECISIVELY WON

Western Titleholder Plays Unbeatable Game, Especially In His Mastery Over His Putter.

Walter Hagen, who was reported to be on the verge of retirement only a few months ago, yesterday proved him in that respect were, like those circulated about Mark Twain, not only greatly exaggerated but exceedingly inaccurate. Playing in the final of the Professional Golfers' Association championship at the Inwood Country Club, Hagen became the possessor of the Rodman Wanamaker Trophy, the diamond medal and the $500 prize by administering a trimming to Long Jim Barnes, the national open champion, that was even more decisive than the 3 and 2 score would indicate.

Seldom has such a brand of golf as he unleashed been seen in any final, and Barnes, with a 71, which is two under the difficult par for the celebrated Inwood course, found himself trailing the Western champion, 1 down in the morning round. Hagen had a 69 for the first eighteen holes, which is only a stroke higher than Barnes's record 68. Going out in the afternoon round, Hagen was cut in 33, four under par, and was 4 up on his rival, who had even pars. But the Pelham pro captured the fourteenth and prolonged the inevitable to the sixteenth green, at which Barnes, by failing dismally on a putt of a little more than a foot, was able to get only a half where he should have had a win. Hagen was thus adjudged the 1921 leader of the Professional Golfers' Association.

It seems impossible for Barnes to win a victory over Hagen in match play, for in all the times they have met the home-bred has yet to bow his head in defeat to Long Jim.

His Third Big Victory.

Hagen's triumph yesterday places him in a position near if not actually at the top of the American golf world, for it was his third big victory of the season. Counting yesterday's performance, two of his victories have been won over the British and American champions. In the recent Western open championship Hagen, starting the final round in a tie with Jock Hutchison, the holder of the British crown, turned in a 71 to Hutch's 76 and became the winner of the Western title. In defeating Barnes in the P. G. A. final he won from the man who outstripped the field in the national open at Washington. Hagen's other performance of the 1921 season was his victory in the Michigan State open championship, a feat that was accomplished in the face of considerable opposition.

Yesterday's victory was the first that Hagen has won in the P. G. A. tournaments, Barnes having been the leader in the first two years of the tournament and Hutchison winning last year, when he defeated the late J. Douglas Edgar at Flossmoor by 1 up.

Trying to bar Hagen's way to the championship yesterday was like attempting to batter down the Rock of Gibraltar. The brilliant Hagen was in one of his unbeatable streaks, one of those streaks which have caused many to regard him as one of the greatest golfers of all time. Barnes, playing almost perfect golf, found himself unable to cope with his great rival. Hagen, in the first nine holes in the morning, had his card embellished with only one solitary 5, that coming at the 502-yard fourth hole. His other marks consisted of six 4s and two 3s. He was even more brilliant on the last nine, where he had three 3s, four 4s and one 5. In the afternoon round Hagen had one 5, which again came at the fourth hole, five 4s, a pair of 3s and a 2. His only mistakes in the final seven holes came at the fourteenth and sixteenth holes, where he was in difficulty.

Wonderful Putting Exhibition.

Hagen's triumph over Barnes was largely the result of two things: His great ability to recover whenever he got into difficulties, which was seldom, and his wonderful mastery over his putter. In the thirty-four holes played against Barnes, Hagen took three putts on only two occasions. On six of these holes he took only a single putt and on thirty-three of them he required only two.

Barnes, although the putting figures showed him to be almost as efficient as his opponent, failed in several pinches, and he was nowhere near Hagen when it came to sinking putts from far distances. It must be added, however, that the Pelham pro was outlucked to a considerable extent, for time and time again his ball rolled true to the cup, stopping at a place where a half a turn would have made the difference of a half or a win.

In the morning round Hagen had 7 birdies and Barnes 5, and in the afternoon he had 4 to 2 for Barnes. The latter was one over the par figures on only two holes in the morning, while, on three, Hagen had an extra stroke. In the last half of the match Hagen was a stroke over par only twice and Barnes three times.

Hagen started at a stiff pace in the morning round immediately after Barnes had won his continuation match from Emmet French, 5 and 4. Hagen took the first two holes with birdie 3s, getting a 25-foot putt down at the first and chipping in from off the edge of the green at the second. The third was halved in par figures, but Barnes cut down his disadvantage by a victory at the fourth with a birdie 4. He squared the match by winning the sixth with a par 3 and became 1 up by taking the seventh in the same figure. Hagen being one over par in both instances. They halved the next two holes, and at the turn Barnes was 1 up, out in 34, to a 35 for Hagen.

Places Barnes on Defensive.

Immediately after the turn, Hagen won four out of the first five holes and placed Barnes on the defensive. He took the tenth with a par 3, lost the eleventh, on which Barnes got a birdie 3, but took the next three holes in rapid succession. He had a birdie 3 for a win at the twelfth and another birdie at the fourteenth. Barnes lost his chances by being out of bounds at both holes. With Hagen leading by 2 up, Barnes got back a hole at the sixteenth, and they halved the next two, the morning round ending with Hagen 1 up. He was home in 34, against a 37 for Barnes, and the total showed Hagen 89 and Barnes 71.

Just as the first two holes proved a hoodoo to Barnes in the morning, so they did in the afternoon, for Hagen captured them both again and became 3 up. Barnes lost the first by hooking his drive into the rough, and Hagen took the second by getting a birdie 3. They halved the next four holes, but Hagen ran down a 40-foot putt for a birdie 2 at the eighth, which left him 4 up at the turn.

From here on it was a desperate struggle, Hagen striving to maintain his lead and Barnes to overcome it. The latter had a few opportunities, but his putts would not go down for him and they halved the first four holes. Hagen missed a rather short putt at the fourteenth, giving Barnes a win, 5 and 6, but the match was concluded after they had halved the next two holes. At the seventeenth, after being twenty feet short of the pin, Barnes barely missed his try by half an inch, but Hagen likewise missed a four-footer and the hole was halved.

The cards:

MORNING ROUND.

Out—
Hagen	3	3	4	5	4	4	4	4	4—35
Barnes	4	4	4	4	3	3	4	4—34
In—
Hagen	3	4	3	4	4	3	5	4	4—34—69
Barnes	4	3	4	5	6	3	4	4—37—71

AFTERNOON ROUND.

Out—
| Hagen | 4 | 3 | 4 | 5 | 4 | 3 | 2 | 4 | 4—33 |
| Barnes | 5 | 4 | 4 | 5 | 4 | 3 | 5 | 4 | 4—37 |
In—
| Hagen | 3 | 4 | 4 | 4 | 5 | 5 |
| Barnes | 4 | 4 | 4 | 5 | 6 | 5 |

October 2, 1921

WALTER HAGEN WINS BRITISH OPEN TITLE

American-Bred Golfer Captures Championship at Sandwich by a Single Stroke.

SCORES 300 FOR 72 HOLES

Jim Barnes and George Duncan Are Tied for Second—Jock Hutchison Is Third.

Copyright, 1922, by The New York Times Company.
Special Cable to The New York Times.

SANDWICH, England, June 23.—The British Open Golf Championship Cup will be taken back to America again tomorrow, when Walter Hagen sails for home. Thus for two years in succession have British golfers failed to withstand the American invaders and prevent the much-coveted trophy from crossing the Atlantic. Hagen is indisputably the finest overseas player who ever contested for the British open championship, Jock Hutchison notwithstanding, and even by leading professionals opposed to him he has been tipped all along as the probable winner. Last year when Hutchison won at St. Andrews after the replay with the amateur, Roger Wethered, local enthusiasts claimed him as one of themselves, since he was born at St. Andrews; or at least they claimed a part share in him. But this year no such contention holds good. Hagen's is an American victory outright.

The leading scores at the end of play were:

Walter Hagen, 76, 78, 79, 72—300.
Jim Barnes, 75, 76, 77, 73—301.
George Duncan, 76, 75, 81, 69—301.
Jock Hutchison, 79, 74, 73, 76—302.
C. A. Whitcomb, 77, 79, 72, 75—303.
J. H. Taylor, 73, 78, 76, 77—304.

The winning score of 300 is good. It had been predicted that a score of four over fours for 72 holes, or an aggregate of 292, would be the winning one, but these prophets had not foreseen the weather conditions that prevailed. Hagen's victory was achieved after a day of thrills during which British hopes ebbed and flowed in remarkable fashion. At the end of the third round the aggregates were: Hagen 228, Duncan 232, Barnes 228, Hutchison 226, Whitcomb 228, Taylor 227.

British hopes in the morning were centred on Taylor and Duncan, but mostly on the latter. Taylor's return of 76 for the third round was good enough and he only needed the same score as he returned in the first round, namely, 73, to be level with Hagen. But Duncan was the cause of many groans. A display of fireworks was expected from him today, but his 81 for the third round was disastrous. A pyrotechnical outburst, however, was surely forthcoming from him in the fourth round, but it was too late. His 69 is one of the most brilliant performances in the history of championship golf. A 68 would have tied with Hagen, but on the last green Duncan's five-yard putt just failed, the ball resting on the lip of the hole.

Hagen's Chances Imperilled.

Like Duncan, Hagen imperilled his chances by his third-round score of 79. He started this round in indifferent fashion, taking three putts on the second green. He made a brilliant recovery by holing a twelve-yard run-up shot at the ninth and after that his good putting saved him from what otherwise would have been a disastrous score. At the fourteenth, for instance, he was first in the rough to the right and then seventeenth he was trapped in bunkers to the left and at the sixteenth and finally he topped his drive at the last hole and was again bunkered.

His card:

Out	4	5	3	5	4	3	5	4	3—36
In	4	4	5	5	4	6	6	4—43—79

In the last round, however, Hagen was at his brilliant best. After starting in moderate fashion he gradually improved and the few mistakes he made on the outward journey were balanced by some wonderful shots on the way home. Reaching the turn in 35, he, for a few holes, did miracles with his putter, holing a three-yarder at the tenth and a twelve-yarder at the twelfth. He missed a five-foot putt at the short sixteenth for a two, however, and a four-yarder at the eighteenth failed to go down.

Hagen played throughout with cheerful determination and with the full knowledge that he had to counteract the two strokes by which Hutchison was leading him at the end of the third round. At the last hole he ought to have had a four. Two superb wooden-club shots landed him on the edge of the green, but once again his putter failed him and he took five.

His card:

Out	5	4	4	5	4	3	3	3	4—35
In	4	3	5	4	4	3	4	5—37—72

Spectators who had crowded round cheered and congratulated him on his fine performance.

Duncan Needs a Four.

Duncan needed a four at the eighteenth hole in the fourth round to equal Hagen's aggregate. Sick over his third round of 81, which seemed to render his task impossible, he nevertheless gritted his teeth and started off from the first tee. By wonderful luck he did the first nine holes in 34. It was known what he had to do, and spectators came out in thousands to watch his progress.

In the second half he picked up a stroke at the thirteenth by using only one putt, and at the short sixteenth he registered a two on his card. A four at the seventeenth left him a four at the home hole to be bracketed with Hagen. Excitement among the spectators was tense as Duncan, who was obviously highly strung, drove a long and accurately placed ball. His second shot with his iron was not favorably treated. The ball kicked off the line and finished up just off the green, but level with the pin. Hagen was there watching, and was, naturally, the most interested of all the spectators. His feelings were expressed in the remark he made to the man next to him:

"Well, I'm going to miss the boat tomorrow. George and I will have to play off."

But Duncan was too nervous with his little chip shot onto the green, and his ball stopped five yards from the pin. He made a great effort to sink it, but it stopped on the edge of the cup, and the championship again went to America. Duncan will never forget the 81 he took for the third round, nor will British golfers, and his 69 in the final round in a big-hearted attempt to bring the cup back to this country will never be forgotten, either.

Started in Deluge.

It should be pointed out that in the morning Duncan started off in a deluge of rain. But Hutchison, for one, had to contend with the same conditions and he went round in 73. Hutchison lost his hold on the cup he won last year at the fourth hole of the final round. His second shot landed his ball in a garden at the back of the green and the error cost him three strokes. It was a great pity, because at the end of the third round strokes and a 74 in the final round strokes and a 74 in the final round would have meant a final tussle tomorrow between him and Hagen for the championship. Hutchison was the man whom Hagen feared most. Before Hagen started on his final round he arranged that he should be kept informed at every hole of what Hutchison was doing. "I wanted to know exactly what I had to do," he said afterward.

Third Hole Wrecks Barnes.

Barnes, whose aggregate is only one stroke less than Hagen's, will have bad dreams tonight over the unhappy adventure he had at the third hole in the final round. This is a short hole of 247 yards, which he did in three in the morning, but in the afternoon he took six for it; it was the only six on his card. His shot from the tee hit the face of the bunker, dropped into the hazard, and he took two to get clear of it.

In the third round Barnes started badly with two fives, and at the fourth and fourteenth holes he took six on his card as a result of poor shots. But in the final round, apart from the unfortunate experience at the third hole, he played perfect golf for eleven holes, with an average of fours, which average he had to maintain in order to be up with Hagen. He dropped a stroke at the twelfth, taking three putts. Three fours followed, and he got back to his average at the sixteenth, which he did in three. Another four followed at the seventeenth. Then came disaster. His second shot at the eighteenth was pushed out into the rough, his third went sailing over the green and finally he managed to secure a five by holing a two-foot putt. The three strokes lost at the third cost him the championship.

Jock's Brilliant Round.

Hutchison's third round of 73 was the result of beautiful accuracy in all departments of the game. His short approaches and putting were deadly. The only blemishes on his card were a six at the fourteenth, where his ball struck the bridge over the canal and glanced off into a bad lie and the missing of a four-foot putt at the sixteenth.

With a lead of two strokes over the rest of the competitors, Hutchison started his fourth round in fine style with 4 4 3 for the first three holes. Then came the 7 at the fourth which destroyed his chances of retaining the championship. It must have heartened Hagen when he heard of it, but it disheartened Hutchison. Nevertheless, he persevered splendidly, the feature of his game again being his uncanny pitching and putting. He holed four-yarders at the eighth and ninth and two-yarders at the thirteenth and sixteenth and finally finished in 76—two strokes too many.

Kirkwood was hopelessly out of it today, with rounds of 80 and 78, his aggregate of 313 being one stroke better than that of Willie Hunter, who had the second best score among the amateurs, Hon. Michael Scott leading him by one stroke.

June 24, 1922

SARAZEN WINS OPEN GOLF CHAMPIONSHIP

Former New York Caddie, 21 Years Old, Scores Great Triumph With Card of 288.

JONES AND BLACK IN TIE

Young Atlanta Amateur and Veteran Coast Pro Even for Second at 289.

MELHORN FOURTH AT 290

YARDAGE AND PAR FOR THE SKOKIE COURSE.

OUTGOING. Hole.	Yards.	Par.	INCOMING. Hole.	Yards.	Par.
No. 1	430	4	No. 10	440	4
No. 2	198	3	No. 11	430	4
No. 3	440	4	No. 12	345	4
No. 4	350	4	No. 13	185	3
No. 5	590	5	No. 14	315	4
No. 6	390	4	No. 15	330	4
No. 7	215	3	No. 16	365	4
No. 8	435	4	No. 17	430	4
No. 9	185	3	No. 18	470	5
Total	3,228	34	Total	3,805	36
Grand total				6,533	70

Special to The New York Times.

GLENCOE, Ill., July 15.—A former New York caddie is the national open golf champion for the year 1922. Competing in the greatest tournament in history, a tournament that included in its list the holding champion and the British champion as well as the amateur and professional golf stars of Great Britain and America, Gene Sarazen, twenty-one year golf professional at the Highland Country Club, Pittsburgh, annexed the year's honors at the Skokie Country Club today with a total score of 288 for the seventy-two holes.

"The new champion, the youngest professional ever to win the greatest laurels that can come to an artisan in the game, was born at Rye, N.Y., of Italian parentage. He took up the game at the tender age of eight years, and served his apprenticeship at the Apawamis Club, near his home. He learned the finer points of the game under George Sparling of the Brooklawn Country Club, for whom he acted as assistant for a period of three years.

"Two years ago he went to the Titusville (Pa.) club and last year transferred to Highland. He won the title in his third bid for the honors, his first appearance in the national championship being at Toledo two years ago when he failed to finish in the money. Last year, at the Columbia Country Club, Washington, he was far down in the list, getting away to a bad start.

"His first achievement of note was his victory over Jock Hutchison, then British open champion and holder of the P.G.A. title in the professionals championship at the Inwood Country Club last Fall. He vanquished the Glenview Scot by the score of 8 and 7, one of the most glaring defeats ever administered to a title-holder. Even before this his bright future was predicted by close followers of the game who saw in him a natural golfer of the calibre of Bobby Jones. During the Winter season he took part in thirteen tournaments in the South and won the Southern open at New Orleans and was placed second in four other events in which he exchanged shots with the best of the American golfers.

Tie for Second Place.

In a tie for second place, with only a single shot separating them from a playoff for the championship, were Bobby Jones, the young Atlanta amateur star, who made his greatest bid for a big title, and the veteran John L. Black from Los Angeles, who practically threw away his chance through a collapse, over the last nine holes. Jones gave his prize money to Black.

William Melhorn, homebred professional at Shreveport, La., who accompanied the American invaders abroad last year, was fourth with 290, while fifth place fell to Walter Hagen, the British open champion, who made a great try to recover a poor second round yesterday, but fell short, finishing with a round of 72, which gave him a total of 291.

George Duncan, former British open champion, who was held as a possible winner when the tournament started, was unable to hit one of his low scoring moods for which he is famed, and was sixth with 296, while Leo Diegel, New Orleans professional, was seventh with 297, his fight today being one of the features of a day that was filled with thrills. Starting out in a tie for thirtieth place, Diegel gave chase to the leaders and finished with a 73 and a 71.

Tied for eighth place were Jock Hutchison, the Glenview professional who captured the British open title at St. Andrews last year, bringing the famous cup to this side for the first time in history, John Golden, homebred professional at the Tuxedo Club, New York, and Mike Prady of Detroit, each with 298 strokes.

Johnny Farrell, another young homebred, who is professional at Quaker Ridge, New York, and Laurie Ayton of Evanston, Ill., were tied for eleventh place with 299, while Bob MacDonald of Bobolink, holder of the metropolitan title, and Joe Kirkwood of Australia were tied for thirteenth position at 300.

Dramatic finishes there have been in this blue ribbon event of golf, but none to compare with that which closed this year's event. At the start of the final round today, only six shots separated the eight leaders. Jones and Melhorn were in the van, with a total of 216, while Black was a stroke behind. Hagen was fourth with 219. Sarazen was fifth with 220, and Evans and Mike Brady of Oakland Hills were tied at 222.

Gallery Eager to Follow Winner.

This was the setting that kept the gallery jumping from pair to pair, eager to follow the winner, but at a loss to know who the leader was going to be. The first of the topnotchers to report was Melhorn, who held the position of honor and looked like a possible winner when he returned a 74, for a total of 290. A few minutes later Sarazen came in with his 68, which tumbled the Shreveport professional out of the honors, and which made him the centre of attraction.

Hagen, Black and Jones were still out, however, each with a chance either to tie the title in a knot and force a play-off or win. The British champion's task was almost an impossible one, for he needed a 69 to tie and a 68 to win. When his return for the first nine holes was flashed the New Yorker was practically counted out of it, for he was 35, and not going any too well.

Both Black and Jones were in the hunt, the Californian needing only a 71 and Jones a 72 to tie. The Atlantian was 36 at the turn and it was felt that here at last he had come into his own. The first three holes going out were what wrecked his chances, for he was a stroke over par at the tenth and a gain at the twelfth and although he played brilliant golf over the remainder of the journey his card showed 289.

played brilliant golf over the remainder of the journey his card showed 289.

It was now do or die for Black, the silent man from the coast, who had come here unthought of as a possible winner and who had held first place for the first 36 holes with a total of 142. He reached the turn in 33, one under par and was traveling as straight as an arrow on the championship way. Then, with the trophy almost in his possession, he crashed.

His first mistake came at the fourteenth hole where he used poor judgment. Of the line with his drive, he attempted to make the pin instead of playing safe and was trapped, taking a 4. He was in trouble at the next when he sliced from the tee, but a great mashie to within a foot and a half of the pin saved him a par 4. Then came his last gasp.

Black Makes Gallant Effort.

Playing through the narrow opening between the trees going to the seventeenth hole, he put a ball out of bounds. He was not yet out of it, for a 5 here and a birdie at the home hole would still give him a tie. But he sent his brassie third over the bank at the right of the green and was too strong coming back, taking a devastating 6.

He could still tie Jones with an eagle 3 at the home hole and no man ever tried harder than did this veteran linksman from the Pacific slope. A tremendous brassie shot sent his ball soaring off on its way to the green, but it was a trifle off the line, leaving him a pitch out of the rough. He had this shot to win. He made a great attempt, but fell short, and, although he got down in a par 4, it was a stroke too many.

The "old master," as this 43-year-old golfer is known out on the coast, was given a great ovation as he stepped off the green, betraying no disappointment over the turn of fate that had lost him a title that was almost within grasp. As great was his ovation as that bestowed upon young Sarazen, who was cheered to the echo when he was presented with the cup which has so much tradition behind it.

In keeping with the affair itself was the day and the crowd which numbered close to 8,000. During the forepart of the day it was broken up into groups that followed the various pairs who were knocking at the doors of the championship. But at the end, when it concentrated on a few, it was a rushing, roaring mob that charged from green to green, seeking every possible vantage point, regardless of the barrage of golf balls that rained down from various points along the way.

Jones, starting his third round in fifth place, was even par for his round. He saved himself at the second hole, where he sank a ten-footer for his par 3 after being far to the right of the green on his drive. He had a fine second at the fourth, which left him an easy 4. Even pars up to the sixth, he lost a stroke by slicing from the tee and then chipping back to within 2 feet of the pin only to lose the putt. He dropped in a ten-footer for his par 4 at the eighth hole and was 35 at the turn.

Going to the tenth, he hooked to the rough on his tee shot, but recovered splendidly with a spoon shot that carried to the green. He wasted a stroke at the second, but recovered it at the next, where he holed a ten-footer for a birdie 3. Two pars followed, although he deserved a birdie at the fourteenth, his putt just curling away from the cup at the last turn. He dropped another ten-footer for a birdie at the fifteenth, but wasted a stroke at the seventeenth. Coming up to the home hole, he pulled his brassie second into the crowd at the corner of the green. He chipped up, but took two putts.

His morning card.

Out ....4 3 4 4 5 4 4 4 3—35
In ....4 4 3 3 4 3 4 5 5—35—70

Short on his approach to the first hole going out, he holed a twelve-foot putt for a par at the first and saved himself at the next by sinking one of eight feet after being trapped off the tee. He was in a trap at the third, the error costing him a disastrous 5. He followed with a 6 at the long fifth, pulling his second into the rough and playing his next into a trap. He played perfect golf for the last four holes, finishing in exact pars although he was in the trap at the ninth.

He was twice in the rough at the tenth, taking a 5, and then overplayed the green at the twelfth. He came back to within ten feet, but missed his try for a 4. He was trapped at the next, but got his par by sinking an 8-foot putt and dropped a twenty-footer for a birdie 3 at the next. On the fifteenth green in 3 he dropped in another ten-footer, but lost his chance at the next two holes.

At the seventeenth he pulled his drive to the left and topped his next, taking a 5. Coming home Jones shoved his second far off the green, approached back to within fifteen feet and almost holed.

His afternoon card:

Out ....4 3 5 4 6 4 3 4 3—36
In ....5 4 5 3 3 4 4 5 5—37—73

Black Misses Putt for Birdie.

Black started out in the morning by narrowly missing a putt for a birdie at the first hole. He holed an eight-footer for a par 4 after being on the third green in two and being short on his approach, and he lost a birdie at the next when his putt, on the line all the way, failed to go down.

Almost home at the 590-yard hole in two screaming wooden shots, he was short on his approach, but sank a 25-foot putt for a birdie 4. He lost a stroke at the next, where he was trapped short of the green and played his second too strong over into a depression at the back. He also lost a stroke at the next when he took three putts, but was out in 36.

After a par 4 at the tenth, a topped drive cost him a stroke at the eleventh and he wasted another at the twelfth when he took three putts. He lost a putt at the next two holes, hooked to the woods at the fifteenth, but got his par 4, just lost a three at the next and finished with a par 5.

His morning card:

Out ....4 3 4 4 4 4 5 3—36
In ....4 5 5 4 4 4 4 5—39—75

Black started out with even pars for the first five holes in the afternoon and holed a putt for a usual birdie 3 at the sixth. He followed with two more 3s, the last for a birdie at the eighth, at which he played his iron within six feet of the pin. He was trapped at the ninth, cost him his chance for the title. A great the first nine. He took three putts at the tenth and was short at the next two although he got pars at each. He overran a two at the thirteenth.

The beginning of the end came in the next where he tried to make the pin instead of playing safe, a mistake that cost him his chance for title. A great recovery to within eighteen inches of the cup gave him a par 4 at the fifteenth and he missed an 8-foot putt for a birdie at the next. Then came the disastrous seventeenth, already described.

His afternoon card:

Out ....4 3 4 5 3 4 3 3 4—33
In ....5 4 4 3 5 4 4 6 4—39—72

Hagen had an auspicious start in the afternoon, just failing to sink a birdie 3 at the first and dropping in a putt from the edge of the green at the second. His trouble started at the third hole, and although he made several great recoveries he was 35 at the turn and took 37 more coming home.

Supporters Desert Sarazen.

Sarazen, tied with Hagen at the start of the morning round, had an inauspicious beginning in the afternoon, and at the end of the first nine holes even his most ardent supporters deserted him, believing that he had flubbed his chances. Short on all of his approaches and putting miserably, his card showed a sequency of four 5's, beginning at the third hole, par 3 affair, and a total of six in all. The other figures were a 4 and two 3's.

He was on the first green in 2, but took three putts from the edge. More disaster followed at the second yard, 193 yards, for he missed a small putt and took 4. Short on his approach to the third hole, he added another 5 to his string and followed with the same figure at the next. He was just off the edge of the green on his third at the long fifth hole and was down in two putts for a par 5. He was in trouble at the next, but almost got his par 4, his stroke rimming the cup and bounding away. He had a par 3 at the next, another 5 at the eighth, and a par 3 at the ninth.

He was one over par for the first three holes coming in and then, after a par 3 at the thirteenth, got a birdie 3 at the fourteenth, his first birdie on the round. He took three putts at the next and finished up 3, 4, 4, the first and last figures being birdies. It was this finish that saved him, for he was 35 for a total of 75, only five over par.

His card in the morning:

Out ....5 4 5 5 5 5 3 5 3—40
In ....4 5 4 3 3 5 3 4 4—35—75

This placed him fifth in the standing, four strokes back of the leader.

It was at this point that the doughty little Pittsburgher started out a round that will go down in history as among the gems of the game. There was nothing sensational about the first hole where he reached the green in 2 and took two putts. He lost a stroke at the second when his iron was trapped at the right. He chipped back to within four feet and just missed the putt. Two birdies followed in succession. He got a birdie at the 440-yard third by dropping a 20-footer into the cup and at the fourth he almost holed out his approach, the ball stopping two feet from the pin.

Makes Great Recovery.

He was off the line with his brassie going to the fifth and the ball was up close to a tree from where he had to waste a shot to get back on the fairway. It took him four strokes to the green and he holed out in two putts for a 6 .a stroke off par. Although he missed his second at the sixth hole he chipped up dead and got his par 4—a fine recovery.

He used a brassie to reach the seventh, and his three-quarter shot landed within fifteen feet of the pin, from where he holed out for a birdie 2. He got away one of the longest drives of the day going to the eighth and got par figures. At the ninth, his iron shot struck the bank, from where he chipped back and holed out in a sizable putt for a par 3. This left him one under par figures at the ninth, out in 33.

After turning, he was over the green with his second and took a 5, but he offset it with a birdie 3 at the twelfth, where he put his second close up to the pin. Five holes in par followed, a great recovery at the fifteenth, where he sliced to the rough saving him and he ended with a magnificent finish at the last hole, where he reached the green in 2 and was down in two putts.

His afternoon round:

Out	4	4	3	3	6	4	3	4	3—33
In	5	4	3	3	4	4	4	4	4—35

July 16, 1922

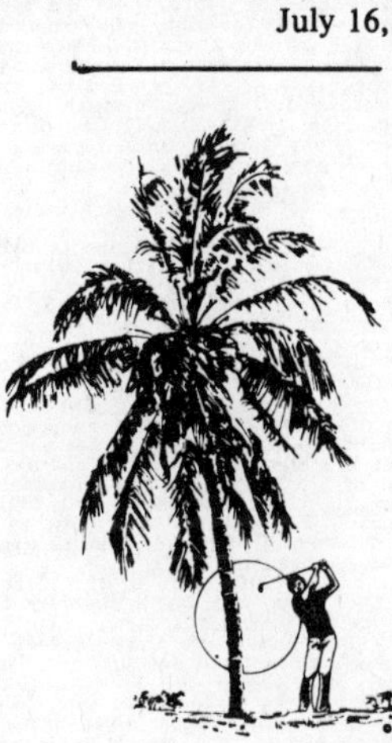

HAGEN IS DEFEATED BY SARAZEN, 3-2

National Champion Comes From Behind to Win Match at Westchester-Biltmore C. C.

TAKES LEAD ON 8TH HOLE

Special to The New York Times.

RYE, N. Y., Oct. 7.—Standing on the sixteenth green of the west course at the Westchester-Biltmore Country Club late this afternoon, Young Gene Sarazen, former Apawamis caddie boy, might well have exclaimed: "I am monarch of all I survey." And the courageous little golfer might have added: "And of some sections beyond my range of vision."

For Gene had just emerged a winner in the final half of his seventy-two-hole match with Walter Hagen, until today America's foremost home-bred and the holder of the British open champion, scheduled as a "world's golf classic" on the admission pasteboards, but really for the "unofficial world's championship." The margin was 3 and 2.

By disposing of the British title-holder, Sarazen bagged his fourth triumph of the year. He entered the contest as the Southern open, national open and P. G. A. champion, and with the defeat of Hagen, the British title-holder, there is little left for him now but a trip to the British Isles to make personal quest of the British crown, an idea he will carry into effect as soon as the Winter's pelt-hunting season through the South closes.

Gene entered today's contest with the British champion leading him by two holes, the result of their initial 36-hole engagement at Oakmont, Pa., yesterday. Spotting Walter Hagen two holes in a 36-hole match is a task that none of them—Barnes, Hutchison, Duncan or Mitchell—relish, but Sarazen did it and then won simply because he outplayed the mighty Walter at the majority of the holes.

Gene Quickly Squares Match.

He won three of the first five holes played to square the match, then, by winning the eighth hole forged ahead for the first time during the two days' play and was never headed thereafter. At the end of the morning half Hagen, by winning the fourteenth and sixteenth holes, cut down Gene's three-hole lead to one hole.

Starting out in the afternoon, Walter, by virtue of a brilliant birdie 3 at the first hole, squared the match, but the youngster was not to be denied. Not once during the entire thirty-four holes did he falter, and even at noontime, when has only 1 up and when various members of the gallery were recalling Hagen's famous come-backs in matches of note, Gene was absolutely unperturbed.

"I'll end this match at the sixteenth green this afternoon," said Gene, assuming the rôle of a prophet. "Watch me in the 'pinches,'" he told his caddie, none other than George Sparling, the Brooklawn professional, "this fellow (meaning Hagen) is cracking!"

It was not braggadocio in the make-up of the little dreadnought of the links; it was simply confidence, the quality which, more than any other, has had to do with the making of Gene Sarazen, super golfer.

His ability to prophesy was emphasised at the sixteenth green. Perhaps that is why Hagen, dormie 4 at the end of the fourteenth, won the fifteenth and stirred up hope in the breasts of his admirers. When Walter captured the 116-yard fifteenth of the round and thirty-third of the day's match by sinking an 8-foot putt for a par 3 after being trapped, there was a flutter of excitement.

Sarazen Calm at Finish.

His great finish against Abe Mitchell on the same course only a few weeks ago was recalled, but it was not Abe Mitchell today. It was Sarazen, a cool, calm, machine-like performer, nevertheless and unflinching. The tide had been only temporarily checked, not stemmed entirely. There was no temerity about his drive or his approach to the sixteenth. His approach putt was a trifle short, but the putt for the half needed to clinch the match and the 55 per cent. share of the $3,000 purse went banging into the cup without a waver.

Thus ended one of the greatest matches in a long time, certainly the greatest of the year and one on which a large chunk of money changed from one pocket to another.

It was not long after the match got under way that the signs began to point to a strenuous day for the British open champion. His rival, undismayed by the fact that he had lost the opening round on his home course and before the eyes of his home folks, lost no time in pointing out that he was prepared to play whatever kind and calibre of golf was necessary to win from the peerless Hagen. His tee shots were straight and true down the fairways, almost always beyond Hagen's and almost always better placed, so far as opening up the hole was concerned. His iron work was not only masterful but brilliant, and when it came to putting he simply left Walter far behind. As a matter of fact, however, Gene's accuracy with his irons left him little work to do with his putter, but whenever the implement was hauled out of the bag it paid strict attention to the bidding of its youthful master.

It must have been a novel experience for Hagen to be outdriven as consistently as he was by Sarazen today, for Walter is not reckoned as a short hitter among the élite of the profession. Perhaps it had something to do with the streak of wildness that Hagen developed early in the day, a streak that had him in trouble on far too many occasions to aid in the cause for which he was battling. Nor was he in his usual form when it came to pitching up shots close to the pin. Gene was inside of him on the green time after time, and to make matters worse Hagen fell down in the department in which he generally excels—putting. On four of the greens, two in the morning round and two in the afternoon round, Hagen was guilty of that guiltiest feeling in golf—three putts. In the morning portion these lapses cost him halves; in the afternoon they cost him holes. Gene was guilty of the misdemeanor only twice, and once it cost him naught, the hole being lost anyway.

Hagen gave every impression of a man overgolfed, while Gene was like a young pony. There was lacking in Walter's play the fire and dash that generally characterize his game. It was evident that the strain of exhibition matches, which have kept him busily engaged, even up to the very day of the match, was exacting its toll. This was made most plain in his putting. Hagen is noted as a golfer who is never short. He always putts boldly for the hole, his motto being "three yards past rather than one foot short." Today he was short of the cup on far more occasions than he was past.

Without subtracting anything from the glory that belongs to the sturdy little Gene, it may be stated that the "breaks" were with him rather than against him. On at least a dozen occasions Hagen's putt traveled straight for the cup and either hopped unhesitatingly over or grazed the rim. It was true on long putts and short putts alike. Only twice did he succeed in dropping those long putts designed to throw consternation into the heart of the enemy. One of these instances was at the tenth hole in the morning, when, 2 down, he took careful calculation of a sidehill roll and dropped a 30-footer for a useful 2, which cut Sarazen's lead down to one hole. He got down a 25-footer at the ninth in the afternoon, but it was wasted, as he already had the hole won.

Sarazen took a hand in the spectacular work in the afternoon when, at the thirtieth hole of the mathc, he dropped a 35-footer, which likewise went to seed. So far as scoring went, the match was unproductive of anything like record-shattering. In the morning Sarazen had a 75, equaling the par of the course, while Hagen had a 77, due to a 36 over the last nine holes. In the afternoon Hagen went out in 39 and Gene in 40, and coming in Walter was even 4s, but lost a hole, Gene being two under 4s when the match ended.

Greens Heavy and Slow.

When they resumed their hostilities this morning, the course was enveloped in a low-hanging fog that made it almost impossible to follow the flight of the ball and that made the greens heavy and slow. Hagen, carrying over from yesterday, had the honor and sent a low-flying ball that carried beyond the green and into the rough. Gene was no better off, his ball stopping short of the green. Both made poor approaches, but Walter grazed the cup on his fifteen-foot try and the hole was halved in par fours.

Sarazen's iron to the 138-yard second was a beauty that stopped five feet from the pin for an easy 2, which reduced Walter's lead to 1 up. Hagen immediately restored his lead by chalking up a birdie 4 at the 485-yard third. His brassie second stopped just short of the green and he played a run-up shot to within inches of the cup. Gene took a 5, after being twice in the rough. Although trapped on his tee shot going to the fourth, Hagen was even with Sarazen on the fourth green, but he lost the hole by taking three putts from thirty-feet, missing a five-footer at the end, while Gene got down in two. This left Walter only 1 up and Gene squared the match by winning the 389-yard fifth hole with a birdie 3. He played a fine iron out of the rough to within a yard of the pin and then sank the putt after Hagen, short of the green on his second and twenty-five feet past on his approach, had holed out for a wasted 4. The next two holes were halved, the sixth in par fives and the seventh in fours, one over. At the sixth, Sarazen after a fine drive, threw away his opportunity with a badly sliced iron second and at the seventh both overplayed the hole and Hagen missed a four-foot putt which would have given him a win.

Sarazen went out in front for the first time at the eighth, which he won with a par 4 after being trapped. Hagen, ahead on the drive, caught a trap with his second and after coming out short just missed holing an 18-footer. Sarazen's run-up from 20 yards short of the green, a favorite shot of his, left him dead to the pin. He increased his lead by winning the ninth. Here Hagen, with a chance for a half, missed a 2-yarder, the ball hanging on the lip of the cup, while Sarazen laid his approach putt dead.

Lead Cut to One Hole.

Walter's long putt at the tenth, a masterly shot from ten yards way, cut Sarazen's lead down to one hole, but the many-titled youngster lost no time in restoring it. He was inside Walter on the eleventh green and came within inches of a 3 while Walter missed an 18-footer. Gene also won the twelfth with a birdie 4, putting him 3 up. They halved the thirteenth, Walter again missing his putt by inches, and then Gene ran into his first really bad hole which cost him a 6, his only 6 of the morning. Here his second was sliced deep into the rough and in an unplayable lie from where he had to drop with a penalty. Hagen succeeded in getting down a 6-yard putt, but it was not needed, as he had two for the hole.

The short fifteenth was halved and then Walter cut down Gene's lead still further by winning the sixteenth with a par 4, Sarazen taking three puts. Hagen saved a half at the seventeenth by means of a great chip shot that left him dead for his par 4 and the home hole was halved in par figures, leaving Sarazen 1 up on the match at the end of the fifty-fourth hole.

The entire afternoon round was played in the rain, which became a downpour toward the concluding stages. Hagen revived hopes with a birdie 3 at the first hole, driving the green and laying his approach putt dead, while Gene was in the rough from the tee. This squared the match and so it remained after the second hole had been played. Here Sarazen's tee shot hit a spectator and rolled down among the traps below the green, while Walter was home in one. The latter, however, took three putts, enabling Sarazen to break even when it looked like a certain loss of the hole. Walter lost his chance for the third when his drive ran into a water hazard, costing him a penalty stroke. Sarazen, home in 2 to Hagen's 3, had to sink a ten-footer for his win. Hagen took three putts at the fourth, costing him the hole and then, after playing a fine second up to within a yard and a half of the pin at the fifth, the British champion failed to get down, giving Gene an undeserved half. Gene dropped back to only 1 up by taking three putts at the sixth, Walter hitting the cup on his approach for a birdie 4.

Sarazen won both the seventh and eighth, Hagen rimming the cup at the former while Gene sank an 8-footer. At the 345-yard eighth, Hagen was twice in trouble, while Gene played two supershots that enabled him to get a par 4, putting him 3 up. Then Gene foozled the ninth, ending up with a 6, Hagen getting down a 25-foot putt for a birdie 4.

The next two holes were halved, Gene dropping down a 10-footer at the tenth, after being a stroke more than Hagen on the green. Sarazen's 25-foot putt at the twelfth placed him 3 up and after halving the thirteenth in 4's, he became 4 up by taking the fourteenth. They were both in traps at the fifteenth, Walter winning the hole with a par 3 after a fine recovery and an 8-foot putt but the match ended at the next hole which they halved in 4's.

The cards:

MORNING ROUND.

Out—									
Par	4	3	5	5	4	5	3	4	5—38
Sarazen	4	2	5	5	3	5	4	4	5—37
Hagen	4	3	4	6	4	5	4	5	6—41
In—									
Par	3	4	5	4	5	3	4	4	5—37—75
Sarazen	3	4	4	4	6	3	5	4	5—38—75
Hagen	2	5	5	4	4	3	4	4	5—36—77

AFTERNOON ROUND.

Out—									
Par	4	3	5	5	4	5	3	4	5—38
Sarazen	4	4	4	5	4	6	3	4	6—40
Hagen	3	4	5	6	4	4	4	5	4—39
In—									
Par	3	4	5	4	5	3	4		
Sarazen	3	4	3	4	4	4	4		
Hagen	3	4	5	4	5	3	4		

October 8, 1922

WOMEN DEFEATED IN MIXED MATCH

Bow to Male Golfers, Five Matches to Two, on Garden City Links.

Special to The New York Times.

GARDEN CITY, L. I., Oct. 8.—In the first team match between the foremost men and women golfers ever played in this country, the men today won a one-sided victory over their fair rivals at the Garden City Golf Club. The men won, five matches to two, after conceding the women six bisques on the eighteen holes played.

Playing in the contest were five women who have at one time or another won the women's national championship and two who have been finalists. For the men only one, Jess W. Sweetser of Siwanoy, was a member of the championship clan, while one other, John G. Anderson of Siwanoy, was twice a runner-up in the national.

The only women who were successful today were Mrs. H. Arnold Jackson of Greenwich, who sponsored the match and who defeated Anderson by 1 up, and Miss Edith Cummings of Chicago, who defeated Max R. Marston of Philadelphia, former New Jersey State champion, by the same margin.

Sweetser, the national champion, proved too strong for Miss Alexa Stirling, the metropolitan champion and former national title-holder, whom he defeated by 4 and 2. Rudy Knepper, Princeton star whose defeat of Tolley was one of the features of the recent Brookline tournament, defeated Miss Glenna Collett of Providence, national women's champion, by 2 and 1.

Grant A. Peacock of Cherry Valley, former runner-up in the metropolitan amateur, defeated Mrs. Ronald H. Barlow of Merion Cricket, Philadelphia, 3 and 2, while Gardiner White, 1921 metropolitan champion, defeated Mrs. Quentin Feitner of the South Shore Country Club. Miss Marion Hollins's conqueror in the White Sulphur Springs tourney, by 4 and 3. Reginald M. Lewis of Greenwich won a closely contested match from Miss Hollins, the match going to the seventeenth green and the score being 2 and 1.

In another match, James D. Standish Jr. of Detroit, Mich., one of the U. S. G. A. Vice Presidents, and Mrs. George Heckscher of Nassau played eighteen holes, the match ending up with the honors all even. Frank Dyer, New Jersey State champion, was supposed to play Mrs. Dorothy Campbell Hurd of Pittsburgh, but failed to make his appearance.

The honor of playing the best golf of the day went to Miss Cummings for the women and to Jess Sweetser for the men. Miss Cummings made the first nine holes in 41 and the last nine in 40, for a total of 81, only 8 strokes more than the men's par for the course. Sweetser was 2 strokes under par, going out with a 35, and he finished the round with a 72 total, 1 under par.

Sweetser was paired against Miss Collett in the original pairings, but owing to the fact that he was carded for an exhibition match in Westchester County in the afternoon, he was unable to wait for the national women's champion and played against Miss Stirling.

Sweetser had a big lead against the former national champion at the end of the first nine holes but as a result of Miss Sterling's using the six bisques allotted to her, the match was all even.

The cards:

Out—									
Miss Stirling...	5	3	4	6	5	4	6	4	5—42
Sweetser	3	2	4	5	4	4	5	4	4—35
In—									
Miss Stirling...	5	5	3	7	5	5	6	5	2—43—85
Sweetser	4	5	3	5	5	4	4	4	3—37—72

Knepper had a 78 for his card against Miss Collett, who took a 90 for her round. The women's champion was off on her game, her card showing a 7 and and an 8. Knepper was 3 up going to the fourteenth, but lost the next hole, where Miss Collett took advantage of her handicap, and the match went to the seventeenth green for a decision.

The cards:

Out—									
Miss Collett...	3	3	5	6	4	5	6	7	6—45
Knepper	5	3	4	5	3	4	6	4	5—39
In—									
Miss Collett...	4	6	4	8	4	5	5	6	3—45—90
Knepper	4	4	4	6	4	5	5	5	2—39—78

In defeating Anderson, Mrs. Jackson had a medal score of 83 against a 75 for her opponent. Mrs. Jackson's card showed nothing worse than 5s.

The card follows:

Out—									
Mrs. Jackson...	5	4	4	5	5	5	5	5	4—42
Anderson	4	3	4	5	4	5	5	4	4—36
In—									
Mrs. Jackson..	5	5	3	5	5	5	5	5	3—41—83
Anderson	4	4	3	6	4	4	6	5	3—39—75

October 9, 1922

JONES, AN AMATEUR, BEATS CRUICKSHANK, PRO, FOR GOLF TITLE

21-Year-Old Georgian Downs Scottish Star at 18th Hole, 76 to 78.

EACH HAS 72 AT THE 17TH

Brilliant Shot Going to Last Green Settles Issue in National Open Play-Off.

10,000 AT INWOOD COURSE

Victor Captures Championship After Three Previous Attempts—Fourth Amateur to Win Honor.

STROKE STANDING AT EACH HOLE.

	1	2	3	4	5	6	7	8	9
Jones	4	8	13	17	22	26	29	33	37
Cruickshank....	5	8	12	17	21	24	28	32	37
	10	11	12	13	14	15	16	17	18
Jones	42	47	49	53	58	63	67	72	76
Cruickshank....	43	48	51	55	59	63	68	72	78

Special to The New York Times.

INWOOD, L. I., July 15.—Robert Tyre Jones Jr. of Atlanta, Ga., 21 years old on March 17 last, is tonight America's national open golf champion for 1923.

In the playoff for the title, necessitated by the fact that Jones was tied yesterday by Robert A. Cruickshank, former Scottish amateur star who came to America and turned pro three years ago, with a score of 296 at the conclusion of the regulation 72-hole test at the Inwood Country Club, Jones was the winner today by two strokes, and it was not until the last hole was played that the question of who was to wear this year's crown was decided in favor of the youthful amateur.

When the Southern youngster, competing in his fourth national open tournament, tapped his putt into the cup for a par 4 on the last hole, it made his total for today's eighteen holes 76, but the issue was decided two strokes previous to that. It was decided when Jones played his second shot coming to the home hole—a truly miraculous shot out of the rough that sped almost two hundred yards and ended less than two yards away from the flapping flag on the eighteenth green. It was a shot that, in addition to proving Jones's capabilities as one of the finest shot-makers in the world and one of the most courageous fighters in the world, will take its place among the epochal strokes that are a part of golf's lengthy history.

Made in the stress of battle, it sealed the fate of the little Scottish gamecock who was Jones's rival for the open crown today, just as it opened up the portals of fame to the man who brought it off. No sooner did the click of iron against gutta-percha and rubber reach the ears of the little professional than he knew that his dreams of fame and fortune were sealed, for this year at least. He didn't even have to glance at the ball to realize that the ambitions that were his when he went to sleep last night, after making his great uphill fight to tie Jones, had gone for nought—at least so far as the present year is concerned.

Victory Fulfills Predictions.

By winning, Jones had finally fulfilled the predictions made in his behalf by ardent admirers ever since he flashed into prominence in 1916, when, a chubby little lad of 14, he led the field in the first day's qualifying round of the national amateur, and then, after putting out Eben Byers and Frank Dyer, was putted into oblivion by Robert A. Gardner, runner-up to Chick Evans. By winning, he gained a coveted title that only three amateurs ahead of him have succeeded in wresting away from the pros—Francis Ouimet in 1913, Jerry Travers in 1915 and Evans in 1916.

World's champion hard-luck golfer, right at the top of the amateur and open field for the last four years, Jones today gave the past a fleeting glance. When he was being acclaimed by the 10,000 rabid golf enthusiasts who braved the prospects of a rainy day and ran hither and thither down the fairways, through the traps and over the greens, Jones made a few brief remarks that spoke volumes.

"I don't care what happens now," he said. For here he was inside the portals at last, after four years of disappointment. Hailed as a probable winner for that four-year period, Bobby had always just fallen short.

Disappointment had followed disappointment until even his most enthusiastic admirers had lost faith in his ability to shake off the jinx that seemed to be pursuing him. Three years ago he had finished eighth in the open, two years ago at Columbia he had finished fifth, last year at Skokie he had the championship almost within the palm of his hand, only to lose his chance by playing the next to last hole badly.

Then yesterday, instead of sewing up the title as he should have done, he spent a costly 6 at the home hole and left the door open to Cruickshank to tie him. Just as he has met with disappointment in the open, so had he failed in the amateur at Oakmont in 1919, for he went to the final round only to meet defeat at the hands of S. Davidson Herron, a golfer of worth but not in the Southerner's class as a shot-maker. In 1920 he passed out of the tournament at the hands of Ouimet in the semi-final round.

At St. Louis, the following year, he lost to Willie Hunter, the then British amateur champion, in the third round, and then at Brookline last years Sweetser beat him by playing the lowest round ever made on the Hub City course.

But everything was forgotten and forgiven today when he finally captured the will-o'-the-wisp-like championship.

Seldom if ever has there been quite such a dramatic ending as that which touched off today's event. Coming to the home hole, Jones and Cruickshank were all even in the matter of strokes and another 18-hole play-off on the morrow was imminent. Having gained a two-stroke lead early in the round, Cruickshank had lost it and then came to the test.

Almost Misses Drive.

Something happened to Cruickshank, for he almost missed his drive to the eighteenth hole completely, topping the ball and sending it into a patch of rough at the left of the fairway. Jones, thinking thoughts of his débâcle of the day before, pushed his own drive well to the right, among the spectators that lined the course, ready for the mad rush to witness the finish. But Jones's drive, although in the rough, was perched up and within striking distance of the green, while Cruickshank had no possible chance of getting home, since his drive measured not more than 150 yards, and the distance between tee and green is nearly three times that.

There was nothing left for him now but to play the ball out through the trees and down the fairway in order to get a chance to play his third for the pin. Not knowing what Jones was about to bring off, Cruickshank put everything he had into the stroke and got a good shot under the circumstances.

It was then that Jones played the shot that sent his fame around the world wherever golf is played. Without a moment's hesitation, Jones drew No. 1 iron out of his bag, took a momentary look at the lie, glanced at the flag and swung. It was a superb shot made by a superb golfer in a superb manner. The ball flew off the face of his club, rose in the air and carried squarely on the green, 190 yards away. A tremendous shout went up as the ball struck on the green, bit its way into the turf, and brought up its journey about two club lengths away from the hole for a possible birdie three.

Cruickshank, fighter that he proved himself throughout the entire tourney, doubtless felt his heart rattling around in the bottom of his boots when he saw his opponent's ball perched up close to the hole, but he didn't show it. He walked a hundred yards down the fairway, measured the distance and then made his last dying effort. Had he been able to get the ball dead to the hole, he could still save his championship for another day. It was a 100 to 1 shot, but he played it for all it was worth. He pulled it off to the left and saw it drop into a trap just at the left of the green.

Nothing remained now but the chance of holing out from where he was. The recovery shot went several feet past the hole and after missing his putt that would have given him a five, he rushed over to Jones and put out his right hand.

The latter took it, then walked over and twice tapped his ball. When it dropped into the cup on the second tap it signalized his first great victory.

Kiltie Furnishes Music.

Then one of the greatest scenes of all was enacted. The crowd, perhaps biased in Jones's favor, since he has always been a favorite, rushed out on the green, two of Bobby's fellow-townsmen who had made the journey all the way from Atlanta to see him win his first title hoisted him on their shoulders and he was borne triumphantly toward the clubhouse. A kiltie, blowing away on the bagpipes, furnished the music. His youthful face wreathed in smiles, Jones was kept busy several minutes accepting the congratulations and plaudits of the golf-mad spectators who had witnessed one of the greatest of all play-offs.

Off in another direction, unattended, except for some of his fellow-countrymen who stood stanchly by, went the other hero of the day, Cruickshank, the stout-hearted little player whose courage, whose shotmaking had made necessary the round of rounds. One was the victor to whom the spoils belonged, the other was the defeated. But after it was all over there wasn't one, even among those who were strong for a victory for the amateur, who did not have a word of praise for the sportsmanship and the fighting qualities of the little Scotsman. There was not one who would not have given him the same ovation had he been the victor.

For the first nine holes of the match today the issue was as completely in doubt as it was until after Cruickshank's bad drive on the eighteenth and Jones's miraculous second shot. The Atlantan had taken the lead through two superb shots at the first hole, only to have Cruickshank draw level through a brilliant second shot which gave him a birdie at the second.

A great approach out of a trap extricated Jones from trouble at the third, but Cruickshank ran down a ten-foot putt for his second consecutive birdie, sending him in the lead. Then Jones, playing out of the rough to within a yard of the pin, a great shot, got another birdie and squared the account. An eighteen-foot putt, which he holed, sent Cruickshank again into the lead when Jones missed a short putt after a great recovery from a trap. Another missed putt at the sixth left Jones two strokes in arrears, but he got one of them back at the treacherous seventh, where he reached the green with a superb iron and was down in two putts, Cruickshank failing to get down a two-yarder.

The eighth hole was unimportant except for a great approach by Cruickshank, which left him with a chance for a birdie three, which he missed, his second costly failure in two consecutive holes.

Jones Even Again.

He could not score better than a 5 at the ninth and Jones, by getting his 4 was again all level, both being out in 37, exactly par.

Then both players began to show signs of cracking. After Jones had won the tenth with a 5, one stroke above par, Cruickshank visited no less than six traps. His iron shots, which had stood him in such good stead, failed him entirely.

That he was saved was only due to the fact that on several occasions Jones joined him in the hazards and once broke the sacred covenant of golf by not keeping his head down. There were several high lights on the incoming nine. One was Jones's pitch for a birdie 2 at the twelfth, another was Cruickshank's good half at the thirteenth and still another was the two second shots played to the fourteenth, especially Cruickshank's.

Then there was Cruickshank's useful

putt for a four at the fifteenth, making matters even again. Jones's second at the sixteenth, where Cruickshank was trapped on the like, gave the southerner the lead once more, but he lost it at the seventeenth. There Cruickshank, after a wild hook and a trapped second, exploded his ball out of the sand to within a yard of the hole and he scrambled his par four, his ball striking the back of the cup and barely staying in. So close was it to coming out that the Scot did a Highland Fling when it hit the bottom of the pin. Finally there was the home hole which told the story.

The card of the day:

Out—											
Jones	4	4	5	4	5	4	3	4	4	37	
Cruickshank	5	3	4	5	4	3	4	4	5	37	
In—											
Jones	5	5	2	4	5	5	4	5	4	39	76
Cruickshank	6	5	3	4	4	4	5	4	6	41	78

Stroke by Stroke Analysis.

Hole No. 1, 343 Yards, Par 4—Cruickshank had the honor and played a low ball that landed on the edge of the fairway and kicked off into a ditch from which he did well to get it out on to the fairway. His second shot was short of Jones's drive which was in the middle of the fairway leaving him an easy pitch to the green. Cruickshank's third stopped four yards to the left of the hole and after Jones pitched a beauty just two yards to the right, the Scottish pro ran past the hole and Jones tapped his ball in for a par 4, giving him an early lead. Jones 4, Cruickshank 5.

No. 2, 371 Yards, Par 4—Jones had ten yards advantage off the tee but Cruickshank discounted it with a great iron second that faded in toward the pin and stopped not more than seven feet above the hole. The amateur pushed his second off to the right and was lucky to escape the water-ditch. As it was he was just on the edge. Jones had a hard approach putt and his ball traveled off to the right, leaving him a yard to hole for his par but he got it after Cruickshank ran down his putt for a birdie 3, putting him all square. As Cruickshank holed out the crowd gave a cheer and he raised his hand in protest, pointing to Jones who still had a putt to make. He dropped it for a par. Cruickshank 3, Jones 4.

No. 3, 522 Yards, Par 5—Cruickshank was dangerously near the rough on the right on his tee shot and Jones's ball was again far ahead. The pro then played a beautiful cleek shot that faded in toward the green but stopped ten yards short. Jones took a brassie and hooked it into a trap on the left, short of the green from where he made a beautiful recovery, his ball stopping only ten feet past the hole. Cruickshank's chip was off the line and about as far away as Jones's, The Southerner was away and putted short after which Cruickshank ran down his second consecutive birdie. Cruickshank 4, Jones 5.

No. 4, 530 Yards, Par 5—Cruickshank's drive was in the rough to the right and Jones's ball trickled off the fairway into the rough on the opposite side of the fairway. Both had hard seconds left but Cruickshank got away a superb wooden shot that ended its journey only ten yards short of the green. Jones hooked his second to the rough to the right of green but made a great all-saving approach to within a yard and got down his putt for a birdie 4. Cruickshank's third was several yards past and his next was half a foot away. Jones 4. Cruickshank 5.

No. 5, 519 Yards, Par 5—Jones's drive was ahead of Cruickshank's and right for the opening of the green, while the Scotchman hooked to the left. Cruickshank's iron second was just short of the green and Jones's brassie off to the right, in a trap. After Cruickshank was wide on his approach, Jones played a nicely calculated shot out of the trap to win six feet. Cruickshank then ran down an 18-footer for a birdie 4, fairly chasing the ball into the hole, after which Jones missed his putt. Cruickshank 4, Jones 5.

No. 6, 177 Yards, Par 3—Cruickshank just made the green with his iron and Jones was not as well off. Both balls were about thirty-five feet away from the hole. Jones overran his try for a 2 by a foot and then missed the putt. Cruickshank was a little off the line but close enough for an easy par, putting him two strokes in the lead. Cruickshank 3, Jones 4.

No. 7, 223 Yards, Par 3—Cruickshank took no chances of going out of bounds and played short of the green, while Jones went for it and reached it. After chipping up to within a couple of club lengths of the hole, Cruickshank's putt for a 3 just grazed past the hole. Jones, from a distance of twenty feet, nearly ran down his 2. Jones 3, Cruickshank 4.

No. 8, 418 Yards, Par 4—Jones again passed Cruickshank off the tee, but the latter played a beautiful shot to within five feet of the hole, while Jones was short of the green and in the short rough off to the left. After chipping up close to the hole, Jones sank his putt for a 4, but Cruickshank missed his short one. He didn't hit the ball firmly and it stopped on the lip. Jones 4, Cruickshank 4.

No. 9, 360 Yards, Par 4—Jones hooked his tee shot to the rough at the left, while Cruickshank played a low ball that grazed the tree and ended up in a fine position for his pitch to the treacherous green. He overplayed his next, the ball landing on the green and bouncing over the mounds at the back. Jones's second stopped twelve feet from the hole, leaving him an easy putt for a birdie. Cruickshank chipped back to a yard—a great shot—but his try for a par 4 was just a hair's breadth off the line. Jones was unable to run down his 3, taking a 4. Jones 4, Cruickshank 5.

Both Show Strain.

No. 10, 295 Yards, Par 4—Both played the hole badly, and showed the first signs of the strain they were under. Jones hooked to a trap on the left, while Cruickshank was in the short rough on the right. Cruickshank's second was a bad shot that went over the green and in among the spectators. Jones, with a hard shot left, played the ball beautifully, but it struck the branches of a tree and dropped back into the rough. He played his third against a mound, and was just on the edge, after which Cruickshank again chipped into the rough on the opposite side of the green. He then ran two yards past, and was off the line on his fifth. Jones narrowly missed his 4 after all his trouble. Jones 5. Cruickshank 6.

No. 11, 421 Yards, Par 4.—The two drives were about even, one on the left and the other on the right. After Cruickshank played his second into a trap at the left of the green, Jones did likewise, and never got close on their recoveries, Jones overplaying and Cruickshank just getting on the green with his explosion shot. The latter had to drop a two-yarder for his 5. Jones 5. Cruickshank 5.

No. 12, 108 Yards, Par 3—Jones played a beautiful pitch to within less than a yard while Cruickshank was off to the left of the hole. At that he narrowly missed running down the putt, the ball being only a few inches off the line. Jones sank his, giving him a two-stroke lead. Jones 2. Cruickshank 3.

No. 13, 420 Yards, Par 4—Cruickshank followed Jones's great drive with a tee shot that just grazed the line of trees between the two fairways. Cruickshank played his next into a trap at the right of the green, while Jones played his second just on the edge. Cruickshank exploded his ball out, twelve feet short, while Jones was only a foot away from a three. Nothing was gained or lost on the hole when Cruickshank sank his long putt for a useful four. Cruickshank 4, Jones 4.

No. 14, 497 Yards, Par 5—Jones was down the middle of the fairway while Cruickshank was on the right, a trifle behind. Both played magnificent seconds that reached the green, Cruickshank being not more than twenty-five feet away and Jones about twice that distance, with a mean approach to calculate. He didn't judge the line and looked a trifle perplexed when the ball skidded several feet past the hole. Cruickshank almost sank his putt for a three, while Jones took two more to hole out, leaving him only a stroke to the good. Cruickshank 4, Jones 5.

Cruickshank Evens Count.

No. 15, 173 Yards, Par 3—Cruickshank was trapped to the left. Jones's ball, after landing on the green, trickled over and stopped in the rough of the downhill slope. Cruickshank's recovery was far past the hole, but he sank a one-yarder for a 4. Jones, looking up as he made his shot, flubbed it and failed to get out, but he stuck his next up close and got the putt, which left the two on even terms. Cruickshank 4, Jones 5.

No. 16, 425 Yards, Par 4—Cruickshank was again in the rough off the tee, while Jones was down the middle. The Scot was again trapped on his second, while Jones played a great second that stopped not more than twenty-five feet from the pin. Cruickshank got well out, but was still fifteen feet short of the pin. He was again short and dropped a precious stroke to Jones, who was down in two putts. Jones 4, Cruickshank 5.

No. 17, 405 Yards, Par 4—Jones hooked to the rough between the sixteenth and seventeenth fairways, while Cruickshank got a bad pull, and was in the middle of the sixteenth fairway. He played a fine shot from there, but his ball rolled into a trap. Here was an opening, but Jones refused to take it, dropping into the same hazard. He played it out short, while Cruickshank made a great pitch to within two feet of the hole. His putt hit the back of the tin and rolled around and the little Scot nearly had nervous prostration until he saw that it stayed in. Jones nearly sank his hard uphill putt, but the ball ran a bit past, making the score all even. Cruickshank 4, Jones 5.

No. 18, 425 Yards, Par 4—Cruickshank topped his drive—the only bad tee shot that was played all day—into the rough at the left of the fairway. There was no chance for him to get home, and he played it out on to the fairway, getting a fine shot from the position he was in. Jones pushed his shot off to the right and into the rough, but it was perched up, and without a moment's hesitation he took out a No. 1 iron and played one of the greatest shots ever seen to within two yards of the pin. Cruickshank, after walking down to study the situation, pulled his mashie into a trap at the left and then ran past the hole on his recovery. After he had missed his try for a 5 he extended his right hand to Jones. The latter, with victory assured, tapped his ball up to the hole and then in. Jones 4, Cruickshank 6.

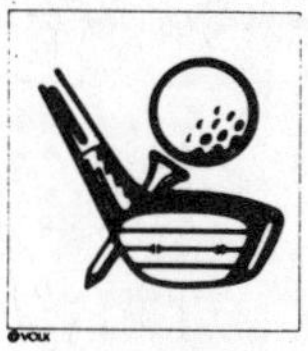

July 16, 1923

SARAZEN TRIUMPHS OVER HAGEN ON 38TH

Captures Thrilling Extra-Hole Match and Retains Pro Golf Title at Pelham.

LOSER MAKES GREAT FIGHT

Is Three Down at Twenty-eighth, but Evens Score at the Thirty-fifth.

For the second successive time, Gene Sarazen, Briarcliff Lodge professional, is the P.G.A. champion. After one of the most thrilling matches ever played, a match that held even his fellow-pros spellbound by its tenseness, Sarazen successfully defended his one remaining title by defeating Walter Hagen on the thirty-eighth green at the Pelham Country Club yesterday afternoon.

The perpetration of one of the cardinal sins of golf, lifting the head, was the ultimate cause of Hagen's downfall, although a wonderful recovery from the rough by Sarazen played a powerful part.

Sarazen, having seen his three-hole lead dwindle to nothing between the tenth hole and the eighteenth in the afternoon round and having had to get down a nervy four-foot putt to save his half at the first extra hole, went boldly for the second hole. He had watched Hagen's tee shot cut the corner of the trees, knowing by the shout of the crowd banked around the green that his rival was somewhere near. There was no indecision on his part when he struck the ball. He pulled the shot a trifle and it just cleared the trees, landing in the heavy rough quite a distance from the green.

Hagen's ball had just escaped a trap and was perched up, leaving him but an easy chip to the hole. Sarazen studied his shot carefully, told his caddy that he was going to put the ball up close and did. It was a magnificent shot that stopped dead, not more than two feet from the hole.

Hagen Misses Chance.

It was now up to Hagen, and instead of having the upper hand, as he had before Gene played his shot. Walter's back was against the wall with the most critical moment of the match at hand. He looked up and flubbed his ball into the trap just ahead. Then, however, as if to prove that he would go down fighting, he almost holed out on his next shot. Sarazen still had his putt to make before his title was safe, but he holed it without wasting more than a second in studying the line.

By defeating Hagen today, Sarazen not only won the P.G.A. title but he also demonstrated that he is the outstanding match play golfer among the professionals. It was the third time that he had defeated Hagen in match day in this country and it transferred to his sturdy shoulders the title that Hagen has enjoyed for several years.

Gene played the course in seventy-three strokes during the afternoon, one under par, the same as did Hagen, but the little champion had birdies at the two extra holes, while Hagen had ony one. The little Italian star was a stroke higher than Hagen in the morning round, having a 77 to 76.

The story of the match hinges on the final round, for at the end of the first eighteen holes the two golf giants were all even.

Starting out the afternoon round with two birdies on the first nine holes and nothing worse than par figures on the others. Gene was 3 up on Hagen by the time the seventh hole was played. He took three putts on the first green in the afternoon. He was short on his approach putt and left himself open for Hagen to lay him a partial stymie so that the hole was halved.

Sarazen Wins Third Hole.

Sarazen made a great recovery from a trap to save his half on the second, but he broke the spell with a birdie at the third hole, where he was home with two beautiful wooden shots, while Hagen was in the rough to the left of the green after pitching onto the green. Hagen hit the cup on his try for a 4, but his ball failed to drop in.

After halving the fourth in par 3s Sarazen holed two fine putts on the next two greens, a thirty-footer for a win at the fifth and a four-yarder for a half at the sixth. Hagen became 3 own by taking three putts at the seventh. The eighth and ninth were solved in par figures.

Hagen rimmed the cup for a 2 at the ninth and his first win came at the seventh, where he played a fine approach and holed a six-foot putt. He was lucky to get his half at the twelfth, for he overplayed the green and his ball was in the rough. He chipped back to five feet and got down the putt. Gene was on in two but could not hole his putt for a 3. Both were close to getting their 3s at the thirteenth, but halved the hole in birdie 4s. The next hole also was halved, as was the fifteenth, in which Hagen almost ran down his putt for a 3.

Sarazen lost the sixteenth, where he was trapped at the side of the green and Hagen squared the match by taking the seventeenth, 5 to 6. Here Sarazen, first to play, sliced to the rough, while Walter hooked out of bounds. Walter then played a great shot to the green and Gene pitched short into a trap, from where he played his next to the green and took two putts. Hagen, although trapped, saved a half at the home hole when he laid Sarazen a partial stymie.

Morning Round.

In the morning round Sarazen lost a chance to square the match at the eighth, which was halved in 5s, by taking three putts. He was home with a fine brassie second while Walter pushed his second off to the rough at the right of the green. The latter pitched out too strong but got down in two putts while Gene was two yards short and then missed his try for a birdie.

Hagen had all the better of the first two shots at the ninth but missed a four-footer for a win, giving Sarazen a half in 4. Gene had a chance to get down a six-foot putt for a win at the tenth, but missed it, but he squared the match a hole later when he played a great stop-shot ten feet short of the flag and Hagen overplayed to the rough over the green and then missed his next stroke completely. He conceded the hole when he failed to get his next down while Sarazen was up dead for a sure four.

Hagen blundered when he attempted to cut the trees too finely going to the long fourteenth and it cost him the hole for his ball hit an overhanging branch and dropped dead. His next attempt did the same thing. But he finally played a superb shot and reached the green. Sarazen was safely home on his third, and Hagen conceded the hole.

Hagen became 1 up by taking the fifteenth with a 4, his second stopping hole high to the left of the pin, two yards away. Gene's second ran over the green into a rough patch, and he overplayed the cup of his recovery, and then failed to hole a four-yarder for a half. Both got down good putts to halve the short sixteenth in threes. Sarazen's recovery from a trap being superbly played.

The seventeenth was halved in fives, but Gene squared the match by winning the home hole 3 to 4, when Walter's drive found a trap and was so close to the bank that he did well in getting it out at all. He made a bold try for his

d, but overran the cup. Gene was only a few yards from the cup with a great tee shot and had an easy birdie 3.
The cards:

MORNING ROUND

Out—
Sarazen ....4 5 5 3 4 5 4 5—39
Hagen ....5 4 5 3 4 4 5 4—38
In—
Sarazen ....3 4 4 6 5 5 8 5 3—38—77
Hagen ....3 5 4 4 6 4 3 5 3—38—76

AFTERNOON ROUND.

Out—
Sarazen ....5 4 4 8 3 4 4 4—35
Hagen ....5 4 5 3 4 4 5 4—38
In—
Sarazen ....3 4 4 1 5 4 4 6 4—38—73
Hagen ....3 5 1 1 5 4 3 5—35—73
Extra holes:
Sarazen 3 4
Hagen 3 4

September 30, 1923

OFFICIALS PUT BAN ON LIVELY GOLF BALL

Manufacturer Produces Pellet Which Adds Fifty Yards to Normal Drive.

CHICAGO, Jan. 10.—While it has not become generally known, a golf ball manufacturer recently perfected a ball that was so lively it could be driven 50 yards further than the best present-day product without any more effort or skill, but the high moguls of golf have decided to ban the ball.

Such a ball might be well enough for the duffer, but, the rulers of golf assert, to allow the use of such a long-distance ball in tournaments by star players would compel the rebuilding of all the golf courses in the country, and that would be prohibitive financially.

During the last ten years all the older links have been rebuilt to keep pace with the increasing sprightliness of golf balls, and the cost has been enormous. On the old links, bunkers that were made to punish poor second shots in the days of the old solid guttapercha ball became hazards for the drive with the rubber cored pellet, and other things were out of proportion in a similar way.

Now, if the balls with the long range were to be allowed, there would be no hole for two full shots in the country, for such long shooters as Jesse Guilford and Bobby Jones would fetch a 600-yard green with a drive and an iron. And if courses were rebuilt to accommodate this far-reaching sphere, they would be too long for comfort, forcing players to travel two or three miles further in an 18-hole round and making women and ordinary male golfers limit themselves to nine holes a day.

The size of a golf ball now is limited to a diameter of not less than 1.62 inch, and to a weight of not more than 1.62 ounces. It so happened that the wonder ball satisfied those limitations, and therefore was eligible. The heads of golf associations have merely told the maker that the new creation would not be allowed, despite its fulfillment of specifications, and that if an attempt should be made to market the pellet the specifications would be changed in some way, possibly by adding one to the effect that the ball must not be more lively than to travel 1.62 furlongs (356.4 yards) under the best blow the best driver could deliver.

January 11, 1924

GOLFERS FACE TASK OF ALTERING CLUBS

New U. S. G. A. Ruling Prohibits the Employment of Grooved or Slotted Sticks.

LEE SENDS OUT WARNING

Before the next golf season makes its appearance golfers who participate in various invitation tournaments held under the auspices of the United States Golf Association have considerable work confronting them. Under the new ruling adopted at the time of the national amateur championship at Flossmoor, grooved and slotted clubs are barred by the association in 1924, which will mean that the faces on many a time-worn and trusty mashie and niblick will have to be filed off before the club will be sanctioned in "official affairs" or else it will be necessary for the golfers to supply themselves with an entirely new kit. In any case it will mean a lot of practice between now and the height of the tournament season to get used to the smooth-surfaced implements of links warfare.

The pros who attended the last British open championship at Troon, having been through the mill, will realize full well what this means, for just previous to the start of the qualifying round at Troon the Royal and Ancient, which controls the game on the other side, posted a ruling to the effect that clubs with slotted, grooved and corrugated surfaces would not be allowed in the championship and Tom Fernie's shop was a busy place for a few hours before the classic started, files and hammers being especially in demand.

The edict in America, although put through last Fall, did not go into effect until Jan. 1, 1924.

Apparently a false impression has gone out regarding the ruling, for Cornelius S. Lee, Secretary of the United States Golf Association, yesterday sent out the following communication to golfers:

"An erroneous impression seems to have been conveyed to golfers from misinterpretation of a remark made during the annual meeting of the U. S. G. A. at the Hotel Astor on Jan. 5, that the new rule with respect to grooved and slotted clubs was not in effect.

"The Executive Committee, during a session at the Flossmoor Country Club, at the time of the amateur championship in September last, unanimously adopted the following ruling, effective Jan. 1, 1924:

"'Club faces shall not bear any lines, dots or other markings, made for the obvious purpose of putting a cut on the ball, nor shall they be stamped or cut with lines exceeding one-sixteenth inch in width, nor less than three-thirty seconds inch apart, measured on their inside edges. Both lines and dot markings may be used, either alone or in combination within the above limitations, provided all rough or raised edges are removed.'

"The attention of all golfers is called to this ruling, which will be strictly enforced in all competitions held under the auspices of the U. S. G. A."

January 13, 1924

HAGEN REGAINS TITLE IN THE BRITISH OPEN

American Leads Whitcombe by One Stroke in 72-Hole Championship at Hoylake.

HAS TOTAL SCORE OF 301

Makes Sensational Finish, Covering Last Nine in 36, to Beat English Golfer.

MAC SMITH TIED FOR THIRD

Shares Place With Ball — Barnes Ties for Seventh, Nichols Is Tenth —Sarazen Well Down.

YARDAGE AND SCRATCH AT HOYLAKE.					
OUT.			IN.		
Hole.	Yds.	Sch.	Hole.	Yds.	Sch.
1	410	5	10	430	5
2	355	4	11	200	4
3	490	5	12	455	5
4	155	3	13	165	3
5	410	4	14	510	5
6	380	4	15	440	4
7	200	3	16	525	5
8	500	5	17	400	4
9	390	5	18	410	4

Distance—Out, 3,290; in, 3,460. Total—750.

Scratch—Out, 38; in, 38. Total—76.

Copyright, 1924, by The New York Times Company.
Special Cable to THE NEW YORK TIMES.

HOYLAKE, England, June 27.—Once again the British open golf championship has gone to an American, and the winner is again Walter Hagen, who captured it two years ago at Sandwich.

It was a well earned victory, but it was not achieved without a struggle that produced many sensational minutes during the day's play, when a good last round by any one of the half-dozen leaders would have gained for him the much coveted laurels.

At the end of the third round this morning the aggregates were as follows: Hagen, 224; E. R. Whitcombe, 224; Macdonald Smith, 227; Frank Ball, 227; George Duncan, 227, and J. H. Taylor, 228.

Hagen's fourth round of 77, with an aggregate of 301, brought him the victory by one stroke better than Whitcombe, whose 78 was not quite good enough. Better scores were expected, but it is recalled that Taylor, when he won his last championship at Hoylake in 1913, took 304 for the four rounds. Moreover, the Hoylake course has been increased to over 6,700 yards in length, and today there was a strong breeze blowing which made low scoring difficult.

Hagen Plays Uphill Game.

In winning the championship by a single stroke Hagen gave a magnificent display of uphill fighting, following an equally courageous effort by Whitcombe. Everybody agrees that Hagen deserved his victory and that, although his golf was not blameless, it was achieved by pure fighting ability. That he has proved his superiority over the best golfers Great Britain can produce is demonstrated by the fact that he won the championship in 1922, and

last year was beaten by a single putt.

When Whitcombe had finished in 302 and Hagen, wanting a 78 to tie, had taken 41 for the first nine holes, the American player appeared to be beaten. He then produced, however, a series of wonderful recovery shots, one after the other, and having pulled the game around, finished like a lion by doing the last nine holes in 36.

Whitcombe in his last round had much the same experience. He made a deplorable start with a 5 and a 6 through visits to bunkers, and he required a 43 to reach the turn. Then he played magnificently, coming home in 35. Like Hagen last year, he can blame himself now because he missed holeable putts to make it 34.

Macdonald Smith, another American—although the Scots claim him as one of their kith and kin—was bracketed third with Ball, both of them having aggregates of 304. Smith played steady golf with nothing particularly exciting about it. His two rounds of 77 each today were not, however, good enough. He found the wind somewhat troublesome, and it was responsible for one or two extra shots that played him out of the running. Incidentally, it may be mentioned that the best score made today was 74, and only three players, namely, Hagen, Ball and Duncan, achieved it.

Barnes, with 79 for his third round, was out of it, and his fourth round of 75 was of no use. Nicholls had an aggregate of 310, and Sarazen, who has been entirely out of form, is well down on the list with 323, having taken 84 and 81 today.

Much praise is given to J. H. Taylor, who made a splendid effort to keep the championship on this side. He already has won the championship five times and he tried for it once more. His first victory dates back to thirty years ago. Despite his 53 years of age he has been persevering manfully, but unfortunately lumbago got a grip on him and he faded away today with rounds of 78 and 79.

The amateurs this year were not in the picture, the first of them being Cyril Tolley with a 314, which mark he shares with James Braid, while Roger Wethered, who tied with Jock Hutchinson for the championship in 1921, retired after finding his first two scores of 82 and 85 made it impossible for him to succeed. Havers also entirely failed to do himself justice, his aggregate being 317 with a third round score of 86.

Hagen and Whitcombe Even.

Hagen finished the morning round in 74 to bring himself level with Whitcombe. One cannot say that it was a great round, for there were many loose shots in it. But Hagen's putting was so uniformly excellent that strokes which went away with wooden and iron clubs were regained on the greens. It must be stated that Hagen had, in the middle of the round, a succession of fours and threes that made 72 seem likely. At one hole, however, he went into the rough, thence into the ditch, thence into a bunker and was fortunate to escape with a 6.

The huge, rushing, trembling crowd, which included many Americans, followed Hagen in his fourth round. He had a calamitous time of it on the way out. He put his supporters in the dumps by beginning with 6, taking another 6 at the third, where he pushed his second into a bunker, and yet another 6 at the eighth, where, after a series of adventures, he holed a putt of five or six yards to save a 7. When he had taken 41 for the first half he knew what he had to do to beat Whitcombe. His sliced second at the tenth looked like the finish for him, but a grand recovery gave him a 4.

Another bunker visitation at the eleventh was perturbing, but a beautiful putt saved him from disaster. At the next hole he cut his second shot far away from the line he intended to take, but recovered with a perfect pitch that laid the ball stone dead.

He almost completely missed his tee shot at the thirteenth and was bunkered, only to lay his next five feet from the hole, and down went a putt again. It was a wonderful series of recoveries that received well deserved applause.

Hagen was now called upon to do the last five holes in 21 to win, and he forthwith stopped making foolish mistakes which needed such marvelous recoveries. Two grand shots got him 4 at the fourteenth, and the same thing happened at the next hole.

Two big hits saw him on the edge of the sixteenth green, but he needed three putts. At the seventeenth hole, which displays all sorts of terrors for the nervous golfer, Hagen hit his second to within three yards of the pin. If he could hole his putt nothing could stop him from being champion. But he did not do so.

Hagen needed 4 at the last hole. He drove straight down the centre and then, taking no risks with the bunker ahead, pitched well up to the pin. The shot was a trifle too strong and the ball trickled just over the green. The run-up was a little short and Hagen had to negotiate a putt of some six feet to be champion. He studied the line carefully and then firmly hit the ball, which went into the hole without a quiver or wabble.

Hagen waved his putter in the air, and America had won the British open championship for the third time in four years.

June 28, 1924

MACFARLANE BEATS JONES BY 1 STROKE FOR OPEN GOLF TITLE

Pro Conquers Amateur in Second Extra Round of Longest Match in History, 72-73.

FIRST 18 HOLES END 75-75

Scot Misses Three-Foot Putt at Home Hole With National Title at Hand.

STAGES A DRAMATIC FINISH

Victor Starts Final Nine With Four-Stroke Deficit but Surpasses Georgian, Who Plays Par Golf.

By WILLIAM D. RICHARDSON.

Special to The New York Times.

WORCESTER, Mass., June 5.—The gods of golf held their fingers crossed for Bobby Jones today, but vainly. After a day of dramatic moments such as no other championship, American or British, has ever witnessed, Willie Macfarlane, the pedagogical-looking Scotsman who presides over the practice tees at the Oak Ridge Club at Tuckahoe, won the twenty-ninth open championship of America. He defeated the amateur champion today by one stroke, his total for the thirty-six holes played to decide the issue at the Worcester Country Club being 147 strokes to Jones's 148.

The end came on the last hole, where Macfarlane took a par 4 and Jones a

Walter Hagen

5, through one faulty shot and another splendid "do-or-die" one that died. With the match all even in strokes, and everything—fame and riches for Macfarlane and a record achievement or Jones—at stake, Bobby sliced his drive into some long grass after Willie had split the fairway. Having to play first, Macfarlane pitched onto the upper tier of the green, about fifty feet from the hole, but facing a treacherous downhill putt to lay dead for his 4.

Then Bobby played. He was resolved to go for the hole, which was cut close to the edge of the green, trapped in the front. Only a miracle shot would place the ball near the hole under the conditions, although the lie was a good one. Bobby made a hasty decision. With Macfarlane's ball in a place where a 4 was inevitable unless he overran, Jones determined to play for either a 3 or a 5 and end the agony then and there.

Jones' Shot That Failed.

The pitch out of the rough kept coming straight for the pin, and for a second or two it appeared as if he had brought off another Inwood shot which gave him the 1923 title in the play-off with another Scot, Bobby Cruickshank. The ball dropped short into the sand, causing a gasp to go up from the gallery banked around the finishing hole. Jones was closer to the hole than was Macfarlane, who had, therefore, to play first.

It was a ticklish situation for the Aberdonian, for the missing of a five-foot putt on the same green had denied him the championship eighteen holes previously. There was no certainty that he would lay the putt dead; there was no certainty that Jones wouldn't hole out from the trap or put the ball up

close for a par 4 which would mean playing on and on ad infinitum.

Willie, to his own annoyance, had missed five and six-footers previously in the round, but he made sure of this one. Showing no outward signs of the tension that must have been his, calmly surveying the line of the putt, he tapped the ball and sent it spinning on its way toward the hole. On it went, getting closer and closer to the hole. A great shout went up. "It's in!" No; it wasn't, but it was perilously close to the hole, not more than a foot away, sitting up for a sure 4—one of the finest approach putts ever made and a wonderful display of nerve and lack of nerves.

And His Last Fatal Putt.

It was now up to Bobby to play. On his next shot would depend whether or not he was to have a chance to equal Chick Evans's record of winning two titles in one year. The Atlantan made a courageous recovery to ten feet beyond the hole and if he could get that one down it meant another tie and another round.

There was a tense silence as he took his stance, glanced along the line of putt, drew back his putter and hit the ball. It started true for a few feet, then swerved off and grazed the side of the hole. Macfarlane had won the championship—the first Scotsman to win the title since 1910, when Alex Smith was crowned.

Thus ended the championship of championships, the greatest struggle between two of the game's giants that the world has ever seen. Never before in golf's history had two men been forced to play two rounds to decide which one of them was to be the cham-

pion. It was a perfect ending to a day of tremendous happenings that forced two thousand mad enthusiasts to dash hither and about, up and over the hills of the Worcester Country Club in spite of a torrid sun that poured down on scorched heads. It was 94 in the shade and there was no shade. In the hills of the far holes and in the woods the heat was stifling, yet it failed to daunt the intrepid followers who could not afford to miss even so much as a single shot in a match such as this.

Macfarlane's wonderful accomplishment in winning the title is best illustrated this way. He tied Jones at the end of the seventy-second hole of tournament play proper. He saw his own good work in the first round of the play-off obliterated by Bobby's almost phenominal run of luck on the middle holes and in the afternoon he began the final nine holes with a four-stroke deficit. In addition, Jones played par golf the rest of the way, another feat that called for superlative golf, and Macfarlane answered that call. In spite of his par golf over the last nine, Jones lost five strokes to his rival and that is how Macfarlane won the title.

Both Play Marvelous Golf.

When consideration is made for the stake involved, the golf that the two played throughout the round was little short of marvelous. Tieing with 75s in the morning, Macfarlane and Jones finished with 72 and 73 respectively in the afternoon, one and two shots over par. There were mistakes here and there, to be sure, but far fewer than one had any right to expect in view of the heat and the physical and mental strain. Macfarlane's main weaknesses during the two rounds were his inability to lay his chips up close when he needed to, to get down putts of four and five feet in a crisis, and his inability to keep on equal terms with Jones off the tee. But his iron work was irreproachable, and it was this that won the title for him just as it was Jones's iron work that cost him the title.

When it was all over one could not help wishing that there could not be two champions, for both golfers deserved to win and neither deserved to lose, taking the two rounds as a whole. But when the truth is told and justice is done to Macfarlane, it must be said that nothing except luck—pure unadulterated luck—gave him the right to play the afternoon round.

He got breaks on the thirteenth, fourteenth and fifteenth holes, particularly the fourteenth, that he did not deserve. They were breaks that would have taken the heart right out of a golfer of less courage than Macfarlane.

Jones Employs Acrobatics.

Going to the short thirteenth hole with a two-stroke deficit and apparently a beaten man, Bobby got his par after being trapped off the tee by dropping a putt of thirty feet or more. That wasn't so bad, for in the first nine his opponent had dropped a few long ones himself, but on the next hole Jones committed robbery. He just missed a trap on his drive, his ball dropping only a foot over the sand. Forced to stand with one foot in the bunker to play the ball, he brought off as respectable a shot as he could make under the conditions. It was to the right of the green and lying in grass nearly a foot high.

Macfarlane, after two beautiful shots, was on the green, in possession of a sure 4 and a possible 3. Bobby then proceeded to hole out from at least sixty yards, the ball dropping on the green, running straight toward the hole and nestling between the flag-stick and the rim. There was a birdie 3 on a hole at which he had played one absolutely bad shot and another that was neither good nor bad, but in between. Macfarlane's deserved two-stroke lead vanished right there.

Then at the next hole Bobby sliced wickedly toward the eleventh tee, found his ball sitting in a perfect spot for a long-iron shot toward the green and got the same as Macfarlane, whose only error was his failure to drop a four-footer.

They alternated strokes at the next two holes, and then the standard bearer of professional golfdom missed what would have been a winning putt on the home green, and the round finished all even.

Starts at a Fast Pace.

Having scraped through that, Jones started the afternoon round as if he intended to eat up his rival. He went out in 35, exact par. One by one his margin increased. He picked up a stroke on the fifth, another on the eighth and another on the ninth. On all these holes it was Macfarlane's approaching and putting that was slipping strokes here and there. Ordinarily these errors would

Macfarlane-Jones Cards in 36-Hole Play-Off And Scores for 72 Holes in Tourney Proper

First Play-off Round.

Out—									
Par 4	5	4	3	5	3	4	3	4—35	
MACFARLANE.									
4	6	3	3	4	3	5	4	5—37	
Strokes—									
4	10	13	16	20	23	28	32	37	
JONES.									
4	5	4	3	5	3	4	4	6—38	
Strokes—									
4	9	13	16	21	24	28	32	38	
In—									
Par 3	4	4	3	4	5	4	5	4—36	
MACFARLANE.									
3	4	5	4	4	5	4	5	4—38	
Strokes—									
40	44	49	53	57	62	66	71	75	
JONES.									
4	4	5	3	3	5	5	4	4—37	
Strokes—									
42	46	51	54	57	62	67	71	75	

Second Play-off Round.

Out—									
MACFARLANE.									
4	5	4	4	5	4	4	4	5—39	
Strokes—									
79	84	88	92	97	101	105	109	114	
JONES.									
4	5	4	3	4	4	4	3	4—35	
Strokes—									
79	84	88	91	95	99	103	106	110	
In—									
MACFARLANE.									
2	4	4	2	4	5	4	4	4—33—72	
Strokes—									
116	120	124	126	130	135	139	143	147	
JONES.									
3	4	4	4	4	6	4	4	5—38—73	
Strokes—									
113	117	121	125	129	135	139	143	148	

Wednesday.

MORNING ROUND.

Out—	
Macfarlane	4 5 4 4 5 3 5 4 4—38
Jones	4 5 5 4 4 5 4 3 5—39
In—	
Macfarlane	3 6 5 3 4 5 3 3 4—36—74
Jones	3 6 5 4 4 4 4 4 4—38—77

AFTERNOON ROUND.

Out—	
Macfarlane	3 5 4 3 4 2 4 2 4—31
Jones	4 4 4 4 4 3 4 3 4—34
In—	
Macfarlane	3 5 4 3 4 5 4 4 4—36—67—141
Jones	3 4 4 3 4 5 5 4 4—36—70—147

Thursday.

MORNING ROUND.

Out—	
Macfarlane	4 6 5 5 5 3 4 2 5—39
Jones	4 5 4 4 4 3 4 3 4—35
In—	
Macfarlane	3 4 5 3 3 5 3 4 3—33—72—213
Jones	2 3 4 3 4 4 5 5 5—35—70—217

AFTERNOON ROUND.

Out—	
Macfarlane	4 5 5 4 5 4 4 4 4—39
Jones	5 5 4 4 5 3 4 3 5—38
In—	
Macfarlane	2 5 5 4 5 5 5 4 4—39—78—201
Jones	2 5 4 3 5 5 4 4 4—36—74—201

not have amounted to anything. Against such a perfect machine as Jones was on those first nine holes, each error counted heavily.

It began to look as though Macfarlane was out of it. Spotting Jones four shots in nine holes and then winning is something that could only be accomplished once in a century. Today happened to be that once. Starting at the ninth, Mac picked up a shot by holing a twelve-foot putt. Three holes after that he picked up two strokes by dropping a twenty-five-footer when Bobby was taking a 4 through a hook to the bank of the green, a fine chip to a little more than a yard and a missed putt.

Two holes later, Bobby was trapped after a great drive and a long second that, had it been a yard or two more, would have been on the green and probably given him the title right there. He failed to get out cleanly and his ball stuck in a fringe of grass on the edge of another bunker five yards ahead. That cost him a six to McFarlane's five and the score was squared again. Six holes before it was almost a dead certainty that the title would again go to Jones. Now MacFarlane was on level terms after one of the greatest uphill fights ever made.

The knowledge that the Scot had made up a deficit that no one believed possible may have had its effect on Bobby's playing of the last hole. Whether it did or not, no mistakin gthe fact that it bolstered up his opponent's nerves, if they needed bolstering. Willie had to play two great chip approaches to get halves on the sixteenth and seventeenth holes, but he played them manfully and the approach putt he made on the home green was a manful shot. It brought him home in 33 strokes, three under par, a champion after the hardest fight that any man ever had to make to win the title.

June 6, 1925

JONES KEEPS TITLE, BEATING WATTS GUNN

CARDS OF JONES AND GUNN.

MORNING ROUND.

Out—	
Par	5 4 4 5 4 3 4 3 5—37
Jones	4 4 4 5 3 3 5 3 5—36
Gunn	4 4 4 3 4 4 4 4 4—35
In—	
Par	4 4 5 3 4 4 3 4 4—35—72
Jones	5 4 5 3 3 4 3 3 4—34—70
Gunn	4 4 5 4 4 5 3 4 6—39—74

AFTERNOON ROUND.

Out—	
Jones	4 3 5 5 4 4 5 3 5—38
Gunn	5 4 3 4 6 4 4 4 6—40
In—	
Jones	4 4
Gunn	5 6

By WILLIAM D. RICHARDSON.

Special to The New York Times.

PITTSBURGH, Sept. 5.—Master outplayed pupil in the final round of the national amateur championship over the Oakmont Country Club course today, when Robert Tyre Jones, the 1924 titleholder, defeated Watts Gunn, his fellow-townsman from Atlanta, 8 up and 7 to play. But for the first fourteen of the twenty-nine holes of the match Bobby's pupil, understudy and bosom companion forced the master to play as fine golf as he is capable of playing.

After that some of the finer points of the game in which his conqueror has been schooling him slipped from his mind and he began making errors that wrecked his chances of succeeding to the throne that Bobby has held for a year and will hold for yet another.

At the age of 24, when Bobby Jones won his second championship out of the eight in which he has competed, he has accomplished a feat which none other has accomplished since 1913, when Jerry Travers repeated at the Garden City Golf Club. It is a feat that only four others besides himself have been able to perform during the twenty-nine years of championship history. H. J. Whigham in the early years of the event, Walter Travers in 1900 and 1901, H. Chandler Egan in 1904 and 1905 and Travers twice.

Gunn Shows His Quality.

Although he went down in a match that ended seven holes before the finishing point, young Mr. Gunn, at the age of 20 years the outstanding figure of the 1925 championship, today served further notice on the golf world at large that he was almost ready to take his place with his masterful mentor at the head of the amateur procession. For five holes he outperformed the champion and for the first fourteen the match was so nip and tuck that no one was able to tell what the outcome was going to be. Then suddenly his perfect timing machinery went askew, he began hooking his tee shots, sending his ball into intriguing traps, and his fate was sealed.

One after another the holes were marked down on Bobby's side of the ledger. Twice trapped playing the last four holes in the morning, Jones came off the field of battle 4 up at noon. Bobby then won the first two played in the afternoon, building his margin up to six.

Still Gunn wasn't finished, for he got two of them back with a sensational ninety-foot chip shot out of a bunker for a birdie 3 on the third and a great birdie 4 on the 536-yard bottle-necked fourth. Back to only 4 down with fourteen holes remaining to be played, Gunn, tiring under the strain of his first championship and discouraged by the withering sample of golf that Jones was playing, again begain mistiming his strokes. From there on to the eleventh green, where the match came to a halt, Gunn was in one or more traps at every solitary hole, Jones winning the last four in a row as a result.

Playing to the last hole with the match standing 7 up and 8 to play in Jones's favor, Gunn, hitting at the top of his swing, hooked into the corner of a trap and had to waste a stroke getting out. Jones, with a well-placed tee shot, then played a superb approach twelve feet to the left of the pin, while Gunn missed his mashie approach into a trap on the left of the green from where he exploded his ball out five yards or more above the hole.

He hit the next putt truly and for a moment it appeared to be headed for the opening. It hit the cup and rolled on for another two feet, and after Bobby putted up dead and then into the cup the pupil extended his hand to the master, slapped him on the back and together victor and vanquished marched off the field of battle, each proud of the other, to resume their friendly feuds on their home links in Atlanta until next year.

Match a Big Strain.

The baptism that Gunn received in his first championship début was one that would have shaken the nerves of any one for against him Jones, forgetting temporarily that he was playing one of his closest friends and a youngster whom he has aided and assisted, schooled and chaperoned, let go of one of the greatest rounds of golf he has ever played and the best round played in the entire tournament.

His medal score was a 70, two under par, which might have been a 68 had he been forced to go after two putts, one on the fifteenth and another on the eighteenth, but he played safe. Gunn had played the round in 74, a scoring feat only a few times equaled during the present championship, and yet he was 4 down.

No wonder then that young Watts playfully said to Jones in the locker room afterward: "Gee, Jones, you're a tough kid." During that first round birdies and eagles flew thick and fast and between them the two finalists had a best ball of 65, seven under par. Jones was out in 35, two under par, while Gunn was 36, one under, and they were all even.

Gunn took a 39 on the homeward half when he was in such an abundance of traps, while Jones came sailing home with a 34, one less than par. They were both a stroke higher than the par figures for the first nine holes in the afternoon and Jones finished with two par 4s against a pair of 5s for Gunn.

Jones's superiority over Gunn was in his remarkable driving, a combination of length and straightness, his fewer mistakes, and his putting, especially in the crises. He was generally out in front of Gunn off the tees and inside on the greens. The vital statistics on the match show that in the morning Gunn was in five traps and in the rough three times, while Jones was in three traps and twice in the rough. On the first round Gunn took 33 putts on the greens, Jones, 32. Each had one three-putt green, Jones taking one more than the conventional number at the sixth hole and Gunn erring on the ninth.

In the afternoon the figures favored Jones by a wide margin, the champion being trapped only three times to Gunn's nine. Bobby was twice in the rough on the last eleven holes, but lost only one hole through it.

When the two Atlanta youngsters started out for their test of ability and strength, there were few who thought that the match would go as far as it actually did, it being the general impression that Gunn would wilt before the master.

Gunn Keeps up the Fight.

No such thing happened, for even near the finish when things began to go so badly for him and when the inevitable end was in sight, Gunn kept on fighting every inch of the way, not giving up until there was no further use to continue.

For the first four holes the match was on an even keel, young Watts getting a good half in birdie 4 figures on the first green by sinking a courageous five-foot putt when he needed it to save himself a half. He got another worthy half on the third when he played a fine chip from the far side of the green to within a foot of the cup after Jones had putted up to within the same distance.

Gunn won the long fourth to give him a lead by playing one of the finest shots of the day. A long iron second that entered the narrow neck of the green and stopped five yards past the hole and less than that distance from a deep bunker. Not satisfied with that exhibition of courage, he holed the putt for an eagle 3, hitting the cup squarely in the centre. It was more than enough to win the hole, for Bobby's second missed the green and went into a trap on the right.

His lead was short-lived, for Bobby ran down a ten-yard putt for a birdie 3 at the fifth. Three putts from the far side of the sixth green cost Gunn the sixth hole and left Jones 1 up. Gunn's approach putt was three yards off the line, while Jones, on at the far left side of the green, twenty yards from the hole, ran his approach practically dead.

Jones's first bad tee shot was played on the way to the seventh, where he hooked off the line to the left and then played his next weakly into a trap short of the green. Gunn was on the green with his second and he left himself a four-foot putt to hole, squaring the match.

Jones then won the eighth, 3 to 4, when Gunn's tee shot was trapped in the shelf-like bunker. Gunn then squarred the match on the ninth, which he won, 4 to 5. Here Jones was lucky when his tee shot, badly hooked, cleaged three traps and landed in the short rough, enabling him to try for the green with his second. He got home, about fifteen yards from the flag, but took three putts, missing a four-footer for a half.

Gunn had a tremendous drive on the hole and his second reached the green, but outside of Jones. Faced with a difficult putt to lay dead, with one down slope and two up slopes to figure, Gunn laid his putt up to within a yard and then holed for a birdie 4 to square the match.

Both were lucky to have their drives, played with a slice, strike in the rough and bounce back onto the fairway enroute to the tenth hole, and Gunn won the hole, 4 to 5, by chipping dead from off the near edge of the green.

Jones Misses His Approach.

Jones missed the green with his approach and then ran his third three yards past the hole, missing on the return voyage. The eleventh was half in perfection figures, as was the twelfth.

The play of the twelfth was less perfect, however, Gunn slicing his tee shot in among the spectators on the right and up against the face of a mound, which forced him to play safe and Jones reaching a trap on the left. Gunn was home on his magnificently played third, while Jones, after reaching a trap with his third, had to hole a ten-footer to get a half.

Still holding the honor, Gunn lost it when he played a poor iron to the thirteenth hole and got trapped on the left of the green for it. It was then that Bobby began creeping away by winning four out of the next five holes. Bobby got a birdie 3 to Gunn's par 4 on the fourteenth, getting off a tremendous drive, playing a pitch-and-run shot twenty feet short and holding the putt. Gunn hooked his drive behind a tree going to the fifteenth and then trapped himself on his attempted recovery out of the rough.

The sixteenth was halved in par 3s, Gunn sinking a five-foot putt for his. Jones got down in ont putt for a birdie 3 and another win on the seventeenth, where Gunn hooked into a trap. Gunn again hooked into a trap playing the final hole in the morning and after falling to get out on in his first attempt he took a 6 to Jones's par 4.

Jones started off with birdies at the second and first holes played in the afternoon round, winning both and becoming six up. Then Gunn won the third by holding out from a trap and he also won the fourth by again reaching the green on his second while Jones was trapped on his lie.

At this point it looked as if the boy would stage a comeback, but then his shots began wandering and except for the sixth, which he halved, and the seventh, which he won, he lost the next five holes. Visitation to bunkers and rought was responsible for each loss.

September 6, 1925

BOBBY JONES WINS BRITISH OPEN TITLE

U. S. Sweeps Event as Watrous Finishes Second and Hagen and Von Elm Tie for Third.

WINNING SCORE IS 291

American Is the Third Amateur to Capture Golf Prize and First in 29 Years.

By ANTHONY SPALDING.

Copyright, 1926, by The New York Times Company.
Special Cable to THE NEW YORK TIMES.

ST. ANNE'S, England, June 25.—For the first time in twenty-nine years an amateur golfer has won the British open golf championship, and the most coveted honor in the game belongs to Bobby Jones, who has also won the deep affection of the British public.

The next three places also went to Americans. Al Watrous was second with a score of 293, two strokes behind Jones, while Walter Hagen and George Von Elm, another amateur, tied for third place with 295 each. Next came two British players, Abe Mitchell and Tom Barber, who were tied at 299.

There were 5,000 persons in an oblong formation, motionless, breathless, while Jones performed the last rites on the home putting green. The ball had nearly disappeared when there burst forth a tremendous shout of joy. Everybody knew his aggregate was 291, leading Watrous by two shots, but Hagen was out at the far end of the course with his teeth clenched in his most hostile and menacing manner. It may sound unsportsmanlike, but the crowd was pulling for his defeat. Hagen had to do 71 to win and 72 to tie. Everybody hoped and believed he could not do it, and when he was ultimately left with a pitch to tie and the pitch raced across the green into the bunker dividing the green from the clubhouse garden everybody heaved a sigh and felt relieved.

Jones Tumultuously Cheered.

Shortly afterward the stage for bestowing the honors was erected, and around this the spectators swarmed like bees. The tension was over and joy abounded. When Bobby Jones came along with Norman Boase, Chairman of the Championship Committee, he got a tumultuous reception. He is the most glorious golfer modern players have seen. He goes about the game without doing anything to the disadvantage of his opponents, he is silent and his cap is homespun and fits his head. That is stuff which appeals to the British attitude to the game.

John Ball and Harold Hilton are the only two other amateurs who ever won this great distinction, and they are historic figures in golf. When presented with the cup by Norman Boase, Jones replied his greatest ambition in life had been to win the cup and have his name inscribed among the illustrious figures in golf—Vardon, Taylor and Braid. He added that he was very nervous all day and felt dazed when putting, and apologized if he had shown himself fidgety.

It was a day brimming with excitement in which the conspicuous figures at the beginning of play were Jones, Watrous and Hagen. Jones and Watrous were partners and it was inevitable that sooner or later the two would lose sight of par figures and the game develop into a personal duel.

This aspect was pleasing to Hagen, who kept watch like a cat ready to pounce on whatever score was put to him. His form was good in parts only and before he reached the ninth he knew what he had to do. Moreover, he began to reel off figures according to schedule and had the bad luck to miss a birdie at the twelfth, where the ball lipped the hole.

Then whatever chance he had of coming back in 35 disappeared. First he missed a two-foot putt on the thirteenth and at the one remaining short hole he was bunkered. One could visualize the championship fading away from his grasp like a picture on a magic lantern slide. He could still tie with two birdies. But though Hagen is a showman he is not a conjurer. The first birdie flew away and not unnaturally he failed to hole his pitch.

There was intense excitement when Bobby and Watrous set forth on the final round, which became intensified when Jones picked up the two strokes he was behind at the fifth. But Bobby was still two in arrears at the turn. He lost a stroke in the trap in the seventh and he went for two at the ninth and took four. He missed a two-footer.

The strain began to tell on both men, especially on Watrous. The first crack came at the tenth, where he pulled behind a sandhill and Bobby regained a stroke. First Watrous was deep in the rough at the long eleventh, but Bobby could not get down under three putts and he was again two in arrears with five holes to play. Then Watrous missed three short putts in a row and Bobby drew level. He led by one stroke at the seventeenth.

Great Crowd Follows Pair.

There was an enormous crowd with the players and another dense crowd was waiting near the clubhouse. Bobby pulled out the necessary extra bit at the last drive, which was long and impeccably straight, with Watrous lying on the loose sand. The crowd closed in and waited in intense silence. Watrous looked long and anxiously before he played and then up came the ball from an evil place to drop on the green and roll into the trap. Bobby steered his ball dead on the pin, four yards past. The people swept forward to watch the putting. Bobby's approach was still, the ball disappeared and he had won the championship. The ovation lasted a couple of minutes.

Bobby's long game and second shots were fine, but his putting was weak. He took thirty-nine putts in the afternoon and 100 putts in the championship. His aggregate was 291, which equals Jim Braid's record at Prestwick in 1908. Watrous, unknown to us, proved himself possessed of grit and if he bent he did not break, his aggregate being 293, while George von Elm's 295 tied Hagen for third.

Watrous and Bobby Jones were early starters in the morning. They set the pace of the day and the pace was cracker. Watrous, whose style and form receive many commendatory notices from British critics, lived up to what had been said. It was he and not Bobby who dominated the situation.

Another day of brilliant sunshine and northwest wind had dried the course and the greens ran very fast, even being disconcerting to the players. Watrous was not enterprising with his approach putts. A trapped iron at the fourth was nearly holed and the only other notable incident was at the ninth where he turned up a deuce. That was the first time he hit his ball without fear and the success gave him much-needed confidence. He was out in 33 and he came back in 36. He missed two holeable putts, but starred with a fifteen-footer and a ten-footer which dropped.

Bobby Not Comfortable.

Bobby Jones was not quite comfortable. The ball ran at a disconcerting pace and trouble began at the third where he overran the green into a bunker, and his second shot entered another trap on the edge of the fourth. He put too much power under an explosion shot and the ball soared over the green into the long grass which also held up his chip.

His start, 3-4-5-6, formed a discordant crescendo, but Bob never struck another wrong note until the ninth. On the way he effected a magnificent recovery out of the deep bunker at the seventh and made his par.

The ninth is a short hole defended by waspish bunkers and the setting reminds one of the shape of a note of interrogation. It puts an unequivocal question to the player as he stands on the tee and demands an answer. Watrous played a deuce; and, a bunker played the deuce with Bobby's score which was 37 out.

Like Watrous, he played fine golf coming back, but the successful putt which gives the sparkle to a game was absent. Bobby did not get down

one respectable putt in the whole round. The ball perversely sat outside or just rolled away and mocked him.

Hagen Plays Well Going Out.

Hagen started the morning round with three and ended with three and some adventures in between. Apart from visiting the traps at the third and fourth, his golf going out was quite good, but the fun began coming back against the wind. He hooked into sandhills at the tenth, played two into the bunker and holed a thirty-foot putt for a 5. He was in the rough at the twelfth, but got par with a pitch and a putt. He missed a five-footer at the thirteenth and was either trapped or in tiger country at the next three holes. His round of 74 put him third.

As the competition proceeded it became more and more evident that the championship had resolved itself into one of purely American rivalry. Freddie McLeod turned up a 76 in the morning and was much disgruntled because his putts would not drop. He took 36 putts. Fred had a bad patch near the turn, where he was trapped, missed a tee shot and was bunkered at three holes in a row. That made his score out 37, and he missed three more putts coming home.

Bill Mehlhorn blew up at the same corner of the course. Before this happened he experienced the thrill of almost holing a brassie shot at the seventh of 543 yards. The ball hit the pin and stopped a few inches away. Two balls flew from the eighth tee over onto the railway tracks and two shots were dissipated in the bunker at the ninth. This made Bill very angry and did not help him any to recover the lost strokes. He went on losing more, and his trail went through traps. His full cup overflowed on the home green, where he missed one of twelve inches.

Von Elm Has Hard Luck.

Joe Kirkwood was out in 35 and broke coming back. George Von Elm played many fine shots, but for the cussedness of things might have handed in a 72, but possible threes turned into fours when it came to putting. Emmett French continued his steady if not brilliant golf with growing confidence, and his third round of 74 was his best.

The first six men at the end of the third round were Americans, with John Henry Taylor, veteran champion, the British leader with 224. He did 71 in the morning; Abe Mitchell had 72, Jim Barnes 72, George Gadd 78, George Duncan 80 and Arthur Havers 82.

The sensation of the day was the disqualification of Archie Compston, who was trapped near the twelfth green. He blasted out into an adjoining plantation which the Championship Committee had expressly declared out of bounds for the tournament, though not out of bounds in ordinary club golf.

The steward in charge of the green informed Compston of the regulation, but, being obstinate, Compston thought he knew better, and so sinned against the light, played out of the plantation and thus committed suicide. He was not doing well at the time of his demise.

Mitchell was himself again and did thirty-six holes in 72 and 71, which was the best performance of the day.

Bobby Jones, Winner of the British Open Golf Title.

Times Wide World Photos.

His aggregate was 299; Barber's, 299 McLeod's, Mehlorn's and Jurado's, Argentine, 301; French, 303; John Henry Taylor and Gaudin, 304, and Armour, 305. Thus America had eight of the first thirteen places.

The par for the course follows:

Hole.	Yds.	Par.	Hole.	Yds.	Par.
1	225	3	10	361	4
2	423	4	11	509	5
3	472	5	12	313	4
4	343	4	13	447	4
5	190	3	14	352	4
6	431	4	15	184	3
7	543	5	16	547	4
8	387	4	17	411	4
9	161	3	18	349	4

Total yardage—6,456. Par—71.

June 26, 1926

HAGEN WINS, 6 AND 5; RETAINS P. G. A. TITLE

Beats Mehlhorn After Great Battle in Chicago and Is Over Par Only Once.

HAS A 67 IN THE MORNING

But Rival Comes Home in Par 70 and Is Just 3 Down After Brilliant Playing.

VICTOR THEN TURNS IN 33

And Is One Under 4s for the Last Four Holes — Chicagoan Has 34, but Fails to Take an Outgoing Hole.

CARDS OF THE FINALISTS.
Morning Round.
COURSE NO. 4.

Out—										
Par	5	4	4	4	4	3	4	3	4—35	
Hagen	3	3	4	4	4	3	4	3	5—33	
Mehlhorn	4	4	5	4	3	3	4	3	3—33	
In—										
Par	4	4	4	3	4	5	3	4	4—35—70	
Hagen	4	4	4	2	4	5	3	4	4—34—67	
Mehlhorn	4	5	5	3	5	5	2	4	4—37—70	

Afternoon Round.
COURSE NO. 3.

Out—									
Par	4	5	3	4	4	4	3	4	4—35
Hagen	4	4	3	4	3	4	3	4	4—33
Mehlhorn	4	3	3	4	4	4	3	4	5—34
In—									
Par	3	4	4	4	4	5	3	4	4—35—70
Hagen	3	4	4	4					
Mehlhorn	3	4	5	5					

By **WILLIAM D. RICHARDSON.**

Special to The New York Times.

CHICAGO, Sept. 26.—Walter Hagen today terminated the greatest week of his golfing career by defeating William Mehlhorn of Chicago, former Western open champion, 6 up and 5 to play, in the final thirty-six hole round of the 1925 P. G. A. championship, played over the Olympia Fields links. By his victory Hagen continues his ownership of the professional golfers' trophy which he was defending and which he has now won three times since 1916, the year it was put up for competition.

Never in his life was Hagen more of a machine than he was against Mehlhorn this morning and again this afternoon. Only once in the thirty-one holes of play was he over par figures at any hole. In the morning round he was 67 against the par of 70, and he might even be conceded a 66, for he didn't hole out on the ninth green, where Mehlhorn sank a twenty-five foot putt for a birdie 3. He was again out in 33 on the No. 3 course in the afternoon and one under 4's for the four holes played after the turn.

Mehlhorn wasn't guilty of many errors, playing the No. 4 course in par during the morning round but finding himself 3 down just the same. He almost matched Hagen for the first eleven holes in the afternoon round, playing the first nine holes in 34, yet failing to take a single hole from Hagen's lead. He finally collapsed under the strain and permitted Hagen to capture two holes in a row with par figures. Rain, which had been threatening, came down hard as the last four holes were played.

Records of the Finalists.

In the course of the tourney Hagen defeated Al Watrous, Grand Rapids, 1 up, 39 holes, in the first round; Mike Brady, Winged Foot, 7 and 6, in the second round; Leo Diegel, Glen Oaks, 1 up, 40 holes, in the third round, and Harry Cooper, Dallas, Texas, 3 and 1, in the semi-final.

Mehlhorn defeated Emmett French, Youngstown, Ohio, 5 and 4, in the first round; Al Espinosa, Chicago, 1 up, in the second round; Tommy Kerrigan, Siwanoy, 7 and 6, in the third round, and Morte Dutra, Aberdeen, Washington, 8 and 6, in the semi-final.

In spite of what appears to be a crushing defeat, viewed solely from the final score, Mehlhorn fought a great battle today and lost a duel that no one in the world could have won. Not only was Hagen in one of his greatest scoring moods, with putts going into the hole from all angles and distances, with his mashie and mashie-niblick sending the ball soaring up close to the pin and his driver behaving the best it has all week, but he had almost every break in the luck. Time and again Mehlhorn had at least reasonable expectation of getting a win or a half when Hagen would kill his hope with some sort of a golfing miracle.

The deciding hole was the third in the afternoon round. Having just won the second with a 30-foot putt for an eagle 3, Mehlhorn reduced Hagen's lead to only two holes. His iron shot to the 235-yard third was a gem, a trifle past the hole, but apparently good for a win after Hagen had missed his tee shot, sending his ball through a trap and up on the fringe of a bunker, still far away from the green and from the pin. Hagen's next shot, a chip, was almost as bad, for he failed to reach the near edge of the green.

Hagen Gets 70-Footer.

Every one, Mehlhorn included, thought that it would be a win for the Middle Westerner, but instead of that the best he got was a half for Hagen holed a putt that was fully 70 feet, and nearly 80, in length. Mehlhorn almost succeeded in dropping his down hill for a putt, but it curled off at the end of its journey and left him 2 down when he might have been only 1 down.

That stroke of fortune, good for Hagen, bad for Mehlhorn, settled the issue then and there. Had he succeeded in winning the hole, as he would have except for Hagen's miraculous putt, the outcome might have been different. It seemed to have tremendous effect on Mehlhorn's subsequent play. To him it must have been conclusive evidence that he was playing against an unbeatable foe. It gave Hagen the mental edge. It made the vast difference between being 2 up and 1 up. Had Mehlhorn won that hole he would have been a much more dangerous foe than he was after the hole was played.

Hagen practically clinched his victory two holes later when he pitched out of the rough to within a foot of the hole for a birdie 3. Mehlhorn, in a furrow on his tee shot, played a spectacular recovery to the green—a stroke that ordinarily would have been good for a half had it not been for the fact that Hagen's ball was snuggling so close to the pin. Hagen was again back to 3 up.

Impending disaster had been avoided and from there on he never once gave his opponent a chance to break through except on the twelfth, where he sliced his tee shot. By then, however, Mehlhorn was at a point where it was impossible for him to take advantage of any opening.

It is doubtful whether, for sheer golf, there ever has been a match that compared with this one over thirty-one holes. Hagen's start in the morning was one that would take the heart out of almost any one, for he holed a thirty-foot putt for an eagle 3 on the first hole and a forty-footer for a birdie 3 on the second. That made him 2 up right off the top and then Mehlhorn took three putts on the next green, presenting Hagen with an unwarned hole, for Walter was short on his approach.

Mehlhorn's Takes Fifth Hole.

The first rift in Mehlhorn's clouds came at the fifth, where he holed a twelve-footer for a 3, reducing Hagen's lead to two holes. Hagen's first putting error came at the short sixth, where with mud on his ball, he missed a one-yarder.

After winning the ninth and losing the eleventh through a badly hooked tee shot—his first one off the fairway—Mehlhorn had another glorious chance to get back to only 1 down playing to the twelfth. Here Walter's mashie was badly shanked, headed apparently for the rough. Instead of hitting the bank of the green and bouncing off to the right, however, it hit a spectator squarely in the back and kicked on to the green, enabling him to get a good position which he did not deserve. Seeing that things were breaking so nicely for him, Hagen then pitched to within eight feet of the pin on the next hole, dropped the putt for a birdie 2, and was again 3 up.

It took Mehlhorn two holes to forget that incident and he lost one of them to become 4 down. He managed to get one of them back, but he finished the round 3 down when his golf didn't deserve that fate. After the fifth hole in the afternoon round he was generally struggling, forcing his game, and failing to get anywhere against the sort of golf that Hagen kept turning on against him.

The figures of the match showed that Hagen had four one-putt greens in the morning against five for Mehlhorn, but Hagen's were more opportune than Mehlhorn's. Mehlhorn was inside Hagen on six holes going out and Hagen inside Mehlhorn on six holes coming in. Hagen played the odd at six holes on the outgoing nine in the morning and at five holes coming in. Mehlhorn played the odd at one hole out and two holes in.

Mehlhorn was in the rough only four times in the morning and in only one trap; Hagen was in the rough on three. In the afternoon Hagen and Mehlhorn each had three one-putt greens, but Mehlhorn had one three-putt green. Hagen was in the rough on four holes and Mehlhorn on six. Hagen played the odd after ten tee shots, Mehlhorn after only one. Hagen was inside on eight greens, Mehlhorn on five.

September 27, 1925

JONES WINS TITLE BY SINGLE STROKE; TURNESA, 294, NEXT

Atlantan Adds Open Crown to the British Open and U. S. Amateur by Great Finish.

HIS PAR 3 SETTLES ISSUE

Gains Lead at 71st Hole When Fairview Pro Takes a 4—Gets Birdie on Last Green.

MEHLHORN TIES FOR THIRD

By **WILLIAM D. RICHARDSON.**

Special to The New York Times.

COLUMBUS, O., July 10. — Bobby Jones, who captured the British open championship only a few weeks ago, won his second American open championship playing over the Scioto Country Club course today, thereby performing an unprecedented golf feat.

Never before in history has one man held both the American and the British open titles at one and the same time.*

As a result of his great victory today, Bobby is tonight the golf monarch of the greater part of the world. The only major crown that has eluded him since he won the American amateur crown at Oakmont last year for the second time, being the British amateur, in which he was beaten by an almost unknown golfer in the semi-final round.

Jones won the 1926 event by a single shot, his winning total for 72 holes being 293 and his rounds 70, 79, 71 and 73. Joe Turnesa, young Fairview professional, had the tournament crown in the palm of his hand, but permitted it to slip through his fingers by faltering on the last few holes.

Leads by Three Strokes.

He led the amateur champion by three strokes at the start of the final round and put another stroke between himself and Bobby by going out in 37 to Jones's 38. Turnesa continued to lead Jones until the seventy-first hole, where he was trapped and took a 4, where Jones, following a few pairs behind, got his par 3.

That settled it so far as his chances and Bobby's were concerned. Knowing exactly what he had to do to win the championship, Jones proceeded to make a finish that sent a shower of thrills up and down the spines of the immense gallery that crowded around the home green—2,000 or more strung out in a gigantic eclipse.

His drive was a screamer that landed 250 yards down the fairway, bounced and rolled another fifty yards before coming to a halt directly in the middle. One hundred and eighty yards ahead lay his goal, a putting green encircled by grass mounds, in the centre of which fluttered a white flag.

There was a breathless hush as the young David of the links took his stance, fixed his gaze at the flag and then at the ball and swung a mashie iron. Up came the ball, on and on, splitting the pin all the way, dropping short of the green and ending up its long journey about four yards past the hole.

Fails to Bag Eagle.

That shot, great considering the circumstances under which it was made, established him as the leader, supplanting Turnesa. He now had two strokes to win, but mindful that every stroke still counted with Diegel, Mehlhorn and Willie Hunter playing in back of him, he tried hard to run down the putt for an eagle 3. The attempt was unsuccessful, but not by much, the ball stopping at the side of the hole, approximately eight inches away.

As it eventually turned out, the 4 was as good as a 3, for one after another his challengers fell by the wayside. The first to fall was Diegel, who needed a 70 to tie, and who appeared to be on a fair road to getting it when he reached the turn in 35 and started home with three 4s, one under par.

All that he required was par for the remaining six holes, but strokes began to slip away from him at the thirteenth and after his 4 on the short hole he was completely out of it.

Mehlhorn, who started the final round two strokes behind Turnesa and one ahead of Jones, lost his chance on the outward nine holes. He took a 39 to the turn, which meant that he would have to come back in 35 to equal Bobby's score.

Twelfth His Downfall.

The twelfth hole was his tomb, for there he needed a 7 to hole out after topping two shots in a row. That left only Willie Hunter to watch. After his third round 69 the former British amateur champion needed only a par round to tie for the title. Three 5s on the out-going nine holes did not make his prospects any brighter and after taking 38 to the turn his entire game went away and he finished with a dismal 79.

The leading returns other than those of Jones and Turnesa were as follows:

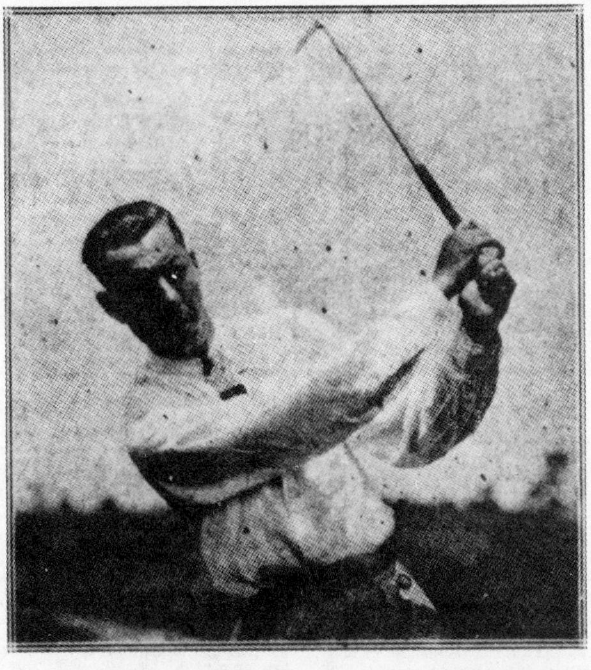

Photo by Edwin Levick.

Joe Turnesa, the Runner-Up for Open Golf Title.

Mehlhorn, Diegel, Sarazen and Farrell, 297; Hagen, 298; Hunter, 300. Sarazen elevated himself by playing the last thirty-six holes in 142 strokes, getting a 72 in the morning and a 70 in the afternoon.

As matters stood when the field squared off for the last and deciding round today, Turnesa, having jolted Mehlhorn out of the lead with a 72 to "Wild Bill's" 73, led the Western professional by two strokes. Mehlhorn was a stroke ahead of Jones; Hunter, who reled off a flashy 69 in the third round, was fourth, with 221; Diegel and Evans, fifth, tied at 223, and Hagen and Farrell tied at 224, the last mentioned duplicating Hunter's feat in the morning session.

Willie Klein, young Wheatley Hills professional, had blighted his prospects by taking 75 for his third round, in which he was Jones's partner, and paid the usual penalty of pairing with Jones by being interfered with by the gallery.

Issue Clearly Defined.

As Turnesa started out to play the last round it was generally agreed that the fight was among himself, Jones, Mehlhorn and Diegel, with Hunter, Evans and Hagen dangerous, but needing a miracle round to win.

Turnesa, followed by a big gallery, started off in shaky fashion, starting out 5, 3, 5 where par is 4, 4, 4. Two more 5s appeared on his card before he got as far as the turn, but he atoned by finishing 3, 4, 3, the 4 being a birdie and a good birdie at that.

He reached the turn in 37 strokes, one over par, and seemed to be riding on his way to victory. Two 4s followed at the tenth and eleventh, and he was still sitting in a seat which only a miracle performance by Jones and Mehlhorn could possibly shake him out of. Then came the crucial hole—the twelfth—crucial for him, crucial for Jones, crucial for Mehlhorn.

Joe invited disaster by hooking his tee shot to the edge of the rough, giving him a hanging lie to play his second from. He failed to get hold of the shot, hooked it, and was again in the rough. He hooked his third and was still in, now stymied by a tree.

He made a good recovery, almost hitting the pin, and going 5 yards past the hole. Missing that, he had to put down a 6, the second 6 that he had to mark down for the entire tournament.

Those mishaps evidently caused him to worry, for he played the next hole badly and the one after that. Having switched from a driver to a spoon for his tee shots, he hit a good long ball to the thirteenth, but his second was short and finished in the rough. He pitched out, about ten feet to the right of the hole, where he had an incline to figure for, and missed the putt.

Two strokes were surrendered to par, and strokes were now increasing mightily in value. Playing to the short fourteenth, he was trapped to the left of the green and played a great shot out to possibly eight feet, only to miss the putt and take a 4.

The situation was now serious for him, and he began to play with less confidence than had been his forte throughout the tournament. He got past the fifteenth with a 4, lipping the cup for a 3, but lost another stroke on the sixteenth through a bad break in luck. His second shot started out nicely and looked likely to finish up somewhere near the hole. It landed on the green, but took a bounce and went over into the rough. His chip was strong, but he failed to get the subsequent putt down for a 4.

Turnesa Calm to the Last.

If he felt the crown slipping from his head, Turnesa gave no indication of it by his play to the last hole. He missed the green on his second shot and had a big mound to pitch over to get near the hole. It looked like a sure 5 but an impossible 4, until he pitched to about ten feet and calmly dropped the putt for a birdie, giving him a 77 for the round and a total of 294 for the seventy-two holes.

As he walked off the green afterward, Turnesa didn't have the appearance of a man who had no fear of the future. A 37 or even a 38 for the incoming nine holes would have put the championship in a place where none of the others could take it from him, but his was a 40.

Even as he stood there reflecting over his neglected opportunities, the lanes were being formed for the arrival of Jones. When he saw Jones's second shot come soaring up to the home green his heart probably sank, for it meant the surrender of a championship that he himself might easily have won, and the flight of fame and riches.

Jones Picks up 5 Strokes.

Just as the twelfth hole was a crucial one for Turnesa, so it was for Jones, for it was the hole on which he picked up five shots on his most dangerous competitors, two on Turnsea and three on Mehlhorn. Bobby got a 4 there, getting home with his second where most of the others were taking 5s. He had now reduced Turnsea's lead from four shots to two, and the outlook was brighter, for there were six holes left on which to make up the difference.

At the thirteenth Bobby had to face a crisis. His second shot landed in a trap to the left of the green and some distance away from the pin. He needed a 4 there and he needed it badly. Instead of taking a chance on pitching, than which nothing is more uncertain at Scioto, he rolled his ball out through the trap and to within two feet of the cup. His 4 was saved and he was still within reach of his prey.

A 4 at the fourteenth, where he was trapped, was disconcerting, but when he got his pars at the next two holes and put his ball on the seventeenth green, twenty-five feet from the hole, he knew exactly where he stood. In his fear of running past the cup he left himself five feet short, but down went the putt. Then came the 4 on the home hole and a 35 for the incoming nine holes.

That 35 was really one of the greatest feats Bobby ever performed and one that was entirely deserving the tremendous ovation it got at the hands of the gallery. Everybody now realized that it was probably Jones's championship, but no one was positive about it, for reports had it that Diegel was burning up the course and that Mehlhorn was still in the running.

Diegel Starts to Weaken.

Diegel, however, began floundering at the thirteenth hole and Mehlhorn at the twelfth, although Bill resuscitated hope by playing the thirteenth and fourteenth in 3s.

None of the other high up, Hagen, Hunter and Evans, chiefly, was able to do the miracle rounds necessary and thus ended one of the strangest championships in modern golf history—a championship that had every one guessing until the last man reported his core.

It was a great one for Jones to win and a hard one for Turnesa and Mehlhorn to lose. The last two had the title as good as won, yet lost it to Jones, who never seemed to have it won until the very end.

A gallery, estimated at 6,000, watched the closing day, which was something more than a three-ring circus. It was a championship marked by unexpected failures and successes. The failure of Hagen, Macdonald Smith, Sarazen, Barnes, Macfarlane, Farrell and Walker, particularly that of Hagen and Smith, was a blow to their backers.

Hagen was in the thick of the fight, however, up to the last few holes, but Mac Smith was never in although his 68 in the third round today was a splendid tribute to his fighting spirit. So, too, was Sarazen's two great rounds and the two 69s of Hunter and Farrell, to bring them up into the money.

The weather, while threatening, held off until nightfall, although there was quite a shower along about noon time.

Sky Heavy in Morning.

The sky was overcast and ominous when the field started out for the third and crucial round this morning. Low hanging, rain-filled clouds threatened every minute to drench the players.

The first of the leaders to leave the tee was George McLean, Grassy Sprain professional and Westchester County open champion, who was tied with Diegel, eight strokes behind Mehlhorn, at the end of the second round.

Out in 37, one over par, George came to grief at the tenth hole, a drive and pitch hole with a creek running in front and along the side. His lot there was a 6 instead of the par 4 he wanted. It all came about through a mashie niblick shot that went wild and into the rough at the right of the green, a failure to get out on the first attempt and two putts after he did manage to get on. That was discouraging and two more 6s further along the line spiked his guns.

One of these came on the thirteenth, where he drove into the rough and then took three putts, and another on the sixteenth, where he was again in the rough and then in the water. He finished with a 79 which brought his total up to 227, too many shots away from the leaders.

Forrester Drops Behind.

The next of the leaders to go plunging downward was Jack Forrester of Baltusrol, who was in a threatening position when he started the round. Like McLean, he too reached the turn in 37, playing par golf at every hole except the second, where he needed a 5. He started back with two 4s and then dropped a stroke on the twelfth. After that he was all right until the last two holes, which he finished in 4, 6 for a total of 77, dropping him from further consideration.

Turnesa, meanwhile, was carrying on in the same steady fashion, clipping a stroke off the par going out and adding one coming in for a total of 72, which, as it turned out, changed him from runner-up to leader.

Joe started fast by holing a tenfoot putt for a birdie on the first green, but dropped the advantage by driving into the rough on the second and taking a 5. From there on to the tenth he played par except at the sixth, where he chipped up for a birdie 4.

He did a rather stupid thing on the tenth, where, after being on the green within eight yards of the flag on his second shot, he took the wrong line to the hole, left himself a difficult yard putt and failed to sink it. That was a 5, where he should have got a 4. Another valuable stroke was permitted to get away at the twelfth, where he missed the green with his third and then failed to chip close enough to hole.

Several persons in his gallery thought that there was no use following him after that, and those who obeyed the impulse missed a treat, for Joe played the next six holes two under par. His finish was 4, 3, 4, 3, 3, 5 and the five was undeserved. As he set himself to play a brassie shot to the home green, the hat of a spectator standing close blew off and dropped near to Turnesa, who topped the shot.

Those figures were not as easily made as one would think. The pars on the finishing holes at Scioto are not easy ones, especially that of the thirteenth, where Turnesa got his 4. He had to use a wood for his second, pushed it off, and his ball ended up in a trap, but his recovery was a corker, nearly holing.

Nor was he on the fourteenth green with his tee shot. Here the par came from a twenty-five-foot putt. His putter did him a good turn at the sixteenth, where it steered a three-yarder into the hole for a birdie 3 and his niblick came to the aid of its master on his hoodoo hole, the short seventeenth.

Not once had he succeeded in hitting the seventeenth green with his iron. This time he was trapped on the left, but came out close to the hole and down went the putt. By duplicating par for the round he assumed the lead with a total of 217.

Shortly after that two of Turnesa's most dangerous challengers, Jones and Willie Klein, Wheatley Hills professional, finished their third rounds, Bobby breaking par with a 71, which brought him only three shots away from the leader where yesterday he was six.

Klein Takes a 75.

Klein was 75—too many from the way things were going to be of any great help to his cause. His worst experiences happened at the sixth hole where he took four to get in from the edge and the ninth where he hooked to the rough and had to play out safe. Fours at two of the short holes and three putts on the sixteenth were bad.

Jones had a really great round, which, except for a few minor mistakes and a number of putts that just wouldn't drop for him, might have been 68 or 69. Bobby had putts for birdies at the fourth and sixth holes that missed by a hair and par on the ninth would have given him a 34. This hole, however, has been his Nemesis and once again he had to put down a 4, one over par.

He played a great iron second for his par at the tenth after using an iron from the tee to avoid getting into the creek, and reeled off a birdie on the long twelfth. The thirteenth was a bad hole for him, costing him three putts, and the fourteenth also.

He just missed birdies on the next three holes and finished grandly with a 4 on the home hole, chipping almost dead for it from off the edge of the green.

Diegel Gets Good Start.

Behind Jones and Klein came Diegel, who played spectacularly for seven holes and then bumped head-on into a 6 at the eighth. Here, after a fine drive and a brassie that only missed the green by a yard or so, Leo, playing out of a trap, sent his ball clean over the green and into another bunker, from where he played a great cut shot out, but was unable to hole the down-hill putt for a 5. He finished the nine with a par 3, which gave him a 36.

He was still even 4s as he started for the thirteenth, but there and at the fourteenth he dissipated strokes. A great recovery out of the long rough gave him his 4 at the fifteenth, and then came a bad hole, the sixteenth, which cost him a 6 and which sent his third round total up to 75, along with Klein's, and left him with a six-stroke deficit.

The third round saw the finish of Danny Williams, Shackamaxon youngster, who started the day in third place, for Danny took an 80, a worse score than his play deserved, and one caused by an absence of a single particle of luck.

His partner, Macdonald Smith, however, got in a long overdue round with a 68, equaling Mehlhorn's record score. The round enabled Smith to jump over the heads of a whole raft of players, but it came too late to be of much use except as a demonstration of what he can do when he puts his mind to it.

Armour Out in 35.

Tommy Armour and Willie Macfarlane were the next pair of interest. The former got off to a flying start with a 35 against the champion's 37, but each finished badly and the reign of the old champion was as good as finished then and there.

Only one other player remained to come home. That was Mehlhorn, leader of the field for the first two rounds. There were rumblings of an impending crash as early as the first hole, where he started with a 6. A good 3 at the second got back one of the wasted strokes, and he finished the first nine in 37, and was tied with Turnesa.

Then came a 5 on the tenth and six holes in par. The last two holes were expensive, costing hi mtwo strokes. He took a 4 at the seventeenth, where he was in a trap and failed to get out, and had to hole a long putt for what he got and a 6 on the home hole, finishing up with three putts after being trapped on his second.

Meanwhile Hagen—"Third Round" Hagen—was thundering around, burning up the course. 4 4 3 2 4 was the way Walter sprinted over the first five holes, turning with a 34 and starting back with a 4 at the tenth. Then came four bad holes to wreck Mr. Hagen's chances.

There was a 5 on the eleventh, a 6 on the twelfth, a 6 on the short fourteenth, where his tee shot was to the right, his third almost a miss, and three putts. Before he succeeded in getting back into his stride he had lost six strokes to par in four holes.

July 11, 1926

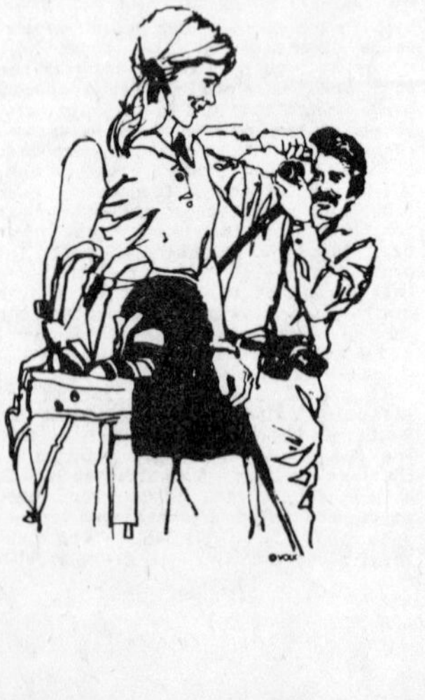

HAGEN SETS RECORD, WINS TITLE 3D TIME

Beats Diegel, 5 and 3, and Takes Pro Golf Crown After Being 2 Up for First Round.

HAS A 69 IN THE MORNING

Stays in Lead From Eleventh Hole and Has Little Trouble Scoring His Victory.

By WILLIAM D. RICHARDSON.
Special to The New York Times.

GARDEN CITY, L. I., Sept. 25.—In spite of the general landslide which has carried throne after throne away from champions in all lines of sport, Walter Hagen won the P. G. A. championship at Salisbury today for the third time running and thus established a new golf record.

He defeated Leo Diegel, former Canadian open champion and at times one of the most brilliant golfers in the world, by the score of 5 and 3 in the final round of the P. G. A. event in which he has been the outstanding player, this making the fourth time that he has captured the crown in the nine years that the event has been held.

Diegel, getting off to a bad start in the morning game, his nervousness indicating plainly that he was unable to rid his mind of the knowledge that he was playing Hagen, was never in front, although once during the match he did manage to get on even terms after being 2 down.

Takes Lead at Next Hole.

That was at the eleventh hole in the morning round, but Hagen went out in front again on the very next hole and from there until the thirty-third hole, where the match ended, he was always out in front. Two down at the end of the first eighteen holes of play, during which Hagen holed the course in sixty-nine strokes and Diegel in seventy-one, there was still a ray of hope that Leo might stage one of his meteoric rounds for which he is noted, but it was not to be.

His complete bobble of the first hole in the afternoon must have made it evident to him as well as almost every one in the gallery that the end would not be long in coming and from then on until the finish there was never any reason for a different appraisal of the situation. After that first hole Diegel was seldom himself and Hagen dominated the situation from then on, slipping occasionally to prove that he was human, but never enough to give the struggling and perspiring Diegel a chance to get his hopes raised very high.

Until his dying day Diegel probably will remember that first hole. It will probably stick in his mind as firmly as does a certain tree on the Worcester course. He was 2 down, it will be recalled, and hit a tee shot that was straight, but not too long—perhaps fifty feet behind the spot to where Hagen drove. The hole is 480 yards on the card and most of the players have reached it easily with irons.

What prompted Diegel to haul a brassie out of his bag no one knows except himself. The fact that the lie was a hanging one and that there was a rather stiff following wind made his choice of club all the more mystifying, but take it he did, with the almost inevitable result—a low hit ball that ran and ran and ran up on the green, over the green and under an automobile that was parked in the road behind.

Ball Lodged in Rut.

The car had to be moved before Diegel could play the shot and after the car was moved there was Leo's ball lying in the wheel-rut. He barely succeeded in moving the ball on his first attempt, sending it out into the rough, a few feet ahead, and lying among pebbles and thickly matted grass. His next attempt moved the ball only four feet, for it hit a stone and the stone shot up to the hole instead of the ball.

Had it been the ball instead of the stone he might have been all right, for the stone was only a yard from the cup. After taking another stroke and not succeeding in getting on the green, he picked up, conceding to Hagen who was three feet away on his third shot. This enabled Walter to become 3 up.

Hagen lost the next hole, 4 to 5, because it happened to be the worst hole he played all day, but he recovered the loss by sending a mashie niblick shot up to within two feet of the pin at the sixth and Diegel was again 3 down. Leo won only one hole after that. It was the very next and in order to lose that one Hagen had to take three putts for his first and only time, his final miss being on a putt of less than his putter's length.

A great run-up shot to within a yard of the flag on the eleventh gave Hagen that hole, restoring his lead to three holes. An elegant pitch from the rough that would have gone into the hole in the thirteenth had the flag been out, gave him a birdie 3 and his lead was now four holes with only five to play. A half at the next and he was dormie, and then Diegel collapsed completely, playing the sixteenth so that Hagen was able to win the hole and end the match in spite of his 5, which is a stroke over par.

Won Where Jones Failed.

It was a rather disappointing outcome for a match that held out the possibilities that this meeting between Hagen and Diegen held out. But before the first drives were hit it was almost assured that Hagen would succeed in his attempt to do the thing that no other golfer in history had done, namely, to win a major championship three times in a row. Bobby Jones tried it and failed; Hagen tried it and succeeded. That ought to start and end a lot of arguments.

Diegel, always a bundle of unbridled nerves, was worse than ever this morning. He was playing the man whom he had almost beaten in the third round of the P. G. A. event at Olympia Fields last year. Diegel was 3 up and 4 to play against Hagen, lost three out of the last four holes and then the match on the fortieth hole. Hagen, on the contrary, was the Hagen of always—the calm, undisturbed, unruffled golfer who takes things as they come in golf with his every thought concentrated on the next shot; none on the one that has been played.

The second shot of the match was the one that foretold the final outcome. Diegel was yards ahead with the green wide open to him and Hagen's second shot in the rough, above the hole on the right. Here was Leo's chance to get the jump on his man. Instead, he topped an iron and did well to get a half. Walter then began to put on the pressure and his pitch to the second was six feet from the hole, and down went the putt for a birdie 3 and Hagen was 1 up.

Diegel momentarily saved his life at the third when, after overplaying the green, he chipped back close and got down in one putt for a half. Then Hagen made two miraculous "saves." Going to the fourth he was only a few feet from being trapped on his second shot and in the rough over the green on his third, while Diegel, from the rough, laid a wonderful mashie niblick shot eight feet from the hole.

It looked as if nothing but a miracle could prevent his squaring the match there, but Hagen, playing his ball off the slope of the green, got back on and holed in one putt, giving him a half when Diegel failed to hole his putt.

Hagen's recovery on the short fifth was even more miraculous and more disturbing to his opponent. His pitch landed in a trap short, while Diegel's stopped in the short rough beyond the edge of the green from where he almost holed, after Hagen had recovered weakly. There was no more than a sixteenth of an inch of daylight between Diegel's ball, lying two inches from the hole, and the line Hagen had to take, but away went the putt and down it dropped.

Those two breaks seemed to nettle Diegel all the more and he missed his tee shot going to the sixth hole, hooking it into the rough, scarcely beyond the 150-yard mark. The hole went to Hagen, 4 to 5, making him 2 up. After that Diegel began to play better golf and from there on his driving improved and his play up to the hole began to compare favorably with Hagen's.

Diegel won the eighth with a twelve-foot putt for a birdie, after Hagen had hit the pin on his approach and missed a three-yarder, and then, after Hagen negotiated a partial stymie successfully for a half at the tenth, Diegel squared the match with a par 4 on the eleventh which Hagen played badly, being twice in the rough on the way to the green and then putting wide of the mark.

Hagen took the honor away almost immediately by pitching to within a yard of the hole for a birdie 3 on the twelfth, and then Diegel was guilty of two errors on the next two holes. His mistake at the fourteenth was being short on his second shot, and at the fifteenth that of being short on a putt for a win. He was again short on his putt at the sixteenth after Hagen had dropped a thirty-five-footer, and by halving the next two in 4s, Hagen finished 2 up.

From there on the title was as good as in Hagen's bag, especially after that first hole in the afternoon. Walter wavered on the second, playing it badly from tee to green, and he wavered a few times thereafter, but never for any period of time did he permit himself to let slip the advantage he already had gained.

What gave him his big advantage over Diegel throughout the day was his uncanny mastery over his mashie niblick. It is doubtful if ever there was any one who pitched them up to the hole so deadly as did Walter with that club today. It was the instrument which he used chiefly to torture Diegel as he tortured Turnesa, Dick Grout, Pat Doyle and Farrell. That and his putter were his main stand-bys throughout the week and never in its charmed life did the putter perform more valiantly than it did today.

Six one-putt greens in the morning round and four one-putt greens in the afternoon tell the story better than words.

Their cards:

MORNING ROUND.

Out—										
Hagen	5	3	4	4	3	4	4	4	4—35	
Diegel	5	4	4	4	3	5	4	3	4—36	
In—										
Hagen	4	5	3	4	4	4	4	2	4—34	—69
Diegel	4	4	4	4	4	4	4	3	4—35	—71

AFTERNOON ROUND.

Out—									
Hagen	4	5	4	4	3	3	5	4	4—36
Diegel	7	4	4	4	3	4	4	4	4—38
In—									
Hagen	3	4	4	3	4	5			
Diegel	4	4	4	4	4	6			

Hagen—5 and 3.

September 26, 1926

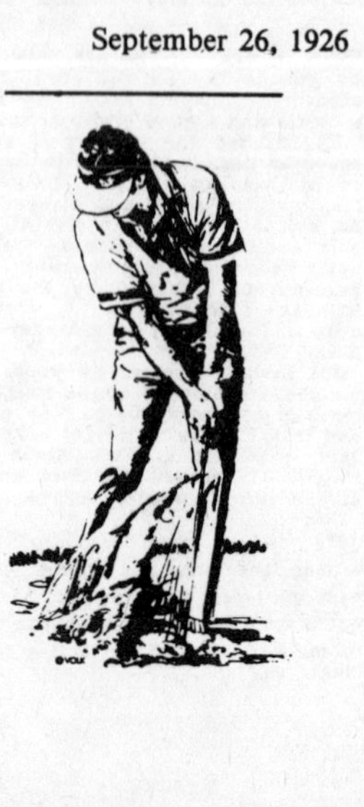

U. S. WINS RYDER CUP FROM BRITISH TEAM

Homebreds Take Six of Eight Singles and Gain Trophy by 9½ to 2½.

CLINCH SERIES AT NOON

Diegel Has Ray 6 Down and Golden's Same Margin Over Jolly Ends All Doubt.

TURNESA IS ONLY LOSER

Bows to Duncan at Last Hole and Sarazen Halves With Whitcombe —Farrell Downs Boomer.

PAR FOR THE COURSE.

Hole.	Yds. Par.	Hole.	Yds. Par.
1	375 4	10	155 3
2	570 5	11	400 4
3	375 4	12	430 4
4	235 3	13	195 3
5	450 5	14	350 4
6	130 3	15	555 5
7	400 4	16	395 4
8	175 3	17	460 4
9	405 4	18	335 4
Total	3,165 35	Total	3,275 35

Grand total—6,440 yards; par, 70.

By WILLIAM D. RICHARDSON.

Special to The New York Times.

WORCESTER, Mass., June 4.—America's homebreds avenged the drubbing that the British professionals gave their pick-up team in England last year by swamping the British professionals in the international matches for the Ryder Cup.

The score was paid off with full interest when the Americans won six of the singles matches at the Worcester Country Club today, halved another and lost only one out of the eight.

Starting with a lead of 3 points to 1 by virtue of their victory in yesterday's foursomes, the homebreds finished the series with a score of 9½ points to 2½. It was not quite as bad a drubbing as the British handed them last year when the score of the first match for the trophy stood 13½ to 1½, but last year England put its full strength into the test while the American side was made up of a number of fill-ins.

Turnesa the Only Loser.

The only member of the American team who went down to defeat today was Joe Turnesa, young Fairview professional, who finished such a close second to Bobby Jones in the open championship at Sciota last year. He lost to George Duncan, the celebrated Scotch star, who won the British open in 1921, but the match went to the last green and Duncan won there by holing a long putt for a birdie 3.

Turnesa led Duncan by two holes going to the twelfth, but a double stymie laid by Duncan there caused the young American to lose a hole that he had won and led to his ultimate downfall on the last green.

The only other match that the British salvaged was the one which Charles Whitcombe halved with Gene Sarazen, or rather Sarazen halved with Whitcombe since the British player was 1

up coming to the thirty-sixth, where Sarazen won with a par 4 to halve the match.

Three of the Americans won by long margins. Johnny Farrell, the debonair Metropolitan champion, crushed Aubrey Boomer, star of the British side, by 5 and 4; Johnny Golden swamped his opponent, Herbert Jolly, by 7 and 6, and Leo Diegel smothered big Ted Ray, the British captain, by 7 and 5.

Watrous Also Triumphs.

Al Watrous, the Michigan professional, who played through the series with a split thumb, defeated Fred Robson by 3 and 2; Hagen, the captain of the American side, won from Arthur Havers, former British open champion, by 2 and 1, and Bill Mehlhorn pulled out a victory over Archie Compston, the Manchester giant, by 1 up.

Conditions under which the final matches of the 1927 series were played today were not nearly as good as they were for the Scotch foursome matches yesterday. Auguring perfect weather conditions in the morning when the matches started, the sky clouded around noontime and the afternoon was cold and raw, with a tricky wind that played havoc with many shots. The gallery, however, was larger than yesterday's and the P. G. A. now has a good start toward its fund to be used in sending a defending team to England next year.

Whatever hopes the British team had of atoning for yesterday's unexpected defeat in the foursomes and pulling victory out of the fire by winning the majority of the singles disappeared at noon, when the first half of the thirty-six-hole matches was finished.

Americans Sure to Win.

Even at that early stage the Americans were assured of victory, for Diegel and Golden, the last two members of the team, had their matches in the bag. Diegel, racing round the course in 70 strokes, equaling par, had Ray 6 down, and Golden had Jolly down by the same number of holes.

Counting those two matches won, the Americans had 5 points to the Britishers' 1, and although the remaining six matches were close, the British would have had to win all six to edge out a victory.

No one, however, not even the British, had any idea of that happening, but not one of the Britons gave up until the final putt was holed, and some of them retrieved holes at such an alarming pace as to cause a few shivers.

The only British players who were on the right side of the ledger at the end of the first eighteen holes were Whitcombe and Robson. Whitcombe was 2 up on Sarazen and Robson 1 up on Watrous. Hagen had a one-hole lead on Havers and Farrell and Boomer and Mehlhorn and Compston were exactly where they started.

America's victory was insured when the Mehlhorn match came up to the last green, for by then Farrell, Golden and Diegel had beaten their men and Bill's narrow-margined victory over Compston lifted their total to 7 points, counting the three points for the foursomes.

The match on which all eyes were focused was that between Farrell and Boomer, and for the first eighteen holes it was a beauty. Boomer, playing gorgeously up to the greens, was more than a match for Johnny through the fairway, but the latter was far superior on the greens.

It was there that he eventually broke Boomer's heart. Time and again the Englishman put his ball inside Farrell's on the greens only to stand by and watch his opponent stroke his putts into the hole with unerring accuracy.

Finally, by reason of a few of those heart-breaking one-putters, Johnny reached a point where he was 2 up, but disaster overcame him on the fifteenth and sixteenth holes, and Boomer was able to catch him and finish all square.

Farrell in the Lead.

Early in the afternoon Farrell stole away to a two-hole lead and the finishing touch came on the short eighth when his ball, pushed out to the right, struck the stone wall running alongside the green and bounced onto the edge of the green. Boomer had a beautiful tee shot himself, but it trickled off the green and into a bunker. The result was that he lost the hole to become 3 down and that was the finish of him.

It was typical of the breaks that went against him time after time. Farrell didn't get many, in fact he didn't need many, for he played really wonderful golf except for the fifteenth and sixteenth holes in the morning and the second hole in the afternoon. Boomer, however, couldn't get a single one to come his way and the sight of Farrell putting those long approach putts dead to the hole and even dropping a few of them had a depressing effect.

Boomer made his own bed by allowing Farrell to win the first hole, although he was only twenty-five feet from the hole in two, while Johnny was in the rough off the tee. After his second Farrell chipped back to within four feet and holed, after which the Englishman missed a one yarder for the half.

Boomer hit the cup for a 3 on the third and squared the match on the fourth when Farrell dumped a spoon shot into a bunker. Farrell was bunkered again on the long fifth and Boomer won that to become 1 up. Then Farrell took the wind out of his opponent's sails by holing a long sixty-footer for a birdie 3 on the seventh after Boomer was close up on his own third from the rough back of the green.

Wins Three in Next Four.

Johnny won three out of the next four holes, Boomer three-putting the tenth from less than seven yards and also the thirteenth. Two down

---

Complete Cards of Players in Ryder Cup Golf Twosomes

FARRELL vs. BOOMER.
Morning Round.

Out—
Farrell .... 4 5 4 4 6 3 3 3 4—36
Boomer .... 5 5 4 3 4 3 4 3 4—35
Match all even.
In—
Farrell .... 3 5 4 3 4 5 6 4 4—38—74
Boomer .... 4 4 5 4 4 4 4 4 4—37—72
Match all even.

Afternoon Round.

Out—
Farrell .... 4 6 4 3 5 3 4 3 4—36
Boomer .... 4 6 5 3 6 3 4 4 4—39
Farrell, 3 up.
In—
Farrell 3 5 4 4 3
Boomer 3 5 5 4 4
Farrell, 5 and 4.

MEHLHORN vs. COMPSTON.
Morning Round.

Out—
Mehlhorn ..... 5 5 4 4 5 4 5 4 4—40
Compston ..... 4 5 3 4 5 4 5 4 5—41
Mehlhorn, 1 up.
In—
Mehlhorn ..... 4 4 4 3 4 5 4 5 4—37—77
Compston ..... 3 4 4 3 4 5 4 4 5—36—77
Match all even.

Afternoon Round.

Out—
Mehlhorn ..... 4 6 4 3 5 3 3 4 4—36
Compston ..... 4 6 3 4 5 2 4 3 4—35
Compston, 1 up.
In—
Mehlhorn ..... 3 5 4 3 5 6 4 4 4—38—74
Compston ..... 4 5 4 4 5 4 4 4 5—39—74
Mehlhorn, 1 up.

SARAZEN vs. WHITCOMBE.
Morning Round.

Out—
Sarazen .... 3 5 4 3 5 3 4 4 4—36
Whitcombe ... 5 4 4 3 4 4 4 4 4—36
Match all even.
In—
Sarazen .... 4 5 5 4 6 5 4 4 4—41—77
Whitcombe ... 3 4 4 3 4 5 5 5 5—38—74
Sarazen, 2 down.

Afternoon Round.

Out—
Sarazen .... 5 6 5 3 5 2 4 3 4—37
Whitcombe ... 5 6 5 3 5 3 5 3 4—39
Match all even.

In—
Sarazen .... 3 4 5 4 4 5 5 6 4—40—77
Whitcombe ... 5 4 4 4 4 5 5 5 5—41—80
Match all even.

HAGEN vs. HAVERS.
Morning Round.

Out—
Hagen .... 4 6 4 4 5 4 4 3 4—38
Havers .... 5 5 4 4 4 3 5 4 4—38
Match all even.
In—
Hagen .... 4 5 4 3 5 4 5 5 4—39—77
Havers .... 3 4 6 3 6 5 6 5 3—41—79
Hagen, 1 up.

Afternoon Round.

Out—
Hagen .... 5 6 4 5 7 2 4 3 5—41
Havers .... 5 6 6 3 6 3 5 2 5—41
Hagen, 1 up.
In—
Hagen 3 5 5 4 4 4 5 5 4
Havers 4 5 5 3 4 6 4 5
Hagen, 2 and 1.

WATROUS vs. ROBSON.
Morning Round.

Out—
Watrous .... 5 4 4 2 4 3 4 3 4—33
Robson .... 4 5 4 3 4 4 4 3 5—36
Watrous, 3 up.
In—
Watrous .... 4 4 5 5 5 6 6 5 5—45—78
Robson .... 3 x 5 4 4 6 5 5 4
Robson, 1 up.

Afternoon Round.

Out—
Watrous .... 4 5 4 5 4 4 4 4 5—39
Robson .... 5 6 4 4 5 4 5 3 4—40
Match all even.
In—
Watrous 3 4 3 4 5 4
Robson 3 5 4 5 4 5 4
Watrous, 3 and 2.

DIEGEL vs. RAY.
Morning Round.

Out—
Diegel .... 4 4 4 2 5 3 4 3 5—34
Ray .... 5 7 4 3 5 3 5 4 4—40
Diegel, 4 up.

In—
Diegel .... 2 4 4 4 4 5 4 5 4—36—70
Ray .... 3 3 4 4 5 5 5 5 4—38—78
Diegel, 6 up.

Afternoon Round.

Out—
Diegel .... 5 4 6 3 4 3 4 3 4—36
Ray .... 4 5 4 3 6 4 4 2 4—36
Diegel, 6 up.
In—
Diegel 4 4 4 3
Ray 3 5 4 4
Diegel, 7 and 5.

DUNCAN vs. TURNESA.
Morning Round.

Out—
Duncan .... 4 4 5 3 5 4 5 4 4—38
Turnesa .... 4 5 5 4 4 4 6 4 4—40
Duncan, 2 up.
In—
Duncan .... 3 4 5 4 5 4 5 4 4—39—77
Turnesa .... 4 4 4 3 4 4 4 4 5—36—76
Turnesa, 1 up.

Afternoon Round.

Out—
Duncan .... 4 6 3 5 6 3 4 3 4—38
Turnesa .... 5 5 5 4 4 4 3 4 4—38
Turnesa, 1 up.
In—
Duncan .... 4 4 5 3 4 7 5 5 3—40—78
Turnesa .... 3 4 6 4 5 5 5 5 4—41—79
Duncan, 1 up.

GOLDEN vs. JOLLY.
Morning Round.

Golden .... 4 6 4 3 5 2 4 4 5—37
Jolly .... 4 6 5 4 5 4 5 3 6—42
Golden, 4 up.

In—
Golden .... 3 4 4 4 5 6 4 5 4—39—76
Jolly .... 4 5 4 3 6 5 6 5 4—42—84
Golden, 6 up.

Afternoon Round.

Out—
Golden .... 4 6 4 3 6 3 4 3 4—37
Jolly .... 4 6 4 3 5 4 x 3 4
Golden, 7 up.

In—
Golden 2 5 4
Jolly 3 4 4
Golden, 7 and 6.

Boomer got back one of his losses by chipping close for a birdie 4 at the long fifteenth and then Farrell had a lost ball on the sixteenth.

The Englishman wasted a fine chance to win the second hole in the afternoon when Johnny drove to the rough and failed to get hold of the ball on his second shot. One of the worst breaks of all came to Boomer in the fifth when he hooked his drive out of bounds. That and the happening on the eighth told him that the wind was against him and Farrell put in the finishing touch by bumping a stymie for a birdie 3 on the fourteenth hole.

It was a great match to watch and a splendid victory for the young Quaker Ridge professional, who more than lived up to the trust his teammates put in him by placing him at No. 1 against the best of the British team.

By taking a 5 and a 6 on the fifteenth and sixteenth holes in the morning round he scored a 74, two strokes higher than Boomer, who had 4s on the same two holes, and Johnny was one under 4s for the fourteen holes in the afternoon.

Mehlhorn and Compston had a nip and tuck fight from start to finish. In the morning they were never more than a hole apart, and the same condition held throughout the day. Finally Compston, having lost the seventh hole of the second round, came out of a bunker to square the match on the eighth and become 1 up.

The ninth was halved in 4s, and Mehlhorn squared by pitching to within six feet of the hole on the tenth. Compston was bunkered, but came out to within four feet of the cup only to miss the putt. Bill won the thirteenth and played a fine chip for his 4 on the fifteenth.

They were still all even playing the seventeenth and Mehlhorn won it to become 1 up with one hole left. The finish was quite dramatic, for after the second shots it looked as if the match would have to go down in the halved category.

Bill was bunkered short of the green. Compston was on approximately forty feet away. Bill came out to about seven feet, while Compston's approach putt went two yards past. Then Bill holed the side-hill down-hiller and Compston dropped his to no avail.

Sarazen and Whitcombe had another touch-and-go battle that ran along on an even keel until the tenth hole, where Gene pushed his drive off to the right and hit a soft approach. That started Whitcombe off on a hole-winning rampage that threatened to wipe Sarazen completely out of the picture.

It went five holes before Gene was able to get hold of himself. He had a very ragged patch, being in trouble on the eleventh and twelfth and losing them to par 4s, missing a two-foot putt for a half on the thirteenth and looking up after overplaying the green on his second shot to the fourteenth.

At that point little Gene was very disgusted with himself and with the world in general. Getting hold of himself, he made a gorgeous recovery out of the woods to win the sixteenth and Whitcombe was bad at the next two, so instead of 5 down or more, Sarazen was able to come out for the second round with only two holes to make up.

There were no signs of this happening until he holed a putt for a 2 on the sixth and won the seventh. From there on it was not only a tightly played but a well played battle. He won the tenth with a 3 after being bunkered, but dropped the twelfth and so they came to the sixteenth all square.

He played the sixteenth badly, being twice in trouble, but holed a good putt for his half there. He also played the seventeenth badly and this time he didn't come off so luckily, for Robson won it, leaving him 1 up. Robson lost his advantage by three-putting the last green, giving Gene a chance to square the match by getting down in two putts from some distance.

Hagen Starts Weakly.

Hagen and Havers played patchy golf in the morning round. Havers twice getting a two-hole lead on the American captain, but each time letting it slip away. Hagen finally got the jump by winning three holes in a row starting at the fourteenth and was leading by 1 up when they finished the morning round.

In the afternoon it was quite different. Now it was Havers who was attempting to hang on. The breaking point came at the fifteenth, and as has been the case generally with the British players it was putting that decided the issue.

Havers was just below the green with his second, within easy pitching distance. Hagen hooked his drive to the rough, topped his second and was in a bunker on his fourth. It was a long-odds bet that Havers would win the hole to square the match. Instead, he took a 6 and Hagen won the hole with a 5 by dropping a four-yard putt.

Two up. Hagen lost the sixteenth when he was in the woods with his drive, short of a trap on his second and past the hole on his third. He on the next one, however, and that ended it.

Watrous Sets Fast Pace.

Watrous, the **Michigan** professional, set **a dazzling** pace for nine holes **against Robson, going** out in 33 and winning four holes to lead his man by 3 holes.

After that he turned face about and took 45 to come in, giving the Briton a chance to not only catch up but take the lead. Al made up the loss by the time they reached the ninth hole in the afternoon and then got a good break when his tee shot to the tenth was kept from going off the green by hitting one of the spectators.

Getting an undeserved half there set him off and he won three straight holes, taking the eleventh when his opponent hooked to the rough, holing a twenty-five-foot putt for a birdie 3 on the twelth and being presented with the thirteenth when Robson missed two shots.

Turnesa, off color, was never up on Duncan during the morning round until the fifteenth hole. At the tenth hole he was 3 down, but got them back by winning the twelfth, thirteenth, fourteenth and fifteenth holes. In the afternoon he was never down until the fourteenth.

Diegel Has Best Round.

For Diegel was reserved the distinction of producing the most brilliant round of the day. Against the veteran Ray he was out in 34 this morning and home in 36 for a notable 70. In the first eight holes Diegel won five and halved three. The stolid Briton struck back gallantly at every opening, but he had to do things like chipping into the cup for a birdie at the eleventh to win a hole.

At the tenth hole in the morning the American played a spectacular shot when he curved his ball around a three-quarter stymie and into the hole for a winning deuce with his mid-iron.

At noontime Diegel was 6 up and Ray could not do better than reduce that margin to five holes on one occasion. For the thirty-one holes Diegel was three shots under even 4's.

Golden had only to play his normal game and let Jolly beat himself. The English professional was playing in his first international match of any consequence and he was quite obviously not up to his normal game. He had an 84 in the morning and was fortunate to find himself only six holes down. At no time did he threaten to cut into the early lead that Golden established and he won only four holes all day.

June 5, 1927

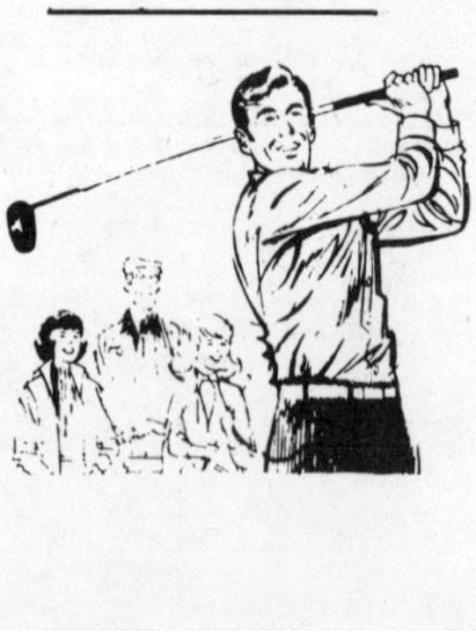

45-FOOT PUTT TURNS MATCH FOR ARMOUR

Great Shot at 15th Ties Count With Cooper and He Gains Two Strokes on 16th.

ADDS ANOTHER AT THE 18TH

By WILLIAM D. RICHARDSON.
Special to The New York Times.

OAKMONT, Pa., June 17.—The same grim determination that enabled Tommy Armour to tie Harry Cooper for the open championship yesterday, carried the 32-year-old Scot through to victory in the eighteen-hole play-off at the Oakmont Club this afternoon.

Trailing the Coast star by two strokes with only six holes left to play, apparently out of the running, Armour staged the same kind of a rally that he did in the final round of the championship proper, and won the title by the comfortable margin of three strokes, the scores for the round being 76 and 79.

The short sixteenth hole, one of the best golf holes on the whole course, was the one that turned the tide of battle in Armour's favor. Up to that point it was nip and tuck, anybody's championship. He and Cooper were tied, going to the sixteenth hole, and whoever succeeded in laying his ball on that green, 234 yards away, would stand a good chance of winning without further adieu, and woe be to him who went into the deep bunker on the right.

Hopes Buried in Bunker.

Using a spoon for the stroke, Armour landed his ball on the green, but it bounced over and trickled half way down the grassy slope behind. Now was Harry's turn and he used a No. 4 iron, pushed it just a trifle in his effort to get close to the pin which was out on the side of the green, and went into the bunker that every one has tried to avoid while the championship was on. That is where his hopes lie buried tonight.

As he was about to play his explosion shot out of the sand, standing there with just the top of his glossy head showing above the level of the green, some one in the gallery on the other side of the bunker shouted: "Down in front."

Harry stopped, looked around and glared. It caused a break in his concentration and he had to start all over again. The effect was shown when he managed to get the ball only half way up the steep slope in front of him.

Now it was Armour's turn to play. It was the time for him to strike the blow that would seal Cooper's doom, and he studied the situation carefully and long. Up came the ball, beautifully onto the green. On and on it rolled, encouraged by the gallery.

Keeps on Its Way.

Traveling at a snail's pace it kept coming on, coming on, until it stopped only four feet away from the hole, leaving him a nice, easy putt for a par 3 and making Cooper's chip shot certainly no easier.

Harry failed to get close to the hole on his third, and then missed his four-yard putt for a 4, taking a 5 and leaving him two strokes to the bad, with only two holes left.

Right then and there the championship was decided. All Armour had to do was play the next two holes safely, while Cooper had to take every chance. Both hit fine drives to the seventeenth. Cooper was in a little better position so far as the hole was concerned, for he was over to the left, with just the corner of a bunker to pitch over. Armour was to the right, with the whole bunker to clear.

The next shot that Cooper played was a shot that proved what a splendid fighter he is. When his ball stopped rolling it was not more than eighteen inches from the hole—a beautiful shot under the circumstances. But Armour, not to be outdone, followed with one that stopped just nine inches away. They were truly magnificent strokes, each of them.

Last Hole a Formality.

After that stroke of Armour's, the playing of the last hole was nothing more than a formality. Cooper's only chance had been for his rival to err on the seventeenth, and when Tommy put his ball closer to the hole than Harry it was an indication to the Coast youngster that this wasn't to be his tournament.

At the last hole, Armour increased his margin to three strokes by getting a par 4 whereas Cooper took a 5 after slicing to the rough and being in the bunker on his second.

Armour thus becomes the thirty-first open champion of the United States and the successor of Robert T. Jones, whose failure to do better than he did proved to be one of the biggest disappointments in modern golf history. Today Bobby had to join the gallery watching two men, one a Scot and the other an Englishman, one 32 years old and the other only 22, battle for the title that he had fought for every year since 1922.

Today's match was somewhat disappointing for the first twelve holes Up to that point it was rather slipshod, each player passing up glorious opportunities to steal away to a good-sized lead? Up to that point, **Cooper had all the best of it and looked to be an easy winner.**

Armour the Under Dog.

Armour was the under dog and playing up to the rôle. Cooper was on top, sailing along jauntily, as is his wont, and apparently headed for the victory which he was denied when Armour played that miraculous second shot and holed that great putt to gain the tie late yesterday afternoon.

Then the tide of battle turned, and it turned on one shot, the No. 4 iron that Cooper played to the thirteenth green and the mongrel mashie that Armour played. Cooper's went into a bunker; Armour's came in beautifully at the finish and after they holed out the black-haired Washington professional had one of his two-stroke deficit made up.

Armour missed a great chance to draw level when he took three putts on the next hole after outplaying Cooper all the way up to the hole, but he atoned for the mistake at the fifteenth, which is perhaps the hardest par 4 hole in the country. There, after being in a bunker on his second shot, Tommy holed a 45-foot putt for his par 4.

Cooper tried desperately to match the putt from only a short yard or so less, but the ball slid past the hole and the match was all level.

That was the putt that did the business, for until it went into the hole, Cooper was sitting in the driver's seat and Tommy was fast coming to the point of giving up the ghost so far as this year's title was concerned. When it dropped, the strain was off Armour and on Cooper and from there on that is where it stayed.

Won on Short Holes.

After all is said and done, it was the short holes—the sixth, eighth, thirteenth and sixteenth—that decided the championship. Armour had four 3s on them and it took Cooper seventeen strokes to play them—five strokes more. Armour won and Cooper lost, bearing out the contention of Aleck Smith that the man who wins the short holes in a championship wins the championship.

And on not one of the short holes was he much better off than Cooper after the tee shots had been played. On the sixth, the first of the four one-shotters at Oakmont, Cooper was just on the green and Armour was bunkered, but Tommy got out with

CARDS WITH PAR.									
Out—									
Par	5	4	4	5	4	2	4	5	5—37
Armour ..	4	4	5	5	4	3	3	5	5—39
Cooper	5	4	6	4	4	4	4	4	4—39
In—									
Par	4	4	5	3	4	4	3	4	4—35—72
Armour ..	5	5	5	3	5	4	3	3	4—37—76
Cooper	4	4	5	4	5	4	5	5	5—40—79

STANDING AT EACH HOLE.									
Holes ..	1	2	3	4	5	6	7	8	9
Armour ..	4	8	13	18	23	26	31	34	39
Cooper ...	5	9	13	19	23	27	31	35	39
Holes ..	10	11	12	13	14	15	16	17	18
Armour..	44	49	54	57	62	66	69	72	76
Cooper ..	43	47	52	56	61	66	71	74	79

a beautifully played cut shot that almost went into the hole, while Harry took three to get down.

On the eighth Cooper was on the green and Armour in a bunker, but the Scot came out and holed a twenty-footer while his rival took three putts. Then, on the thirteenth, Armour stayed on the green, whereas Cooper was bunkered, and on the sixteenth Armour was just over and the Coast youngster again in a bunker.

What was surprising in today's play-off was the manner in which Armour outdrove Cooper from the tees. Only once or twice was Cooper, rated as one of the longest hitters in the country, past the District of Columbia star on the drives. That, and his ability to recover out of trouble, was what gave Armour a great advantage and what aided him in beating the youngster who earned his spurs by playing Hagen a tight match in the semi-final round of the P. G. A. championship two years ago.

Ball Hits a Spectator.

Breaks had something to do with determining which way the battle would go, and if anything, Tommy was slightly favored in that respect, especially in playing the tenth hole. There his second shot, a gorgeous mongrel-mashie pitch out of the rou, skidded off the top of a mound near the green and was kept from going into trouble by hitting on of the spectators who was at the pack of the green. If it had ever got by it would have gone several yards over and might have cost him any number of strokes.

The rough was terrible only a few yards behind where it stopped, and there were rocks and trees and trouble galore. As it was, he lost only a stroke to Cooper, when he might have lost several if the ball had gone on where it was headed for.

Toward the finish of the match, especially on the last few holes, Cooper began to break down under the strain and made serious errors that cost him dearly, while Armour seemed to improve the further the match went.

The new champion is a finished golfer, one of the very best in America today in spite of his failure to win anything of a major sort until now. And Cooper, the youngster, is destined to greater things, for he has the game and he has what is most needed, superb confidence in himself.

Fully 4,000 persons witnessed today's play-off, which was held under threatening conditions. Early in the day it looked as if the match would have to be played in rain, but the weather held off until play was ended.

June 18, 1927

JONES AGAIN WINS BRITISH GOLF TITLE; SCORE 7 UNDER PAR

Scots Try to Carry 'Dour, Braw Lad' Off St. Andrews Links After He Makes a 285.

MARVEL AT 6-STROKE LEAD

Applaud Wildly When American Amateur Asks Them to 'Keep the Cup' for Him.

Copyright. 1927, by The New York Times Company
Special Cable to THE NEW YORK TIMES.

ST. ANDREWS, Scotland, July 15.—Bobbie Jones, with four rounds aggregating 285, retained his British open golf championship here today, and all Scotland seems to be rejoicing over the feat. The scene, when Bobby holed his final putt on the last green this afternoon, will dwell forever in the memory of every one who witnessed it.

Bobby, seized by the enthusiastic crowd of Scots, was hoisted shoulder high and was carried off the green with difficulty amid the plaudits of 20,000 spectators. They demanded a speech and Bobby opened his mouth, but whether he said anything cannot be recorded, for the pandemonium of cheers and shouts drowned out all other sounds.

For ten minutes everybody in St. Andrews wanted to congratulate the young American and pat his shoulders. The Scots who had him on their shoulders and those surrounding him were shouting in their own tongue "atta boy," and Bobby smiled.

Singing Is Drowned Out.

Several lads started singing "For he's a jolly good fellow," but their efforts were drowned in the general din.

A number of women got caught in the press of people crowding around Bobby and it looked as if they might get hurt. Bobby, traveling precariously on the shoulders of his admirers, saw the situation and appealed to the crowd to fall back. It obeyed him and Bobby waved his thanks.

Andra Kirkaldy, the famous Scotch golfer who presides over the last green of St. Andrews, then came to the rescue. The Scots know Andra and know also that he won't be denied. With the use of his hefty elbows and commanding voice he cleared a path for Bobby, who finally reached his hotel—still on the shoulders of his Scottish henchmen.

After he had disappeared the crowd of some thousands waited outside the hotel hoping he would appear on the balcony to say a few words to them, but Bobby had had a very trying time and knew anyway that he would be expected to make a speech when the presentation of the cup took place.

Performs Notable Feats.

In winning the championship, Jones performed a number of notable feats, among them the following:

His score of 285 was three under even 4s;

Seven strokes under par;

Six strokes under the previous record of 291, set by James Braid in 1908 and tied by himself last year;

One stroke lower than the best American Open score ever turned in, a 286 by Chick Evans in 1916.

He had 17 birdies.

And one eagle during the seventy-two holes of tournament play.

He was the first to win the championship two years in succession since Braid triumphed in 1905 and 1906.

Such is the record of the twenty-five-year-old Atlanta amateur who is being hailed through all Scotland tonight as the world's greatest golfer.

He finished the tourney six strokes better than Audrey Boomer, English pro at the St. Cloud Country Club in France, and Fred Robson, British pro, who tied for second with 219 strokes each.

Kirkwood Leads Others.

Joe Kirkwood led the other Americans with his 293, but he had to share fourth place with Ernest Whitcombe, a British pro. Jim Barnes was next best among the entrants from the United States when he scored a 301. Tom Stevens had a 302 and Walter Kennett a 306.

It was said at the seventeenth hole yesterday that Bobby almost was overcome with sickness. If he felt any physical disability today he certainly did not show any signs of it. As a matter of fact, Bobby says physical fitness counts only 10 per cent. in golf—always providing the player isn't a cripple.

Jones is a dour player who appeals to the Scots, and today he allowed himself to smile only toward the end of the second round, when he knew he was certain to retain the cham-

pionship. It was then that he could permit himself to watch the behavior of the crowd and listen to the many who called him a "braw lad."

Cup Presented to Jones.

This evening a crowd sixty deep, numbering probably 20,000 persons, gathered around the clubhouse to witness the presentation of the cup to Bobby—or at least the return of the cup to him. Colonel Bethune, handing the cup to Bobby, said: "The open golf competition started in 1860. For the first ten years Scotland managed to retain the trophy—which then was a belt—but in 1871 it was taken over the border to England.

"Now, however, the tourney has become an international event. It has been won once by a Frenchman, Arnaud Massy, in 1907, and in 1921 the cup was taken across the Atlantic for the first time by Jock Hutchison. Since then it has made many journeys to and fro."

This caused laughter, as the Americans have won it six times in the last seven years. Colonel Bethune added that he had great pleasure in handing the cup to a member of the Royal and Ancient Club of St. Andrews, although that member resided in the United States.

After the presentation Bobby, who was made a life member of the Royal and Ancient last year, was called upon to make a speech. Amid great cheering he said: "This is the happiest moment of my life, as it has been the ambition of my life to win the championship at St. Andrews. I want to thank everybody for their kindness to me. Every one has been so nice to us I ever experienced happened on the last green.

Leaves Cup Behind.

"I have one request to make and I hope I will be pardoned since I have asked so much from the St.

Bobby Jones, Who Set New Record in Winning British Open Title.

Andrews people. I would take it as a great honor if they would mind the cup for me at St. Andrews."

This compliment to the natives was greeted with great cheering, and Colonel Bethune, on behalf of the Royal and Ancient Club, granted the request.

The other winners then received their prizes. Among the pros to win checks was the famous old Scot Sandy Herd. He was the oldest player in the championship and won the title at Hoylake in 1902.

In response to the demands for a speech Sandy said as an old St. Andrews boy he would have liked to have seen a Scotsman or an Englishman win, but since it was not to be he was glad it had been won by such "a thorough gentleman and sportsman as Robert T. Jones, one of the greatest players of all time," to whom he offered his sincere congratulations.

As an instance of Bobby's popularity, what happened at the sixteenth, the railway, hole this morning should be recorded. Bobby was on the green in two just as an excursion train was stopped by an adverse signal. Those aboard saw what had happened. At least half of them dropped out of the train onto the tracks and scampered over the fence to the green. There were whole families of them and one, an athlete, sought a vantage point by climbing up a signal post.

Crowd Is Rewarded.

Bobby rewarded them by sinking a four-yard putt for a 3. The engineer blew his whistle triumphantly and the crowd almost drowned it with cheers.

Never in the memory of the oldest inhabitant of St. Andrews has there been such a huge crowd following a golf champion as today. Thousands of persons tracked Bobby all the way around. That he managed to play the perfect golf he did is little less than a miracle. The stewards had great difficulty clearing the way for him and sometimes he had to wait ten minutes before he was able to play.

As soon as he struck the ball and while it still was in the air the crowd would surge forward and Bobby would be engulfed in it. Those who were ahead, waiting on the green, kept their eyes concentrated on the immediate vicinity of the hole, and Bobby's ball invariably landed somewhere near. He was playing with the greatest of confidence and if he had any nerves he never let any one know it.

This afternoon Bobby missed a seven-foot putt for a 3 at the first hole. At the second he pulled his drive into a bunker and just got out and on the green in 3. Then he had to take two putts.

Gets in a Bunker.

At the third he was in a bunker at the left of the green after his second shot. He failed to get out on his next, but got another 5 when he holed a ten-foot putt. He got his par 4 at the fourth, but at the fifth, 530 yards long, he was short of the green with his second shot. He then had a poor approach and took two putts.

At the sixth he was on the green with his second shot and then he holed a four-yarder. At the seventh he got his 4, but at the short eighth, 150 yards, he pulled his tee shot and barely got on the green. To make matters worse he had to take three putts. At the ninth he holed a fifteen-footer for a neat 3.

The tenth, which is 312 yards long, was reached with a drive and from the edge of the green he was down in 2. At the short eleventh he got a 3, after having just missed a 25-yarder for a 2. At the twelfth a beautiful second pitch shot put him a yard from the pin and he was down in one putt.

At the thirteenth he missed a 5-yard putt for a 3, but at the long fourteenth he was just short of the green with his second. He made a good approach and needed only one putt. He easily made the fifteenth in par 4.

Slices to the Right.

The sixteenth saw Jones drive well, but he sliced his second to the right of the green. It went into the crowd and landed a yard from the railway fence. He made a poor approach and required two putts.

Bobby Jones's Complete Cards In British Open Golf Tourney

The cards of the tourney for Bobby Jones:

Par for Course.

Out .4 4 4 4 5 4 4 3 4—36
In ..4 3 4 4 5 4 4 5 4—37—73

First Round.

Out .4 5 4 4 3 3 4 2 3—32
In ..4 3 4 4 5 4 4 4 4—36—68

Second Round.

Out .5 4 4 4 5 3 4 3 5—37
In ..3 2 5 4 4 4 4 5 4—35—72—140

Third Round.

Out .4 4 4 5 4 4 5 3 5—38
In ..3 3 5 4 4 4 3 5 4—35—72—213

Fourth Round.

Out .4 5 5 4 5 3 4 4 3—37
In ..3 3 3 4 4 4 5 5 4—35—72—285

Bobby then knew he had the championship in his pocket again. Playing pawkily, he hit his second for safety with an iron at the seventeenth and then took a 5. At the eighteenth he got a par 4 after narrowly missing a 30-yard putt for a 3. The first putt finished only a few inches from the hole.

Further testimony of the popularity of Bobby with the youths of St. Andrews was shown tonight when a number of them besieged the clubhouse, hoping he would come out. They cried, "Bobby! Bobby!" in chorus, and some even invaded the almost sacred club premises, but Bobby had had enough excitement f the day and preferred to enjoy a well-earned dinner.

Bobby did rounds of 73 and 72 today, but his morning efforts showed nothing remarkable until he reached the fourth hole, where he took three putts. At the fifth he had a drive of 275 yards, and his second, a pitch shot, landed him eighteen feet from the pin. Then he took two putts.

Is Close to the Pin.

At the sixth he was fifteen feet from the pin and had to take two putts. At the seventh it is estimated that he drove 290 yards. He chipped his second into a trap, exploded out, and was down in two putts. The short eighth hole found him fifty feet from th pin with his tee shot, but he got a 3. On the ninth he took three putts.

One putt at the tenth gave him a 3, and he got another at the short eleventh. He was short at the twelfth with his second and then his third and he required two putts. The thirteenth produced a normal 4.

The fourteenth, 527 yards long, found him short of the green with his second, but he was down in two more. The fifteenth produced a par 4. At the sixteenth he pitched his second three yards from the pin and was down in one putt.

The seventeenth required a 5, owing to his being short with his second, and the eighteenth was a normal par 4.

While Jones looked like the winner all day, Jim Barnes, who took a 301, seemed on the verge of making a bid for the championship. He had a 72 in the morning and a 33 for the first nine holes in the afternoon, but taking a 5 at the short eleventh rather unsettled him and cost him 44 coming home, including two 6s.

Kirkwood's two scores today were 75 and 74. He missed a yard putt on the eighteenth to take undivided fourth prize. Tom Stevens did well this morning with a 74, but two 6s this afternoon in his round of 79 spoiled his chance. Walter Kennett of Florida had rounds of 75 and 78.

July 16, 1927

HAGEN KEEPS TITLE; BEATS TURNESA, 1 UP

Wins Fourth Pro Golf Crown in Row, New Record for U. S. Championship Play.

WAGES AN UPHILL FIGHT

1 Down at Turn in Afternoon, He Wins 12th and 14th as Turnesa Falters, Taking Match.

By WILLIAM D. RICHARDSON.
Special to The New York Times.

DALLAS, Texas, Nov. 5.—Walter Hagen made new golf history here this afternoon when he defeated Joe Turnesa, young Elmsford Country Club professional, 1 up, in the final round of the 1927 Professional Golfers' Association championship.

Today's was the fourth straight victory that Hagen has won in this event, which holds an equal place with the open championship. Never before in the history of the game of golf has any one succeeded in doing anything equal to what Hagen has done in this yearly grind at medal and match play.

Two bad slips by Turnesa on the last nine holes of the thirty-six hole match that they fought over the fairways and greens of the Cedar Crest Country Club cost the young Westchester professional the championship.

The first came when he took three putts on the twelfth hole in the afternoon round and the second when he made three bad shots playing No. 13.

Before that Turnesa had played Hagen stroke for stroke, holding his own for the most part and even outplaying the defending champion. He had turned 1 up and seemed to be in a fair way to take the champion into camp and win his first major title.

Hagen Squares Match.

Hagen squared the match by winning No. 12 with a birdie 3. Playing the next hole Walter was short of the green on his tee shot, while Turnesa's iron shot finished its journey on the extreme right-hand side of the green, less than a foot from being in a bunker.

Hagen was short and by no means certain of holding the next, and then Turnesa lost his chance by putting so far past the hole that he couldn't sink the next one. Hagen missed also, and so Turnesa got a half, but halves were not what he was after at this stage of the match.

Turnesa's next tee shot reflected the frame of mind that the missed putt put him in. It was a poor drive and left him a long journey away from the green, so far, in fact, that when he came to play the shot he missed the green entirely and had to play his off hard ground. He recovered strong and had to putt his fourth before Hagen, well on the green in two, putted his third. The result was a 4 for Hagen and a 6 for Turnesa.

Hagen was now 1 up and from there on Walter hung on to that lead for dear life, his faultless play keeping Turnesa in his place. Walter had a great chance to clinch the match on No. 15, where he missed a short putt for a 3 after Joe had left himself short and failed to hole a five-footer, but it made no difference.

Last Three Holes Halved.

The long sixteenth was halved in 5s, the seventeenth in 4s and the last hole in 4s. Turnesa had chances to square the match on both the seventeenth and eighteenth, but his putter, which had worked like a magic wand all day, failed him in the crisis.

At the seventeenth his second shot out of the rough left him a seven-foot putt uphill to make for his 3, and he had an even shorter one for a victory on the last hole, but neither one went down and Hagen was again the P. G. A. champion.

Great credit is due Turnesa for the grand fight he put up against the old master. It was a fight that would have rewarded him against almost any one else. He holed the course in 71 in the morning round and had Hagen 2 down at noon.

After Turnesa won the first hole in the afternoon to make him 3 up indications pointed strongly toward the crowning of a new champion. Hagen, however, fought like a tiger from then on.

He began to play his old game, which is that of waiting for the breaks to come and seizing them. He got back two holes by winning the second and third to be only 1 down, lost the fourth when his drive hit a spectator and went into the rough, making him 2 down again, but holed a fine putt to win No. 7 and then squared the match by holing out for a birdie 3 on No. 11.

Not for a second did Hagen show the slightest sign of giving up even though the tide of battle seemed to be going against him. He was always trying for everything, making the breaks when he could and taking full advantage of every opportunity that his opponent gave him.

It was a great final, certainly the outstanding final since the one in which Hagen and Sarazen clashed at the Pelham Country Club in 1923. Incidentally that was the last time that Hagen has been beaten in a P. G. A. event. He has now won four years running and has set up a record that has not only made history but may never be equaled again. The Hagens in golf come few and far between.

Turnesa Nervous at Start.

Turnesa, appearing a trifle nervous at the outset of the match, practically presented Hagen with the first hole. His mashie niblick pitch was hooked into a bunker at the corner of the green and he went over on his third, taking a 5. Hagen came out of the rough to within ten feet and won the hole with a 4.

Neither was close at the short second hole, which was halved in par, although Turnesa lipped the cup from thirty-five feet on his try for a birdie.

Walter became 2 up by winning the third with a par 4, pitching his second thirty feet below the hole and getting down in two putts, while Turnesa overplayed the green on his second and was weak on his chip back. The next two holes were halved, the fourth in 4s and the next in 5s. Turnesa was in the rough on his drive to the fourth and had to play a spoon to reach the green.

Turnesa was again in the rough on his drive to the fifth hole and had a long third shot left to the green. He pitched to within four yards and got a half when Hagen, who was up near the bunker in 2, chipped weakly.

By this time Turnesa had got his nerves under control, and for the remainder of the round played Hagen better than even.

Starting at the sixth hole, Joe won three holes in succession to take the lead away from Hagen. Both were bunkered at the short sixth, Turnesa on the right and Hagen on the left. Joe came out to within six feet, but Walter, attempting to lift the ball, failed to get it out of the sand, and was six yards from the pin when he did succeed, so that Joe won the hole with a 4, 1 over par.

Walter Hagen, Who Retained P. G. A. Title.

Photo by P. and A

Hagen Hooks Tee Shot.

His failure to extricate himself nettled Hagen, and Walter played the next hole badly, hooking his tee shot to a place where he had to play his second through some trees, with practically no chance of reaching the green. He made the shot all right, but was bunkered at the left of the green, and again recovering poorly, finished up with a 6. Turnesa was on the green in 2, twenty yards from the pin, and approached up dead for an easy 4, squaring the match.

Turnesa then played a beautiful shot to No. 7, 167 yards, the ball stopping six feet from the hole. After Hagen had missed a six-yard putt, Turnesa holed out for a birdie 2 to become 1 up.

The next hole was one of the most spectacular of the entire match. After good drives by each, Turnesa pitched to within ten feet of the pin and holed out for a birdie 3, forcing Hagen, within five feet, to sink the putt for a half. Turnesa was out in 35, equaling par, and Hagen in 38 as a result of those 6s on six and seven.

Walter squared the match by getting down in one putt for a birdie 4 on the tenth. After playing a beautiful spoon shot over the trees for his second, he pitched on to within twelve feet. Turnesa's ball was five feet nearer the hole, but he failed to run it in for a 4 after Hagen had made a beautiful side-hill putt on

which he had to borrow at least two feet.

The eleventh was another spectacular hole on which Hagen again had to sink a five-footer down hill to save his half after Turnesa had run down a ten-footer for a birdie 3. Hagen lost the short twelfth, 3 to 4, permitting Turnesa to take the lead again. Walter was bunkered short of the green and came out poorly, while Turnesa was on from the tee.

Turnesa Loses Chance.

Joe lost a chance to hold the lead when, after a fine drive to No. 13 hole, he pitched far to the right of the pin and failed to lay his approach putt close, the ball sliding about three and a half feet past. With Hagen's ball dead for a 4, Joe, missed, taking three putts.

Hagen wasted no time throwing the advantage away. His drive went into the trees on the right and he hit a tree trying to reach the green. Before he finally managed to reach the green he had played five and was not close even then. He finally conceded the hole to Turnesa who was on in two.

Although he was on the fifteenth green off the tee, while Turnesa was short, Walter lost the hole by taking three putts from thirty feet, while Joe managed to get down in one putt after playing a fine chip shot to within four feet of the cup.

The long sixteenth was halved in perfect figures and so were the next two. Both narrowly missed holing

difficult side-hill putts for 3s on No. 17 and both had putts for birdies on the eighteenth. Turnesa's score for the incoming nine was 36, giving him even par for the round, while Hagen was 39 on the inward half for a 77, leaving him 2 down.

Turnesa Takes First Hole.

Although bunkered on his second shot to the first hole in the afternoon, Turnesa won the hole, 4 to 5, exploding out to within four feet and sinking the putt after Hagen, in the rough on his drive, missed his second and took three to reach the green. Joe failed to get home on his mashie shot to the second hole and Hagen won it, 3 to 4.

Joe played the third badly, driving to the rough and pitching short of the green, but it made no difference for Walter pitched the ball a yard from the flag and had a certain 3. Both played bad second shots to the fourth, Hagen slicing into the trees at the left of the green and Turnesa following suit. Before Hagen finally holed out he had an approximated 7 on his card, while Turnesa got a 5 by chipping on and getting down in two putts.

From then on, except for two three-putt greens, Walter played flawless golf. Although his drive to the fifth was not what it should have been, he got an easy 5, while Joe was lucky to have his second shot, badly hooked, stop in a place where he could reach the green on his third instead of being down in among the trees.

Hagen, after a beautiful second shot to the seventh, holed an eighteen-foot putt for a birdie 3 which won the hole and left him only 1 down. The short eighth was halved in par 3s and the ninth in 4s. Turnesa's putt for a half hanging on the lip of the cup for a few seconds before finally dropping in.

Turnesa Evens Tenth.

Turnesa had to lay a long approach putt for his half at the tenth, and then Hagen outplayed him to win the eleventh with a birdie 3. There Walter took the short cut over the trees and pitched to within two yards, while Joe played safe and went thirty feet over the hole on his second. The remaining holes of the match have been already described. The cards follow:

Morning Round.

Out—
Turnesa ...5 3 5 4 5 4 4 2 3—35
Hagen ....4 3 4 4 5 6 6 3 3—38
Turnesa 1 up.
In—
Turnesa ...5 3 3 5 4 3 5 4 4—36—71
Hagen ....4 3 4 4 7 4 5 4 4—39—77
Turnesa 2 up.

Afternoon Round.

Hagen ....5 3 3 7 5 3 3 3 4—36
Turnesa ..4 4 5 5 5 3 4 3 4—37
Turnesa 1 up.
In—
Hagen ....5 3 4 4 4 4 5 4 4—37—73
Turnesa ...5 4 4 6 4 4 5 4 4—40—77
Hagen 1 up.

November 6, 1927

PAR FOR THE COURSE.

Out.	Yards	Par.	In.	Yards	Par.
1...	445	4	10...	335	5
2...	410	4	11...	335	4
3...	350	4	12...	217	3
4...	465	5	13...	391	4
5...	525	5	14...	388	4
6...	215	3	15...	182	3
7...	430	4	16...	551	5
8...	167	3	17...	315	4
9...	374	4	18...	335	4
Total.				**Yards.**	**Par.**
Out				3,686	36
In				3,385	35
Grand total				**6,571**	**71**

WHAT MAKES HAGEN A GREAT PLAYER?

Not Luck, but Headwork, Confidence, Nerve and an Ability to Forget Bad Shots.

MAKES AIDES OF OBSTACLES

Once, When Leaves Impeded Putt, He Removed All but Two, Using Them as Markers.

By WILLIAM D. RICHARDSON.

What is there about him that makes Walter Hagen such a marvel when it comes to match play? Is it that he is so far superior to his fellow-professionals? Was he born under a lucky star? Does he bear a charmed life?

Questions such as these have been asked and discussed since Hagen won the P. G. A. championship for the fourth year in succession at Dallas recently. Walter has always been an interesting figure in golf, but never the outstanding man he has become through that triumph over men and nature at the Cedar Crest Country Club.

Not often has it happened that in a game fraught with so many uncertainties as golf one man is able to dominate his field the way Hagen has his for the past four years. In fact, never before has there been an instance where the same man has won a major title four times running, especially at match play.

Having followed Hagen's career through those four years, having been in a position to watch him play many notable matches down that stretch of years and to talk with him about them afterward, the writer feels qualified to set down a few observations that may shed some light on some of the questions Hagen's recent triumph has brought.

Hagen's main asset, we are inclined to think, is his head. Others, his mechanical equals, maybe superiors, have to give way to him when it comes to headwork on the links. An incident that happened in the course of one of Hagen's matches in Texas will serve to illustrate the point.

He was faced with a difficult putt on a green with a double roll. It being Autumn, the ground was covered with leaves, and Hagen, instead of picking up each and every one that was between his ball and the hole, as most golfers would do, left two as "markers." By so doing he knew exactly where to aim.

Cruikshank, watching the match, was quick to observe the strategy. "What do you know about that?" he asked. "Did you see him use those leaves as markers? Had I been in that situation there wouldn't have been a leaf left on the green, and here the Haig uses them as sights. We live to learn new tricks every day."

Confidence—Second Asset.

Now for a second asset—confidence in himself. Hagen is a great believer in Hagen. Not that he is a braggart. He isn't. He is a swagger. His swagger on the links is nothing more nor less than a pose designed to mask his own inward feelings and emotions and, if possible, to have an effect on the man he happens to be playing against. No matter how the tide of battle happens to be running, whether it is with or against, you'll always see Hagen stamping forward —long, big, confident strides; chest out, head up.

We saw him at Olympia Fields in 1925 when he was 3 down to Diegel with four holes left to play; more recently we saw him when he was apparently beaten by young Jack Farrell in the first round at Cedar Crest and by Espinosa in the semi-final. Against Diegel and Espinosa he had every reason to believe that his end had come, but did his face show it? No. Not once in all the time we have trailed after Hagen have we ever seen him evince a single outward sign that betrayed doubt of his ability to pull through somehow.

In this same connection it is interesting to learn from Hagen how he came to defend his title at Dallas. It illustrates not only his self-confidence, but his sense of fairness.

Few persons know that up to within two weeks or so of the P. G. A. event Hagen had definitely decided to let his title go by default. He had played little if any golf between then and the time he won the Western open in September. He was out of shape physically and not in playing form.

"I had figured that the odds were all against my winning the championship again and decided to rest on my oars and let it go at that," he told me on the way back from Dallas. "I'd won the thing four times, three years in succession, so why flirt with trouble?

"And then I happened to look at it another way. I looked at it from the point of view of the fellow who would win without me in it and I decided it was only fair for me to come and take my medicine and let the winner take all the glory there was coming to him."

Walter was perfectly sincere about it all. With him away, the victory would be a more or less hollow one for the next champion, for there would always be those who would say: "Well, Hagen wasn't there. If he had been, So-and-So might not have won."

Having checked up and found that the facts were exactly as Hagen had stated them, we returned with a greater feeling of admiration for Hagen than we have ever cherished before.

Having decided to defend his title and, as he was prepared to do, to sacrifice himself in order that the man who won might receive full credit, did Hagen repair at once to the nearest golf course and begin to practice? He did not. Instead he went up into the north woods of Wisconsin and began getting himself in shape physically.

He went to Dallas, therefore, out of practice, but decidedy keen, more keen, perhaps, than anybody else who was there. The others had spent weeks preparing for the ordeal. Hagen played only one practice round prior to the championship and then stepped out on the qualifying day and led the field by three strokes.

There is still another attribute which Hagen has in abundance—nerve. He can play the game safely if he has to or if it serves his purpose best, but let the match get tight and he's as bold as a pirate. Look at those second shots he played on the last two holes against Espinosa if you don't believe it—the one at the thirty-sixth hole and the other at the thirty-seventh.

Each one was right at the flag, not below it. What mattered it to Hagen if the holes were cut on the upper side of the green and if the slightest miscalculation would send his ball into the rough and cost him the match? Not a thing. He gave the ball a chance. He always does that. The one thing that seems to annoy him in a golf match is cowardice on a pitch or an approach putt. He knows full well that the hole, being stationary, cannot meet the ball half-way.

The Case of Mitchell.

A great deal has been written concerning Hagen's baiting his opponents. He has been accused of divers acts of unsportsmanship designed to get an opponent's "goat." He was severely censured for causing Abe Mitchell to wait on the tee for such a long period in their now famous 72-hole match in England that poor Abe was in a state of nervous exhaustion when Hagen finally did appear.

Although late-arrival at the tee is a breach of etiquette that cannot be condoned we are inclined to think that the mere thought of Hagen as an opponent had as much to do with Mitchell's collapse as Walter's delay, which, it has been shown, was not his fault but that of some officials.

Lastly we come to Hagen's main asset—his ability to forget to remember a bad shot or a series of bad shots.

When he goes out to play a round of golf, be it in match or medal play, Hagen resigns himself to the thought that he is bound to make some errors, that he is certain to miss some putts and that all the breaks will not be in his favor. He figures the adversities first and then, when they come, as they generally do, he is not put out by them.

Break For His Rival.

At a critical point in the final match of the P. G. A. tourney, Turnesa, his opponent, hit a crooked second shot and the ball was prevented from doing a disappearing act into the woods only because it happened to strike a spectator standing at the green. It was a good break for Turnesa, a bad one for Hagen. It meant that instead of winning the hole he might not even get a half, for Joe's ball was closer to the hole than his was in spite of the fact that he had played a fine second.

Instead of gnashing his teeth and pulling his hair, Hagen holed the long putt for a birdie 3 and won the hole anyway.

Playing any round of golf, Hagen makes up his mind in advance that he is going to get four 5s. "What does it matter," he asks, "whether they come on the first four holes, in the middle or at the end of the round? If I happen to start out with four 5s I simply figure that I've used up my quota. I forget them and start out on a new tack.

"Another mistake golfers often make is to figure their scores by nines. If they take 40 going out they become panic stricken over the thought that they've got to come home in 35 or less in order to get a good score. Or, if they go out in 34, they become equally panic stricken over the thought that they may take 40 coming in.

"Why make the ninth hole the one where all reckoning takes place? If I have some good holes to start with I figure that I have some bad ones due me and make allowance for them; if I get a bad start I don't wait until the ninth hole to start a rally. What's the matter with the sixth or the seventh?"

What can you do with a fellow possessing such a philosophy as that? Ask Diegel, Barnes, Espinosa, Mitchell, Jones, Watrous, Turnesa, Armour and all the rest. Maybe they know!

November 13, 1927

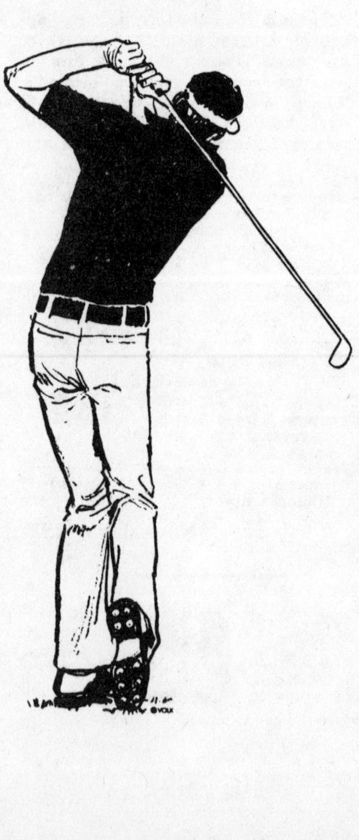

BRITISH GOLF TITLE WON BY HAGEN'S 292

His Third Open Victory Marks Seventh Time in Eight Years U. S. Has Taken Crown.

PRINCE PRESENTS THE CUP

Sees Sarazen Gain Second Place With a 294 and Compston Third With a 295.

VICTOR REGISTERS TWO 72S

Great Triumph Comes After 18-and-17 Defeat in Compston Match —Jurado Finishes in 80.

ST. GEORGE'S PAR.

Hole.	Yards.	Par.	Hole.	Yards.	Par.
1	440	4	10	375	4
2	325	4	11	380	4
3	247	4	12	340	4
4	423	4	13	439	4
5	406	4	14	510	5
6	182	3	15	457	5
7	484	5	16	160	3
8	197	3	17	420	4
9	397	4	18	434	4
Total	3,101	35	Total	3,515	37

Grand total, 6,616 yards; par, 72.

By HENRY C. CROUCH.

Special Cable to THE NEW YORK TIMES.

SANDWICH, England, May 11.—Walter Hagen has won the British open golf championship, and for the seventh time in the last eight years the title goes to the United States.

It is a humiliating record for British golf, but today's result was not unexpected; in fact, it was thought that the final honor must go to either Hagen or Gene Sarazen.

The Argentine star, Jose Jurado, led the field by three strokes, it is true, when play began this morning, but apart from the luck that came his way, there was a general belief that he would crack under the ordeal of the grueling last two rounds—and he did. His scores of 76 and 80 today bracketed him with Aubrey Boomer and Jim Barnes for fifth place with a score of 301.

Taylor Had Predicted Score.

Hagen's aggregate of 292 for the four rounds was the exact figure, it is interesting to note, which J. H. Taylor had predicted would win the championship. Next to Hagen came Sarazen with a 294—a score which easily might have been five strokes less.

Archie Compston occupied third place with a 295 and Percy Alliss came next with a 298. Jim Barnes had the best score of the day, a 71, but the effort came too late. Bill Mehlhorn, falling away from his first day start, had rounds of 76 and 77 today and occupies eighth place.

Analysis of the eight leading scores shows that two Americans are first and second; an Englishman, Compston, is third; another Englishman, Alliss, who has gone to Berlin to seek his fortune, is fourth; Aubrey Boomer, a British subject born on the Channel Islands, who is a professional at a French club, is tied for fifth place with Jurado and Barnes, and finally there comes Mehlhorn with his aggregate of 302.

Hagen has won the British open championship three times out of seven visits to this country. His first victory was scored here in 1922, when he had a total score of 300 for the four rounds. His knowledge of the course served him in good stead and he openly confesses that had he been playing on a less familiar course he probably would have been one of the "also rans."

Felt Nervous During Tourney.

After the tourney he said, "In general I am never nervous about my shots. Ordinarily I can go up to the ball and hit it without hesitating, but owing, I suppose, to lack of practice on the other side of the ocean, I felt no better than a four-handicap player in this tourney. I was compelled to think all during the play of what I might do wrong."

Sarazen, only two strokes removed from Hagen, has no regrets or excuses to make. "Things didn't always come my way," he said tonight, "but I am glad that one of our boys won. I will certainly come over here again and I hope that I will do better. Anyway, I have had a grand time and the people have treated me fine."

The Prince of Wales followed Hagen's fortunes this morning, but this afternoon he turned his attentions to Sarazen, walking in company with Hagen, who, having finished his rounds, was watching his compatriot's progress. The Prince chatted with both Americans and showed much interest in golf. He also made many inquiries about mutual friends in the United States.

Hagen had two rounds of 72 today, which meant that he was even 4s for the thirty-six holes. He was out in a remarkable 33 in the morning, although he took three putts at the first hole. At the second he almost holed a 10-yard putt for a 3. He was over the 247-yard third with his tee shot, but he pitched back beautifully and sank a two-yarder for a 3.

Gets Two Pars in Row.

At the fourth and fifth he registered par 4s and the short sixth gave him an encouraging 2 when he sank a pretty putt of six yards. The seventh caused him great concern. He was bunkered with his second and then decided he would have to play safe for a 5. He shot the ball to within six yards of the pin and then dropped the putt for a 4.

This set his heart working steadily and at both the eighth and ninth he almost holed long putts. Anyway a 33 was good enough. Then he became somewhat timorous with his second shots, perhaps because he now had the eyes of the Prince of Wales on him, and possible 4s became 5s.

Coming in he had four 5s at the first six holes, but he steadied himself and finished grandly in 3—4—4. In the afternoon he was out in 36 and back in the same figures for a total of 72. He played the first three or four holes in a mechanical sort of way and he should have had a 3 at the third, where he took a 4 after missing a four-foot putt.

Moderately short putts at the fifth and sixth missed their mark and by the time he reached the seventh he was two over 4s as a result. But the eighth brought him to the top of his game. A perfectly hit drive here, followed by a nicely negotiated putt, gave him a 2 and then a 4 at the ninth took him out in even 4s.

Coming in he registered four 4s in a row, the first three of which represented par golf. At the 439-yard thirteenth he was over the green with his second and into some very bad rough, but the occasion produced the man who could deal with it. With a dexterous use of his mashie niblick he planted the ball just a foot from the hole and another 4 went down on his card.

His 5 at the fourteenth was due mainly to a badly hooked second into a bunker. The ball shot over the green and it looked as though a 6 were going to be put down on his card, but again a fine chip put him near enough to the pin for him to hole out in 5.

Complete Cards for Hagen In British Open Golf Play

QUALIFYING ROUNDS.

First Eighteen.

Out -- 4 4 3 5 4 4 6 4 3--37
In — 4 4 5 4 4 4 5 5 4—39—76

Second Eighteen.

Out — 5 4 4 4 4 3 5 3 4—36
In -- 3 4 5 5 6 5 5 3 5—41—77—153

CHAMPIONSHIP.

First Round.

Out — 5 4 4 4 3 3 5 4 5--37
In — 4 3 4 5 5 5 3 4 5—38—75.

Second Round.

Out — 5 4 4 3 5 3 5 3 4—36
In — 4 4 4 5 5 4 2 4 5—37—73

Third Round.

Out — 5 4 3 4 4 2 4 3 4--33
In — 4 5 4 5 5 5 3 4 4—39—72

Fourth Round.

Out — 4 4 4 5 4 4 5 2 4—36
In -- 4 4 4 4 5 4 3 4 4—36—72—292

He was in trouble again at the fifteenth when his second shot visited a bunker, but for the third time he planted the ball within holing distance although he had to get down an 8-foot putt for a 4.

The sixteenth produced nothing more than an ordinary par 3, but at the seventeenth Hagen played what probably was his best shot of the day. Using an iron he planted a long second within five feet of the hole only to have the putt look in the tin without dropping. The eighteenth found him short with his second, but he rolled the ball up to the pin and got his par 4.

Sarazen on Hagen's Trail.

Pursuing Hagen was Sarazen. At the end of the third round this morning Sarazen, with his 73, was one stroke worse than Hagen and by the time he had completed the round he knew taht he would have to shoot a 70 to win. But luck wasn't with him.

This morning his 73 was marred by a 6 at the very first hole where he missed a fifteen-inch putt after sending his second shot into a bunker. At the second he pulled his drive and at the short third hole he hit a weak tee shot, but sank a four-yard putt for a 3. He missed a four-yard putt for a 3 at the fourth.

He then retrieved himself. At the fifth a five-yard putt found its home and at the sixth he put a seven-yarder to bed for a handsome 2. The seventh was poorly played and cost him a 5, but another seven-yard putt at the eighth got home for another 2 and he was out in 34.

He came back in 39 for a round of 73. At the tenth he took three putts from a distance of eighteen yards. His tragic 6 at the thirteenth was the result of a duffed iron shot, a poor approach, and three putts. He lipped the hole at the fourteenth for a 3 and his 5 at the next was due to a trip into a jungle.

Misses a Two-Yard Putt.

At the short sixteenth he missed a two-yard putt for a 2 and at the seventeenth he found more rough. As a result, he had to mark down another 5. But the eighteenth was beautifully played. A fine drive and an even better second brought him within two yards of the hole and a single putt gave him a par 3.

In the afternoon Sarazen turned in another 73. He was off with five 4s in a row, the ones at the first two holes representing ordinary golf, but the one at the short third should have been a 3. He pushed his tee shot to the right and that brought about his trouble.

He missed a 3 at the fourth by an inch, but a single putt for a 4 at the fifth encouraged him. At the short sixth he was on the green with his mashie but was too strong with his first putt, finally getting down a three-yarder with his second. Then misfortune befell him. His second shot, a brassie, was badly topped and his third with a mashie was over the green. His fourth sped past the hole and he then missed a three-yard putt.

Fortune favored him, however, at the ninth, where a five-yard putt went in for a 3. Then Gene knew he would have to make the homeward half in 34 in order to win. He gritted his teeth and set out on the voyage with the greatest determination. Dame Fortune, however, had deserted him, although the Prince of Wales had come along to encourage him.

Putt Refuses to Drop.

At the eleventh a two-yard putt refused to enter the tin, but a bit of luck brought him a 3 at the twelfth. The thirteenth was quite sensational. From a good drive, Gene topped his brassie and his second went into a bunker in a nasty lie. He played a magnificent shot to within fourteen yards of the pin and then holed out in 4.

There was a great outburst of applause from the large gallery over this feat. Gene was so flabbergasted at seeing the putt drop that he fell over backward on the green, much to the amusement of the Prince and the gallery.

Then at the fourteenth he had to mark down another 5, which meant that he would have to perform miracles to tie with Hagen. And then another 5 at the fifteenth further darkened the outlook. Gene just missed a putt for a 2 at the sixteenth.

He hit the tin for a 3 at the seventeenth, but the ball refused to stay in and he finished the day with a 4 at the eighteenth, two strokes behind Hagen.

Compston had two rounds of 73 today. He played some wonderful golf and for a long time, especially during the last round, he was a real menace to Hagen. But a 7 at the second hole in the morning practically put him out of the running.

In the second round, Barnes, with no one following him, burned up the course, but he knew it was no use. A feature of his game was his accurate and splendid putting.

Mehlhorn, who had as good a chance as any of winning the championship, was in anything but his best form today and after the first few holes it was evident that he was not going to be a factor in the final round.

Some of the cards:

Gene Sarazen.

THIRD ROUND.

Out ....6 4 3 4 4 2 5 2 4—34
In ....5 4 4 6 4 5 3 5 3—39—73

FOURTH ROUND.

Out ....4 4 4 4 4 3 6 4 3—36
In ....4 4 4 4 5 5 3 4 4—37—73

Jose Jurado.

THIRD ROUND.

Out ....4 5 4 4 5 3 5 3 4—37
In ....5 4 4 4 5 4 3 4 6—39—76

FOURTH ROUND.

Out ....4 5 5 5 5 4 5 3 5—41
In ....5 4 4 5 5 5 3 3 5—39—80

Jim Barnes.

THIRD ROUND.

Out ....4 3 4 4 5 3 4 3 6—36
In ....4 5 4 5 5 5 3 5 4—40—76

FOURTH ROUND.

Out ....5 4 3 5 5 3 4 4 4—37
In ....5 4 3 4 4 4 3 3 4—34—71

May 12, 1928

HAGEN OF U. S. WINS BRITISH GOLF CROWN SECOND YEAR IN ROW

Takes Open Championship for the Fourth Time by Scoring 292 in Scotland.

BRITONS ARE LEFT BEHIND

Farrell and Diegel, Americans, Are Second and Third With Scores of 298 and 299.

VICTOR MAKES FINE FINISH

Comes From Behind on Final Day With Two 75s—Two Britons in First Ten.

By HENRY C. CROUCH.

Special Cable to THE NEW YORK TIMES.

MUIRFIELD, Scotland, May 10.—Walter Hagen won the British open golf championship here today for the fourth time in his career and for two years in succession. The British golf experts are saying tonight, "We deserve it, and the Americans will go on winning until we take golf seriously. The whole story is that the Americans practice and we don't. We are too casual about it and that won't do."

Not only did an American win, but second and third on the list also were Americans. In fact, among the first fourteen performers were ten from the United States.

Hagen's total was 292 and was the same score that won the championship for him at Sandwich last year. Johnny Farrell, six strokes worse, was second at 298 and Diegel was third with 299. Then came two Englishmen, Percy Alliss and Abe Mitchell at 300 to break the American procession, but Bobby Cruickshank started it again with his 301 and Jim Barnes followed with a 303.

Sarazen and Watrous Next.

Gene Sarazen and Al Watrous each got a 304 and Tommy Armour a 305. Arthur Havers of Great Britain made 306 and Archie Compston, who took a 7 at the ninth in the morning as a result of being out of bounds, scored 307. Jimmy Thomson and John Golden turned in 308.

Altogether, the result is disagreeable to the British golfers and they admit it. They heartily congratulated the Americans on their performances and they meant what they said, but tonight they are going back to their homes in anything but a jubilant mood.

Hagen's victory and the performances of his compatriots are all the more creditable, because the last two rounds of the championship today were played in weather conditions that were regarded entirely favorable to the natives. A howling gale was blowing in the morning with occasional showers and the local experts were exulting. It was thought the elements were entirely in favor of the British players, because the idea was that the Americans were unable to control the ball in the wind.

Why this idea generally should be accepted as correct is beyond comprehension. Hagen and Farrell, as well as Diegel, have proved very conclusively they could direct the ball in the right direction whichever way the wind blew, and one American, not speaking at all boastfully, said today's gale was a mere zephyr compared to the tornadoes he had played in on the other side. But at the same time Farrell, who finished second, and Diegel, who was third, both confessed the wind was troublesome and set them guessing.

Are Weak on Putting.

They reached the greens all right, it would seem, but were weak when it came to putting. For instance, Diegel, who led Hagen by two strokes when he started out this morning, took three putts on five greens. Tonight he asked, "Can you tell me why I can cheat the wind on a 200-yard shot and yet let the wind get the better of me on the greens? It's simply disgraceful.

"I am going to give away my putter and I will be glad to see the last of it. I don't think I can come over next year, but I believe I shall be here again and with the determination to do better."

As a matter of fact, many experts were predicting Diegel would crack under the strain. A number of times he showed "nerves," especially while putting. He admits he has a decidedly unorthodox way of putting and that at the back of his mind he has the troublesome idea that everybody is watching him and is criticizing his method as being altogether impossible.

Farrell, although six strokes behind Hagen, wasn't dismayed. He said, "I think this trip here is going to do me a lot of good. It taught me one or two things which I hope to take advantage of when I defend my United States open title in June. I haven't played bad golf here, but regret the last two holes of this afternoon which cost me 5 apiece. Still, with 6 at the ninth a 75 wasn't bad."

Has Two Great Rounds.

Hagen's two magnificent rounds of 75 a piece provided the great sensation of the day. Before he had finished his morning round everybody was certain he was going to take the cup back to America again. While the native-born players were struggling with little success against the wind, Hagen pursued his way with the utmost confidence that the weather could not beat him. He just played low shots all the time and did not give the wind much chance to blow the ball into many difficulties.

He admits the conditions puzzled him and he was set guessing on many occasions. He thinks using his iron for several approaches where ordinarily he would have taken a mashie niblick, saved him a few strokes.

While he did not escape trouble entirely, he showed that he is a master at recovering from all traps. On a number of occasions today one putt from such a recovery sufficed.

In the morning Hagen was out in 37, which represented superlative golf, considering the weather conditions. A birdie 4 at the fifth made him go on his way rejoicing. At the short seventh the wind blew the ball into a bunker and he took a 4. A 6 at the fourteenth gave Hagen food for thought, and at the eighteenth a visit to a trap with his second caused him perturbation. Another stroke of genius, however, got him out of his trouble.

Out in Score of 35.

In the afternoon Hagen was out in 35 and then was ten strokes better than the nearest British player, and the galleries already were proclaiming him as the champion.

From first to last it was just inspired golf which simply amazed the natives and at the same time depressed them, owing to the fact they had to confess their own countrymen were altogether outclassed.

Hagen missed an eagle 3 at the sixth hole, 485 yards long, by an inch, and at the seventh he took three putts from twelve yards.

There were two incidents during the round which were extensively discussed. On the green at one hole Hagen was about to address the ball when it oscillated. It made an almost complete revolution, but then turned back again to its original position. As it turned out, it didn't matter, but Walter was eager to know whether he lost a stroke or not. The consensus was that he didn't.

The other incident was at the ninth, where Walter, with his second, hit a boundary wall and the ball bounced back a few inches. To the amazement of the spectators, Walter took his putter and, playing lefthanded shot the ball nicely onto the fairway.

Club Idle for Years.

"It's funny," he said afterward, "but I've carried a left-handed mashie in my bag for years and never found any use for it."

When he got to the eighteenth green he received a great ovation since it was obvious nobody could beat him.

At the presentation of the cup at the end of the day he made a happy speech. "I am the proudest man in the world today," he said, "and perhaps the luckiest. I've been fortunate enough in winning this championship four times, but I would like to mention that some of the British veterans of the game have won it more times than I have and I take my cap off to them. I am thinking of Jimmie Braid, Harry Vardon and J.H. Taylor. There's a triumvirate this country should be proud of.

"However, I am hopeful of equaling their record and I shall come over every year, not only for that object but because I love meeting all you boys. You have been very good to me and I hope I have done nothing to offend you. If so, believe me, I never intended it."

The hugh crowd of some 7,000 persons burst into applause that could be heard for miles. "Good old Walter" they yelled, and then, with the heartiest utterance, gave three cheers for the victor on this great occasion.

Saves One of Two Cups.

Interviewed afterward, Hagen said: "Well, the loss of the Ryder Cup was a severe smack in the eye for us. We brought two cups over with us and we didn't want to leave both of them here. As it is, it's fifty-fifty. The British boys have won one and we've retained the other.

"As a matter of fact, I was lucky today because everything went all right for me and I was rather surprised myself with the steadiness of my game. It was blowing a gale when I went out this morning, but I managed to reach the greens in comfortable figures and luck was good to me when putting, because the greens, with the wind and rain, were very treacherous.

"My putting lately has been very weak, but during this championship it certainly saved me. In the last round this afternoon I knew I ought to have strokes to spare from the next man, so I tried to shoot another comfortable 75 and, fortunately, I got it."

Cruickshank, Barnes, Sarazen, Watrous, Armour, Thomson and Golden, although among the fourteen leading players, were displeased with their performances today, and it was the same old tale of visits to traps and missed putts.

Cruickshank disappointed the hopes of the local Scots, but his play didn't inspire much confidence in the experts nor did that of Mac Smith, whose shortness on his drive surprised everybody.

Alliss weakened and finished at 300 because he could not defeat the elements, and Mitchell, at the same figure, struggled vainly to win his first championship. "Is Abe able?" was featured in one newspaper. It turned out Abe was not able, mainly because of his bad health, which is such a great handicap to him.

To conclude, it has been a great day for America and an unhappy one for this country and, it seems, there is no British golfer in view who can prevent the succession of American victories continuing.

"These Americans," said a famous old Scottish golfer, "have got us licked. We are not in the same class with them. Just think of it—ten of them among the first fourteen and eight among the first ten. Old Tom Morris would have wept bitter tears over it all."

May 11, 1929

AMERICAN GOLFERS BEAT BRITISH, 10-2, TO KEEP WALKER CUP

Capture 7 of the 8 Singles in Final of Tournament Over Links at Sandwich.

JONES LEADS THE WAY

Upsets Rival Captain, Wethered, 9 and 8—Moe, 7 Down, Rallies to Take His Match.

MISS COLLETT IS DEFEATED

By W. F. LEYSMITH.
Special Cable to The New York Times.

SANDWICH, England, May 16.—America has kept the Walker Cup. As a result of a smashing victory, 7 points to 1, in the singles matches over the St. George's course today, Bobby Jones and his men will bring the trophy, which Great Britain has never won, back to America for another two years. Having won, 3 matches to 1, in the foursomes yesterday, the total tally of the contests is 10 matches to 2 in America's favor.

Somewhat offsetting the blow to Britain's golf hopes, however, was the news from Formby, where a 19-year-old girl, Miss Diana Fishwick, defeated Miss Glenna Collett, the American champion, in the final of the women's British championship, 4 up and 3 to play.

The result was a startling upset. Miss Collett, striving for a title which no American has ever captured, had been considered almost a certain winner because of her convincing triumphs in earlier rounds. But that tournament is a story in itself.

The Walker Cup victory, sterling as it is, fades somewhat in comparison with the individual performance of Donald K. Moe, 20-year-old amateur from Oregon, who, pitted against J. A. Stout, one of England's finest match players, in fifteen holes turned a deficit of 7 holes down to a victory by 1 up on the last green. And if he had been asked to sink an easy, straight line putt of under five feet he probably would have lowered the record of this 6,551-yard championship course, which has stood for nineteen years, with a score of 67.

Moe Tells His Own Story.

Here is Moe's own story, told as the smiling young giant forced his way from the last green through a wildly cheering crowd of close to 6,000:

"I lost the first three holes of the afternoon round to Stout, which brought him 7 up. Then I seemed to get going with a long putt on the fourth green which dropped nicely—a birdie 3.

"We halved the fifth in par 4s. I then won the sixth in par 3, the seventh with a birdie 4, the eighth with a par 3 and the ninth with a birdie 3. I was then out in 33 and 2 down on the match.

"My sixth consecutive win came to me at the tenth in par 4 and we halved the eleventh also in par 4. I won the twelfth with a birdie 3 to bring the match all square.

"A par 4 at the thirteenth put me 1 up, but I didn't get out of a bunker at the fifteenth too well and was 5 to Stout's par 4. Then, all square, we halved the sixteenth and seventeenth in par 3s and par 4s and I was lying pretty good for a birdie 3 at the last hole when Stout, who had chipped short and then played two more shots, gave me the match. When Stout walked across to me on the eighteenth green it was the most thrilling moment of my life."

Great Iron Shot Decides.

Moe won his match with a great iron shot played from in close and on a sloping lie on the eighteenth fairway. His heroic comeback would have gone for naught if that shot had followed a brisk crosswind.

He played it like a master. The ball flew like a bullet dead on the pin all the way down an avenue formed by the black massed crowd, to rest within easy pin distance.

Stout, who stood figuratively "at the back door" to keep the match square at the last hole, made a determined effort but the ball overran the green.

After two more shots he removed his cap and walked across the green with extended hand to where the young victor stood.

The Walker Cup had been won long before.

Commanding Lead at Lunch.

At lunch the United States was standing in a reasonably safe position, with a commanding lead in four games and square in one. Harrison Johnston had got in front of Cyril Tolley, who was none too sure of his game. Jones, running away from Roger Wethered at the ninth by winning six holes in a row, was 7 up on the opposing captain.

George Von Elm had come in all square with young Rex Hartley, who had been hitting home great shots. George Voigt, who was robbed of a certain half on the home green through a spectator stopping the New Yorker's second shot with his neck just as it was falling on the green, was 6 up on Sir Ernest Holderness, and Roland Mackenzie, gaining a steady ascendancy over the Scotsman, William Campbell, from the jump, was 8 up.

On the other side of the ledger, Dr. O. F. Willing was 1 down to John Nelson Smith, who had given the doctor rough passage. Francis Ouimet had more than met his measure in T. A. Torrance, who was around in 70 and in addition had presented Ouimet with a hole at the fifteenth when he obligingly sank the American's ball.

Stout Plays in Great Form.

Young Donald Moe was 4 down to Stout, but that was hardly Moe's fault. He went out in 33 and was 1 down from the third hole. Stout had four 3s running, and the best thing Moe could do with this rocket was to hang onto its tail, waiting in the hope of his opponent's energy expending itself.

After lunch the Americans' supporters were not kept long in suspense. With Wethered put out by Jones, 9 and 8, Holderness out by 10 and 8 to Voigt and Tolley mastered by Johnston to the tune of 5 and 4, the United States required only one more triumph to keep the trophy. And both Mackenzie and Von Elm were well set for it.

Hopes of Von Elm's opponent, Hartley, faded in a bunker at the fifteenth, where a par 4 put Von Elm dormie 3, and with a half at the next hole the Walker Cup remained in America's keeping. About the same time the crowd learned that Mackenzie had knocked out Campbell, 6 and 5.

Francis Ouimet had already disappeared from the contest at the hands of Britain's lone victor, Torrance, in a 7 and 6 match, but with Dr. Willing, dead tired, but fighting off his younger opponent all the way to a 2-to-1 victory, America's job was well done.

In the top match of the morning Johnston played far better golf than Tolley. The United States amateur champion was always going straight for the pin and had Tolley 3 down at the fifth hole. Tolley got the sixth back owing to Johnston lifting his head on his approach, and they halved the seventh in par 4s.

To keep apace Johnston was confronted with a number of long putts which simply had to go down, and to

TWO OF THE WINNERS IN WALKER CUP GOLF.

Times Wide World Photo.
Don Moe, United States.

Times Wide World Photo.
T. A. Torrance, Great Britain.

his credit they went.

Tolley Erratic but Gets a Half.

The ninth hole provided another instance of the way Tolley went all around the mulberry bush to get to the green, while Johnston, going all the time straight for the pin and playing all shots like a real golfer, could get nothing better than a half.

Johnston turned 2 up, having had only one putt on five greens and being outdriven by the Englishman some times as much as fifty yards. His lead was reduced to one hole by a missed putt on the tenth—the first putt which Johnston played badly. Tolley then played three bad shots in succession and Johnston was 2 up again.

Tolley at this stage was causing the English critics much concern by putting off the toe of his aluminum putter with his heel cocked in the air. This undoubtedly enabled Johnston to halve the thirteenth which was a truly remarkable hole for him. The American underclubbed his second shot, then playing a forcing shot with a mashie, rushed the ball out—a long wallop which finished in a deep sand trap guarding the right of the green. It took a hefty hack with a niblick to lift the ball which flew across the green and finished on the reverse sloping bank in long grass. A magnificent chip brought the ball dead to the cup.

But all this time Tolley had been lyin in easy putting distance in 2. The Englishman's first putt was a foot short and his second seemed to slip off the toe of his putter and they called it a half. That just about represented Tolley's style of play all the way in, with the British amateur champion hitting prodigious shots into the rough and making equally prodigious recoveries.

Jones All Square at Turn.

Jones and Wethered turned all square at the ninth in the second match without much blood being spilled on either side, but from then on Bobby Jones became Bobby Jones.

Wethered, who had had several chances of putting a hole or two in his pocket, now had none and when Jones sank a thirty-yard chip shot with the flag still in the cup at the thirteenth hole, the American was 4 up.

Wethered now could not keep out of the crowd. He hit spectators at the thirteenth and fourteenth and at the fifteenth knocked a man unconscious. Jones should get credit for a 4 at the fourteenth for he had so many strokes in hand that he merely rolled the ball toward the cup and actually took three putts where two ordinarily would have sufficed. That would make his gross score 69 instead of 70.

The English captain was 5 down at the fourteenth and at the sixteenth had lost six holes in a row. He was so erratic at this stage that the stewards found it impossible to control the gallery and the crowd of about 3,000 stood around in groups hoping the ball would fall between them.

A par 3 at the sixteenth stopped the rout for the Englishman but Jones walked off the seventeenth green 7 up in sixty-five shots. The only blemish on his card was a five at the eighteenth, where he put his second shot in a bunker to the right of the green. He got out well but missed a short putt, although the ball lipped the cup.

Wethered could make no impression against his rival captain in the second round and did no more than relieve the pressure on the other matches by drawing away the crowd. The score just about represented the difference between their play and Jones has every reason to be happy about his prospects in the forthcoming British amateur championship which he is so keen to win.

In the third match Von Elm just went out to show that he is not the spent force that some English critics, who have compared his play with that of four years ago, have declared he is. He had the measure of his younger opponent all the way. He was getting his body into his shots with the club meeting the ball in the exact centre and much needed length was the result.

Results of Singles Matches In Walker Cup Play Abroad

Robert T. Jones Jr., United States, defeated Roger Wethered, 9 and 8.

Harrison R. Johnston, United States, defeated Cyril Tolley, 5 and 4.

Roland Mackenzie, United States, defeated William Campbell, 6 and 5.

Dr. O. F. Willing, United States, defeated John Nelson Smith, 2 and 1.

George Von Elm, United States, defeated Rex Hartley, 3 and 2.

Don Moe, United States, defeated J. A. Stout, 1 up.

T. A. Torrance, England, defeated Francis Ouimet, 7 and 6.

George Voigt, United States, defeated Sir Ernest Holderness, 10 and 8.

Voigt on Bad Terms With Putter.

Voigt in the fourth match was not at all on good terms with his aluminum putter against Holderness and has decided to change it before competing in the open and amateur championships and other events. It was unquestionably this instrument which saved Holderness from complete extinction in the morning round.

Despite so many slipped putts Voigt was out in 35 and home in 39,

but the match up to this stage was so onesided that Voigt really had no occasion to extend himself.

After his victory Voigt said he had found the greens "terribly hard—the most difficult I have ever experienced." He added that he had no fear of not coming back on his short game as soon as he got on another course. "It is purely a mental phase," he declared.

Willing in the fifth match did a good turn to Britain in bringing out the good qualities in Nelson Smith's golf. But there is not much to be added to the game between Ouimet and Torrance except to say that the former hero of St. George's course seems to be getting along.

But Mackenzie's match against Campbell will long be remembered for an extraordinary incident at the last hole in the morning. The American took a full punching iron for his second shot, but pushed it out among the spectators lining the fairway to the right about 180 yards from where the ball was struck.

"I hope I have not killed anyone," said Mackenzie as he ran forward "That ball was traveling."

The commotion around that spot, however, was not caused by any injury to a spectator but from the fact that the ball could not be found.

"Where did it hit you?" asked a marker.

"Here," said a spectator, pointing to his side.

There was another search then suddenly the spectator cried:

"Here it is! It's in my jacket pocket."

May 17, 1930

rounds of 70, 72, 74 and 75.

Leo Diegel and Macdonald Smith, American professionals, tied for second place with 293. Horton Smith of the United States and Fred Robson of England tied for fourth with 296. Jim Barnes, American pro, and Archie Compston and Henry Cotton of England were tied at 297. Thus the first three places and five out of the first eight were filled by United States players.

At the end of the third round today Compston had broken the record of the course with a 68 and was leading Jones by one stroke. Diegel, with 71, was two strokes behind Jones—within easy striking distance. It was a desperately exciting situation.

Horton Smith's aggregate of 296 was not one to frighten Jones. Don Moe had come to grief, so had Robson. Cotton's 71 had arrived too late and could not affect the issue. So Jones was left to set the pace for the last time to Compston, Barnes, Diegel and Macdonald Smith, with Compston and Diegel as the greatest dangers.

Bobby started with a 4 and a 3. At the second he pushed his drive. The ball was bound for some very thick rough, but it dropped full pitch on top of a man's head and bounced into the bunker guarding the fourteenth green. The ball lay clear on hard, firm sand. Bobby played a perfect pitch to the green and holed his putt for a 3.

To the long third he hit two magnificent shots to the edge of the green, then unfortunately took three putts. He required three putts at the short fourth hole also, which meant two valuable strokes lost. However, he rose to the occasion and did the next three in 4, 4, 3. Then came disaster—he took a 7 at the eighth hole, which was almost unbelievable.

Two good shots left his ball on an upward slope of a soft, grassy bank. He tried to run up his third. It was

BOBBY JONES WINS BRITISH OPEN TITLE

Becomes Only Golfer Who Ever Has Held Three National Crowns at One Time.

DIEGEL, MAC SMITH NEXT

Tie Two Strokes Behind Winning Score of 291—Five Americans Among First Eight.

By Major GUY C. CAMPBELL.

Special Cable to THE NEW YORK TIMES.

HOYLAKE, England, June 20.—To all his other laurels Bobby Jones today added the crown of British open golf champion, thus equaling John Ball's achievement of 1890 by winning the British amateur and open titles in the same year.

The incomparable Jones also became the first man in the history of golf to hold three major titles at the same time—British open, British amateur and United States open—and he is the only golfer ever to wear the open crowns of both nations at the same time, a feat he achieved previously, in 1926.

One after another of the great golfers from both sides of the Atlantic challenged him and fell. Playing not only against the strongest field of golfers ever pitted against him and against a testing course, he was fighting himself as well—for throughout this tournament he was never at his best.

He was never confident, and I have no doubt there were times when he never was quite sure where his shots would finish. Undoubtedly it was his greatest performance—this winning of two titles, amateur and open, within a month. His aggregate was 291 strokes for seventy-two holes—

WINNER OF BRITISH OPEN GOLF TITLE.

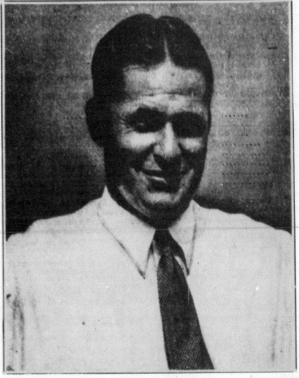

Bobby Jones.

P. & A. Photo.

Cards of Some of the Leaders at Hoylake

By The Associated Press.

BOBBY JONES.
Third Round.
Out ....4 5 6 3 4 4 3 4 4—37
In ......3 3 4 3 5 5 5 5 4—37—74—216
Fourth Round.
Out ....4 3 5 4 4 4 3 7 4—38
In ......4 4 4 4 4 5 4 4 4—37—75—291

LEO DIEGEL.
Third Round.
Out ....4 3 4 3 4 4 3 5 3—33
In ......4 3 5 3 6 4 5 4 4—38—71—218
Fourth Round.
Out ....4 4 5 3 5 4 4 5 4—38
In ......4 4 3 3 5 4 6 4 4—37—75—293

MACDONALD SMITH.
Third Round.
Out ....4 5 5 3 4 4 4 5 3—37
In ......4 4 5 3 4 4 4 5 5—38—75—222
Fourth Round.
Out ....4 4 5 3 5 4 3 4 4—36
In ......4 3 4 3 5 4 4 4 4—35—71—293

HORTON SMITH.
Third Round.
Out ....6 5 4 3 4 4 4 5 5—40
In ......5 3 4 3 5 4 6 4 4—38—78—223

Fourth Round.
Out ....4 4 5 4 5 4 4 3 7 4—39
In ......4 2 4 3 5 4 4 4—34—73—296

JIM BARNES.
Third Round.
Out ....5 4 5 3 4 4 5 4—39
In ......4 4 4 3 5 4 3 3 3—33—72—220
Fourth Round.
Out ....5 4 4 4 5 3 5 4—38
In ......4 4 4 3 5 6 5 4—39—77—297

ARCHIE COMPSTON.
Third Round.
Out ....4 3 4 2 6 4 3 4 4—34
In ......3 3 3 2 5 4 6 4 4—34—68—215
Fourth Round.
Out ....5 5 5 4 5 5 6 4 6—43
In ......4 4 4 4 5 4 5 5 4—39—82—297

DON MOE.
Third Round.
Out ....5 6 4 3 5 4 4 5 4—40
In ......3 3 5 3 5 4 5 4 4—36—76—223
Fourth Round.
Out ....5 4 4 3 5 6 5 4 5—41
In ......5 4 5 3 4 5 4 5 4—39—80—303

P. & A. Photo.
MACDONALD SMITH,
Who Finished Second With 289,
Two Strokes Behind Jones.

P. & A. Photo.
HORTON SMITH,
Leader at Half-Way Mark, Who
Finished Third With 292.

short. He pitched his fourth, was short again, went eighteen inches past with his putt, and then—horrors —missed one back. A 4 at the ninth gave him 38 going out.

Coming back it was a hard fight. Five 4s meant two more strokes dropped. Three putts on the short eleventh and a bunker at the thirteenth did the damage. Then he showed his real worth.

The last five holes, in a west wind and changed conditions, were real tests. He got a fine 4 at the fourteenth. At the fifteenth he played a poor run-up, but chipped dead and got his 5. At the sixteenth he played a stroke which I believe won him the championship.

Bobby's long second found a pot bunker biting into the left of the green. From here with his concave niblick he flicked the ball out of the depths and got his 4. It was the stroke of a master. Two 4s followed, the one at the seventeenth the result of a great putt. That meant a 75 and total of 291. Good, but not unbeatable.

Compston's Game Collapses.

Meanwhile, news had been filtering in that Barnes and Compston were doing badly and that Diegel was go-

ing strong. Compston's game had, in fact, collapsed. Actually he had taken 43 to reach the turn, and after the thirteenth hole he was seven over 4s—a stroke a hole more than in the morning.

Diegel went out in 38 but with 4, 4, 3, 3 to start home, it was evident he could win if he could finish with five more 4s. The fourteenth cost him 5, but he scored a 4 at the lake hole, then drove into a bunker at "The Dun," and after reaching the green in 3 with a fine brassie shot, took three putts.

Eventually Diegel was left with a full iron shot to the hole for a 2 at the last hole to tie. He sent the steward to the flag and played a fine shot, but could do no better than a 4.

Only Macdonald Smith remained. He started well with 4, 4, 5, 3, and reached the turn in 36. That meant he needed 33 home to tie. Macdonald reeled off 4, 3, 4, 3, but a 5 at the fourteenth made his task hopeless, and although he finished in 35, for a splendid 71, he could not displace Jones, who came into possession of his third British open championship.

June 21, 1930

JONES WINS U.S. OPEN FOR THE FOURTH TIME AS 10,000 LOOK ON

Atlantan Finishes With a 75 for 287, Leading Macdonald Smith by 2 Strokes.

By WILLIAM D. RICHARDSON.
Special to The New York Times.

MINNEAPOLIS, July 12.—So long as Bobby Jones still has strength enough left in his sturdy arms and shoulders to swing a golf club he probably will keep on winning golf championships.

Today, at the Interlachen Country Club, the Atlanta barrister gained

his third major title of the year and his fourth American open with a score of 287, which is only a stroke above the record score made by Chick Evans at Minikahda in 1916.

He should have shattered that record, for his last round was 75 and in it he had 5s on three of the four short holes. Those six wasted strokes made the difference between a 75 and a 69, which would have given him a 72-hole total of 281.

Bobby won today, but not without giving his gallery, numbering close to 10,000 at times, a great thrill and his well-wishers great anguish. For after seemingly clinching the title as a result of a record-smashing 68 in the third round, his final round was a curious and nerve-racking mixture of great golf such as he alone is capable of producing and golf that would have caused a duffer to give up the game.

Enters Final With 5-Stroke Lead.

When he started out on his fourth round with a lead of five strokes on Harry Cooper, who tied with Tommy Armour for the championship at Oakmont three years ago, and six strokes on Johnny Golden and Hor-

ton Smith, it looked as if he could breeze home to victory.

Even after he took 38, two over par, on the first nine, there appeared to be nothing to worry about. But when he started the last half of his final journey around the Interlachen course 4, 5, 5, 5, the race began to tighten, for Macdonald Smith, unheeded when he started his fourth round seven shots behind, had picked up four strokes on him, and it was conceivable that he might catch Bobby and perhaps pass him on the inward journey.

But where Jones clinched his victory was on the home green, where he demonstrated what a really great golfer he is. He had just lost two precious strokes to par by pushing his tee shot into the parallel water hazard on the seventeenth. He had opened the doors to Smith, and he plainly showed his annoyance for he had played the same hole just as badly in the morning round.

Forced to Putt Over Mound.

And then the real Jones asserted himself. Any other golfer might easily have cracked right there. Not Jones. After his second shot to the home green he was left with a putt of some forty feet to hole over a mound. Now was this the time for Calamity Jane, his renowned putter, to deliver a telling blow and deliver it did. His ball went up the hill, over the top and into the hole for a birdie 3 which left Mac Smith with the impossible to do.

As Bobby's ball made its way toward the hole there was utter silence, but when it disappeared into the tin a shout that could be heard to the utmost limits of the course went up. Jones had won again—the only man in the history of the game to gain the two British championships and one of the two American championships in the same year. All that now remains for him to do in order to accomplish a feat that probably will never be equaled in golf is to win the American amateur at Merion next September, and after what he has done already there is little likelihood of his failing there.

Mac Smith, finishing with a brilliant 70, came in second, two strokes behind Bobby, to lead the professionals. That was a great round of golf for the veteran who, twenty years ago, tied for the title. And all that prevented him from throwing the championship into a tie was that long putt Jones holed on the home green and his own 4 on the short thirteenth hole, where Bobby took one of his 5s.

Horton Smith finished in third

place, five strokes behind, with a 74 on his last round after a 76 in the morning for a 292 total. Harry Cooper was fourth with a score of 293; Johnny Golden, fifth, 294; Tommy Armour, sixth, 297; Charles Lacey of Pine Valley, seventh, 298; Johnny Farrell, eighth, 299; and Bill Mehlhorn and Craig Wood, tied for ninth, 300.

Has Broken 70 Only Twice.

If there is any round of a championship where a 68 comes in handiest it is the third, for that is considered the crucial round, and it was the round that gained Bobby his second consecutive title.

Only twice before during all the years that Jones has taken part in championships has he broken 70. Once was at St. Andrews, Scotland, where he won the British open for the second time in his career with a score of 285, and the other was at Winged Foot last year.

At St. Andrews three years ago Jones shot a 68 to break the record for the old course, but the round he shot today was a far more perfect exhibition of golf than that one was. It was Calamity Jane that did the business at the shrine of golf; it was Jones, the shot-maker, who bore the brunt of his slashing attack on par at Interlachen.

This morning his putter did little indeed to help him for although he had nine one-putt greens, the longest putt he holed was a ten-footer on the first hole. At all the others it was his mashie niblick that did the bulk of the work. Generally he was so close to the pin with his approaches that Calamity Jane had nothing to do except tap the ball in.

Misses Chance to Score 66.

As a matter of fact Bobby's round should have been 66, even with Calamity Jane doing no more than expected, for he lost a stroke to par on each of the last two holes where par figures would have given him a round of 33-33. Then, too, he took a 5 on the ninth hole where, under today's playing conditions, it was not difficult to get a 4.

There was considerable discussion over the ruling made on Jones's ball on the seventeenth hole, which was the seventy-first of the championship. Bobby sliced the ball badly and, aided by the same cross wind that

Jones During a Practice Round at Interlachen.

P. & A. Photo.

had helped carry it into a bunker in the morning round, it struck the branches of a tree and was never found, although hundreds of people following the twosome tramped around in the long marsh grass in an effort to locate it.

According to spectators who were standing near the spot where the ball struck, it bounded into the parallel hazard, and Prescott S. Bush, secretary of the U. S. G. A.,

ruled that he could drop another ball in the fairway with a one-stroke penalty as provided in the rules of golf.

It is perhaps just as well that Jones didn't get his 66 in the morning. For in that case the afternoon round would have been far less interesting than it was and Mac Smith might not have received the credit which was due him for playing that fourth round the way he did.

Horton Smith, tall Missouri prod-

uct and a golfer whose praises many more would now be singing were it not for the fact that there is only one Jones, had the lead when the day's play started. He had moved Bobby out of first place by getting a 70 yesterday while Jones was taking a 73.

His thirty-six-hole total was 142, while Jones, Cooper and Charles Lacey were tied for second, two shots back. After them came Mac Smith, three strokes away; then Tommy Armour, Johnny Farrell and Whiffy Cox, four strokes behind, and Walter Hagen and John Golden, five strokes behind.

They were the only ones in the field conceded a chance and everything tended to favor Jones and Horton Smith. Just before Bobby started there came a sprinkle of rain, but it was only a light shower and soon passed over.

Jones Outdistances Field.

By the time the morning round was finished Bobby's 68 had outdistanced them all. It had apparently closed the gates to the others and locked them tight. Of those in the race when the round started, the only one who succeeded in playing anywhere near his figures was Golden, who produced a 71 to tie with Horton Smith, who had taken a disastrous 40 on the last nine holes for a round total of 76. Cooper had moved into second place with a 73, leaving him a stroke ahead of Horton Smith and Golden and five strokes behind Bobby.

Then came Farrell and Mac Smith, with a 73 and 74, respectively, to tie for fifth place. Craig Wood had shoved himself up into the fight for second place with a 72, but all the others—Lacey, Armour, Cox and Hagen—had definitely finished themselves.

And so, when Jones began his final round, it looked more like a romp than anything else. It was just as if he were playing an exhibition match. The gallery, feeling the same way about it, trailed him and no one else. He started with a 4 and then went three strokes over par on the next two holes, taking three putts from the edge of the second green, bunkering himself in front of the third green and just getting out.

Almost Holes Out From Sand.

A birdie on the fourth, where he put his second shot almost on the green and then chipped dead, followed by a par on the short hole,

left him only one over 4s. Then he pulled his mashie niblick into a bunker only to play one of the greatest shots of the entire tournament— an explosion from the depths of a deep trap that almost holed out. From there on his only mistake was one of judgment in the use of the club for his second shot to the ninth.

He had used a spoon off the tee to make sure of not going into the lake and then took the same club for his second shot without noticing that the wind had changed from a cross to a following one. The result was that he overplayed the green by some forty yards and landed his ball on the practice putting green, from where he took 3 to get down.

Mac Smith Starts Pursuit.

In spite of all that he was out in 38, only two over par, which meant that he still had plenty of margin to play with. But when he started back 4, 5, 5, 5 things began to look dubious. Mac Smith, pounding off a brilliant 34 on the first nine, had picked up four strokes on him and was now only three in arrears. Furthermore, he had an excellent opportunity to pick up those three on the next four holes, one of which was a par 3 and two of the others possible 4s, although 5s on the card.

The 5s that Jones got on the second and third after the turn were pars. But the 5 on the short hole, where he got into another bunker and took two to extricate himself, was.

But by getting down a ten-footer for a birdie 3 on the fourteenth and pitching to within four feet of the flag on the sixteenth Jones offset the error he had made previously, and a 3, 4 finish would still give him a round of 74 and make it impossible for any one to nose him out.

However, he didn't get his 3 on the seventeenth. Instead he took a 5, so that now almost anything could happen. But not after that 3 on the home hole. Neither Mac Smith nor any one else could win now. He was safely in. The championship was his and his alone. The show was over.

When Smith was going to the fifteenth hole he had par left for a 70. And as he was trudging along the fairway to where his drive landed the roar that came echoing across the hills and dales of Interlachen told him that Jones had finished with a 3 and that par wouldn't be good enough. He had to get one birdie to tie and two to win.

The veteran, whose showing in the .

Walter Hagen Driving From the First Tee in National Open Tourney.

P. and A. Photo.

Jones's Cards for Four Rounds Of National Open Golf Tourney

First Round.

Out ....4 4 3 4 3 4 4 4 4—34
In ......5 5 5 3 4 4 4 3 4—37—71

Second Round.

Out ....5 4 3 4 2 4 4 4 4—34
In ......4 5 5 4 4 6 3 4 4—39—73—144

Third Round.

Out ....4 4 3 4 3 3 3 4 5—33
In ......4 4 4 3 4 4 3 4 5—35—68—212

Fourth Round.

Out ....4 5 5 4 3 4 4 4 5—38
In ......4 5 5 5 3 4 3 5 3—37—75—287

tournament was one of the big features of the event, did the best any man can expect to do. He finished with five pars to come within two strokes of Bobby and established himself in second place, ahead of Horton Smith, of Armour, Farrell, Cooper, Golden and Wood—men younger than himself. He had simply left himself just a little too much to do on his earlier rounds with a golfer of the calibre of Jones in the field.

After the round Jones declared that he has hit his shots better in this championship than in any other he had ever played in. He was not at all disgruntled over those 5s he had taken, simply saying that in one or two instances the wind had changed to fool him and that in others he had not allowed for his tendency to pull his irons.

Jones Starts Well.

The story of Jones's great round—the best he ever shot in an American open championship—started with the holing of a ten-foot putt on the first green. He was just a short distance from home on his second, but failed to get his chip close and had to work to save par figures.

He hooked his drive into the rough playing the second hole and gave the gallery a thrill by coming out to within four yards of the hole and lipping the cup on his try for a birdie 3.

He took a mashie for the short third and reached the right hand side of the green, from where he took two putts to be still all even with par.

Has a Fine Drive.

Bobby had a fine drive to the first of the long par 5 hole, reached the top of the hill and then pulled a No. 2 iron slightly to the left so that he had to pitch over a bunker onto a down slope. The shot came off beautifully and left his ball about two yards from the hole, from where he tapped it in for the first of his six birdies.

It looked as if he would squander a stroke to par when he pulled his mashie shot into the edge of a bunker on the short No. 5 hole, but he holed a four-footer for par figures after chipping a bit strongly.

Then came two scintillating holes, one after the other. His mashie niblick pitch to the sixth finished two feet from the hole, leaving him an easy birdie 3, while the same club lifted his ball out of the rough less than two yards from the hole on the seventh for another birdie.

After getting his par 4 on the eighth he had a 4 left at the ninth to be out in 32, four under par. He didn't get it, however, for after placing his drive in a nice position for the second shot across the lake he used a light spoon where his heavy one would have left him better off.

He failed to allow enough for the wind, which was coming from the right, and his ball wound up in a bunker on the left hand corner of the green, where he almost left it in his attempt to lay it close. It just managed to get over the top of the bunker and the momentum it got when it hit the down slope carried it to within twenty-five feet of the hole. His putt was never on the line and he had to put a 5 down for himself.

Just the same he was out in 33, which is anything but bad considering the strain there is on the third round of a championship. After a beautiful drive to the tenth his pitch was a little too strong for him to go after a birdie, but he got his par 4.

Then came two birdie 4s on the holes that have balked him until today. He was just short of the eleventh green with a driver and a heavy spoon, chipped up to two feet and almost failed to hole the putt. It just managed to get to the lip of the cup and topple in.

His good judgment in playing the twelfth was rewarded. The wind was behind today and at least one or two of the long hitters managed to reach the green with their seconds. But it was a chance-taking method and Bobby disdained to use it. After driving approximately 300 yards, he took out a No. 2 iron and hit the ball up close to the green and safely out of the way of the traps, and then pitched up to within four feet of the hole for another 4.

The thirteenth is both tricky and dangerous, and Jones played it just a little too safe, his iron leaving his ball in the short rough to the right. His next was not an easy shot to lay dead, but he played it perfectly, pitching onto the edge of the green, where the downslope carried his ball to within less than a yard of the hole for a well-saved par 3.

Another Long Drive.

He had another tremendous drive, with the wind at his back to help him on the fourteenth, and his No. 4 iron shot left him putting for another birdie. He couldn't quite hole the putt, however.

Mindful of the pain and misery the No. 15 hole gave him yesterday, when getting into the rough off the tee cost him a 6, he used his light spoon off the tee this morning and pitched a gorgeous No. 4 iron shot on the green, hole high to the left, about twelve feet away. He didn't get it down, but on the next hole he chipped a mashie niblick so close that there was nothing for Calamity Jane to do but tap his ball in from six inches for a birdie 3.

That left him gunning for a par 3 and a par 4 for a 66. The 3, though, is one of the hardest pars to get on the whole course. The hole measures 262 yards and the fairway falls away to the right. To make matters more complicated today there was a cross-wind blowing from the left.

Bobby used his light spoon, did not aim quite enough to the left and put his ball into a bunker short of the green. It was lying well, but he had a difficult stance, having to perch himself on the bank of the bunker. His line was perfect, but his judgment of distance was a trifle poor and his ball stopped twelve or fourteen feet short of the hole. It looked as if he might hole it, but the ball slid pass the side of the hole and he took a 4.

Slices Into the Rough.

His drive to the last hole was one of the poorest he hit on the whole round. It was sliced and dropped into the rough, among a clump of trees. There was no chance to go for the green and he merely chopped it out onto the fairway. He used a mashie niblick for the next, pitched over the green slightly and almost holed the next one coming back, so that he again went a stroke over par.

Still he had a 68 that might easily have been a 66, for in addition to those two over-par holes at the finish he had two or three putts that went so far as to take a peep at the hole without dropping in for him.

July 13, 1930

JONES WINS, 8 AND 7, SWEEPING TO FOURTH MAJOR TITLE OF YEAR

Beats Homans to Become First to Hold All British and U. S. Crowns at Once.

BREAKS TRAVERS'S RECORD

PAR FOR THE COURSE.

Hole.	Yds.	Par.	Hole.	Yds.	Par.
1	360	4	10	335	4
2	523	5	11	378	4
3	195	3	12	415	4
4	595	5	13	125	3
5	435	4	14	412	4
6	427	4	15	370	4
7	335	4	16	435	4
8	350	4	17	215	3
9	170	3	18	455	4
Total	3,390	36	Total	3,140	34

Grand total, 6,530; par, 70.

By WILLIAM D. RICHARDSON.

Special to The New York Times.

ARDMORE, Pa., Sept. 27.—When Gene Homans's ball grazed the side of the cup on the twenty-ninth hole at the Merion Cricket Club today, Bobby Jones not only became the national amateur champion for 1930 but the holder of a record that probably will survive through the ages.

At 28, this rarely-gifted golfer from Atlanta, who defeated Homans 8 up and 7 to play in today's final and who has come closer to mastering the intricacies of the game than any one else, has performed a feat that no one hitherto had considered possible.

Within the short span of five months, Bobby has played in the four major golf events—the British amateur and open championships and the American open and amateur—and won them all, outscoring the professionals at their own game in the two open tournaments and out-stripping all his fellow amateurs in the others.

Moreover he is the first man in the history of American golf to win the National amateur five times, he and Jerry Travers, who was in the gallery that followed the marvelous Atlantan today, having been tied at four victories each until this afternoon.

It was no more than appropriate that all these honors should be spread at Bobby's feet on the same golf course where, as a boy of 14, he made his début in championship golf in 1916 and where, eight years later, he broke his spell of failures in the amateur by beating George von Elm, 9 and 8.

No one in the great throng of fully 18,000 spectators, who made a great human fringe around the green and a solid mass packed in the fairway that Jones had just played from, could help but feel that here was golf history being made.

Regret for Homans, who had put up a resistance that looked weak beside the finished golf of the world's greatest golfer, was overbalanced by the joy of seeing the Southerner make his record, for certainly Bobby will never try to repeat it and almost certainly no one can ever break it.

It was an epochal moment, and the demonstration that came after it was one that will never be forgotten. Playing the hole, a two-shotter with two level fairways and an island green tucked away back in the woods, Jones was dormie 8. But a moment before he had missed a chance to close out the match on the previous hole by misjudging a little pitch shot out of the rough and putting his ball into a bunker alongside Homans's.

Both sides of the fairway were lined with persons ten and twelve rows deep as he and Homans drove off. It was Gene's honor, Bobby having conceded him a birdie 2 on the No. 9 hole. The ex-Princeton star, realizing by now, of course, that it was all over, drove to the left.

Having nothing to lose, Bobby lit into his drive and sent his ball flying down the fairway. It was a long drive, almost reaching the edge of the little stream that runs across the fairway near the 300-yard mark. Homans had to play first and sent a beautiful mashie shot onto the green, a trifle beyond the hole. A moment later Bobby's ball came sailing on, stopping short of the pin.

Onlookers Are Tense.

Despite the fact that all those thousands were standing as close as they could get, the dropping of a pin in the grass would have been heard as Bobby, looking a little haggard and drawn, walked over to his ball after his caddie had handed him his pet putter, known the world over as Calamity Jane. One of those quizzical glances that he gives the hole, the familiar cocking of the Jones head, a slight movement of the wrists as they brought the club back and then forward.

The ball started on its journey up to the hole over the closely cropped grass. He didn't quite have the line, but it stopped so close to the side of the hole that Homans would have had to sink his in order to prevent the match from ending there and then. Knowing full well that it was all over Gene took comparatively little time over his own putt, hit the ball and, almost before it passed by the side of the hole he was over wringing Bobby's hand.

Immediately a great shout was sent up, then the tumult that reverberated for miles. It lasted for several minutes. There was a wild rush toward Jones who, had it not been for the presence of a squad of marines, would have been crushed.

It was some moments before order was restored and an opening made through which Jones and Homans could walk over to the number 12 fairway and begin their journey back to the clubhouse. And over the entire distance Jones was cheered on as triumphant a journey as any man ever traveled in sport.

Today's match was far more of a spectacle than it was a contest. As a matter of fact there was not much contest to it. It was merely an exhibition on Jones's part, a parade to victory.

Jones Soon Draws Away.

Starting by winning the very first hole played, Bobby, taking advantage of his opponent's wildness and his proneness to get into bunkers, and likewise his inability to hole winning putts, gradually built up a lead that became three holes at the fourth, eight holes at the sixteenth seven holes at the finish of the morning round, 9 up after the first four holes had been played in the afternoon and, finally, 8 up and 7 to play.

Yesterday, playing against young Charley Seaver, budding Californian, Homans was 5 down at noon, 2 down and 4 to play and yet he pulled the match out of the fire by his sheer nerve.

But it is one thing to start Charley Seaver 5 up and beat him and quite another thing to start Bobby Jones 3 up on the first four holes and 7 up in eighteen. It simply can't be done nowadays. There may have been a time when it could, but those days seem to have gone.

Bobby wasn't flawless today. During the round he was in enough trouble to disprove the generally accepted theory that he is a machine and not a human being, but only on few occasions was Homans able to capitalize on the mistakes.

Gene can play better golf than he played against Jones and Bobby can play better golf than he played against Gene. But what happened to Homans is the same thing that would probably have happened to

Bobby Jones Putting on the Fifth Green During Final of National Amateur.

any one else in his shoes.

None of them, not even the professionals, are able to play their own game against the invincible Atlantan who has carried everything before him this year. His reputation, a reputation that has been earned only after years of bitter experience, seems to overawe them, and is not at all strange.

Homans's Fate Sealed Early.

Jones won the match on the first few holes. When he took 3 over par on the first nine and still was 2 up on Homans no one expected the match to go any further than it did. On the second nine Jones traveled at a par pace and added five more holes to his total. After the fourth hole in the afternoon he was 9 up and the match should have ended even before it did.

Homans got off to a bad start when he was in bunkers on the first three holes. Jones should have been 3 up right there but on the second, after two tremendous wooden shots into the wind up near the green, he played a weak mashie-niblick pitch and took three putts on the terraced green.

Despite the fact that he put his drive into a bunker on the fourth, Bobby got his par 5 and won the hole when Homans took three putts. On the fifth both hooked into the rough, but this time it was Bobby who three-putted to give Homans a half.

Homans got nearer to the hole with his approaches on the sixth and seventh and won the seventh to reduce Bobby's lead from three holes to two when Jones again three-putted. Then, playing the ninth, Homans pitched his tee shot into the water and the penalty stroke cost him the hole, leaving him 3 down at the turn.

Homans Again Finds Bunker.

Homans was bunkered again on the tenth and lost it on Jones's par 4 and then, on the eleventh, Jones holed an eighteen-foot putt for his first birdie in the round. It was right after that that Jones began picking up holes almost as fast as he came to them. Gene got halves on the next two, but Jones won the fourteenth, fifteenth and sixteenth, Homans hooking on the fourteenth, putting his second into a bunker on the fifteenth and taking three putts from an excusable distance on the sixteenth.

The only hole on the last nine which Jones failed to get par on was the seventeenth, where he hooked to the rough and even then almost got

Jones Receiving Cup From Findlay S. Douglas, President of U. S. G. A., After Victory Over Homans (Right).

his par for he came back to within seven feet and missed the putt. To prevent himself from being 8 down instead of 7 at noontime Gene had to drop a fifteen-foot putt on the last green.

Homans was wild off the tee on the first two holes in the afternoon, but escaped with halves. It looked as if he might win the third when Jones fell short into a bunker while he was on, but he took three putts, and Bobby, coming out almost dead, won the hole. Bobby also won the fourth, Gene's drive going into a bunker. Except for the seventh the next four holes were well played. On the seventh both went over the green on their approaches, but the green was hard to hold.

Bobby was bunkered on the ninth or he might have been dormie. But he failed to get out at all close and Homans, who was nicely on, won the hole to reduce Bobby's advantage back to eight holes instead of nine.

Jones missed a fine opportunity to finish the match on the tenth by pitching into a bunker and taking two to get out. Gene was in the same bunker and pitched out over the green into another, and so the hole was halved in 6s, two over par. Then came the finish.

Solid Jam of Spectators.

Some idea of the size of the crowd may be gathered from the fact that in the afternoon round both sides of the fourth hole from the tee to the green were solidly lined with spectators. The hole is 595 yards in length.

For the first time during the championship the wind was a real element to be considered. It blew across the course from the west, making it a factor in calculating direction on both the first and second holes. Homans found a trap at the first green through making too strong an allowance for this factor. Both players steered a course to the left at the second, even though the wind was sweeping across from right to left.

When Jones missed a putt of less than three feet for his four at the fifth and thus allowed Homans to get a half in 5s, the break seemed to hearten the Englewood boy. He played the next two holes faultlessly, whereas up to that point he had made at least one mistake on each hole.

The fifth hole was supposed to be something of a hoodoo for Jones, but that did not keep him from holing a long curling putt for a par 4 in the afternoon against Homans.

On the other hand the fourth hole, which had been something of a favorite with Homans in his earlier matches, played him false in the final test. He took 6 on both rounds, losing it each time. In the morning he took three putts and in the afternoon he was trapped on his drive and needed four to reach the green.

Jones's three putts on the fifth hole was his first error of the morning round. Up to that point the Atlantan was a perfect golfing machine.

Homans really got into the final through a great tee shot he made at the 215-yard seventeenth in his final round against Seaver on Friday and he duplicated his good work in the morning round against Jones. His tee shot pulled up no more than nine feet from the hole. He didn't have to hole out since Jones missed the green with his tee shot and after pitching on was still away, following which he missed his 3 and conceded the hole.

Generally speaking the crowd was remarkably well handled, but it was inevitable that some mishaps were bound to creep in. Homans was the victim of such a break at the tenth in the morning round. His approach shot rolled just over the green into a trap. Spectators standing along the edge of the green moved out of the way in time to avoid actually stopping the ball which rolled into a heel print, making the recovery very much more difficult. He lost the hole.

In spite of the fact that the wind was more with than against, neither player hit a particularly long drive at the eighteenth in the forenoon. Homan's second, a low hit, scurrying shot, struck short of the green but ran over the far side. He holed a good long one for his half in four, after chipping back.

Homans Reveals Spirit.

Homans's tee shot to the ninth in the afternoon revealed his rugged fighting spirit. He was almost hopelessly outdistanced at the time, but when Jones pushed his tee shot into

Times Wide World Photo.

Crowd Following the Finalists From the First Tee at Merion Cricket Club.

a trap Gene stuck a full iron up within eight feet of the pin. Jones conceded the hole after recovering from the trap and missing his 3.

A small dog was making merry near the green on the tenth hole as Jones drove from the tee far back in the wood across a ravine. The ball struck so near the canine galleryite that it scared him and he scampered for safety.

A narrow sector of a trap to the left of the green at the tenth intervened between Homans's ball and the hole after his drive. At that stage there was nothing for him to do but shoot for the pin. The ball fell short.

into a trap. It appeared likely that Jones would wind up the day then and there, but he, too, cut his distance too short and found the trap. An eventful half in 6s sent them on to the eleventh.

The marines and other branches of the constabulary found a man-sized job in rescuing Jones from the mob when the match ended at the eleventh. In spite of the fact that its location makes it most inaccessible, a huge crowd had pushed up as closely as possible, and when Homans, after failing to get his putt for a 3 to win, rushed over to congratulate Jones, the full force of the onrush converged on the two of them

about the centre of the green.

An aviator circling overhead near the clubhouse as the players were ready to start the afternoon round, went through his paces with a few loops and other fancy stunts, but he drew scant consideration. The gallery was more intent on jockeying into a position to see what was going to happen on the green turf of that testing first hole.

THE CARDS.
Morning Round.

Out—
Jones ....4 6 3 5 5 4 5 4 3—39
Homans ....5 6 4 6 5 4 4 4 5—43
Jones, 3 up.

In—
Jones ....4 3 4 3 4 3 4 4 4—33—72
Homans ....5 4 4 3 5 5 5 2 4—37—80
Jones, 7 up.

Afternoon Round.

Out—
Jones ....4 5 3 5 4 4 5 4 4—38
Homans ....4 5 4 6 4 4 5 4 2—38

In—
Jones 6 4
Homans 6 4
Jones wins, 8 and 7.

September 28, 1930

MISS COLLETT WINS NATIONAL GOLF TITLE

Triumphs Over Miss Van Wie, 6 and 5, to Capture Her Fifth United States Crown.

THIRD VICTORY IN 3 YEARS

Champion Closes Match on 31st Green, Despite Opponent's Determined Struggle.

By The Associated Press.

LOS ANGELES, Oct. 18.—Miss Glenna Collett, the wonder girl of American golf, reached new and brilliant heights today when she stroked her way to her fifth national women's title with a 6 and 5 victory over Miss Virginia Van Wie of Chicago in the 36-hole final of the 1930 classic.

As calmly as though out for a

couple of practice rounds, the defending champion of the last two years pitted her mastery of the woods and irons against the challenge of her younger rival. Oblivious to everything, including frequent applause from several thousand spectators, Miss Collett set a steady pace that produced the best golf of the tournament.

Pressed only during the first nine holes, which she finished one up on the Chicago contender, the champion set out to make history in the second half of the morning round. Three birdies and a spectacular eagle followed. She finished the morning round in 76, five under men's par for the sharply trapped, rolling north course of the Los Angeles Country Club.

Six Below Par for the Day.

Her first nine card read 40, one over par, but she trimmed half a dozen strokes off par for the second nine. For the thirty-one holes she played, she was six under par. Miss Van Wie, comparatively poor off the tee and erratic in her putting, turned the morning round in 41, 42—83.

Five holes to the good, Miss Collett was forced to bow to better golf on the nineteenth and twenty-first, but at the twenty-fifth she had won back the two, and at the twenty-eighth increased her margin to 6 up. Miss Van Wie made a last desperate effort and won the thirtieth, but her par 5 on the thirty-first was not good enough for the birdie 4 posted by the champion.

Miss Collett's par-shattering morning round disheartened the Chicago

girl. The first three holes were halved in 5s. Miss Van Wie went into the lead for the only time of the match when she won the fourth with a birdie 2 after putting her tee shot two feet from the pin on the 175-yard hole.

Champion Squares the Match.

The champion squared accounts by winning the fifth with a par 5. It was the turning point of the match. They halved the next two holes in par 4s, and Miss Collett went one up on the eighth, with a birdie 5. Miss Van Wie being stymied. The ninth was halved in 4s.

Three birdies in a row put Miss Collett 4 up. She won the tenth with a 4 and the eleventh and twelfth with 3s. A stymie cost Miss Van Wie the tenth, while on the twelfth the champion sent a beautiful full iron second shot spinning to within three feet of the cup.

The Chicagoan had a birdie on the thirteenth with a 4, but Miss Collett posted an eagle 4 to win the 530-yard fourteenth. Her third, a fine spoon shot, left her ball 18 inches from the cup. They halved the next two holes in 4s and Miss Collett went 5 up at the seventeenth. She had a birdie 4 after laying a chip shot from heavy grass near the green, two inches from the cup. The Eighteenth was halved in par 5s.

Miss Van Wie won back a hole when she dropped an eight-foot putt for a birdie 4 on the nineteenth. They halved the twentieth and Miss Van Wie cut her rival's lead to 3 up with a par 4 on the twenty-first. Miss Collett three-putted the green. The next was halved in par 3s, and the twenty-third in 6s.

Par 4s on the twenty-fourth and twenty-fifth gave Miss Collett a 5 up lead again. Each had a birdie 5 on the twenty-sixth, Miss Collett missing an eagle by four inches. They halved the next hole in 4s and Miss Collett went 6 up with a birdie 4 on the twenty-eighth. Birdie 3s halved the twenty-ninth.

Challenger Bears Down.

The challenger bore down at the thirtieth, winning it with a par 4, to become 5 down. Miss Collett hooked her second into the crowd and was forced to play her third from beneath a small tree. Her approach was strong, forty feet over, and her fine putt for a possible half stopped an inch short of the hole.

A brilliant recovery shot, after her topped second had traveled seventy-five yards, left Miss Collett a ten-foot putt at the thirty-first. Miss Van Wie had sliced badly on her drive, but she had a great second and her third was twelve feet from the pin. Her putt was weak, the ball stopping ten inches from the hole.

Miss Collett stepped up and putted boldly. The ball rolled true into the hole.

Although her earlier rounds were not as spectacular as followers had hoped for, Miss Collett's finish left nothing to be desired. Her game today was sound and what few poor shots she made from the tee were quickly made up for by sparkling work with the irons and a bold putting touch that sent the ball holeward with no uncertainty.

Miss Van Wie experienced difficulty with her woods on the morning round and after she had corrected

Times Wide World Photo.

Winner of Women's National Golf Title.
Miss Glenna Collett, Who Defeated Miss Virginia Van Wie in Final Round of Tourney at Los Angeles.

this trouble in the afternoon she faltered on the greens.

As a girl of 19, Miss Collett won her first national title in 1922, and she repeated in 1925. Since 1928 she had ruled America's women golfers with an iron hand. Today's match was the second meeting of Miss Collett and Miss Van Wie in the national final, the former winning, 13-12, two years ago.

Halve First Three Holes.

After halving the first three holes in the morning with 5s, Miss Van Wie became 1 up at the 175-yard fourth. Hitting a beautiful tee shot Miss Van Wie sent her ball to the green, two and one-half feet from the pin, and sank her short putt for a birdie 2.

Miss Collett squared it at the next, however, after both drives and seconds were even, straight down the middle. Miss Van Wie pitched over the green and chipped back eighteen feet past the cup. Miss Collett's third was fifteen feet past the pin and she too putted for a birdie 4. Miss Van Wie missed her putt and was down in 5.

They halved the sixth and seventh, then Miss Collett went 1 up at the eighth, taking a birdie 5 after laying Miss Van Wie a dead stymie. The ninth was halved, but at the tenth Miss Collett increased her lead to 2 up with a 4 to Miss Van Wie's 5. The Chicago girl's twenty-five-foot putt rolled three feet past the cup.

Miss Collett Scores Birdie.

At the eleventh hole Miss Collett drove fifty feet short of the pin, while Miss Van Wie's tee shot was fifteen feet to the left of the hole. The champion putted five feet past the cup, while the Chicago stylist putted five feet short. Miss Van Wie missed her next, taking a 4, while Miss Collett holed out for a birdie, going 3 up.

Miss Collett shot her third successive birdie to go 4 up at the twelfth, but Miss Van Wie took the next with a 4 to reduce the champion's margin to 3.

An eagle 4 gave Miss Collett her advantage of 4 up again on the fourteenth. She had a fair drive and a strong brassie. Her third, a great spoon shot, nearly holed out. They halved the fifteenth and sixteenth. At the seventeenth Miss Van Wie hooked her second. Miss Collett's second was ten feet short of the green in high grass. She chipped two inches from the cup, while the Chicago girl was out of the rough ten feet past the pin. She missed her putt and conceded the hole, giving the champion a 5-up lead, which remained by virtue of halves on the eighteenth.

At the nineteenth hole Miss Van Wie hooked to the right into a trap on her drive, but had a nice out, 175 yards down the fairway, and pitched eight feet from the pin. She holed out for a birdie 4, cutting the lead to 4 up.

A six-foot putt allowed Miss Collett to halve the twentieth in 5s, then Miss Van Wie cut the champion's lead to 3 up on the twenty-first with a 4. She outdrove Miss Collett thirty yards and just got on the green with a No. 3 iron, twenty feet to the left of the pin. Miss Collett's approach stopped on the back edge of the green. Her putt ran six feet past the whole, but was short coming back, forcing a fifth shot. Miss Van Wie two-putted to win.

They halved the twenty-second and twenty-third, the latter being 450 yards long. Here Miss Van Wie matched Miss Collett's drive and second, and then placed her third eight feet past the hole. The New Yorker's ball was thirty-five feet past the pin, off the green. She chipped two feet past the cup. The Chicago girl's putt rolled past the cup, forcing a six, allowing her to halve with Miss Collett, who also two-putted.

Miss Van Wie Finds Rough.

The heavy rough caught Miss Van Wie's tee shot hooked to the left of the fairway at the twenty-fourth, while the champion banged the ball straight down the lane. The Chicagoan was out nicely, her ball landing on the bank short of the green. It rolled into a trap. Miss Collett's second was ten feet from the pin and she two-putted for a par four. Miss Van Wie had a nice out of the trap, also two-putting for a bogie, to move down again.

At the twenty-fifth Miss Collett won with a par 4 after a thirty-five-foot approach putt left her three feet from the cup. Miss Van Wie was short on her second and third and missed a ten-foot putt for a half.

Miss Collett was outdriven by the Chicago girl by 20 yards, but she retaliated with a fine brassie. Miss Van Wie duplicating. They halved the hole in 5s.

The twenty-seventh was halved in 4s, each playing the hole poorly with three putts. At the next Miss Collett strengthened her lead by taking a birdie 4 to her opponent's par. She sliced the first and was in the rough

with her second, while Miss Van Wie was on the edge of the green in 2. Then the champion chipped nicely five feet past the pin and holed her putt. Still unable to make her putter behave, the Chicago girl took three shots on the green for a 5.

Miss Van Wie Keeps Up Fight.

Fighting gamely, Miss Van Wie matched the champion's birdie 3 on the twenty-ninth. Miss Van Wie rallied again on the thirtieth, getting a par 4 against the champion's bogie 5.

Miss Collett took a birdie 4 on the thirty-first to win. She was straight down the middle with her drive. Miss Van Wie sliced into the rough. The champion topped her second, the ball dribbling 75 feet. She pitched the third ten feet past the pin and holed the putt. The challenger missed a twelve-foot putt for a half.

THE CARDS.
Women's Par.
Out ....5 5 4 3 5 4 4 6 3—39
In ....5 4 4 5 6 3 5 5 5—42—81

MORNING ROUND.
Out—
Miss Collett ...5 5 5 3 5 4 4 5 4—40
Miss Van Wie...5 5 5 2 6 4 4 4 6 4—41
Miss Collett, 1 up.
In—
Miss Collett ...4 3 3 3 5 4 4 4 4 5—36—40—76
Miss Van Wie...5 4 5 4 6 4 4 5 5—42—41—83
Miss Collett, 5 up.

AFTERNOON ROUND.
Out—
Miss Collett ...5 5 5 3 6 4 4 5 3—41
Miss Van Wie ....4 5 4 3 6 3 5 5 4—41
Miss Collett, 5 up.
In—
Miss Collett 4 3 5 4
Miss Van Wie 5 3 4 5
Miss Collett wins, 6 and 5.

October 19, 1930

JONES QUITS GOLF; ACCEPTS FILM OFFER

Announces Retirement After Signing for Series of Instructional Pictures on the Game.

WORK MAY NET $250,000

Demands of His Law Business Prompt Him to End Competitive Play, Champion Says.

By WILLIAM D. RICHARDSON.

Bobby Jones, winner of the four major golf championships during the past season and generally regarded as the greatest golfer the world has ever known, has announced his retirement from competition.

In a carefully prepared statement, made public yesterday on Jones's behalf by H. H. Ramsay, vice president of the United States Golf Association, in which Bobby is a member of the executive committee, the famous Atlantan gave the details of his withdrawal from competitive golf.

He has signed a contract with Warner Brothers to make a series of twelve one-reel motion pictures dealing with the instructional side of golf. The series will be issued under the general title, "How I Play Golf," and will illustrate the champion's shot-making methods.

Will Go to Coast March 1.

He will leave for the West Coast

studios of the company on March 1, and it is expected that the films will be ready for release at two-week intervals beginning April 15.

It is understood that the champion will receive a flat guarantee as well as a percentage of the profits. While no statement was made as to the amount Jones would receive for his work, estimates placed the figures at approximately $250,000.

The statement, which Jones prepared following his conference with officials of the Warner firm here on Thursday and Friday of last week, follows:

Text of Jones's Statement.

Upon the close of the 1930 golfing season I determined immediately that I would withdraw entirely from golfing competition of a serious nature. Fourteen years of intense tournament play in this country and abroad had given me about all I wanted in the way of hard work in the game. I had reached a point where I felt that my profession required more of my time and effort, leaving golf in its proper place, a means of obtaining recreation and enjoyment.

My intention at the time was to make no announcement of retirement, but merely to drop out quietly by neglecting to send in my entry to the open championship next Spring. There was at that time no reason to make a definite statement of any kind, but since then, after careful consideration, I have decided upon a step which I think ought to be explained to the golfers of this country, in order that they may have a clear understanding of what the thing is and why it is being done.

Pictures to Be Educational.

On Nov. 13, 1930, I signed a contract with Warner Brothers Pictures to make a series of twelve one-reel motion pictures, devoted entirely to exhibiting and explaining the methods which I employ in playing the various shots ordinarily required in playing a round of golf. These pictures are to be purely educational in character, and it is the ardent hope of both parties that they will be of some value, first by improving the play and thereby increasing the enjoyment of the vast number of people already interested in the game, and second by creating an interest where none exists now among the many who may find enjoyment and beneficial exercise on the golf course.

The talking picture, with its combination of visual presentation and demonstration, with the possibility of detailed explanation, appeals to me as the ideal vehicle for an undertaking of this nature.

Of course, the matter of monetary compensation enters into the discussion at this point, and it is for numerous reasons that I wish to be perfectly understood on this score. The amateur status problem is one of the most serious with which the United States Golf Association has to deal for the good of the game as a whole.

Contrary to Amateur Spirit.

I am not certain that the step I am taking is in a strict sense a violation of the amateur rule. I think a lot might be said on either side. But I am so far convinced that it is contrary to the spirit of amateurism that I am prepared to accept and even endorse a ruling

that it is an infringement.

I have chosen to play as an amateur, not because I have regarded an honest professionalism as discreditable but simply because I have had other ambitions in life. So long as I played as an amateur there could be no question of subterfuge or concealment. The rules of the game, whatever they were, I have respected, sometimes even beyond the letter. I certainly shall never become a professional golfer. But, since I am no longer a competitor, I feel free to act entirely outside the amateur rule, as my judgment and conscience may decide.

When these pictures have been made, I expect to return to the practice of my profession, unhampered by the necessity of keeping my golf up to championship requirements.

Ramsay Praises Career.

Asked to comment on Jones's retirement, Mr. Ramsay said:

"He has unquestionably during his career made the greatest competitive record in the history of the game. Aside from that, though, his character and personality are such that he has become a popular world figure. His withdrawal will be greatly regretted by every one."

No one who has been at all closely associated with golf was surprised at Jones's retirement, for it was generally understood that this year would be his last and that henceforth he would concentrate on his law business and play golf for pleasure.

Indeed, even before the amateur championship at the Merion Cricket Club, where Bobby became the first golfer in the world to win the four major titles in the same year, the writer learned from his closest friend, O. B. Keeler, that this year would be his last.

While Jones would not admit his intention of retiring, neither would

High Lights of Jones's Competitive Career

1911 (Age 9)—Won junior championship cup of Atlanta Athletic Club.
1912 (Age 10)—Lost in semi-final round of junior championship of Atlanta Athletic Club.
1913 (Age 11)—Played his first round in 80 strokes at East Lake course.
1915 (Age 13)—Qualified in Southern amateur, but lost in second course.
1916 (Age 14)—Won Georgia State amateur championship. Qualified in playing in his first national amateur tourney, losing in third round, at Merion.
1917 (Age 15)—Won Southern amateur championship.
1918 (Age 16)—Played in Red Cross exhibition matches.
1919 (Age 17)—Finalist in national amateur tourney. Finished in tie for second, Canadian open. Played in first national open, placing with 299, four strokes behind the winner, Ted Ray.
1920 (Age 18)—Won Southern amateur. Tied for eighth place, national open. Medalist in national amateur, beaten in semifinals.
1921 (Age 19)—Lost in third round, national amateur. Tied for fifth in national open. Withdrew from British open at St. Andrews; lost in fourth round of British amateur.
1922 (Age 20)—Tied for second place, national open. Lost in semifinal, national amateur. Won Southern amateur. Won both matches in Walker Cup contest.

1923 (Age 21)—Won national open, Inwood, after play-off with Bobby Cruikshank. Won medal after play-off in national amateur, but lost in second round.
1924 (Age 22)—Won national amateur at Merion. Runner-up to Cyril Walker in national open. Won singles, lost foursome match in Walker Cup contest.
1925 (Age 23)—Won national amateur at Oakmont. Lost to Willie Macfarlane in play-off for national open.
1926 (Age 24)—Won British open, St. Anne's. Won national open, Scioto. Won medal in national amateur, but lost in final. Won both matches in Walker Cup contest. Lost in quarter-final, British amateur.
1927 (Age 25)—Won national open. Finished in quadruple tie for eleventh place in national open. Won national amateur, Minikahda. Won British open, St. Andrews, with record score, 285.
1928 (Age 26)—Won national amateur, Brae Burn. Lost in national open play-off with Johnny Farrell. Won both matches in Walker Cup series.
1929 (Age 27)—Tied for medal in national amateur; lost in first round. Won national open after play-off with Al Espinosa at Winged Foot.
1930 (Age 28)—Won British open at Hoylake. Won British amateur, St. Andrews. Won both matches in Walker Cup series. Won national open, Interlachen. Won national amateur, Merion.

Times Wide World Photo.

BOBBY JONES.

he deny it. The belief that he was through with competitive golf was strengthened when he defeated Gene Homans in the final.

Monarch of His Field.

With that victory he had accomplished his last objective. He has achieved something that no one even dreamed possible, golf being the uncertain game that it is. At the age of twenty-eight he was monarch of all he surveyed; he had been through fourteen years of championship storms; he had won the national amateur title five times, the national open four times, the British open three times and the British amateur once. He was ready to call it enough.

No doubt his victory at Merion had a great deal to do toward helping him make his decision. It is the firm belief of the writer that Bobby for some time had his heart set on winning the four major championships in a single year.

He knew too much about the vicissitudes of golf to think a great deal of his chances until he returned from England in possession of both British titles, and then, with his goal in sight, he worked as he never had worked before. His last barrier seemingly was hurdled when he won the national open at Interlachen, but he continued to work like a Trojan at Merion, even going so far as to hold a long driving session between rounds in his final match with Homans, when he was 7 up.

Revival of Interest Seen.

Just what his retirement will mean, so far as the championships are concerned, is not known. The general belief is that while his withdrawal will hurt the attendance for the time being, it will result in an upbuilding of interest in these events—interest that has been on the wane ever since Jones's superiority became so marked.

This will be especially true in the case of the national amateur, in which the Atlantan has been preeminent ever since 1924, when he managed to break the spell of ill-luck that had held him back for eight years.

Between 1924 and 1930 he met with only two reversals in the amateur, one at Baltusrol in 1926, when George Von Elm defeated him in the final round, and again at Pebble Beach in 1929, when Johnny Goodman, young Omaha star, eliminated

him in the first round.

In every other year he has emerged the victor. It came to be a legend that, once safely past the first two eighteen-hole match-play rounds, he would be the winner. And so, with his attractive personality—a personality that is admired in all parts of the globe—his fine sportsmanship and his almost bashful modesty made him as popular a figure as sport has ever seen, his continual triumphs had the effect of lowering the standards of the competitions. It came to a point where there was no competition.

Effect Felt in Open, Too.

To a large degree the same thing was true in regard to the national open championships. Between 1922, when he finished second to Gene Sarazen, and the present time he has been either first or second every year except one, that being in 1927, when he was off his stride. During that period he has been a constant thorn in the flesh of the professionals, it being estimated that his four victories have cost them at least $200,000, based on the fact that the value of an open championship to a professional is $50,000 a year.

But despite that the professionals are his stanchest admirers. All acclaim him as the greatest golfer that ever lived. There is not one who does not recognize the fact that Jones has added many times $200,000 to their business by popularizing the game to the extent that he has.

What made Jones the idol he became was the fact that his road was not always as rose-strewn as it has been in late years. He went through many trials of adversity, and he did so at a period of life when adversities are hardest to bear.

It will be recalled that it took Jones five years to win his first title, despite the fact that even then he was perhaps as good a shot-maker as he is now. But he possessed, as do most boys between the ages of 14 and 21, a fiery temper. It was not until he learned to control his temper that the control of his shots began producing results.

Set Par as His Goal.

After winning the open championship in 1923 he conceived the idea of playing against par instead of his opponent in match-play events, and once that happened there was no stopping him.

Honors have lain lightly upon his

shoulders. They failed to produce any changes in him. He was the same Bobby Jones at Merion this year that he was at the same place in 1924, when he won his first national amateur.

Moreover, he has upheld the dignity of golf. He has done nothing that savored of commercialization, and it is typical of him to take the stand he has in this instance. He probably has had more temptation placed in his way than any other amateur sportsman in the world, and turned his back on it.

Witness the case when his fellow-Atlantans, proud of the distinction he had brought to his city, wanted to show their appreciation by presenting him with a house. He refused the kindly proffer. The only way in which he has realized on his career has been in writing for a syndicate, and one of the stipulations of that contract was that he would write his own stories. Incidentally, his articles constitute the finest instructional series on golf that has ever been written.

Jones has been erroneously called a "machine." There is nothing machine-like about him. He errs, far more than do many of the professionals, but he is the most consistent scorer who ever played the game. His withdrawal from competition will be a decided loss to the game, but his retirement comes at the right time—while he is still on the crest.

November 18, 1930

BURKE WINS U.S. OPEN, DEFEATING VON ELM BY STROKE AT TOLEDO

28-Year-Old Greenwich Pro Scores 148 in the Second 36-Hole Play-Off.

TRAILS AT END OF FIRST 18

Lead Switches Constantly, but Victor Virtually Clinches Title on 34th Green.

5,000 FOLLOW THE MATCH

Burke's Great Work With Irons Is Highlight as Longest Tourney in History of Event Ends.

By WILLIAM D. RICHARDSON.
Special to The New York Times.

TOLEDO, July 6.—At the end of the longest trail ever followed in thirty-five years of championship history, Billy Burke, 28-year-old professional at the Round Hill Club in Greenwich, Conn., former steel mill worker, has stepped into Bobby Jones's shoes as the national open golf champion.

After 144 holes of golf, the longest stretch ever played in a championship of major importance, the stolid son of the Nutmeg State was crowned king of golf for 1931 today at Inverness, where eleven years ago Ted Ray, the big Englishman, won the title.

His victory over George Von Elm, business-man-golfer, was won by a narrow margin of a single stroke, although it might have been two had the occasion warranted. Coming up to the final green, set, in a hollow that gave the 5,000 members of the gallery a stadium-like view of the "kill," Burke had a two-stroke advantage over his rival.

Play Second Shots Boldly.

Both played their second shots boldly and the two balls stopped not far apart, Billy's perhaps eight yards from the flag and George's a trifle further. Each had to putt over a knoll and Von Elm, putting first, didn't allow quite enough and curled off, stopping four feet from the hole.

Burke now had chances galore and took them, putting his first carelessly and running it five feet past the hole, from where he missed the next one after his adversary had holed his 4. He got his 5 however, and it made him a winner by one stroke, his total for the day being 148, while Von Elm's was 149.

Thus ended the longest championship play in history—a contest in which Burke and Von Elm had tied at 292 for the seventy-two holes of the championship proper and then tied again in the first thirty-six-hole play-off with scores of 149.

Although Burke was never behind from the first hole this morning until the eighteenth, where he dubbed a niblick approach shot, and then never behind again after catching Von Elm at the second hole this afternoon, today's two rounds were so closely fought that the outcome was in doubt right up until the last three holes.

Burke Gains Edge on 34th.

Where Burke got the edge that carried him through successfully was on the No. 16 hole, a 398-yarder, in the second round. Leading his opponent by a stroke coming to that one, the thirty-fourth in today's match, Burke had a stroke lead, having picked it up two holes before.

His second shot just got to the edge of the green, in fact, it was just off the edge, while Von Elm put his own shot thirty-five feet from the pin. Playing the odd, Billy used a putter and rolled up a beauty within six inches of the cup for an easy par 4. Von Elm, trying desperately for a birdie 3, ran his ball only a few inches past the hole, not more than fifteen at the very outside, and, then, to the surprise of everybody who saw it, missed the next one.

It was the third putt of less than a yard that he had failed to drop during the day. One was only nine inches long, the other perhaps as much as thirty inches. Both came on the short eighth hole.

Neither of these, however, did as much damage as the one on the sixteenth this afternoon. That one practically killed off Von Elm's last chance of victory and brought an end to one of the greatest battles ever witnessed in the championship.

Burke Has Medal Round of 71.

The three putts that Burke took on the home green did nothing more than take the edge off a great round. Had Burke succeeded in getting down in two putts he would have had a round of 70. As it was he had a 71 this afternoon, against Von Elm's 73.

At the end of the morning round Von Elm, due largely to two holes on which Burke used bad judgment, the twelfth and the fifteenth, led by a shot, scoring a 76 to Burke's 77.

Burke might easily have lost the championship on the last of these two holes, where, after hooking to the side of a bunker, he tried to play a brassie to the green and pushed his ball far to the right, almost into the creek. Luckily the ball missed the water and wound up on the bank, from where he at least could hit it without being penalized. As it was he took a 6 on the hole and dropped two strokes to Von Elm, leaving the match all even.

Where Burke clinched the championship was on the first four holes in the afternoon round. As he finished the morning round Burke looked exceedingly tired. There was considerable doubt whether he would be able to withstand the pressure of the afternoon round.

Burke Shows Evidence of Strain.

Burke had played some pretty ragged holes at the finish of the round and his long irons were beginning to stray, tell-tale indications of a tired golfer.

Moreover, not once had he succeeded in getting past the first two holes with pars. This time he did, however. His start on those first four holes, par on which is 4, 4, 3, 4, was 4, 3, 3, 3, and might easily as not have been 3, 3, 2, 3.

He was within five yards of the flag with his approach to the first one after lunchtime, but missed his attempt for a birdie; dropped a fifteen-foot putt for a birdie 3 on the second hole, just missed a putt for a 2 on the short third from about the same distance, and then put a No. 2 iron within inches of the hole for an easy 3 on the 431-yard No. 4 hole, where the second shot is all carry.

It is a testimonial to Von Elm's fighting ability that he lost only three strokes to that sort of withering golf. Two of these came on the No. 4 hole. George stuck manfully by his guns, however, squared the match three times afterward, but finally tossed it over his shoulder by missing that wee one on the thirty-fourth.

Burke Superb With Irons.

Today, as indeed all through the tournament, Burke's chipping and putting were marvelous. This afternoon Billy had only thirty putts, while Von Elm had thirty-six. Burke's only three-putt green was the last, while George had two, one on the eighth hole and the other on the sixteenth.

Burke got away to a bad start this morning, dropping three strokes on the first two holes when Von Elm got into the rough playing the fifth, while he knocked in a fifteen-footer for a birdie 3.

Getting a two-stroke advantage when George came out of one bunker into another playing the short thirteenth, Billy threw it away on the fifteenth and then, with 5s on the last two holes, finished the morning round with a one-stroke deficit.

The first half of today's match was give and take, only five of the eighteen holes being halved.

Great Golf Almost All the Way.

It is too bad that one had to lose in such a match as Burke and Von Elm played at Inverness today. It was great golf practically all the way, with comparatively few badly played holes and a great many brilliantly played ones.

Both Von Elm and Burke had many breaks that played important rôles in determining which one of

Times Wide World Photo.

BILLY BURKE.

them was to be the next open champion. Whether the luck ran more against one than the other is hard to say, but one thing is certain: both men are great golfers and courageous fighters and the duel that they waged for this year's title will be remembered by golfers for many, many years to come.

Back a few years ago, Macdonald Smith and Gene Sarazen had to play 126 holes before one of them won the metropolitan open, but that cannot compare with this.

In addition to the first prize of $1,000 Burke received $750 from the U. S. G. A. this afternoon, while Von Elm received $250 in addition to the $750 that goes to the runner-up.

July 7, 1931

U. S. G. A. ADOPTS HEAVIER GOLF BALL

1.55-1.68 Sphere Replaced by One of 1.62 Ounces and 1.68 Inches Diameter.

GOES INTO EFFECT JAN. 1

Marks Culmination of Controversy Over "Balloon" Ball in Use During Past Year.

"Effective for play Jan. 1, 1932, the size of the golf ball shall not be less than 1.68 inches in diameter, and the weight shall not be greater than 1.62 ounces avoirdupois."

With that short statement, agreed on at the meeting of the executive committee Thursday and released yesterday for publication, the United States Golf Association has disposed of one of the most annoying problems with which it ever has dealt.

The statement means that the 1.55-1.68 ball, adopted a year ago and used during the current season, supplanting the 1.62-1.62 ball which was the official sphere from 1921 to 1931, at last is out of the picture.

Decision Not a Surprise.

The news, despite its being official, took no one by surprise, for long ago it was known that a change was intended and at the time when the professionals were playing their championship at Providence, the U. S. G. A. made a definite announcement that the weight would be increased. This, however, was the first official announcement of what the new weight would be.

Nothing that the U. S. G. A. ever has done evoked such a controversy as did the adoption of the 1.55-1.68 ball. Brought out as an attempt to curb long-driving and to prevent old courses from becoming obsolete as a result of the 1.62-1.62 ball's constantly increasing ballistic properties, the new sphere, quickly dubbed the "balloon" ball, immediately aroused a storm of criticism.

There was a general feeling among golfers throughout the country that the "balloon" had been thrust upon them by the controlling body and that feeling persisted, although at the end of the season it was not as violent as it was at first.

Curiously enough, the ball that was supposed to curb length, reward skill and bring back the use of clubs that were coming to be neglected, such as the spoon and the mashie, did nothing of the sort. The skillful hitters began getting even more length down wind with it than they had with its predecessor and even with the wind adverse the loss of distance was negligible.

But the duffer and the dub suffered, or at least imagined he did. It was all well and good for others to inform him that whatever distance he lost or fancied he lost from the tee would be recompensed by the way the ball sat up, begging to be hit, through the fairway. The 1.62-1.62 ball had got him off the tee and nothing else mattered.

Bemoaned Loss of Distance.

In a great many cases, perhaps most, those few 150, 175, even 200 yard drives that he had been getting with the 1.62-1.62 ball brought the only thrill of the game, and to take that away left nothing, or next to nothing. He complained lustily and the U. S. G. A. officials heeded.

It is doubtful, however, if the failure of golfers generally to approve the "balloon" ball had as much to do in bringing about the change to the 1.62-1.68 ball as had something else.

In adopting the 1.55-1.68 ball, the U. S. G. A. no doubt had some inkling at least that the Royal and Ancient Golf Club, which controls golf abroad, would join hands, maybe not at once, but eventually.

No such thing happened. Moreover, it is doubtful if it ever could happen, playing conditions being what they are abroad, with so many seaside courses wind-swept. The result was that two standards were set up, Great Britain adhering to the 1.62-1.62 ball.

Now, however, there is at least a chance for agreement which will make for a ball that is again standard wherever the game is played. Opposed as they were to a ball so uncontrollable in high winds, the British golfers may not be averse to adopting a ball which has the same weight as the one they are now playing and which is only .06 inch larger in diameter.

Already Being Manufactured.

It is understood that a quantity of the 1.62-1.68 balls, which, by the way, manufacturers already have been making, have been sent to certain leaders of the game abroad with this hope in mind. But no agreement possibly can be reached for another year or so.

Whether the 1.62-1.68 ball succeeds in becoming more popular than the one it supplants is as yet speculative. The impressions gathered are varying. Some have expressed approval, while others, declaring that it took something more of a hit to get it away, have gone back to the "balloon" ball.

Of course, the new specifications give manufacturers greater freedom of action than they had with the 1.55-1.68. The weight, it will be noticed, need not necessarily be 1.62 ounces. That is the maximum weight permitted, just as 1.68 inches is the minimum diameter permitted.

This is the third time in the game's history that the specifications of the ball have been changed by legislation. Prior to 1921, when 1.62-1.62 was fixed as the standard, the use of any ball was permissible. "Gibson's choice" was the rule.

November 21, 1931

Sarazen Wins the British Open Golf Title; Lowers Bobby Jones's Record by 2 Strokes

By W. F. LEYSMITH.
Special Cable to THE NEW YORK TIMES.

SANDWICH, England, June 10.—Smashing golf championship records with almost every swing of his clubs, Gene Sarazen won the coveted British open crown today, leading by five strokes another American, Macdonald Smith, who had 288.

Sarazen's aggregate of 283—on rounds of 70, 69, 70, 74—was two shots better than Bobby Jones's famous record of 285 at St. Andrew's in 1927 and for the first three rounds he eclipsed Jones's performance by no fewer than four strokes.

Arthur Havers, in a courageous effort to overtake Sarazen, broke the record at the Prince's course in the third round with a brilliant 68, but requiring a 70 to tie, the last Englishman to hold the championship faltered in the afternoon and fell into third place with his total of 289.

Mac Smith's last two rounds, 71 and 70, produced the best aggregate performance today, but a tragic 7 on the first hole of the second round yesterday, followed by a 5, ruined his chance.

So, for the ninth consecutive year the championship cup crosses the Atlantic. When called to the balcony of the Prince's clubhouse to receive the cup from the hands of the chairman of the club, Sir Henry Mallaby Deeley, before a great gathering of golfing enthusiasts, Sarazen's happy grin broadened from ear to ear.

"I really am the happiest man living today," he said, "and my only regret is that my wife, who has accompanied me so often, is not here to share the honor." Then, glancing at the names on the cup, he added, "I only hope I shall be a champion as worthy as those whose names are on this cup. I am coming back next year to do my best."

Sir Henry was wildly cheered when he said "the best man has won," and Havers, on the behalf of British professionals, appealed to the American to come again. "There is no record that can't be broken," he added.

The Prince of Wales, very lame and leaning heavily on his shooting-stick, watched Sarazen complete his final round, after which Lady Astor rescued the little American from a group of autograph hunters and whisked him away.

Sarazen has won the affections of British sportsmen not only as a great golfer but as a great personality, and late this afternoon, when obviously tiring and with a vast, enthusiastic crowd surging around him on the last few holes, he showed not the slightest sign of impatience, although one false shot might have ruined his lifetime ambition.

He won the championship largely because he could recover from bad positions without losing his head and possessed the courage to sacrifice a stroke and play back when an emergency arose in a difficult trap, as on Wednesday. His talisman was a necktie, the gift of his wife, which was adorned with a large question mark, and his answer to that was to shoot seventy-two holes in five under an average of 4s.

"The prospect of his visit here next year will keep British golf alive," was the comment of one of the authorities.

Regarded yesterday as British "hopes," Percy Alliss, Archie Compston, Charles Whitcombe and W. H. Davies all failed early today. But Sarazen, out in 33 for the third round, played throughout better than he did yesterday, when, with several large slices of luck, he tied the record of Prince's with a 69.

Never Off the Course.

He never was off the course and played a really great shot at the eighth, over the Himalayas, hitting the pin with his second iron and holing an eagle 3. He three-putted the fifteenth, then got a birdie 3 at the sixteenth, which put him three under 4s. His long putts were not dropping and he had to tap the ball into the cup for a 5 at the seventeenth and again for a 4 at the eighteenth.

"Anyway," he said, "that's far better than my usual 78 for the third round of a championship." Then, after a long look at the question mark on his necktie, he said, "The fourth round? Well, I am enjoying myself. The crowds are good to me—there are no signs of a depression here."

Havers was not in when Sarazen commenced his final round, and the American started eight strokes ahead of any competitor. For the second time today a glorious second shot over the Himalayas got him on the eighth green against a rising wind and he holed a 15-yard putt for an eagle 3.

His putt from the edge of the green almost dropped for a birdie 3 at the ninth and he turned the corner in 35. Runners then brought the news that Havers, in a valiant effort to overtake the American, had broken the record. This put him only four strokes behind on the third round.

Seemingly affected by the news, Sarazen became erratic. He pulled his drive, which gave him a bad lie at the tenth, and he took 3 to reach the green and two putts. He mistimed his drive at the eleventh and the ball, luckily for him, came to rest in a lone clump of grass amid the wilderness of hazards on the very peak of the Himalayas.

Sends Ball Near the Pin.

With the ball twelve inches above his feet, Sarazen hit a courageous mashie over a dozen gaping traps to a point near the pin. Such luck, combined with club mastery, would win any championship.

Still unsteady, Sarazen found the rough again with his drive at the twelfth and put his second into the rough left of the green. Chipping short, he took two putts for a 5. At the thirteenth he got in the rough with his drive and his second iron found a bad lie to the right of the green, but he chipped dead for a 4.

His high spirits returned at the short fifteenth, when he sank a 20-foot curling putt for a birdie 2 and blew a kiss after the ball. At this point he had one-putted on four greens, but at the fifteenth, when running one under 4s, he three-putted for a 5, passing the cup five yards with his approach putt.

Sarazen now seemed pale under his tan, and after putting the ball in the rough to the right of the green with his second iron at the sixteenth, he fluffed it completely with his niblick, taking a 5.

The gallery of 4,000 following him and the waits between shots were trying to the mercurial temperament of the man with the championship in his hands and the bogey of Havers behind him. "He's had nearly enough," was his sympathetic caddie's remark.

Plays Seventeenth Shrewdly.

It took five minutes to settle the crowd for the critical dog-legged sev-

PAR FOR THE COURSE.
By The Associated Press.

Hole.	Yards.	Par.	Hole.	Yards.	Par.
1	382	4	10	386	4
2	460	5	11	408	4
3	154	3	12	456	5
4	399	4	13	411	4
5	217	3	14	202	3
6	436	4	15	335	4
7	391	4	16	416	4
8	453	5	17	516	5
9	408	4	18	460	5
Total	3,300	36	Total	3,590	38

Grand total—Yards, 6,890; par, 74.

GENE SARAZEN.

Times Wide World Photo.

SARAZEN, WITH 286, WINS THE U. S. OPEN; SCORE TIES RECORD

Cards 66, 2 Under Course Mark, on Final Round to Triumph by 3-Stroke Margin.

10,000 ACCLAIM VICTORY

Ovation Resounds as He Adds Title to British Crown, Duplicating Jones's Feat.

PERKINS, CRUICKSHANK TIE

Are Deadlocked at Second at Fresh Meadow—Burke, Defending Champion, Bracketed at Seventh.

PAR FOR THE COURSE.

Hole.	Yards.	Par.		Hole.	Yards.	Par.
1	437	4		10	385	4
2	395	4		11	413	4
3	391	4		12	155	3
4	188	3		13	448	4
5	578	5		14	219	3
6	428	4		15	424	4
7	412	4		16	587	5
8	435	4		17	373	4
9	143	3		18	404	4
Total	3,407	35		Total	3,408	35

Grand total—6,815 yards, par 70.

By WILLIAM D. RICHARDSON.

With two smashing finishing rounds, unquestionably the greatest ever played in any golf championship, Gene Sarazen yesterday added the United States open title to the crown he annexed only a few weeks ago in Great Britain.

Undaunted by the fact that he was five strokes behind the two leaders, Phil Perkins and Jose Jurado, at the end of the second round and that he was not hitting the ball particularly well, Sarazen went out on the Fresh Meadow Country Club course, his old stamping ground, and won the title by three shots, his winning total being 286, a figure equalled only once in the thirty-six years of championship history.

By coming home in 32 yesterday morning, Gene played himself into a gorgeous position with a 70 to equal par and then, later in the day and in full knowledge of what had to be done, he went out again and brought home a 66, shattering the course record, held by Leo Diegel, by two strokes to win the championship in a walk.

Almost in Perkin's Grasp.

He literally snatched the title out of the grasp of Perkins, former British amateur champion who recently left the amateur ranks and who appeared to have it won when he turned in a great 70 earlier in the afternoon for a total of 289, a mark that was tied later by Bobby Cruickshank, the wee Scot who, nine years ago, at nearby Inwood, lost the title to Bobby Jones in a play-off.

Despite the fact that six men were within two strokes of one another going into the last round, no one else in the field was anywhere close to the three leaders who put on the greatest exhibition ever witnessed on the closing day of a championship.

Leo Diegel, who was tied with Sarazen and Jurado for second place, one stroke behind Perkins, going into the last round, finished fourth with a 72-hole total of 294; Wiffy Cox was fifth, one stroke back; Jurado, sixth, and Billy Burke, the defending champion, Harry Cooper and Olin Dutra, tied for seventh with totals of 297. Only one other man in the field broke 300. That was Hagen, who had 298.

Excitement Proves Intense.

Never has there been such a last-round drive as took place over the Fresh Meadow course yesterday and at the finish there wasn't a person in the gallery who was not completely overcome by the excitement of it all.

The afternoon was a series of thrills which began when Perkins, playing superbly, refused to crack under the terrific strain of a championship, and posted his brilliant 70 to give him a seventy-two-hole score of 289.

At the time it looked as if that mark would make Perkins the champion and provide one of the greatest achievements in the history of the game. Knowing full well how much trouble the course had given so many of the stars, no one believed it would be possible for any one to equal his mark.

But suddenly, out of nowhere, Cruickshank hobbed into the picture with a score of 33 on the outgoing nine holes, a score that left him with par to tie Perkins for the lead. And then came word from the front that Sarazen was burning up the course.

Reaches Turn in 32.

By the time he reached the turn in 32, giving him a 64 for the last nine holes in the morning and the first nine in the afternoon, Gene had topped Perkin's and Cruickshank's fifty-four hole totals by two strokes.

All he had to do then in order to win was to play the last nine holes in 36 strokes, and after watching his golf for a few holes no one ever had any doubt of his ability to do that.

One look at Gene was all that was necessary to convince any one that there was the new open champion, the man who would soon join hands with Bobby Jones as the only two men ever to win the two major titles in the same year.

It was the Sarazen of old out there on the course. The same kind of a bold, flashing player who as a boy had won the United States open at Skokie ten years back. The only difference was that he was a far better shot-maker now than then.

Title No Longer in Doubt.

After the first six holes on the last nine, the title was as good as won so far as he was concerned. Not once was Sarazen over par figures on that final nine holes and at no time was he in any serious trouble. He was driving the ball a tremendous distance, putting his second shots up on the greens with putts for birdies on almost every hole.

A tremendous gallery, perhaps 10,000 wild-eyed enthusiasts, crowded around the home green as Sarazen came up to play the final hole. It was so dense and so unruly a crowd that even the players had a hard time getting onto the green to finish.

enteenth, which Sarazen played shrewdly. Placed rather too far to the right with his drive, he took a No. 1 iron and played short, safe from the yawning traps guarding the narrow entrance to the green. He chipped on with his niblick and got a 5.

A grand drive at the eighteenth carried him far down the fairway past the wall-faced bunker which had been his nightmare since the first day. "Club?" asked his trusted caddie, Ernest Daniels. "No. 3," came the prompt reply.

It was a peach of a shot, pin high, leaving a straight six-yard putt. But it failed to drop and Sarazen tapped it in with his seventy-fourth stroke. This left Havers with a 69 to win. The Englishman started with a 5, then lipped the cup for 3s at the tenth, eleventh and twelfth, three-putted at the thirteenth, and was left to get 3, 3, 4 for the last three. A 5 at the sixteenth was the end of his battle for this year's championship.

Breaks Par on Three Rounds.

SANDWICH, England, June 10 (P).—Gene Sarazen, with his 70, 69, 70, 74 for the seventy-two holes, shattered par on every round but the last one this afternoon. He finished 13 strokes better than regulation figures for the championship layout, a long, treacherous par 74 course laid out on the edge of the English Channel.

Sarazen led from start to finish and not only lowered the tournament record of 285 but surpassed the best mark ever made in the Ameri-

can open, 286, by Chick Evans.

Mac Smith's 71, 76, 71, 70—288 was good enough to win any other British open in history save Jones's 285, but was hopeless today. Arthur Havers's rounds were 74, 71, 68, 76—289.

A discouraged figure, buried well down the list, was Tommy Armour, the "black Scot" from Detroit, and defending champion. He faltered on the final eighteen, taking an 83 for a 72-hole aggregate of 75, 70, 74, 83—302.

W. L. Hope, with 299, was the lowest of the amateurs.

THE CARDS.

GENE SARAZEN.

Morning Round.

Out ...... 4 4 3 5 3 4 3 3 4—33
In .... 4 4 4 5 3 5 3 5 4—37—70—209

Afternoon Round.

Out ...... 4 4 3 4 4 4 5 3 4—35
In .... 5 4 5 4 2 5 5 5 4—39—74—283

MACDONALD SMITH.

Morning Round.

Out ...... 4 4 3 4 3 4 3 5 4—34
In .... 4 4 4 4 3 5 4 5 4—37—71—218

Afternoon Round.

Out ...... 4 4 3 3 4 6 5 4 3—34
In .... 3 4 5 5 3 4 3 4 5—36—70—288

ARTHUR HAVERS.

Morning Round.

Out ...... 4 4 2 4 3 4 4 4 4—33
In .... 3 4 4 4 3 4 5 4—35—68—213

Afternoon Round.

Out ...... 5 4 3 5 3 4 4 5 4—37
In .... 4 4 4 3 5 3 3 5 5—39—76—289

TOMMY ARMOUR.

Morning Round.

Out ...... 3 4 4 5 4 4 4 5 3—36
In .... 4 4 4 4 3 4 4 5 6—38—74—219

Afternoon Round.

Out ...... 4 4 3 5 5 5 5 5 5—41
In .... 4 5 5 4 4 4 5 6 5—42—83—302

June 11, 1932

Times Wide World Photo.

Gene Sarazen With Trophies He Won In the United States and British Open Tournaments.

Gene's second shot, following a perfectly placed drive, went a bit too far to the right and dropped into a bunker, from where, almost without waiting for quiet, he pitched out roughly, eight feet wide of the pin.

Sarazen had that putt for a 66, something almost unheard of in a championship, and when the ball rolled straight and true right into the cup, he was engulfed in a throng that swept him away, paying not the slightest attention to the expensive green on which they were tramping.

Receives Historic Trophy.

Sarazen was borne away to receive the historic cup, the $1,000 first prize that goes to the winner, and fame and glory.

Thus finished the most thrilling day of any championship the writer has ever witnessed, a finish that made one almost forget the courageous exhibition of Perkins, who was never out of the lead until Sarazen came along to grasp the laurels, and Cruickshank, who had played the last two rounds in 137 strokes, tying the 36-hole record for the course, made by Diegel in 1930, and yet failed to finish better than second.

As the third round started, there were eight players who were considered likely candidates for the honor won a year ago by Burke after the memorable play-off with George von Elm. They were Perkins and Jurado tied at 145; Dutra, 146; Diegel, 147; Hagen, 148, and Cooper, Sarazen and Craig Wood, 150.

And when it was over, the only victims of that critical round of the championship were Hagen and Wood, each having taken 79's. Perkins's 74 had given him the lead at 219, with Jurado, Diegel and Sarazen tied for second at 220 and Dutra joined by Cruickshank in a tie, two shots behind the leader.

It now looked as if the championship lay somewhere among those six men. Perkins was the first out and when he reached the turn in 35, even par figures, he had put two strokes between himself and Jurado and outdistanced Dutra and Diegel, the former having taken a 7 on the fifth hole to be 37 out and the latter out in 38. As Perkins turned, Cruickshank and Sarazen were just about starting out.

A tremendous gallery was trekking after Perkins as he rounded the turn, when the question was raised: "Can he stand up under the strain?" It was a question he answered by the way he played the last nine holes.

Although bunkered on his drive, he got a gorgeous par on the tenth hole and another par on the eleventh. Then down went a twenty-foot putt for a birdie 2 on the twelfth, making him one under par on the round.

His First Three-Putt Green.

Perkins's first three-putt green in the championship came on the sixteenth hole, where, getting above the cup with his pitch, he failed to lay his down-hill approach putt dead and missed the next one.

Then he hooked his drive to the rough near a bunker playing No. 17, pushed his second to the right of the green and plumped his next one into a bunker. "There he blows," said some one in the gallery. But there was no "blowing" by the bespectacled British player, as he demonstrated by exploding out and getting down in one putt for a good 5.

And then came a gorgeous finish—the finish of a champion. He was on the green five feet from the cup in 2 and sank the putt for a birdie 3

and a 70 for the round.

In that moment he was hailed as the new champion, no one suspecting that Cruickshank possibly could tie him or that Sarazen would eventually come along to snatch the hard-won honors out of his very hands.

The first intimation of Cruickshank's threat came with word that the little Scot had gone out in 33 notwithstanding three putts on the second green and trouble on his drive to the seventh.

That 33 put him out in precisely the same total as Perkins's, 254 strokes for sixty-three holes. He started back 4, 4, 3, 5, two more strokes than the tall young Englishman had taken, caught up to him by getting a birdie 3 on the fifteenth and getting his par on the sixteenth. Par on the last two holes would put him into a tie, and he got them by dint of great shots on both the seventeenth and the eighteenth.

The shot on the seventeenth was in the rough and that on the eighteenth in the rough also, but this time menaced by a tree. That last one put his ball four feet from the hole, leaving him that putt to take the lead away from Perkins provided he succeeded in getting it down.

It wouldn't go in, however, and the two of them were tied at a score that would have been good enough to win nine out of ten championships, especially on this course.

But there was Sarazen still to be reckoned with. About the only thing that made Sarazen a feared man up to today was the name and the knowledge of what he had done in the British open, where he won with a score of 283, to beat by two strokes the record held by Bobby Jones.

Sarazen Appears Ill at Ease.

When Gene took 38 on the first nine holes this morning he had all the appearance of a man ill at ease. Even to do that he had to hole a 2 on the ninth. That was the turning point so far as Sarazen was concerned.

With three birdies in succession, each one the result of a good iron shot, which left him within easy putting range, little Gene romped home in 32 for a 70 to tie for second.

There was no stopping him after that, and the chances are that if he had had to do a 62 on the final round he would have done it. Only at the second hole on that final round did he waver even the slightest. There he was bunkered and the mistake cost him a 5. After that he had only two other 5s, each of them on par five holes.

Putts of six and seven yards found the bottom of the tins on the third and fourth greens for birdies. Another birdie dropped on the sixth and still another on the ninth, where his putter rammed down a fifteen-footer.

Those four birdies put him out in 32 and left him in the happy position of having to do only a 36 on the last nine in order to tie Perkins, who was now in the clubhouse wondering whether he would be the winner. For one in the inspired mood he was in yesterday afternoon a 36 was easy for Gene, and when he got safely past the next six holes he was in a position of being able to play the last three holes each in one over par figures and still tie for the title.

Throws Caution to the Winds.

He did far better than that, almost holing his 4 on the long sixteenth, playing which he threw all caution to the four winds and lashed out one of the longest balls hit, getting his par on the seventeenth and then coming out of the bunker for his final 4 on the eighteenth.

It was a great exhibition on the part of the dark-skinned little Italian-American who burst into fame by winning the title at Skokie in 1922, when he nosed out Bobby Jones and John L. Black, and who romped away with the British open title at

Sandwich early in the month.

In closing, one cannot help but say a word concerning the man who was the hero of the championship a year ago—Burke. Although he was never in the race from start to finish, playing well enough, but putting poorly, Burke put on a championship finish by reeling off a 71 yesterday to finish among the first ten.

June 26, 1932

GOLFERS' PARADISE READY FOR OPENING

Only 22 Traps on the New Augusta National, "Course for Forgotten Man."

PREMIUM IS ON ACCURACY

Layout Designed by Jones and Dr. MacKenzie Represents Georgian's Ideal.

LORD DECIES TO ATTEND

Officials, Champions and Other Notables Will Be Present at Inaugural of Links Jan. 13-15.

PAR FOR THE COURSE.

Hole	Yds.	Par.	Hole	Yds.	Par.
1	430	4	10	400	4
2	435	4	11	535	5
3	150	3	12	350	4
4	480	5	13	190	3
5	435	4	14	440	4
6	485	5	15	185	3
7	145	3	16	340	4
8	400	4	17	500	5
9	410	4	18	430	4
Total	3,350	36	Total	3,350	36

Grand Total—6,700 yards, par 72.

By WILLIAM D. RICHARDSON.

Strange and unbelievable as it will appear to golfers who have spent half their lives down in bunkers and the other half cussing the men who constructed them, there is to be opened, in the near future, a course that has on it only twenty-two traps.

We expect that statement will be challenged. "Surely," we can hear one of those unfortunates whose Saturdays, Sundays and holidays have been ru"ned by excessive use of the niblick remark: "You mean 122. Or perhaps twenty-two on one hole. But not twenty-two bunkers altogether!"

That's just what we mean. If you were to get into every single bunker on the course (which most of us manage to do) you would only have visited twenty-two. That is all there are on the whole course.

Idyllic Conditions Exist.

For fear the pointing out of that feature will cause wholesale resignation from other clubs and a golfers' migration to these Elysian Fields, we hasten to state that the course where these idyllic conditions exist is a private one, that membership is by invitation only.

It is the Augusta National Golf Club in Georgia, a new golfing paradise laid out by Robert Tyre Jones Jr. and Dr. Alister MacKenzie, famous architect who designed Cypress Point and other noted California links, and its opening, on Jan. 13-15, will be an occasion of international import.

Among those who will take part in the affair is Lord Decies, chairman of the British Sportsmen's Club, and a delegation of golf officials, golf champions and leaders in the business world. Thus far acceptances have been received from H. H. Ramsay, president of the United States Golf Association; G. Herbert Walker, former president of the organization and donor of the Walker Cup; Charles H. Sabin and John G. Jackson, both officials of the national body.

Douglas to Make Trip.

Others scheduled to make the trip to Augusta by special train, leaving New York at 3:30 in the afternoon of Jan. 12, are Francis Ouimet and Jess W. Sweetser, former champions and Findlay Douglas, former national champion and former president of the U. S. G. A.

Also M. H. Aylesworth, Kent Cooper, Matthew C. Brush, Walter Case, William L. Chenery, Reuben S. Crispbell, Frank Crowninshield, Julian W. Curtiss, Boykin C. Wright, Frank A. Willard, W. Alton Jones, George M. Gales, Jay R. Monroe, A. C. Beane, Fred N. Shepherd, William A. Willingham, Donald Mackay 2d, William Randolph Hearst Jr., Walton H. Marshall, Grantland Rice and Clifford Roberts.

On the reception committee to greet the guests when they arrive in Augusta are William H. Wallace Jr., Eugene G. Grace, George G. Bourne, Thomas Barrett Jr., Alfred S. Bourne, Fielding Wallace, Devereux Milburn, John W. Herbert, Henry P. Crowell, Harry M. Atkinson, Colonel Robert P. Jones and Robert Tyre Jones Jr., who is president of the club.

Competition Is Likely.

It is not known as yet just what form the opening will take, but there probably will be a competition of some sort for the club is first, last and always a golf club without embellishment other than a superb course, laid out in beautiful surroundings.

The writer has seen the man who is most responsible for the creation of the course in many ebullient moments such as the time he won his first major championship after long years of bitter disappointment, the time he won his first amateur championship—his heart's desire—and the time he completed his cycle of four major titles in the same year, a hitherto unaccomplished feat, but never did he seem quite so enthusiastic as he was one day last Fall when he first told the writer about this Augusta project.

Sprawled out on the floor of his suite in the Hotel Vanderbilt the day after the national open, with a huge contour map in front of him, the ordinarily placid Georgian fairly radiated enthusiasm as he described the progressive stages by which the course was built.

Four Requirements Listed.

It represents his conception of what the "ideal" golf course should be. To be ideal, in his opinion, a course must fulfill at least four requirements. It must give pleasure to the greatest possible number of players, in the first place. It must require strategy as well as skill, otherwise it cannot be enduringly interesting.

It must give the average player a fair chance and at the same time require the utmost from the expert who tries for sub-par scores. Finally, all natural beauty must be preserved, natural hazards utilized and a minimum of artificiality introduced.

Luckily for the builders they found a tract of land that was ideally adapted to their purpose. It was a tract originally held by a Belgian Baron by the name of Berckmans, an ardent horticulturist who landscaped the entire property beautifully and skillfully.

Terrain Mildly Rolling.

It was a large tract on which stood towering pines and a large variety of other trees. It was crossed by streams, the terrain was mildly rolling and the soil was rich. All that remained for Messrs. Jones and MacKenzie to do was to design a layout that would take full advantage of what man and nature had endowed them with.

The result is the Augusta National, a course I like to term "a golf course for the forgotten man" for the simple reason that in its conception Bobby has gone out of his way to espouse the cause of the golfer whose scores range between 95 and 130!

For him Bobby has done something that others frequently disdain to do. He has not only eliminated bunkers to a large extent, using them only wherever they have a specific purpose, but he has everywhere offered the "forgotten man" an alternate route. For every one, be he expert or duffer, there is always the shot that is within his range.

Sound Judgment Stressed.

In Bobby's opinion the great thing in golf is accuracy, and in his construction of holes he has put a premium on accurate hitting, plus sound judgment.

The course, using the championship tees, plays 6,700 yards, with two evenly balanced nines, and its par is 72. The use of the regular tees cuts off 370 yards.

A hole-by-hole description, which illustrates the care that has been exercised to provide a "way around," and likewise the premiums offered for accuracy follows:

No. 1, 420 Yards—Par 4.

An excellent get-away hole, comparatively easy and downhill. There is a large spectacular bunker guarding the green on the left which makes a difficult second shot for the player who has placed his drive on the left side of the fairway. The player who has taken

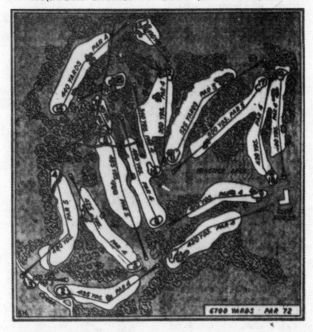

'AUGUSTA NATIONAL' GOLF CLUB COURSE.

6700 YARDS · PAR 72

the correct line over a succession of hillocks on the right-hand side is presented with an easy second shot into an opening that leads to a nature-made punch-bowl green.

No. 2, 455 Yards—Par 4.

Another two-shotter, with the green situated in the bend of a stream. The approach has a marked tilt upward from left to right, so that the longer and more accurately the drive is placed the easier becomes the second shot. This is a most interesting hole, without a single bunker.

No. 3, 150 Yards—Par 3.

A pitch shot to a long, narrow green immediately across a stream—a very testing hole, calling for an accurately hit ball.

No. 4, 480 Yards—Par 5.

This hole has some of the features of the seventeenth at Cypress Point. It is a dog-leg hole, played diagonally over a stream that constitutes a continuous hazard. The long hitter may go for as large a carry as he wishes and thus reach the green with a long second shot, but the less powerful driver can play out across the stream, play his second up the fairway and his third on the green without encountering any trouble. Here's another hole without a bunker.

No. 5, 425 Yards—Par 4.

Here some of the features of the sixth hole at St. Andrews (Bobby's favorite course) are embodied. A long drive skirting or played over a bunker on the right will give a visible shot to the green. If the drive is to the left, however, the green will be only semi-visible and a run-up approach required over a succession of hillocks and hollows.

No. 6, 485 Yards—Par 5.

Here again we see boldness and accuracy rewarded. The design of the hole gives assistance to the big hitter who has driven far and accurately, for a large hillock has been built to the right of the loop of the stream which assists him in pulling his second shot around to the green. The hole has certain characteristics of the first hole at St. Andrews.

No. 7, 145 Yards—Par 3.

Somewhat similar in design to the seventh hole at Stoke Poges in England, but better in that the green will be more visible and the background more attractive.

No. 8, 400 Yards—Par 4.

This green is something like the famous fourteenth at St. Andrews reversed. It will be necessary to attack the green from the right and play a run-up second shot, the aim of the builders being to make the turf of such a texture that an indifferent pitch shot will not hold on the green.

No. 9, 410 Yards—Par 4.

Again a premium on accurate driving, for the tee shot must be to the right, since the approach to the green is bunkered heavily on the left.

No. 10, 400 Yards—Par 4.

Here, again, is the drive stressed.

No. 11, 535 Yards—Par 5.

The "alternate route" is again emphasized. The long hitter can reach home on his second shot, while the more timid souls can make their pars with safety-first tactics.

No. 12, 350 Yards—Par 4.

The second shot is the important shot here, for the left-hand side of the green is narrow and the right-hand side wide. It will not be difficult to hit the wide side, but in nine times out of ten the hole will be cut in the left-hand side.

No. 13, 190 Yards—Par 3.

Very similar to the Eden hole at St. Andrews.

No. 14, 440 Yards—Par 4.

Here again one comes across the St. Andrews influence. It is very much like the famous road hole there, with a group of trees forming a corner of the dog leg instead of the station master's garden, and the green itself is situated on a similar plateau to its prototype. Unless the tee shot is properly placed the second shot is a blind one fraught with danger.

No. 15, 185 Yards—Par 3.

This hole reminds one of the redan hole at North Berwick, Scotland, only here the visibility is greater than at the original redan.

No. 16, 340 Yards—Par 4.

One sees here a certain similarity to the finishing hole at St. Andrews, with the second shot preferably of the run-up type.

No. 17, 500 Yards—Par 5.

A three-shotter uphill to a punch-bowl green something like Muirfield's seventeenth.

No. 18, 420 Yards—Par 4.

A Cape type finishing hole played slightly downhill, with the placing of the drive essential.

No. 19.

Just what type this hole will take depends to a large extent upon what Congress does!

January 1, 1933

U. S. TEAM DEFEATED IN RYDER CUP GOLF

British Stars Break Even in Singles to Capture the Series, 6½ to 5½.

DRAMA MARKS THE FINISH

Easterbrook Beats Shute on Last Hole of Last Match to Provide Margin.

RESULTS OF SINGLES MATCHES.

Gene Sarazen, United States, defeated Alfred Padgham, 6 and 4.
Walter Hagen, United States, defeated A. J. Lacey, 2 and 1.
Craig Wood, United States, defeated W. H. Davies, 4 and 3.
Horton Smith, United States, defeated Charles Whitcombe, 2 and 1.
Abe Mitchell, Great Britain, defeated Olin Dutra, 9 and 8.
Percy Alliss, Great Britain, defeated Paul Runyan, 2 and 1.
Arthur Havers, Great Britain, defeated Leo Diegel, 4 and 3.
Syd Easterbrook, Great Britain, defeated Densmore Shute, 1 up.

Special Cable to THE NEW YORK TIMES.

SOUTHPORT, England, June 27.

Great Britain took the Ryder Cup away from America today by a single point, gained by the last putt in the last match on the last green.

Th putt was two feet long and Syd Easterbrook had to sink it to beat Densmore Shute. The Prince of Wales and 20,000 others—the biggest crowd ever seen on a British golf course—waited tensely while the young Bristol professional tapped the ball firmly into the cup to give the British the victory in the international golf series, 6½ to 5½.

The crowd remained cheering and shouting long after the Prince handed the trophy to J. H. Taylor, non-playing captain of the British team.

How narrow was the margin of victory may be judged by the story of that last hole. The roaring, rushing thousands saw Easterbrook drive into a bunker. But with the green wide open to him, Shute put his second shot into another bunker. Both were on the green in 3.

Shute Runs Past Hole.

Easterbrook putted to within two feet, but Shute gave the hole a chance and ran four feet past it, then missed his return putt. Amid a deathly hush Easterbrook sank his.

Earlier, the British had been in a tight fix, for they had to win three matches in a row to regain the cup. All three matches had trembled in the balance all day and might have gone either way.

The gentleman on the megaphone again harangued the crowd, introducing a novel topic—the presence of pickpockets. It seemed prophetic, for in the match between Walter Hagen and A. J. Lacey a perfectly innocent spectator picked up Lacey's ball from the rough and had to be pursued and brought back, thoroughly frightened, by an escort of stewards armed with lances bearing red and white flags.

Gene Sarazen and Alfred Padgham, after a formal introduction in Lancashire dialect, set the first match going, both playing magnificently, with Padgham having something the better of it from the tees.

Sarazen Has Putting Streak.

He was 1 up at the tenth, but Sarazen then had a spell of fine putting until at the eighteenth Padgham, amid ecstatic squeals, holed one from back of the green and was only 2 down, the scores being 71 for Sarazen and 72 for Padgham.

After luncheon Sarazen went great guns and, playing with serene confidence, gradually drew away to win comfortably by 6 and 4.

The Prince of Wales, who arrived by airplane, came out between 3 and 4 o'clock to watch the play. There are seven hills near the sixteenth green, each crowded with people, and across the flatter parts of the links could be seen seven or eight separate armies moving against a background of glittering cars in the car parks. Crackles of applause broke out like rifle fire here, there and everywhere. It was impossible for any one to see much and reports generally were untrue.

Dutra Is Overwhelmed.

Abe Mitchell, who, his friends hope, will win his first championship this year, was the hero of the British team, beating the massive Olin Dutra by the day's widest margin, 9 and 8. From the eleventh, where he was 3 down, he won every hole to go to lunch 5 up. After losing the first hole in the afternoon he had another string of five victories to be 9 up on the bewildered American.

A huge mob followed Hagen and Lacey, one of the key matches. Lacey fought back well to square the match in the afternoon at the thirteenth. But Hagen's finishing power again was in evidence. He went ahead again to be 1 up at the fifteenth. Young Lacey made a terrible mess of the sixteenth, taking four to hole out from fifty or sixty yards. That settled it, and Hagen won at the next hole by 2 and 1.

Other victories for America were scored by Horton Smith and Craig Wood. Smith, after gaining a 5-hole lead on Charles Whitcombe in the morning round, played grimly in the afternoon to eke out a triumph by 2 and 1.

Wood Defeats Davies.

Wood, in his first appearance in Ryder Cup singles on this side, played steadily, to turn back W. H. Davies by 4 and 3.

The two other invaders who met defeat were Leo Diegel and Paul Runyan. Runyan was brilliant in the morning with a 70, but unfortunately for him his rival, Percy Alliss, was in unbeatable form. Alliss countered with a 68, 5 under par. Although the match was close all the way in the afternoon, the Britisher finally prevailed, 2 and 1.

Diegel was able to hold his opponent, Arthur Havers, all even in the morning round, but eventually succumbed by a score of 4 and 3.

An even break in the singles today was not enough for the Americans, as they had trailed at the finish of the foursomes yesterday, 2½ to 1½.

The British now lead in the Ryder Cup series with three victories to two, including the first informal match held in 1926 and won by the British. Since that year there have been four formal tests, with each country twice victorious.

June 28, 1933

Times Wide World Photo.

Gene Sarazen.

SARAZEN TRIUMPHS IN FINAL, 5 AND 4

Beats Goggin, San Francisco Golfer, to Capture P. G. A. Title at Milwaukee.

CLOSE DUEL IN MORNING

Victor, Only 1 Up Despite His Sub-Par 69, Widens Margin in Afternoon Round.

By The Associated Press.

MILWAUKEE, Wis., Aug. 13.—Storming over the fairways and greens of the Blue Mound Club with magic irons and a putter that routed par by four shots, Gene Sarazen won the national professional golf championship for the third time in his illustrious career today. He submerged the stout-hearted Willie Goggin of San Francisco, 5 and 4.

Sarazen's triumph, clinched by a great afternoon finish after the 200-pound, 6-foot professional of a municipal golf course had held him to a single hole advantage after a hard battle in the morning, came exactly ten years after he won his last P. G. A crown. He captured that by beating Walter Hagen in a memorable thirty-eight-hole overtime match at Pelham.

The victory of Sarazen not only assured him of escaping a shut-out in major championship competition this year after his open conquests of the United States and Great Britain in 1932, but it gave him more satisfaction than any other title.

Receives $1,000 Prize.

"Pretty good for a washed-up golfer," he said with his cocksure victory smile as he received possession of the cup and first prize money of $1,000 for the third time.

His reference to a "washed-up" golfer referred to the blast fired by Tommy Armour of Chicago before the tournament in which he said Sarazen was "all washed up" as a championship contender for threatening to pass up the big show of American professional golf.

That remark by Armour fired a greater competitive spirit in the jaunty little ex-caddy from New York. All week, as he romped on his way to the crown, dropped by Olin Dutra of Los Angeles, he clenched his fists and said he was going to win.

Goggin, who arose from the ranks of golf's unknowns this week in his march to the final, gave Sarazen a great battle this morning, only to fade in the afternoon before a charging gallery of 5,000 spectators.

Only 1 up at noon despite a 69, one under par, Sarazen came right back with even better golf and held Goggin to a one-hole victory as he picked up five. Then he clinched the struggle by matching a birdie 4 on the thirty-second green with the aid of a trusty putter. He required only fifty-one putts for the thirty-two holes.

But for a pair of three-putt greens, Goggin would have led Sarazen instead of trailing him at the end of the morning 18, which saw both hooking wildly from the tee frequently and strolling through the rough.

Sarazen started his victory march on the second hole as Goggin dubbed a niblick shot and lost the hole with a 5. They played evenly until the sixth, but there Goggin squared the duel by holing a forty-foot putt down a treacherous incline for a birdie 3.

Sarazen bounded 1 up on the short eighth. His putter responded on an eight-footer for a deuce. Goggin evened it up again on the 400-yard tenth by parking a mashie shot from 120 yards three feet high for a birdie 3.

Hits Great Spoon Shot.

Three putts by Goggin on the thirteenth sent Gene 1 up again, but back came Goggin to square it for the third and last time with a great spoon shot on the fourteenth. It carried his ball 225 yards over the traps and on the green to produce an ultimate birdie 4.

Gene drilled in a birdie 3 and a par 3 on the next two, hauling his colors up to stay. He gallantly overlooked a dead stymie on the seventeenth hole to concede a half to his stout-hearted rival.

Willie's last threatening salute came on the home green, where he smashed a 200-yard approach seven feet from the cup for a birdie 3, trimming Sarazen's lead to only one hole.

Goggin's only winning hole in the afternoon came on the twenty-fifth, another birdie 3 produced by a fifteen-foot putt. That, however, came after Gene had won three of the first five holes with sub-par golf.

Sarazen ended the match in brilliant fashion with a pair of birdies. Four up at the three-quarter turn and playing for halves on the next three in par, he arched a spectacular approach for the rough to only three feet of the pin and sank his putt for a 3.

Has Chance for an Eagle.

On the final hole, Goggin, tossing all caution to the winds, hit a remarkable wood shot more than 200 yards. It sent his ball ten feet past the cup to give him a chance for an eagle. Sarazen, short with his second, rolled his approach six feet beyond the cup and sank it for a half in 4.

THE CARDS WITH PAR.

```
                        Par.
Out .........4 4 4 3 4 4 4 3 3—35
In ..........4 4 3 4 5 4 3 4 4—35—70
            Morning Round.
Out—
Sarazen .....4 4 3 4 4 4 2 4—34
Goggin ......4 5 3 4 3 4 3 4—35
    Sarazen, 1 up.
In—
Sarazen .....4 4 4 4 5 3 3 4 4—35—69
Goggin ......3 4 4 5 4 4 4 4 3—35—70
    Sarazen, 1 up.
            Afternoon Round.
Out—
Sarazen .....4 4 4 3 4 4 3 4—34
Goggin ......5 4 5 3 4 4 3 4 5—37
    Sarazen, 4 up.
In—
Sarazen .....4 4 3 4
Goggin ......4 4 3 4 4
    Sarazen wins, 5 and 4.
```

August 14, 1933

Golf Decreed a National Sport by Nazis; Club Fees Are Limited to 2 Marks a Year

By The Associated Press.

WIESBADEN, Germany, Feb. 19.—Golf, by Nazi decree, is to be a national sport of Germany.

Acting under orders from Berlin, Karl Henkel, chief of the German Golf Clubs Unions, and Gustav Schaefer, leader of the Gymnastics and Sports Association, announced plans to popularize the royal and ancient game and bring it within the price-reach of the lowliest German.

New and better golf courses are to be built, Herr Henkel said; the price of equipment is to be lowered and membership in golf clubs limited to two marks a year for adults and one mark for juniors under 18 years of age.

A national tournament is to be held May 10, Ascension Day, open to all amateur men and women players, and a full program of international matches, juvenile championships, professional and mixed championships will be drawn up for later in the year.

All that remains now is for some professor to give the Germans a golfing vocabulary. The game has never been as popular in Germany as in many other countries, its two oldest tournaments going back only to 1907. During the war the game almost went out of existence and to the man in the street it is almost a complete mystery.

The 1933 Golfers' Handbook lists only forty-two golf clubs in Germany as compared with an estimated 5,800 in the United States, and some 2,000 in England and Scotland. In addition, the United States and Great Britain are dotted with municipal and semi-public courses.

February 20, 1934

SMITH, WITH 284, WINS BY A STROKE

Posts 72 on Final Round of Augusta Golf—Wood Is Second With 285.

JONES GETS 72 FOR 294

Bobby Denies Plan to Return to Title Play—Runyan and Burke Card 286.

PAR FOR THE COURSE.
By The Associated Press.

Hole.	Yards.	Par.	Hole.	Yards.	Par.
1........	430	4	10........	400	4
2........	515	4	11........	525	5
3........	150	3	12........	350	4
4........	480	5	13........	190	3
5........	425	4	14........	440	4
6........	485	5	15........	185	3
7........	145	3	16........	340	4
8........	400	4	17........	500	5
9........	420	4	18........	420	4
Total..	3,350	36	Total..	3,350	36

Grand totals—Yardage, 6,700; par 72.

Special to THE NEW YORK TIMES.

AUGUSTA, Ga., March 25.—There was a long roar late today as a four-foot putt dropped on the home green at the Augusta National Club for a par 72 and Horton Smith stood an all and grinned. He had won the masters' invitation golf tournament and the $1,500 first prize with a score of 284 for seventy-two holes.

The tall Missourian, pro at the Oak Park Club at Chicago, had held up under tremendous pressure put on him by Craig Wood's 285, posted early in the day, and Billy Burke's 286, which was in just ahead of him.

Later Paul Runyan of White Plains, N. Y., returned a 71 for a total of 286 to tie Burke for third.

In a tie for thirteenth place was Bobby Jones, grand-slam champion of 1930, who returned to competition for this tournament. Jones finished with a par 72, his second in as many days, for a total of 294, ten strokes behind the winner.

Lowest Since 1927.

Not since 1927 at Oakmont, when he finished eleventh, has Bobby been so far down the list.

But at that he found himself, after four years without competition, in a tie with such noted linksmen as Densmore Shute, the British open champion, and Walter Hagen, twice national open and four times British open champion.

Jones began the tournament erratically, his wood and heavy iron game as steady as ever but weak on his putting and chipping. He scored 76, 74, 72, 72, even par on the last thirty-six holes.

Jones, finishing the tournament, congratulated the winner, who was the last man to defeat him in open competition, and then announced that he was not returning to competition in any national event.

The report had been that Jones, finding his game not to his liking, would come back to the national open at Merion this Summer.

Bobby Tells His Plans.

These rumors flew like wildfire about the course the last two days. Sought out in the clubhouse after the tournament had ended, Bobby emphatically denied the report.

"I have no idea of returning to open competition," he said. "I hope to have this masters' tournament an annual affair and I will limit my competition to playing in it for the fun I get out of it."

Charlie Yates, a fellow townsman of Bobby's, who has twice qualified in the national amateur, was the low amateur in the tournament, scoring 76, 72, 77, 72—297.

He was nine strokes ahead of George T. Dunlap Jr., the national amateur champion, and fourteen strokes ahead of C. Ross Somerville of Canada, the national amateur champion of 1932. Walter Emery, the national intercollegiate champion, had 319.

Spectacular Shot by Wood.

Craig Wood's 285, which brought him second money, was in by noon. He had shot a rather remarkable round. His 4 on No. 1 was spectacular.

Wood steered his tee shot into the pines on the right. His out shot struck a tree and bounded far back into the forest. His third dropped within a foot of the cup, which was 150 yards away, and he holed out for his par.

Ed Dudley, the resident professional, duplicated his opening-day score of 74 and this wiped out, in some measure, the gain derived from his 69 of Friday and his 71 yesterday. He finished in fifth place with 288.

Horton Smith drove in this tournament better than ever before in his career. He was using a club strange to him, a Bobby Jones model driver borrowed from Runyan the day the tournament began. He knew what he had to do to win today and his performance, under this pressure, was highly creditable. Smith felt that he had a chance when he had a par at No. 9 and a birdie at the par-4 tenth.

Makes Difficult Putt.

He consistently had played those two holes in poor fashion. Today his second shot at the ninth was in the trap in front of the green. A half-explosion shot sent him ten feet past the cup. It was a downhill putt and one which necessitated a breaking twist, but he made it.

Smith was one under par when he went to the fourteenth green. Near the green with his second, he chipped over a hazard and then missed a four-foot putt to wipe out the advantage of his birdie on the tenth.

Smith now needed even par to beat Wood and one over par to tie. He went one over on the fifteenth, a par-3 hole. He was too anxious on his tee shot and had a long down-hill putt. His approach putt left him a four-footer, which he missed.

His cause appeared in danger, but the Missourian began to fight back. On the sixteenth he got his par with a good putt.

Smith's chances appeared to be lost on the seventeenth when a seventy-five-yard approach pitch on the third shot failed to run as far as he expected and left him with a ten-foot putt. But he rammed it home for a birdie 4. It was a dramatic moment.

The eighteenth saw him blast a long shot from the tee, a tremendous wallop, and then pitch to within twenty-five feet of the pin. He was a bit short with his putt and left himself a four-footer.

Drops Vital Putt.

It meant the difference between victory and a tie. But Smith, after studying the lie coolly, dropped it in for the 284, which gave him a 1-stroke margin over Wood.

"I feel that I am back on my game after three years of trying," said Smith when it was over.

Smith never has won a major tournament. His victory today probably is his greatest one. He beat Bobby Jones at Savannah in 1930 by one stroke, but the next week he lost at Augusta to Bobby, the margin being thirteen strokes.

The tragic figure of the day was Burke, 1931 open champion. His score with a little luck, would have been a 283, and the first place money his. On the sixteenth, seventeenth and eighteenth greens Burke's putts hung so close on the lip of the cup that the crowd each time yelled for him to wait for a breeze to blow the ball in.

Each time the ball seemed to be looking down into the cup. There was a wind blowing, but it never seemed to strike the ball. Each time Burke was forced to tap the ball in.

If just two of them had dropped, he would have had a tie, had three of them fallen, he would have been the winner. But that is golf.

Runyan in Brave Finish.

Runyan, the pre-tournament favorite, along with Jones, scored 74, 71, 70, 71—286. He finished strongly today, but a first nine of one over par hurt his chances.

Hagen, again paired with Jones was erratic, along with Bobby. Both had poor first nines, Bob with 37, Walter with 40. Jones was three over par on the first three holes. Hagen two over.

Jones rallied for a 35 coming in but the best Hagen could do after three rounds of 71, 76, 70 was a 77. He finished just out of the first twelve sharing in the money.

The money winners besides Smith were Wood, $800; Burke and Runyan, $550 each; Dudley, $400; Willie Macfarlane, $300; Harold McSpaden, Al Espinosa, Jimmy Hines and Mac Smith, $175 each; Mortie Dutra and Al Watrous, $100 each.

The tournament was a tremendous success. The course, modeled after several in England, tested the players very well.

Ties Record with 69.

McSpaden, Kansas City pro, shot a 69 today to equal the competitive course record. His 69 was the third under 70 during the tournament. Ed Dudley and Craig Wood also had 69s previously.

Tremendous crowds tramped after Bobby Jones on each round, with scores advising him, slapping his back, asking questions, urging him on. It was a wonder the Georgian was able to play as well as he did.

March 26, 1934

OLIN DUTRA SCORES 293 TO WIN IN U. S. OPEN GOLF; SARAZEN A STROKE BACK

FINISH IS SPECTACULAR

Coast Ace, Eight Strokes Behind, Shoots 71 and 72 to Take Title.

THREE DEADLOCK AT 295

Cruickshank, Cox and Cooper Finish in Tie for Third Place at Merion Club.

RESULT A GREAT UPSET

Sarazen, Pace-Setter at Three-quarter Mark, Among Favorites to Falter.

By WILLIAM D. RICHARDSON.
Special to THE NEW YORK TIMES.

ARDMORE, Pa., June 9.—Olin Dutra, massively-constructed Californian, won the thirty-eighth national open golf championship today by playing his last two rounds on the wind-swept Merion Cricket Club course in 71 and 72, only three strokes over par figures. His total for the seventy-two-hole test was 293, giving him the title by a stroke.

Gene Sarazen, twice a winner in the event, wound up in second place with 294, a disastrous 7, three strokes above par, on the treacherous No. 11 hole, robbing him of the title and enabling the 230-pound Californian to coast home.

Not even considered in the running when the last round started, Dutra, playing with W. Lawson Little, the British amateur champion, as the last pair in the field of sixty-four players, went the majority of the way unaccompanied by any gallery.

It was not until he was three holes from the finish that the huge gallery, following the fortunes and misfortunes of the various contenders, became aware of the fact that Dutra had played himself into a position where he could scarcely lose.

Wins Despite Putting Lapses.

As it was, he won in spite of two three-putt greens at the finish. Coming up to the last hole of the long grind, Dutra was fully conscious of the fact that he could take a 5, one over par on the hole and still win. His drive, although far behind the gigantic wallop of his long-hitting partner, was well placed and he reached the green safely with his second shot.

Just on the front edge of the green, fully forty feet away from the pin and fame, Dutra played cautiously and with good judgment. He didn't go for the hole and was four feet short of it after his first putt. He then trickled the next one up beside the hole for an easy 5.

Two of the three contenders, Little Bobby Cruickshank of Richmond, Va., and Wiffy Cox of Dyker Beach in Brooklyn, finished in a tie for third place with Lighthorse Harry Cooper of Chicago, their totals being 295. Macdonald Smith of Nashville and Billy Burke of Cleveland tied for sixth with 296.

Perfect Spot for an Upset.

Dutra, whose forebears were among the first Spanish settlers of the Monterey Peninsula in California, was in a perfect position to win the championship in the spectacular manner that he did.

Starting the final round of the tournament with a total of 221, he was in fourth place through his great third round of 71. He had been far back, eight strokes behind the pace-setter, at the start of the final 36 holes.

Although he was the winner of the National P. G. A. crown in 1932 and also the Metropolitan of that same year, he was not considered as having even the remotest chance of overhauling the leaders. It was all well and good to play one such round as he had, but to tack another on it was believed to be impossible.

For one thing there was even more wind in the afternoon than in the morning and for another the strain would probably be too great.

The championship, according to all the best minds, lay among Sarazen, now leading the field as a result of the 73 he made in the

Times Wide World Photo.
OLIN DUTRA WITH TROPHY.

morning, and closely pursued by Cruickshank and Cox. Sarazen's total going into the final round was 218. Cruickshank, falling off badly in the crucial third round, which it took him 77 strokes to play, was 219 and Cox, coming up with a 74, was 220.

Leaders Have Slipped Before.

By now the race seemed to be among those three and those three only. While it was generally admitted that past events had proved that leaders can slip or even sometimes collapse on the last round of an event on which so much is at stake, it seemed impossible that all three of the leaders would slip badly enough to be caught.

Long before any of the leaders went out to play the final round in a light spattering of rain that failed to materialize, Cooper, who lost the title to Tommy Armour after a play-off at Oakmont in 1927, posted a 71 to give him a grand total of 295. At that he had finished three strokes above par on the last four holes.

When Cruickshank and Cox arrived at the turn in the afternoon the former, having played the first half of the final round in 37, one over par, was leading his rival by two strokes, Bobby's sixty-three hole total being 256. Shortly afterward, when Sarazen came along to the same point, he and Cruickshank were tied and when Dutra arrived at the half-way mark he was still three strokes back of the two leaders.

It was to be a race to the finish, all right, with every possibility of a tie and a play-off tomorrow afternoon.

Sarazen Falters on No. 11.

The No. 11 hole, the hole on which Bobby Jones finished off Gene Homans in winning the national amateur championship here in 1930, decided the fate of Sarazen, and the one after that wrote finis to the prospects of Cox, the former sailor from Brooklyn.

Playing the eleventh, Sarazen, still tied with Cruickshank for the lead, received a jolt even more severe than the one he got in the British open a year ago. Inclined toward wildness in playing his tee shots, Gene selected the worst possible hole on the course to hit a bad one.

His ball, badly hooked, landed in the creek, forcing him to drop out and not only lose a stroke but have a difficult shot left to the green. After he had dropped his ball, he had almost the same type of shot to play as he had yesterday when he hooked to the same place but not in the water. Yesterday he got a birdie 3; today he took a 7.

The shot, not perfectly executed, was pulled, went through the branches of a tree and dropped in the rough, short of the green. A good recovery might have earned him a 5, but the recovery was not good. His ball trickled over the back of the green and lodged in the rough from where he chipped back four feet short and missed the putt.

Plays Six Holes in Par.

It was a heart-breaking blow for Gene at that stage of the championship, but even then he fought as only he can. Playing the next six holes in even par, Sarazen came to the last hole with a 4 for 293. If he had made it, the championship's ending might have been different from what it was, but he didn't, taking a 5 for 294 to edge out Cruickshank, Cox and Cooper.

On the same hole that Sarazen went amiss, Cruickshank had a "break" that he should have capitalized. His second shot to the No. 11 hole was poorly hit, and his ball, landing in the creek that runs in front of the green, sent up a high splash of water. A groan from the huge gallery following him, and rooting hard for either Bobby or Wiffy to win, turned into a wild cheer as the ball bounced up onto the green. It had hit a rock and been saved from its watery grave.

"That's the break Cruickshank needs," some one in the gallery said. "He's destined to win now."

Instead of being credited with a 6, as it appeared he would when the ball made its splash, Cruickshank got a 4 and he was now leading Cox by two strokes with seven holes to go.

Beginning of the End.

But Bobby, twice thwarted in his effort to win the championship, once getting into a play-off and then losing to Jones, had begun to slip. His drive to the next hole landed in the rough near where the fairway bends to the right. His next went into a bunker on the right and he missed an eight-foot putt for his 4 after playing a fine recovery out of the sand.

That was the beginning of the end so far as Cruickshank was concerned.

Only twice in the next six holes was he able to make a par. He began slipping on the No. 15, where he had a 5, and kept slipping for the next two holes.

Just as the No. 11 hole was a Waterloo for Sarazen, so was the No. 12 hole for Cox. His chance for the championship vanished right at that point when a pushed tee shot went into the trees and landed in the rough, just outside the woods.

His next shot from the rough deserved a better fate than it got. The ball, well hit, landed on the sloping green, well below the hole, and kept bouncing and running until it rolled over the green, down into the road out of bounds.

His second ball almost did the same thing and he took a 6. Although he finished in masterful fashion, playing the last six holes in one over par figures, the best he was able to get was the tie for third.

Dutra Goes Out in 38.

By the time the others had passed the turn, Dutra, the winner, was playing the ninth hole. A 4 there put him out in 38, and he was still three strokes behind. By holing a seven-foot putt for a 3 on the No. 10 hole, he picked up one shot on them and by the time he had passed the fourteenth hole he was all even with Cruickshank, a stroke ahead of Sarazen and two ahead of Cox.

Where he really clinched the title was on the No. 15 hole. Fully cognizant of the situation confronting him and the opportunity that lay ahead, he hit a tremendous drive to the hole that perches up in the corner of the Merion property, following it up with a pitch that dropped over the yawning bunker on the right and stopped twelve or fifteen feet from the flag. He got that one down for a birdie 3 and by doing so jumped two strokes ahead of Cruickshank and Sarazen.

The only question now was whether or not he would hold out. There is terrible pressure on a man in the spot he was in, but if he felt any it was not apparent from the way he played the quarry hole.

His drive was perfectly placed and he sent a No. 2 iron shot up on the green, the ball falling limply on the front edge and just crawling up to the top of the second elevation. His next putt was a poor one and it left him six or eight feet from the hole, but he got it down and the championship was his beyond all question.

By now Sarazen was home with 294 and Dutra could putt his way in and beat that. As it eventually turned out he needed all the margin he had, but it seemed as if he took no gamble on the two finishing holes.

After a fine, low-flying wood shot to the No. 17 green, his ball stopped short, rolling back into the gully in the front side. He was left with a long approach putt, which he rolled up within a yard and missed.

Where a 3 there would have left him in the comfortable position of knowing that he could take 6 on the last hole and still win, now a 5 was required. There was never

Cards in Merion Golf Tourney

THIRD ROUND.

GENE SARAZEN.										
Out	5	5	2	6	5	4	4	3	3	—37
In	3	4	4	3	4	5	5	3	5	—36—73—218
BOBBY CRUICKSHANK.										
Out	4	5	4	5	5	5	4	5	3	—40
In	4	4	4	3	4	4	5	4	5	—37—77—219
WIFFY COX.										
Out	3	6	3	5	4	5	4	4	4	—38
In	4	5	4	3	4	4	4	4	4	—36—74—220
OLIN DUTRA.										
Out	4	5	3	5	4	4	3	4	4	—36
In	4	4	4	3	4	4	4	3	5	—35—71—221
RALPH GULDAHL.										
Out	4	4	3	5	4	4	5	4	2	—35
In	4	4	5	3	5	3	5	2	4	—35—70—221
BILLY BURKE.										
Out	4	4	3	6	5	6	5	4	3	—40
In	3	5	4	3	5	4	4	3	6	—37—77—224
HARRY COOPER.										
Out	3	5	4	5	5	5	4	4	3	—38
In	4	5	4	3	4	4	5	3	4	—36—74—224
LEO DIEGEL.										
Out	5	6	3	5	4	4	4	4	3	—38
In	5	4	5	3	6	5	4	4	4	—40—78—225
HORTON SMITH.										
Out	4	5	3	5	4	4	4	4	4	—37
In	5	6	5	4	5	5	4	4	4	—42—79—226
MACDONALD SMITH.										
Out	4	7	3	5	6	5	4	4	3	—41
In	4	5	4	3	5	4	4	3	5	—37—78—226
JOHNNY REVOLTA.										
Out	4	6	4	4	4	4	4	6	3	—39
In	4	4	5	3	6	4	4	4	4	—38—77—226
ZELL EATON.										
Out	5	5	3	4	4	4	4	4	3	—36
In	4	5	5	3	5	5	5	5	5	—42—78—227
JIMMY HINES.										
Out	4	4	4	7	4	6	3	3	3	—38
In	4	5	4	3	5	5	4	4	5	—39—77—227
RODNEY BLISS Jr.										
Out	5	6	3	4	4	4	8	4	5	—43
In	4	5	4	3	5	5	5	3	5	—39—82—229

THIRD ROUND.

TOM CREAVY.										
Out	5	6	3	5	4	4	5	4	3	—39
In	4	7	4	3	5	4	5	3	4	—39—78—233
JOHNNY GOODMAN.										
Out	4	7	4	5	4	5	5	4	4	—42
In	4	4	4	4	6	5	6	4	4	—41—83—236

FOURTH ROUND.

OLIN DUTRA.										
Out	4	5	3	5	4	5	4	4	4	—38
In	3	4	4	3	4	3	4	4	5	—34—72—293
GENE SARAZEN.										
Out	4	5	4	5	4	4	4	5	3	—38
In	4	7	4	2	5	4	4	3	5	—38—76—294
HARRY COOPER.										
Out	4	7	3	5	4	3	4	3	2	—35
In	4	4	4	2	4	5	4	4	5	—36—71—295
WIFFY COX.										
Out	4	5	2	6	4	5	5	4	3	—38
In	4	4	6	3	4	4	4	3	5	—37—75—295
BOBBY CRUICKSHANK.										
Out	4	5	4	5	4	4	4	4	3	—37
In	4	4	5	3	5	5	5	3	5	—39—76—295
BILLY BURKE.										
Out	4	5	3	5	5	3	4	3	3	—35
In	4	5	4	4	4	5	4	3	4	—37—72—296
MACDONALD SMITH.										
Out	4	6	3	4	4	4	4	4	3	—36
In	3	4	4	3	5	3	4	3	5	—34—70—296
TOM CREAVY.										
Out	3	5	3	5	4	4	4	3	3	—34
In	3	3	4	3	4	4	4	2	5	—32—66—299
RALPH GULDAHL.										
Out	3	8	3	5	4	5	4	3	4	—39
In	4	5	5	3	4	4	5	4	5	—39—78—299
JIMMY HINES.										
Out	4	6	4	5	4	4	4	4	3	—38
In	4	4	4	3	4	5	4	2	4	—34—72—299
JOHNNY REVOLTA.										
Out	4	5	3	5	4	4	4	4	3	—36
In	3	4	4	3	5	5	4	4	5	—37—73—299

PAR FOR THE COURSE.

Hole.	Yards.	Par.	Hole.	Yards.	Par.
1	360	4	10	335	4
2	555	5	11	378	4
3	195	3	12	400	4
4	595	5	13	133	3
5	425	4	14	443	4
6	435	4	15	395	4
7	360	4	16	445	4
8	367	4	17	230	3
9	185	3	18	458	4
Total	3,477	36	Total	3,217	34

Grand total—6,694 yards; par 70.

much doubt of his ability to get that. Again he drove perfectly and so far, even against the wind, that he could use an iron for his second shot and still reach the green.

That is what he took and his ball dropped short of the green and rolled upon the front edge.

With three putts for the title he took no foolish chances and made no attempt to be spectacular. Two putts left his ball within inches of the hole and he tapped it into the cup to become the new national open champion, supplanting Johnny Goodman, the Omaha amateur who outstripped the professionals last year.

Creavy Shoots a 66.

So uncertain and breathlessly exciting was the finish to today's championship that even the sensational finish of Mac Smith and Bill Burke and the record-breaking accomplishment of Tom Creavy, Albany pro and former P. G. A. champion, were lost in the shuffle.

Creavy broke the record for the Merion course with a round of 66, a figure that equalled Sarazen's finishing round in the championship which he won at Fresh Meadow in 1932. That score constituted a championship record at the time and now Creavy is a coholder.

Smith, too far behind after the third round to be anywhere in the running for the title, finished with a 70, while Burke, winner of the 72-hole championship play-off against George Von Elm at Toledo in 1931, came strong at the finish with a 72 that put him up with the leaders.

Sarazen Goes to Front.

With the third round completed about 3 o'clock in the afternoon, Sarazen had wrested the lead from Cruickshank by scoring a 73 to make his fifty-four-hole total 218. The little Scot, struggling most of the time, finished three over par on the last three holes to bring his score up to 77, making his three-round total 219.

Cox, in third position, four strokes behind Cruickshank at the end of the second round, held that place as a result of his 74. He was two strokes back of Sarazen and one behind Cruickshank.

Two others had elevated themselves into a contending position with spectacular rounds of 70 and 71. They were Guldahl, the man who chased Johnny Goodman to the last green at North Shore a year ago, and Dutra.

Both were well out of the running when the day's play started, Guldahl being well back with his thirty-six-hole score of 151 and Dutra only one stroke better off. The former, however, equaled the par of the course in a brilliant round to jump him over the heads of all but the three leaders. They were tied for fourth with totals of 221, three strokes ahead of any one else.

Cooper, dashing young Chicago professional who started eight strokes behind Cruickshank as he began his third round, returned a 74 to make his fifty-four-hole score 224 and tied with Billy Burke, former national open champion, at that notch.

Only two others in the field appeared to have even an outside chance at this stage of the proceedings, Diegel and Johnny Golden, the former dropping back by taking a 78 and the latter holding his own, but gaining no ground with a 74.

It was still an unconclusive championship, which left everything up to the last round.

The only thing that had been decided by the third eighteen holes of play was that the last remote chances of Horton Smith, Diegel and Rodney Bliss, young Omaha amateur, all of whom were in a position to strike when the round started, had disappeared and that they could be dismissed from mind. Others now out of the race included Kirkwood, Macdonald Smith and young Ciuci, now too far back to have any hope of catching up.

The three leaders began their third round not only bunched together so far as scores went but also in their starting times. Cruickshank, playing with Cox, was only six pairs ahead of Sarazen, making it possible to keep pretty good track of what they were accomplishing.

Cox Starts With Birdie.

Cruickshank began by almost getting a birdie 3 on the first hole, his ball just rimming the cup. Cox actually got a 3 there, and he was now within three strokes of his partner. But he gave the stroke back on the second hole when he got into trouble off the tee and took a 6 while Bobby was making a spectacular 5. Cruicky was in a bunker on the left, twice in the rough between there and the green, yet got on and down in one putt.

Cox picked up two strokes on the next three holes. He got a par on the short third, where Bobby took a 4 after getting into the long grass, a great 5 on the long third despite a poor pitch shot into the bunker behind the green, and a 4 on the fifth. Cruickshank had an orthodox 5 on the fourth, but three-putted the fifth for a 5.

Between there and the turn they played all even, Cruickshank taking a 5 on the eighth to Cox's par, but getting a par on the ninth, where Cox missed a short putt after coming out of a bunker to within a yard of the hole.

For a moment it looked as if Cruickshank was in for serious trouble playing the eighth hole. His drive just cleared a bunker on the left, leaving his ball in the rough and in a hanging lie. He just got it out, pitched his next shot over the green and then nearly holed out, his ball just missing the hole.

Picks Up Two Strokes.

Out in 38 to Cruickshank's 40, Wiffy had picked up two strokes on his partner and was only two shots behind him in all.

They came home in 36 and 37, Cox getting the 36 despite a 5 on the eleventh, where he took two strokes getting out of a bunker, and then holed a twenty-footer, and a 4 on the seventh.

Cruickshank played the first six holes in par figures and had three pars left for a 74 only to lose a stroke on each of the finishing holes, his scores being 5, 4, 5 for a 77 and a total of 218.

Sarazen, who was three strokes behind Cruickshank at the half-way point, picked them all up on the first nine, the ex-champion going out in 37. He started badly by taking a 5 on the first hole, got a great 5 on the second after being bunkered and then got himself squared away by holing a twelve-foot putt for a deuce on the third.

The fourth hole was costly, for he three-putted that green, missing a short one at the end. He added further to his discomfiture by pulling his second shot to the fifth hole into the creek that borders the fairway on the left. He had a 5 there after dropping back for a penalty of one stroke; had 4s on the next two holes, and then started a string of 3s that made it appear as if he intended to sew the championship up right there

He began by getting a 3 on the seventh. A beautifully played pitch shot that just cleared the bunker and stopped less than four feet from the pin enabled him to hole a tricky downhill putt for a birdie on the eighth. He had his par on the ninth and stuck his approach shot within easy holding distance on the tenth.

Four more pars left Gene playing for a 70 that probably would have clinched the championship by enabling him to start the final round with a four-stroke lead on the field.

The fifteenth hole cost him a 5 as did the sixteenth and eighteenth. On the sixteenth he pushed his second shot into a trap and failed to come out close enough for him to hole the next, while on the eighteenth the same thing happened.

Mrs. Vare Gains 6th Title By Vanquishing Miss Berg

Triumphs, 3 and 2, in Women's U. S. Golf Final, Ending 17-Year-Old Rival's Great Bid After Fine Recovery From Rough.

By WILLIAM D. RICHARDSON.
Special to THE NEW YORK TIMES.

HOPKINS, Minn., Aug. 31.—By finishing with two birdies, one of them for a half and the other for the match, Mrs. Edwin H. Vare Jr. of Philadelphia, the former Glenna Collett, today gained the national women's golf championship for the sixth time to set a record that may never be equaled.

It was on the thirty-fourth hole of their match at the Interlachen Country Club, scene of the 1930 national open, which Bobby Jones won, that the most proficient woman golfer America has yet produced finally defeated Miss Patty Berg, 17-year-old home-town girl, who is the darling of Minneapolis galleries, by 3 and 2.

Leading the plucky little youngster, who has been playing golf only the last four years, her attention before that being given to rougher sports, such as baseball and football, by two holes, Mrs. Vare finally staved off a closing rally by pitching out of the rough to within six feet of the pin and then holing the putt she needed to win the match.

A few minutes before the youngster had taken two holes from Mrs. Vare, reducing her lead from four holes with six to play to a point where she was only 2 up and 4 to go. Miss Berg accomplished this by some of the most accurate putting ever witnessed in a championship.

Miss Berg had just run down a ten or twelve foot putt on the thirty-third green to snatch a half from Mrs. Vare, who got home with two beautiful shots. Having the honor, the youngster played out to the right, a trifle too far, although her ball did not reach the heavy rough.

Mrs. Vare's drive was several yards ahead but in the rough also. Although she had a comparatively easy shot to the green, Miss Berg pushed her ball over the heads of persons standing around the green. Right after that Mrs. Vare pitched the ball seven feet or so from the pin, and it seemed to every one that the match was at last over.

Sinks Difficult Putt.

Miss Berg, however, had different ideas. Although she had to play her third shot from the rough, off a downward slope, and chipped a good fifteen feet past the hole, she banged the putt in, forcing Mrs. Vare to hole out in order to finish the match.

Although never a great putter, Mrs. Vare dropped this one, and the championship that appeared to be hers from the inception of the tournament actually became hers.

No gallery in recent years has ever received so many thrills as did this one of 5,000 or more persons today, especially on the last few holes of the match. There wasn't much to become excited about until the thirtieth hole, which is where Miss Berg began her rally—a comeback that threatened to bring disaster to the ex-champion, who was

winning her fifth title when Miss Berg started playing golf.

Starting at the third hole this morning, Mrs. Vare began to open ground between her and the youngster. She didn't get a substantial lead until Miss Berg made one mistake after another playing the ninth and reached the turn 2 down.

Still 4 Up at Twenty-sixth.

Gradually Mrs. Vare's lead increased until it became four holes when they finished the first eighteen. She was 4 up again after they finished the twenty-sixth hole of the match in the afternoon.

And when Miss Berg three-putted on the No. 12 green, the twenty-ninth hole of the match, to give Mrs. Vare a half she wasn't entitled to, it looked as if Miss Berg would be beaten by a big margin.

One began to feel sorry for the youngster who, after a week of sensational golf, during which she had eliminated such top-notchers as Miss Ada Mackenzie, Canadian champion, and Miss Charlotte Glutting, New Jersey champion, seemed to have run out her string.

It wasn't that she was playing badly, for she wasn't. But she wasn't quite hitting her shots the way she had hit them in her previous matches. Then, too, she was up against a golfer to whom playing in finals of the National was an old story. Moreover, Mrs. Vare was playing fine golf, scoring a 79, only one over par, in the first round and being out in 39, only one over par in the afternoon. With that kind of golf Mrs. Vare was not offering many openings.

But suddenly the match, instead

of turning into a rout, tightened to a point where there is no telling what might have happened if Mrs. Vare had not holed her putt for a 3 on the thirty-fourth green.

Miss Berg's spurt, belated as it was, started on the thirtieth hole, where, after being short of the green on her third, she played a beautiful pitch almost dead to the hole to prevent herself from going 5 down. Mrs. Vare's third was hole high, just off the edge, an almost sure 5, when the youngster looked the situation over before playing her approach.

That half seemed to inspire her, for she dropped her tee shot on the next green twenty feet from the flag and won the hole after Mrs. Vare, off to the left, putted four feet past the hole.

Mrs. Vare had all the better of it playing the 420-yard Number 14 hole, while Miss Berg was far short of the green in the same number of shots. But the persistent Patty did not merely get her half; she won the hole by dropping a 6-yard putt for as good a 4 as was ever made while her opponent, who had made a poor chip shot, took two to get down from twenty-feet.

The Minneapolis girl was only 2 down now, and there was still a chance left when she sank that putt on the thirty-third green to prolong the match.

It didn't prolong it much, however, for that iron shot by Mrs. Vare on the thirty-fourth hole spelled victory and brought her her sixth title in a career beginning in 1919 at Shawnee.

But it also emphasized the fact that Miss Berg is one of the grittiest little battlers that the game has ever seen—a girl who no doubt will win the title before many more years roll past. She has everything it takes to make a champion—the game and temperament.

Even against the kind of golf Mrs. Vare shot today, Miss Berg won one more hole than she lost playing the last sixteen of the match. Only two holes were decided in the first nine this afternoon. Miss Berg winning the first when Mrs. Vare three-putted and the champion taking the eighth with a birdie 4 when Miss Berg three-putted trying to get around a partial stymie.

Mrs. Vare got a great half on the ninth hole the second time around

the course after she pushed her tee shot into the trees. She got another half on the tenth hole when Miss Berg played a poor recovery shot after pushing an iron into the long grass below the green.

But as it turned out, the crucial hole in the match was the long No. 11, where the second shot is all uphill. If Miss Berg had not taken three putts there, missing a short one for a 5, it is doubtful whether Mrs. Vare would have won at all.

While Mrs. Vare was still 4 up there, the loss of two holes later would not matter so much. But if instead of being 2 up and 4 to play, it had been only 1 up, the memory of what happened to Miss Glutting in her defeat by Miss Berg yesterday might have had an important bearing on the match.

It was perhaps just as well that the match turned out as it did, for Mrs. Vare deserved to win and Miss Berg did all that one could expect of a girl playing in her first national.

She no doubt earned her place on the team that will go to England for the international matches next year and certainly she earned a place in the affection of every one who likes to see a real competitor in action, whether it be in golf or another field.

THE CARDS.
MORNING ROUND.

Out—
Mrs. Vare...5 5 3 5 4 4 4 4 5 5—40
Miss Berg...5 5 4 6 3 4 5 4 8—44
Mrs. Vare, 2 up.
In—
Mrs. Vare...4 5 6 3 5 4 4 4 4—39—79
Miss Berg...5 5 5 4 6 4 4 4 4—41—85
Mrs. Vare, 4 up.

AFTERNOON ROUND.

Out—
Mrs. Vare...6 4 3 5 3 4 4 4 5—39
Miss Berg...5 4 3 5 3 4 5 5 5—39
Mrs. Vare, 4 up.
In—
Mrs. Vare...5 6 5 4 5 4 3
Miss Berg...5 6 5 3 4 4 4
Mrs. Vare wins, 3 and 2.

PAR FOR THE COURSE.

Holes.	Yds.	Wo-men's Par.	Men's Par.	Holes.	Yds.	Wo-men's Par.	Men's Par.
1....	479	5	5	10....	338	4	4
2....	337	4	4	11....	452	5	5
3....	152	3	3	12....	534	5	5
4....	450	5	5	13....	185	3	3
5....	130	3	3	14....	420	4	5
6....	338	4	4	15....	405	4	5
7....	345	4	4	16....	325	4	4
8....	390	4	4	17....	220	3	4
9....	460	5	5	18....	385	4	4
Tot.3,081		37	38	Tot.3,264		36	40

Grand total—Yardage, 6,345. Men's par, 73. Women's par, 78.

September 1, 1935

MRS. GLENNA COLLETT VARE PUTTING AT INTERLACHEN.

MANERO'S RECORD-BREAKING 282 WINS U. S. OPEN GOLF

FINAL 67 CLINCHES TITLE

Dark Horse, Four Below Tourney Mark, Clips All Major Figures.

COOPER SECOND AT 284

First to Beat 20-Year Record, but Manero Rushes Past Him With New Low at Baltusrol.

GREAT ROUND FOR VICTOR

Shoots Ahead on Last 9 Holes —Clark Third With 287, Mac Smith Fourth With 288.

By WILLIAM D. RICHARDSON
Special to The New York Times.

SPRINGFIELD, N. J., June 6. — Racing from behind to set a new world's record for a major seventy-two-hole title tournament, Tony Manero, slightly built former Westchester caddie, today won the United States open championship in a manner that gave one of the largest galleries of all time a thrill such as few golfing crowds have experienced in the forty-year history of the event.

Back in a tie for fourth position, four strokes behind Light Horse Harry Cooper, the leader, going into the final round, the 31-year-old Manero produced a new Baltusrol Golf Club course record score of 67 on his final dash.

That 67, five strokes under par for the layout, made his seventy-two-hole total 282, which broke the old standard for the United States open by four strokes and clipped one from the record total for the British open. The former mark for the American open was 286, established by Charles (Chick) Evans at Minikahda in 1916 and equaled by Gene Sarazen at Fresh Meadow in 1932.

Sarazen also set the record in the British open of 1932, when he won at Sandwich with 283, a figure that Henry Cotton duplicated over the same course in 1934.

Cooper First to Better Mark

Manero, a medium-sized youth, dark of complexion, a heritage of his Italian ancestry, won the event by two strokes, leading Cooper, who was the victim of Tommy Armour in the play-off at Oakmont in 1927, after the latter had eclipsed the old record by posting a score of 284.

By finishing with a round of 72, Clarence Clark, burly Bloomfield (N. J.) pro, snatched third place with a score of 287, a total that

National Open Victor and His Wife

Times Wide World Photo.

Mr. and Mrs. Tony Manero with the trophy that the former Westchester caddie won at the Baltusrol Golf Club. His seventy-two-hole total of 282 broke the old record for the United States open by four strokes and was one better than the standard for the British open.

ordinarily would have won the championship, while the veteran Macdonald Smith of Glendale, Calif., took fourth with 288, his closing bid being a 70, which followed a 72—a great feat for a man who tied for the open title twenty-six years ago.

Ky Laffoon, whose ancestors were members of a Cherokee tribe, finished in a triple tie with Wiffy Cox, former Dyker Beach professional who is now located near Washington, and Henry Picard, Hershey (Pa.) pro, who was one of the favorites to win. Their totals were 289. After them came Ralph Guldahl of the Pacific Coast, who was second to Johnny Goodman at North Shore in 1931, and Paul Runyan, tied at 290.

The finish was a bitter experience for the English-born Cooper, who twice has seen a major title he had won snatched out of his hands at the last moment. Out at Oakmont nine years ago Armour tied him by laying a long iron shot a dozen feet or so from the hole, sinking the putt for a birdie 3 and then beating him in the play-off the next day.

Today Cooper, one of the greatest golfers of the present era, appeared to have things his own way until Manero, a "dark horse" if ever there was one in advance of the tournament, came along to pass him by playing one of the greatest pressure rounds ever witnessed in the championship.

Missed Putt Costly

The missing of a putt less than a yard long on the No. 14 hole, the sixty-eighth in the championship, cost Cooper the title he so richly deserved to win. It started him on a series of mistakes that cost him two more strokes before he was through playing and might have cost him even more.

Despite the fact that Manero, hitting all his drives down the middle of the course, playing his irons like a master and putting with a beautiful touch, had reached the turn in 33, three strokes under par, Cooper still led him by two strokes at the final turn.

After three more holes the dashing Cooper, who got the name Light

Horse, from his speed in playing and walking, had further safe-guarded his lead by getting a birdie 3 on the No. 12 green. Par from there on would have made his total 281.

He got a par 4 on the No. 13 hole, almost dropping a long downhill putt from the back edge of the green into the cup for a birdie 3. A few more feet and it would have been in. It must have been disappointing not to have it drop, especially since the approach shot Cooper hit landed less than five feet from the flag-stick and had no right to jump and roll as far beyond as it did.

At that point, however, it didn't seem that it would make the slightest difference in the outcome of the championship. Cooper was playing like a champion and had been getting a champion's "breaks."

Then came the fatal No. 14, where, after pitching a superb approach shot to follow a perfect drive almost to the top of the hill, not more than ten feet beyond the cup, he putted hurriedly to the right of the hole and then missed the next. It couldn't have been a yard long.

The missing of that putt undoubtedly had a disastrous effect on the morale of a player as high strung as he is. At any rate, he pitched into the bunker at the next hole and took a 4, got his par 4 on the No. 16, had to scramble for his par 5 on the No. 17 and then took another 5, one over, on the finishing hole.

Even then almost everybody in the gallery of 3,000 or 4,000 spectators who had followed him home regarded him as the next national open champion.

But suddenly came word via the grapevine that Manero was coming along with the speed of a race horse and was certain to surpass Cooper's score. And so there was a mad chase out to where he was coming, playing with Sarazen, who was open champion in 1922 and again in 1932. Out of the race himself, little Gene proved himself something of a godfather to the lad who started his career the way he did, caddying on a Westchester course.

Thanks to the mistakes Cooper made on the No. 14 and 15 holes, Manero had the championship won by the time he came through that point on the course. By knocking a twenty-five-foot putt into the cup for a birdie 3 on the No. 13 hole, Manero picked up one stroke on Cooper there and needed to pick up only one more to be even with the Chicagoan with five holes to play.

He made that one when he pitched to within four yards and got down in two putts for a par 4 on the fourteenth hole of the round, but was still tied when he bunkered himself on the short No. 15 and took a 4, just as Cooper had done.

Sets Himself Easy Task

He forged ahead on the No. 16, the seventieth hole in the championship, when he dropped a ten-foot putt for a birdie 3, and after that the title was in the bag for him. He could finish with a 5, which is par on the No. 17, and a 5, one over, on the No. 18, and still win the crown.

There was no difficulty at all attached to his 5 on the next-to-last hole. As a matter of fact he almost got a birdie 4 there, his approach shot after two perfect woods going a dozen feet to the left, and he just missed holing out from there.

There was a long delay on the No. 18 tee and he had to wait while two other pairs drove off. It was a tantalizing wait for a golfer with as much at stake and one so highly strung, but if it affected his nerves he gave no sign of it when he finally hit his drive. The ball fairly whistled as it left the clubhead and split the fairway right in middle.

And then, with some 12,000 or 15,000 spectators forming an oval that extended from behind him to the back edge of the green almost 200 yards away, the man who will be known as champion for at least another year, successor of Sam Parks Jr., who was eliminated yesterday when the field was cut, hit a screaming iron shot that just managed to get over the bunker on the left-hand side of the fairway, and left his ball on the magic carpet fifteen yards or so from the pin, but as safe as Gibraltar, unless he were to four-putt.

Firmly Hit Putt Drops

There was no chance of that happening after he putted six feet short of the pin and rammed the next one in with such determination and confidence that it almost broke the back of the cup.

The race for the title narrowed down after the first three rounds to Cooper, leading with 211; Victor Ghezzi, Deal professional, who was two strokes behind; Denny Shute, former British open champion, who was three strokes in the rear, and two quartets tied at 215 and 216. Among those at 215 were Picard, Laffoon, Clark and Manero, while in the group a stroke behind were Guldahl, Herman Barron, Ray Mangrum and Charley (Chuck) Kocsis of the University of Michigan, Big Ten champion.

It wasn't long after the start of the last round, however, that the race was between Cooper and Manero. Shute took 38 to go out and blew up completely when he had a 7 on the No. 11 hole. Ghezzi, who started slipping in the morning, needed 40 to get out, while Picard, Laffoon and Clark were unable to close the gap.

A Native New Yorker

Picard gave his supporters a ray of hope when he went out in 35, but he took 39 to come in. One by one the others fell, leaving the field clear first to Cooper and then to Manero.

The new champion was born in New York City on April 4, 1905, and has been a coming figure in the golf world ever since he started his tournament career by winning the Catalina open in 1929. The following year he won the Pasadena and Glens Falls opens, his score in the last-mentioned event, 276, being one of the lowest ever made in a seventy-two-hole event.

He was victor in the Westchester open in 1932, when he was at the Fairview Country Club. Some of his other links triumphs include the General Brock Hotel open, the North Carolina open and the Southeast P. G. A. championship. He has been pro at the Sedgefield Country Club in Greensboro, N. C., for the last three years and barely managed to qualify for this year's open.

The end of the third round, generally considered to be the crucial phase of an open championship, found Cooper on top by a margin of two strokes. The Chicagoan, a stroke behind the two leaders, Ghezzi and Mangrum, when the field teed off this morning, produced a gorgeous round of 70, two under par, to lead the field with a total of 211.

Par for the Course

Hole.	Yards.	Par	Hole.	Yards.	Par.
1	471		10	158	3
2	423	4	11	602	5
3	186	3	12	340	4
4	390	4	13	365	4
5	385	[illegible]	14	400	4
6	439	4	15	140	3
7	216	3	16	439	4
8	538	5	17	563	5
9	346	4	18	465	4
Total	3,394	36	Total	3,472	36

Grand totals—6,866 yards; par 72.

Ghezzi, going along in great style in his first real bid for a national title, came to grief on the last three holes when he took two strokes over what par calls for. His troubles began on the sixteenth when his drive went into the rough to the right and his second caught a bunker near the green. The 5 on the seventeenth was par for the hole but on the eighteenth he took three putts from approximately fifteen yards.

Pars on two of those holes would have put him in a tie with Cooper going into the final round. As it was, he finished the third circuit in second place with a fifty-four hole total of 213.

Shute, whose brilliant 69 in the second round yesterday put him in a tie with Johnny Revolta, Picard and Cooper for third place, only a stroke away from the two leaders at the midway mark, required 73 strokes this morning and was in third place then with a score of 214, still in a commanding position to overtake Cooper in the event the flashy little Chicago star let down.

Slumps at Fifth and Sixth

The Massachusetts pro, who beat Craig Wood in the play-off for the British open crown in 1933 had two serious mishaps early in the round. They came in the form of a pair of 5s on the fifth and sixth holes. Up to there he was one under par. On the fifth his tee shot found a bunker and he was short of the green in 2. On the sixth his second shot was bunkered.

These two mistakes dropped him a stroke behind par at the turn and he finished that way after getting a birdie 4 on the long eleventh, where he dropped a twenty-foot putt and offsetting it by losing a stroke on the short fifteenth, where his tee shot was buried in a trap short of the green.

One stroke behind Shute came a quartet composed of Picard, Laffoon, Clark and Manero. Tied for third, a stroke behind the leaders at the outset this morning, Picard, the tall Hershey professional, had only a mediocre third round, taking a stroke over par on each nine for a 74, which made his three-quarter total 215. His play was unsteady and he missed five greens, was in three bunkers and was off the fairway ten times.

Laffoon, who started five strokes behind, got himself into a contending position when he produced a 70, one of the best rounds of the morning. This warrior made a sensational dash after reaching the turn in par figures. He was never over regulation figures and had birdies on the eleventh and seventeenth, where he knocked in six-foot putts.

Clark Out in 34

Clark, the New Jersey giant, made his bid on the first nine by going out in 34. He slipped by taking 5s on the thirteenth and fourteenth but came back with a birdie 2 on the fifteenth and was home in 37, one over, for a 71 which made his total 215.

After the seven leaders at the three-quarter pole came Barron, Mangrum, Guldahl and Kocsis, tied at 216; Cox and Tom Kerrigan, tied Smith, Willie Goggin, Jimmy Thomson and Gianferante, bracketed at 218, and Walter Hagen and several others in a group at 219.

Revolta, one of the heavily backed favorites, began to show signs of a general breakdown at the seventh hole. He was one under par up to there and got into a bunker which cost him a stroke. He lost another stroke on the ninth when he was bunkered near the green and missed a four-foot putt.

Back on even terms with par when he dropped a twenty-foot putt for a birdie 3 on the twelfth, he lost five strokes between there and the finish, his chief trouble coming on the seventeenth, where, in a fine position for his third shot to the green, he hooked badly. It was so poor that he even went beyond the bunker. He didn't miss it with his next shot, however. He left the ball in on his first attempt to get out and then had to get down in a single putt for his 7.

Concludes Round With 5

He concluded with a 5 and that looked like his finish, so far as the championship was concerned.

Mangrum did much the same thing. Playing with Mac Smith, the man who has brought more than one winner home in the open, the Texas product was even with par for three holes, but from then on he was constantly struggling. Over the green on his approach shot to the fifth hole, he took a 5, one over, and followed that by three-putting on the sixth. He got out in 38, two over par, but started back with five pars and one birdie, on the fourteenth, where he dropped a 5-yard putt.

A bunkered second shot cost him a stroke on the sixteenth. He was in trouble with his second on the home hole also, came out too cleanly and went over the back edge of the green, down among some bushes, from where he approached back weakly and wound up with a bad 6, which to all intents finished him as a contender for the 1936 honors.

June 7, 1936

DRASTIC CUT MADE IN GOLF EQUIPMENT

By WILLIAM D. RICHARDSON

"The game of golf shall be played with not more than fourteen clubs beginning Jan. 1, 1938."

Thus does the United States Golf Association, final ruling authority of the ga e in this country, announce one of the most drastic regulations it has ever made in the matter of implements of golfing warfare.

The announcement was made yesterday by Frank M. Hardt, secretary of the American body, who stated that the rules of golf committee of the Royal and Ancient Golf Club of St. Andrews, Scotland, is taking steps in the same direction.

In order to make the restriction effective, the preamble to the Rules of Golf has been amended to read as follows:

"The game of golf consists in a ball being played from the teeing ground into the hole by successive strokes, with clubs (not exceeding fourteen in number) and balls made in conformity with the directions laid down in the clause on 'Form and Make of Golf Clubs and Balls.'"

In giving reasons for the limitation of clubs the executive committee of the U. S. G. A. stated that it will bring relief to caddies from unfair burdens, reduce delays in play since the players will spend less time in deciding what club to use and give players who cannot afford an unlimited supply of clubs an opportunity to compete with others on a more even basis.

The question of reducing the number of clubs has been under consideration for some time, especially since the vogue was started for several wooden clubs, ranging up to five or more, and irons of various range, from the No. 1 down to the No. 9s, with many gradations for each number.

It first came to notice last year when, at the annual meeting, the executive committee noted that "it viewed with concern the growing increase in the number of clubs."

As a result of inquiries made, the announcement states, "the conclusion is supported that limiting the number of clubs will tend to re;.:re to the game individual shotm.:.:ng skill lost through the intr.:.u:tion of an excessive number of clubs in finely graduated and matched sets."

Mechanical Trend Involved

"The committee feels," the announcement goes on, "that a multiplicity of clubs tends toward a mechanization of a game, one of whose chief virtues lies in the opportunity it affords for full individual skill.

"In earlier days players sometimes changed their swings to execute varied shots. The tendency in recent years has been to change only the club.

"It was felt that, as a former president of the association said, players should not buy their shots in the professional's shop, but should develop skill by their own effort."

The reason for not making the rule effective at once, it was stated, was to give both players and manufacturers ample opportunity to make necessary adjustments.

Although there have been numerous instances of changes in the golf ball, starting with the introduction of the rubber-cored ball and ending with the adoption of the present one two years ago, and various legislation with respect to individual clubs such as the putter and the wedge, this is the first time that any legislation dealing with numbers has ever been undertaken.

It has been known for a long time, however, that the U. S. G. A. was watching with considerable alarm the gradual increase. Each year saw something new developed and added to the kit which caddies had to carry, some players loading their bags with as many as thirty clubs, including spares.

The bags of the pros were especially bulky, although gradually amateurs began to follow suit.

There developed two schools of thought, one claiming that the game, being so difficult anyway, nothing should be done to reduce the number of clubs. The contention of the other was that clubs were mechanizing the game.

It is a well-known fact that Chick Evans, one of the great masters of all time, winner of the U. S. open and amateur and eight times triumphant in the Western amateur, limited his clubs to seven or eight in number.

The ruling, naturally, will have no effect whatsoever on the ordinary golfer who does not participate in championships. So far as he is concerned, the sky has been and will continue to be the limit.

January 1, 1937

BRITISH WIN WALKER CUP FROM U. S. FOR 1ST TIME, 7-4

KYLE GOLF VICTOR

Clinches Triumph Over Americans, Beating Haas, 5 and 4

THOMSON HALTS GOODMAN

Yates, Fischer and Ward Gain U. S. Points—Ouimet Hails First British Success

By W. F. LEYSMITH
Special Cable to THE NEW YORK TIMES.

ST. ANDREWS, Scotland, June 4.—Great Britain at long last has laid the hoodoo of the Walker Cup, and Anglo-American golf will be a better game for it.

Starting with a lead of 2—1, gained in the Scotch foursomes yesterday, when one match was halved, the British team, with Cecil Ewing substituted for Harry Bentley, today won five singles matches to three by the United States, thus making a grand total of 7—4. This brought the first British victory in the series that began in 1922.

Among the heroes of this epic encounter is held to be the British selection committee, which put precedent aside and held a series of special trials, picked the team purely on merit and then turned it over to the single captaincy of John B. Beck.

Beck caused a furor last night by dropping Bentley instead of Alex Kyle from the singles line-up. It is revealed now that he did so on a hunch that Bentley had played himself out in the foursomes with young Jimmy Bruen of Ireland against Johnny Fischer and Charles Kocsis and that Kyle was just coming into his game.

Ewing's Task Made Easier

It was a masterly stroke, because with America late in the afternoon needing only the last two matches for victory and with Ewing tottering on the brink of defeat, it was the long-hitting Kyle who fired a succession of birdies at unlucky Freddie Haas to win, 5 and 4, and clinch the victory for Britain before the worst could befall her and lift a dead weight from the now drooping shoulders of Ewing.

Charles Yates, Johnny Fischer and Marvin Ward played memorable parts for the United States. Yates, the new British amateur champion, had the measure of the young Irish star almost from the first tee and won, 2 and 1; Fischer played a terrific round in the afternoon to beat Leonard Crawley, 3

and 2, in a match that at lunch time had seemed lost, and Ward, facing Frank Pennink, one of the toughest and most experienced members of the British side, let loose a tornado. He took the thirty-six hole match by 12 and 11.

When the enormous galleries that throughout the day's rainstorms had blackened the sandy slopes around the course like overcrowded bleachers at a ball game finally surged before the gray stone building of the Royal and Ancient Club, Francis Ouimet, American non-playing captain, paid his tribute in ungrudging terms.

Acts for Duke of Kent

"All good things must come to an end," he said before a crowd of 12,000. Colonel B. G. M. Skene, who was acting as deputy for the Duke of Kent, club captain, handed the cup for the first time in its history to Britain.

"I can safely say in behalf of my American playmates and the Amer-

ican people at large that we are delighted. We did our best but we weren't good enough. We faced one of the greatest golf teams which has ever been assembled.

"If you have liked us, we feel our business among you has been well worth the time."

A skirl of bagpipes and a roll of drums from a kilted Highland band drowned out his closing words as all St. Andrews started to make whoopee.

Among the many cables of congratulations that have been received from the United States was one from George H. Walker, donor of the cup.

After Kyle sealed the British triumph, Ewing made it more decisive by beating Ray Billows, 1 up. The other British points in singles today were scored by Hector Thomson of Scotland, who won from Johnny Goodman, United States amateur titleholder, 6 and 4; Charles Stowe of England, victor over Kocsis, 2 and 1, and Gordon Peters, a Scot,

who routed Reynolds Smith, 9 and 8.

With the minimum task set of winning one singles match and halving the remaining seven to retain the cup or, instead, winning five, America set out in a mizzling rain, with the new British amateur champion, Yates, pitted against Bruen.

At lunch time, with only one ond when his opponent's ball was deeply buried in the rough from a cut drive.

Kocsis had been shaky going out, but, coming home, sank long putts on the twelfth, thirteenth, fifteenth and sixteenth. He thought a twenty-footer had dropped for a birdie on the eighteenth and made a gesture of surprise when the ball wabbled around the rim and stayed out.

Ward put up one of the most extraordinary performances of the day against the English champion, Pennink, who never won a hole. Ward's first drive landed in Swilken brook. He picked up, with the loss of a stroke, pitched to the green and sank a nine-footer, rattling the Englishman so that he three-putted and lost the hole.

Seven times in this round Ward rolled three shots into two, and although Pennink was out in 37, he was four down to the American, who had the amazing score of 32. At the fourteenth Pennink missed from two feet to halve the hole, at the fifteenth Ward pitched out of a green trap and holed his putt and at the seventeenth he repeated that feat, both times for victories. Poor Pennink was so badly shaken he three-putted the eighteenth to increase Ward's margin to nine holes.

Billows had Ewing in his pocket at the fifteenth, where the Irishman, tymying himself, took three putts from five feet.

Peters wore down Smith by sheer physical strength, and the player from Texas went, somewhat crestfallen to lunch with his deficit increased to three holes after he missed a three-footer on the eighteenth.

Against Haas, Kyle did not miss a single putt under two and a half feet and the American was hard put to it to recover from a position 3 down at the turn. At the seventeenth he hit his second shot poorly —it looked as if it had been done with a driver—the ball scurried around all obstacles four feet past the pin and Haas holed it to win. He then sank a difficult seven-footer to take the eighteenth.

Cards of Walker Cup Matches
By The Associated Press.

KYLE vs. HAAS
Morning Round

Out—									
Haas	5	4	4	5	5	4	3	3	4—39
Kyle	4	5	5	4	4	4	4	2	2—36
Kyle 3 up.									
In—									
Haas	4	3	4	6	4	4	4	3—36—75
Kyle	4	3	4	4	4	4	4	4—37—72
Kyle 1 up.								

Afternoon Round

Out—									
Haas	4	4	4	5	5	4	3	5—38
Kyle	4	4	4	4	5	4	3	4—36
Kyle 3 up.								
In—								
Haas	4	4	3	5	4			
Kyle	4	3	3	4	4			
Kyle wins, 5 and 4.							

EWING vs. BILLOWS
Morning Round

Out—									
Billows	4	4	4	4	4	4	3	3	4—37
Ewing	3	6	4	4	5	4	3	4—40
Billows 1 up.								
In—								
Billows	3	3	4	5	5	4	5	4—38—75
Ewing	3	3	4	5	5	6	3	5	4—38—78
Billows 1 up.								

Afternoon Round

Out—									
Billows	5	4	4	4	5	4	3	4—37
Ewing	3	4	4	4	4	4	3	3—33
Ewing 2 up.								
In—								
Billows	4	3	3	4	3	4	5	4—35—72
Ewing	4	3	4	4	4	4	4	4—37—70
Ewing wins, 1 up.								

THOMSON vs. GOODMAN
Morning Round

Out—									
Goodman	4	4	4	5	5	4	4	3—38
Thomson	4	5	4	4	4	4	3	3—35
Thomson 3 up.								
In—								
Goodman	4	3	4	6	5	4	5	4—39—77
Thomson	4	3	4	3	4	4	4	4—34—69
Thomson 6 up.								

Out—									
Goodman	4	4	4	3	5	4	4	3—34
Thomson	4	4	4	5	3	3	3	3—33
Thomson 7 up.								
In—								
Goodman	4	3	4	4	6			
Thomson	4	4	4	5	5			
Thomson wins, 6 and 4.							

STOWE vs. KOCSIS
Morning Round

Out—									
Kocsis	5	4	4	5	4	3	4	3—37
Stowe	4	5	4	4	4	3	4	3—35
Stowe, 2 up.								
In—								
Kocsis	4	5	3	3	6	3	4	5—37—74
Stowe	4	4	5	4	5	4	5	3—39—74
Stowe, 1 up.								

Afternoon Round

Out—									
Kocsis	4	5	3	4	4	4	4	4—36
Stowe	3	3	3	5	4	3	4	4—37
Match even.								
In—								
Kocsis	3	3	6	6	4	5		
Stowe	3	3	3	4	5	4	5	
Stowe wins, 2 and 1.								

PETERS vs. SMITH
Morning Round

Out—									
Smith	4	5	5	4	4	4	4	4—39
Peters	5	5	4	4	5	3	5	3—38
Peters, 1 up.								
In—								
Smith	3	3	5	5	5	4		
Peters	4	4	4	5	4	4	4	3—37—75
Peters, 2 up.								

Afternoon Round

Out—									
Smith	4	5	4	5	4	5	4	5—40
Peters	4	4	4	4	3	4	3	4—34
Peters, 9 up.								
In—								
Smith	4							
Peters	4							
Peters wins, 9 and 8.							

YATES vs. BRUEN
Morning Round

Out—									
Yates	4	4	4	4	3	3	2	3—32
Bruen	4	4	5	4	4	3	3	3—34
Yates, 1 up.								
In—								
Yates	4	4	4	4	5	4	4	5	3—37—70
Bruen	3	4	4	5	6	4	4	5	4—39—73
Yates, 3 up.								

Afternoon Round

Out—									
Yates	4	4	4	5	4	4	4	4—37
Bruen	4	3	5	4	4	4	4	4—36
Yates, 2 up.								
In—								
Yates	4	4	4	5	4			
Bruen	5	2	4	5	4	4		
Yates wins, 2 up.								

WARD vs. PENNINK
Morning Round

Out—									
Ward	4	4	3	4	3	4	4	3—32
Pennink	5	4	4	4	4	4	3	5—37
Ward, 4 up.								
In—								
Ward	3	3	4	4	5	4	4	4—35—67
Pennink	4	3	5	5	5	4	5	5—40—77
Ward, 9 up.								

Afternoon Round

Out—							
Ward	4	4	3	6	4	4	
Pennink	4	4	5	4	6	4	5
Ward wins, 12 and 11.							

FISCHER vs. CRAWLEY
Morning Round

Out—									
Fischer	4	3	4	5	5	4	4	4—36
Crawley	4	3	4	4	6	4	4	3—36
Match even.								
In—								
Fischer	4	3	4	5	5	4	6	3—39—75
Crawley	4	4	4	3	5	4	5	3—35—71
Crawley, 4 up.								

Afternoon Round

Out—									
Fischer	4	4	3	4	4	4	3	3—33
Crawley	4	5	4	4	4	4	3	4—37
Match even.								
In—								
Fischer	3	3	3	3	5	4	4	
Crawley	4	4	4	4	5	4		
Fischer wins, 3 and 2.								

Patty Berg, often one of the Ladies' Professional Golf Association's leading money winners, had a championship career that spanned three decades.

Yates clung tenaciously to his three-hole lead through the afternoon's rainstorm until the twenty-ninth, where Bruen sank another twelve-footer down-hill for a birdie to win.

The Atlantan then hit the ball off the heel of his putter at the thirtieth, missing a chance for the hole from three feet, and after this lucky escape Bruen missed the chance of his life at the thirty-first when his body lurched as he was putting for a victory from two feet. He was on the point of cracking.

Bruen Misses Opportunity

With this gift from the gods, Yates left the thirty-second green wide open for Bruen, who again failed to take his chance, and Yates, now making no mistake, went on in steady par to clinch his victory on the thirty-fifth. Bruen had been short with every approach putt from the twelfth hole on.

Fischer's performance against Crawley in the afternoon rivals that of his compatriot, Don Moe, in the 1930 series. He won seven holes from the heavily built schoolmaster, and when the match ended at the thirty-fourth green the Ameri-

can needed two par 4s for an incoming 33. He had been 4 down when they went to lunch.

Yet, against that avalanche of 3s, Crawley did not wilt. Immediately after lunch Fischer set about pulling him back from the lead, and by the twenty-third he had the Briton's margin down to one hole. At the twenty-fourth Crawley saved himself by holing a ten-footer and on the next hole Fischer came within an ace of 3, putting with his aluminum club.

They were square at the turn and at the thirty-fourth Crawley had seen a 4-up lead vanish to 3 down. Meanwhile, Thomson had completed the demolition of Goodman and, taking the foursomes into account, the matches stood at 3-all.

Kocsis In Battle

Then along came Kocsis. He had squared his match with Stowe at the twenty-fourth, where both were in the heather, but Kocsis played a better shot out and held his opponent in check until the twenty-seventh.

June 5, 1938

Patty Berg Vanquishes Mrs. Page For National Golf Title, 6 and 5

Minneapolis Girl, 20 Years Old, Dethrones Champion, Shooting Fine Game in Face of Wind—2 Up After 18 Holes

By WILLIAM D. RICHARDSON
Special to THE NEW YORK TIMES.

WILMETTE, Ill., Sept. 24.—Little Patty Berg's fourth attempt to lift the women's national golf crown was successful today.

Playing invincible golf, the best she has shot all week, the 20-year-old Minneapolis redhead avenged the setback she received from Mrs. Estelle Lawson Page of Chapel Hill, N. C., in the final of the championship at Memphis last year by dethroning her opponent, 6 and 5, over the thirty-six-hole route at the Westmoreland Country Club.

Despite the fact that the course was swept by a strong northeast wind that had a chill in it and made the going the roughest it has been all week, Miss Berg played the first eighteen holes in women's par to be 2 up, went out in 37, only two over men's par, in the afternoon and was three strokes under women's par for the day's play when the match ended on the No. 13 green, thirty-first hole of the match.

Miss Berg had a chance to end the unequal contest at 7 and 6, the margin by which Mrs. Page beat her last year, when she teed off to play the thirtieth hole 7 up, but a hooked drive into the rough, a shot into a bunker on the opposite side of the fairway and a mediocre recovery enabled her opponent to win the hole, the first she had won since the thirteenth in the morning.

Both got fine drives into the wind playing the 205-yard No. 13 hole, Mrs. Page's ball stopping on the green, about forty feet from the cup, and Patty's just short of the putting surface. A chip that sent her ball within a yard of the hole, followed by a putt that went down for a birdie 3 gave her a half as

Times Wide World
Miss Patty Berg

Mrs. Page's approach putt missed the cup.

No sooner had the youngster's putt dropped than the vanquished champion ran over to her, kissed her on the cheek and offered congratulations.

Great Year of Golf

Today's triumph for the freckle-faced girl who sprang into the limelight at Interlachen in 1935 when she went to the final round in her first national, losing to Mrs. Glenna Collett Vare, was the climax of one of the greatest years any woman golfer ever enjoyed. It was Miss Berg's thirteenth tournament and her tenth victory, the Western, Western Derby and Trans-Missis-

sippi being the other major crowns that fell to her lot.

In the final analysis, it was Miss Berg's superior work around and on the putting greens that gave her the title, for which she was twice runner-up. Her chipping was nothing short of miraculous; it was something marvelous that she needed only thirty-one putts in the morning and had seven one-putt greens out of thirteen holes in the afternoon.

Mrs. Page, on the other hand, averaged one over 2s in the first eighteen and was only one under 2s in the afternoon.

The Southern girl got off to a bad start when she three-putted the first green in the morning, leaving herself an eight-footer to start with, and from then on was green-shy. The only firm putt she hit in almost the whole round was on the third hole in the afternoon when she ran down a curling twenty-footer, but that was wasted, for Miss Berg holed a six-footer to win the hole and go 3 up.

3,000 Watch Finalists

The match had not progressed far before it was evident to almost everybody in the gallery numbering close to 3,000 that this was to be little Patty's day. In most of her other matches, especially those against Miss Jean Bauer, Miss Eva Shorb and Miss Dorothy Traung, she had to come from behind, but today she was down only once.

After losing the first hole and being denied a chance to square the match when Miss Berg set her a stymie at the second, causing her to miss a two-foot putt, Mrs. Page got on even terms by winning the third, 4 to 5, when she pitched a No. 7 iron within twenty inches of the cup.

A poor approach shot that overran the green and went into the rough cost her a bad 6 on the fourth, where Patty had a conceded 4. Following two halves in orthodox figures, Mrs. Page again squared the match when she propelled two great wood shots home on the 440-yard eighth hole and got a birdie 4, Miss Berg taking a 5 after being in the rough on her second shot.

Bunker Costs a Hole

Mrs. Page couldn't stand prosperity, however, and gave Miss Berg an unexpected half on the ninth by three-putting for the third time, missing a putt of less than a yard for a half.

A bunkered tee shot cost Mrs. Page the tenth hole and put her 1 down again and from then on she was always behind. Miss Berg won the twelfth, 4 to 5, going 2 up by chipping to within thirty inches, but lost the thirteenth by bunkering her drive and taking a 4, while Mrs. Page, hole high, got down in

two putts for a birdie 3.

Patty wasted no time getting the hole back, taking the fourteenth, 4 to 5, when Mrs. Page's tee shot caught the heavy rough on the right, from where she was unable to get home. Miss Berg saved a half on the fifteenth with another brilliant chip shot and got another on the sixteenth because Mrs. Page missed a five-foot putt after playing a fine bunker shot.

Miss Berg's par-equaling score for the first eighteen holes was 79, while Mrs. Page needed an 82, her worst round of the entire tourney.

Mrs. Page's prospects of repeating last year's triumph ebbed further when she lost the third hole in the afternoon. That was the one where she dropped a 20-foot putt, apparently making up for two visits to the rough until Miss Berg knocked in the 6-footer.

Takes Two Straight

Patty had to get down in 2 from off the green to get a half on the No. 4 hole and was still only 3 up when they halved the short No. 5 hole in 4s, one over par. The young Minnesota girl had a chance to win the hole and go 4 up when she missed a 4-footer, but took the next two. She got down in one putt for a 4 on the No. 6 while Mrs. Page three-putted, and won the No. 7 with a 4, Mrs. Page taking a 6 after being bunkered.

The next two were halved, then Miss Berg stepped out, winning the No. 10 with a birdie 3, after holing a 5-yarder and the eleventh with a par 5 when Mrs. Page played a poor third and fourth.

Then came the hole that Mrs. Page won, a success that merely postponed the inevitable.

THE CARDS
By The Associated Press.
MORNING ROUND

Out—										
Miss Berg	.4	5	5	4	3	4	5	5	5—40	
Mrs. Page	.5	5	4	6	3	4	4	4	6—41	
Match all even.										
In—										
Miss Berg	.4	5	4	4	4	5	4	4	5—39—79	
Mrs. Page	.5	5	3	5	3	5	4	4	5—41—82	
Miss Berg, 2 up.										

AFTERNOON ROUND

Out—										
Miss Berg	.4	4	4	4	4	4	4	4	5—37	
Mrs. Page	.4	4	5	4	4	5	6	4	5—41	
Miss Berg, 5 up.										
In—										
Miss Berg	.3	8	6	3						
Mrs. Page	.4	6	5	4						
Miss Berg wins, 6 and 5.										

PAR FOR THE COURSE

Out			In		
Hole.	Yds.	Par.	Hole.	Yds.	Par.
1........	341	4	10........	350	4
2........	391	5	11........	484	5
3........	445	5	12........	385	5
4........	361	4	13........	205	4
5........	177	3	14........	370	4
6........	350	4	15........	525	5
7........	320	4	16........	415	5
8........	440	4	17........	150	3
9........	420	5	18........	410	5
Total..3,245		39	Total..3,294		40
Grand total—Yards, 6,539; par 79.					

September 25, 1938

Score of 279, Record for Masters' Golf Tournament, Wins for Guldahl

By WILLIAM D. RICHARDSON
Special to THE NEW YORK TIMES.

AUGUSTA, Ga., April 2.—Thwarted in his two previous attempts to win the Masters' tournament, one of golf's most coveted honors these days, Ralph Guldahl, national and Western open titleholder, today played one of the greatest rounds of all time to capture the event.

Finishing with a brilliant 69 on the famous Augusta National course, built as a sort of memorial to Bobby Jones's past achievements in the golf world, the big, droop-shouldered pro snatched the victory away from Sam Snead of White Sulphur Springs, W. Va., by a 1-stroke margin with a record-shattering seventy-two-hole total of 279.

Until today the record for the 6-year-old tournament stood at 282, the figure at which Gene Sarazen and Craig Wood tied in the event's second year. Today two broke it in Guldahl and Snead, who finished with 280. Two tied it—Billy Burke, Cleveland veteran, and Lawson Little, former king of the amateurs.

Wood Finishes Sixth

Sarazen, maker of the famous double-eagle here in 1935, when he played off with Wood, finished fifth today with 283, while Wood, the new Winged Foot pro who captured second money in 1934 and 1935, was sixth with 284.

After them came Byron Nelson of Reading, Pa., winner two years ago, with a total of 287; Henry Picard, last year's winner, with 289; Ben Hogan, young assistant pro at the Century Country Club, with 290, and big Ed Dudley of the home club and Tony Penna of Dayton, Ohio, tied for tenth with 291.

The last to finish in the money were Tommy Armour of Chicago, Harold (Jug) McSpaden of Winchester, Mass., and Victor Ghezzi of Deal, N. J., whose totals for the four rounds were 293.

Jones, the man in whose honor the tournament is staged annually and who confines his competitive golf to this one event, tied for thirty-third place with a score of 304.

Bobby was in good company, however, his companions being Light Horse Harry Cooper, Walter Hagen and Jimmy Demaret, the Texan.

The best round Jones had in the entire tournament was the last when he came home in 34 for a 73. His other rounds were 76, 77 and 78.

At the conclusion of the third round this morning six of the leading shot-makers in the land—Guldahl, Sarazen, Snead, Nelson, Burke and Little—were practically blanketed.

Guldahl with a 70, for a three-round total of 210, had a one-stroke advantage over Sarazen, who needed a 72. The other four were bracketed at 212, Little playing himself up into a contending position with a 68.

By this time it was evident to most of the 8,000 spectators in attendance from near and far that the tournament honors would go to one of the six mentioned. A 76 had thrown Picard overboard.

In the afternoon Burke was the first of the six contenders to round the final turn and his 37, one over par, looked to be too high for further consideration.

Nelson 3 Over Par

When Nelson came to the tenth with a 39, three over, everyone knew that his goose was cooked. And so, by this time, it was pretty much of a certainty that the battle would be between Snead and Guldahl, with Little as a threat.

By the time Guldahl reached the turn Snead had finished with 280 and so the big man, who had won two of his last three tournaments—the Miami four-ball when he had Snead as his partner, and the Greensboro open — knew exactly what he had to do on the final nine in order to win the laurels that he had tossed away by a careless tee shot to the No. 12 hole here in 1937.

By this time, however, Little, his

playing partner, had popped up as a candidate. As a matter of fact, Little, the reformed amateur, and he were tied teeing off to play the tenth hole for the final time, their 63-hole scores being 246, one more than Snead had at that point.

Where Guldahl shut Little off was at the tenth when he pitched his second close enough to the hole for a birdie 3, while Lawson had to put down a 5 after missing a putt of approximately one yard for his 4.

From there on Guldahl really put on a golf show. His second shot to the No. 11 hole hit a yard from the flag and bounced to the far edge of the green from where Guldahl almost got a 3, his putt lacking only six inches from being in the cup.

On the twelfth hole, over the water—the hole that cost him the tourney in 1937 when his ball landed in the water and forced him to take a 5 while Nelson came along and got a 2—he hit a beautiful pitch up to within six feet, only to miss that one.

And then came the shot of shots, one that will go down alongside the brassie that Sarazen played into the hole for a 2 on the par 5 No. 15 back in 1935. On the No. 13, a dogleg of 480 yards, Guldahl's drive was none too long.

In order to get home in two,

PAR FOR THE COURSE

Hole	Out Yards.	Par.	Hole	In Yards.	Par.
1	400	4	10	470	4
2	525	5	11	415	4
3	350	4	12	155	3
4	190	3	13	480	5
5	440	4	14	440	4
6	185	3	15	485	5
7	370	4	16	145	3
8	510	5	17	400	4
9	430	4	18	425	4
Total	3,400	36	Total	3,400	36

Grand total—Yards, 6,800; par, 72.

which he knew he had to do in order to make sure of catching Snead, he had a terrific carry of 230 yards to make to clear a deep ravine in front and one on the side on which the hole was cut.

Without a moment's hesitation, Guldahl whipped out a No. 3 wood, took the ball off a side-hill lie and sent it whistling home and up to within six inches of the cup.

That was the shot of a master and the shot that won the tournament for him. It was a big gamble, of course, but he never flinched for a moment. It was rewarded a moment later when he holed a curling putt for an eagle 3.

68 on His Last Round

Par from there in would give him a two-stroke margin over Snead, who had finished with birdies on two of the last four holes for a 68 and a 280 total.

Guldahl had to work for his par at the No. 14, where he was forced to get down in two from the front edge of the green. He almost snagged another 3 on the par 5 No. 15, and made only one mistake from there on. That was on the No. 17, where he pitched over the green and missed a five-foot putt for a 4 after getting back on.

So now a 4 on the last hole would win and a 5 would tie Snead since Little, taking 5s on the thirteenth and fourteenth, was out of it. A perfectly placed drive to the right-hand side of the last fairway left him with a No. 3 iron shot to the green and, although he was a little strong, sending his ball to the back edge of the green, he putted back to within a foot or so and tapped in the putt that made him the winner.

April 3, 1939

Nelson Rallies to Defeat Snead

EX-OPEN CHAMPION GAINS 1-UP VICTORY

Nelson, 1 Down at 16th Tee, Bags Two Birdies and Par to Triumph Over Snead

SAM MAKES GAME STAND

Shoots 73 and 68 to Rival's 71 and 70—Winner 2 Up After Morning Round

By WILLIAM D. RICHARDSON
Special to THE NEW YORK TIMES.

HERSHEY, Pa., Sept. 2—With a gem of a finish—two birdies and a par—Byron Nelson of Toledo, former holder of the United States open golf crown, today snatched victory out of the jaws of defeat in

the final round of the P. G. A. championship.

One down to Slammin' Sam Snead of Shawnee with only three holes left to play, Nelson fired three almost perfect iron shots at the Virginian—a No. 7, a niblick and a No. 3—that gave him his first victory in the pros' championship by a margin of 1 up.

It was a hard match for Snead to lose, but in losing he gained almost as much prestige as if he had won. Trailing by as much as 3 down in the early stages of the battle which brought a gallery of more than 4,000 spectators to the Hershey course, Sam stuck gamely to his guns and never for a moment showed signs of cracking.

Three Birdies in a Row

As a matter of fact, it was Nelson who betrayed those signs toward the finish of the match when Snead, playing the finest golf seen here during the entire week of the championship, began to overtake him and then finally passed him by shooting three consecutive birdies.

When the round was over Snead had a 68, five under par. The only trouble was that he had hung too heavy a millstone around his neck in the morning round when,

through his ineffectual putting, he spotted the tall, gaunt Texan a two-hole lead.

The kind of golf the pair played in the final day of the seven-day grind is best told by reciting the medal rounds of the two players, Nelson having a 71 and a 70 and Snead a 73 and a 68. And this was in spite of several short putts that each one failed to get down.

The real drama of the match came in the last ten holes, for prior to that Nelson was always in front. Byron was 2 up at the ninth, still 2 up at the end of eighteen and 2 up with only ten holes left to play.

Nelson Begins to Falter

Up to there and especially after the No. 8 hole, twenty-sixth in the ding-dong match, where Sam took three to get in from off the right-hand edge of the green, it didn't seem possible that Nelson would allow the match to go much further.

But with victory almost in sight, Nelson's game began to crumble. He lost three holes of the next six and the entire picture had been changed. He went from an almost sure winner to an almost sure loser in that short stretch.

Over that part of the course Snead played as brilliant golf as has ever been played in this colorful event that is now past its twenty-third milestone. He had won back holes when the winning counted most and he seemed to be on the

Times Wide World
RALPH GULDAHL

P. G. A. FINALISTS WITH TROPHY THAT WENT TO THE WINNER

Byron Nelson, the victor; Tom Walsh, P. G. A. president, and Sam Snead at Hershey yesterday.

Times Wide World

past the side of the hole.

There was not much chance for Snead on the last hole. With Nelson's ball snuggled just behind the hole, Sam was off the carpet where even his holing out might not have helped.

The first half of the match, while well played, was by no means brilliantly played. There were three stymies in the course of the first eighteen holes, all against Nelson.

Unlucky on the Greens

During the first half of the match Snead was having the worst kind of luck with his putts. The only one of any length that he holed was a fifteen-footer at the fifth for a half.

Nelson drew first blood in the match when he won the sixth by bowling in a long one for a birdie 4 and he became 2 up when Snead made him a present of the ninth by three-putting, missing a two-footer for a half. Nelson pitched five feet from the hole for a birdie on the eleventh, making him 3 up, and the only hole he lost from there in was the fifteenth, where he was stymied.

Snead rimmed the cup on a five-footer at the sixteenth and just grazed the side of the hole on a twelve-footer at the seventeenth.

He held that advantage until the seventh where Snead put down a seven-footer for a birdie 3, only to lose it by taking three putts on the eighth. It was right after that that the battle started—as stirring a duel as has ever been waged in the championship. And so when they started the afternoon round Snead was 2 down, a deficit he reduced to only one by winning the first hole with a fifteen-foot putt that went in for a birdie 3. Snead had a bad set-back when he lost the third hole to Nelson by missing a four-foot putt after Nelson had holed a much longer one. That put Nelson right where he was when they started out, 2 up.

September 3, 1940

Cattle Grazing on Site Of Noted Masters Golf

By The Associated Press.

AUGUSTA, Ga., Jan. 7—Fifty head of cattle are now grazing on the greens and fairways of the Augusta National Golf Club course, scene of the annual masters tournament.

Club members last April decided to discontinue the tournament for the duration.

"The course wasn't doing any one a bit of good—just idle ground," explained Bobby Jones, former emperor of golf and now a captain in the Army Air Force, "so we thought we would add it to grazing lands available for the war effort." Jones laid out the course.

January 8, 1943

brink of capturing his first major crown.

But then Nelson, as determined a fighter as golf has ever had, thwarted his hopes with those three iron shots, the No. 7 at the sixteenth hole to within a yard of the cup, the niblick at the seventeenth to within five feet and the No. 3 at the eighteenth to perhaps six feet behind the pin.

Half Is Good Enough

He didn't roll the last putt in for his third consecutive birdie, but he didn't have to. A half was all that was required to deliver the championship he lost to Henry Picard on the thirty-seventh green at Pomonok last year.

As a matter of fact, what Nelson did to Snead here today was almost what Picard did to him last year. At Pomonok the Chocolate Soldier squared the match with a birdie on the thirty-sixth hole and then won the championship with another birdie on the thirty-seventh.

Where Nelson started to waver to-

day was at the ninth hole in the afternoon. He pulled his tee shot into the trees, the ball finally dropping into a trout pond. Snead didn't even have to putt out there, although he was nowhere near the hole himself. That error, wiping out the mistake made by Snead when he three-putted the hole before, left Nelson only 1 up with nine holes to play.

Right after that Nelson lipped the hole on two comparatively short putts. On both those holes, the tenth and eleventh, he had easy chances to close Snead entirely out and when he didn't it looked pretty evident to nearly everybody present that he never would.

Match Is Squared

This appeared even more certain when he was guilty of a poor approach shot on the long twelfth hole. Snead won with a birdie 4 to square the match for the first time since Nelson took the honor by winning the sixth hole in the morning round.

The all-important hole, as it finally turned out, was the thirteenth. Nelson came out of a bunker and holed a putt of eight feet to get a half with Sammy, who had pitched out of the sand on the other side of the green to within four feet.

If he had lost that hole Nelson would have been 2 down when Snead put a superb iron shot six feet from the cup at the short No. 14 and dropped the putt for a deuce. As it was, however, he was only 1 down and the approach shots on the next two holes did the rest.

But even at the sixteenth, where Nelson was up so close, Snead almost got a half, his putt from fifteen or eighteen feet hitting the cup and jumping away. Sam also had a chance for a half on the seventeenth hole. He was only six feet away after a magnificent shot out of the rough, but the ball slipped

Hole-by-Hole Golf Score

MORNING ROUND OUT						AFTERNOON ROUND OUT					
Hole	Yds.	Par	Nelson	Snead		Hole	Yds.	Par	Nelson	Snead	
1	329	4	4	4	Even	1	329	4	4	3	N. 1 up
2	441	4	4	4	Even	2	441	4	4	4	N. 1 up
3	565	5	5	5	Even	3	565	5	4	5	N. 2 up
4	480	4	4	4	Even	4	480	4	4	4	N. 2 up
5	212	3	3	3	Even	5	212	3	3	3	N. 2 up
6	579	5	4	5	N. 1 up	6	579	5	4	4	N. 2 up
7	372	4	4	4	N. 1 up	7	372	4	4	3	N. 1 up
8	320	4	4	4	N. 1 up	8	320	4	4	5	N. 2 up
9	191	3	3	4	N. 2 up	9	191	3	5	3	N. 1 up
Tot.	3,489	36	35	37	N. 2 up	Tot.	3,489	36	36	34	N. 1 up
IN						**IN**					
Hole	Yds.	Par	Nelson	Snead		Hole	Yds.	Par	Nelson	Snead	
10	587	5	5	5	N. 2 up	10	587	5	5	5	N. 1 up
11	343	4	3	4	N. 3 up	11	343	4	4	4	N. 1 up
12	521	5	5	5	N. 3 up	12	521	5	5	4	Even
13	522	5	4	4	N. 3 up	13	522	5	4	4	Even
14	189	3	3	3	N. 3 up	14	189	3	3	2	S. 1 up
15	401	4	5	4	N. 2 up	15	401	4	4	4	S. 1 up
16	417	4	4	4	N. 2 up	16	417	4	3	4	Even
17	358	4	4	4	N. 2 up	17	358	4	3	4	N. 1 up
18	190	3	3	3	N. 2 up	18	190	3	3	3	N. 1 up
Tot.	3,528	37	36	36	N. 2 up	Tot.	3,528	37	34	34	N. 1 up

Grand total—7,017 yards, par 73.

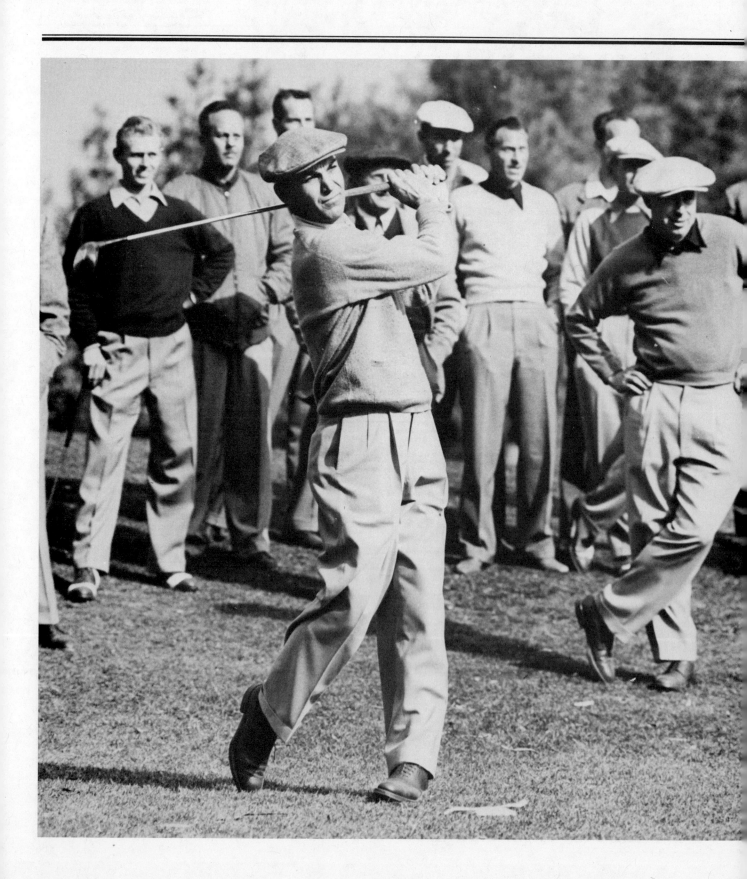

CHAPTER 2

THE ERA OF HOGAN AND SNEAD

One of the great sports stories of the last fifty years tells of the dramatic performance of Ben Hogan in the 1950 Los Angeles Open. Only eleven months after a brush with death in an auto accident, Hogan returned to the fairways in championship form.

MANGRUM ANNEXES OPEN GOLF LAURELS

Beats Nelson and Ghezzi by a Single Stroke in Two-Round Play-Off at Cleveland

---

TIED AT 72 ON FIRST 18

Lloyd Duplicates Score on Second Tour While Rivals Falter at End for 73s

---

By WILLIAM D. RICHARDSON
Special to The New York Times.

CLEVELAND, June 16—Lloyd Mangrum, the dapper 31-year-old Texan who saw some rugged action during the war, won the forty-sixth National Open championship today after a double-round play-off on the well-groomed and exacting Canterbury course. After he and his two opponents, Byron Nelson and Vic Ghezzi, who had finished the 72-hole event in a triple tie with four-under-par totals of 284, had tied again in the first 18-hole play-off this morning, Mangrum, who now makes his home in Los Angeles, finally gained the highest honor in golf when he beat them by a single stroke this afternoon.

Mangrum managed to get around in another 72, which gave him a total of 144, even par, for the day, while his two frustrated adversaries had to be content with a 73 each, making their two-round total 145.

It was a battle that went on to the bitter end, the issue being in doubt right up to the final moment, when, with lightning flashing all around and the rain coming down, Mangrum put down a two-foot putt that gave him a 5 on the eighteenth after Ghezzi had missed an eight-footer for a 4 that would have brought the two of them back for another session tomorrow.

When they came to the eighteenth tee Mangrum had a one-stroke lead on Ghezzi and a two-stroke margin on Nelson, who had tossed his chance overboard by flubbing an approach shot. Which meant that all Mangrum had to do was to hold his own with Ghezzi on the last hole—a task he accomplished only because the tall Ghezzi, a New Jersey-born product, failed to sink the eight-footer.

Many Dramatic Moments

Although none of the three turned in a performance that could be called brilliant, the play-off fairly reeked with drama as first one and then the other appeared on the road to victory.

Naturally, most of the excitement centered on the play at the last hole, where Mangrum's drive wound up in the rough to the left, leaving him with anything but a simple second shot to get to the green, since he had to avoid a tree that stuck out in the fairway close to his line of play. He didn't quite pull it off, and his ball stopped on the up-slope of a bunker short of the green, only a few inches from an overhanging ledge.

Ghezzi's second shot from the

Lloyd Mangrum
Associated Press Wirephotos

fairway overran the green and stopped in the rough, barely out of a bunker, while Nelson's ball stopped just short of the green. Being furthest away, Mangrum took too much sand and his ball, while reaching the green, was several yards short of the hole.

It was there that Ghezzi, who had lost the one-stroke lead he had enjoyed over the other two leaving the thirteenth green, had a chance to make up lost ground. After he played his chip shot it looked as if he had done just that, for his ball ran straight for the hole, but with enough speed to carry it past a distance of approximately four feet.

If he could hole that one and if Mangrum missed his, which was a good distance away, Ghezzi and Mangrum would be tied. There was a breathless silence in the gallery of about 4,000, few having sought shelter from the rain, as Ghezzi lined up his putt after Mangrum's bid for a 4 stopped two feet away.

Putt Missed by Inches

Vic failed to apply enough power and the ball stopped inches away from the hole. After he had tapped it in Mangrum holed out and with the lightning flashing and the rain pouring down, became the new national open champion and a right worthy one, too, for he had displayed great courage right down to the last.

As an indication of how close the match was throughout the day it might be mentioned that the lead changed eleven times in the course of the 36 holes of competition.

After they had finished on even terms in the morning, Mangrum went out in front at the first hole in the afternoon when he sank a wedge shot from four yards off the green for a birdie 3 while both his opponents took 4's.

His advantage disappeared on the next hole, however, when he took a 5 after missing the green with his second shot and failed to run down a 7-foot putt. Ghezzi was the only one to hit the green at the short third, but all got 3's, Mangrum and Nelson getting down in one putt, while Vic took two.

All had 4's on the fourth, leaving accounts all square, but at the fifth Mangrum ran down a 15-footer for a birdie that put him back in front of both Nelson and

Ghezzie by a shot. At the long sixth Nelson and Ghezzie had birdie 4's by getting down in one putt, while Mangrum had a 5 after being twice in the rough on the way to the green, and then lipping the cup from ten feet away.

Byron Cards a Deuce

That left them just where they had started early in the morning. It didn't take Nelson long to change the situation, however. On the short seventh he holed a ten-footer for a deuce, one of the few times during the day's play that Lady Luck was on his side on the putting greens.

There was no change until the ninth hole, where Ghezzi got on even terms with Nelson by holing a twenty-footer for a birdie 4 while Nelson needed a 5 and Mangrum a 6. As it turned out, that could easily have been the hole that gave Mangrum the crown, for he had driven out of bounds for a stroke-and-distance penalty and when he finally got onto the green his ball was a good sixty feet from the pin and he was putting for a 6.

Fortunately for him he got it. His ball, hit a little too violently, raced for the hole, hit the back of the cup, jumped a foot into the air and dropped in to stay there. It was a great break, for if the ball hadn't hit the cup it must have gone several feet beyond, leaving him with 8 in prospect. Even the 6 was bad enough, for it meant that he was two strokes behind, with 36 to 34 for the other two, at that critical juncture of the struggle.

All had par 4s on the tenth, although Nelson had to make a fine recovery from the rough at the right of the green after being guilty of a badly hit approach shot from the left-hand side of the fairway. His recovery was so good that it almost holed out.

Lloyd Misses 3-Footer

Neelson dropped a stroke to each of the others playing the short eleventh, although after the tee shots he was in the best position of all. He was short on his first putt and took two more to get into the hole, while Ghezzi came out of the sand and got down in one putt and Mangrum chipped out of the rough to within inches.

That put Ghezzi a stroke ahead of Nelson and two ahead of Mangrum. After the next hole, the twelfth, Ghezzi still led Nelson by a shot and Mangrum by two as he and Lord Byron got their 4's while Lloyd was taking a bogey 5 through the missing of a three-foot putt after chipping strong from off the back edge of the green.

The next three holes were good ones for Mangrum. He got birdies on two of them, while Ghezzi was taking two bogies and Nelson one. On the thirteenth, which is the hole where Nelson suffered a costly penalty stroke when his caddy stepped on his ball during the third round of the championship proper, Mangrum chipped up to within easy putting distance and sank a four-footer for a birdie 4, while Ghezzi needed two putts to get in from six yards away and Nelson a 6 as a result of three putts, missing one of less than three feet for his 5.

As things stood now Mangrum and Nelson were tied at 52 strokes, two more than Ghezzi had played through that point. But the next two holes, No. 14 and 15, were bad ones for the ponderous New Jersey pro who now represents a Knoxville (Tenn.) food concern, for after they had been played he

and Nelson were tied and Mangrum was ahead of both by a shot.

A bad chip cost Ghezzi a 5 on the fourteenth, where Mangrum and Nelson each had 4's as a result of using only one putt each. And on No. 15, another easy par 4, Ghezzi had to mark down another bogey 5 where Nelson had a 4 and Mangrum a birdie 3 as he rolled in another long putt, this one approximately a fifteen-footer.

The slightly-built but powerful Mangrum added another stroke to his lead when he rolled in another putt, one of six or seven feet, for a birdie 4 on the long sixteenth where Nelson and Ghezzi were able to do no better than 5, which is par.

So, with two holes to go, Mangrum had two shots apiece on his two rivals. He lost one of them to Ghezzi, at the short seventeenth where he put his tee shot to the left of the green, down the hill into the rough, and was unable to get close enough on his approach to save his par. Ghezzi was the only one on and got his 3. Nelson duplicated Mangrum's mistake and took a 4 after playing a chip shot so ineffectually that he showed his displeasure by wrenching his putter out of his bag and then slamming it back after taking two putts.

Then came the denouement previously described—the play at the final hole, which was played almost in darkness due both to the lateness of the hour and the overhead clouds. Nelson was ahead only twice during the morning round.

The 1939 champion, who, incidentally had won his title in the same sort of three playoff, found his putter as unfaithful to him as it had been during the regular competition. Byron took thirty-two putts in the morning round against twenty-eight for both Mangrum and Ghezzi. Byron led only twice during the entire thirty-six holes, at the second and twenty-fifth, his longest putt, a 12-footer, falling at the latter.

Ghezzi, who, like Mangrum, had never come this far in the big show, played well until the final nine holes, when his putter went cranky on him, and he began to miss his tee shots. Vic had joined with Mangrum in taking a two-stroke lead over Nelson in the morning, each collecting 34's to Byron's 36.

Nelson was three down after No. 10. Mangrum took a two-stroke lead on the twelfth, where his second shot from the spinach struck a hard spot in the turf near a trap and bounded on to the green for an easy birdie.

Ghezzi needed a 5 here, but came back with a 4 on the long thirteenth, where Mangrum's ball hit a spectator, and he wound up with a 6. Nelson hounded par to the finish after matching Ghezzi's birdie on the same, and matters were square as they arrived at the eighteenth, where all earned par 4.

Open Golf Cards

MORNING ROUND

	Out	In	
Par	443 445 345—36	434 544 534—36—72	
Nelson	433 445 345—36	534 444 534—36—72	
Mangrum	442 535 245—34	433 654 544—38—72	
Ghezzi	442 435 444—34	435 445 634—38—72	

AFTERNOON ROUND

	Out	In	
Nelson	4 4 3 4 4 4 2 4 5—34	4 4 4 6 4 4 5 4 4—39—73	
Mangrum	4 4 3 4 4 4 3 6—34	4 3 5 4 3 4 4 4—36—72	
Ghezzi	4 4 3 4 4 4 3 4 4—34	4 3 4 5 5 5 5 3 5—39—73	

Babe Didrikson Zaharias was probably the greatest woman athlete of the century. She is remembered as much for her heroic fight against cancer as for her athletic accomplishments in golf and track. In this 1953 photo, Betty Dodd and Patty Berg watch her tee off.

Lloyd Mangrum won the U.S. Open in 1946 by beating two challengers in a double-round playoff amidst thunder, lightning and a steady downpour.

Cary Middlecoff was the only major tournament winner entitled to be called ''Dr.'' He had studied dentistry but decided to drill golf balls rather than teeth.

$1,500 Goes to Mangrum

CLEVELAND, June 16 (AP)—Here's how they split up the prize money in the national open golf championship:

Lloyd Mangrum, $1,500.

Byron Nelson and Vic Ghezzi, tied for second, $875 each.

Ben Hogan and Herman Barron, tied for fourth, $550 each.

Ed Oliver and Jimmy Dem-aret, tied for sixth, $350 each.

Dick Metz and Chick Harbert, tied for eighth, $225 each.

E. J. Harrison and Lawson Little, tied for tenth, $175 each.

Clayton Heafner, Ed Furgol and Henry Picard, tied for twelfth, $150 each.

Toney Penna, Claud Harmon, Steve Kovach and Chandler Harper, tied for fifteenth, $125 each.

Gene Kunes, Sam Snead, Paul Runyan, Harry Todd, Lew Worsham, Johnny Bulla, Henry Ransom, Mike Turnesa, Leland Gibson, Ellsworth Vines, Harold McSpaden, Toby Lyons, $100 each.

Medals to Marvin Ward and Smiley Quick, tied for low amateur.

June 17, 1946

NEW P. G. A. NATIONAL CHAMPION RECEIVES HIS TROPHY

Ed Dudley (left), president of the association, presenting the award to Ben Hogan as Ed Oliver, the runner-up, looks on in Portland, Ore.

Associated Press Wirephoto

Hogan Sets Back Oliver by 6 and 4 To Take the National P. G. A. Title

Ben, Staging Rally, Triumphs in Tourney at Portland, Ore.—Loser, 3 Up After First Eighteen, Falters in Afternoon

PORTLAND, Ore., Aug. 25 (AP)—Beltin' Ben Hogan, the 135-pounder from Hershey, Pa., with the big golfing wallop, won the 1946 National Professional Golfers Association championship today with a 6-and-4 victory over Ed (Porky) Oliver of Wilmington, Del.

Hogan, leading money winner of the year but never a serious challenger for this title before, proved that a good little man can beat a good big man in golf. Oliver, 207 pounds, never had a chance after the nineteenth hole.

The victor fired a five-under-par 30 on the third nine, winning four holes in a row to wipe out Oliver's morning-round lead of 3 up.

Putts Find the Cup

Hogan shot the fourteen holes played in the afternoon in eight under par. His putts, which failed to drop in the morning, ran into the cup as if magnetized.

Oliver, whose two-under-par score of 70 on the Portland Country Club course in the first round had given him his 3-up lead and his followers' hopes he would score a startling upset, in contrast played badly in the afternoon.

Ed continually pushed his drives on second shots to the right and missed putts that most average players could make. Hogan's wobbly morning round had left him with a one-over-par 73.

Hogan, with $3,500 first money slipping away, turned on the steam as they teed off for the final round. Lengthy putts won him four holes in a row, from the twentieth through the twenty-third, two of them for birdies. He finished the third nine with another birdie at the twenty-seventh, carding a five under 30 on the nine and was 2 up at that point.

By this time the poker faced Hogan was like a bloodhound at the scent of prey. He bagged the twenty-eighth and twenty-ninth holes with birdies, coming out of a trap for a two-foot putt on the former and sinking a ten-footer on the other, to make the count 4 up. He made it 5 up on the thirtieth, when Oliver's drive landed in a trap and he was short on the out.

Crowd Senses End

They halved the thirty-first, but the crowd, estimated variously from 6,000 to 7,500 fans, realized that the end was near. Oliver had a chance here, but his putt from eighteen feet away was timid and stopped short.

Hogan hung the clincher on the thirty-second. He pitched No. 8 iron shot to within three feet of the cup, being there in 2. Oliver, twenty feet away, missed the putt and walked over to congratulate the new champion.

When they teed off for the championship, Hogan was the favorite. At the eighteenth, 3 down, Ben looked like a bad bet. The roly-poly man from Delaware seemed headed for another big upset, just as when he eliminated the defending champion, Byron Nelson, 1 up, in the quarter-finals.

Hogan merely gritted his teeth and began the tough uphill climb. This was the first time he had gotten past the quarter-finals in the big PGA event. He made it all the way.

As the runner-up, Oliver picked up $1,500. In defeat he had little to be ashamed of. In his first competition in the tournament he reached the final.

THE CARDS

MORNING ROUND

Out—										
Par	5	4	4	3	4	4	4	3	4—35
Oliver	5	4	4	3	4	4	4	3	4—35
Hogan	4	5	4	3	4	5	4	3	4—36

Oliver, 1 up.

In—										
Par	5	4	3	4	4	5	4	3	5—37—72
Oliver	5	4	4	4	3	4	4	3	5—35—70
Hogan	5	5	3	4	4	5	4	3	5—37—73

Oliver, 3 up.

AFTERNOON ROUND

Out—									
Oliver	4	4	5	3	5	3	4	3	5—36
Hogan	4	3	4	2	4	3	4	3	3—30

Hogan, 2 up.

In—					
Oliver	5	4	4	4	4
Hogan	4	3	3	4	3

Hogan wins, 6 and 4.

August 26, 1946

U. S. OPEN BARRED TO MRS. ZAHARIAS

Rules Amended to Read 'for Men Only,' and Her Informal Entry Is Declined

Politely but firmly, the United States Golf Association advised Mrs. Babe Didrikson Zaharias yesterday that her presence is not desired in the national open championship at the Riviera Country Club, Los Angeles, June 10-12.

Mrs. Zaharias said some time ago that she would like to be the first of her sex to compete in the classic. The golfing fathers, taking alarm, have amended their rules to read "for men only."

"As the championship has always been intended to be for men, the eligibility rules have been rephrased to confirm that condition," says a communication from the association's office.

"Applicants must be men who are either professional golfers or amateurs with handicaps not exceeding three strokes. Thus, the U. S. G. A. has declined an informal entry submitted in behalf of Mrs. George Zaharias."

The qualifying rounds on June 1 will be played in twenty-nine sections this year, three more than in the past. The Pacific Northwest will have two sections, at Seattle and Portland. So will Texas, at Lubbock and Fort Worth. Salt Lake City and Honolulu have been added, while the Middle Atlantic section has been dropped.

As usual, the qualifying rounds will be at thirty-six holes stroke play. Except at Los Angeles and Honolulu, all will be held June 1. Honolulu's date is May 25, and at Los Angeles play will be spread over two days, May 27 and 28.

More qualifying places will be open than ever before, due to a reduction in exemptions. Only the twenty low scorers and ties for twentieth in last year's open will qualify automatically, instead of the low thirty and ties. Others eligible for exemption are former open champions, the 1947 winners of the United States amateur, the P. G. A., the British open and amateur, and the Riviera professional.

After the sectional eliminations, the field at Riviera will number 171. The field for the final thirty-six holes will be reduced to the lowest fifty scorers and ties, where formerly the low sixty and ties played through.

Every entrant in the qualifying rounds this year will have to say definitely whether he intends to play in the open if he is successful.

Getting additionally tough, the U.S.G.A. also stipulates that every player eligible for the open must register at Riviera by noon two days before the start of play, or send an excuse in advance. Any player who fails to do so will find he has made a long trip for nothing.

Finally, all applications must reach the U.S.G.A. office here by 5 P. M. on May 17, accompanied by $5, the notice says.

April 7, 1948

WILL NOT BAR NEGROES

P. G. A. Revises Attitude, Suit by 3 Pros Is Dismissed

MARTINEZ, Calif., Sept. 21 (AP) —The attorney for three Negro professional golfers barred from the Richmond, Calif., Open last January said today he had won a pledge of no further "discrimination" by the Professional Golfers Association.

Jonathan Rowell, representing Madison Gunter, Bill Spiller and Ted Rhodes, said he was satisfied with yesterday's dismissal of his clients' $325,000 suit against the P. G. A. in the court of Superior Judge Hugh Donovan.

He said P. G. A. representatives had pledged there would be no rule against Negroes in the future and declared his clients filed the suit not for financial redress but to "break down racial barriers."

The P. G. A., through Attorney Dana Murdock, declared in Judge Donovan's court that it would not discriminate or refuse tournament-playing privileges to anyone because of color.

September 22, 1948

Hogan Reported in 'Fair' Condition At Texas Hospital After Collision

The Golf Star Suffers Fractured Pelvis, Other Injuries as His Car and a Bus Crash

EL PASO, Tex., Feb. 2 (AP)— Ben Hogan, king of the golfers, suffered a fractured pelvis, broken collar bone and possible fracture of a rib in a collision of his auto and a bus today.

His injuries were enumerated in an official bulletin issued by physicians at 6:25 P. M. (Mountain Standard Time) today. The physicians expressed confidence that Hogan would be able to play golf again, but would not venture a guess as to when.

The bulletin said Hogan was now out of shock and much improved. It listed his condition as "fair."

The bantam of the links, leading money winner of the nation, was hurt in the collision of his automobile and a bus near Van Horn, Tex., 200 miles southeast of here, this morning.

Open and P. G. A. Champion

They call Ben golf's little giant. His links magic brought him the National Open and National PGA titles last year.

Hogan's wife, Valerie, said his injuries might have been worse had he not thrown himself across her to protect her. This got him out of the way of their 1949 Cadillac's steering wheel, which was jammed back into the driver's seat.

Mrs. Hogan suffered minor injuries. She was at the hospital a while tonight, then left for the hotel where she plans to stay.

Ben Hogan

Hogan's attending physicians are David Eron, D. L. Feeney and Leopoldo Villareal.

Hogan was conscious but "suffering from shock" when he was brought to the Hotel Dieu, an El Paso hospital, by ambulance from Van Horn.

When the accident occurred he was on his way to his home in Fort Worth from Phoenix, Ariz., where he played in the Phoenix Open.

Ben's brother, Royal Hogan, an amateur golfer, flew here from Fort Worth. Ben Hogan had sent word that no announcement of his condition was to be made until his brother arrived.

Accident Occurs in Morning

The accident occurred 29 miles east of Van Horn at 8:30 A. M. Hogan and his wife were rushed here, reaching El Paso about 1 P. M.

Hogan, last year voted "Golfer of the Year" by the PGA, resides in Fort Worth, although he plays golf out of Hershey, Pa.

Mrs. Hogan said she saw an approaching bus, traveling the opposite direction from their car, start to pass a truck shortly before the accident. Her husband tried to avoid a collision but could not because of a culvert, she recounted, and the two vehicles met squarely.

She said there was some ground haze despite bright sunshine at the time. The impact hurled the engine of the Hogan car back into the front seat, Mrs. Hogan said.

Contrary to first reports, none of the bus passengers was injured, authorities here said. They proceeded in a relief bus which reached El Paso about 1:30 P. M.

Company officials here said the bus driver, L. H. Logan of Van Horn, remained with his crippled vehicle, on which the front wheels were damaged. He was understood to have accompanied it back to Van Horn.

Mrs. Hogan said it was 90 minutes after the crash before an ambulance arrived to pick up her husband. Confusion in the crowd which gathered for the delay, several believing that others already had summoned an ambulance from Van Horn.

Pro Golfers Concerned

TUCSON, Ariz., Feb. 2 (AP)—The professional golfing brigade, here to take part in the Tucson open, expressed deep concern today over the injuries suffered by Ben Hogan.

"The entire Professional Golfers Association is deeply grieved and we are anxiously awaiting the doctor's final report," said George Schneiter, PGA tournament chairman.

"We are praying that his injuries will not be permanent," Schneiter said. "The loss of Hogan in the tournament world could leave a gap that would be extremely difficult to fill. He is one of the most loved champions in the history of the game."

Jimmy Demaret, a fellow-Texan and friend of Hogan and his closest competitor in the 1949 winter tour, said: "It is a very unfortunate thing. Any golfer would be tickled to death to do anything to help him out."

February 3, 1949

Snead, Displaying Brilliant Putting, Annexes Masters Golf With Card of 282

W. VIRGINIAN FIRST BY THREE STROKES

By LINCOLN A. WERDEN
Special to THE NEW YORK TIMES.

AUGUSTA, Ga., April 10—Samuel Jackson Snead of White Sul-

phur Springs, W. Va., often called luckless because of his inability to sink short putts when titles were at stake, today forgot all about such misfortunes and won the thirteenth Masters golf tournament with a concluding-round 67 for a seventy-two hole total of 282.

The likable 35-year-old Virginia-born professional banged in long putts with the accuracy of a sharp-shooter, using thirty during his round, and ended by annexing this blue ribbon event over the Augusta National Golf Club course before one of e largest galleries in Southern history by a margin of three strokes.

Fully 15,000 trailed over this picturesque 6,750-yard layout that has been associated with the name of Bobby Jones since its construction. The famed golfer, still convalescing from an operation, fol-

lowed much of the play in an automobile and was in on the finish as Snead completed his spectacular round that kept the big crowd constantly yelling, "That a boy, Sammy."

Second 67 in Row

Trailing by a stroke at the beginning of the last round, Snead's five-under-par burst, his second 67 in succession, enabled him to pass Johnny Palmer of Badin, N. C., the leader, at the end of fifty-four holes, and finish four strokes ahead of the North Carolinian, who had a par 72 today.

Tied for second were Lloyd Mangrum of Niles, Ill., leading money winner of the season, who finished with a 70, and Johnny Bulla of Pittsburgh, former commercial air pilot, at 285. Tall, rangy Bulla put together another 69 on the last round. Palmer and Jim Turnesa of Briarcliff Manor, N. Y., deadlocked at 286.

Paired with Snead, Turnesa gained a momentary edge in the duel that developed between them until he reached the par-3 twelfth hole. Snead had a one-stroke advantage starting the round and he was out in 33 to Turnesa's 34. When Snead went over par with 5s at both the tenth and eleventh while Turnesa rolled in par 4s, they were exactly even.

The picture changed entirely after the water hole twelfth. Turnesa dropped one into the pond, his next failed to hold the green and he ended with a 5. Snead, however, sighted his twelve-footer and stroked the ball into the cup for a birdie 2.

Thrills Crowd on 18th

After that Snead added a birdie 4 at the thirteenth, another birdie 4 at the fifteenth and had pars at the fourteenth, sixteenth and seventeenth. Then he gave the big crowd, with which he proved extremely popular, a thrill by rolling in an eighteen-foot putt for a birdie 3 at the home green for his inward 34.

With thousands, including a group of convalescing soldiers from near-by Oliver General Hospital, banked around the eighteenth, Snead preceded that mighty putt with a superb No. 7 iron from the rough near the trees that put the ball on the putting surface.

Turnesa had driven in deeply and had just cleared the evergreens with his second, before shooting to the green for a final 5 and a 70. But Snead had clearance to swing his club and sent the ball on a long arc, leaving him six yards away from the flag for the final putt.

By virtue of a 68, Lew Worsham of Oakmont, Pa., who won the United States Open crown in 1947 when he beat Snead in a play-off as Hapless Sam missed a tiny putt, took sixth with 289. In seventh place was Joe Kirkwood Jr., of Hollywood, Calif. The blond-haired motion picture actor and son of the well-known trick shot golfer posted a final 75 for 290.

Then came the group at 292 which included Jimmy Demaret of

Ojai, Calif.; Byron Nelson of Roanoke, Tex., who comes out of partial retirement each year to play here, and 230-pound Clayton Heafner of Charlotte, N. C.

Claude Harmon of the Winged Foot Club of Mamaroneck, N. Y., who won last year with a record-equalling 279, had a final 72 for 293, which Herman Keiser of St. Andrews, Ill., matched. Bobby Locke, South African star, Herman Barron of White Plains, N. Y., and Leland Gibson of Kansas City, Mo., formed the trio at 294.

From the moment that Snead holed a twenty-footer for a birdie 3 at the first hole, it seemed that the former British Open champion and P. G. A. titleholder would be the man to reckon with. He won the P. G. A. crown in 1942, incidentally, by beating Jim Turnesa,

A MASTER'S TOUCH ON THE GREEN AT AUGUSTA

Sam Snead sinking a putt at the third hole for a par 4 yesterday   Associated Press Wirephoto

with whom he was paired.

Although Snead may minimize his ability on occasion, he gave a remarkable exhibition of shot making. Dubbed Slammin' Sam because of the tremendous distances he gets with his drives, he started with two birdies. The 4 at the second came after his No. 1 iron trickled onto the green at the 535-yard par-5 hole.

He bagged a par 4 at the third and then sank a fifteen-footer for a deuce at the fourth. Bunkered at the fifth, he was down with a 5 and followed with a par 3 and a par 4. At the eighth, his second went to the left but he pitched up well and holed a ten-footer for a 4, his fourth birdie.

His putting style, which he changed prior to winning the Greensboro Open, worked splendidly once more on the ninth; he

got down a seven-footer for a 4 after being short with his second. That put him out in 33 and set the stage for the final dash.

Palmer lost ground, despite the fact that he was out in 36, when he took a 6 at the long eighth where his second hit a tree. At the short twelfth, which ruined Turnesa, he also took a 5, being at the water's edge on his tee shot and bunkered on his second.

Mangrum, out in 34, matched par for the next five. Then at the fifteenth his second shot hit a spectator and fell back onto the green where he holed out for a birdie 4. At the short sixteenth, his tee shot fell into the water and, after the penalty stroke, he dropped a ten-footer for a 4, finishing with an incoming 36.

April 11, 1949

MIDDLECOFF, WITH 286, TAKES NATIONAL OPEN GOLF TITLE

SNEAD TIES FOR 2D

By LINCOLN A. WERDEN
Special to The New York Times.

CHICAGO, June 11 — A young man who chose to become a golf professional two years ago instead of practicing dentistry won the United States open title over the

rugged Medinah Country Club's No. 3 course today.

Pride of Memphis, a 6-foot-2 athlete, Cary Middlecoff posted a four-round total of 286 that withstood the challenge of the late finishers.

Assuming the lead at the end of the third round this morning with a 69, he had a stroke margin to spare at the end of a long wait in

the clubhouse for one of the game's greatest competitors, Samuel Jackson Snead, to complete his round.

While the minutes ticked away, ever so slowly to the 28-year-old Tennesean and his wife, who sat beside him, Snead, with two pars left to gain a tie, tossed away his chance by going over par at the seventeenth, a 3 over water. A 4 there and a 4 at the eighteenth,

while thousands hemmed in the home green, brought Snead a final 70 for a 287 to tie for second with Clayton Heafner of Charlotte, N. C.

Mrs. Middlecoff in Tears

When the official report reached the Middlecoffs, seated now in the press room, Mrs. Middlecoff could not help bursting into tears of joy.

Only two days ago Cary had

Sinking His Final Putt to Take the United States Open Crown

Cary Middlecoff just after playing his shot on the eighteenth green at the Medinah Country Club. Leaning on his club and watching is Buck White.

Associated Press Wirephoto

toured about Chicago seeking a can of black paint. Somewhat superstitious, and disappointed with the way he was stroking the ball on the first round on the greens, he decided to administer a coat of this black paint to his putter for luck. And that was the shade of the clubhead that was in his bag for the last three rounds.

Playing with O'Neal (Buck) White, formerly of Memphis, to whom Middlecoff credited much of his knowledge of the game, and Heafner, Middlecoff found them to be among his most formidable rivals. Heafner had a chance to tie, too, but missed a six-footer for a birdie at the eighteenth and he had a final 73 for his 287.

When Middlecoff closed with a 75, White went out in a 41, ruining his chances of overtaking Cary, and finally tumbled back in the race with an ultimate total of 290, the same aggregate posted by Dave Douglas, the tall Delaware pro. Jim Turnesa of Briarcliff Manor was ahead of them with a 289.

Johnny Palmer was farther down the list at 291 along with Claude Harmon of Winged Foot and Pete Cooper of Ponte Vedra Beach, Fla.

One of the game's longest drivers, Middlecoff, who succeeds the convalescing Ben Hogan, victor in Los Angeles a year ago with a record winning score of 276, was greeted by Charles (Chick) Evans after it was all over. It was Evans back in 1916 who won the crown with the same 286 total, so there was an occasion for more congratulations.

For a time, however, Middlecoff admitted he was somewhat "scared." That was when he carded a 6 at the seventh hole after

his second shot hit a spectator and Middlecoff then pitched his approach into a spot in a bunker. After that he three-putted for a 5 at the eleventh but had pars at the other eight holes for what proved to be the winning score.

Brosch Registers 293

Al Brosch, the Long Islander who had enjoyed the leader's place at the conclusion of the first 36 holes and was three strokes back starting the last round, closed with a 79, running into trouble with a 43 for the outgoing nine on the last round that just about blasted his hopes. Brosch's score of 293 put him back of Eric Monti, the Californian, and Hershel Spears of Birmingham, Ala., who had 292.

Brosch's playing partner, Bobby Locke, the South African, who was among the last to come into the clubhouse, had a par 71 for 289 to tie Turnesa for fourth.

The drama of the last round when White and finally Heafner failed to catch Middlecoff was supplied by Slammin Sam. Winner of the P. G. A. championship that Hogan held last year, as well as the Masters, Snead was regarded as the man to watch.

With two rounds of 73, he had his first par equalling round this morning with a 71. By the time the sixty-three hole mark had been passed, Middlecoff and Heafner had 250, Turnesa 252, White and Snead 253 and Ellsworth Vines, former tennis champion, 255. Vines finally came in with 294 that tied Skee Riegel, low amateur, Lloyd Mangrum, Johnny Bulla and Harry Todd.

While Turnesa failed to hit the birdie trail coming back, Snead, one of the late starters, collected two on two of the first three holes of the inward nine. Then he set

up his place as Middlecoff's potential rival with three more pars. All that was needed now for Sam was to get three additional pars to tie. He got one, but then came the seventeenth hole of the course.

Snead got his tee shot over the pond but the ball fell to the right and stopped off on the fringe below the green. Selecting a putter he moved the ball to within five feet.

Some of the critics said he used the wrong club, but the shot was made. Snead failed to hole the ball with the remaining putt for a 3 and took a 4.

He needed a birdie now to tie. The eighteenth has danger lurking on right and left in the trees. Snead drove into the rough on the left and then pitched his second to the left in the grass off the green.

He chipped up well but not into the cup on his third shot and the resulting 4 left him one stroke away from the title that still eludes him.

Middlecoff, classed as a touring pro inasmuch as he has no affiliation with any golf country club, said he intended to play the circuit "as long as he could win tournaments." When asked if he had decided to quit dentistry, he said, "No. If I ever stop playing in tournaments, I'll go back to being a dentist."

Today's victor has plans to compete in the British Open. He won his first tournament in 1937, the Tennessee State High School competition, and annexed the North and South Open as an amateur in 1945. The Tennessee star went to the quarter-finals of the 1946 National amateur championship.

At the end of the morning round, or fifty-four holes of play, Middlecoff had moved into the lead. Starting one stroke back of the Long Islander, Brosch, who topped the competitors yesterday with a two-round total of 141, Middlecoff

had his second consecutive burst of sub-par golf with a 69.

That put the Memphis pro at 211, while another Tennessean, Buck White, was 212. Heafner followed at 214, with Brosch. Then came the former tennis champion, Ellsworth Vines, making a serious bid for golf's biggest plum, at 216.

Monti moved into the race with a 70, so that he had an aggregate of 217. Harmon was in at that figure, along with Jim Turnesa, who followed yesterday's 69 with a 70, while the Delaware golfer, Douglas, posted a 70 for 217. The P. G. A. champion, Snead, came through with a 71, after two earlier 73's, to be at 217 also.

Snead had a 6 at the fourth and then, with a chance to break par, he took a 5 at the sixteenth, where his drive landed almost against a tree. Nevertheless, Snead pulled ahead of Palmer, Worsham, Cooper, Spears, Mangrum and Locke, all of whom had 218.

Delays at Short Holes

Because of the delays that developed at the short holes, especially the second, where Joe Kirkwood Sr., the trick-shot artist, took a 7 this morning, the fourth round started late. Some, like Brosch, Locke and Horton Smith, who played together, had only three or forty minutes' allowance for lunch and a brief rest before beginning the arduous fourth round.

Cary started with three birdies that were the foundation of his good scoring, short putts being responsible for the 3's at the first and third, and he had one of about ten feet for his deuce at the second. Another birdie 4 at the fifth made him four under but this phenomenal speed did not continue.

Middlecoff was over par at the next, where he faded an iron shot into a bunker. He collected a birdie at the seventh, then missed the green at the short eighth and went over par there with a 4. His second caught the rough at the ninth for, a 5, and he was out in 34, two under. When he three-putted for a 6 at the tenth, his early advantage was further reduced. But he followed this with successive pars until he dropped an eight-footer for a deuce at the short fourteenth. He had a try for a birdie at the next, but didn't get it, and closed with pars at the last three for 35 and a two-under-par 69.

Brosch, with a big gallery trailing, went over par at the fourth when he carded a 6, but he promptly set his chances on the right trail with successive birdies at the next two. His next bit of woe came at the seventh, where he hit a tree with his second shot at this long par-5 hole, winding up with a 6. Two additional pars enabled him to get by the turn in 37.

Another birdie fell to his lot at the eleventh, but then at the thirteenth, a dog-leg hole with an elevated green, his second landed to the right and he had to pitch up for a 5.

Brosch had a short putt for a birdie at the next, but didn't get it and, though he sailed through with pars to the eighteenth tee, he

U. S. Open Cards and Scores

Cards of the Leaders

THIRD ROUND

CARY MIDDLECOFF
Out .... 3 2 4 3 4 4 5 4—34
In .... 5 4 4 4 2 4 4 3 4—35—69

GEORGE FAZIO
Out .... 4 3 3 4 5 5 5 3 4—36
In .... 5 3 4 3 3 5 3 4 4—34—70

ERIC MONTI
Out .... 4 4 5 4 4 4 5 3 3—36
In .... 4 4 4 4 3 3 5 3 4—34—70

LLOYD MANGRUM
Out .... 3 3 4 4 5 3 5 5 4—36
In .... 4 4 3 4 4 4 3 4 4—34—70

BUCK WHITE
Out .... 3 3 4 4 5 4 5 3 4—36
In .... 5 4 4 5 3 3 3 3 4—34—70

DAVE DOUGLAS
Out .... 4 3 4 4 4 5 3 5 5—37
In .... 5 3 3 4 2 5 4 3 4—33—70

LEW WORSHAM
Out .... 4 5 4 4 5 4 5 4—38
In .... 5 4 4 4 4 2 4 2 4—33—71

CLAYTON HEAFNER
Out .... 3 3 4 3 5 4 5 3 4—34
In .... 5 4 4 4 3 5 4 3 5—37—71

ELLSWORTH VINES
Out .... 4 3 4 4 5 4 4 4 4—36
In .... 5 4 4 5 2 5 4 3 4—35—71

SAM SNEAD
Out .... 4 4 4 5 4 6 4 3 4—37
In .... 5 4 3 4 2 5 4 3 4—34—71

JOHNNY PALMER
Out .... 4 2 4 4 5 4 6 3 3—35
In .... 5 5 4 5 4 4 4 2 4—37—72

AL BROSCH
Out .... 4 3 4 6 4 3 6 3 4—37
In .... 5 3 4 5 3 4 4 4 3 5—36—73

BOBBY LOCKE
Out .... 3 3 4 5 5 4 5 2 4—35
In .... 5 5 3 4 3 4 5 3 6—38—73

CLAUDE HARMON
Out .... 4 3 4 6 5 3 3 3 4—38
In .... 5 3 4 2 4 4 2 5—36—74

FOURTH ROUND

SAM SNEAD
Out .... 4 3 4 4 5 4 4 3 5—36
In .... 5 3 3 4 3 4 4 4 4—34—70

BOBBY LOCKE
Out .... 3 4 3 6 5 4 4 3 5—37
In .... 5 4 4 4 4 5 3 4 4—34—71

JIM TURNESA
Out .... 4 2 4 4 4 4 5 1 4—35
In .... 5 4 4 4 4 3 4 4 5—37—72

DAVE DOUGLAS
Out .... 4 3 4 5 4 4 5 3 5—37
In .... 5 4 4 5 3 3 4 3 5—36—73

CLAYTON HEAFNER
Out .... 4 2 5 4 5 4 5 3 4—36
In .... 5 4 6 3 4 4 4 3 4—37—73

JOHNNY PALMER
Out .... 3 3 4 4 4 3 5 5 4—35
In .... 5 4 3 4 5 4 4 4 3—33—73

CLAUDE HARMON
Out .... 3 3 4 4 5 4 3 3 5—34
In .... 5 4 5 4 5 3 4 3 4—35—74

CARY MIDDLECOFF
Out .... 5 3 4 5 4 4 6 5 3 4—39
In .... 5 4 4 3 3 3 4 6 3—35—75

BUCK WHITE
Out .... 5 3 4 4 4 6 7 5 3—41
In .... 5 3 3 5 3 5 5 3 4—37—78

AL BROSCH
Out .... 4 4 3 5 6 4 6 4 5—43
In .... 5 4 4 4 3 3 4 4—36—79

PAR FOR THE COURSE

Hole	Yards	Par	Hole	Yards	Par
1	385	4	10	542	5
2	182	3	11	412	4
3	415	4	12	369	4
4	442	4	13	415	4
5	525	5	14	163	3
6	525	5	15	316	4
7	444	4	16	445	4
8	200	3	17	193	3
9	443	4	18	395	4
Total	3,616	36	Total	3,320	35

Grand total—6,936 yards; par 71

struck a concluding 5. His tee shot fell into bushes at the left, and he chipped out before reaching the green and getting down in two putts for the 73.

Middlecoff's Net $11,999

CHICAGO, June 11 (AP)—Cary Middlecoff boosted his golf earnings to $11,999.57 this year with his $2,000 victory in the National Open. That put him second only to Sam Snead who has earned $13,860.83. It was Middlecoff's fifth tournament victory of the year.

June 12, 1949

Louise Suggs Takes Women's U. S. Open Golf Championship by 14 Strokes

GEORGIAN POSTS 291 FOR 72-HOLE EVENT

Miss Suggs Cards 70 on Last Round and Mrs. Zaharias Gets 80 for 305 Total

CAROL DIRINGER IS THIRD

Ohio Girl Top Amateur of the Tourney With 306—Dorothy Kielty, Patty Berg at 310

From a Staff Correspondent

LANDOVER, Md., Sept. 25 — Finishing in a blaze of glory with another par shattering round, Miss Louise Suggs, 26-year-old Carrollton, Ga., professional, won the fourth annual 72-hole United States open medal play golf championship today. A 36, 34—70 gave her a grand total of 291 at the Prince George's Golf and Country Club.

Miss Suggs, winner of the recent All-American open championship at Tam-o'-Shanter, was competing in this event for the first time as a pro. In her first round on Thursday she carded a record six-under-par 69, held the lead through Friday and Saturday and finished 14 strokes ahead of the defending champion, Mrs. Babe Didrikson

A WINNER ON LINKS

Miss Louise Suggs
Associated Press

Zaharias of Grossinger, N. Y.

Only once in the 72-hole struggle for the $7,500 prize money was Mrs. Zaharias close to catching up with her rival. That was at the end of 54 holes when she trailed by four strokes.

The Babe was decidedly off her game in this tournament, her first round 74 was her best effort. When she played the first nine today in 40 the large gallery that came out expecting a photo finish soon deserted her for Miss Suggs, who was burning up the course again. The Babe finished with another 40 for 80 and a grand total of 305.

The weather was ideal today

with the result that twenty of the players, the majority of whom are amateurs, broke 80.

The top amateur, 23-year-old Miss Carol Diringer of Tiffin, Ohio, had rounds of 75, 76, 77, 78 for third position in the field with 306.

Miss Dorothy Kielty of Long Beach, Calif., runner-up in the national amateur at Merion last week, posted 77 for a total of 310 and the second amateur prize.

This figure was tied by Miss Patty Berg of Savage, Minn., president of the newly organized Women's P. G. A. when she sank a 40-foot putt on the eighteenth for a 75 to take third money among the pros.

There was a four-way tie at 311 among amateurs. They were Miss Beverly Hanson of Riverside, Calif., who jumped to 83 today after rounds of 72, 81, 75; Miss Frances Stephens of Liverpool, England, who carded even par 75 to add to earlier rounds of 75, 81, 80; the 23-year-old Vermont champion, Miss Mae Murray, who got a 76 to add to 78, 88, 79, and Miss Marlene Bauer of Los Angeles, 15-year-old star, who three-putted the eighteenth for an even 80. Her previous rounds were 75, 78, 78.

Miss Riley Registers 312

Other amateurs to top the pros were Miss Polly Riley of Fort Worth, Tex., open champion, at 312; Miss Helen Sigel, Philadelphia, 313; Miss Marjorie Lindsay of Decatur, Ill., state champion, 314, and Miss Grace Lenczyk of Hartford, Conn., 315.

The ten professionals in the tourney all were winners as far as prize money was concerned, namely Miss Suggs, $1,500; Mrs. Zaharias, $1,000; Miss Berg, $800; Miss Betty Hicks of Detroit, $700, for 315; Miss Betty Jameson, $600 for 317; Miss Sally Sessions of Muskegon, Mich., $500 for 320; Miss Helen Detweiler of Indio,

Calif., $400 for 322; Miss Katherine Hemphill, $300 for 329; Mrs. Betty Mims White, $220 for 332, and Miss Marilyn Smith, $100 for 337.

THE LEADING SCORES

*Louise Suggs, Carrollton, Ga.	69	75	77	70—291	
*Babe Didrikson Zaharias, Grossinger, N. Y.	74	76	75	80—305	
Carol Diringer, Tiffin, Ohio	75	76	77	78—306	
Dot Kielty, Long Beach, Calif.	74	83	76	77—310	
*Patty Berg, Savage, Minn.	73	84	78	75—310	
Mae Murray, Urtland, Vt.	78	78	79	76—311	
Beverly Hanson, Riverside, Calif.	72	81	75	83—311	
Frances Stephens, Bootle, England	75	81	80	75—311	
Marlene Bauer, Los Angeles	75	78	78	80—311	
Polly Riley, Fort Worth, Tex.	75	83	79	75—312	
Helen Sigel, Philadelphia	79	75	79	80—313	
Marjorie Lindsay, Decatur, Ill.	80	81	76	77—314	
Grace Lenczyk, Hartford, Conn.	77	80	80	78—315	
*Betty Hicks, Detroit	76	80	82	77—315	
Claire Doran, Cleveland	79	80	79	78—316	
*Betty Jameson, Chicago	78	86	73	80—317	
Peggy Kirk, Findlay, Ohio	78	81	83	75—317	
Mary Agnes Wall, Menominee, Mich.	79	84	77	78—318	
Maureen Orcutt, Englewood, N. J.	76	82	83	78—319	
*Sally Sessions, Muskegon, Mich.	79	83	83	75—320	
Bee McWane, Birmingham	73	84	86	79—322	
*Helen Dettweiler, Indio, Calif.	81	84	76—322		
Shirley Spork, Detroit	80	79	85	79—323	
Betty MacKinnon, Texarkana, Tex.	84	83	80	79—326	

*Denotes pro.

September 26, 1949

Hogan Gets 73 in Return to Tourney Golf

LITTLE TEXAN TIRES AFTER 9 HOLES IN 34

But 9,000 at Los Angeles Pay More Heed to Hogan's 73 Than to Better Scores

---

FURGOL 68 IS 3 UNDER PAR

Vines and Barber Next at 69 —Snead and Ferrier Need 71s, Middlecoff a 73

LOS ANGELES, Jan. 6 (AP)—Golf's mechanical man returned to the championship picture today, a little rusty and a little crusty.

The little man was Ben Hogan, launching a comeback in top-flight competition in the $15,000 Los Angeles open. He was good enough to make a fight all the way through a long first round of 18 holes at the Riviera Country Club.

He had par whipped in a miraculous exhibition for nine holes, but he tired on the final nine for a creditable 73, two shots over par and five back of the leader.

The leader was dark-horse Ed Furgol of Royal Oaks, Mich., with a three-under-par 68 that in other years would have set the spectators buzzing.

But Furgol and the remainder of the players, except Hogan, were unknown today. Nearly killed in an auto-bus crack-up eleven months ago, Hogan had returned to tournament golf.

No one in the crowd seemed to care what national open champion Cary Middlecoff did, although he tied at 73 with Hogan, Jimmy Demaret, Jimmy Turnesa and several others.

Sam Snead was ignored as he went around in 71 strokes, the same as Bob Hamilton, Otto Greiner, Jim Ferrier and other familiar touring pros.

This was Hogan's day on Hogan's course — the same Riviera where the little Texan had won the national open in 1948, where he had scored two of his three triumphs in this richest of the winter golf tourneys.

Hogan wasn't quite the same. His irons cracked like a rifle in the sunshine. He appeared the same cool Hogan as ever but he was off on the greens.

Things that never had bothered Hogan seemed to get to him. There was the sound of a hammer, with its dull, distant thud from a home construction high above the seventh green. That annoyed him.

An occasional airplane rumbled overhead. The old Hogan wouldn't have noticed. There was a voice in the stillness beside one tee. Hogan was disturbed, and pulled his shot into the rough. On the fifteenth he drove to the left and hit a girl spectator.

BEN HOGAN STARTS ON COMEBACK TRAIL IN CALIFORNIA

The golfer on the Riviera Country Club course in the Los Angeles Open. The sign reading "No cameras" was carried at the request of Hogan, who asked that photographers refrain from taking pictures while he was shooting.

Associated Press Wirephoto

The photographers worried him, more so than ever. Once he objected. One camerman thought he heard Ben say he'd quit if the cameras didn't quit. Hogan denied this afterward. He explained he meant he couldn't shoot while the cameras were shooting.

For the first time a man carried a large placard behind the threesome. It warned that no photography would be permitted on this threesome—Hogan, Johnny Bulla and Eric Monti.

Cameramen Fear Wider Ban

There was fear that all threesomes would demand the same placard. Halfway through, the card disappeared. Hogan later said he just wanted to be assured that all cameras, amateur and professional, were silent until he had made his shot.

For 12 holes, Ben outdrove Bulla and Monti. Then he began to tire. On the thirteenth he went one down to par for the first time. He couldn't rally and finished with another bad hole on the eighteenth, hooking his tee shot to the side of a hill.

On other holes, it was Hogan as golfers know him. His amazing recovery on the thirteenth was an example. He was in the rough off the tee, but he spanked a shot through a narrow space between trees and took a one-over-par 5.

He used an iron on No. 2 and drove 180 yards within one foot of the pin, barely missing an eagle 2. Conversely, on the tenth, he rammed a putt thirty feet within two feet of the cup and then missed.

Hogan admitted he was "sort of tired" at the finish, but he'll be back for the second round tomorrow.

After one round, Furgol was ahead by one stroke. Just back were two Pasadena shotmakers, Ellsworth Vines and Jerry Barber. Even with par 71 were Snead, Ferrier, Bob Gajda of Detroit and Hamilton.

Seven Golfers Tied at 72

Seven players were tied at 72 and eleven were listed in the 73 bracket with Hogan. Included was his threesome partner, Monti of Los Angeles. Bulla landed in the 74 class, along with six others.

Little Ben got a warm reception when he stepped up to the first tee at noon. There was a tenseness as he warmed up with a few swings. Announcer D. Scott Chisholm, clad in the plaid kilts of his homeland in the Scottish highlands, bellowed:

"This is the greatest event in the history of the Los Angeles open. But Ben Hogan has asked that I limit my introduction to—Ben Hogan, on the first tee."

That signaled the comeback of the slim, grim champion from Fort Worth. Some months ago, when Hogan lay near death, many feared he would never play a round of golf again.

Hogan, whose threesome was followed by most of the 9,000 spectators, said he was 10 or 15 pounds overweight, but it was hardly apparent. His legs gave the most concern. A blood clot developed after the surgery that followed the accident, but, leg cramps or not, Hogan was hoping to play the full 72 holes.

Just as Hogan was starting, Furgol finished his 36, 32—68, a strange round that listed seven birdies and four holes over par. Furgol, a fine player despite an arm crippled as a youth, was one over par going out this morning and had an erratic but low-scoring return trip with six birdies and two over par holes.

Early starters were hampered by greens virtually frozen by the cold. They had high scores, but improved them as the sun warmed the course.

Sidelined by a shoulder injury and operation, Lloyd Mangrum, last year's winner, was among the spectators.

January 7, 1950

Snead Defeats Hogan by Four Strokes in Los Angeles Golf Play-Off

WEST VIRGINIA ACE TOPS RIVAL, 72 TO 76

Snead Gains Lead on 1st and Never Trails to Beat Hogan In 18-Hole Play-Off

EDGE AT TURN 2 STROKES

Gallery of 7,500, Fog, Haze Hamper Golfers—Victor Gets Prize of $2,600

LOS ANGELES, Jan. 18 (AP)— Ben Hogan's gallant come-back to golf creaked slowly to a walk and then was stopped cold by Sam Snead today. The titans of golf met in a delayed, dramatic eighteen-hole play-off medal match, and the result was soon evident.

Snead, matchless today, sank Hogan's dreams of victory in his initial return to the golfing wars by a convincing four-stroke margin.

The long-slamming pro from West Virginia carded a 36, 36—72 and Hogan a 38, 38—76. Snead was one over par and Hogan five over. Those were the cold scores posted in the low-hanging fog enveloping the play-off scene at the Riviera Country Club.

They gave Snead undisputed claim to first prize of the recent $15,000 Los Angeles Open, leading money of $2,600. They gave Hogan the runner-up honors, $1,900 in cash—and the belated finale to a wonderful return to the links for golf's mighty mite.

Hurt in Crash

Hogan lost, and was, it seemed, never a threat. Snead won, and gave a masterful demonstration under adverse conditions in doing it.

The gallery was never too obviously in favor of Little Ben, but all the spectators knew the story of his courageous comeback. Just last February his broken body was lifted from the wreckage after his car collided with a bus in West Texas. For a time Ben had a 50-50 chance of living. His chances of ever playing golf again were much less.

But Hogan came back to enter the Los Angeles tourney, richest on the winter tournament swing, and he was good enough to hit the finish line in what for a few minutes looked like a clear-cut triumph.

But, this was a week ago yesterday. Snead came from behind and tied the count on the eighteenth and last green. The rivals were set for the play-off last Wednesday. It was rained out.

Snead did not wait for the eighteenth green today for his triumph.

He moved in front on the first hole. He held a two-stroke lead at the end of nine and he wheeled on to capture the play-off by four solid strokes.

There was no gambling man in Sam today. He played Riviera's long, heavily trapped, 7,020 yards of golfing challenge in conservative fashion. He had only one bad hole, the fourth.

Ben Pulls up Even

That was when Hogan made his only true bid to go past Sam. He pulled up even.

But Sam rammed home a 10-foot putt for a birdie 3 on the eighth and from then on it was not so much a question of Snead whipping Ben as of Ben defeating himself.

Hogan, the nation's 1948 golf king, and Snead, his successor while he was gone in 1949, attracted a swarming, overanxious gallery of more than 7,500 spectators.

There were some who thought Hogan lost the play-off when he missed a two-foot putt on the ninth green. Others thought the turn came when Snead sank his 10-footer on the preceding hole. Or, perhaps it came when Hogan belted a ball into the crowd and the trees on the eleventh fairway and wound up with a one-over 6.

The break the other way could have come on the fourth, where Snead whacked into a trap and failed to blast out and took a two-over par 5.

It is more possible that the break came on the very first tee, and Snead doubtless knew he had "the little man" this day.

Hogan's first tee shot was to the left—out of bounds. Hogan doesn't drive out of bounds from the first tee. Not steel-nerved Hogan. But he did.

He recovered in amazing style to get his par 5 on the hole, but Snead posted a birdie and was off. Hogan, appearing more grim and taut than at any time during play in the tournament, three-putted the second for five strokes. Hogan has been accustomed to birdies on the early holes, at least, before fatigue set in.

Misses 5-Foot Putt

There was Hogan on the difficult, slanting green of the fifteenth. He twice sank 50-foot putts there last week. Today he missed a 5-footer.

Snead outdrove him on almost every hole, while Ben was wild off the tee. Snead had 32 putts, Hogan 35. Hogan rimmed the cup from 30, 40 feet out on at least three greens. Snead sank putts from 10 and 11 feet, but generally they were much shorter.

This was hardly the Hogan who put together rounds of 73, 69, 69, 69 for his 280 last week. This was the Snead who brought on the deadlock with rounds of 71, 72, 71, 66.

The slowness of the match was attributed to three factors—visibility limited to approximately 165 yards by the fog, the hard to corral gallery and the cautiousness of the players in their drive down the stretch.

Hogan won the event three times dating from 1942, and Snead triumphed once, in 1945. Snead missed an excellent chance to tie Hogan and Jimmy Thomson in 1942, but—and he probably recalled it today—he took eight strokes on the eighteenth green and bowed out of the picture.

Hogan appeared at the course an hour or more before the scheduled start. He immediately went to the practice tee to hit a few balls and later practiced on the putting green.

Snead appeared more relaxed, joshing with the veteran announcer, D. Scott Chisholm, while Hogan, aside from a quick smile and a handshake with Sam as cameras clicked, was all business.

Hogan allowed himself a chuckle when he was introduced as hailing from his home town, Fort Worth. "Hershey, Pennsylvania," Hogan corrected as the crowd joined in the laughter. Hogan's professional address is Hershey.

Marshals were forced repeatedly before the tee-off to wave wandering groups of spectators off the fairway, 300 yards away.

They tossed for the honor of teeing off first. Snead won. Approaching the first green, Snead's ball hit a spectator. It was a lucky hit because the ball seemed headed for trouble.

An early morning fog blanketed the course. By noon it had become a heavy haze and then the sun peeped through. From then on it was a merry battle between the haze, the fog and the sun.

Snead will play in the Long Beach Open this week-end. Hogan will go to Palm Springs for a rest.

Sam Snead, right, receiving the good wishes of Ben Hogan   Associated Press Wirephotos

January 19, 1950

Players and P. G. A. End Dispute Over the Operation of Tourneys

By The Associated Press.

AUGUSTA, Ga., April 8—Touring golf stars won their fight with the P. G. A. tonight for more say-so in operating tournaments. They will remain in the P. G. A.

Once threatening difficulties between the two groups were ironed out in adoption of a series of proposals which P. G. A. Executive Secretary Tom Crane said virtually will provide the players "with complete self operation of tournament affairs within the structure of the association.

George Schneiter, ousted last Monday as P. G. A. Tournament Bureau Manager, will not be included in the set-up in any capacity other than as a tournament golfer.

A temporary committee was appointed at a meeting of P. G. A. officials and the golfers to supervise the tournament bureau until the executive committee meets in Columbus, Ohio, between June 20-27.

Its P. G. A. members are Joe Novak of Los Angeles, P. G. A. president; Horton Smith of Detroit, secretary, and Harry Moffitt of Toledo, treasurer. Player members are Lawson Little, Jimmy Demaret, Clayton Heafner, Toney Penna and Chick Harbert.

The golfers were selected by a board of governors which had acted on behalf of the displaced shot-makers.

Within the next three months, the entire player group will elect a permanent committee to serve from June to the end of the year. A new election then will be held.

At the annual meeting of the association in November a series of amendments to the P. G. A. constitution will be presented to give the players additional authority in tournament affairs.

Novak is chairman of the committee and a co-chairmanship arrangement was agreed upon whereby members of the committee can act while tournaments are going on from Florida to California.

Little was named the first co-chairman.

The players' board of governors first convened last winter and held spasmodic conferences with P. G. A. officials. The "board," including such stars as Sam Snead, Ben Hogan, Cary Middlecoff, Little and Demaret, was headed by Schneiter.

The player bid for power came to a head this week. Schneiter's firing in Chicago opened the week and tonight's meeting concluded it.

Among controversial points were P. G. A. plans to change the distribution of purse money in both $10,000 and $15,000 tournaments. Another issue involved where autographed golf clubs can be sold.

Home club pros. who form the bulk of the P. G. A. membership of 2,800, wish to sell the clubs only in their shops. The players for whom the clubs are named wish them sold in department stores and sports shops as well.

There was no comment from either side on what was decided on either of these issues.

April 9, 1950

Demaret Sets Record by Taking Masters Golf Third Time With 283

TEXAS-BORN PLAYER WINS BY 2 STROKES

Demaret, Clad in Green, Fires 69 for 283 to Gain Third Augusta Links Victory

FERRIER FINISHES SECOND

Falters on Final Six Holes— Snead Next at 287—Hogan and Nelson Tie at 288

By LINCOLN A. WERDEN
Special to The New York Times.

AUGUSTA, Ga., April 9—In a flamboyant Easter outfit, Jimmy Demaret, a native Texan, won the Masters tourney over the Augusta National Golf Club course today with a final 69 and a four-round aggregate of 283.

Smiling Jimmy, who selects his wardrobe with as much care as he does his clubs, chose an ensemble that reflected the greens of the pines and shrubbery that border this beautiful course. Chartreuse slacks, a green and white sweater, a light green cap and suede shoes of a deeper verdant hue identified the Houston-born professional, whose unexpected triumph in this event was his third—a record in itself.

But his taste in clothes did not affect his good judgment in playing the last nine in 34 when it seemed unlikely that he would emerge the winner. Nor did it detract from his sportsmanship as he said, "I

A MASTER GETTING OUT OF A TRAP ON GEORGIA LINKS

Jimmy Demaret playing to the seventh green in championship tournament yesterday

Associated Press Wirephoto

got a lucky break," when pace-setting Jim Ferrier, former P. G. A. champion, faltered badly on the last six holes and finished with 75 for 285, with a 41 on the incoming nine.

Just when it seemed that Ferrier had the tourney in his hand, the title slipped away in incredible fashion. The big fellow, born in Sydney, Australia, lost five strokes to par on the last six holes. He three-putted the home green but managed to save second place as last year's winner, Sam Snead, closed with an even-par 72 for 287.

Little Ben Hogan, essaying the role of chief challenger to Ferrier in the second and third rounds, could do no better than a 76 for 288, which put him in a tie for fourth with another Texan, Byron Nelson.

Following them was Lloyd Mangrum with the day's best round, a 68, for 291, while Clayton Heafner, Charlotte, N. C., pro, added a 72 for 292 to be bracketed with the United States Open champion, Cary Middlecoff. Lawson Little was next at 293 and Gene Sarazen and Fred Haas Jr. had 294's. Top amateur was Frank Stranahan, erstwhile British Amateur champion, with a four-round 71 for 297.

Once Ferrier passed the ninth with a 34, two under, there were few who believed he could be beaten. Next to last to start in the field, he was well aware, as the afternoon wore on, of just how his score stood in relation to the others.

Hogan, off to an early getaway and trailing Ferrier by only two strokes at 212 as the fourth round started, was filled with confidence. He was determined to win his first Masters title. Hogan's comeback in the sport gave added interest to the tourney.

18,000 Trudge Fairways

Some 18,000 trudged the fairways on this beautiful day and Hogan had a partisan crowd trailing him. But as he failed to keep to a par pace on the first five holes, there was no denying he had a real job ahead if he hoped to carve out a low enough score to give Ferrier something to shoot at. He was two over par at the fifth, as he missed two greens. Being bunkered at the seventh, he dropped another to par with a 5. However, he sank a birdie 4 at the eighth and made the turn in 38.

But Hogan never did strike the sub-par stretch that everyone awaited. He went over on the eleventh, and the dog-leg thirteenth of 480 yards, that was to

prove disastrous also to Ferrier later, cost Hogan a 6, after his second fell into the creek and he was charged with a penalty stroke before playing to the green.

A birdie at the fifteenth was a help, but he went over again at the sixteenth and three-putted the seventeenth. There was some solace in the five-footer Ben dropped for a closing birdie 3 at the home green but his 76, his highest round of the tourney, could not pay real dividends.

Meanwhile Demaret, paired with Norman Von Nida, Australian visitor, playing three duos back of Hogan, was steadily putting together a good solid round.

A 5 at the first where he drove into the woods was the only hole at which he went over par going out and he compensated with a 4 at the eighth, where he rolled in an eighteen-footer, and a birdie 3 at the ninth where his No. 8 iron second hit the flag and stopped six inches from the cup. That gave Demaret a 35 and, as it proved, a real chance.

Two Important Birdies

Down went a fifteen-footer for a par 4 at the tenth, and then at the thirteenth he snared a birdie 4 at the green where he had registered eagle 3's on his last two rounds. Demaret momentarily faltered at the fourteenth, three-putting for a 5. However, two important birdies followed.

A 4 at the picturesque fifteenth, where he chipped to within a yard, and a deuce at the sixteenth helped him to wrap up the $2,400 first-prize money. The "two" came as a result of a sturdy chip from the back fringe of the green that sent the ball in. With 4's at the last two holes, Demaret was in with a 69 for 283, which he hoped would take second honors.

Ferrier and Middlecoff were playing the twelfth hole when Demaret ended his bid for the honors

that also went to him in 1940 and 1947.

Big Jim, a 198-pounder, whose short game is excelled by few, gave the gallery something to cheer about early in the round. Running in a prodigious putt some sixty feet across the sixth green, he holed a deuce to be one under par. He followed with a fifteen-footer for a second consecutive birdie 3 at the seventh.

With this sort of golf and two pars for a 34 out, it was little wonder then that it looked as if he could win handsomely with par golf the rest of the way. In fact, a 38 on the back nine for a 72 would have clinched the event for him.

After a 4 at the tenth, he got down in one putt at the eleventh and twelfth for two more pars. Then came the blow that started the trouble. He hooked his drive into the woods off the thirteenth fairway. By local rule, he was permitted to drop out two lengths in on the fairway with a one-stroke penalty.

Reaches Corner of Green

However, he played his third short of the brook guarding the green, but sent his subsequent approach well past the pin and finally holed his second putt for a 6. At the par-4 fourteenth his second reached the corner of the green, but he three-putted for a 5. He had to chip from the fringe of the putting carpet at the fifteenth, but he gained his par 5 there.

This was the only par in the ruinous six-hole span that he collected. For at the water hole sixteenth he overplayed from the tee and then chipped four feet past the pin, missed the putt for a par coming back and took a 4. By now he had lost the advantage, and he needed two parts for a tie.

At the seventeenth his second failed to clear the bunker and the ball dropped into the sand, forcing him to a 5 instead of a precious 4.

A birdie 3 at the eighteenth still could save a tie, but Ferrier's second was some thirty-five feet beyond the pin, leaving him a tricky downhill putt. The ball went by the cup and stopped some five feet below. And he missed on his try for a 4, thus taking the third putt for a 5 and as costly a 41 as this tourney has ever seen.

Demaret not only has a sense of humor but is a baritone who likes to entertain his fellow pros. He could not avoid an opportunity when Bob Jones presented the prizes to sing into the microphone, "How Lucky You Are?" That was Demaret's theme song and the way he modestly explained his victory when he scored 70, 72, 72, 69 to win one of golf's most coveted honors.

FOURTH-ROUND CARDS

LLOYD MANGRUM

Out			
.... .4 4 4 4 3 5 2 3 5			3—33
In 4 3 4 5 4 3 4 4			4—35—68

JIMMY DEMARET

Out			
.... .5 5 4 3 4 4 3 4 4			3—35
In 4 3 4 5 4 2 2 4			4—34—69

CLAYTON HEAFNER

Out			
.... .4 4 4 4 5 2 4 4 4			4—35
In 5 4 3 5 5 4 3 5			3—37—72

SAM SNEAD

Out			
.... .5 5 4 3 4 4 3 5 3			4—36
In 4 3 4 5 5 4 4 4			5—36—72

CARY MIDDLECOFF

Out			
.... .4 4 4 4 4 3 4 4 4			4—35
In 4 4 3 4 5 4 3 4			4—36—73

BYRON NELSON

Out			
.... .4 4 5 4 3 5 4 5			4—38—74
In 4 4 3 5 5 4 4 5			4—38—74

JIM FERRIER

Out			
.... .4 4 5 3 4 2 3 5			4—34
In 4 4 6 5 6 4 4 5			5—41—75

BEN HOGAN

Out			
.... .4 5 5 3 5 3 5 4 4			4—38
In 4 5 3 6 4 4 4 5			3—38—76

PAR FOR THE COURSE

OUT			IN		
Hole.	Yards.	Par.	Hole.	Yards.	Par.
1........	400	4	10......	465	4
2........	535	5	11......	415	4
3........	350	4	12......	155	3
4........	220	3	13......	480	5
5........	440	4	14......	425	4
6........	185	3	15......	485	5
7........	370	4	16......	190	3
8........	520	5	17......	400	4
9........	430	4	18......	435	4
Total..3,450		36	Total..3,450		36

Grand total—6,900 yards; par 72.

April 10, 1950

Hogan Wins U. S. Open Golf In a Remarkable Comeback

By LINCOLN A. WERDEN
Special to THE NEW YORK TIMES.

ARDMORE, Pa., June 11—The man they said never would be able to play again regained the United States open golf championship today at the Merion Golf Club.

Ben Hogan, who miraculously survived an automobile smash-up in February, 1949, and returned to tournament competition last January, defeated Lloyd Mangrum and George Fazio in an eighteen-hole play-off for the game's biggest honor by scoring a 69, four less than Mangrum and six below Fazio.

In a dramatic finish, Hogan completed one of the outstanding feats in the annals of sports to win the trophy he captured for the first time at the Riviera Country Club, Santa Monica, Calif., in 1948.

A year ago he sent the trophy back to the United States Golf Association because a blood clot in one of his legs threatened his life. He told the U. S. G. A. he regretted

his inability to defend his laurels. He was convalescing when the 1949 open championship was played at the Medinah Country Club outside Chicago, being content with putting on the rug in his Fort Worth, Tex., home while listening to radio reports of the tourney.

When he returned to tournament golf in the Los Angeles open in January over the same Riviera course that is now known as "Hogan's Alley" because of his numerous victories there, he stunned the followers of the royal and ancient game as well as sports adherents everywhere by finishing in a tie in his first test of the comeback trail. Sam Snead overtook him and then beat him in a play-off.

Starts The Road Back

But Hogan was not discouraged. His customary determination was in evidence as he slowly rebuilt his health, aided by his wife, Valerie, who had escaped serious injury in the automobile crash with him. Then came his decision to recreate

Ben Hogan with the championship trophy

ON THE FINAL GREEN IN EXTRA ROUND OF THE U. S. OPEN AT ARDMORE

Ben Hogan (wearing dark sweater) playing at the eighteenth hole of the Merion Golf Club yesterday   Associated Press Wirephoto

the mechanical perfection of his great golf game. It was one thing, colleagues admitted, to regain health, quite another to regain the timing and coordination of a super-expert after a long lay-off and a nerve-testing ordeal.

Yesterday his challenge to the disbelievers was on the line. He had a chance to take the title outright with a finish of pars on the last four holes. But he went over regulation figures at two of these and posted a 72-hole aggregate of 287, the same as Mangrum, champion in 1946, and Fazio, the Norristown, Pa., born pro.

Today, in a duel that approached the bizarre with an incident at the sixteenth green, Hogan came on to win. Perhaps a bit tired at the conclusion of his first thirty-six holes of play in one day yesterday since he resumed his tournament schedule, he warded off those who proffered words of encouragement.

"I feel fine," Hogan insisted, with a trace of annoyance that anyone would dare suggest his legs might be bothering him during the championship grind.

He reiterated this statement as he sat in the locker room before starting out in this crucial three-way play-off in golf's golden jubilee championship today. But at the fifteenth hole this afternoon, almost four hours after the three professionals, followed by some 10,000 wildly enthusiastic spectators, had started, Hogan had a lead of one stroke over Mangrum and three over Fazio.

Then came the play at a hole that is perhaps without equal in the fifty years that golfers have been battling for the cup. Mangrum drove into the heavy rough and his rivals were out in the fairway with their drives. This is the famed quarry hole that has since been "softened," but still has a series of bunkers below the green amidst trees and sand. Mangrum realized that he had almost an impossible second shot to the elevated green. Trees blocked his way. He played a safety shot to

the fairway for his second.

Mangrum pitched his third to within fifteen feet of the pin. Fazio's second was at the back edge and Hogan hit a perfect iron to within six feet of the pin. Fazio played up for a certain 5. Mangrum replaced the ball on the spot from which he had lifted while Fazio was playing.

Then a strange thing happened. After sighting the line of the putt, he picked up the ball, blew on it and replaced it on the green, rolled it in for what would have been a 4. Hogan putted, missed his chance for a birdie and sank the par 4. Most of those huddled about the green, still thought Hogan had only one stroke advantage over Mangrum.

But soon the signboard carried by an attendant to indicate the progress of the play-off indicated that something was amiss. Mangrum had a 6 there instead of a 4. Isaac Grainger, chairman of the United States Golf Association rules of golf committee, along with three other executives, had been sitting back of the green, as interested as any of the fans who had been following the stroke by stroke battle.

Mangrum had broken a rule, in fact two, since competitors are not permitted to lift a ball that is in play under penalty of two strokes. Neither are they permitted to "clean" a ball, without suffering a penalty. Mangrum had inadvertently done just that by blowing a bug off the ball.

Questioned later, Mangrum said he did not realize that his action had been an infraction and that he was not familiar with the ruling. Coming as it did at a crucial stage in the match, it caused a stir in the crowd surrounding the seventeenth tee as the players started down the hill to the green. Few realized what had happened and on all sides questions were being asked.

Would Hogan coast in because of a rule infraction?

His lead was now three strokes over Mangrum, but there was still

uncertainty among the gallery. Hogan dispelled all that soon after. His shot to the seventeenth green stopped on the lower level of the putting surface. He sighted it carefully and hit it well, the ball running up and over a ridge and on into the cup for a deuce.

"That's the way to win," shouted an overjoyed bystander.

Fazio and Mangrum had par 3s there and now Hogan was four strokes in front, or two without the penalty.

The long eighteenth was lined with spectators sensing the tenseness of the finish. Another incident might change the picture. All three players hit the green on their second shots, but they did not hold the green.

Fazio chipped up for a 5 after Mangrum and Hogan approached well, Hogan having less than a six-footer for his par. Mangrum sank his 4 and then Hogan's putt curled in for the championship. There was a mad crush and several persons were knocked down in the melee. A cordon of police saved Hogan from the happy jam of well-wishers.

Fazio Putting Brilliant

Over the outgoing nine Fazio had proved the better putter. He was constantly bringing cheers by his recoveries, and, at the turn, Hogan and Mangrum were deadlocked at 36 to the former Canadian open champion's 37. Fazio had used only thirteen putts during that stretch, Hogan sixteen and Mangrum seventeen.

Before starting out Hogan had joshed with Dick Chapman, former National Amateur champion and recent finalist in the British amateur. "No, Dick," he said, "I'm not a good putter. I've had thirty-six on every round of the championship so far." "Don't tell me that, Ben," replied Chapman. "You're one of the best in the game."

For a long while, though, it seemed that Hogan was allowing opportunity to slip by. He was putting short. Only once on the outgoing half did he snare a birdie and that was when he sank a four-

footer at the seventh for a 3. He had seven pars, and the only one over par was at the eighth, where he drove into a bunker and took a 5. Mangrum had a birdie 4 at the second, where his fine second stopped three feet from the pin. He got a 4 at the short third after chipping from the back edge and having his putt for the par rim the cup. Fazio one-putted the second, fourth, fifth, eighth and ninth greens.

On the tenth Mangrum drove into a bunker at the right, standing in the hazard below the ball to make his recovery shot. But after the 5 there he birdied the eleventh when he ran in a seven footer.

At the twelfth Mangrum hit a No. 5 iron too strongly as the breeze faded and the ball flew over the crowd, going out of bounds to the road back of the green. Hogan then led Mangrum by a stroke. Hogan was 2 ahead with a 4 at the fourteenth, where Mangrum was bunkered and took a 5. At the next hole Mangrum sank a fifteen-footer for a birdie 3, and Hogan had to be content with a 4.

Then the bug alighted on Mangrum's ball at the sixteenth, and the penalty for handling the ball sealed the victory for Little Ben

Par for the Course

Hole.	Yards.	Par.	Hole.	Yards.	Par.
1	360	4	10	335	4
2	535	5	11	375	4
3	195	3	12	400	4
4	595	5	13	133	3
5	425	4	14	443	4
6	438	4	15	395	4
7	360	4	16	445	4
8	367	4	17	230	3
9	185	3	18	458	4
Total	3,177	36	Total	3,217	34

Grand totals—6,694 yards; par 70.

THE CARDS

Out—										
Hogan	4	5	3	5	4	4	3	5	3—36
Mangrum	4	4	4	5	4	4	4	3—38
Fazio	5	4	3	5	4	5	5	3—37

In—									
Hogan	4	4	4	3	4	4	4	2—33—69
Mangrum	4	3	5	3	5	6	3	4—37—73
Fazio	4	4	4	3	5	5	3	3—38—75

Sports of the Times

BY ARTHUR DALEY

An Anti-Climax of Sports

ARDMORE, Pa., June 11—It was inevitable, of course, that there would be something of an anti-climax to the open championship in today's play-off. There usually is to every play-off. But what set this one apart from all the others was that, in some respects, it was reminiscent of the Los Angeles Open of last January. You remember that, don't you?

Little Ben Hogan at that time was meeting his first test in his long uphill climb from the valley of death. Learned doctors had said after his terrifying auto smash-up that he would be lucky to live. Never again would his torn body be able to carry him around a golf course. Of that they were sure. The chances were that he would be unable to play even for fun. Working at his trade once more was much too insane a thought for serious consideration.

But Blazin' Ben made his return in the Los Angeles Open, and the gallant mite finished in a tie with Sammy Snead. He lost that play-off, which was not particularly important. The electrifying news was that Hogan was back in the thick of the fight, getting there on sheer grit and determination.

The experts, who can be just as wide of the mark as anybody, were pretty well agreed before this tournament started that the tenacious Texan might score well in the first two rounds, but they were equally certain that the marathon finish of 36 holes in a day would buckle his tortured legs and have him popping osselets all over the course.

The Pace That Kills

"Ben just can't do it," said the outspoken Gene Sarazen with a sympathetic shake of his head. "Thirty-six holes in one day will kill him." It was a reasonable assumption. This was only Hogan's seventh tournament since his brush with death, and in none of the others had he been forced to jam in two rounds in the one day. Yet the healthy stars faltered in the homestretch yesterday and the iron-willed, square-jawed scrapper from Texas finished in a tie.

Ben was chatting in the hotel lobby this morning. It was idle chatter. But in the course of it he dropped a couple of sentences which were highly significant.

"The trouble with Merion," he drawled, "is that it always has you on the defensive. There's no way you can take the offensive against it."

His jaw jutted grimly. It was obvious that he favors attack, even against something as inanimate as a golf links.

Appearances Are Deceiving

After studying Merion's treachery for four days, however, one can't help but wonder if this fiendish device for playing pasture pool is as inanimate as it looks. It has a par of 70 and measures only 6,694 yards, both sets of statistics being slightly on the skimpy side. Yet there is no getting around the fact that there were only fourteen sub-par rounds out of the first 434 completed.

The opening day fooled a lot of people. When an unknown like Lee Mackey tears Merion apart with a record 64, no one could be blamed for snorting, "Huh, that can't be so tough." Everyone more or less expected that par of 280 for the 72 holes would be shattered. But Mackey soared up to 81 on the second round. Non-golfers have since asked, "Why did everyone immediately disregard Mackey as a contender in spite of his record 64?"

It's a good question. The answer is simple. Some unknown rookie can hit a longer home run than Babe Ruth ever hit. But it's consistency over the long pull which marks the true champion. That rookie still hasn't hammered out sixty homers in a full season of play. That's why the kid from Alabama had no chance of ever being more than a one-day sensation.

Much Too Defiant

Merion can be licked once, but it has the resil-

lency of a rubber-ball or the recuperative powers of the champion who can bounce back off the floor after being knocked down and belt the other guy's block off. Unlike an ordinary golf course, it does all of the attacking.

Cary Middlecoff, for instance, was in a fine spot just before the final round to repeat as champion. He had three rounds of 71, and, as later events were to prove, only needed an ordinary 73 to win. But his luck was inordinately atrocious. Whenever his playing partner, Hogan, hit a spectator with a drive or approach, the victim helped him by keeping the ball from heading for impending disaster.

But whenever the young dentist from Memphis hit a spectator, it meant a major extraction. The ball invariably caromed in the wrong direction. Toward the end he just ceased to care and performed mechanically. That, naturally, led him into further difficulties and an eventual score of 79.

It was on the sixteenth, though, that Merion gave him a ghoulish horse-laugh—and the business. Just before the green and in a deep gully in front of it is an abandoned rock quarry, now covered with jungle growth. The second shot is across the rock quarry.

Middlecoff's second fell into the gully behind a twenty-foot rock-faced cliff. He had to play safe and, as its last ironic jest, Merion forced him to chip into a sand trap, the only spot in the gully from which he could reach the green. When safety play requires a fellow to shoot into sand traps—well, that gives you an idea of what this course is like.

Perfect Ending

If Battling Ben had lost this play-off, no one could have blamed him. After all, he had done miraculously well in dragging his wearied legs this far. Yet this was such a gushily romantic setting, and he was such an overwhelmingly sentimental favorite, that it would have been cruel indeed for him to have wavered. So the little Texas bulldog, who had defied the doctors, took it upon himself to defy the laws of probabilities and to defy Merion's constantly outrageous challenge.

He beat Lloyd Mangrum. He beat George Fazio. And as a final flourish he also beat Merion's par. A fifty-foot uphill putt of incredible accuracy on the seventeenth brought the birdie that did it. This was the cushion which handed him outright victory beyond question, one untainted by Mangrum's two-stroke penalty on the sixteenth. He was to win by a margin of four strokes.

This is a sport success story without parallel. All hail Ben Hogan, a champion among champions!

June 12, 1950

Locke Takes British Open

South African Keeps Golf Crown
On Last-Round 68 for Record 279

Mrs. Zaharias' card, with women's par:

Out—		
Women's par	.... 4 5 4 5 4 3 4 4 4	3—38
Mrs. Zaharias	.... 4 4 3 4 4 4 4 4	3—34
In—		
Women's par	.... 4 3 4 5 5 4 3 5 4	—37—75
Mrs. Zaharias	....4 4 5 5 4 3 3 4	4—36—70—291

October 2, 1950

Locke Clips Sarazen Mark—
Stranahan Cards a 66 and
Is Low Amateur at 286

TROON, Scotland, July 7 (AP)—Bobby Locke, walking as if the Troon fairways were carpeted with eggs, shot a fourth-round 68 today to win the British open golf title for the second straight year and lowered a scoring mark that had stood since 1932.

The South African, widely known in the United States' golfing circles, totaled 279 with rounds of 69, 72, 70, 68 over the par-70 course. His aggregate excelled the previous low of 283 posted by Gene Sarazen eighteen years ago.

Only because it retained the championship for Locke did his hot round overshadow a sensational 66 which Frank Stranahan of Toledo fired in a vain attempt to place the open trophy beside the British amateur award he had won earlier this spring.

Stranahan finished with 286, the best of the three-man United States contingent. The Ohio muscleman really lost his title chance in the first round when he needed 77 strokes to tour the tiny fairways of this 6,583-yard layout on the seacoast.

Johnny Bulla of Pittsburgh scored 288 and Jimmy McHale of Philadelphia posted 290.

Bulla Ties for Fourteenth

Stranahan's showed rounds of 77, 70, 73, 66, while Bulla did 73, 70, 71, 74 and McHale 73, 73, 74, 70. The Ohioan finished in a threeway tie for ninth place, but was low amateur. Bulla shared fourteenth place and McHale tied for seventeenth.

Roberto de Vicenzo of Argentina, second with 281, also broke Sarazen's record. Before the afternoon round, Locke and de Vicenzo were tied with Dai Rees of Wales for the lead at 211.

Two others bettered Sarazen's old mark. They were Fred Daly of Ireland and Rees, who tied for third at 282. Daly shot 75, 72, 69, 66 and Rees 71, 68, 72, 71.

Even with the former record of 283 and deadlocked for fifth were Eric Moore, South Africa, 74, 68, 73, 68, and Max Faulkner, England, 72, 70, 70, 71. Two English golfers, Fred Bullock, with four 71s, and Arthur Lees, 68, 76, 68, 72, shared seventh place at 284.

At the start of the morning round, Locke was third, two strokes off Rees' 139 pace. He had dropped back yesterday when he needed six strokes on the par 3 fifth hole.

Locke figured then he was out of the running for the title, "but I just swallowed the pill—and it was a hard one—and determined to forget it."

Forget it he did. He was a cold, merciless competitor. He never smiled after a good shot. He never frowned after one of his rare bad ones. His routine always was the same. A shot, a quick march down the fairway like a church deacon making the Sunday collection, a brief inspection and then another shot.

He was on the fourteenth tee

Bobby Locke
The New York Times (London Bureau)

when he heard that De Vicenzo had finished with 281, two below Sarazen's mark. He answered the challenge by slapping an iron tee shot within six feet of the pin and sinking the putt for a deuce.

Stranahan's blazing finish included three 3s and a 2 over the last six holes. He covered that stretch in nineteen strokes, four under par. His 66 was two strokes below the amateur record for the course.

The Ohioan went out in 35 and returned with a 31. Daly, who annexed this title in 1947, also scored a 66. He shot 33, 33.

Bulla, twice runner-up in this event, was only three strokes off the pace at the start of the final round, but his game crumbled on the last nine. McHale ran into all sorts of trouble in the morning with a 74.

THIRD-ROUND CARDS

	PAR		
Out	........4 4 4 4 3 5 4 3	4—35	
In	........4 4 4 4 3 5 4 3	4—35—70	
	FRANK TRANAHAN		
Out	........4 4 4 4 3 5 5 3	4—36	
In	........4 5 5 4 4 4 3 3	3—37—73—220	
	JOHN BULLA		
Out	........3 4 4 5 2 4—5 3	5—35	
In	........4 4 4 5 3 4 5 2	5—36—71—214	
	BOBBY LOCKE		
Out	........4 4 4 4 3 5 4 3	4—33	
In	........5 4 4 5 3 4 5 3	4—37—70—211	
	JIM McHALE		
Out	........5 4 4 3 3 5 5 2	5—36	
In	........4 4 5 5 4 4 4 3	4—38—74—220	
	ROBERTO DE VINCENZO		
Out	........4 4 4 4 3 5 4 2	4—34	
In	........3 4 4 4 3 4 5 3	4—34—68—211	
	ARTHUR LEES		
Out	........4 3 4 4 3 5 3 3	4—33	
In	........4 3 4 4 4 5 4 4	4—35—68—212	
	DAI REES		
Out	........4 3 5 4 3 4 3 3	4—33	
In	........4 4 6 4 2 5 6 4	4—39—72—211	

FOURTH-ROUND CARDS

	JIM McHALE		
Out	........4 4 4 4 3 4 3 4	4—34	
In	........5 5 4 4 3 5 3	4—36—70—290	
	ROBERTO DE VICENZO		
Out	........3 4 4 4 3 4 4 3	4—33	
In	........5 3 6 3 5 4 2	4—37—70—281	
	BOBBY LOCKE		
Out	........3 4 4 4 3 4 4 3	4—33	
In	........4 4 5 4 2 4 5 3	4—35—68—279	
	FRANK STRANAHAN		
Out	........5 3 4 4 3 6 4 3	3—35	
In	........4 4 3 4 2 3 3	3—31—66—286	
	JOHN BULLA		
Out	........4 4 4 4 3 5 4 3	4—35	
In	........6 5 4 5 3 4 4 3	5—39—74—288	
	DAI REES		
Out	........4 4 4 4 3 4 4 2	4—33	
In	........4 4 5 4 4 5 3	4—38—71—282	
	ARTHUR LEES		
Out	........5 4 4 5 5 4 5 4 3	4—39	
In	........4 3 4 4 3 4 5 2	4—33—72—284	

July 8, 1950

LINKS HONORS WON BY MRS. ZAHARIAS

She Finishes With 5-Under-Par 70 to Take National Open With Record-Tying 291

WICHITA, Kan., Oct. 1 (AP) — Mrs. Babe Didrikson Zaharias won her second women's national open golf tournament today with a five-under-par 70 for a seventy-two-hole score of 291, tying the record for the event.

The fabulous Babe, playing out of Prairie View, Ill., boosted her money earnings to $14,200 as she beat her nearest competitor, amateur Miss Betsy Rawls of Austin, Tex., by nine strokes. Mrs. Zaharias took $1,250 of the $5,000 payoff today. Miss Louise Suggs of Cincinnati was third with 302 strokes after a one-under-par 74. Miss Suggs set the tourney record in winning the open at Landover, Maryland, last year.

Miss Helen Dettweiler of Indio, Calif., shot the windy, wet Rolling Hills Country Club course in 76

and wound up with a 304 for third place among the professionals and fourth in the field.

Miss Berg Is Fifth

Miss Patty Berg, the Minneapolis redhead who won the first open in 1936, had a sparkling 72 for a 307 total that pulled here into fifth place.

Mrs. Zaharias, winner of every blue ribbon offered women golfers, shot her second successive 70 under weather conditions that made the going extremely difficult.

The Babe's long game was the pay-off. Her seven birdies, four out and three in, were mostly on short putts.

Mrs. Zaharias played the 6,203-yard, hilly course in 34, 36, two strokes under men's par.

Marlene Bauer at 308

Miss Marlene Bauer of Midland, Tex., finished with a 77 and 308 for a tie with the national amateur champion, Miss Beverly Hanson of Indio, Calif., for sixth and seventh places.

Miss Betty Bush of Hammond, Ind., who started the day with a 227, second to Miss Rawls in the amateur group, blew to an 87 for 314, one more than amateur Miss Helen Fay Crocker of Montevideo, Uruguay. Miss Crocker played in 76 strokes today.

Miss Rawls scored an even par 75 as she played consistently on both nines.

HONORS IN POLL GO TO MRS. ZAHARIAS

Louise Suggs, Patty Berg and Betty Jameson Also Named to Golf Hall of Fame

AUGUSTA, Ga., April 8 (AP)—The four best-known women professionals of present-day golf were elected to the women's golf Hall of Fame today by the board of selectors for the hall.

Mrs. Mildred D. (Babe) Zaharias was the No. 1 choice to join the group of six amateurs named last year for charter membership. Mrs. Zaharias, winner of every important title in women's golf, polled nine votes of a possible nine.

Mrs. Zaharias is a Texan by birth but now owns a golf course in Tampa, Fla.

Miss Louise Suggs of Carrollton, Ga., was second with eight votes; Miss Patty Berg of Minneapolis was third with seven and Miss Betty Jameson of San Antonio was fourth with four votes.

The Women's Professional Golf Association is sponsor of the hall. Last year the board of selectors elected as charter honorees: Beatrix Hoyt, Margaret Curtis, Alexa Stirling, Dorothy Campbell Hurd, Virginia Van Wie and Glenna Collett Vare.

The board of selectors is made up of Grantland Rice, N. A. N. A., chairman; Bob Harlow, Golf World, vice chairman; Sterling Slappey, Associated Press, secretary; Charles Bartlett, Chicago Tribune; Bert Prather, Atlanta Constitution; Lincoln A. Werden, NEW YORK TIMES; Chuck Curtis, Los Angeles Times; Russ Newland, Associated Press.

Also Herb Graffis, Golfdom and the Chicago Sun-Times; Linde Fowler, retired golf writer for Boston Transcript; Kerr Petrie, retired New York Herald Tribune golf writer, and Ed Miles, Atlanta Journal, serving for the late O. B. Keeler.

April 9, 1951

Hogan Captures Masters Golf for First Time, Beating Riegel by 2 Strokes

TEXAN'S 68 FOR 280 BEST AT AUGUSTA

Hogan Plays Steadily, Safely on Final Round as Riegel Registers 71 for 282

SNEAD FALTERS, GETS 291

Mangrum, Worsham Tie for 3d at 286—Douglas Is Fifth as Coe Tops Amateurs

By LINCOLN A. WERDEN
Special to THE NEW YORK TIMES.

THE VICTOR MISSES A BIRDIE ON THE SECOND GREEN

Ben Hogan rises from his stance just after his ball rolled past the cup in final round of Masters golf at Augusta yesterday. Lew Worsham is on the left.

Associated Press Wirephoto

AUGUSTA, Ga., April 7—Ben Hogan, the man who came back last June to win the United States Open Golf championship after they said he would never play again, captured the Masters tourney over the picturesque Augusta National course today with a 72-hole score of 280.

With 10,000 of a gallery of 15,-000 following him in the warm sunshine, Hogan accounted for a 4-under-par 68 on this concluding round that gave him the honors for the first time by a margin of two strokes.

The little Texan, trailing by one shot at the start of the final 18, played a safe, steady game and when he came to the home green, hemmed in by the enthusiastic gallery, he needed only a bogey 5 to beat Robert (Skee) Riegel, former United States amateur champion, who shared the lead with Sam Snead after yesterday's third round. But Ben got his par 4 for the victory.

When it was all over, Hogan was asked what other golf title he would like to win now.

"If I never win another, I'll be satisfied," he said. "I have had my full share of golfing luck."

Hogan never willingly refers to the automobile accident in 1949 that almost caused his death or the long months in which he recovered from his injuries and got back to his game.

A disastrous 80 by Snead today eliminated the former Masters and P. G. A. champion from contention and he finished in a tie for eighth place with 291. Snead and Riegel had carded 211 apiece for 54 holes and Hogan was a stroke back of them.

Riegel was in the clubhouse two hours before Hogan completed his final round, with a one under par 71 that clinched second place at 282, four strokes ahead of Lloyd Mangrum, who got 73 for 286 to tie Lew Worsham.

Worsham, paired with Hogan, had some unusual experiences, especially in getting a deuce at the short twelfth, where his ball bounded onto the green after splashing in the pond. He sank a 45-foot putt there.

Dave Douglas, the slim Delaware pro threatened with a 34 out. But Dave, who had been three shots back of Hogan beginning the fourth round, took 39 home and finished fifth at 288, or even with par. Lawson Little, despite a par 72, was sixth at 289, while Big Jim Ferrier, a pre-tourney favorite, could do no better than 72 for 290.

Then came Byron Nelson, twice Masters champion, with a 74 and John Bulla, who came back in 40 for a 75 to be grouped at 291 with Snead. Snead carded an 8 at the 415-yard eleventh, where the pond was widened to the left of the green this year. Sam's second ran over the putting carpet into the water. After a penalty stroke, he pitched into the water in front of the green, finally holing out after being on in 6. He had more trouble at the par-5 fifteenth where he popped his approach into the creek guarding the green, for his third penalty of the round, and finally marking down a 7 for the hole.

Nelson Escapes With 6

Nelson escaped with a 6 at the eleventh where he also had a ball in the water, but his partner, Billy Goodloe, Valdosta, Ga., amateur, ran into an 8 there as well. Goodloe, who had four-putted one green going out, could not extricate himself from various degrees of misfortune, since he followed the 8 with a 6 and a 7 for an 88. This put him far back at 305. He had been tied for tenth when he teed off for the fourth round.

Amateur honors thus went to Charlie Coe, the Oklahoma City star and U. S. Walker Cup player, who had 293 to tie Gene Sarazen and Cary Middlecoff. Dick Chapman was second among the amateurs at 297 and Sam Urzetta, national amateur titleholder, posted 298.

With ill luck besetting his rivals, it was little wonder that Hogan decided to play safe on the last nine. He had completed the initial stretch with a three under par 33 and realized his opportunity. Riegel had already posted his 282, Snead had faded as Hogan walked to the tenth tee. He had a fine drive and after a stunning second that sailed by the pin and stopped some six feet away, the crowd roared approval. He took two putts for a 4.

At the tricky eleventh he played his second shot carefully to avoid the mound on the right and the water at the left. He had to chip with a No. 6 iron on his third but he put the ball four feet from the pin and holed the putt for a par 4. Hogan bagged a par at the twelfth, where Worsham's hop, skip and jump tee shot resulted in a deuce. Bobby Jones was out to see this and was reminded of his famous shot that skimmed the water and lily pads at Interlachen when he won the 1930 U. S. open.

"It wasn't quite like this one, though," he said, referring to Worsham's luck.

Hogan met another challenge at the dog-leg par 5 thirteenth. Worsham had hit a second that landed on the wooden bridge over the creek surrounding the green. Hogan decided to use a No. 6 iron after he had pulled a No. 4 wood from his bag. Ben was short of the hazard in two, pitched to within seven feet in three and holed a birdie. Play was delayed some ten minutes when Worsham asked for permission to lift from the bridge without penalty. His plea was granted.

4 Under and 5 to Go

Hogan was now four under par. He needed only par on the next five holes to insure the title.

In the 1950 tourney Ferrier had wrecked his chances by losing five strokes to par on the last six holes. Hogan remembered that.

The 4 at the fourteenth was comparatively easy for Ben. But at the fifteenth, a par 5, where Sarazen in 1935 holed his spoon shot for the famous double eagle, Hogan had to choose once more between gambling or playing conservatively. Using a No. 4 iron for his second at this 485-yard hole, he kept the ball short of the water that cuts across the fairway near the green.

He pitched on well and was down for his 5, after two putts. Then came a par 3 at the short sixteenth, two shots to the green at the seventeenth for another 4. He was thirty feet from the pin and down in two putts. It was almost over. Hogan played deliberately short at the home hole, using a No. 6 iron for his second that left him below the green. But he pitched his third to within four feet and ran in the final putt for the 4 that sealed his 68. His 280 total was only one above the all-time mark of 279 set by Claude Harmon. The 280 matched his score in 1942 when he and Nelson

tied for first and Hogan lost in a playoff, 69 to 70.

After the war, Hogan finished second to Herman Keiser, who won the 1946 tourney with 282 to Ben's 283. It was 283, incidentally, that brought Jimmy Demaret the crown for the third time last year. But Demaret got a 71 today and was tied for thirtieth place at 299.

Jones, at presentation ceremonies in front of the clubhouse,

called Hogan's comeback in golf as one of the greatest in sports history.

Hogan thanked the gallery and praised the course, remarking with a laugh, of the "improvements" at the eleventh hole where so many of his rivals met disaster today.

April 9, 1951

HOGAN GOLF VICTOR

TEXAN TOTALS 287

Hogan Retains U.S. Open Title by Shooting Keen 67 on Final Round

HEAFNER SECOND ON 289

Locke 4 Strokes Behind Links Victor—Mangrum and Boros at 293—4 Get 294s

By LINCOLN A. WERDEN
Special to The New York Times.

BIRMINGHAM, Mich., June 16 —Ben Hogan is still the champion. In another great comeback, the little Texan retained the United States open golf title by closing with a 67 at the Oakland Hills Country Club to finish with a 72-hole aggregate of 287.

Trailing the leader, Bobby Locke of South Africa, at the end of the second round yesterday by five strokes and co-leaders Locke and Jimmy Demaret after the third this morning by two, Hogan won in a smashing finale by two strokes.

With a large sector of the record crowd of 17,500 hemming in the eighteenth green to view another phase of his courageous bid to keep the crown, Hogan rolled in a 14-foot putt for a concluding birdie 3. Surrounded by a cordon of police he made his way to the clubhouse amid the cheers of the spectators who had witnessed another stirring chapter in the golfing story of Hogan.

Then Hogan, the man who returned to the game after an almost fatal accident in 1949 to triumph in the historic play-off at Merion a year ago in one of the greatest of all sports comebacks, had to wait 1 hour and 45 minutes before he knew his claim on the trophy was secure.

Fourth Unsuccessful Try

Clayton Heafner, the 200-pound Charlotte, N. C., pro, came in

The Winner and Still Champion

Ben Hogan (right) with his caddy, Dave Press, after he carded a three-under-par 67 for the final eighteen holes at Birmingham, Mich., to retain his national golf crown.   Associated Press Wirephoto

with a one-under-par 69 for 289 and then Locke, the British open champion who now has tried unsuccessfully on four occasions to take golf's highest honor across the seas, came home with a 73 for 291 and third place.

Locke, who appeared to have mastered the 6,927-yard course, the most difficult in the fifty-one-year history of the tourney, could not hammer out the 32 that he needed to tie, since he had completed nine holes of his last round when Hogan had finished.

Until Hogan did the trick, no one among the 162 who started play here Thursday had been able to beat the controversial par 70 of the course. Heafner did it later,

but he and the famed golfer from Fort Worth proved the only successful two in the championship.

"Under the circumstances," stated Hogan as he sat in the locker room patiently awaiting the latest news of Locke's progress, "it was the greatest round I have played. I didn't think I could do it. My friends said last night that I might win with a pair of 69's. It seemed too much on this course. It is the hardest course I have ever played. I haven't played all the courses in the world, but I don't want to, especially if there are any that are tougher than this one."

He started Thursday with a 76, a bit ruffled by his failure to solve

the course. Neither was he satisfied yesterday with a 73, nor his morning with a 71. He blamed himself for overclubbing, for making mistakes. "I guess all of the boys are making more," he confessed.

But the 71 this morning was something in the way of an inspiration for the thrill-hungry crowd. All week they had heard reports of or seen for themselves the narrow fairways with strategically placed traps, the greens of rolling contours and two par-4 holes that many thought should have been rated at 5. And no one was under par! Hogan changed this attitude completely as he played the first nine in 32.

Victor Appears Determined

Hogan seemed determined to "beat" the course. He looked grim. He was concentrating. In fact, on the final putt for the 67, he stood over the ball at least 30 seconds before stroking. He wanted to do his best and he did.

But there were stumbling blocks. After the 32, for example, on the morning tour, he failed to get a par at the fourteenth after chipping from the rough. Then came his most discouraging experience of the day—a 6 at the fifteenth, where the trap is in the center of the fairway.

Hogan avoided the bunker but he had to play a second shot from the rough and the clubhead, he said later, caught in the tangled grass. From there the ball went across to the other side of the fairway. He pitched to the green but the ball struck a hard spot and bounded into the trap at the left. Extricating it, he added two putts before he holed out.

Once more "par" seemed to get the better of the argument. That was at the seventeenth where he used a No. 1 iron from the tee and was short of the green. A 4 resulted at this par 3, but he saved his 4 at the home hole after overplaying.

After the third round, Locke and Demaret were 218; Julius Boros and Paul Runyan, the 140-pounder, were 219, and Hogan, Dave Douglas, who was second yesterday, and Heafner were grouped at 220. Al Besselink, former Florida College golfer and now pro at Mount Clemens, Mich., was deadlocked with Sam Snead, first-day leader who played in his first open on this course in 1937 and who hoped to crash through this time after many disappointments, with 221.

Runyan Proves Amazing

But one by one as the players came in from their fourth rounds, it looked as if Hogan and Locke were the ones to beat. Lloyd Mangrum clinched a tie for fourth with Boros, the ex-Connecticut amateur, after a 70 for 293. Boros had a 71 this morning and a 74 later. Then Douglas with a final 74 followed at 294, along with 28-year-old Fred Hawkins of El Paso. Runyan and Besslink also posted 294's.

Runyan, who stayed in the running despite the fact that he is a short hitter, proved one of the amazing performers of the competition, depending on a reliable "spoon," the former Arkansas farm boy and twice P. G. A. champion did his best to solve the scoring problem. Out in 34 this morning he came back in 38. But this afternoon, he faltered on the outward trip with a 39 and ended with a 36 back for 75.

Snead closed with a 74 to be bracketed at 295 along with Al Brosch, Long Island's principal contender, Skee Riegel and Smiley Quick. Demaret finished with a 78 for 296, which also was Lew Worsham's total.

Francis (Bo) Wininger, the Philadelphian who was third yesterday, took a 77 and 79 for 302; Roberto De Vicenzo, the Argentine pro, and Sam Urzetta, United States amateur champion, also had 302, while Chuck Kocsis was the low amateur as the former Walker Cupper finished with 72 for 297.

It was Hogan and Locke then as the day wore on. Hogan was out in 35. Then came his 32. "A 32 this morning out and a 32 back this afternoon. We'll have to break up Hogan," joshed Claude Harmon, "just as we'll have to do with the Yankees."

Hogan said his greatest shot of the round was the No. 2 iron to the tenth green as he started back on the road to victory. It left the ball five feet from the pin and he holed his 3. A 15-footer that went in for a deuce at the thirteenth helped, too, but he was over par with a 5 at the fourteenth.

Where he took 6 this morning at the fifteenth, he ran in a birdie 3 as he used a No. 4 wood from the tee and a No. 6 iron to the green, before rolling in a 5-footer.

Now two under par, Hogan sank his par 4 at the sixteenth, after a tremendous drive almost to the edge of the lake. A wedge here stopped five feet from the flag and the crowd moaned as his putt for a birdie ran by. Then he added a par 3 at the seventeenth before the fine birdie 3 for the 67 at the eighteenth.

Locke Bunkered 8 Times

Locke, bunkered eight times on his morning round as he had a tendency to hook nevertheless was still sharing the lead after Demaret's third-round 70. A 6 at the tenth this morning hurt Locke's chances, but he said "the fifth hole ruined me." He had a 5 there this morning and this afternoon.

On the afternoon round, he was one under par for the first three holes with a birdie at the second. He drove into the rough for bogey 5 at the fourth. Then came the fifth where a good drive was three feet off the fairway into a trap. Recovering from the sand he had to chalk up a 5. A push drive close to a tree resulted in a 5 at the sixth and although he holed a 20-footer for a 3 at the seventh, he was out in 37.

When he started with a fine 3 at the tenth, by corralling a 20-footer, he still had a chance. He had pars at the next two, but missed the green at the short thirteenth and took a 4. He was down in one putt for a 4 at the next and, although bunkered at the fifteenth, holed a 4 there, too. At the six-teenth, his chances went glimmering when he was bunkered on his second back of the green.

Hogan has won the last three open championships in which he has competed. His record-breaking 276 accounted for the laurels in 1948 at Los Angeles. He was unable to compete in the 1949 tourney and his victory in the 1950 play-off brought him his most sought-after title.

Today, he became the third to win this championship three times. Ralph Guldahl is the last to win successively in 1937 and 1938. Only Willie Anderson, who won in 1903, 1904 and 1905, as well as in 1901, and Bobby Jones, who scored in 1923, 1926, 1929 and 1930, have exceeded Hogan's record.

The Leading Cards

THIRD ROUND

JIMMY DEMARET		
Out 4 4 3 4 5 4	3—36	
In 4 4 4 3 5 3 4 3	4—34—70	

BEN HOGAN		
Out 3 4 3 4 4 3	3—32	
In 4 4 5 3 6 4 4 4	4—39—71	

JULIUS BOROS		
Out 4 5 3 3 4 4 4	3—34	
In 4 4 5 4 5 4 3	5—37—71	

PAUL RUNYAN		
Out 4 5 3 4 4 4 4	2—34	
In 4 5 5 4 4 4 4 3	5—38—72	

SAM SNEAD		
Out 4 5 3 4 5 4 4	4—37	
In 4 4 4 3 5 5 4 3	3—35—72	

CLAYTON HEAFNER		
Out 4 5 3 4 4 4 4	4—37	
In 4 4 5 3 5 4 4 3	4—36—73	

BOBBY LOCKE		
Out 4 4 3 5 5 5	4—37	
In 3 4 5 4 5 4 5 3	4—36—73	

DAVE DOUGLAS		
Out 4 4 3 6 4 4	3—37	
In 4 5 5 3 5 4 4 3	3—38—75	

LEW WORSHAM		
Out 4 5 3 5 5 4 4 4	2—35	
In 5 3 4 3 5 5 7 3	5—40—76	

AL BROSCH		
Out 4 5 3 5 5 5 4 4	3—39	
In 4 4 5 4 5 4 5	5—37—76	

FRANCIS WININGER		
Out 4 5 3 4 5 5 4 5	4—39	
In 4 5 4 4 5 4 5 4	5—38—77	

FOURTH ROUND

BEN HOGAN		
Out 4 5 3 4 5 4 4	3—35	
In 3 4 5 2 5 3 4 3	3—32—67	

CLAYTON HEAFNER		
Out 4 5 3 3 4 4 4 5	3—35	
In 4 4 5 3 4 3 4 3	4—34—69	

LLOYD MANGRUM		
Out 3 5 4 5 6 4 4	3—35	
In 4 5 5 4 4 4 3 3	4—35—70	

FRED HAWKINS		
Out 4 5 4 5 4 4 3	3—37	
In .... 4 3 5•3 4 4 3	5—34—71	

AL BROSCH		
Out 4 5 3 5 4 4 4	3—37	
In 5 5 5 3 4 4 4 3	4—37—72	

AL BESSELINK		
Out 5 4 3 5 4 4 4	4—37	
In 4 5 4 3 4 4 4 3	5—36—73	

JULIUS BOROS		
Out 5 4 3 5 5 4 4	3—38	
In 5 4 5 3 4 4 4 3	4—36—74	

DAVE DOUGLAS		
Out 4 5 3 5 5 4 4	4—39	
In 5 4 6 3 4 4 3 3	5—37—76	

SAM SNEAD		
Out 5 4 3 5 5 4 4	4—39	
In 4 5 4 3 5 5 4 3	4—35—74	

PAUL RUNYAN		
Out 5 5 3 5 5 3 4	3—39	
In 5 4 5 3 4 4 4 3	4—36—75	

ROBERTO DE VINCENZO		
Out 4 6 4 5 4 4 4	4—39	
In 5 5 4 4 4 4 4 3	5—38—77	

June 17, 1951

Snead Easily Turns Back Burkemo in Final to Capture Third P. G. A. Title

WEST VIRGINIA PRO TRIUMPHS, 7 AND 6

Snead Takes Lead With Eagle 3 at First Hole and Has 5-Up Edge After Six

---

BURKEMO 3 DOWN AT 18TH

Rallies on 2d Nine of P. G. A. Final, but Winner Takes First 3 in Afternoon

---

PAR FOR THE COURSE

	OUT			IN	
Hole.	Yards.	Par.	Hole.	Yards.	Par.
1	483	5	10	470	4
2	343	4	11	372	4
3	428	4	12	598	5
4	544	5	13	161	3
5	384	4	14	363	4
6	183	3	15	458	4
7	375	4	16	234	3
8	253	3	17	392	4
9	480	5	18	462	4
Total ..	3,473	37	Total ..	3,409	35

Grand total 6,882 yards, par 72.

By LINCOLN A. WERDEN
Special to The New York Times.

OAKMONT, Pa., July 3 — Sam Snead, one of the game's greatest stylists, scored a significant triumph in the final of the Professional Golfers Association championship as he defeated Walter Burkemo, Detroit competitor, 7 and 6, today at the Oakmont Country Club.

When the West Virginia pro won after thirty holes of play against his 32-year-old rival, it meant that only one other golfer in the thirty-three-year history of the event had surpassed Snead's record. Snead tied Gene Sarazen's mark of three victories by his brilliant golf that was featured by keen putting. Only Walter Hagen, with five triumphs, bettered that total.

The 37-year-old Snead took the lead at the start, chipping in from the edge of the green at the first hole for an eagle 3. Burkemo, competing in his initial P. G. A. championship, could never overcome the advantage and Snead led by 5 up after the first six holes.

Burkemo Shows Courage

Burkemo, winner of the Purple Heart in World War II and hospitalized for eighteen months in France, left no doubt in the minds of the spectators that he was a fighter. But it was finesse around the greens that counted and Snead had it today.

By dint of an incoming 34, which included seven one-putt greens, five on the last five holes, Burkemo was able to reduce Snead's advantage so that Snead was only 3 up at the conclusion of the first eighteen.

When they started out for the second tour of the course, many in the gallery expected that Burkemo would rally. The former caddie and victor in the 1950 Michigan Open, who won some $405 in tournament prize money during the past season, compared to more than $5,000 that went to Snead, showed no signs of nervousness or annoyance at the effectiveness of his opponent's game.

Snead won the first three holes of the afternoon round to become 6 up, but Burkemo came back to take the fourth. They halved the next two with pars, but at the twenty-fifth Snead forged farther ahead with a par 4 since Burkemo was bunkered.

Snead Goes 7 Up

Burkemo was trapped again at the left on the twenty-sixth, a testing par 3, but Snead sank his 3 to become 7 up. At the twenty-seventh, however, Snead pushed his second to the right of the green in the grass, while Burkemo pitched to within a yard of the flag and carded a birdie 4 to cut Snead's margin to 6 up. Snead was under par with a 35 for that stretch which he had played in 34, 2 under, this morning.

Any hopes of a last-minute bid by Burkemo vanished at the twenty-eighth as he three-putted. Seven up once more, Snead halved the next with a 4, despite Burkemo's effort to sink a fifteen-footer.

At the thirtieth, Burkemo had a final chance, needing a four-footer for a birdie 4, but his putt ran by the cup and his subsequent 5 halved the hole and ended the match.

Snead's share of the purse was $3,500. Burkemo received $1,500. Snead won first in 1942 when he beat Jim Turnesa at Seaview. Then at Richmond in 1949 he turned back Johnny Palmer in the final. He was in the 1938 and 1940 finals also, losing to Paul Runyan and Byron Nelson, respectively.

Snead scored a fantastic birdie 3 at the fifth. He hit his second into the right-hand bunker guarding the green. Burkemo failed to hit his ball farther to the right and it landed on the down slope beyond the trap. He had to stand below the ball to hit it after finally locating it in the high grass.

Burkemo chopped away at it and the ball moved about three feet. From there he hacked it to the far edge of the green, then ran his putt up close. Snead then holed out from the sand, a distance of about thirty feet. Burkemo was charged with a 6.

THE CARDS
MORNING ROUND

Out—
Snead	3 4 4 4 3 3 4 4	5—34
Burkemo	4 5 4 5 4 4 4 4	5—41

Snead leads, 5 up.

In—
Snead	4 4 5 3 4 4 3 3	5—36—70
Burkemo	4 3 5 4 3 4 4 3	4—34—75

Snead leads. 3 up.

AFTERNOON ROUND

Out—
Snead	4 3 4 5 3 4 3	5—35
Burkemo	5 4 5 4 4 3 4	3—38

Snead leads, 6 up.

In—
Snead	4 4 5	
Burkemo	4 4 5	

Snead wins 7 and 6.

July 4, 1951

P.G.A. Committee Votes to Ease Tourney Ban on Negro Players

Action to Help Admit Them to Co-Sponsored Events Effective at Once, Smith Says— Kroll's 206 Leads in San Diego Open

By The United Press.

SAN DIEGO, Calif., Jan. 19—The tournament committee of the Professional Golfers' Association today voted to approve participation by Negroes in P. G. A.-co-sponsored golf tournaments.

Meanwhile Ted Kroll, fighting off stage fright before a throng of 4,000, clung to his lead in the $10,-000 San Diego open as he played a steady par round of 72 for a fifty-four hole total of 206.

Horton Smith, president of the P. G. A., said the action was effective immediately and he hoped some Negroes would be allowed to play in the Phoenix and Tucson open in the next two weeks.

Smith completed a ballot of the P. G. A. tournament committee today. He spoke to six of the seven members and received affirmative votes from them all. The only man he was not able to reach was Dave Douglas.

Voting approval of the drastic change in P. G. A. rules were Smith, Jackie Burke Jr., Clayton Heafner, Leland Gibson, Harry Moffitt and Chick Harbert.

"I hope that this action will allow Negro participation in both the Phoenix and Tucson open," said Smith. "Otherwise I will feel that most of my efforts have been in vain."

The Negro golf committee here, headed by Joe Louis, an amateur, and professional star Bill Spiller, still have some other obstacles to clear before they will be allowed to play.

They face the same rules that affect all golfers who are not regular tournament players. In other words, they would have to be invited as one of the ten players exempted from qualifying or ten others invited to attempt to qualify.

Smith said this puts the Negroes on the same basis as the other non-touring professionals. If the time comes when a Negro becomes a touring professional he may receive a different status, he said.

It is expected that new by-laws will be written into the P. G. A. constitution at its next national meeting in November to take care of the loosely drawn program that was outlined today by Smith.

Smith said that Phoenix had been approached about the possibility of inviting two or three Negroes to its tournament and was considering the proposal.

The P. G. A. president will get a list of top Negro golfers in this country, from each of the five members of a Negro steering committee. In this group are Spiller and Louis; Chairman Ted Rhodes of Nashville, Tenn., Howard Wheeler, Philadelphia, and Eural Clark of Los Angeles.

The tournament committee's loosely worded proposal, which is an "added clause" to the P. G. A. by-laws on players and playing procedure, provides that accredited amateurs (handicap 5 or less) and professional golfers of recognized standing and ability may be designated by the sponsor of a P. G. A. co-sponsored tournament as "approved entries" under the following conditions:

1. Such players must be specifically invited by the sponsor and approved by the club or clubs where the event is played.
2. Such players must also be approved or endorsed by the P. G. A. tournament committee.
3. Such players and their entries shall be subject to all other P. G. A. tournament regulations.

"It is understood, informally," said Smith, "that the steering and advisory committee, as far as this new clause applies to colored golfers is concerned, shall, until later organization is developed * * * assist both the P. G. A. tournament committee and the sponsors in every way when called upon to do so in connection with this new clause in the P. G. A. tournament regulations.

"It must be pointed out that the P. G. A. tournament rules have undergone a most basic change during the past year or so, in philosophy, equality of opportunity for the deserving, etc., and that the P. G. A. actually is a guest at wherever tournaments are played and must necessarily be governed by rights of local sponsors and clubs.

"We are endorsing a half-dozen amateurs and professional Negroes for the Phoenix tournament—men who will be recommended to the P. G. A. tournament committee by the Negro steering committee."

January 20, 1952

Snead Wins Augusta Golf 2d Time Record High Score

Sam Snead

CARD OF 72 FOR 286 FIRST BY 4 STROKES

Snead Gains Second Masters Crown With a Final-Round Par—Burke Totals 290

18,000 FANS SET RECORD

Bolt, Ferrier and Besselink at 291—Hogan in 293 Tie— Wind Hampers Golfers

By LINCOLN A. WERDEN
Special to The New York Times.

AUGUSTA, Ga., April 6—A par-equaling 72 today brought Sam Snead the Masters crown for the second time at the Augusta National Golf Club. He completed the 72-hole test under unfavorable conditions with a score of 286.

The battle of Snead against the rugged course, as well as against Ben Hogan, with whom he was tied beginning the fourth round, went to the P. G. A. titleholder after one of the most unusual final days since the inception of the tournament in 1934.

Bobby Jones declared, while presiding over the presentation ceremonies shortly before dusk in front of the big clubhouse, "conditions today were the most difficult we have ever had."

A cold wind continued unabated from early morning and the greens were so slippery that only three in the stellar field of professionals and amateurs clipped par, while four others matched it.

Snead's winning total, compiled as a record gallery of 18,000 spectators attended, was the highest in the sixteen-year history of the tournament, while Hogan, with whom he was tied at 214 this morning, played one of his highest rounds, a 79, in major competition in recent years.

Nothing Hogan could do on the greens proved satisfactory and he used forty putts for his round, which did not include a birdie. This in itself was such a rare performance for one of the game's great players that Hogan could not recall a previous similar experience.

Snead's comment was, "I guess Hogan is human after all."

Hogan, United States open champion and winner of the 1951 Masters, with a 40 on the incoming half finished in a tie for seventh at 293, seven strokes back of the victor.

The tournament officials doubled

the prize money and Snead's share was $4,000.

Jack Burke Jr., winner of four winter tournaments, carried off second place with 290, four strokes back of Snead. Burke, who was tied for eleventh place going into the last round, went around in 69, three under par, aided by a keen touch on the ultra-fast greens.

Tommy Bolt, the Durham (N.C.) driving range instructor, tossed away an opportunity, after being tied with Snead with four holes left to play, by three-putting three of the last four holes. Bolt ended in a tie for third at 291.

Bolt had a 5-footer for a birdie 4 at the fifteenth green, but instead of bagging it he finished with a 6 as he failed to sink the 1-footer that curled around the cup for a par 5. This upset "Thunder," who included two eagles on his last round of his first Masters.

Jim Ferrier, who lost a chance to win here in 1950 on the concluding nine holes, finished with a 72 for 291, while Al Besselink, the 205-pound, 6-foot, 3-inch Chicago professional and former Southern intercollegiate champion, turned in a one-under-par 71, despite a 6 at the eighth hole, for 291 also.

Lloyd Mangrum, with a 7 at the thirteenth, where his approach fell into the creek, nevertheless carded a 72 for 292. Joining Hogan in the group at 293 were Fred Hawkins and

Julius Boros, both of whom had 71's, and Lew Worsham, former United States open champion who had a fourth-round 74.

Cary Middlecoff, after playing the course in 72 three times, required 78 for 294, and John Palmer was next at 295. John Revita, ex-P.G.A. titleholder, had 296.

Snead Won in 1949

After Snead, victor here in 1949, played the short twelfth hole, he said "I guess I'm not licked yet." After holing a 4, he had every reason for that deduction.

Sam had been out in 37, one over par, after three-putting at the eighth and chipping up for a 5, one over par, at the ninth.

He sank a 22-footer for a birdie 3 at the tenth and then came to the "terrible triangle" of the course, the eleventh, twelfth and thirteenth holes. The White Sulphur Springs (W.Va.) pro three-putted for a 5 at the eleventh and then came the twelfth.

Using a No. 5 iron from the tee, Snead knocked the ball into the water. He walked back, dropped another, after taking a penalty stroke, and then pitched the ball into the bank of the green, just clearing the pond. What happened next helped to assure him that he was still in the fight. Using an 8-iron, he pitched the ball into the cup for a precious bogey 4.

Hogan was playing some seven holes back and didn't fully realize

what that 4 meant to Snead. With a No. 1 Iron on his second shot, Snead reached the par-5 thirteenth green in 2 and sank an important birdie 4 to be only one over par at that point.

Snead played the next four holes in par, holing a crucial 5-footer at the seventeenth. Then at the eighteenth he hit a No. 7 iron to within 7 feet of the pin and sank the putt for a birdie 3 that gave him his 72.

Hogan three-putted five greens in all, three on the first five holes. He hit a good second to the ninth green but the ball rolled back. A 4 there put him out in 39—three over par. As it turned out he needed a 33 to tie Snead.

But after pars at the next four holes Hogan three-putted the fourteenth. He chalked up a 6 at the fifteenth, after hitting a brassie shot over the green and finding the ball in the rough.

Then, to the consternation of the gallery, Hogan took three putts for 4 at the short sixteenth. After a par at the seventeenth, Hogan added a 5 at the home green, where he failed to get home in 2, carding a 40 back for a 79.

LEADING FINAL-ROUND CARDS

SAM SNEAD

Out .... 4 5 4 2 4 3 4 6 5—37
In .... 3 5 4 4 4 3 7 3—35—72—306

JACK BURKE JR.

Out .... 5 4 3 3 4 3 4 5 3—34
In .... 4 4 3 4 4 5 3 4—35—69—290

April 7, 1952

Miss Suggs Captures National Open Golf by 7 Strokes With Record 284 Score

Associated Press Wirephoto

Louise Suggs kissing trophy after record-breaking victory on links.

GEORGIA GIRL GETS 75 ON FINAL ROUND

By LINCOLN A. WERDEN
Special to The New York Times.

PHILADELPHIA, June 29 — A 28-year-old Georgian, Louise Suggs, set a record in winning the women's national open golf championship today when she completed the seventy-two holes of play with a total of 284 for a margin of seven strokes.

Not only did she smash the tourney mark of 291, but Miss Suggs bettered the seventy-two-hole scoring record set by Mrs. Mildred (Babe) Zaharias in winning the 1951 Tampa open with 288.

The Bala Golf Club course over which this seventh open championship was staged, as a benefit for The Philadelphia Inquirer charities, is considerably shorter than the Florida layout. Bala, where accurate approaching and putting are essential, is 5,460 yards with a par of 69. Five of the holes are par 3's.

Winner Becomes Fatigued

Miss Suggs, however, probably was less concerned than the 4,000

fans who watched the final round and discussed the merits of her "world's record."

"I wasn't thinking of any record on the last few holes," the winner said. "I was getting pretty tired. In fact, at the seventeenth tee I handed my driver to a marshal. I was concentrating so much that I mistook him for my caddie."

A last round of 75 for Miss Suggs was her highest of the four, following a 70, 69 and a 70. At the fifteenth she hooked her drive almost to the fence and out of bounds to go 5 over par. She went over par again at the seventeenth, but scored a final par 4 at the home green after chipping up well and sinking a 5-footer.

Miss Suggs, who last won this title in 1949, was followed by Betty Jameson of San Antonio and 18-year-old Marlene Bauer, who tied for second at 291. Miss Jameson, who also posted 75, was the runner-up yesterday, but Miss Bauer succeeded in moving up in the list with a final 71.

Out in 38, despite a 6 at the eighth, Marlene came back in 33. Her last three rounds, incidentally, could be considered something of a record since she had a 70, 67 and 71.

Miss Suggs collected $1,750 to bring her winnings for the year to $6,899.25.

Beverly Hanson, former national amateur champion, carded the day's low round with 35, 34—69 to

finish fourth at 293. Then came Peggy Kirk, whose concluding 73 tied her at 295 with Betty Mackinnon, who had a final round of 76.

Betsy Rawls, winner of the last three tournaments on the professional circuit and the defending champion, shot a 75 and finished with 297. Alice Bauer, older sister of Marlene, had the second low round with a 70 for 298.

Patty Berg, first-day leader, finished with 299, while Mrs. Mark Porter of Philadelphia led the amateurs with 300. Marilynn Smith, who tallied a record 67 only to have Marlene Bauer equal it during the tournament, finished with 301.

The old 72-hole record for this championship was established in 1949 by Miss Suggs. Mrs. Zaharias equaled it the following year.

Miss Suggs was 4 over par with a 38 out today, overplaying the short sixth and then taking bogey 5's at the next two before holing a 3 at the ninth where her tee shot hit a spectator and the ball fell in the rough off the green. The winner played the next five in par but then began to show signs of fatigue and the hot weather when she hooked her drive at the fifteenth.

Mrs. Charles Spalding of Greenwich, Conn., scored a hole in one at the 160-yard ninth, using a No. 2 iron. She finished with an 80 for 350.

June 30, 1952

Hogan Captures Masters Golf Event Second Time With Record 274

12,000 SEE TEXAN WIN BY 5 STROKES

Hogan Posts Fourth-Round 69 to Break Mark at Augusta by 5 Shots With 274

OLIVER FINISHES SECOND

Mangrum Gets 282, Hamilton 283 — Storm Halts Before Masters Victor Plays

By LINCOLN A. WERDEN
Special to The New York Times.

AUGUSTA, Ga., April 12—Ben Hogan became the Masters champion again today and a gathering of 12,000 at the Augusta National Golf Club agreed that his new title fitted him well.

For many of them watched the Texan tally a 69, three under par, on his fourth round and thereby break the seventy-two hole scoring mark for the event with an aggregate of 274. Hours after the rains had ceased, Hogan played the 6,950-yard course in the sunshine and finished with five strokes to spare over his nearest challenger.

"It was the best I have ever played for seventy-two holes," said the 40-year-old golfer, who has won three United States open championships and the 1951 Masters, among other links honors. His score was five under the previous record, jointly held by Ralph Guldahl, who triumphed in 1939, and Claude Harmon, 1948 victor.

Ben Also Holds Open Mark

Hogan, fourteen below par for the four rounds, now holds two important major records. His 276 stands as the best anyone ever has done in the United States open.

For a golfer who has not played a seventy-two-hole tournament since the United States open last June, his performance during the last four days here was all the more remarkable. What did Hogan think of it? At the presentation ceremonies on the green before the clubhouse, where Bob Jones, a golfing star of yesteryear, presided as president of the club, Hogan had a few observations to make.

"I am quite sure God was with me as I avoided the two storms that swept the course, and I pray that he will be with Babe Zaharias (the champion woman golfer who is gravely ill at Beaumont, Tex.)."

Hogan had praise, too, for Ed (Porky) Oliver, who finished second with a 279 that equaled the previous mark of the seventeenth Masters. Oliver gamely tried to wrest the advantage from Hogan, but even with a 70, the heavyweight ace, who had trailed Ben by four shots going into today's round, was one more further back tonight.

"I hope to come back next year and play the same caliber of golf," commented Hogan. "If you do," said Byron Nelson, Hogan's playing partner today, "you'll be playing here all alone."

Storm Cuts Attendance

A storm marred the morning play and reduced the attendance. Those who came after 1 o'clock, however, enjoyed a bright, clear afternoon. The $7.50 admission price set a new high for golf, but the tournament committee was unable to decide whether this price would reduce the size of the crowds—their original intention. The weather was the big factor in keeping the gathering from reaching unmanageable proportions.

While interest centered about Hogan, who was out in par 36, and

Ben Hogan

the effort of Oliver, who had 35 for the first nine, Lloyd Mangrum moved into third place with a 69 for 282. Bob Hamilton, the former P. G. A. champion, who was an outstanding contender through the tournament, finished with a 73 for 283. Tommy Bolt, with a final 71 for 285, tied with Chick Harbert for the next spot.

Harbert, the first-day leader, had difficulty at the fifth hole, where his ball struck a spectator and landed in a bad spot. Harbert failed to dislodge the ball on the subsequent attempt and ended with a 7. He was out in 38 and took a 74 for the round.

Ted Kroll, with a 72, had 286 and Jack Burke, second a year ago, scored 71 for 287 to complete a group of eight, who were under par for four rounds. Al Besselink followed at 288, while the national open champion, Julius Boros, was in the bracket at 289 after a 70.

The low amateur honors were divided between Harvie Ward of Atlanta, current British amateur champion, and Frank Stranahan, the muscular Ohioan. They were paired together and had an interesting duel. Each had a 75 to finish in a deadlock at 291.

Snead in 292 Bracket

Sam Snead never did get going and carded a 75, which put him in the 292 bracket. Winner last year, Snead tied with Milon Marusic, Dick Mayer, Earl Stewart, Jim Ferrier and Charlie Coe, a former national amateur champion.

The prize money was doubled all along the line, bringing the purse to $20,000 and Hogan's share to $4,000. Hogan will play in the Pan-American, Greenbrier and Colonial tournaments before he makes another bid for the United States open at Oakmont in June.

Hogan said the damp weather bothered his leg, injured in an automobile collision in 1949, but he credited the fine condition of the course to the rains.

Several incidents today illustrated his game and his golfing ability. One of these came at the long second hole, where his drive was slightly to the left. Tall pines prevented a clear shot to the pin that was at the left side of the green. Hogan played a No. 4 wood from a downhill lie and hooked the ball onto the putting carpet. It was one of his best shots of the tourney and he subsequently took two putts for his opening birdie.

Two holes later, at the par-3 fourth, he hit a No. 3 iron within ten inches of the flag. He sank a deuce and declared this was the shot he liked best, because he hit the ball "the way I wanted to."

On the short sixth, his No. 5 iron to the green landed to the left and the ball stopped on a spectator's raincoat that was stretched out there. Hogan replaced the ball after removing the coat, as was his privilege, and three-putted for

a 4. Three putts at the par-5 eighth gave him the only 6 he had in the entire tournament.

On the incoming nine, Hogan holed a birdie 4 at the dogleg thirteenth, where the creek runs parallel to the fairway on the left. He smashed a fine drive of approximately 275 yards, then hit a No. 4 iron into perfect position just over a ditch, 12 feet below the pin. Two putts gave him a birdie. He said later he thought victory was within sight about that time.

Another birdie came at the fifteenth, where he intentionally played short of the creek that bisects the fairway and sank a 6-footer for a 4.

Hogan finished like the champion he is with a curling 8-footer that went in for a birdie 3, giving him an incoming 33 and a 69 that established a scoring record that may stand for years.

The Leading Cards

FINAL ROUND

BEN HOGAN
Out .... 4 4 4 2 4 4 4 6 4—36
In .... 4 4 3 4 4 4 3 4 3—33—69

LLOYD MANGRUM
Out .... 5 5 4 3 4 3 4 5 4—37
In .... 4 4 3 4 4 4 2 3 3—32—69

ED OLIVER
Out .... 4 4 3 3 4 3 4 5 5—35
In .... 4 5 3 4 4 4 3 4 3—35—70

JULIUS BOROS
Out .... 5 4 4 3 3 4 3 5 4—36
In .... 4 4 3 4 3 4 5 3 4—34—70

TOMMY BOLT
Out .... 4 4 4 3 4 3 4 5 4—35
In .... 5 4 3 4 4 4 5 3 4—36—71

JACK BURKE
Out .... 4 5 5 2 5 3 4 5 4—37
In .... 4 4 2 5 4 4 2 5 4—34—71

TED KROLL
Out .... 4 5 4 3 4 4 4 4 5 4—35
In .... 4 4 3 4 4 4 4 4 4—35—72

BOB HAMILTON
Out .... 5 5 4 3 4 2 4 5 4—36
In .... 5 4 3 6 3 5 4 3 3—27—73

AL BESSELINK
Out .... 4 7 3 3 5 3 4 4 4—37
In .... 5 3 3 4 5 5 3 4 4—5—37—74

CHICK HARBERT
Out .... 4 5 4 3 3 7 3 4 5 3—38
In .... 6 4 3 5 4 5 2 3 4—36—74

SAM SNEAD
Out .... 4 5 4 4 5 3 4 4 5 5—39
In .... 5 4 3 5 3 5 3 4 4—36—75

April 13, 1953

3,265,000 Reasons For Playing Golf

That many devotees find as many ways to say it relaxes, saves marriages, aids business.

By ARTHUR DALEY

NOT since Herbert Hoover made the medicine ball an American institution has any President given a sport as much of a fillip as Dwight D. Eisenhower, who can take his golf but can't leave it alone. The game has been booming for years, but the chances are that the golfing President has done it even more good than might normally have been expected. He has even revived the interest of House Republican leader Charles Halleck, who is digging divots again after having given up the game for a number of years. Vice President Nixon has lately become a former non-golfer. Since January, he has clipped twenty strokes off his score, but still can't break a hundred. Ike's golf has given rise as well to one of the better cocktail-party gags in Washington: it is said of the Treasury Department, which is having refunding trouble with the national debt, that it is likely to break 90 before Eisenhower does.

Just what is the appeal of golf, anyway, that gets more than 3,000,000 Americans out? "Golf means many things to many people," says Joe Dey, the executive secretary of the United States Golf Association. He was not trying to be cryptic. He merely was stating facts. The appeal of the sport almost defies definition or explanation but its grip on the vast army of golf fanatics is unmistakable and unshakable.

"Doggone," drawls Slammin' Sammy Snead, twice the professional champion, "ain't that a silly question? I like golf 'cause—well, I reckon I jes' loves to play the game."

The President is considerably more articulate on the subject. He expressed his feelings in a letter he wrote to

"Golf has preserved countless marriages."

the Professional Golfers Association for use in the program at the forthcoming P. G. A. championships. Said Ike:

"While I know that I speak with the partisanship of an enthusiast, golf obviously provides one of our best forms of healthful exercise accompanied by good fellowship and companionship.

"It is a sport in which the whole American family can participate—fathers and mothers, sons and daughters alike. It offers healthy respite from daily toil, refreshment of body and mind."

THAT is probably as neat an explanation of the sport's appeal as anyone could devise. Generalized as it is, however, it still doesn't reach out quite far enough. Golf, you see, means many things to many people.

"Why do I like golf?" repeated Ben

Hogan, three times winner of the United States Open title. Ben looked surprised. The Texan probably is the greatest competitor the game has produced in ages. He's great because he's thorough. He thought carefully before he answered. "I like golf, I guess," he said, "because golf is my business, my livelihood. I've devoted my entire life to it and I want to be the top performer in my field. I'm never satisfied with anything less than perfection."

But is there perfection in golf? The answer is no, of course. If a Hogan shoots a record round in 66 strokes, he thinks back to a shot that could have brought his score down to 65. If a Dwight D. Eisenhower shoots an 86, he mourns over the wasted strokes that could have given him an 84. If a John Q. McDuffer hacks his way around in 148, he grieves over missed putts or sliced drives which might have brought him home in 142.

MUCH of golf's appeal lies in the persistent, relentless challenge it offers in the endless search for perfection. Historians will tell you that the nearest approach to it was achieved by Bobby Jones in the British Open of 1926 over the rugged and testing Sunningdale course. The Britons and the Scots are always jealous of par figures, par being an arbitrary norm of excellence. When they established a par of 72 strokes for Sunningdale, they felt it would withstand any assault.

In the qualifying round at Sunningdale, Jones ripped off an unbelievable 66, six strokes below what was considered a "perfect" round. That was extraordinary enough in itself. But what left the Britishers goggle-eyed was that he shot the first nine in 33 and the second nine in 33. He had 33 putts and 33 other strokes. His card did not show a 2 or a 5, just 3's and 4's. Here was consistency at its uniform best. Was Jones satisfied? Probably not. After all, he did flub several five-foot putts which he should have been able to drop with his eyes closed. Golf's challenge never ends.

Some deep-thinking philosopher once described the game thus:

"It's an ineffectual endeavor to put an insignificant pellet into an obscure hole with entirely inadequate weapons."

Joe Cook, the once-famous vaudeville comedian, balked all golf's frustrations in quite ingenious fashion. He built himself a tee-to-green hole on his

"Golf is a sport a man can pursue to his dying day."

Drawings by Ajay

estate near Lake Hopatcong. The green was constructed like a funnel so that any ball landing thereon promptly trickled into the cup for a hole in one. It was a good gag but only a gag. Golfers prefer their frustrations.

JUDGING by the statistics, it would seem that they are preferring them in ever-increasing numbers. Herb Graffis of the magazine Golfdom made a survey last year and produced these figures: 3,265,000 golfers played 63,-000,000 rounds over 5,045 courses whose value was $1,015,000,000.

Manufacturers of sports equipment estimate that 40 per cent of their wares go to golfers. In one year, they sell more than 4,000,000 golf clubs and almost 3,000,000 *dozen* golf balls. Most of that equipment, by the way, is used for very horrible golf because the hackers outnumber the experts in about the same proportion that poor people outnumber the rich.

It is significant also that golf already has lost both of its earliest derisive designations. Once upon a time, it was called "an old man's game" and also "a rich man's game." It now is neither. In fact, that represents much of its appeal. It can be played by anyone from 9 to 90, male or female. A baseball player is ancient at 35. A golfer becomes too old only when he no longer has the strength to swing a club.

A football player has to be big and brawny; a basketball player has to be tall; a jockey has to be small; a boxer has to be tough. Every sport, it seems, has certain physical requirements. Golf has none. Golfers can be tall or short, fat or lean, young or old, fast or slow, strong or weak, hard or soft.

Although a fellow had to be at least a junior size millionaire to afford golf a half century ago, that situation no longer holds true. It still isn't as inexpensive a form of exercise as bouncing a rubber ball off a brick wall, but swank and exclusive country clubs are the exceptions these days rather than the rule.

THE new trend is toward public courses, most of them municipally owned, where the green fees are modest and the golfer carries his own bag. A surprisingly large number of these public courses are only nine holes in length instead of the regulation eighteen. But they spread the gospel just as driving ranges (a bucket of balls for a quarter or a half dollar) spread it.

Male golfers fume and mutter unkind words at the invasion of their once completely masculine domain by the female of the species but the dolls can't be ruled off the course. What makes women play golf? "When I was a small girl," explains Maureen Orcutt, a top-flight woman golfer, "I was extremely interested in sports. My field of activity, naturally, was limited. I tried tennis, but there were always arrangements to be made for partners. But golf I could play by myself. Furthermore, I had no critical eyes watching me while I was learning, no one to give me that embarrassed or flustered feeling. In that respect, golf is the ideal game for a girl."

There are other women who are driven to the links in self-defense. Married to golf nuts, they become "golf widows." The smarter ones learn how to swing a club and then accompany hubby. Countless marriages have been preserved that

"It's a marvelous help in business."

way. There are other women who have other reasons. Here's the way one of them explained her motives:

"Let's face facts," she said. "I'm not as young as I used to be and I have to fight to keep my figure. The most pleasant way I know to battle increasing weight is to play golf. It forces me to walk a couple of miles on every round and I swing a club often enough—much too often to score well—to wear away the pounds."

MORE and more schools and colleges are supporting golf teams these days. The major sports still are football, baseball and basketball. But undergraduates are becoming aware of the fact that most of them will leave their athletic careers on the campus when they depart. But golf is a sport each can pursue to his dying day.

It can be pursued with profit, too. Here is a random cross-section of reasons given by post-graduate golfers:

"I play golf only for the exercise."

"I like the cameraderie it gives me."

"It's a marvelous help in business. When I play a customer, formality drops away and he becomes extremely approachable."

"I like golf because it demands so much concentration that my cares and worries are forgotten for the couple of hours I'm on the links."

"The constant challenge every golf shot offers me is too intriguing to resist."

GOLF actually helped Jack Westland get elected to Congress. He never planned it that way. In 1931, Westland was the runner-up to Francis Ouimet for the United States Amateur title. He never dreamed that he'd be that close again. But he got even closer. Last year, at the age of 47, he won the championship.

While the tournament was under way, Westland was running for the House of Representatives. His campaign slogan was, "You can trust Westland." There is something about a golfer which inspires trust. Westland was elected.

Why do folks trust golfers? There are cheats and chiselers on the links just as there are cheats and chiselers everywhere. But when a man fails to count a stroke, the fellow he fools worst is himself. He can say that he shot an 89 in order to claim that he broke 90 at long last. Deep in his heart, though, he knows better. He gets no satisfaction from it.

In the United States Open one year, Bobby Jones prepared to address his ball in an

"Golf is an ineffectual endeavor to put an insignificant pellet into an obscure hole with entirely inadequate weapons."

awkward lie in a bunker. Jones took his stance carefully so as not to disturb the ball. He shot to the green and holed out.

"A 4 for you, Bob?" intoned the official scorer.

"No," said Jones. "Better put me down for a 5. The ball moved as I made ready to address it."

THE movement was almost imperceptible. Only Jones saw it. But true to the golfers' code, Bob called a stroke on himself and that extra stroke put him into a tie. He won the playoff. But he could just as well have lost it.

Another thing about golf is that the world's worst duffer

can beat a Jones or a Hogan or a Snead because the sport provides a unique handicapping system.

No middle-aged man would dare fight Rocky Marciano even if given a free swing at Rocky's jaw first. There couldn't possibly be any fun in batting against Allie Reynolds, the Yankee pitcher. It would be a miserable mismatch to play tennis against Jack Kramer or Frank Sedgman, even if spotted five games a set. Each set still would wind up by a 7—5 score in favor of the champion.

GOLF is the great leveler A Ben Hogan and a Dwight Eisenhower can battle away merrily down to the last hole

on a handicap basis. Folks can even make a family party out of a round of golf, the head of a household conceding so many strokes to his wife, so many to his little son and so many more to his grandmother.

The competition golf offers is boundless. A fellow can compete in a tournament against hundreds. Or he can wander off by himself and compete against par alone

Golf is like that. Maybe Sam Snead's answer is the most accurate and the most general: "I reckon I jes' loves to play the game."

May 31, 1953

HOGAN, WITH A 283, TAKES FOURTH U. S. OPEN GOLF TITLE

SNEAD'S 289 SECOND

He Soars to 76 in Last Round as Hogan Closes With 71 at Oakmont

By LINCOLN A. WERDEN
Special to The New York Times.

OAKMONT, Pa., June 13—Ben Hogan stepped to a new place in the history of American golf today by winning the United States open championship for the fourth time.

The 40-year-old Texan finished the seventy-two-hole tournament at the Oakmont Country Club with a brilliant closing streak that gave him a score of 283. He had a final 71 after a third-round 73.

As the cup, symbolic of victory, went to the dark-haired suntanned golfer, it marked the first time that a home-bred professional had carried it off on four occasions. Only two others before him, Willie Anderson, Scottish-born professional star of the early days of the game on this continent and the amateur from Atlanta, Bob Jones, had ever accomplished a feat of similar magnitude.

Anderson won in 1901, 1903, 1904 and 1905. Jones scored his victories in 1923, 1926, 1929 and 1930, the year of his grand slam.

Closes With Birdie 3

Hogan, the sturdy challenger as the tourney got under way, once more demonstrated the qualities that rank him among the world's greatest shotmakers on a golf course. Leading the indomitable

Associated Press Wirephoto
SMILE OF WINNER: Ben Hogan, the only American pro to take U. S. Open four times, tips his cap to crowd's ovation at Oakmont, Pa., yesterday.

Sam Snead by one stroke at the conclusion of fifty-four holes, after Snead had a similar edge over Hogan after forty-five, Hogan played the concluding nine in 33, two under par. He had a birdie 3 to finish his bid in dramatic fashion while thousands cheered in approval.

Although thrilled and smiling by his triumph here over a course that in other years proved an enigma to those who sought to smash par, Hogan said, "I'm not so sure that I will play next year to try to make it five."

He plans to leave for Scotland within ten days to begin practice for the British open championship at Carnoustie, one major golfing honor he has not tried to capture. His success here unquestionably will spur him on in a year that has been marked by achievements in four of the five tournaments in which he has competed.

Hogan won the Masters at Augusta in April and then went on to take the Pan-American in Mexico City and the Colonial at Fort Worth. He did lose in the Greenbrier open at White Sulphur Springs, West Va., where Snead was the winner.

It was Snead who took up the task of trying to stop Hogan today. Snead was making his thirteenth quest for his first open title, the one big golf plum that has eluded him. Only one stroke separated them as they went into the last round this afternoon.

Both were 38 over the next nine holes, but Snead needed another 38 in and took a 76, four over par, finishing second with a total of 289, six strokes back of Hogan.

Tourney Won 'On Greens'

Snead conceded that Hogan won this tournament "on the greens."

Others who tried to overtake the Texan were Lloyd Mangrum, who finished with 292; George Fazio, who had rounds of 77 and 76 today for 294, and Jimmy Demaret, who went four over par on the last trip, after a 71 this morning, for 294.

Pete Cooper of White Plains, N. Y., had two eagles and the low two rounds of the day with a 71 and a 70 for 294. He sank a 20-footer at the first hole of the final round and then a wedge shot for a deuce at the fourteenth.

Dick Metz, 45-year-old Kansas

rancher, who was Hogan's partner today, had 295, as did Ted Kroll. Jay Hebert, the young Pennsylvania pro, in his first open, posted 296, deadlocking Marty Furgol.

Julius Boros, who won at Dallas a year ago, when Hogan finished third back of Ed Oliver, had a pair of 76's for his efforts today and was down the list at 299, the same figure returned by Clarence Doser, Jim Turnesa and Bill Nary. Bill Ogden and Fred Haas were at 297, while E. J. Harrison and Jack Burke had 298's.

Frank Souchak of Oakmont, a former Pitt football star, closed with a 74 to lead the amateurs with a score of 296. Bobby Locke, British Open champion, with a final 76, had 298.

Hogan matched the triumph of Jim Barnes, who won the title in 1921, by leading all the way. Oakmont's four-round scoring record of 294, credited to Willie MacFarlane in winning the Pennsylvania open in 1934, also went by the boards.

As far as he was concerned, Hogan did not try to catalogue this victory. He was satisfied, he explained, to chalk it up along with his first United States open triumph in 1948 at the Riviera Country Club in Santa Monica, Calif.; his second at Merion, Pa., in 1950, which marked his comeback after an automobile accident, and his third in 1951 at Oakland Hills, Birmingham, Mich., where he closed with a scintilating 67.

Snead, who finished second in 1937, lost in the play-off for the title in 1947 to Lew Worsham, after missing a tiny putt, and tied for second in 1949, had a tremendous crowd with him as he started out after lunch. He and Jimmy Demaret were paired and Hogan was an hour ahead of them on the course.

"I had opportunity after opportunity," commented Snead, who three-putted at crucial junctures. This morning at the eighth green of the course he three-putted from eight feet. He had been two under par until then. This afternoon, while Hogan was pressing on, his

FOURTH TIME WINNER: Ben Hogan, who captured the U. S. Open yesterday at Oakmont, Pa., with a 283 score, lifts ball in a shower of sand to blast from eighth-hole trap in the homestretch round of the fifty-third edition of the tourney.

goal in sight, Snead, after being one over par, three-putted at the twelfth green and again at the fifteenth.

There were two other chances, Snead believed, where he could have saved strokes—on the first green this afternoon and two holes later, where chip shots brought him within three feet and he could not sink the putts for important 4's.

The feature of Hogan's fourth round came over the rugged last three holes. Earlier he had said he would not envy anyone who was trying for birdies over this route. After he had taken a bogey 5 at the fifteenth, where he pulled a No. 2 iron ("too much club," he said later) into a trap, his words almost seemed prophetic. With that 5 he was one over par for fifteen holes.

Would Oakmont finally gain some sort of revenge for the sub-par rounds in his championship? The famed course had given way only in the 1927 and 1935 tournaments to four men who were below regulation figures. But since then the course has been materially changed.

Some sixty traps have been eliminated. The fairways have been widened a bit, but the greens today were almost in the traditional pattern, fast and on such undulating surfaces that the more timid putters might describe them as treacherous. Snead was having his troubles on them and here was Hogan with three more holes to go. Could he hold them with his approaches?

The answer almost came from Hogan's play thereafter. He smashed a brassie to the green, 234 yards away, at the sixteenth. Trying to select his "outstanding shot," he named this one hours afterward. But on the course those who saw him play to the center of the green, avoiding the pitfall on the right where the pin was placed, tantalizing perhaps to the player who might gamble, but acting as a signal to Hogan to beware of the trap off to the right side. They realized it was a key stroke. Hogan got down in two putts for a par 3 there.

Drives for 17th Green

After that Hogan decided to hit his drive at the 292-yard seventeenth with all his power. Usually he had driven purposely into the rough and tried for a par 4, since traps hem in the putting surface at the hole that calls for perfect placement to a green uphill. Hogan

hit it and on the ball flew, rolling on and stopping thirty-five feet to the left of the pin. Two putts and he had his birdie 3—almost a 2 as the try for a deuce stopped inches away. Now all even with par for the round Hogan uncorked another long drive at the eighteenth or seventy-second hole of the round.

This was a 462-yarder and Hogan had a No. 5 iron left for his second. He hit beautifully amid almost complete silence, notwithstanding that there were thousands lined on both sides of the fairway and encircling the green. When the ball came to rest it was some eight or ten feet from the pin. After Metz had putted out, Hogan lined up his putt and stroked the ball in for a concluding birdie 3, a finish of 3, 3, 3, and a 71, his third sub-par round.

Going out Hogan had a birdie at the first and after five pars, three-putted for a 5 at the seventh. At the eighth his No. 4 wood shot from the green carried over into a trap and he had another bogey when he sank a 4 there. At the ninth hole, he was trapped in 2, recovered well and

sank a par 5 to be out in 38.

Hogan had thirty-four putts on his last round and the most unusual of these was the 18-footer that ran over a ridge in the green and fell into the cup for a deuce at the thirteenth. He hit the cup with putts for birdies that rimmed but stayed out at the twelfth and fourteenth. At both these holes he had pars.

Hogan Composed at Lunch

Hogan started the final round before Snead had finished the morning session. The man from Texas was composed as he ate a light lunch of vegetables and fruit and conducted an informal press interview at the same time.

His chief comment concerning his prospects and those of the others in the field was that anyone needing a birdie on one of the last four holes would be in a dangerous spot. "That's the toughest part of the course," said Ben.

Because of his 73 this morning, Hogan was able to maintain a lead of one stroke since Snead carded par 72 and had a total of 213 to Hogan's 212. Next was Mangrum with a 74 at 217, while Fazio soared to a 77 and as a result he, Hebert and Demaret were in the 218 bracket. Demaret, who was paired with Snead, had another 71. He started with a 71 on Thursday and carded a 76 yesterday.

Metz, who returned to the golf circuit a year ago, after several years' absence during which he concentrated on ranching, finished with a 6 at the eighteenth, after a fine round, for a 74. His aggregate of 219 was the same as Haas'. Fred took a 72 after going two over par on the last four holes. Burke and Kroll were tied at 221.

Locke, the British open champion, holed a birdie 3 at the eighteenth for a 74 to score 222 the same as Souchak who had a third round of 76.

A crowd estimated at 10,000 formed early, a good share of the spectators trailing Hogan and Metz, while Snead and Demaret attracted most of the others. When word was spread that Snead was two under par at the end of four holes, thousands raced to get a glimpse of the Virginia-born star, one of the game's favorites.

"Why are you rooting for Snead?" asked one bystander of another as Sam and Demaret approached the ninth green. "He's never won, that's why I'm for him," was the reply.

Snead, however, tossed away a golden opportunity at the eighth, where he three-putted from eight feet, leaving his putt for a birdie 2 some two feet short, and then he failed to drop the ball the remaining distance on his next attempt.

He had played beautifully with a birdie 4 at the first, a birdie 3 at the next on a 14-footer and a birdie 4 at the long fourth, where he recovered from a trap and sank a 3-footer. He was trapped also at the sixth and took a bogey 4.

The long-hitting ability of Snead was in evidence at the uphill ninth, where he was home with a No. 2 iron and netted a birdie 4 after two putts to be out in 35, two under. Hogan, playing ahead, had taken a 38 there, so at that stage Snead was the leader with 176 to Hogan's 177 for forty-five holes.

Snead Hurts Chances

Coming in, however, Snead injured his chances further by three-putting at the seventeenth. Snead laced out a drive that reached the green there which is uphill from the tee, but three-putted from within thirty feet for a bogey 4.

Snead drove into the rough and took a bogey 5 at the tenth and he was trapped to lose a stroke to par at the short thirteenth. After playing the other six holes of the nine in par he came to the eighteenth of his third round as a huge gallery formed from tee to green. To their delight he unleashed a tremendous drive. He pitched his second to the green and two-putted for an incoming 37, two over, and his 72.

Hogan's third round found him driving off the fairway at four holes. The fifth hole cost him a bogey 5, as it did yesterday, and sent him one over at that stage. He recovered well from a corner of the trap at the eighth for par 3 and he pitched from the rough at the left of the ninth for par 5 and an outgoing 38, one over par.

On the inward nine he was even with par, aided by a 20-footer he sank for a birdie 4 at the twelfth.

Hogan ran into his first 6 of the tourney when he drove into the side of a bunker at the fifteenth. He recovered from there, only to knock his third into a trap before getting to the green. Where Snead later was to three-putt at the seventeenth on this round, Hogan chipped to within two inches of the pin and carded a birdie 3. At the eighteenth, Hogan had a 4 for his 73.

Boros, the defending champion, had a ruinous finish of 6, 2, 4, 6 on the last four holes this morning for a 76. He was trapped for the first 6 and overplayed on his recovery. He found his drive at the eighteenth in a small declivity and was trapped on his second, finally going over the green before holing out.

Fazio, who needed a 77, was off to a disappointing start when he three-putted the first green this morning. He missed a putt of eighteen inches for a birdie 4. The Pine Valley pro was out in 39 after three-putting the eighth and he was unable to stay even with par, taking 38 on the inward trip, missing the green at both the tenth and eighteenth holes.

Mangrum had a 6 at the fifteenth that put him off stride. He was one under par before that hole. His drive landed in a muddy spot and he subsequently used three wedge shots before reaching the green. A 5 at the seventeenth lost another valuable stroke and his 38 back for a 74 left him five strokes back of Hogan.

The Cards

THIRD ROUND

JIMMY DEMARET
Out ....4 4 4 5 4 4 4 3 4—36
In ....4 4 4 3 5 5 3 3 4—35—71

SAM SNEAD
Out ....4 3 4 4 4 4 4 4 4—35
In ....5 4 5 4 4 4 3 4 4—37—72

JACK BURKE
Out ....5 4 4 5 3 4 5 3 6—39
In ....4 4 5 3 3 4 3 3 4—33—72

FRED HAAS
Out ....4 4 4 4 4 2 4 2 6—34
In ....4 5 5 3 4 5 3 4 5—38—72

BEN HOGAN
Out ....4 4 5 5 5 3 4 3 5—38
In ....4 4 4 3 4 6 3 3 4—35—73

DICK METZ
Out ....5 4 4 5 3 3 4 4 5—37
In ....4 4 4 3 4 5 3 4 6—37—74

LLOYD MANGRUM
Out ....4 4 4 5 4 3 5 3 4—36
In ....4 4 4 3 5 6 3 5 4—38—74

JULIUS BOROS
Out ....5 5 5 4 4 3 4 3 4—37
In ....5 4 5 3 4 6 2 4 6—39—76

GEORGE FAZIO
Out ....5 4 4 5 4 4 4 4 5—39
In ....5 4 5 3 4 6 3 3 5—38—77

FOURTH ROUND

PETE COOPER
Out ....3 4 4 4 4 2 5 3 6—35
In ....4 5 5 3 2 4 4 3 5—35—70

BEN HOGAN
Out ....4 4 4 5 4 3 5 4 5—38
In ....4 4 5 2 4 5 3 3 3—33—71

FRANK SOUCHAK
Out ....3 4 5 4 4 4 5 4 5—38
In ....5 4 5 2 4 5 2 4 5—36—74

LLOYD MANGRUM
Out ....5 5 4 5 3 3 4 3 4—36
In ....4 4 5 4 5 4 5 4 4—39—75

SAM SNEAD
Out ....5 4 5 5 4 3 5 3 4—38
In ....4 4 6 3 4 5 4 4 4—38—76

GEORGE FAZIO
Out ....5 5 4 5 4 3 4 4 5—39
In ....4 5 5 3 4 6 3 3 4—37—76

JIMMY DEMARET
Out ....5 4 4 6 4 3 4 3 5—38
In ....4 4 5 3 4 7 3 4 4—38—76

JULIUS BOROS
Out ....4 4 6 4 5 3 4 4 5—39
In ....4 4 5 3 4 4 3 5 5—37—76

June 14, 1953

Hogan Wins British Open Title in His First Try as Stranahan Ties for Second

CARNOUSTIE, Scotland, July 10—Gallant Ben Hogan, in one of the most dramatic finishes ever witnessed in this staid old birthplace of golf, shot a record 68 on the ancient Carnoustie course today to win the British open championship.

Fighting back weariness in his aching limbs, the little, 40-year-old Texan once again lived up to his role as one of the world's greatest competitive golfers by winning the coveted British title in his first try with a seventy-two-hole total of 282 strokes.

A crowd of 20,000 Scots, most of whom had trailed him through the alternating wind, rain and sunshine that accompanied today's final thirty-six holes, gave Hogan a tremendous cheer as he received the championship trophy.

Hogan, the icy-nerved, unsmiling automaton, had won despite unfavorable weather, the relatively unfamiliar Carnoustie layout, the smaller, more difficult-to-control British ball and the tremendous pressure through two qualifying rounds and four championship rounds.

'Tired But Happy'

"I'm tired but I'm happy," he said as he wearily walked off the eighteenth green with his wife, Valerie, who had followed him throughout the tournament.

His victory made him the third player in history ever to win both the British and the United States open titles in the same year. The immortal Bobby Jones turned the trick in 1926 and 1930 and Gene Sarazen in 1932.

Hogan, who started today's play two strokes behind first place, finished four strokes ahead of four players who were deadlocked for the runner-up spot, including Amateur Frank Stranahan of Toledo, Ohio. The other three at 286 were Dai Rees of Wales, Peter Thomson of Australia and Antonio Cerda of Argentina.

Lloyd Mangrum of Los Angeles and Niles, Ill., the only United States entrant besides Hogan and Stranahan to qualify for the final thirty-six holes, had a total of 301, carding rounds of 74 and 76.

Hogan, whose golfing career nearly was ended by an auto crash in February, 1949, was exhausted when he finished his final round. He kept the crowd waiting for ten minutes while someone got him a coat to keep warm in the chill air during the presentation ceremony.

Rallies With Birdies

"Ben doesn't feel well," said an American friend. "This has been an exhausting effort for him. I wish they'd cut this short so that he can get somewhere and warm his feet."

For a while in the rain-soaked morning round, when he had trouble making his iron shots stick on the wiry greens, it looked as if Bantam Ben might not make it. But each time he faltered, he battled back immediately with birdies, and he finished the morning eighteen holes with a two-under-par 70 that put him in a first-place tie at 214 with Roberto De Vicenzo of Argentina.

After lunching alone with his caddie from a box lunch taken to him by his wife, Hogan set out in sunshine for the final round.

"I didn't think I had a chance to win before I came over here," he had told his caddie, "but now I think I have. Let's go out there and do it."

He proceeded to shoot one of the most remarkable rounds of his brilliant career. Not once on the final round did Hogan stray beyond par, and he shot birdies on four holes. His performance was machine-like as he split the fairways with his drives and chipped close enough to the hole so that he never took more than two putts.

After matching par for four holes, he made one of the most dramatic shots of the tournament on the fifth. In playing his second shot to a sloping green, Hogan's ball rolled back to the foot of a bunker. He studied the shot for five minutes before chipping in a 50-footer for a birdie 3.

34 on Outgoing Nine

He added another birdie on the long sixth, where he reached the green in 2, ran the ball to within 4 feet of the cup and holed out for a 4. That gave him a 34 for the outgoing nine.

Ben repeated his birdie performances on the short thirteenth, when he hit his tee shot 15 feet from the pin, and on the long eighteenth, where he reached the green in 2 and two-putted for a 4.

By that time, his closest pursuers in the earlier rounds had faded. De Vicenzo, who had shot a third-round 71 to gain a tie with Hogan, carded a final-round 73 and finished with a 287 that put him one stroke behind the runners-up.

Stranahan, who started the final round three strokes off the pace after a 73, returned with a superb 69 on the fourth round, but it was not enough to overcome his deficit. The muscular Ohioan, the only amateur among the forty-nine final qualifiers, finished far better than most had expected.

After shooting a 37 on the outgoing nine of the final round, Stranahan came home in a 32, a new competitive course record for the last nine at Carnoustie. He one-putted the last six greens and sank a 30-foot putt for his second eagle of the day on the eighteenth.

Rees, who shared a thirty-six-hole lead with Eric Brown of Scotland, shot a 73 and 71, while Thomson, the young Australian champion who was only one stroke

Ben Hogan after adding the British Open to his previous victories in United States Open and the Masters at Augusta, Ga.

off the pace entering today's play, carded a pair of 71's.

One of the biggest disappointments in the tournament was the defending champion, Bobby Locke of South Africa, who had won the title three times in the last four years. Locke had 74 and 72 as he finished in eighth place at 291. One stroke ahead of him was Sam King of England, who carded 72 and 71.

Brown fell from the lead when he shot a third-round 75 and repeated that score on the last round to finish at 292 in a tie with Peter Allis of Britain.

THIRD-ROUND CARDS
PAR FOR THE COURSE

Out	4	4	4	4	4	5	4	3	4—36	
In	4	4	3	4	3	4	3	4	5—36—72	

ANTONIO CERDA

| Out | 3 | 3 | 4 | 4 | 4 | 5 | 4 | 3 | 5—35 | |
| In | 3 | 3 | 5 | 4 | 4 | 4 | 3 | 4 | 4—34—69 |

BEN HOGAN

| Out | 4 | 3 | 4 | 5 | 5 | 4 | 3 | 3 | 4—35 |
| In | 3 | 4 | 5 | 2 | 4 | 4 | 3 | 6 | 4—35—70 |

ROBERTO DE VICENZO

| Out | 4 | 4 | 4 | 4 | 4 | 5 | 4 | 4 | 4—37 |
| In | 4 | 3 | 5 | 3 | 5 | 4 | 3 | 4 | 4—34—71 |

PETER THOMSON

| Out | 4 | 4 | 4 | 4 | 5 | 4 | 3 | 4 | 4—36 |
| In | 3 | 4 | 4 | 3 | 4 | 5 | 3 | 4 | 4—35—71 |

LLOYD MANGRUM

| Out | 5 | 4 | 4 | 4 | 4 | 5 | 3 | 3 | 5—37 |
| In | 4 | 4 | 4 | 3 | 4 | 4 | 4 | 3 | 4—36—73 |

FRANK STRANAHAN

| Out | 4 | 4 | 4 | 4 | 4 | 5 | 4 | 3 | 5—37 |
| In | 4 | 4 | 3 | 6 | 5 | 3 | 4 | 3 | 4—36—73 |

DAI REES

| Out | 4 | 4 | 4 | 4 | 4 | 4 | 4 | 4 | 4—36 |
| In | 4 | 4 | 3 | 4 | 3 | 4 | 5 | 4 | 4—37—73 |

BOBBY LOCKE

| Out | 4 | 4 | 5 | 4 | 4 | 5 | 3 | 5 | 3 | 4—37 |
| In | 4 | 4 | 3 | 5 | 3 | 5 | 3 | 4 | 4—37—74 |

ERIC BROWN

| Out | 4 | 4 | 4 | 4 | 4 | 5 | 4 | 3 | 4—35 |
| In | 6 | 4 | 5 | 4 | 5 | 4 | 4 | 4 | 4—40—75 |

FINAL-ROUND CARDS
BEN HOGAN

| Out | 4 | 3 | 4 | 4 | 4 | 3 | 4 | 4 | 4—34 |
| In | 4 | 4 | 4 | 2 | 5 | 4 | 3 | 4 | 4—34—68 |

FRANK STRANAHAN

| Out | 4 | 3 | 5 | 5 | 4 | 5 | 3 | 3 | 5—37 |
| In | 4 | 4 | 4 | 3 | 4 | 3 | 3 | 4 | 4—32—69 |

PETER THOMSON

| Out | 4 | 4 | 4 | 4 | 4 | 5 | 4 | 3 | 4—36 |
| In | 4 | 4 | 4 | 3 | 4 | 4 | 4 | 4 | 4—35—71 |

ANTONIO CERDA

| Out | 4 | 3 | 4 | 3 | 4 | 5 | 4 | 4 | 4—35 |
| In | 4 | 4 | 5 | 3 | 4 | 4 | 4 | 4 | 4—36—71 |

DAI REES

| Out | 4 | 3 | 5 | 4 | 4 | 6 | 4 | 2 | 4—35 |
| In | 5 | 3 | 4 | 3 | 4 | 5 | 4 | 4 | 4—36—71 |

BOBBY LOCKE

| Out | 4 | 4 | 4 | 5 | 5 | 5 | 4 | 2 | 5—37 |
| In | 4 | 3 | 5 | 2 | 5 | 5 | 3 | 4 | 4—35—72 |

ROBERTO DE VICENZO

| Out | 5 | 5 | 4 | 5 | 4 | 5 | 5 | 3 | 5—38 |
| In | 4 | 3 | 5 | 3 | 4 | 4 | 4 | 4 | 4—35—73 |

ERIC BROWN

| Out | 5 | 5 | 4 | 4 | 4 | 5 | 4 | 4 | 4—39 |
| In | 5 | 4 | 4 | 4 | 4 | 4 | 4 | 3 | 4—36—75 |

LLOYD MANGRUM

| Out | 5 | 4 | 6 | 5 | 4 | 5 | 4 | 4 | 5—42 |
| In | 3 | 3 | 5 | 3 | 4 | 3 | 4 | 4—34—76 |

July 11, 1953

Snead Beats Hogan in Play-Off for His Third Masters Golf Title

VICTOR SHOOTS 70 FOR STROKE EDGE

Snead Outdrives Hogan and Putts Well at Augusta— 13th Hole Turning Point

By LINCOLN A. WERDEN
Special to The New York Times.

AUGUSTA, Ga., April 12—Sam Snead beat the champion today to win the Masters golf title for the third time. In the eighteen-hole play-off, necessitated because he and Ben Hogan deadlocked after seventy-two holes at 289, Sam was the winner, 70 to 71.

"Those two players are the two finest golfers in the world—and that is a statement you can prove," commented Bob Jones, president of the Augusta National Golf Club where the extra-round test decided the tourney's eighteenth winner.

Some 6,500 were in attendance on a warm, sunny day as Snead overcame a putting lapse that had marred his rounds during the tournament proper.

The long-hitting White Sulphur Springs, W. Va., professional had thirty-two putts during the round. He didn't need any at the tenth, where he chipped in from the back of the green for a birdie 3. This shot of approximately sixty-five feet came at a crucial time. Hogan and Snead had played the first nine on an even basis, since both were out in 35, one under par.

The spectacular chip, coming at the tenth, put Snead ahead. Earlier, Hogan, seeking to retain his Masters crown, had taken the lead at the fourth where Snead three-putted. Then Sam drew even at the sixth where he dropped a seven-footer for a deuce.

Rivals Even at Twelfth

Hogan came back, however, at the twelfth with a par 3, where a bogey by Snead made them all square in strokes once more. However, the thirteenth—the azalea hole—that had proved so vital throughout the first four rounds, once more became a turning point.

Hogan was meeting Snead for the first time since the Los Angeles open play-off of 1950, which was Ben's first tournament following his almost fatal automobile crash of 1949.

Hogan today tried desperately to beat Snead. When he didn't, he smiled and said, "I met Sam in 1950 and the outcome was the same as it was today. I'm a little younger than Sam (Hogan and Snead were both born in 1912, but Hogan is three months younger) and if I keep trying, maybe I'm going to win against him."

And one of the reasons why he didn't was that Snead was able to bag a birdie 4 at the thirteenth, while Hogan, the British and United States open champion, played safe and took a par 5.

Snead had the advantage with his drives. He was constantly ahead of Hogan from five to ten yards off the tee.

Sam's powerful iron play was demonstrated at the thirteenth, a 470-yard hole.

A Bold Iron Shot

After Hogan used a No. 4 iron and played short of the creek at this par 5 hole, Snead walloped a No. 2 iron that flew the ball over the ditch and onto the green. Sam's resulting birdie 4 to Ben's 5 gave him a lead he never relinquished.

Three holes later, Hogan, regarded as one of the steadiest putters in the game, failed to sink a three-footer for a par 3.

Snead had been "outside" on their tee shots, but Hogan, despite the fact that he had hit his iron to within fifteen feet, still was shy of the cup by a yard on his first putt. Then after surveying the line considerably, he failed to get the short one in and consequently carded a 4.

That gave Snead a two-stroke edge, since Sam had sent his approach putt close and tapped in a par 3.

Hogan's task, with two holes remaining, appeared hopeless. He was closer to the pin than Snead at the seventeenth, even though he did have to chip. The flag was at the back edge and Ben attempted to sink the fifteen-foot approach, but the ball stayed out.

Once more, Snead had laid his approach putt close with deadly accuracy and he safely tapped in a par 4. Hogan made no headway when he rolled in his 4 there.

Sam Lands in Trap

As the gallery trudged uphill to the home green there were few spectators who anticipated a sudden form reversal. However, there was some excitement, for Hogan hit his second to the green while Snead pushed his shot into a trap.

Sam said later he had "tried to cut" his No. 3 iron. At any rate, he was in the sand some seventy-five feet from the pin. He pitched out nicely to within five feet of

the flag. Hogan was twenty feet away in two. Ben made an effort to hole out for a birdie, but the uphill putt missed. Snead then took two putts, but still won the crown by a margin of one stroke with his concluding 5.

With Snead two under par and Hogan one under, this completed the third play-off in the Masters history. Hogan was also in the last one, in 1942, when he bowed to Byron Nelson after both had 280 for four rounds. The other play-off occurred in 1935 when Gene Sarazen defeated Craig Wood in thirty-six holes.

Clifford Roberts, tournament chairman, announced before the players started this afternoon, that should another tie result it was planned to continue with another eighteen-hole round tomorrow.

Hogan congratulated Snead

and said he not only played "good golf for the gallery's pleasure but gave them a few chuckles, too."

"However, he didn't give me any chuckles," explained Hogan. Snead, who thus joins Jimmy

Demaret as the only one to have won the Masters three times, was quick with a response. "I was a little luckier than Ben today. I hope it's the same way in the U. S. Open."

Sam, despite the fact that he has carried off almost every title, has never won that one. He triumphed in the Masters in 1949 and in 1952.

Hogan reaffirmed his intention of adhering to his original plan to compete in only three major 1954 championships. Although thwarted today in seeking to re-

Play-Off Cards

Out—		
Par	4 5 4 3 4 3 4 5 4	—36
Snead ...	4 4 4 4 4 2 4 5 4	—35
Hogan ...	4 4 4 3 4 3 4 5 4	—35
In—		
Par	4 4 3 5 4 5 3 4 4	—36—72
Snead ...	3 4 4 4 4 4 3 4 5	—35—70
Hogan ...	4 4 3 5 4 4 4 4 4	—36—71

tain the Masters laurels, Ben asserted the setback would not alter his campaign. He said he would not go to Britain for the British Open, but would compete only in the Colonial invitation in his native Fort Worth next month and in the U. S. Open at Baltusrol in June.

"I putted badly," he added. "The greens were slower today, but I never did have the touch. I hit back of my putt at the sixteenth."

Snead said he looked forward to the U. S. Open, but he had no intention of trying his luck in the British championship. "It seems to me," he said with a twinkle, "that maybe the sun doesn't always shine on the same fellow. Just say, I am really looking forward to being present at Baltusrol."

From the standpoint of statistics: both Hogan and Snead, were in two traps. There are twenty-seven on the course. Hogan had two birdies, at the par 5 second and par 5 fifteenth. He went over par at one hole, the sixteenth. He had fifteen pars. Snead had three bogeys, the fourth, twelfth and eighteenth. He had five birdies, the second, sixth, tenth, thirteenth and fifteenth. He had ten pars.

April 13, 1954

ED FURGOL TAKES U. S. OPEN

CARD OF 284 BEST

By LINCOLN A. WERDEN
Special to The New York Times.

SPRINGFIELD, N. J., June 19 —Ed Furgol, who overcame a physical handicap in becoming a golfer, won the United States open championship at the Baltusrol Club today.

While Ben Hogan, the defend-

ing titleholder, fought vainly to retain the trophy and become the first man in history to win the title for the fifth time, Furgol came through to an unexpected triumph.

The 37-year-old teaching pro from Clayton, Mo., took the lead this morning after the third round. Then with a closing 72, after an unusual experience at the seventy-second and last hole, he posted an aggregate of 284.

This total won by one stroke.

Shortly after Furgol had completed his final round, Gene Littler came to the last green needing a birdie 4 for a deadlock. While thousands watched from vantage points in front of the clubhouse, Littler's putt for a birdie from 4 feet missed the cup and with it went his chance as he closed with 285.

The winner of the national amateur title last fall at Oklahoma City and a professional only for the last six months,

Littler was competing in this tournament for the first time.

Mayer, Mangrum at 286

Dick Mayer, 29-year-old blond-haired professional from St. Petersburg, Fla., tied for third with Lloyd Mangrum, the 1946 champion, at 286. Mayer spoiled his bid with a 7 at the final hole.

Needing a par 5 to tie, Mayer, former New York State and Westchester amateur champion, pushed his drive into the pine trees on the right. He realized his predicament immediately and drove a provisional ball.

As it turned out, the first one was so far in it was unplayable. Consequently, he elected to put the other into play, with the penalty, so that he was then lying 3. After playing this one out from the rough, he eventually sank a twelve-footer for the 7. He had a 73 for the round.

With a closing 70, Bobby Locke, the South African star, finished fifth at 288, one better than Hogan's total. Hogan, after a third-round 76, one of his highest in championship play in six years, turned in a fourth-round 72.

Patton in 289 Group

Billy Joe Patton, the 32-year-old amateur from Morganton, N. C., who led in the initial round, contributed some startling recoveries in the morning for a 71. He then added a 73 to tie for sixth with Hogan, Tommy Bolt, Fred Haas and Shelley Mayfield at 289.

Amid considerable excitement, and with the attendance close to 14,000, establishing a four-round open record of 39,600, Furgol emerged with golf's highest honor.

The victim of a fall from crossbars in a playground as a 12-year-old, Furgol's is a story of persistence.

In the accident Furgol sustained a shattered left elbow.

"It never set right, even after two operations," he said today, "but I wanted to be a golfer and a pro. Why? Well, I figured I'd have a chance—everyone does—if you just want to. So I exercised to strengthen my hands. I used my shoulder muscles because there's no strength in my left arm."

At first he caddied near Utica, N. Y., and turned pro in 1945. He has a brother who is also a golf professional.

After he had won the first prize of $6,000, Furgol said he would give $1,000 to his caddie as a bonus.

Ed is 5 feet 11½ inches and weighs 155 pounds. He is married. His best showing in the open previously was in 1946, when he finished five strokes back of the three who tied for the title.

At the eighteenth hole of the last round, he hooked his drive into the trees. He noted a clearing toward the adjoining eighteenth fairway of the club's upper course. He lost no time in hitting a No. 7 iron out to safety.

He pitched just short of the green as thousands milled about wondering how he would save his par and clinch the crown. He chipped to within 4 or 5 feet of the pin and sank the put for par 5 and a 72 that meant the championship.

Furgol's earlier rounds were 71, 70 and a 71 this morning that gave him a one-stroke margin over Mayer at the three-quarter mark.

Snead Misses Again

Hogan predicted at luncheon that Furgol would win. Ben then was trailing by five strokes and

Associated Press Wirephoto

Ed Furgol raises his arms in victory after winning the U. S. open with a card of 284

was in the 217 bracket, along with Sam Snead.

Snead, who has made fourteen attempts to win this title, closed with a 73 for 290 to tie with Cary Middlecoff.

Rudy Horvath of Windsor, Ont., the only Canadian entrant, and Al Mengert, Winged Foot Club assistant, followed at 291. Jack Burke and Claude Harmon had 293's.

Hogan, who last year joined Bob Jones and Willie Anderson as a four-time winner of the crown, did not say definitely that he would try again at San Francisco next year.

Ben began the last round with a 5 and then took three putts for a 5 at the third hole, which did not help. However, the defending champion stayed close to par with a 35 out. He needed a last-round 67 to tie Furgol but the birdies did not fall as he played the last nine in 37.

Three-Putts Two Greens

On the last round, Furgol was out in 36, two over par, chiefly because he three-putted at both the seventh and eighth greens. Trapped at the ninth, he recovered for a par.

The steadiness with which Furgol played the next seven netted pars and when his second shot kicked through the trap at the seventeenth, he went on for a par 5. Then came the eighteenth.

After three rounds, Furgol was leading with 212. The Missouri

pro capped a 71 this morning by sinking a 40-foot putt at the home green for a birdie 4.

Furgol's total gave him a stroke edge over Mayer, who returned in 33 for a 70. Behind Mayer, at 215, were Mangrum and Middlecoff, who had 72's, and Littler. The leader after thirty-six holes with 139, the Californian carded a 76.

Mengert, who two years ago was a finalist in the national amateur in which he bowed to Jack Westland, finished with birdies at the seventeenth and eighteenth holes for a 73.

His total of 216 put him in a deadlock with Patton, the North and South amateur champion who has been one of the sensational figures in both the Masters and this tourney. Paired with Hogan, Patton posted a 71.

Hogan found himself down the list in a tie for eighth place after his 76 for 217. The defending champion was only two strokes back of Littler starting the third round, but his score, his highest in this event since the opening round in the 1951 championship at Oakland Hills, Mich., left him

a long, rugged road to his goal.

Tied with Hogan were Jay Herbert, Woodmere, L. I. pro who had his second consecutive 70; Snead, with a 72; Haas, 71, and Bolt, 73.

Burke followed at 218, along with Locke, Horvath and Leland Gibson, who had a 69. Bob Toski soared to a 78 for 222, back of

Bill Campbell and Dick Chapman, amateurs, who had 221's.

Furgol began with a 5 at the first hole this morning after being trapped. He compensated by dropping a twenty-foot putt for a birdie 3 at the second. He was trapped at the sixth and ninth. At the latter hole he dropped a stroke to par with a 4. At the sixth he carded a par 4.

After a one-over-par 35 he went over regulation figures only once in the next six holes, when he was trapped on a second shot. His next mistake happened at the sixteenth, where he three-putted for a 4 from a distance of sixty feet. He holed a ten-footer for a birdie 4 at the seventeenth and scored another birdie at the eighteenth, after being trapped, for a 36.

Hogan was away to a poor start, for him, over the first nine.

At the opening hole he was trapped as his No. 3 iron approach bounced into a trap. At the second he sank a six-footer for a birdie 3. But at the next Hogan's second caught the trap at the right, where he found the ball buried in what he described as "a crater."

After a 3 at the water-hole fourth, Hogan missed par again at the fifth. Hogan three-putted for a 5, while Patton, who had been on one fairway in the first six holes, sank a 4 after driving near a tree.

95

EYES RIGHT: Billy Joe Patton smacks one out of the rough on the sixth hole during the third round of open on Baltusrol links. The Morganton (N. C.) amateur got 71 on this round.

Associated Press

A 5, one more over, followed at the sixth for Hogan. Finally, after pars at the seventh and eighth, he was trapped on the downslope of the hazard and carded a 4.

On the next three Hogan had pars. His drive drifted into the rough at the thirteenth and he marked down a 5. Running in a six-footer, he holed a birdie 3 at the fourteenth. The big gallery that trailed in the hot sun found him over par for the seventh time when he was trapped at the short sixteenth. His troubles were not over for he ran into a 6 at the long seventeenth, where he found his ball in a tuft of grass. His par at the eighteenth brought him back in 38.

Cards of the Leaders

ED FURGOL

THIRD ROUND
Out ......5 3 4 3 4 4 4 4 4—35
In ....4 4 3 4 5 4 4 4 4—36—71—212

FOURTH ROUND
Out ......4 4 4 3 4 4 5 5 3—36
In ....4 4 3 4 4 4 3 5 5—36—72—284

GENE LITTLER

THIRD ROUND
Out ......5 3 5 3 3 5 4 5 4—37
In ....5 4 3 5 5 4 3 5 5—39—76—215

FOURTH ROUND
Out ......4 4 4 3 4 5 4 4 3—35
In ....4 3 3 4 3 4 4 4 5 5—35—70—285

DICK MAYER

THIRD ROUND
Out ......4 7 4 3 3 4 4 5 3—37
In ....4 3 2 4 4 4 3 4 5—33—70—213

FOURTH ROUND
Out ......5 4 5 3 4 4 5 4 2—36
In ....4 4 3 3 4 4 3 5 7—37—73—286

LLOYD MANGRUM

THIRD ROUND
Out ......4 4 6 3 5 4 5 3 3—37
In ....4 5 3 3 4 4 2 5 5—35—72—215

FOURTH ROUND
Out ......4 4 4 2 6 4 5 4 3—36
In ....4 4 3 4 4 4 3 4 5—35—71—286

June 20, 1954

Mrs. Zaharias Tallies 291 For Third Open Golf Title

By LINCOLN A. WERDEN

Special to The New York Times.

PEABODY, Mass., July 3—Mrs. Mildred (Babe) Didrikson Zaharias completed her comeback bid by winning the United States women's open golf championship today. Over the Salem Country Club course the famed woman all-around athlete, who underwent an operation for cancer in the spring of 1953, regained the title she held in 1948 and 1950 with a seventy-two-hole score of 291.

Visibly tiring on the last six of the 36 holes that she played today, Mrs. Zaharias admitted that this triumph was one of the highlights of a long athletic career. A member of the Olympic track team and winner of two events in the 1932 games, Mrs. Zaharias has competed in many sports and was declared the "greatest woman athlete of the half century" in an Associated Press poll several years ago.

After receiving a thunderous ovation upon holing the final putt of her fourth round for a 75, following a 73 this morning, Mrs.

Zaharias declared that "my prayers have been answered.

"When I was in the hospital I prayed that I could play again. Now I'm happy because I can tell people not to be afraid of cancer. I've had over 15,000 letters from people and this victory today is an answer to them—it will show a lot of people that they need not be afraid of an operation and can go on and live a normal life."

Those who followed Mrs. Zaharias on the concluding day of the championship were anxious to see how the physical strain might affect her in this arduous tourney. She proved equal to it all.

'I really wanted to win this one," the Babe explained, "and I'm glad I could hold my concentration. Winning my first tournament, the Serbin Open, after

Associated Press Wirephoto

THREE-TIME WINNER: Mrs. Mildred (Babe) Didrikson Zaharias holding cup awarded for women's U. S. open golf championship. She regained title she held in 1948 and 1950.

my operation and this big one today makes me feel wonderful. That's right, now I don't expect to retire for twenty years," she said to a group of interviewers.

Betty Hicks of Durham, N. C., with 75 and 77 for her closing rounds, finished second at 303. Mrs. Zaharias' 12-stroke advantage was one of the widest victory margins in history. The record is the 14-stroke edge enjoyed by Louise Suggs in 1949. Miss Suggs posted a closing 76 for 307 today.

Betsy Rawls of Spartanburg. S. C., the defending champion, took an 80 in the fourth round. At 308, she tied with the 19-year-old California girl, Mickey Wright, who had a 76 this afternoon. Mrs. Jacqueline Pung, the Hawaiian star, followed at 309 and Beverly Hanson, the former amateur champion, trailed at 310.

Pat Lesser, Seattle amateur, posted a 310 after a fourth round of 80.

Mrs. Zaharias, who started with a 72 and a 71 for a 7-stroke margin, equaled her winning total of 1950, the best for a course over 6,000 yards. Miss Suggs holds the scoring record, 284, at the Bala Golf Club, but that course measured only 5.460 yards when the tourney was held there in 1952.

Mrs. Zaharias, an absentee from this tourney in 1952 and 1953 because of illness, not only drove steadily until the last stage today but she chipped and putted well throughout the championship. She became the center of attention by the proficiency of her game.

Out in 36 with Miss Wright as her partner today, Mrs. Zaharias did not show signs of fatigue until the thirteenth this afternoon.

Posts 5 at Thirteenth

Until then she was even with the par of a course that offered trouble for those who veered off line. At the thirteenth, she was short with her second shot and took a 5. She sank pars at the next two, but then she faltered a bit on her drive and the ball went into the rough on the right.

This resulted in her losing one stroke to par and carding a 5. At the seventy-first hole, she hooked her tee shot and then overplayed the green. She took a 5 there.

At the seventy-second, she pushed her drive into the trees. She didn't elect to play safe, but boldly pitched through an opening to the fairway. From below the hill, she pitched her third shot to the green and was down in two putts for a 5. The Babe doffed her straw hat in response to the applause of the crowd.

Statistics revealed Mrs. Zaharias was over par at fourteen holes during the championship and had eleven birdies. She went over par at five holes and had two birdies in the last round.

The first United States woman golfer to win the British championship, a title she captured in 1947, Mrs. Zaharias has now won four of twelve tournaments since

Highlights in Golf Career Of National Open Winner

1935—Began playing golf.
1940—Won Western and Texas opens.
1945—Voted woman athlete of year by The Associated Press; won Western and Texas opens.
1946—Won United States amateur championship.
1947—Won Women's British amateur.
1948—Won "world's championship" tourney and National open.
1949—Won "world's champion-ship" tourney and finished second in National open; voted greatest woman athlete of half-century by The Associated Press.
1950—Won National open; voted woman athlete of year by The Associated Press.
1951—Won "all-American and world's championship tournaments; finished third in National open; led women pros in money winnings.
1952—Won Augusta titleholders tourney and Texas open.
1954—Won Serbin open; Sarasota open; Landover (Md.) open and National open.

she underwent her operation at Beaumont, Tex., in 1953.

Mrs. Zaharias was declared to be the "greatest woman athlete in the world" by Isaac Grainger, president of the United States Golf Association as he presented the championship cup and the check of $2,000 that goes to the first professional. Grainger paid high compliment to the stamina of the new champion and her "wonderful mental attitude in fighting against what many would consider an insurmountable handicap."

July 4, 1954

Middlecoff Triumphs in Masters Golf, Beating Hogan by Record 7 Strokes

WINNER CARDS 279 ON AUGUSTA LINKS

Middlecoff Has 2-Under-Par 70 on Last Round—Snead Finishes Third at 287

By LINCOLN A. WERDEN
Special to The New York Times.

AUGUSTA, Ga., April 10—Cary Middlecoff won the Masters golf tournament today by a record seven strokes.

With a closing two-under-par 70 at the Augusta National Golf Club, the former dentist from Memphis took the first prize of $5,000 with a 279 aggregate.

In second place was Ben Hogan, twice Masters victor and four-time United States open titleholder, who finished with a 73 for 286. It was Hogan who officially inducted Middlecoff into the "Masters Club" at the ceremony in the rain in front of the clubhouse this evening.

Bob Jones, the club president, recalled he once had been asked by Cary's father, Dr. H. F. Middlecof, to dissuade his son from becoming a professional golfer. Jones said he gave that advice to Cary, but it was not heeded.

"The way he filled those seventy-two cavities during the last four days makes me think maybe I was wrong," commented Jones.

Sportsmanship Is Hailed

Jones then told how Cary had turned down a bid to become a member of the United States Walker Cup team of amateurs at a time he was contemplating joining the professional ranks in 1947. "That certainly was an act of sportsmanship," Jones said.

While this was Middlecoff's first Masters triumph, he had been a competitor here nine times previously. He played as an amateur in 1946. He also played the course as an Army lieutenant in the Dental Corps when he was assigned to near-by Oliver Hospital.

Middlecoff, the winner of the United States open in 1949, said he was nervous before the start of the concluding round. "From the time I awoke this morning to my starting hour of 1:42, it seemed like a week," he d.

To most of the gallery that saw the final stages of the nineteenth tournament in the light rain, it seemed certain that Middlecoff would capture the honors long before he actually holed out at the home green.

Starting with a four-stroke lead over Hogan, the same margin he had after his spectacular second-round 65, Middlecoff widened the gap. One of the late starters, he played today's first nine in 34. Hogan, out ahead of him, had 36.

Trapped at Tenth

Middlecoff's enthusiastic adherents had a slight setback when he ran into a 6 at the tenth. Trapped there, he failed to recover on his first attempt. But when he sank an eight-footer for a 4 at the eleventh and an eighteen-footer for a deuce at the twelfth they sighed with relief.

"No wonder," said Middlecoff later, "that I kissed my putter after getting those important putts."

Middlecoff elected to play safe at the thirteenth that had proved so disastrous to several players. Jack Burke, the opening-day leader, had a 9 there today. Sam Snead had an 8 there on the first day and injured his scoring chances. Snead finished in third place with a 287.

Middlecoff's policy paid off. The 6-foot 2-inch Tennessean had a par 5 at the thirteenth by playing his second short of the creek.

He used the same tactics at the water-hole fifteenth. Short of the small pond with his second, Middlecoff pitched his approach so close that he had a four-foot putt left. He sank it for a birdie 4.

In a fitting ending, Middlecoff ran in a three-footer for a birdie 3 at the eighteenth after a bogey 5 at the seventeenth. His closing 70 followed rounds of 72, 65 and 72 for a nine-under-par total.

Middlecoff scored previously this season in the Bing Crosby tournament and the St. Petersburg open. In 1948 he finished second in the Masters to Claude Harmon, trailing by five strokes.

Hogan, in one of his few scheduled tournament appearances, failed in his efforts to win the Masters for a third time largely through the lack of a putting touch.

Snead, with a 70, had one of the best fourth rounds. The defender by virtue of defeating Hogan for the 1954 honors in a play-off, Snead had his best round of the tournament. He had birdies at the par-5 holes on the second nine for a 34 after a 36 out.

Three Tied for Fourth

In a three-way tie for fourth place was 28-year-old Bob Rosburg of San Francisco, a former Stanford University star. After three rounds of 72, Rosburg finished with a 73 that included a last nine of 34. Mike Souchak, the leading pro money winner, had his second 72 in a row to enter the 289 deadlock. Julius Boros, who had a 71 on the opening day, had another for his 289.

Lloyd Mangrum followed with a 291. Stan Leonard, the Canadian open champion, was among the 292's, together with Harvie Ward, a member of the United States Walker Cup team. Ward was the leading amateur, having a closing 71. Lieut. Joe Conrad of San Marcos, Tex., was second among the amateurs with a score of 297.

Arnold Palmer, the 1954 national amateur champion, a newcomer to the pro ranks, turned in a 69, the day's best round, for a 293 total. That put him in the same bracket with Dick Mayer, who sank a hundred-yard eagle 2 at the seventh on the way to a 71, and with Byron Nelson.

Dick Chapman, former British and United States amateur champion, did not post a score after inadvertently playing the wrong ball at the sixteenth.

Burke, after his disastrous 9 at the thirteenth, had an 80 for 294.

Hogan three-putted one green

on the first nine. He failed to get pars at the tenth and eleventh. He had one birdie after that and six pars.

One of Middlecoff's stellar shots was his No. 3 wood second to the green at the second. It paved the way to his first birdie of the round.

Middlecoff drove into a trap at

the fifth for a bogey 5, but was two under par at the turn. He sank a twelve-footer for a deuce at the sixth and a tricky ten-footer for a birdie 3 at the seventh.

He had thirty-one putts today, but his long driving was a feature of his game throughout the tournament. "It's one of the so-

lutions to playing this course well," he said.

CARDS OF LEADERS

Out—		
Middlecoff	444 352	354—34
Hogan	454 353	444—36
Snead	354 344	454—36
In—		
Middlecoff	642 544	353—36—70—279
Hogan	553 445	344—37—73—286
Snead	443 444	344—34—70—287

April 11, 1955

Jack Burke Captures Masters Golf With 289 as Venturi Soars to 80 for 290

FINAL ROUND OF 71 DEFEATS AMATEUR

By LINCOLN A. WERDEN
Special to The New York Times.

AUGUSTA, Ga., April 8— Jack Burke, a 33-year-old Houston professional, won the Masters golf title today in a surprising finish.

While some of the most bizarre golf in the tournament's twenty-year history marked the concluding round, Burke came through with a sub-par 71 for a 72-hole aggregate of 289.

This enabled him to beat Ken Venturi, 24-year-old San Francisco amateur who had been the pacemaker for three rounds, by one stroke. Burke started the round eight strokes behind the leader. A gallery estimated at 15,000 followed the proceedings at the Augusta National Golf Club somewhat in amazement.

Attention had been centered on Venturi and Cary Middlecoff, the defending champion, for the greater part of the tournament and again today. But Venturi soared to an 80 and Middlecoff, who used four putts on one green and had a 6 at the seventh, carded a 77 for 291.

Thus, Middlecoff placed third, while Sam Snead, Venturi's playing partner, got the other sub-par 71 of the day and moved into a tie for fourth with Lloyd Mangrum at 292.

Barber and Ford at 294

Jerry Barber and Doug Ford shared the 294 bracket while Ben Hogan, Shelley Mayfield and Tommy Bolt were grouped at 296.

Burke, who had not won a tournament since the Inverness open in 1953, had a 218 at the start of the round. After playing his final eighteen holes, Jack returned to the clubhouse believing he had overtaken Middlecoff, but not Venturi, who was still on the course.

Venturi was visibly nervous on the incoming stretch after he had taken 38 for the first nine. The same score was credited to Middlecoff and it was three more than appeared on Burke's card. Ken went over par at seven of the last ten holes.

Snead said: "He didn't crack, he just misread the greens." Venturi, whose 66 in the opening round brought him the lead over

Middlecoff by one shot, got a 69 on the second day. He was ahead of Middlecoff then by four strokes. After the gales yesterday he was still in front of Middlecoff by four shots with 210.

"It seemed like I was moving away from Cary," said the saddened Venturi, "but I got hit by the door. I tried my best and I will be back next year trying just as hard."

The unexpected triumph for Burke followed an announcement several weeks ago that he might retire from tournament golf. The victory was worth $6,000 to him.

He finished second to Snead in the 1952 Masters. Last year he was off to a good start, leading the Masters field with a 67. But he did what Venturi did in the last round—shot an 80—and ended with 294 as Middlecoff won with 279.

Total Ties Record High

The score of 289 ties the record high and was caused chiefly by the weather conditions prevailing for the last three days.

As far as the scoring today was concerned, Venturi three-putted at three greens going out. Expected by many to be the first amateur winner, he remained cool and confident until his putting lapse continued.

Middlecoff, out ahead of him, was having his own troubles and Burke was not considered by the gallery until the last nine as Venturi began to slip, stroke by stroke.

Venturi was bunkered with his second at the tenth, chipped out and missed a 3-foot putt for a 5. At the eleventh, he had to chip from off the green. Down went a 5 as his first putt stayed out of the cup.

At this stage the spectators became aware that Burke was in the midst of what had been regarded as a two-man bid for the crown.

Burke had started back 4, 5, 2, the deuce coming at the short twelfth, the hole Venturi subsequently played in 4. Venturi's ball was over the green on a sandy patch and he failed to reach the putting surface with his chip. Ken showed signs of the pressure he was under by tossing his putter in disgust.

But at the thirteenth, he seemed to save a chance after driving into the pines at the right and recovering with a fine iron. A 5 at this hole was the first par since the eighth

hole for him. But a pushed drive followed by three putts at the fourteenth green put Venturi in a precarious position again.

Then Venturi took a 6 by overplaying the fifteenth. He sank a par 3 at the sixteenth.

Burke was in with his score as Venturi went to the seventeenth. Ken still could win with a birdie and a par, or tie with two pars. Venturi overplayed the seventeenth for a 5. He left himself a 15-footer for a birdie at the home green for a deadlock with Burke but failed to hole the putt, sinking the second putt for a final 4.

Burke did not start like Middlecoff, who had birdies at the first two holes, but Jack had

twenty-nine putts, and this accounted for most of his success.

The big one came at the seventeenth hole, a 15-footer for a birdie 3. At the eighteenth, after being trapped to the right of the green, he sank one that was just under 5 feet for a par 4 and an incoming 36.

Burke bagged a 6-footer for his par at the first hole. He two-putted for a birdie 4 and followed with six pars, hitting each green and getting down in two putts.

At the eighth his try for a birdie went in and out of the cup and stayed out. At the ninth he was short of the green in 2, chipped to within 5 feet of the flag and sank the putt for a

Jack Burke, eight strokes out of first place at the beginning of the final round of the Masters tournament, hits from under tree along fifteenth fairway at Augusta, Ga.

par 4 to be out in 35, one under par.

Coming in, Burke's keen touch was in evidence as he rolled in a 10-footer for a par 4 after he was trapped on his second. He went over par at the eleventh where he took a 5. But at the short twelfth, he knocked his tee shot to within a yard of the pin and ran in a deuce.

After playing the thirteenth cautiously for a par 5, he went over par again at the fourteenth.

There he drove into the pines but recovered well for a 5.

He had to hole a 5-footer for his par 5 at the fifteenth after he wen into the trees on his third. He putted up for a par 3 after being 60 feet from the pin on his tee shot at the short sixteenth.

Burke sank his long putt for the birdie 3 at the seventeenth and holed out with a 4 at the home green after being trapped.

CARDS OF THE LEADERS

JACK BURKE

Out	4 4 4 3 4 3 4 5 4—35	
In	4 5 2 5 5 5 3 3 4—36—71—289	

KEN VENTURI

Out	3 5 4 3 5 4 3 5—38	
In	5 5 4 5 5 6 3 5 4—42—80—290	

CARY MIDDLECOFF

Out	3 4 4 4 6 3 6 5 3—38	
In	4 5 4 4 4 4 4 5 4—39—77—291	

LLOYD MANGRUM

Out	4 5 4 3 4 4 4 5 4—37	
In	4 5 4 5 4 4 4 5 3—37—74—292	

SAM SNEAD

Out	5 4 3 3 5 3 5 4 4—36	
In	5 4 3 5 4 4 2 4 4—35—71—292	

April 9, 1956

Stranahan had final rounds of 36, 36—72 and 38, 38—76. He, too, had trouble with his putting and his rounds were marked by brilliant recovery shots.

FINAL SCORES AND CARDS

By The Associated Press.

Peter Thomson, Australia...146.	72 74—286	
Flory Van Donck, Belgium..145	70 74—289	
Roberto de Vicenzo, Mexico.141	79 70—290	
Gary Player, South Africa..147	73 71—291	
John Panton, Scotland......150	72 70—292	
Enrique Bertolino, Argentina.141	76 76—293	
Henry Cotton, England......153	71 74—293	
Antonio Cerda, Argentina...153	68 73—294	
Mike Souchak, Grossinger.		
N. Y..................148	74 72—294	
Harry Weetman, England...148	75 72—295	
Christie O'Connor, Ireland...151	74 70—295	
Frank Stranahan, Toledo....148	72 76—296	
Bruce Crampton, Australia..153	72 72—297	
Dai Rees, Wales...........150	72 75—297	
Angel Miguel, Spain........145	75 77—297	
John R. M. Jacobs, England.150	72 76—300	
Ricardo Rossi, Brazil......152	72 76—300	
Al Balding, Canada.........150	76 74—300	
Jack Hargreaves, England..152	75 73—300	
Charlie Ward, England......148	78 74—300	
David Thomas, England.....153	75 73—301	
Gerry De Wit, Holland......149	74 78—301	
Ken Bousfield, England.....150	76 75—301	
Ted Lester, England........146	77 78—301	
Laurie Ayton, England......152	78 72—302	
E. Moore, South Africa.....151	77 74—302	
Jimmy Adams, England.....151	76 75—302	
Dennis Smalldon, Wales....146	78 78—302	
Syd Scott, England.........152	74 77—303	
Ken Adwick, England.......153	74 76—303	
Alfonso Angelini, Italy.....153	76 75—304	
Bernard Hunt, England.....148	81 75—304	
Chen Ching Po, China......152	77 76—305	
Roberto Salas, Chile.......153	75 77—305	
Marion Gonzalez, Brazil....153	77 75—305	
Michio Ishii, Japan.........151	77 78—306	
*Joe Carr, Ireland.........150	79 77—306	
Christy Greene, England...151	79 76—306	
James Martin, England.....153	78 75—306	
Bill Shankland, England....150	79 77—306	
Carlos Celles, Spain.......153	78 76—307	
Sebastian Miguel, Spain....150	84 73—307	
T. H. T. Fairbairn, England.153	81 74—308	
Harry Bradshaw, Ireland...152	81 76—309	
Frank E. Miller, England...150	78 81—309	
Trevor Wilkes, South Africa..152	85 75—312	
Jack Wilkshire, England....151	85 77—313	
Martin Pose, Argentina....151	85 —†	

*Amateur. †Withdrew at end of third round because of injury.

July 7, 1956

Thomson Takes British Open

AUSSIE'S 286 WINS BY THREE STROKES

HOYLAKE, England, July 6 (UP)—Peter Thomson of Australia today won the British Open golf championship for the third consecutive year.

Although he was 4 over par for the final rounds today when he shot 72 and 74, he won the title by three strokes with a seventy-two-hole total of 286.

Flory Van Donck of Belgium was the runner-up with 289. Mike Souchak of Grossinger, N. Y., had a 294 and Frank Stranahan of Toledo, Ohio, finished twelfth with 296.

This was the first time since the Open became a seventy-two-hole contest in 1892 that a golfer had won the title three years in a row. Walter Hagen and Bobby Jones couldn't accomplish the feat. Both Hagen and Jones won twice in a row.

Other golfers have won the Open three times, but not in succession. Among them are Henry Cotton of England, who finished in a tie for sixth place today with 293, and Bobby Locke of South Africa, who failed to qualify for the final thirty-six holes of play.

Holding a one-stroke lead over Roberto de Vicenzo of Mexico City and Enrique Bertolino of Argentina going into the third round this morning, Thomson carded a 35, 37—72 to increase his lead to three strokes with an aggregate of 212. Van Donck shot a 1-under-par 33, 37—70 to take second place with a total of 215, while de Vicenzo and Bertolino fell out of the running, shooting 79 and 76, respectively.

Thomson was 2 over par with 37 in the final round when he learned that Van Donck had finished with a 74 for a total of 289. That meant Thomson could shoot a 3-over-par 39 on the back nine and still win.

But he came back in 37 for his winning total. Thomson was so careful that on the fifteenth hole, when a six-foot putt stopped on the lip of the cup,

he walked around for minutes hoping it would drop in. Finally he tapped it in for a bogey—one of six he had on the round against only three birdies.

With a gallery of 8,000 following him on the final holes, he put his second shot on the eighteenth green, but his putt of twelve feet rolled a foot beyond the pin. He sank his second putt for a par to close out the round.

De Vicenzo carded a 70 on the fourth round to finish in third place with a total of 290, while Gary Player, a 21-year-old South African, was fourth with 291. John Panton of Scotland was fifth with 292, while Bertolino and Cotton were tied for sixth. Souchak and Antonio Cerda of Argentina were deadlocked for eighth.

Harry Weetman of England and Christie O'Connor of Ireland were next in line with 295's, followed by Stranahan.

Souchak shot a 38, 36—74 on the third round this morning, the third straight 74 he had carded, and then finished with a 37, 35—72.

Trigonometry Finds 'Sweet Spot' For the Golf Club to Meet the Ball

By STACY V. JONES
Special to The New York Times.

WASHINGTON, March 15—An engineer has used trigonometry to find the proper point of impact, or "sweet spot," for a golf club.

Irons embodying the principle were patented this week for A. G. Spalding & Bros., Inc. Company officials believe the clubs are already lowering America's golf scores.

Thomas O. Brandon, a con-

sultant for Spalding and inventor of the clubs, concluded after a study that the old system of placing the "sweet spot" the same distance above the ground on all the clubs in a set was wrong. He found that when the height was calculated separately for each club by the angle of its face and the diameter of the ball, the player got a uniform "feel" as well as maximum power and control.

Spalding uses Mr. Brandon's

formula in producing its "Synchro-dyned" clubs. The patent (No. 2,784,969) explains that if the "loft angle" of the face of a No. 2 iron is 20 degrees and a standard golf ball is used, the height of the "sweet spot" should be a little over one-half inch (.553 inch). It must also be exactly in line with the club shaft.

March 16, 1957

MISS RAWLS GOLF VICTOR, PUNG IS DISQUALIFIED

CARD ERROR CITED

By LINCOLN A. WERDEN
Special to The New York Times.

MAMARONECK, N. Y., June 29—Betsy Rawls of Spartanburg, S. C., became the United

States Golf Association's women's open champion after the apparent winner, Mrs. Jacqueline Pung of San Francisco, was disqualified today.

Miss Rawls, winner in 1951 and 1953, posted a seventy-two-hole total of 299, finishing with

a fourth round of 76 over the East course of the Winged Foot Golf Club. However, Mrs. Pung, a 35-year-old Hawaiian-born player, had come in with a concluding 72. She was hailed by the spectators as the new titleholder with a total of 298.

The 235-pound jovial matron, accompanied by her 15-year-old daughter, was applauded generously by the crowd and interviewed by the press for several minutes in the scoring tent after finishing as "the new champion."

However, no card was posted for her beyond thirteen holes in the scoring tent. Mrs. Pung and her playing partner, Betty Jameson, had both attested their scores.

A short while later it was announced by Joseph C. Dey Jr., executive director of the United States Golf Association, that Mrs. Pung and Miss Jameson both had been disqualified for turning in incorrect scores.

This involved the par-5 fourth hole, where both players incorrectly had marked down "5's instead of 6's." However, Mrs. Pung had the correct total of 72, which included a 6 there, while Miss Jameson had an 85.

The U. S. G. A. regulation states that if a competitor turns in a score for any hole lower than actually played "he shall be disqualified."

The case is not without parallel in U. S. G. A. championships. Jack Burke turned in a lower score for one hole during the 1956 United States Open at Rochester. He got a two-stroke penalty at the time. Golf's ruling body has reversed the policy and announced the more severe penalty would be applied in future cases.

Today's incident was compared to the 1940 United States Open, when Ed Oliver was disqualified after apparently winning. He had started before his regular starting time.

Mrs. Pung in Tears

Mrs. Pung was in tears after learning of the decision. "It was an awful mistake and it is due a great deal to the excitement. Both Betty and I knew we had 6's and concentrated on our score. I knew I had a 72, including that 6. My mistake and Betty's was in not repeating to each other what we had at that hole and seeing it was on the card."

"Of course, I'm heartbroken. I thought I won this tournament. It means a lot to me and my family. I would have won $1,800 besides a bonus from the manufacturing company I represent. Now I have absolutely nothing for play here this week."

Miss Jameson was also greatly disturbed by the outcome, blaming the error to tournament pressure.

Miss Rawls stated later that she felt badly about Mrs. Pung. But she admitted it was "nice to be a winner."

The effect of Mrs. Pung's disqualification marred the closing hour of the competition. Members of the press blamed themselves for being in a hurry to interview Mrs. Pung in order to make deadlines. They whisked her off for an interview while she could have been rechecking her card in leisurely fashion.

A drive was started to raise a fund for Mrs. Pung by reporters covering the tournament.

At a late hour yesterday, friends of Mrs. Pung had contributed a purse of $2,367 for the San Francisco player. Mrs. Ellis Baum of Winged Foot made the presentation at the club.

Overshadowed by the turn of the last round, Patty Berg moved into contention with rounds of 73 and 75 today for an aggregate of 305. Betty Hicks, with a final round of 80, was next at 308, along with Louise Suggs, the Ladies Professional Golfers' Association champion.

Betty Dodd added an 82 for her fourth round to bring her aggregate to 310. Jo Anne Prentice of Birmingham was in the bracket at 311, along with Alice Bauer and her sister Mrs. Marlene Bauer Hagge.

Alice, who tied for the lead at 72 on the first day with Marlene, led after thirty-six holes at 145. Her game collapsed this morning with an 87 and she took a 79 on the fourth round. Mrs. Hagge had an 81 this morning and a 77 this afternoon.

Miss Rawls Starts Well

Barbara McIntire, the Toledo amateur who lost the championship last year in a play-off with Mrs. Kathy Cornelius, was the low amateur with a score of 313. Mrs. Cornelius had 83 and 83 for her rounds today to end with 328.

Playing some eighteen minutes ahead of Mrs. Pung, Miss Rawls began at a sub-par clip. She birdied the first two holes, but then overplayed the short third for a 4. A damaging blow came at the next par 3, the sixth, where she hit her iron from the tee close to a tree, failed to recover on the next shot and two-putted for a 5. This meant she was one over par for the round.

Miss Rawls was trapped on her second at the seventh for another 5 to be two over. After a par 5 at the eighth, she rolled in a thirty-five footer for a birdie 3 at the ninth. That put her out in 38, one over for this half of the course.

Betsy reeled off pars at the next three, but was trapped at the short thirteenth. Retrieving the ball from the sand, she three-putted for a 5.

After this setback, Miss Rawls settled down to par golf. She had to play through the trees with her second at the sixteenth, but secured her par 3. At the short seventeenth she was on with her tee shot and two putted for a 3. Another par fell to her lot at the last hole for a 76.

Mrs. Pung was two under par for the opening three holes also. A four-footer for a 4 at the second and a fifteen-footer for a deuce at the third sent her under regulation figures after an opening par 4. She drove into the rough at the fourth and was short in 3, taking a 6. Mrs. Pung scored pars at the next three, but rolled in a birdie 4 at the eighth. She was just short of the trap by the green in 2, pitched to within four feet and sank the putt. She three-putted the ninth green for a 5 to be out in 36, one under par.

With nine holes to go, Miss Rawls was still ahead of Mrs. Pung by one stroke. Mrs. Pung, however, knocked a No. 7 iron to within thirty inches of the flag at the tenth and dropped the putt for a birdie 3. At that point, she drew even with the former champion.

Although Mrs. Pung carded pars at the next three, the thirteenth hole was important, for there she had a par 3, where Miss Rawls had taken a 5. That meant the Hawaiian-born golfer had gained a two-stroke edge at this hole.

With 4's at the fourteenth and fifteenth, Mrs. Pung then played cautiously, on the advice of her caddie, at the long sixteenth. At first she selected a No. 4 wood for her second, but she put it back into the bag and took a No. 2 iron instead. She hit the ball to the edge of the green, pitched her next shot on and two-putted for a 5.

At the short seventeenth, she missed the green, pitched on and two-putted for a 4. She now needed a 4 to beat Miss Rawls' score. On the 2, Mrs. Pung knocked in a four-footer for her second putt and a 4 that apparently clinched the title.

The aftermath was sudden and unexpected. The press tent scoreboard showed a 6 at the fourth hole, which caused the disqualification of Mrs. Pung.

Alice Bauer Gets 87

After enjoying a two-stroke lead at the half-way mark, Alice Bauer trailed by nine strokes at the end of the third or morning round. The slim player, who shared the lead with her sister at 72 after the first eighteen, took an 87, fourteen over par. This was a tremendous scoring reversal.

Alice couldn't get her game under control and the winds that were blowing up to 30 miles per hour, didn't help. She was hooking badly and finished the outgoing half with a 7-6-6 for a 47. She improved on the inward half with a 40.

Alice's fifty-four-hole total of 232 put her in a tie for seventh with Miss Suggs, who had a 75 this morning.

The leader after fifty-four holes was Miss Rawls, who had been in second place at the start of the day at 148. She stayed even with par going out and was two over coming back for a 75. She went over par at the tenth and fifteenth and three-putted the sixteenth green.

Miss Rawls failed to hit the seventeenth green from the tee and carded a 4 there. But she finished with a flourish by knocking a No. 6 iron second to within two feet of the pin at the eighteenth.

She tapped in the putt for the 75 that put her ahead of the field.

Mrs. Pung was only one over par through the first nine, then came back in 35 for one of the two 73's recorded this morning. She was hewing well to the line with her powerful drives and seconds, collecting eight pars and one birdie on the inward half.

The birdie 4 came at the sixteenth, where she was just short of the green at the 450-yard hole chipped up and sank a putt. Miss Hicks, who had a 76 after being out in 35, and Miss Dodd, with a 76, also shared the next place at 228.

Then came Miss Jameson at 229. Miss Berg's 73 put her into contention at 230, while Mrs. Hagge could do no better than equal her 81 of yesterday. Mrs. Hagge had a 42 to the turn and a 39 on the back nine.

Mrs. J. Douglas Streit, the former Marlene Stewart, who won the United States amateur crown at Indianapolis last September, led the amateurs with a 75 at 233. Beverly Hanson was also in the 233 bracket. Mrs. Cornelius, the defending champion, took a third round of 83 for 243.

Miss Berg was trapped at the first, but holed a twenty-footer for a par 4 to start. She found her ball buried at the sixth, but succeeded in sinking a fifteen-footer for a par. "And I holed a fifteen-footer for a birdie 3 at the fifteenth," smiled Patty, after she had walked off the eighteenth. "That wasn't too bad, was it?"

Miss Prentice took a 84 on her third round after a 75 and 78 on her previous rounds. Miss Prentice's brother, Charles, is a professional at Columbia, S. C., and he also played in the recent United States Open at Inverness. The Prentices have the distinction of being the only sister and brother to participate in the two United States open championships this year.

June 30, 1957

Ford Takes Masters Golf With 66 for 283, Beating Snead by Three Strokes

Associated Press Wirephoto

Doug Ford blasting ball out of trap on 18th hole and into cup in winning Masters at Augusta, Ga.

DOUG 6 UNDER PAR IN HIS LAST ROUND

By LINCOLN A. WERDEN
Special to The New York Times.

AUGUSTA, Ga., April 7—Doug Ford holed out from a bunker at the eighteenth green of the Augusta National Golf Club today. As the ball fell into the cup for a 66, Ford's cap and sand wedge went into the air and so did Ford. He had clinched victory in the Masters golf tournament with a 72-hole score of 283.

Not since the tournament began in 1934 had any player finished with a six-under-par card as the 34-year-old professional from Yonkers did on the last eighteen holes. A cheer went up from the spectators, part of a record crowd of approximately 18,000.

"It was the greatest shot I ever played," asserted Ford, and no one was inclined to argue. Ford had been a stroke back of the leader on the first day and trailed by three after thirty-six holes. Beginning the fourth and

final round in bright, sunny weather with Harvie Ward, the national amateur champion, as his playing partner, Ford was still three strokes back of the pace-setter, Sam Snead.

One of the fastest players in the game, Ford quickly indicated he meant business. Snead began an hour later and he was soon aware that Ford was pouring in birdies up ahead. Ford clipped two from par with a 34 for nine holes, then bagged four birdies on the incoming half for a sparkling 32.

Snead, a three-time winner of Masters honors, had all sorts of misadventures. He took three shots from the edge of the eighth green and was trapped on the ninth. The result was a 5 on each hole for an outgoing round o⁻ 35.

Two more 5's dotted Sam's card on the tenth and eleventh. Then, after a par 3 at the twelfth, he went into the creek twice for two penalty strokes at the thirteenth and took a 6. Three putts came at the fourteenth for a 5. With Ford shattering par, that just about wrecked Snead's hopes of becoming the first four-time Masters champion.

Snead finished with birdies on three of the next four holes, for a 72 and second place at 286. But Sammy had played the

twelfth, thirteenth and fourteenth holes in fourteen strokes compared to Ford's ten. That made the difference.

Forty-six-year-old Jimmy Demaret closed with a two-under-par 70 to take third with 287. Then at 288 came Ward, who had tried so hard to become the first amateur to win this tourney.

Ward was one of three players who had started the day a stroke behind Snead at 215. The others were Stan Leonard, five-time Professional Golfers Association champion of Canada, and 27-year-old Arnold Palmer, an ex-national amateur titleholder. But Leonard took a 78 for 293 and Palmer a 76 for 291.

Peter Thomson, the British open champion whose native city is Melbourne, Australia, topped the foreign entry with 289 after a fourth round of 71. Ed Furgol's bid was marred by two 6's on the first nine after the former United States Open champion had been among the leaders for three rounds. Furgol's 74 left him with an aggregate of 290.

Jack Burke, who was the hero of the fourth round a year ago when his 71 enabled him to finish first, tied for seventh place at 291 with Dow Finsterwald and Palmer. Jay Hebert, formerly of the metropolitan district, posted 292, while Marty Furgol's

293 put him into the bracket with Leonard.

Ken Venturi, who as an amateur finished second to Burke last year with a closing 80, was ten strokes better today with a 70. The Californian, now a professional, had 294, which equaled the score of a 38-year-old dentist and amateur from Uplands, Calif., Dr. Frank (Bud) Taylor. Taylor won considerable praise for a 69, the best of any amateur in the tourney. Also at 294 was Henry Cotton, a former British open champion, who used 76 strokes.

Ford, who won the P. G. A. championship in 1955, said he thought the shot that did the most for him today was a spoon second that he slammed over the guarding pond to the green at the 520-yard fifteenth.

The large gallery, mindful of Ford's chances, waited with interest as he deliberated the shot. He had debated with his caddie whether "to go for it" or play short of the hazard and be safe. Ford chose the wood club from his bag, then an iron. Finally he took the wood again.

Before he addressed the ball, the spectators applauded. They knew he had decided to gamble and they appreciated his boldness. Ford swung and hit cleanly. The ball arched over the water, onto the bank and rolled up the green some forty feet to the left of the flag. There was a ripple of hand-clapping again. Ford, by then four under par, had a chance for another birdie.

Two putts and Ford had carded a 4 for his fifth birdie. He chipped to secure a par 3 at the short sixteenth and sank a par 4 at the seventeenth. Now he was ready for the home hole, the seventy-second and last in the big tournament.

Ford hooked a No. 7 iron second into the sand and found the ball partly buried. He walked into the hazard, whisked out his sand wedge, whacked into the sand and out flew the ball. It trickled over the green and into the cup. Up went Ford's cap and club. And up went Ford.

After he had turned in his score and been whisked away by a cordon of police, he telephoned the good news to his wife. When he appeared later for a press interview he was wearing the green jacket symbolic of the Masters championship.

"How did you get a coat so quickly that fits you?" he was asked.

"Shucks," he laughed, "I had it made for me last week."

CARDS OF THE LEADERS

	Out—								
Par	4 5 4	3 4 3	4 5 4	—36					
Ford	3 5 4	3 4 3	4 4 4	—34					
Snead	5 4 4	2 4 3	3 5 5	—35					
Demaret	4 5 4	3 4 2	4 5 4	—35					
Ward	4 5 5	3 4 2	4 5 5	—37					

	In—								
Par	4 4 3	5 4 5	3 4 4	—36—72					
Ford	4 4 2	5 3 4	3 4 3	—32—66—283					
Snead	5 5 3	6 5 4	2 4 3	—37—72—286					
Demaret	5 4 3	4 4 4	3 4 4	—35—70—287					
Ward	4 5 4	4 4 5	3 4 3	—36—73—288					

April 8, 1957

CHAPTER 3

THE TELEVISION AGE

Two of the greatest players ever to tread the fairways, Jack Nicklaus (shown here) and Arnold Palmer, dominated the game in the 1960's.

Palmer's 284 Beats Ford and Hawkins by a Stroke in Masters Golf

WINNER CARDS 73 ON SOGGY COURSE

Ruling on 12th Green and an Eagle at 13th Help Palmer —Venturi, Leonard at 286

By LINCOLN A. WERDEN
Special to The New York Times.

AUGUSTA, Ga., April 6— One of the game's young stars, Arnold Palmer, earned the Masters title today with a closing 73 at the Augusta National Golf Club.

The husky 28-year-old athlete from Latrobe, Pa., who won the National Amateur crown in 1954 two months before he joined the pro ranks, finished with a total of 284. Then he waited two hours for assurance that victory was his.

When Doug Ford, the 1957 winner, and Fred Hawkins, the slim star from El Paso, failed to bag birdies at the home green that would have forced a deadlock, Palmer was safely in.

Ford made an exciting bid with one of the two sub-par rounds recorded on the soggy course. He raced around with a 70 that almost closed the gap. Hawkins had a 71, but he, too, failed to catch Palmer. His birdie putt at the eighteenth hole swerved off the cup and stayed out, sending him into a tie with Ford for second place at 285.

Venturi, Snead Falter

Under sunny skies, and with a crowd estimated at 20,000, Ken Venturi, the leader for two rounds, and Sam Snead, who shared the pace-setter's role with Palmer yesterday, fell back in the competition for top honors.

Venturi three-putted three holes in a row starting at the fourteenth, after going out in 35. The Californian, paired with Palmer, equaled the par of 72, but it proved two strokes too high.

Venturi's 286 tied Stan Leonard, the Canadian Professional Golfers' Association champion from Vancouver, B. C., for fourth place. Leonard posted a 71 after a scorching 33 for the first nine.

Snead finished badly. At the first hole, the Slammer's No. 2 iron shot landed on soggy ground and Snead needed three more strokes to move the ball to the green. He holed out with a 6. Snead went to the turn in 38 and was back in 41. He

Associated Press Wirephoto

ON WAY TO VICTORY: Arnold Palmer watching flight of ball from the third tee during yesterday's final round of Masters tourney in Augusta.

ended with a 290 for the seventy-two holes.

The weather helped set the stage for a dramatic experience by Palmer at the water-hole twelfth. Because of an all-night storm and a cloudy morning, there had been doubts at breakfast time whether the fourth round could be completed today.

Rules Cover Weather

Under United States Golf Association regulations applying to weather conditions, the ball can be cleaned on the greens without penalty. An imbedded ball "through the green" also may be lifted and cleaned without penalty, then dropped as near as possible to the original lie. "Through the green," by definition, is the whole area of the course, except the tee, the putting green or any of the hazards.

After the eleventh hole, Palmer was leading Venturi by one stroke. Palmer knocked his tee shot over the pond to the green and the ball bounded up a slope short of the sandy trap beyond the putting surface. Venturi's tee shot stopped on the back edge of the green.

Spectators are not allowed to cross the newly dedicated Ben Hogan Bridge that spans the creek to the green. Viewers consequently stayed on a bank some 200 yards away to witness the action that then took place. It was almost as if the principals were engaged in pantomime as far as the onlookers were concerned.

They saw Palmer go into a huddle with one official and later with another. He talked to Venturi, too. Then he stroked his ball about two feet into casual water at the base of the mound. He picked it up, dropped it over his shoulder, chipped to the green and two-putted for a 5.

But to the amazement of the crowd, Palmer went back, placed the ball a few inches from where it had been originally on the slope, chipped close to the pin and sank a 3.

Mystery to Spectators

The confusion of the spectators was compounded when a 5 was posted for Palmer on the scoreboards. But as the Penn-sylvanian was playing the fifteenth hole, he was advised officially that his score at the twelfth was 3 and not 5.

It was disclosed later that he had had an imbedded ball in the moundside and was entitled to a free lift under today's playing conditions. But Palmer said he had been originally advised by one of the officials that he could not "lift" at that point.

On the thirteenth, even before he knew what his twelfth-hole score would be, Palmer turned in a prodigious 3 for an eagle.

He walloped a No. 3 wood to the green at the 475-yard par-5 hole over the meandering creek and sank a twenty-foot putt.

Venturi was still in contention but his putting difficulties beginning at the fourteenth smashed his hopes. He missed two-footers at the fourteenth and fifteenth.

Palmer wavered a bit, too. He was trapped at the short sixteenth and took a 4. He carded a par 4 at the seventeenth, but three-putted from the back of the eighteenth green for a one-over-par 5. He was taken to a committee room and waited eagerly for reports on the progress of Ford and Hawkins.

Art Wall finished with 74 to tie Cary Middlecoff at 287. Middlecoff, twice the United States Open champion and the Masters winner in 1955, tossed away an opportunity after starting at 4, 4. A 6 marred his card at the third where he hooked his second shot and needed three more to get close to the pin. Middlecoff turned in 38, 37 for a 75.

Billy Joe Patton of Morganton, N. C., was the low amateur with 288. Patton had 74 for his fourth round.

Disaster struck Francis (Bo) Winninger, who put two balls into the pond at the eleventh and ran up a 9. This contributed to an inward 43 and a 79 finish for 292. Bill Casper, the leading money-winner before the tourney started, also had a 9. This came at the thirteenth and he took a 74 for 293.

Claude Harmon was the other 70 scorer. He placed at 289, along with Billy Maxwell, Al Mengert and Jay Hebert. Ben Hogan had 291, the same total as Jimmy Demaret and Mike Souchak.

FINAL-ROUND CARDS

ARNOLD PALMER

Out	4	5	4	3	5	3	4	4	4—36		
In	5	4	3	3	4	5	4	4	4—37—73—284		

DOUG FORD

Out	4	4	3	4	3	3	5	4	4—34	
In	4	4	3	5	4	5	3	4	4—36—70—285

FRED HAWKINS

Out	4	4	3	4	4	3	5	5	3—35	
In	5	5	3	5	4	3	3	4	4—36—71—285

KEN VENTURI

Out	3	5	4	2	4	4	4	5	5—35	
In	4	4	3	4	5	6	4	4	3—37—72—286

STAN LEONARD

Out	4	5	4	3	4	3	3	4	3—33	
In	5	4	3	5	5	3	4	4	4—38—71—286

April 7, 1958

GOLF EQUIPMENT FIRST IN '57 SALES

Manufacturers Group Lists $163,279,859 in All Sports, $60,711,924 on Links

By LINCOLN A. WERDEN

More than $60,000,000 was spent for golf equipment in 1957 although no one can guess how much of this went for lost golf balls.

Figures disclosed yesterday by the Athletic Goods Manufacturers Association at the annual meeting of the industry at the Yale Club showed that golf accounted for $60,711,924 of a total $163,279,859 for all sports equipment. These figures are at the manufacturer's level, or factory selling price.

Theodore Bank, president of The Athletic Institute, asserted that this sales volume reflected the business of 80 per cent of the industry. He predicted that "1958 would be as good a year saleswise as 1957."

"If there is a recession, athletic goods are the last to feel it," he said. "Most people with more leisure time on their hands usually turn to sports."

$32,127,399 for Golf Clubs

The sale of golf clubs totaled $32,127,399, the manufacturers reported. Wholesalers disposed of 3,046,808 dozen golf balls valued at $21,111,608.

Although golf sales topped the list, the manufacturers pointed out that their recapitulation did not include expenditures on such pastimes as fishing, hunting, bowling or boating.

Second in the standing was "baseball and softball equipment" at $33,074,046. Sales of athletic shoes amounted to $22,073,466. The total for "inflated goods," which include basketballs, footballs and volleyballs, was $15,127,632.

Tennis racquets, badminton, squash equipment and the like accounted for $8,359,231. Athletic clothing, including pants, jerseys and uniforms, amounted to $7,450,235. "Miscellaneous items" were listed at $10,279,169.

Boxing Glove Sales Low

Boxing glove sales were reported at $300,523, considerably below items used in other contact sports such as football, where $5,903,633 was expended on football helmets and pads.

The Athletic Institute, a nonprofit organization, aims to promote sports, recreation and physical education.

H. T. Frierwood of the National Council of the Young Men's Christian Association reported that many schools were cutting down on physical education in favor of science.

"We mustn't forget," he warned, "that scientists and science teachers will have to be physically fit to do their jobs, too."

April 23, 1958

THOMSON IS VICTOR IN OPEN PLAY-OFF

Aussie Takes British Golf Title, Beating Thomas by 4 Strokes With 139

By United Press International.

ST. ANNE'S-ON-THE-SEA, England, July 5—Peter Thomson, a 28-year-old Australian, turned on the pressure on the last nine holes of a thirty-six-hole play-off against Dave Thomas of England today to win his fourth British open title in the last five years.

Leading by only a stroke after twenty-seven holes, the methodical Thomson, although bothered by a body rash, shot a par 36 on the final nine to beat the 23-year-old British professional by four strokes.

Thomson carded a three-under-par 68 on the morning round against Thomas' 69 and then got a 71 on the afternoon eighteen for a total of 139. Thomas shot a 74 in the afternoon for an aggregate of 143.

Thomas Cuts Deficit

They had tied for first at the end of the regulation seventy-two holes of play with record totals of 278. Thomson led by four strokes after the first eleven holes today, but Thomas, picking up three strokes on the last five holes, cut his deficit to one stroke when they went to lunch.

Each carded a 35 on the first nine of the afternoon round, leaving Thomson only one stroke in front. But then the Australian went to work.

He birdied the next two holes, picking up three strokes as Thomas went one over par on the twenty-eighth and parred the twenty-ninth. That gave Thomson a four-stroke lead, which he maintained to the finish.

Thomas got one of the strokes back when Thomson went one over par on the thirty-second, but Thomson went four strokes up again on the thirty-fourth with his third birdie of the nine. He increased it to five strokes as Thomas missed par on the thirty-fifth, but on the final hole Thomson carded a one-over-par 5 to reduce his winning margin to four strokes.

Thomas' putter, which had kept him in the running until the final nine holes, deserted him in the stretch run. He took a 39 on the final nine.

Thomson's victory continued his virtual monopoly on the British open. He has won or finished second every year since 1952.

THE CARDS
MORNING ROUND

Out—										
Par	3	4	5	4	3	4	5	4	3—35	
Thomson	3	3	4	3	4	4	4	3—31		
Thomas	3	4	5	4	3	4	5	3—34		
In—										
Par	4	5	3	4	4	4	4	4—36—71		
Thomson	4	4	3	3	5	5	4	4—37—68		
Thomas	4	5	3	4	4	4	3	5—35—69		

AFTERNOON ROUND

Out—									
Thomson	3	5	4	4	3	4	5	4	3—35
Thomas	4	4	3	4	3	4	5	5	3—35
In—									
Thomson	3	4	3	4	5	4	4	5—36—71—139	
Thomas	5	5	3	4	4	5	4	5—39—74—143	

July 14, 1958

Associated Press Radiophoto

VICTOR IN BRITISH GOLF PLAY-OFF: Peter Thomson, 28-year-old Australian, holds trophy after winning the British open title at St. Anne's-on-the-Sea, England. Thomson defeated Dave Thomas, 23, of England.

PATTY BERG'S 288 TAKES OPEN TEST

She Scores at Minneapolis With a Final 72—Miss Suggs Is Runner-Up

MINNEAPOLIS, July 13 (UPI)—Patty Berg fired her fourth straight sub-par round, a 72, for a 72-hole total of 288 and a victory in the $7,500 American women's open golf tournament at the Brookview Country Club today.

Patty had five birdies and was over par only once during her final round.

In second place was Louise Suggs, who had a five-under-par 71, the best round of the day, for a total of 296. The Atlanta had five birdies and thirteen pars on her 37, 34 final round.

Fay Crocker of Montevideo, Uruguay, trailed Miss Berg by three strokes going into the final. However, she slipped to an 83 to finish with a 302.

Betsy Rawls of Spartansburg, S. C., and Joyce Ziske of Milwaukee tied at 297. Mrs. Marlene Bauer Hagge of Delray Beach, Fla., and Bonnie Randolph, Naples, Fla., were a stroke behind.

Miss Ziske sunk a 150-yard No. 7 iron shot at the sixteenth hole for an eagle 2, the best shot of the tournament.

Mrs. Ann Casey Johnstone, a member of the United States Curtis Cup team, took amateur honors with a three-over-par 307. Mrs. Johnstone of Mason City, Iowa, had a final round of 75.

THE LEADING SCORES

Patty Berg, Minneapolis .72 71 73 72—288
Louise Suggs, Atlanta ...73 72 80 71—296
Betsy Rawls Spartans-
burg, S. C. ....75 75 73 74—297
Joyce Ziske, Milwaukee...74 74 74 75—297
Mrs. Marlene Bauer
Hagge, Delray Beach,
Fla. ....73 76 75 74—298
Bonnie Randolph, Naples,
Fla. ....77 74 72 75—298
Beverly Hanson, Fargo,
N. D. ....74 72 74 79—299
Mickey Wright, Bonita,
Calif ....78 74 73 75—300
Wiffi Smith, St. Clair,
Mich. ....76 79 74 75—300
Mrs. Kathy Cornelius,
Lake Worth, Fla. ....72 77 74 79—302
Fay Crocker, Montevideo,
Uruguay ....75 72 73 83—302
Betty Jameson, San An-
tonio ....76 76 73 77—302
Mary Lena Faulk, Thom-
asville, Ga. ....73 73 76 81—303
Marilyn Smith, Wichita,
Kan. ....77 75 76 78—306
Betty Dodd, San Antonio.81 76 75 74—306
Wanda Sanches, Baton
Rouse ....77 77 76 77—307
*Mrs. Ann Casey John-
stone. Mason City, Iowa.79 77 76 75—307
Mrs. Jackie Pung, Hono-
lulu ....78 78 74 78—308
*Denotes amateur.

July 14, 1958

GARY PLAYER WINS BRITISH OPEN GOLF

He Triumphs by Two Shots With 284—Van Donck and Bullock Share Second

MUIRFIELD, Scotland, July 3 (UPI)—Gary Player of South Africa became the youngest winner of the British open golf championship in modern history when he put together two brilliant rounds today for a winning total of 284.

The 23-year-old son of a Johannesburg dairy farmer started the final thirty-six holes eiht strokes behind the pace-setting Fred Bullock of England. He picked up four strokes on Bullock with a two-under-par 70 in the morning round and capped his comeback with a 68 during his final tour of Muirfield's rugged, 6,806-yard layout.

Bullock, an unheralded English pro who held or shared the lead from the start, finished with a 286 to tie Belgium's Flory Van Donck for second place. Bullock had a pair of 74's and Van Donck finished with a pair of 73's.

GARY PLAYER'S CARD
THIRD ROUND
Out—
Par ......4 4 4 3 3 3 4 3 1—29
Player ...4 4 4 3 3 3 3 3 1—37
In—
Par ......5 4 4 3 4 4 3 5 4—36—73
Player ...5 4 4 3 4 3 4 3 3—33—70—284

FOURTH ROUND
Out—
Player ...4 4 4 3 4 3 4 3 5—34
In—
Player ...3 4 4 3 5 4 2 4 6—34—68—284

July 4, 1959

NICKLAUS DEFEATS COE ON 36TH HOLE OF AMATEUR FINAL

Youngster Gets Birdie 3 to Dethrone Champion After Trailing Most of Day

By LINCOLN A. WERDEN
Special to The New York Times.

COLORADO SPRINGS, Sept. 19—Sinking an 8-foot putt for a birdie 3 at the thirty-sixth green, 19-year-old Jack Nicklaus of Columbus, Ohio, won the United States amateur golf final by 1 up today.

With this one sweep of the putter, he turned back Charley Coe, the defender from Oklahoma City, at the Broadmoor Golf Club. He thus became the second youngest player ever to win the coveted cup in as dramatic a finish as any in the history of this championship.

Coe sat by and watched his youthful rival win. Charley had failed to hole a chip shot for a birdie on the thirty-sixth by the slim margin of a turn of the ball.

Three Straight Birdies

It was Coe who scored a 69 in the morning round, two under par, over this fine course that is set in the foothills of the Rocky Mountains. He led by 2 up then after having been 3 up at the conclusion of ten holes.

A string of birdies at the first three holes had sent Coe on his way. Charley, the winner of the championship in 1949 as well' as at San Francisco last fall, had hoped to join the select circle of three who have triumphed three times or more in this event.

For most of the day it seemed that he would achieve this goal, but he realized at the outset that this husky challenger, 6 feet tall and weighing 190 pounds, was a bold and courageous player. Nicklaus never played safe. He gambled and hit with full power when caution sometimes seemed desirable.

And when the 35-year-old Oklahoman fired those opening birdies, Nicklaus allowed him to win only one of the three holes, which proved an indication of what Coe would face all through the match. It was Nick laus who staged a comeback with a 69 this afternoon to Coe's 73.

Defender Retains Lead

Soon after the luncheon recess, it was evident that Coe could not afford to relax or hit a bad shot. He drove into the trees and lost the nineteenth. Then he was short and lost the twenty-first.

As quickly as that the match was on an even keel. Coe didn't allow it to stay that way. He sank a 9-footer for a birdie at the twenty-fourth and went 1 up. It was not much, but as the match wore on, it loomed as a worthy margin.

Nicklaus went to the turn in 34; and Coe, with a 36 or par, held his lead of 1 up.

When they played the tenth, Coe seemed headed for disaster. He hooked his drive badly, then played a provisional ball. He found the first one close to a pond, some 3 feet within bounds. Six African geese enjoying the water cackled widly as Coe selected a club for his recovery. Charley whacked the ball to the green, and with two putts got his 4 for a halve.

Coe drove into the rough at the next, and he three-putted at the thirtieth. This enabled Nicklaus to square matters once more. But although Charley drove into the rough again at the thirty-first, the error he made at the thirty-second was more costly. There he pulled his drive into a wide trap and blasted to the rough across the fairway near a path.

Nicklaus banged a 4 iron second through the pines onto the elevated green. In two putts Nicklaus had his winning 4 and went 1 up for the first time in the match, on the thirty-second hole.

Both had 4's at the thirty-third. They halved the thirty-fourth, and now Nicklaus was 1 up with two to go. Later, he admitted he was "a bit nervous" on the seventeenth tee of the course, the thirty-fifth hole of the match. At any rate, he "closed the face" of his driver; and when he hit the ball, it zoomed far off-line into the pines.

Ball Strikes a Stake

He hit from a difficult spot along a roadway, and the ball struck a stake post to which the fairway rope was attached. The ball kicked left onto the practice area. Nicklaus then tried to clear the trees about 100 yards in front of him, and failed. However, he recovered well to the edge of the green from there. He was on in four.

Coe had played safely, using an iron second from the rough, and pitched to the green with his third. He sank a tricky 2-footer for his 5 and won the hole, making them all even for the third time during the afternoon.

The prospect of an extra-hole decision seemed almost imminent after both hit fine drives, splitting the fairway at the thirty-sixth. They had played so even. Coe was "away," however, and he pitched an 8 iron to the green, at the dogleg to the right over the pond. The ball dropped on but bounded beyond into the heavy grass some 35 feet from the flag.

Nicklaus, observing what happened to Coe, then chose a 9 iron. He hit it gracefully; and after it arched high in the air, the ball fell lazily onto the green. Applause from those around the green indicated that it was close. The ball was 8 feet short of the pin. Then came the suspense.

Coe finally chipped his ball delicately. It rolled onto the green that slopes downhill. On it went; and then as the crowd groaned, the ball hesitated and stopped, an inch or less from tumbling into the cup. Coe

The Cards

MORNING ROUND
Out—
Coe ....3 3 4 3 4 4 4 3 5—33
Nicklaus ....4 3 4 3 4 5 5 3 4—35
Coe leads, 2 up.
In—
Coe ....3 4 3 5 4 5 3 5 4—36—69
Nicklaus ....4 3 4 4 4 4 4 5 4—36—71
Coe leads, 2 up.

AFTERNOON ROUND
Coe leads, 1 up.
Out—
Coe ....6 4 5 3 4 3 4 3 4—36
Nicklaus ....4 4 3 4 4 4 4 3 4—34
Coe leads, 1 up.
In—
Coe ....4 4 4 4 4 4 4 5 4—37—73
Nicklaus ....4 4 3 4 4 4 3 6 3—35—69
Nicklaus wins, 1 up.

took his folding chair and sat down to wait.

Nicklaus conferred with his caddie. Finally, he grasped his hickory-shafted putter, made for him last spring in North Berwick, Scotland. He has been using it for five weeks. Crouching over the ball, he drew back the putter, hit the ball, and it went into the cup.

Coe doffed his cap. He walked over and shook hands with the new champion vigorously. "It was great; you were great; my congratulations, Jack," he said.

Only one other golfer, the late Robert A. Gardner of Chicago, who carried off the title fifty years ago as a Yale undergraduate, was younger than Nicklaus when he won the championship. Gardner scored at the age of 19 years and 5 months in 1909. Nicklaus is 19 years old and 8 months. Louis N. James of Chicago won in 1902 when he was 19 years and 10 months old.

Bob Jones, who first played in this tourney at the age of 14, was 17 when he went to the final against S. Davidson Heron at Oakmont in 1919. Jones was 22 when he captured the first of his five amateur crowns, in 1924.

September 20, 1959

Palmer Wins Masters Golf Tourney With Birdies on Last 2 Holes for a 282

By LINCOLN A. WERDEN
Special to The New York Times.

AUGUSTA, Ga., April 10 — There was room at the top of the Masters field for Arnold Palmer again today. With birdies on the last two holes, the 30-year-old professional squeezed past Ken Venturi and won with a 72-hole score of 282.

Palmer, the leader in each of the three previous rounds at the Augusta National Golf Club, closed under pressure with a 2-under-par 70. The sturdy young man from Pennsylvania's steel region came through after it appeared that Venturi had victory in his grasp.

Venturi finished about an hour ahead of Palmer. He had shot a 283. Palmer, who had won the tournament in 1958, needed a birdie to tie the Californian and two birdies to beat him. He had six holes to go.

As an amateur in 1956, Venturi had led the Masters for the first three rounds, only to lose by a stroke to Jack Burke when he took an 80 on the fourth and final round. Today he watched on television in the clubhouse as Palmer set out to overtake him.

37 Feet for a Birdie

Palmer, who turned professional after winning the national amateur campionship in 1954, ran in a putt of some thirty-seven feet at the seventeenth hole for a 3. That was birdie No. 1.

Now he needed only a par 4 to tie Venturi or birdie No. 2 to beat him. A picture of confidence, Palmer smashed a No. 6 iron for his second shot to the sloping home green.

For a moment as it crossed the green, it seemed the ball would go into the cup. Then it stopped less than six feet away. While the thousands around the green fell silent, Palmer stroked the ball into the cup for a winning 3.

Palmer had been the pretourney favorite. In leading after each round, he equaled a feat last accomplished here by Craig Wood in 1941. Already the leading money winner on the pro tour this year, Palmer received $17,500 of the $87,050 purse for a 1960 total of $42,797.

He had a two-stroke margin with a 67 on the first round and a one-stroke lead after his second-round 73. After a 72 yesterday, Palmer still was first,

UNFORGETTABLE MOMENT: The Pennsylvanian, left, receives medal and plaque from Art Wall, 1959 winner. Wall didn't play this year because of a kidney ailment.

a stroke ahead of Venturi and four other players.

The other second-placers at the start of play this morning were Ben Hogan, Julius Boros, Bill Casper Jr. and Dow Finsterwald. With Venturi, they stood at 213.

Beaten by a 5

Paired with Venturi, Finsterwald played him stroke for stroke on most of the eighteen holes, then carded a damaging 5 at the eighteenth for 71 and 284.

As it turned out, Finsterwald was beaten by an error he had made in the first round. Inadvertently he had taken a practice putt at the fifth hole after holing out there. The next day his attention was called to a local rule prohibiting such practice. He was penalized two strokes.

Finsterwald's final score included that two-stroke punishment. Without it his score would have been 282. For fin-

ishing third, he collected $7,000. Venturi's prize was $10,500.

Casper at 287 and Boros at 288 were fourth and fifth, respectively. Then came Hogan, who could do no better than a 76 for 289. He was tied by the British open champion, Gary Player of Johannesburg, South Africa, and Walter Burkemo of Franklin, Mich.

Player, losing strokes around the greens, posted a 74. Burkemo, a former Professional Golfers Association champion, had a 73.

Topcoat Weather

Weather in the 40's did not reduce the attendance. Estimates placed the crowd between 35,000 and 40,000. Topcoats were in order and some of the women wore furs. Clear skies made the setting pleasant.

While Palmer stayed even with par for the first nine holes Venturi was 3 under for that stretch with a 33. He had birdies

at the second and third and dropped a 20-footer for a deuce at the sixth.

But he hurt his chances with a damaging second shot at the eleventh. He hooked the ball into the water and took a 5. He safely passed the short water-hole twelfth by chipping closely for a par 3. And he played conservatively short at the long thirteenth and fifteenth holes to get his pars.

Palmer stayed with par going out, watching the scoreboards along the way to see how those ahead of him were doing.

Never once did he give up, although the signs indicated that Venturi was en route to victory. He never hesitated at the par-5 thirteenth and slammed a No. 3 wood second shot over the creek, defying the hazard. The ball traveled so far it landed in a trap beyond the green. Two putts gave him the par.

Once more came a demonstration of Palmer's will to win. There was no caution in the manner he tried for a birdie at the fifteenth in an effort to close in on Venturi. He had to hook a wood second, but he didn't worry about the water below the green.

The shot didn't work as planned. The ball landed near the trees and scoreboard on the right and Palmer didn't get his birdie. But he hadn't played it safe. He spent some time considering his third shot. It was a pitch and run to within seven feet of the flag. He took two putts and carded a par 5.

At the short sixteenth he hit the pin from about thirty feet on another birdie bid. The ball stayed out and he sank a par 3. Then came the birdies. They made Palmer the winner, just as he had been here in 1958.

FINAL ROUND

ARNOLD PALMER	
Out ....3 5 5 3 5 3 4 4 4—36	
In ....4 4 3 5 4 5 3 3 3—34—70	
KEN VENTURI	
Out ....4 4 3 3 4 2 4 5 4—33	
In ....4 5 3 5 4 5 3 4 4—37—70	
DOW FINSTERWALD	
Out ....4 5 4 3 4 3 4 4 3—34	
In ....4 4 4 5 3 5 3 4 5—37—71	

April 11, 1960

The Caddie— A Non-Alger Story

The bag-toting situation is not up to par. Good times and automation have thinned the ranks of yesteryear's 'Rabbits.'

By GAY TALESE

" * * he found himself glancing at the four caddies who trailed them, trying to catch a gleam or gesture that would remind him of himself, that would lessen the gap which lay between his present and his past."*
—F. SCOTT FITZGERALD.

THE hero of Fitzgerald's short story, "Winter Dreams," is a former caddie who, at a very early age, dreamed of beating the pro, becoming rich and having someone else carry the bag. He eventually did become rich, and someone else did carry the bag, but he never forgot his caddie days. For him, and for thousands of other young dreamers, the caddie job was the point where the dream began. But it isn't any more.

Caddies have changed. The caddie today is more likely to be an older man, unmarried, perhaps a drifter; or, if he is a boy, he certainly is not the Fitzgeraldian hero who treks through "the fairways of his imagination" with lofty thoughts. No longer do most great professional golfers come from caddie yards. No longer is caddying often the first job for a self-made tycoon of the future.

Although a record number of 5,000,000 Americans are now playing golf, the number of caddies has dropped from 400,000 a generation ago to about 200,000 today. In large part they have been replaced on the nation's 5,000 courses by 50,000 electric cars and 250,000 two-wheeled hand carts. But it isn't only automation that has produced the twilight of the caddy. Many

boys, in these days of affluence, are reluctant to tote a bag and chase some duffer's hook shots into the woods for a paltry $3 or $4 a round.

TO be sure, it is not really important that many boys no longer wish to caddie, or that the carts nowadays make some country clubs look like supermarkets. What is important, so far as professional golf goes, is that ex-caddies usually make the most exciting golfers. As caddie-turned-champion Willie Turnesa says, "If we don't keep young caddies interested in golf, where will we get our future Walter Hagens, Gene Sarazens, Sam Sneads, Ben Hogans, Byron Nelsons?" (All are former caddies.)

Caddies in the old days, in addition to being just plain interested in the game, were often (by their own admission) the brains of the golfer. The first mental giant on record to carry clubs was a man named Andrew Dickson, hired in Scotland in 1681. He rarely lost a ball, conceded all five-foot putts and became immensely popular with his patron, the Duke of York. In those days the caddie — the word is the Scottish spelling of the French *cadet,* meaning "little chief"—held a position similar to that of a squire to the knight. He is still the only person to whom, under the rules, a player can go for advice on choice of clubs or strategy.

IN America, some of the early great caddies were Joe Horgan, who caddied for a half century; Jack Allen, a confidant of Bobby Jones; and Leggy Ahearn, who knew which clubs Walter

Hagen hit best when he was hung-over and which when he was not.

"Back in the Open in 1919, Haig had been drinking the night before, and had a couple of cocktails at noon," recalls Ahearn, who is now 55 and still caddies occasionally at the Winged Foot Country Club in Mamaroneck. "On the fourteenth hole, Haig wanted to use a mashie. He was even at the time with Mike Brady. He pulled the mashie out, but I said, 'No, no, Haig, go to a midiron.' He did. And he hit it up stiff, inches from the pin. He holed out for a birdie 3. And that one-shot edge beat Brady. Haig gave me $160. We got along well. But when I used to see him come to the clubhouse in the morning wearing a tuxedo, I knew we were in for a bad day."

Gene Sarazen gave his caddie much credit for his triumph in the British Open in 1932. Lawson Little was so grateful to his caddie for helping him win the National Open in 1940 that he sent him to college. And when Ed Furgol won the Open in 1954, he gave his caddie $1,000. Snead also has always leaned heavily on a caddie's advice.

BUT there are times (as one out of ten caddies will admit) when a golfer would be a lot better off without a caddie. In 1946, Byron Nelson lost the National Open by a single penalty stroke because his caddie accidentally kicked his ball.

GAY TALESE of The Times staff regularly puts the caddie before the cart in an effort to re-establish golf's historic "farm system."

CHANGING FAIRWAYS—Above, when the caddie was king; below, two products of the automation age that have moved in on him.

Those were the days — during the war and immediately after it — when the quality of caddying reached its nadir. Older teen-agers were in the Army, drifting men were making more money in factories, and so caddie masters were left with incompetents who often knew nothing about the game at all. Once

CADDIE-CHAMP—The great Sam Snead in his bag-carrying days.

Jack Burke, undecided on what club he should use to reach the green, asked his caddie, "What do you think I need to get home?" "Get home?" repeated the caddie. "Man, I don't even know where you live."

THE caddie characteristic of the present days falls (or trips) into various categories, although all caddies are united in their contempt for bad tippers ("stiffs"), slow, bad players ("choppers"), and players who own heavy bags filled with extra clubs, shoes, practice balls, umbrellas and jugs (a "house and lot").

One category of caddie is the "Matinee Caddie." He refuses to get up before noon and fastidiously avoids ladies' tournaments because, he says, ladies tip poorly, play slowly, expect extra service and will not concede each other a one-foot putt.

A second type is the "Mad Looper." He loves to walk, will carry anybody's bag, and will make two or three loops (rounds) a day. But he is not very smart. He is of little help to conscientious golfers who depend on a caddie's judgment regarding distances. He is a "bag-toter," as distinguished from a caddie.

Then there are "Vagabond Caddies." These are the best caddies, and they wander about the country, following the sun and money. In the winter they're working for a golf course in Florida, or perhaps in Arizona. They'll work during the summer in the plush clubs of Westchester County, or perhaps spend week-ends at clubs at East Hampton or Montauk Point. They're anywhere from 21 to 60, and can average over $100

DISCRIMINATING

It has long been characteristic of some caddies to take credit for all a golfer's triumphs, but to disclaim any part in his failures. If a golfer shot into a trap, the caddie would say, "Too bad, you're in a trap." But should the golfer blast beautifully out of the trap, the caddie would pipe up with, "Boy, we sure got out of that one!"

---

a week (much more when they caddie in tournaments).

The fourth type is the "Rabbit." Rabbits are beginners with enthusiasm. Golf was once overrun with these youngsters, and they were the boys who often became famous pros. Caddies who learn golf early in life develop what is called a "caddie-house swing," a natural, rhythmic swing easily distinguished from the jerky motions of business men whose golf began with an expense account.

Though scarce, some Rabbits are still around, and caddie masters always try to give them lots of experience. The usual procedure when a foursome is going out is to send along one older, seasoned caddie (who will carry two bags) and two Rabbits.

"In this way, the older caddie can keep the Rabbits from messing up the game," explains Gene Hayden, a caddie master for three decades in Westchester County. "Rabbits alone would mess around out there, lag behind, whistle. There's an old saying among caddie masters—if you send one boy, you have a boy; if you send out two boys, you have half a boy; if you send out three boys, you have no boys at all."

The absence of great numbers of Rabbits in recent years has meant that golf's tournament professionals have come mainly from college campuses.

According to Charles Price, editor of Golf Magazine, only one of the top twenty-four money-winners in 1959 was a former caddie: Doug Ford. The twenty-three others were college boys.

WHILE the college boys are fine golfers, none of them has electrified the nation in the way ex-caddies like Snead & Co. did in their prime. The college boys, say some former caddies, are a pack of conformists. None of them would be caught dead in such polka-dot shirts and fancy hats as Jimmy Demaret (an ex-caddie) used to wear. They do not fling clubs like Tommy Bolt (an ex-caddie) used to do. They do not show up in the morning wearing tuxedos.

All this may be fine with some people. But is the game itself as exciting, other golf devotees wonder, as it was when the fairways were crawling with Rabbits who had, secretly vowed one day to surpass the masters they served?

June 12, 1960

PALMER'S 280 TAKES U. S. OPEN GOLF BY TWO STROKES

NICKLAUS SECOND

By LINCOLN A. WERDEN
Special to The New York Times

DENVER, June 18 — Golf's man of steel won the United States Open championship today.

Refusing to concede defeat when he trailed by seven strokes going into the final round, Arnold Palmer scored an incredible closing 65 for the greatest winning finish anyone has made in the game's top tournament.

While thousands cheered him at the Cherry Hills Country Club, the 30-year-old Ligonier (Pa.) professional brought his 72-hole total to 280. He won by two strokes.

In a dramatic fourth round, Palmer played the first nine holes in 30. That equaled the Open record set by Jimmy Mc-Hale, a Philadelphia amateur, in 1947. It also turned Palmer from an also-ran into a challenger.

Palmer started the round with four straight birdie 3's.

A tremendous bid by 20-year-old Jack Nicklaus, the National Amateur titleholder from Columbus, Ohio, fell just short. Nicklaus finished with a par 71 for 282 and runner-up laurels.

No amateur since Johnny Goodman in 1933 has carried

Associated Press Wirephotos

MOMENT OF VICTORY: Arnold Palmer jumps for joy on sinking final putt to win the U. S. Open golf championship.

off this title. But the score by Nicklaus, an Ohio State University junior, is the lowest ever by an amateur, including Bob Jones, in this championship.

Souchak Finishes at 283

Six pros tied for third place at 283. They were Mike Souchak, Dutch Harrison, Julius Boros, Dow Finsterwald, Jack Fleck and Ted Kroll. Souchak led for the first three rounds but took a 75 for the final 18-hole tour.

At 284 were Ben Hogan, Jerry Barber and Don Cherry, an amateur. Bill Casper Jr., the defender, finished at 286 with George Bayer and Paul Harney.

Nicklaus was caught in the midst of tremendous interest because his playing partner on the last two rounds was Hogan. The 47-year-old Texan made his bid when Souchak started to falter.

Hogan reached the brink of a fifth championship, a feat never achieved in this tournament. But the seventy-first and seventy-second holes smashed his fondest hopes.

Hogan was 4 under par until then. But he slipped to a 6 and 7 on these holes for a 73.

At the moat-hole seventeenth Hogan tried valiantly for a par 5. His third shot fell close to the edge of the water guarding the green. Hogan took off his right shoe and sock, stood in the water and splashed the ball to within 18 feet of the pin. He two-putted for a 6.

Hogan Drives Into Lake

With excited spectators lining the eighteenth, where the lake borders the fairway on the left, Nicklaus drove into the rough on the right. Hogan, intending to put the ball in position on a level part of the fairway, hooked it the least bit. It fell into the lake.

Hogan hit another ball. His subsequent approach fell short below the crest of the green. After he chipped 4 feet by the pin, Hogan failed to sink his first putt. He ended with a 7.

Playing back of Nicklaus and Hogan, Palmer learned what was happening ahead and adhered to pars on the last four holes for the victory. It brought to him a first prize of $14,400.

One by one, the others among ten players who were within two strokes of each other with nine holes to go saw their chances fade. None faded quite as badly, however, as Souchak, who had a seven-stroke advantage over Palmer beginning the fourth round.

Camera Upsets Souchak

Souchak was upset this morning at the eighteenth when an amateur camera man started taking movies just as Mike was on the backswing of his drive. Startled by the noise, Souchak drove the ball out of bounds and took a 6 for a 73.

A par 4 would have made a big diference. But Souchak, who had a 68 and 67 in the earlier rounds, was still the leader by two strokes after the morning round.

"I would have had a four-stroke lead if it weren't for that 6 this morning," Souchak said. But his last round of 75 was even more disappointing to him.

Souchak was off to a bad start in the afternoon and never regained his stride of previous rounds. He used a driver instead of a No. 4 wood on the first hole and knocked the ball into the meandering creek on the right, which cost him a penalty stroke.

He had an unplayable lie at the ninth as he hooked a drive into a pine tree. This, too, resulted in a 5. At that, he was out in 36.

But the race had tightened at this stage of the championship. Souchak's score then was 244. Nicklaus had 243, Fleck 244, Hogan 245, Palmer 245, Boros 245, Finsterwald 246, Barber 246 and Cherry 246.

Souchak Drops Back

Then "everything happened," as Souchak put it later.

The ex-football end from Duke went over par when Palmer was making his bid. Souchak, who tied for third in the 1959 Open, dropped back.

The chief trouble came at the short twelfth, where Souchak dropped his tee shot into the pond for a 5. And he three-putted for a 5 at the seventy-second green.

Palmer is a determined fellow on a golf course. He is the son of a professional and grew up in a golfing atmosphere.

After winning the Masters in April, he said his goal this year would be to win here. But the British Open and the Professional Golfers Association championship. Those who know him think that the task is not necessarily too big for Palmer.

Palmer was confident as he drove the first green and started his string of birdies. He had thirteen birdies in earlier rounds of 72, 71 and 72 and bagged seven more in the final eighteen holes.

'I Never Lost My Desire'

"I never lost my desire to win here. But you must have the breaks, too," Palmer said after he had won.

The turn of the tide, he said, came at the second hole. There.

he chipped in from about 30 feet for a birdie.

This acted as a spur, he said, and on he went, "fired up." A putt of less than a yard went in for a 3 at the third. A 20-footer for a 3 followed at the fourth. Then came a par 5 at the fifth.

"I hit a No. 7 iron to within 25 feet of the pin at the sixth and sank it. That was sweet," Palmer said.

At the seventh hole, Palmer dropped a 6-footer for a birdie 3. He was trapped at the short eighth, blasted from the sand and took two putts for a 4. This was the only time he went over par. Palmer hit over the ninth green with a No. 6 iron, pitched to about 8 feet away and got a 4 for his 30.

A par followed at the tenth. Then, with a drive and a No. 4 iron, he reached the green at the 563-yard eleventh. Two putts there resulted in a birdie 4.

Pars the Rest of the Way

At the twelfth, where Souchak had trouble, Palmer two-putted for a par 3. He got pars the rest of the way for an incoming 35.

Palmer drove with a No. 1 iron at the eighteenth, where Hogan had met disaster earlier. Palmer was safe and with a No. 4 iron was 80 feet to the left of the pin on his second. He chipped to within a yard and ran in the putt for a 4.

The only other closing rush to the title that approached Palmer's was a 66 by Gene Sarazen as he triumphed in 1932 at Fresh Meadow.

Palmer, who attended Wake Forest College, won the National Amateur in 1954 and subsequently joined the pro ranks, a life-long ambition. This was his eighth appearance in the Open championship. He tied for fifth in his best previous performance last year at Winged Foot.

Doug Sanders, who was in second place at the start of the day, finished in a tie for forty-sixth place. He closed with rounds of 82 and 77 for 297.

Palmer will leave New York by plane Sunday night for the International Trophy and Canada Cup matches at Portmarnock, Ireland, next week-end. He and Sam Snead will represent the United States. After that, Palmer will play in the 100th British Open at St. Andrews, Scotland.

Snead, a perennial contender but never a winner in the United States Open, finished in a tie for nineteenth palce at 289. His closing rounds were 73 and 75.

Al Feminelli of New York City, N. Y., shot a hole-in-one on the 212-yard twelfth hole in the third round—for a par 3. His first shot went into the water, which also cost a penalty stroke. His next shot went into the cup. His final score was 290.

Other metropolitan golfers were well back. Al Mengert finished with 294, Jim Turnesa at 297 and Bob Watson at 302.

One Putt for Three Holes

Chick Harbert had one putt at the first three holes in the morning. He rammed in an 18-footer at the first for a 3. He sank an 80-yard recovery from a trap for a 3 at the second. Then he chipped in from 50 feet for a 3 at the third. He played in more orthodox fashion after that and scored a 69 for 215.

Fleck proved ambidextrous at the fourth hole in the third round. His ball nestled below a spruce back of the green. The 1955 champion then straddled as if he were playing croquet and with a putter knocked the ball between his legs to within 15 feet of the pin. He took two putts for a 5.

Souchak and Sanders were playing partners. Never previously in the Open had the competitors who were first and second after thirty-six holes been paired for the final two rounds.

Snead Takes a 7

Snead was out in 38 with a 7 at the ninth hole in the morning. He drove into the rough and had to crouch against a bush to play his second shot. Then he knocked the ball across the fairway into the heavy grass and from there went into a trap.

June 19, 1960

MISS WRIGHT'S 292 BEST BY 3 SHOTS

Californian Gets 71 in Last Round and Wins Second Ladies P. G. A. Crown

FRENCH LICK, Ind., July 4 (AP)—Mickey Wright of San Diego, Calif., posted a three-under-par 71 today and won the Ladies Professional Golf Association championship with a 72-hole total of 292.

Miss Wright's score cut four strokes from the Sheraton Country Club par for the distance. In winning, Miss Wright became the first player to capture the L. P. G. A. prize twice.

Louise Suggs of Atlanta, starting the final round one stroke back, matched shots with Miss Wright for twelve holes, but slipped to a 73 and finished with 295 in second place.

The defending champion, Betsy Rawls of Spartanburg, S. C., the only other player in contention for the title entering the fourth round, soared to 78, but held third place with a 301. Patty Berg of Chicago posted a 306 for fourth place.

Miss Wright got off to a fast start with a 20-foot birdie putt on the first hole. She had three birdies on the front nine, two on the back nine and was over par on only two holes.

July 5, 1960

Gary Player Wins Masters by Stroke When Palmer Takes 6 on Last Hole

SOUTH AFRICA PRO POSTS 74 FOR 280

Player Slumps but Gets Top Award of $20,000—Coe Ties Palmer for Second

By LINCOLN A. WERDEN
Special to The New York Times.

AUGUSTA, Ga., April 10—Gary Player of South Africa became the Masters golf champion today after shooting his weakest round of the tournament—a two-over-par 74.

This was five strokes worse than any of his other rounds, which had been 69, 68 and 69 in that order. However, with the pressure also affecting his chief rival, it was good enough to enable Player to emerge as the first foreigner to win here.

The Johannesburg professional staggered home in one of the most hectic finishes in the twenty-five years of the tournament.

Player, who had taken a four-stroke lead into the final eighteen holes, weakened in the late stages. His 74 gave him a total of 280.

But Arnold Palmer, with victory within his grasp, suffered an even more dramatic and costly blow-up. He went two over par on the par-4 last hole, taking a 71 for 281 and a second place tie with Charley Coe.

Player, a dejected figure when he finished, suddenly found himself the champion. Actually, he became the title-holder while watching the action on television.

Palmer needed only a par on

Arnold Palmer dancing with joy after he sank putt yesterday for a par 5 on fifteenth to send him ahead of Gary Player.

Associated Press Wirephotos

Player is grim-faced as he blasts out of sand on eighteenth. Palmer took a 6 here and gave the South African the victory.

the eighteenth hole of the Augusta National Golf Club to win with 279. A one-over-par 5 would have meant a tie.

But then the unexpected developed. Palmer exploded too strongly from a trap and proceeded to take a 6.

Bidding for his third Masters victory and his second in a row, he had to settle for the second-place tie. Coe, 36 years old, closed fast with a 69 and narrowly missed becoming the first amateur to win the tournament.

Emotions, along with the scores, changed rapidly because of Palmer's experience at the final hole. Whereas disaster had struck Player at the thirteenth hole, where he took a 7, Palmer had been on the verge of another characteristic dramatic spurt to victory.

A 12 he took last January at the last hole of the Los Angeles Open had focussed attention on Palmer. His 6 today was so unexpected that it left the gallery amazed.

Arnold Palmer became a celebrity known to millions in the age of televised golf. His followers, some of whom may be seen in this photo, became known as "Arnie's Army."

Gary Player, one of the top competitors of the last ten years, has often had his career overshadowed by protests against the racial policies of his native South Africa.

Winner Embraces Wife

"I thought sixes only happened to other people," said Palmer.

Player and his wife Vivienne embraced when they saw Palmer take his costly 6.

Mrs. Player had followed her husband every step of the way along the course. A 2-handicap golfer herself before their marriage, she was sometimes critical but always calm about Gary's fluctuating fortunes.

"That was a nasty little putt he missed," she said when he failed to sink a 3-footer for a par 5 at the fifteenth.

After that error, most of the 15,000 spectators were ready to count Player out.

It was Palmer's gallery, of course, cheering continuously. Some of the cheers were for Coe's birdie putts at the thirteenth and fourteenth.

Palmer was some thirty minutes astern of the South African, or three pairs back. Out in 33 to Player's 34, he had gained a stroke at that point.

Player needed only eleven putts over that stretch. Palmer had recovered well from two traps.

Palmer collected a par 4 at the tenth. Player had taken a 5 there. Palmer matched Player's 4 at the eleventh.

Then, at the water-hole twelfth, where a 6 in the 1959 Masters had ruined his hopes, Palmer was confronted with another problem. His tee shot over the pond sailed to a rough slope at the back above a trap.

Palmer bided his time and made a careful survey. Then he putted the ball down through the heavy grass and it stopped three feet from its goal. Palmer tapped the ball in. The spectators roared their approval.

Crowd Becomes Tenser

The thirteenth, a picturesque 475-yard dogleg, now awaited Palmer. The crowd tensed with anticipation. When Palmer split the middle with his long drive, there were more cheers.

Ahead, Player had taken his 6 at No. 15. The crowd knew it and some enthusiasts shouted the news to Palmer.

"Palmer might sew it up right here," said one fan. Palmer did hit the thirteenth green with his No. 3 wood second. A birdie here would be vital. But he three-putted from seventy feet for a par 5, after leaving his birdie putt short by some eight feet.

It was this thirteenth that had cost Player a 7. Gary had pushed his drive into the pines. There were five giant ones a bit to his right and three equally tall ones ahead of him as he went to address the ball. The ball was lying on pine needles. He hit a recovery with a No. 2 iron. But the ball rolled across the fairway into a creek.

That cost Player a penalty stroke. He dropped another ball over his shoulder to play. He sent his iron, his fourth stroke, to the back of the green. Then he rolled his first putt past the cup about eight feet. He missed it coming back by two feet. Then he knocked in his 7.

After that, the usual jovial Player was morose. A par followed at the fourteenth. Then came the 6 at the fifteenth, where his pitch was short of the green but over the water. It was there that the "nasty little putt" refused to drop for a par. Player admitted later he had been disturbed and worried after that fifteenth.

However, he putted well for pars at the last three holes.

Palmer, meanwhile, coasted along for four straight pars after the thirteenth. He was confident as he teed off at the eighteenth.

"I never for one minute thought I was going to lose," he said afterward.

The gallery didn't, either.

Wasn't this the man whose 65 in the last round had won the 1960 United States Open?

Hadn't he won here a year ago with a birdie-birdie finish?

He had, indeed. But today, his second at the eighteenth was trapped to the right. The ball was partly buried. His recovery went over the green and nestled in the grass, some thirty feet from the pin as the crowd milled around.

Next, he putted the ball fifteen to twenty feet past the cup. Then he missed his try for the 5 that would have meant a tie.

Player's first prize was $20,000, the largest slice of the $99,500 that proved a record for the event. The money increased Player's winnings in the United States since 1957 to $95,217. This far exceeds the earnings of his colleague, Bobby Locke of Johannesburg, who won $62,179.16 in eight years of touring here.

Bob Jones considers him one of the greatest of all foreign

stars to challenge the home-breds. In fact, Player's victory in the Masters is the outstanding triumph by a foreigner since Ted Ray of Britain won the United States Open in 1920.

The South African said he would vacation on an island off the Carolinas with his family for at least a week. He intends to resume the tour and stay for the United States Open, if he qualifies. He also will compete in the Canada Cup matches in Puerto Rico and in the British Open.

Palmer received a $12,000 check for the second prize; Coe, as an amateur, was awarded a medal.

Tommy Bolt closed strongly with a 68 that included a 6 at the last green. This spurt gave him 285 and tied Don January, whose final round was 71.

Paul Harney had 286 and won fifth money of $4,800. Jack Nicklaus, a 21-year-old senior at Ohio State University, was in the group at 287. Nicklaus, an amateur, had 72 today. Bill Collins, Jack Burke and Bill Casper, who had a 69 today, were bracketed at 287.

Bob Gardner, the Metropolitan amateur from New York, played the incoming nine in 34 for 71 and a 288. Walter Burkemo, Doug Sanders and Ken Venturi also were 288. Sam Snead, Gene Littler, Stan Leonard and Bob Rosburg had 289. Ben Hogan, with a closing 79, had 293.

April 11, 1961

THE LEADING CARDS

GARY PLAYER

Out ......3 4 3 4 3 4 5 ←34	
In .....5 4 3 7 4 6 3 4 ←40—74—280	

ARNOLD PALMER

Out ......4 4 3 4 3 4 4 ←33	
In .....4 4 3 5 4 5 3 6 ←38—71—281	

CHARLES COE

Out ......4 4 4 4 4 4 5 ←35	
In .....4 5 3 4 3 4 3 4 ←34—69—281	

TOMMY BOLT

Out ......4 4 3 4 3 2 4 5 ←32	
In .....5 4 2 4 4 4 3 6 ←36—68—285	

DON JANUARY

Out ......4 4 4 3 5 3 4 4 ←35	
In .....4 4 3 5 4 3 5 4 ←36—71—285	

PAUL HARNEY

Out ......5 4 4 4 4 3 4 4 ←38	
In .....4 4 3 5 4 5 3 4 ←36—74—286	

P.G.A. WILL SHIFT '62 TOURNEY SITE

HOLLYWOOD, Fla., May 17 (UPI)—The executive committee of the Professional Golfers Association withdrew its 1962 national championship from Los Angeles for racial reasons today and recommended that the P. G. A. eliminate racial restrictions on membership.

The thirteen-member committee, ending a three-day, mid-year meeting, unanimously passed a resolution to wipe the "Caucasian clause" from the P. G. A. constitution. The resolution will be submitted to the P. G. A.'s annual meeting here Nov. 2-10.

Present P. G. A. regulations limit membership to "professional golfers of the Caucasian race, residing in North or South America."

The resolution came after the committee pulled its 1962 championship out of Los Angeles, apparently as a result of a feud with California Attorney General Stanley Mosk. Mosk said the P. G. A. constitution violates California law because it restricted membership to Caucasians. He said also the tournament could not be played in California if the ranking Negro professional, Charles Sifford, were not allowed to participate.

Tournament Chairman Edwin Carter had explained earlier that Sifford was not eligible to play because he was not a P.G.A. member "and under our constitution, if he were approved today, he could not become a member for at least four years."

Lou Strong, the P.G.A. president, said in announcing the executive committee's action, "Under present conditions in California, the P. G. A. did not feel that it would be possible to conduct a successful tournament of the magnitude of the P. G. A. championship in that state." He said a new site for the tournament would be chosen.

The Los Angeles Junior Chamber of Commerce later announced it would hold a seventy-two-hole Los Angeles open tournament Jan. 4-8 in place of the P. G. A. tournament.

May 18, 1961

PALMER TAKES BRITISH OPEN

284 FIRST BY SHOT

By The Associated Press.

BIRKDALE, England, July 15 — Arnold Palmer won the British Open golf championship by a stroke today with one of his patented late surges and became the first American to win

the title since Ben Hogan did it in 1953.

The Latrobe (Pa.) professional started the rain-splattered day one stroke off the pace. Then came one of his typical dramatic charges. He blazed over the soggy front nine of the Birkdale course, where par is 36, 36—72, in 32. That carried him to a third-round 69 and put

him in front. A 72 in the fourth round brought him the title.

His card for the four rounds read 70, 73, 69, 72—284. That was four under par, astounding under the miserable weather conditions that prevailed.

On Wednesday the weatherman had cooperated. But on Thursday heavy rains and terrific winds did thousands of

dollars worth of damage to the course and clubhouse besides wrecking the scores of some of the world's best golfers.

Blankets Blot Greens

Yesterday's scheduled final thirty-six holes of play had to be postponed because of the rains. Today's shower-spotted program saw workmen with buckets and blankets, which were used as blotters, stationed at every green.

Dai Rees of Wales, the captain of the British Ryder Cup team, shot a 71, 72 and finished with 285. Last year it was Palmer who failed to win the crown by one stroke in his first try for the honors.

Rees, playing in the twosome behind Palmer, stepped up to the eighteenth tee knowing that he needed an eagle 2 to tie the soft-spoken American. He made a heroic effort but his second shot halted twelve feet from the flag. He sank it for a birdie to become the runner-up.

Paul Runyan of La Jolla, Calif., the recently crowned seniors' champion of Great Britain and the United States, was the only other American in the forty-eight-man field that qualified for the last two rounds. He had a 75, 72 today for a 299 total.

Second Shot Is Topped

Not only did Palmer have to stave off the charges of his rivals, but he had to conquer a jinx on the sixteenth hole.

In the second round he had been penalized a stroke and took a 7 there. In the third he had to play one of the shots of his life to salvage a par 5 and in the last round he managed to get another 5 after topping his second shot.

"One day I would like to play that hole well," he told wellwishers after receiving the trophy. "I don't know how to do it now."

Christy O'Connor, the fighting Irishman, shot a 67 in the third round and finished in a tie for third place with Neil Coles of England. O'Connor had rounds of 71, 77, 67 and 73 for his 288. Coles posted 70, 77, 69 and 72.

Eric Brown of Scotland carded 73, 76, 70, 70—289. The defender, Kel Nagle of Australia, finished with 68, 75, 75, 71—289.

Gary Player Withdraws

Gary Player, the South African who deposed Palmer this year as the winner of the Masters tourney, had to withdraw after five holes in the third round because of a stomach ailment.

While the British Open title is one of the most cherished in all golf, the prize money is on the meager side. Palmer's victory in the 101st playing of the tournament was worth only $3,920. Rees received $2,800.

Palmer appeared headed for victory on the 517-yard fourteenth in the last round. He got a birdie 4 on the tricky hole that bends to the right with the green on a plateau.

The American had a difficult 8-footer to sink there after being short of the green in 2. He

Associated Press Radiophoto

ON TO VICTORY: The gallery follows iron shot by Arnold Palmer of Latrobe, Pa., during the final round of British Open golf tournament at Birkdale. Palmer was winner.

CARDS OF THE LEADERS
THIRD ROUND

Out—										
Par	5 4 4	3 4 5	3 4 4—36							
Palmer	4 4 4	3 3 4	2 4 4—32							
Rees	7 4 3	3 4 4	3 5 3—36							
Runyan	5 5 4	4 4 5	4 4 4—39							
In—										
Par	4 4 4	3 5 4	5 3 4—36—72							
Palmer	4 4 5	3 5 4	5 3 4—37—69							
Rees	4 4 4	2 5 4	5 3 4—35—71							
Runyan	5 4 5	3 4 4	4 3 6—36—75							

FOURTH ROUND

Out—										
Palmer	5 4 4	4 4 4	3 4 4—36							
Rees	5 5 3	4 4 6	3 4 4—38							
Runyan	5 4 4	3 5 5	3 4 4—37							
In—										
Palmer	4 4 4	4 4 4	5 3 4—36—72—284							
Rees	4 4 4	4 5 3	4 3 3—34—72—285							
Runyan	5 4 3	3 5 3	3 3 4—35—72—299							

examined the putt with the eye of a surgeon. Then he stroked the ball in smoothly and easily.

"That was the turning point," Palmer said afterward. "I felt then that if I could just keep on level 4's I would win—not that I could ever seem to get under 4's on that back nine."

And More Rain

Players and spectators kept their fingers crossed as more rain poured down when Palmer reached the thirteenth green in the morning. Officials had warned that if the two rounds were not completed today the championship would be voided. It could not be put off another day because the law does not permit paid admissions to contests on Sundays. Most of the golfers had other commitments that barred play thereafter.

Pools of water started to form on the fairways this morning. But the sandy seaside links soaked up the water, the rain stopped and the sun came out

in the afternoon.

A great shot saved Palmer from disaster at the sixteenth in the third round.

He was in the rough off the tee and on the slope of a bank. He hacked out to the fairway and then overclubbed a five iron to the top of a hillside, under a bush and in deep scrub above the green. Bushes surrounded him and the out-of-bounds fence was only a few

feet behind him.

A 7—or even 8—seemed likely. But Palmer, surrounded by anxious fans, selected a wedge. He popped the ball through one little opening, sent it sailing forty feet up and watched with relief as it plopped eighteen inches from the cup. He miraculously saved his par.

July 16, 1961

NICKLAUS WINS

MARGIN IS 8 AND 6

Nicklaus Takes U. S. Amateur Golf Title, Downing Wysong

By LINCOLN A. WERDEN
Special to The New York Times.

PEBBLE BEACH, Calif., Sept. 16—Jack Nicklaus, only 21 years old, became the amateur golf champion of the United States for the second time today.

The Ohio State University senior, a resident of Columbus, Ohio, played through fog, rain and sunshine to beat Dudley Wysong of McKinney, Tex., 8 and 6, in the scheduled 36-hole final over the Pebble Beach course.

It was the widest margin in a final since 1955, and Nicklaus seemed completely relaxed. He gave a tremendous demonstration of long hitting through the morning eighteen, when rain and fog engulfed the finalists, as well as during the brief afternoon session as the weather cleared.

When the match ended at the

SYMBOL OF SUPREMACY: Jack Nicklaus, right, of Columbus, Ohio, holds cup awarded the winner in the National Amateur golf tourney at Pebble Beach, Calif. With him is Dudley Wysong, McKinney, Tex., whom he defeated.

thirtieth hole, Nicklaus was five under par for the day. He led by 4 up after eighteen following a three-under-par 69. Few finalists have played at such a pace in the sixty-one years the championship has been staged.

The outcome was highly edifying to Nicklaus, who already had won the National Collegiate and Western titles this year. And it was equally gratifying for his caddie, 58-year-old Al Gonzales.

This was the second triumph for Gonzales, too. He also carried the bag of Harrison (Jimmy) Johnston of Minneapolis when Johnston won the championship on this course in 1929.

Nicklaus played so well that Gonzales puffed away on a cigar between shots. He says he always does that and usually consumes five to eight, "depending on how tough the match is —the tougher the match, the more I smoke."

Caddie Under Par, Too

But Nicklaus' fine golf and the rain this morning forced Gonzales to cut down his quota. He was under par, too. He smoked only three cigars in the morning and one during the afternoon.

The husky, 205-pound Nicklaus joined thirteen others who have twice won this tournament. When he triumphed in 1959 at Colorado Springs, Nicklaus became the second youngest to do so. At that time he was four months short of 20.

Nicklaus widened his gap to 8 up at the twenty-second hole, but his 22-year-old opponent, the son of a physician, never gave the impression of giving up.

In 1954 Wysong sustained a back injury in a train wreck. But his fine solid swing here gave no evidence of that. And his courage against Nicklaus won continuous commendation from the gallery.

Wysong won only two holes this morning. In the afternoon round he ran in winning deuces twice.

But it was an uphill struggle because Nicklaus' burst of birdies on the opening four holes after luncheon increased his lead quickly. Nicklaus won four in a row, beginning at the nineteenth, to become 8 up.

A 2 by Wysong won him the twenty-third, but he lost the next with a 6. The Texan rolled in a 6-footer at the twenty-fifth for a second deuce, and a winning 4 at the following hole reduced Nicklaus' margin to 6 up.

Nicklaus won the twenty-seventh with a par 4 and was out in 34, two under par, to Wy-

TOO SHORT: Dudley Wysong of McKinney, Tex., strokes a 12-foot putt within two inches of the cup on the third green in the final of the National Amateur at Pebble Beach, Calif. Opponent is Jack Nicklaus of Columbus, Ohio.

song's 32. Nicklaus went over this same span in 33 this morning.

Nicklaus was trapped and lost the twenty-eighth. Then he crashed his iron to within eighteen inches of the pin for a certain birdie 3 at the twenty-ninth. That brought him a 7-up margin.

The match ended at the next green. Both were trapped, but Wysong was twenty feet from the pin on his recovery. Nicklaus left himself about five feet away after he had played from the trap. After putting, Wysong walked over and conceded Nicklaus the final par 3 that clinched the championship.

Rain Trousers Needed

Both changed into rain trousers for the afternoon round. Officials delayed the start some fifteen minutes so the players could get into dry clothes following their morning soaking. Then the mist cleared suddenly for the remainder of the match. Wysong didn't have an umbrella when the rain struck and Nicklaus offered him the shelter of his. They walked together down the fairways after that, trying to stay out of the rain.

It wasn't until the thirteenth that the Texan captured a hole. Here, for the first time during the round, Nicklaus hit his drive off line. It went into a trap on the left and then he smashed his recovery from the sand so far that the ball went over the green.

Nicklaus chipped weakly from the heavy grass and took a losing 5 to Wysong's 4.

Nicklaus went 4 up again at the fourteenth. Both were trapped short of the green at this dogleg, par-5 hole. But Wysong knocked the ball from the

hazard over the green to the sixteenth tee.

Wysong chipped back short and later conceded Nicklaus a winning birdie 4 after the latter had come out of the trap nicely.

The second hole Nicklaus lost was the fifteenth. Once more his power brought him beyond the green. His second ran into a trap at the back edge. Wysong, extremely cool under pressure, hit a fine iron to the putting surface and won the hole with a par 4.

Wysong's best shot came at the sixteenth, where a gully and trees are in the bend of the right dogleg. His drive dropped into a trap near this danger zone, but he hit a marvelous No. 6 iron from there to within ten feet of the pin.

Nicklaus then sank a 40-foot putt for a birdie 3. Wysong rolled his in for a birdie 3 also.

Nicklaus went 4 up at the seventeenth after both were trapped. His 12-foot putt went in for a winning par 3 but Wysong had been trapped at the green.

Although Wysong's drive at the eighteenth was close to a pine tree near the center of the fairway, he matched Nicklaus' par 5.

Nicklaus Starts Well

Shortly after the start, it appeared the match would be a runaway because Nicklaus had winning birdies at two of the first four holes and had a chance for another at the third.

He went 1 up at the 497-yard second hole, where his iron second carried over the ravine and stopped in the trap at the back of the green. Wysong, who used a wood for his second shot, was off the green in 2.

Nicklaus recovered from the

sand to within four feet of the flag and sank a winning birdie 4.

The Ohioan had a chance for a birdie at the third green but his putt went past the cup. Nicklaus had only a 2-foot putt to sink for a birdie 3 at the fourth.

Now 2 up, Nicklaus tried for another birdie at the fifth, where his tee shot left him six feet from the flag. But he couldn't get this one in. He secured a half there and another at the long sixth, where he outdrove Wysong by 50 yards.

A deuce at the seventh hole, which is a photographer's delight because the green juts out into the bay, enabled Nicklaus to go 3 up.

Using a No. 1 iron cautiously from the eighth tee, Nicklaus sent his second to the left just off the edge of the green. He pitched to within six feet of the pin and got a 4. Wysong, after playing from the edge, had a 4 there also.

Nicklaus was home with an iron at the 450-yard ninth for a 4, while Wysong chipped to within four feet of the flag and sank his 4 to be out in 36. Nicklaus had a 33, three under par, for that stretch.

After Wysong chipped well for a 4, Nicklaus tried for a birdie at the tenth from twelve feet away. He failed to get it

THE CARDS

MORNING ROUND

```
Out—
Nicklaus . 4 4 4 3 3 5 2 4 4—33
Wysong . 4 5 4 4 3 5 3 4 4—36
    Nicklaus leads, 3 up.
In—
Nicklaus . 4 4 3 5 4 5 3 3 5—36—69
Wysong . 4 5 3 4 6 4 3 4 5—38—74
    Nicklaus leads, 4 up.
```

AFTERNOON ROUND

```
Out—
Nicklaus . . . . . . . 3 4 4 3 3 5 3 5 4—34
Wysong . . . . . . . . 4 6 5 4 2 6 2 4 5—38
    Nicklaus leads, 7 up.
In—
Nicklaus . . . . . . . . . . 5 3 3
Wysong . . . . . . . . . . . 4 4 4
    Nicklaus wins, 8 and 6.
```

and tapped in his 4. Decidedly outdriven going uphill to the eleventh, Wysong dumped his second into a trap and lost the hole to a par 4 by Nicklaus.

Both had 3's at the par-3 twelfth before Nicklaus left his winning stride for the first time at the thirteenth.

The Man Enjoyed Himself

At the presentation ceremony, Nicklaus said:

"I certainly have enjoyed myself here this year. It's the first occasion I have ever been able to have to play the course."

He paid high compliments to Wysong, whom he described as a "giant killer for being able to beat Harvie Ward, twice a champion, and Joe Carr, the Irishman who three times has won the British championship."

A few minutes after receiving the championship trophy, Nicklaus was talking about next year's golf campaign.

"I intend to try for the British Open next summer," he said. "What would I like to win next? Well I'd like to win everything I play in 1961, and that includes the Masters and the United Open.

Nicklaus, who finished second in the 1960 United States Open and tied for fourth last June, said he preferred stroke play to match play. His immediate plans, he said, were to get back to the classroom a week from Monday.

"My next tournament will probably be here in the Bing Crosby event in January," he said.

Did he intend to become a professional? The reddish-haired collegian said:

"I have no plans whatsoever to become a pro."

September 17, 1961

Palmer Beats Gary Player by 3 Shots, Finsterwald by 9 in Masters Play-Off

PRO, 32, RECORDS A 68 AT AUGUSTA

Palmer, 3 Shots Back After 9 Holes, Rallies for 31 and Earns Purse of $20,000

By LINCOLN A. WERDEN
Special to The New York Times.

AUGUSTA, Ga., April 9 — Arnold Palmer proved again today to be an amazing golfer as he won the Masters tournament for the third time.

Palmer won with a rally over the closing nine, which he played in 31. He turned back his two challengers in the three-cornered 18-hole play-off with

a final 68. This four-under-par performance gave him a three-stroke edge over the 1961 Masters winner, Gary Player of South Africa, and nine strokes over Dow Finsterwald.

Palmer's victory netted him the top prize of $20,000 from the total purse of $109,100, the largest in golf history. It had added significance because it made Palmer the game's greatest official money-winner.

Since late 1954, when he turned professional after winning the National Amateur championship in Detroit, Palmer has won $298,739.09. This, of course, does not include sums earned from unofficial tourneys, exhibitions and various sources of income he now enjoys as the No. 1 man in the game.

Doug Ford and Cary Middlecoff had led Palmer in official earnings until the 32-year-old Latrobe (Pa.) professional reeled off his sensational golf

at the Augusta National Golf Club this afternoon.

15,000 See Play-Off

After nine holes, Palmer trailed Player by three strokes but had a three-stroke lead over the tiring Finsterwald. The Ohioan's 65 on the third round was the low score of the 72-hole competition that ended yesterday in the first three-way tie in Master's history.

But as Bob Jones, the club president, who presided at the presentation ceremonies, had pointed out earlier, the measure of a good golfer is his ability to score well after he is not playing at his best. This certainly was true of Palmer.

A glance at his scoring over the second nine during the tourney gave his admirers in the crowd of 15,000 something to anticipate. On the way to his four-round total 280, he had been twelve under par for four rounds on the back nine.

In the fourth round yesterday, in characteristic fashion, he never gave up. He punched out birdies on two of the last three holes to force his way into the play-off with a 75 after going out in 39.

In the play-off, he scorched that back nine again. Player, attempting to become the first to win twice in a row here, three-putted for a 5 at the tenth. Palmer calmly rolled in a 12-footer for a birdie 3.

Player's Lead Vanishes

Right here Palmer chopped two strokes from the Johannesburg professional's lead. Finsterwald, failing to get his game under control, had gone out in 40 but took a 4 at the tenth.

After Palmer and Player had posted par 4's at the eleventh, Palmer resumed his birdie streak. He had a deuce at the water-hole twelfth, his nemesis in 1959 when it cost him a 6.

The Cards

Out—									
Palmer	4	5	4	3	4	3	5	5	4—37
Player	3	4	4	3	5	2	4	5	4—34
Finsterwald	5	4	5	4	3	5	5	5	5—40
In—									
Palmer	3	4	2	4	3	5	2	4	4—31—68
Player	5	4	4	5	5	4	3	4	3—37—71
Finsterwald	4	5	3	4	4	6	3	4	4—37—77

The deuce sent him into the lead after Player had three-putted for a 4.

The vitality that marks Palmer's golf was evident again at the dogleg, par-5 thirteenth of 475 yards. There he slammed an arcing No. 1 iron second shot to the left side of the green, two-putted for a birdie 4 and led Player by two shots when Player took a 5.

Palmer sealed his victory at the par-4 fourteenth hole. On this green, with its rolling terrain, Palmer stroked in a 15-footer for his third straight birdie and his fourth in five holes. Player, at the back of the green, used three putts for a 5. That built Palmer's advantage to four strokes.

A birdie 4 at the fifteenth by Player momentarily stopped Palmer's rush. He had to be content with a 5 at this hole.

Palmer 4 Strokes Ahead

The gap was widened at the sixteenth, a picturesque par 3, as Palmer ran in a 12-footer for a deuce. Yesterday, he had a 2 there also when he chipped in a 40-footer. Palmer was now four strokes ahead of Player with two holes to go.

Both had 4's at the seventeenth. Palmer's drive caromed off a pine tree on the left, but the ball fell safely to the fairway.

At the eighteenth, there was less drama than marked the tourney finale there a year ago. In 1961 Player sat in the clubhouse and waited while Palmer, needing a 4, took a surprising 6 and finished in a tie for second with an amateur, Charlie Coe.

Today, Player slipped in a 15-foot putt for a concluding birdie 3 and a 71. Palmer was on the

green safely in 2, carefully avoiding the danger of the trap on the right that caught his second shot in 1961.

When he took two putts for a 4 it meant his third Masters victory. Palmer also won here in 1958 and 1960.

Palmer plans many more championship appearances. "The idea of a grand slam is certainly still in my mind," he said, after leaving the course.

That means he is gunning again for the United States and British Opens and the Professoinal Golfers Association championship this year. He is the British Open titleholder and will defend July 9 through 13 at Troon, Scotland.

His next major target is the United States Open at Oakmont, Pa., June 14 through 16. In 1960 he won that title in sensational fashion with a closing round of 65.

With both the Masters and United States Open to his credit that year he failed to complete the slam by finishing second in the British Open to Kel Nagle of Australia. He tripped badly later in the P. G. A.

That disappointment rankles Palmer, and he wants to capture this crown July 19 through 22 at Newton Square, Pa. It is the only major title of the big four that has escaped him.

Besides being a remarkable competitor, Palmer has the determination to strive for perfection plus an ability to tie a lucrative business career to a golf career.

No accurate figures on his income have been released. But he is associated with a dozen or more companies, in some of which he is the principal stockholder.

Tycoon of the Links

He has his own attorney and manager, a Yale Law School graduate, on hand at most tournaments. They confer constantly between rounds, checking on

new deals, endorsements and a schedule that has taken Palmer around the world on exhibition tours and will resume shortly.

Some estimates place Palmer's over-all income at $300,000 a year. And he is expected to expand a profitable insurance business and may market his own line of golf equipment soon.

If this is unusual for most golfers, it must be realized that Palmer is far from the ordinary in everything he does. He has an obsession to tinker with clubs. According to the manufacturer who supplies them, Palmer makes long-distance calls several times each month to keep up to date on what is being designed or made.

"He is always asking questions and constantly wants to improve," said the company representative. This man had a brief scare when he saw Palmer tee off on the fourth round. He caught a glimpse of Palmer's backswing as Arnold drove from the first tee.

A Happy Mistake

"Oh, no, is that a new driver he's using?" exclaimed the startled manufacturer. He quickly worked through the crowd for a closer look and discovered he was in error.

"I'm glad I'm wrong," he said, "but it wouldn't have surprised me if Palmer was trying a new driver, even in the midst

of a championship. No other golfer would dare such a thing."

Palmer did change his No. 5 iron by "shaving off part of the heel" after the first round. It worked better after that, he said.

That's the kind of fellow the son of Deacon Palmer, the professional at the Latrobe Country Club, is.

Previously, Palmer won the Phoenix open by twelve strokes and the Palm Springs (Calif.) open on the winter tour. His next stop is Greensboro, N. C., this week-end.

Player said he was going home for a visit. The South African, a father-to-be, will be back for the major tourneys on the spring and summer calendar. Finsterwald, who has not won a tournament since the 1960 New Orleans open, received $8,000 as third prize to $12,000 for Player.

Dow had a great chance yesterday until a 5 at the seventeenth spoiled his hopes. Subsequently, while waiting for the others to finish, a valet suggested that he be fitted for the green jacket given to the Masters victor. Finsterwald declined.

Today, he never had a chance. He trailed after Player got birdies on the first and second holes while he took 5's at each.

April 10, 1962

Palmer's Money-Winnings

Year	No. Tourneys	Won	In Top 5	Official Winnings	Total Winnings
1955	31	1	2	$7,958.32	$8,225.90
1956	31	3	4	16,144.66	20,043.85
1957	22	4	9	27,802.80	31,703.81
1958	33	3	10	42,607.50	45,607.93
1959	31	3	11	32,462.14	38,674.87
1960	27	8	17	75,262.85	80,968.06
1961	26	5	16	61,091.49	65,001.67
1962	10	3	4	35,408.33	36,136.40
Total	221	30	73	$298,738.09	$326,362.49

Nicklaus Beats Palmer by Three Strokes in Play-Off for U. S. Open Title

SUPERIOR PUTTING GIVES OHIOAN A 71

By LINCOLN A. WERDEN
Special to The New York Times.

OAKMONT, Pa., June 17— Jack Nicklaus, a 22-year-old rookie professional, beat Arnold Palmer by three strokes in an 18-hole golf play-off today and won the sixty-second United States Open championship. Nicklaus scored a par 71, Palmer a 74.

Although the husky 200-pounder from Columbus, Ohio, learned at the age of 16 how to outscore professional golfers by winning the Ohio open, the triumph this afternoon over the 6,894-yard Oakmont Country Club course was his first since he left the amateur ranks last November.

The two-time United States amateur champion won only $33 in making his professional debut in the Los Angeles open six months ago. Today he received $15,000 in first-prize money and a bonus check for $2,500 from the United States Golf Association.

Palmer also received a $2,500 bonus for his participation in the play-off, in addition to

$8,000 for finishing second. His earnings for the year now are $70,581. Nicklaus increased his earnings for the year to $45,698.

In beating the favored Palmer, Nicklaus became the first man to take the Open in his initial season as a pro.

The extra session proved a surprise to a partisan gallery of 11,000, which called constantly, "Come on, Arnie." But the crowd failed to rattle Nicklaus, who outdrove his illustrious rival and outputted him on the undulating greens of this rugged course. At the end of six holes, Nicklaus had a four-stroke lead.

Presently, however, as almost everyone expected, Palmer put on one of his characteristic rallies. This one accounted for birdies on the ninth, eleventh

TENSION IN THE TRAP: Jack Nicklaus, left, watches as Arnold Palmer blasts from a sand trap on the fourth hole of the play-off round for National Open Golf championship.

was 19 when he won in 1895 at Newport R. I. Bobby Jones was 21 when he won the first of his four Opens in 1923.

Even though many were aware that Nicklaus had been a money winner in seventeen circuit tournaments, Palmer was the decided favorite leaving the first tee. Minutes later, Palmer took three from the fringe of the first green for a 5. Nicklaus, playing deliberately on the slippery surfaces, went ahead immediately with a par 4 after taking two putts.

Palmer might have expected to be outdriven by Nicklaus, but he didn't anticipate that his putting touch would leave him. Three-putting at three greens today increased Palmer's total of three-putt greens during the championship proper and the play-off to ten.

After each had 4's at the third and fourth, Nicklaus increased his lead to two strokes at the fifth. Nicklaus had driven into the rough at this par-5 hole. Palmer was trapped at the green in two. Palmer recovered from the sand to within six feet of the pin. But the man from Latrobe, Pa., couldn't sink this important putt. Nicklaus, on in three, got his 4-footer down for a birdie 4.

The biggest break in favor of Nicklaus came at the short sixth, where Palmer three-putted from twenty-five feet for a 4. When Nicklaus stroked in a 5-footer for a deuce, he had his astonishing four-stroke margin over the man who is currently the British open champion, who won the Masters title at Augusta, Ga., three times and who is still the leading money winner of the year.

Palmer Starts Rally

After each competitor had a 4 at the seventh and eighth, Palmer rolled in his first birdie at the ninth, dropping a 4-footer for a 4. Nicklaus had taken a 7 at this hole in the opening round and he played it cautiously today for a par. He was on the surface in three and two-putted in orthodox fashion. Palmer lashed a wood second to the grass atop a bunker, then pitched close before getting the putt.

Out in 38 to 35 for Nicklaus, Palmer then matched the 4 Nicklaus had at the tenth. At the eleventh, his second stopped four feet from the flag after clearing the trap.

Nicklaus drove into the rough and was twelve feet from the pin in two. Palmer seemed impatient as he waited for Nicklaus to putt. When Palmer made his birdie 3, a whoop went up and crowd surged forward.

At the par-5 twelfth, Nicklaus again was in the rough off the tee. The big difference at this hole was that Palmer smashed a wood shot from the fairway, some twenty yards short of the green, while Nicklaus played his second from the heavy grass.

Palmer pitched his third to the sloping green and the ball rolled on and on and finally stopped a yard or so from the flag. Once more, the crowd yelled approval. Palmer then

and twelfth holes and reduced Nicklaus' margin to one stroke. Unfortunately for Palmer, who won the 1960 Open at Denver when Nicklaus was second as an amateur, the rally could not be sustained.

Nicklaus Appears Calmer

Nicklaus and Palmer had ended the regulation seventy-two holes yesterday tied for first with scores of 283. Today, there were some moments of confusion, but Nicklaus appeared to be calmer and more relaxed in what was a duel that tested emotions as well as golfing skills.

Some of the tension was shown at the eighteenth, where Palmer conceded Nicklaus the title before the latter had holed out. Nicklaus had called for a ruling after driving into the rough when he found his ball lodged in a bad spot. He was ordered to continue, and did so after Palmer had knocked his second short of the bunker to the right, below the green.

After a recovery wedge, Nicklaus pitched a No. 9 iron to the green and putted close. Palmer, on with his third, then putted and missed. After he again knocked his ball toward the cup, Palmer picked up the coin that Nicklaus had used to mark his place on the green and offered congratulations to the new champion.

As Nicklaus was surrounded by well-wishers, Joseph C. Dey Jr., the executive director of the United States Golf Association, reminded him that he had not holed out.

The happy Ohioan complied by going back and tapping in a tiny putt for the 5 that officially made him one of the youngest champions ever to win the game's most cherished honor.

In the ninety holes he played here, Nicklaus three putted only one green.

There was one other incident, which went almost unnoticed, in the closing stages. It happened at a time when Nicklaus was hanging to a one-stroke edge.

At the par-3 thirteenth, Pal-

mer's tee shot landed seventy-five feet from the pin. Nicklaus had hit his to within twelve feet. Palmer putted boldly but could get no closer than six feet. He marked his spot on the green and picked up his ball.

Nicklaus failed on his bid for a deuce and had a 4-inch putt left, which he stroked in for his par 3. Palmer was about to address the ball, on his second putt, when he suddenly looked up and turned to an official. He had inadvertently put the ball down in the wrong spot.

The official told Palmer he had been about to call his attention to it. It's a two-stroke penalty if the ball is not replaced properly.

Palmer then putted, but missed his par. His three putts for a 4 there sent him two strokes back of Nicklaus again. This was the edge Nicklaus held until his 5 to Palmer's 6 at the eighteenth put the final margin at three.

Despite his youth, Nicklaus isn't the youngest to win this title. That honor went to Horace Rawlins, the first winner, who sank the putt for a birdie 4 while Nicklaus had to be content with a par.

But that proved the limit of Palmer's rally. Nicklaus regained one stroke at the next green and had pars at the next three, as did Palmer. At the uphill seventeenth, the crowd stood in anticipation. Would Palmer drive it again? Would he bag another spectacular eagle 2 here as he had in the third round?

Palmer pulled his drive a bit, avoiding the small pine trees, but the ball fell to the left of the green, in the rough. Nicklaus was closer to the green but in the heavy grass, too. Each pitched well and the officials had to measure with a

long string to decide which player was away.

It was Palmer. He had a putt of ten feet but he didn't get his needed birdie. After topping in a par 4, Palmer sat down on his golf bag somewhat dejectedly to see what Nicklaus would do. A birdie for Nicklaus now would virtually seal the decision, with one hole left. Although he took infinite care, Nicklaus failed to run the ball in and took a 4.

THE CARDS

```
Out—
Nicklaus ..4 4 4 4 4 2 4 4 5—35
Palmer ...5 4 4 4 4 4 4 4—38
In—
Nicklaus ..4 4 5 3 4 4 4 3 4 5—36—71
Palmer ....4 3 4 4 4 4 3 4 6—36—74
```

June 18, 1962

A Serious Driver

Jack William Nicklaus

IN the pressure-cooker world of professional golf, where men throw clubs and fits with some regularity, Jack William Nicklaus sinks climatic putts with the outward aplomb of a tea-taster.

Aside from being one of the sport's coolest competitors, Nicklaus, who slams balls over trees instead of fences, is the Mickey Mantle of golf—possibly the hardest hitter in the game. When the new National Open champion tees off and connects solidly, his drives generally travel 270 to 300 yards. Mantle's 420-foot homers are merely wedge shots by comparison.

Man in the News

Though he is only 22 years old, Nicklaus has been belting them long and hard since he was scarcely as tall as a driver. He started playing the game when he was 10 years old. At 16, he won the Ohio State open championship. Three years earlier, he had won the state's junior championship, qualified for the national junior championships—and learned an important lesson.

"In the nationals," he recalled, "I sauntered to the tee leisurely and was promptly told I was late. I was warned that I was only a few seconds from being penalized one hole. Since then, I have always been on time."

He is so serious about his

game, in fact, that his fiancèe was afraid he would miss their wedding. On July 23, 1960, his wedding day, Nicklaus and three ushers played a round before the afternoon ceremony. Only after he had practiced his swing, his putt and his wedge did he leave the course to marry the former Barbara Bash. He was on time, too. They have a 9-month-old son, Jack 2d.

Nicklaus, who was born in Columbus, Ohio, and still lives there, began playing the game through a twist of an ankle. Jack's father, Charles, suffered an ankle injury in a volleyball game and his physician ordered him to walk at least two hours a day.

The elder Nicklaus, a former president of the Ohio Pharmacy Board, prescribed golf for himself. He took Jack with him, and that is the way at least one National Open champion got his start. As an amateur—he won the United States Amateur crowns in 1959 and 1961—he was considered the best since Bobby Jones.

The 5-foot-11½-inch 200-pound Nicklaus has light short-cropped hair, blue eyes and enormous thighs and calves. He dieted away some thirty pounds before competing in the Open. As a man who learns from good (and profitable) experience, he probably will continue to watch his calories. He earned $17,500 in the Open, his first victory since he turned pro last November.

Nicklaus, born on Jan. 21, 1940, spent a typical childhood in Columbus. Although his 19-year-old sister, Marilyn, says he was "a great big

brother," she adds that he was "a great big mischief-maker." He studied the piano until he rebelled when his teacher told him that he couldn't count. He once spilled a glass of milk in Marilyn's face in an argument over comic books, and the family lost a maid because of him.

"One day," his sister said, "Jack came home after playing football and, trying to practice what he learned, tackled the maid. She almost fell down the cellar steps. She quit."

Through his teens and while completing three years toward a Business Administration degree at Ohio State, Nicklaus was an excellent student. And though all he could say after winning the Open was, "I'm just so elated I just can't say anything," he never was at a loss for words. In fact, his glibness once got him a spanking.

"Dad locked him in the closet once for being ornery," Marilyn said. "He cried and cried and finally stopped. Dad investigated and found that Jack had climbed to the top of the closet and turned on the light. Dad removed the light bulb and and locked him in again. He cried some more. Finally mom said, 'Oh, Charlie, let him out.' Jack came out with a triumphant look and said:

"'Hmph. Thought I'd cry you into it.'"

The future National Open champion couldn't sit down for a week.

June 18, 1962

Palmer Cards 67 and 69 to Win British Open by 6 Shots With Record 276

U. S. PRO STAGES BRILLIANT RALLY

Palmer Wins His 2d British Open in Row—Nagle Is 2d, Rodgers 3d, Snead 6th

By FRED TUPPER
Special to The New York Times.

TROON, Scotland, July 13—Arnold Palmer, the defender, shot fantastic rounds of 67 and 69 today amid unruly mob scenes to win the British Open by six strokes with a final total of 276. In the process, he broke the 18-hole course record, the championship record at Troon and the British Open golf championship record.

The Pennsylvanian's 67 this morning, when it counted most, was the lowest on this newly stretched-out course, and his 276 was two strokes better than any British Open total since the tournament was first held over seventy-two holes seventy years ago. Altogether, the tourney is 102 years old.

Peter Thomson of Australia had posted a 278 at Hoylake in 1958 and Kel Nagle of Australia had beaten Palmer by one stroke with a 278 at St. Andrews in 1960.

Nagle scored a 282 to finish second to Palmer today. Phil Rodgers of La Jolla, Calif., and Brian Huggett of England tied for third at 289.

Snead Posts a 292

Fifth was Bob Charles of New Zealand with a 290. Peter Thomson of Australia and 50-year-old Sam Snead of White Sulphur Springs, W. Va., who won this title way back in 1946,

tied for sixth with 292's.

Palmer picked up £1,400 ($3,920) for first prize, and a handful of pounds for low scores on individual days to send his season's winnings to around $75,000.

Palmer could have written this scenario before it started. It reads as it almost always does with him. He went off the tee last this morning, leading his partner, Nagle, by two strokes after the first thirty-six holes.

A lead rests uneasily on Palmer's shoulders, however, and he didn't have it long. The 41-year-old Nagle, a former caddie from Australia's outback, was at him like a tiger.

Nagle dropped a 20-footer for a birdie 3 on the first hole. Then he rolled in a 15-footer for a birdie 3 on the second as Palmer's putt hit the cup and bounced out. With everything even, Nagle missed an 8-footer for another birdie at the third,

where Palmer also got a par.

Nagle finally went into the lead with a par 5 at the fourth when Palmer hooked into a bunker and took a 6. Palmer had lost three precious strokes in four holes, but it seemed to be what he had been waiting for.

A 2 For Palmer

He lofted his pitch onto the 210-yard fifth hole and rapped in a 10-foot putt for a birdie 2 while Nagle took a 4. Now one stroke ahead, Palmer gained another on the interminaly long 580-yard sixth, reaching a greenside bunker with two tremendous woods, splashing out and then sinking his putt from four feet for a birdie 4.

Nagle's tee shot on the eighth bounced off a handy mound onto the green and he made the putt for a birdie 2. The Australian was 34 at the turn to Palmer's 35, and the Latrobe (Pa.) pro led by a single stroke, 175 to 176.

United Press International Radiophoto

Palmer blasts out of a trap on sixth hole during the third round, which he finished with a course record of 67.

Associated Press Radiophotos

The Latrobe (Pa.) golfer then posted a fourth-round 69 to clinch trophy emblematic of the British championship.

A huge crowd had gathered momentum during the morning and was now breaking in tidal waves over the humps and hillocks. Palmer they had heard of and Palmer they were going to see, preferably as close up as possible.

Then Palmer went wild:

¶On the twelfth, he blasted out of a bunker to within fifteen feet and rolled in the putt for a birdie 4. On the thirteenth, he holed out from five feet for a birdie 3. On the forteenth, he got his par 3.

¶On the fifteenth, he hit the shot of the day—a deliberately hooked iron shot that swung into the green and fetched up six feet from the cup. Palmer got it down for another 3.

¶On the sixteenth, he pitched stiff from seventy yards and sank a 20-foot putt for a birdie 2.

That settled it. He came down the stretch with a gorgeous 32 to finish with 67 to Nagle's 70, and led by five strokes as they recessed for lunch.

No One Else Is Close

A glance at the scoreboard showed that nobody else had made an impression on the leaders. Palmer had a 207, Nagle 212, Charles 215 and Rodgers 217.

Throughout this tourney Palmer had played the back nine to perfection. This afternoon, he played the first nine in a brilliant 33 under difficult conditions.

Some 15,000 persons were running amok on the course now, ignoring the stewards' signals, yelling when the players were striking the ball and knocking one another down in wild scrambles. Both Palmer and Nagle repeatedly asked for silence and refused to hit until they got it.

There were shots to savor in Palmer's outgoing nine this afternoon. He slouched into his famous putting stance on the second green and bagged a 15-footer for a birdie. He posted another 2 on the fifth, this time from ten feet.

They will be reminiscing for years about his shots on the sixth hole. It's nearly 600 yards with a steep climb uphill at the end, and this afternoon the wind was diagonally against Palmer.

His tee shot was 300 yards down the middle, and he chose to go for the flag. He smacked a No. 3 wood an enormous distance right on the green. Then his long putt came up to the hole and looked in.

Palmer was not quite through. He gave one more lesson — on how to play the treacherous eleventh, a 484-yarder that has been the bugaboo of this fine field all week

This time, he hit two irons to the green for a birdie 4. He was ten strokes up on Nagle. now. There seemed nothing left that he hadn't already done in ʼhe grand manner.

Nagle gave it a last fine try. He made an excellent approach on the twelfth to get his birdie 4, put his tee shot against the flag for a 2 on the fourteenth and got another 2 on the seventeenth with a 15-footer that was true all the way.

They came down the last hole together, almost obliterated from sight by the mob. Nagle hit his second shot onto the green twenty feet from the flag, Palmer was twelve feet away.

As the crowd engulfed Palmer, the police pushed and pushed harder. For a few moments, there was no sign of him. Then he forced his way through, struggling.

As a gigantic roar went up, Nagle dropped his long putt for a 3. Then Palmer dropped his to make history.

All in all, it was a day to rememember.

"I don't know if I ever played better over four rounds," Palmer said later. "I'll be back again if they do something about the crowds."

"I'll wear a suit of armor," said Nagle.

One more note about that eleventh hole. Jack Nicklaus was in trouble there today. He hit one in the gorse. He fanned. He hit out of the gorse. He hit out of bounds. He reached the green in 8. He got down in 10.

THIRD-ROUND CARDS

PAR FOR THE COURSE

Out	444 535	434—36
In	454 434	534—36—72

ARNOLD PALMER

Out	444 624	434—35
In	454 333	424—32—67—207

KEL NAGLE

Out	334 545	424—34
In	454 434	534—36—70—212

PHIL RODGERS

Out	444 435	434—35
In	454 534	534—37—72—217

SAM SNEAD

Out	344 545	434—36
In	454 434	534—36—72—221

JACK NICKLAUS

Out	444 635	334—36
In	465 435	434—38—74—226

DON ESSIG

Out	443 534	434—34
In	754 744	734—45 79—227

FOURTH-ROUND CARDS

ARNOLD PALMER

Out	434 524	434—33
In	445 445	433—36—69—276

KEL NAGLE

Out	444 545	524—37
In	454 424	523—33—70—282

PHIL RODGERS

Out	344 534	434—33
In	444 534	546—39 72—289

SAM SNEAD

Out	453 535	435—37
In	444 435	424—34—71—292

JACK NICKLAUS

Out	344 535	443—35
In	5 10 5 435	534—44—79—305

DON ESSIG

Out	445 547	444—40
In	564 444	634—41—81—308

July 14, 1962

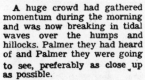

Gary Player Takes P. G. A. Title by a Stroke Over Goalby With 70 for 278

PALMER FINISHES AT 8-OVER-PAR 288

Trails Player by 10 Shots in Tying for 17th—Bayer and Nicklaus Third on 281's

By LINCOLN A. WERDEN
Special to The New York Times.

NEWTOWN SQUARE, Pa., July 22—Gary Player of Johannesburg, South Africa, today became the first non-resident of this country to win the Professional Golfers Association championship.

The 26-year-old Player withstood a closing 67 by Bob Goalby and triumphed by one stroke with 278.

The 5-foot-7-inch 150-pounder thus made further international golf history. When he won the British Open in 1959, he was the second youngest ever to do so. Then in 1961, he became the most successful foreign star to invade the United States golfing circuit.

He won the Masters at Augusta, Ga., the first non-American to do so, and became the leading money-winner of the year with $64,540.45.

On the Aronimink Golf Club course today, where he equaled par with a 70 after rounds of 72, 67 and 69, Player joined Arnold Palmer as a winner of three of the world's major golf titles. Player has yet to capture the United States Open. He placed second in 1958 at Tulsa.

Palmer, meanwhile, has yet to win the P.G.A. championship.

The 32-year-old Pennsylvanian, who took the British Open at Troon, Scotland, tied for seventeenth place here.

Three-putting at two greens on the first nine and failing to get down a birdie putt of less than three feet, Palmer had a concluding 72 for 288. In five P.G.A. championships, Palmer has done no better than a tie for fifth.

Nicklaus Ties for Third

Jack Nicklaus, the 22-year-old United States Open champion, remained in the race until the end. Rallying for his lowest round, a 67, Nicklaus finished in a tie for third with the long-hitting George Bayer at 281. This was the first P.G.A. title event for Nicklaus.

Doug Ford, the 36-hole leader and a former champion, had a 71 for 282. Bobby Nichols followed at 283. Then came Paul Harney, Dave Ragan and Jack Fleck at 284. Jay Hebert had 285, and Julius Boros, Chick Harbert and Dow Finster-

wald were bracketed at 286.

Palmer was in the clubhouse well ahead of the late contenders. Though the spectators gathered early in anticipation of a characteristic rally, Palmer was unable to produce one.

"I'm going to take a rest," he said after playing the back nine in 35 and posting his score. "I'm tired mentally. After you miss a couple of putts it makes you more tired."

Palmer said he intended to reduce the number of events in which he will compete next year.

"I want to concentrate on the big championships, including this one," he said. "I want to win it. However, this one was scheduled too close, as far as I am concerned, to the British Open. I'll have to decide whether I'll play in the British or this one in another year. I won't say now."

The Latrobe (Pa.) stylist said he would go to the West Coast in a few weeks to complete a television series of matches with Player as a partner. Gary said he would go to Montreal next week for the Canadian open. Palmer is passing up this one and intends to compete in only four or five more tournaments this year.

Rain Enters Picture

A fifteen-minute rainstorm shortly before 4 P.M. threatened to upset the program.

Player, Goalby and Bob McCallister, the 28-year-old Claremont (Calif.) golfer, were on the ninth green when the downpour came. After putting on a rain suit, Goalby was the last of the three to hole out.

He did so by running in a 5-footer for a birdie 4 and a 35 that helped set the stage for his concluding surge.

Player said he had seen a streak of lightning and had momentarily halted while McCallister went for shelter to the clubhouse porch.

J.E. Riley of Salt Lake City, the chairman of the P.G.A. Rules Committee, supported Player, saying he also had noticed a lightning flash. Most of the others proceeded, however, in the rain.

Player attributed his success to his decision to use a No. 4 wood at a majority of the par-4 holes.

"I've learned to play golf my own way here," he explained. "In my world tour with Palmer, I have been accustomed to trying to hit as far as he. By the time I'm 30, I hope to have the muscles he has. You need them. But I decided to rely on my No. 4 wood, which I can use as effectively as my driver, and I had the face lofted a bit."

Player's best shot of the tournament was a No. 2 iron from the rough to the green at the eighteenth yesterday that capped a 69 for 208 and made him the 54-hole leader by two strokes.

THE LEADING CARDS

COURSE PAR												
Out	4	4	4	4	3	4	4	3	5—35			
In	4	4	4	4	3	4	5	3	4—35—70			
GARY PLAYER												
Out	4	4	4	4	2	4	5	4	5—36			
In	4	4	4	3	3	4	5	3	4—34—70—278			
BOB GOALBY												
Out	4	5	4	4	3	4	4	3	4—35			
In	4	3	4	4	2	4	4	3	4—32—67—279			
JACK NICKLAUS												
Out	5	3	4	4	3	3	4	3	4—33			
In	4	5	4	3	3	4	3	4	4—34—67—281			
GEORGE BAYER												
Out	4	4	5	5	2	4	3	4	5—36			
In	4	3	4	3	3	4	4	3	5—35—71—281			

This was Player's first triumph since the 1961 Masters, where Palmer finished second after taking a 7 at the last hole. In the British Open at Troon, Player failed to qualify for the final thirty-six holes.

"My putting was most satisfactory there," said Player. "I didn't have a three-putt green in this championship until the seventh this afternoon. Then I followed that with another three-putt at the eighth hole."

Despite these errors, Player was out in 36. Realizing that Goalby was closing in on him, Player studied the greens with particular care.

He downed a 40-footer for a 3 at the thirteenth, his only incoming birdie. He recovered well from a trap to get down in one putt on the par-3 fourteenth. His 4 at the fifteenth where he drove in to the rough, also came after one putt.

The pressure increased and the gallery grew as he played the sixteenth. His par rolled in there. So did his par putts, the seventeenth and eighteenth for his 34.

Goalby, who had tied for second with Doug Sanders in the 1961 United States Open, fired birdies at the eleventh and fourteenth. At the fifteenth, he was still two strokes behind the South African.

His putt for a birdie rimmed the cup at the fifteenth and stayed out. He said later that this was the turning point.

At the long sixteenth he recovered from a trap to snare a birdie 4 and reduce Player's advantage to one stroke.

"Had I got that one at the fifteenth, it might have been a different story," the 31-year-old native of Illinois said.

He won $6,700, while Player received $13,000.

Goalby now needed one birdie on the last two holes to catch Player. The water-hole seventeenth of 213 yards and the uphill eighteenth of 423 yards are not rated birdie holes.

Goalby matched Player's par at the seventeenth. But at the last hole, he had a 25-footer left for a 3 to tie. Player's second shot was thirty-five feet out and he putted to within two feet.

Goalby's ball then went two feet past the cup. He sank it for a 4 and Player ran his in for the championship.

The last foreign-born golfer to

win the P.G.A. event was Jim Ferrier of Australia, who was a naturalized United States citizen when he captured the title in 1947 at match play by defeating Harbert, 2 and 1, in the final at Detroit.

English-born Jim Barnes, now living in New Jersey, won the first championship in 1916 and repeated in 1919.

July 23, 1962

Texan Shoots Round of 55, Lowest in U. S. Golf Annals

LONGVIEW, Tex., Aug. 20 (UPI)—A former University of Houston golfer, Homero Blancas, shot a fifteen-under-par 27, 28—55 yesterday and registered the lowest competitive round ever in the United States.

Blancas fired the round on the short 5,002-yard Premier golf course and clipped five strokes off the previous course record. His 72-hole total of 256 gave him the club championship six strokes ahead of Fred Marti, another University of Houston product.

Blancas had one eagle and thirteen birdies on his record round. The only other 55 recorded in golf annals was by an Englishman, A. E. Smith, who had a 29, 26—55 on the 4,248-yard Woolacombe Bay course. The lowest previous competitive score in the United States has been a 59 by Sam Snead and Earl Fry, who each did it on short courses.

August 21, 1962

Nicklaus Cards a 286 and at 23 Becomes Youngest Golfer to Win Masters

LEMA SCORES 287 ON AUGUSTA LINKS

Nicklaus Gets Final-Round 72 to Win—Snead Shares 3d With Boros at 288

By LINCOLN A. WERDEN
Special to The New York Times

AUGUSTA, Ga. April 7—Jack Nicklaus, the 23-year-old United States Open champion, gained further stature as a golfer today by winning the Masters tourney.

Registering a closing 72 for 286, the reddish-haired, husky player from Columbus, Ohio became the youngest golfer to win here. Bobby Jones, president of the Augusta National Golf Club, who presented Nicklaus with the first prize of $20,000, had tried to persuade Nicklaus to remain in the amateur ranks in November, 1961. But Nicklaus decided otherwise and since then has compiled an enviable record.

As a professional he won more than $100,000 last year.

While excitement was packed into the closing stages, 29-year-old Tony Lema of San Leandro, Calif., made the greatest bid to overtake Nicklaus, who had taken the lead yesterday after 54 holes.

Lema, known as "Champagne Tony" because of parties he has given, rolled in a 25-foot putt at the 72d hole for a birdie. It was a tremendous thrill for those of the 25,000 spectators encircling the 18th green. But Nicklaus, playing in the second pair back of Lema, was coolness personified.

A birdie at the par 3 16th helped Jack clinch the title by one stroke. Lema was second.

Sam Snead, the 50-year-old three-time Masters champion, was one of those in the thick of the battle down to the wire. Snead's 71, one under par, brought him 288, despite the fact that he went over par at two of the last three holes. Sam shared third with Julius Boros.

Spectator Gets a Chance

Dow Finsterwald, who was in the three-way playoff of 1962, had 289 to tie with Ed Furgol and Gary Player.

Player, the 1961 champion, also came close to overtaking Nicklaus in the scramble of the closing hour. But he, too, went over par at the critical junctures. Gary had bogey 5's both at the 17th and then at the

18th, where he was trapped.

Bo Wininger followed at 290, while Arnold Palmer the pretourney favorite and defender, trailed Nicklaus by five with a 291 that put him in a bracket with Don January. Palmer had given his followers some encouragement with a 34 out.

Some of "Arnie's Army," his band of faithful rooters, went into action at the 10th. There Palmer hooked his drive into the pines. An anxious spectator retrieved it and tossed it out to a more playable spot on the fairway.

When Palmer reached it, he promptly picked it up and dropped it near its original location. "Maybe I need more guys like that," he said jokingly. Palmer nevertheless took a 5, one over par.

After that Palmer tried to get closer to par and holed a birdie at the par-5 13th. At the other par 5 on the incoming stretch—the 15th—he knocked his second into the crowd to the right of the green. He carded a par there, although he sought a birdie.

Pars followed at the next two, but his hopes fell when his second missed the 18th. A 5, one over, resulted and Palmer was convinced he was defeated in his efforts to win two Masters in a row.

Poise Under Pressure

Nicklaus had a variety of experiences that might have frazzled the nerves of a less complacent player. Careful and analytical, even under the greatest pressure, Nicklaus used all his talents to achieve this tremendous success.

The winner of the National Amateur at the age of 19, Nicklaus carried off the World Amateur crown a year later with a fabulous score of 269 at the Merion Golf Club, Ardmore, Pa. There he showed some of the poise he displayed today. Once when a gust of wind blew off his cap as he was about to putt at Ardmore, he stood still, let the headgear go and holed the putt.

And today, since the course still showed effects of yesterday's downpour, he geared himself to meet emergencies. He knows the rules, too, and on four occasions his knowledge stood him in good stead.

Since it was permissible to lift without penalty if the ball was embedded in casual water, Nicklaus showed a nationwide television audience and some 28,000 spectators here how to act under tournament fire.

Perhaps the most dramatic of these incidents came after he hooked his drive at the 18th. All he needed was a par to clinch the title. The ball landed in an area of mud. It was off to the left of the fairway and

had been well trod by gallery-ites all day.

Nicklaus wasn't baffled. He made certain he had an official ruling and was advised to drop the ball freely at the edge of the fairway, away from the mire. After that he knocked his second to the green and two-putted for the closing par 4. He had about a 3-footer remaining for his second putt.

Once the ball was in, he tossed his cap wildly and was greeted by a group that included his father, a Columbus (Ohio) druggist. Jack has a junior pharmacist license.

$112,500 Purse a Record

The purse for the tournament reached a record $112,500. This keeps it the biggest money tourney in golfdom.

Nicklaus became the leading money winner of the tour as a result of his victory, lifting his total to $36,715.

Player is next at $27,502, Lema third at $26,831 and Palmer trails at $25,025. Nicklaus also is assured of a place in golf's World Series, a competition staged for television. Last year, Nicklaus won the $50,000 first prize at Akron, Ohio, and will be back again Sept. 7-8, he said.

He will also make a bid for both the British Open and Professional Golfers Association championships in addition to defending his United States Open crown at Brookline, Mass., in June.

Nicklaus had rounds of 74, 66, 74 and 72 and indicated throughout the power of his long game and an uncanny touch on the greens. The 200-pounder three-putted at the second green after reaching the green at this 555-yard hole in 2. His second glanced off a spectator's folding chair and stopped at the edge of the putting surface.

Nicklaus went over par at two holes, the first being the uphill eighth. He played to the left and his apooach caught in the heavy grass. He chipped to within six feet of the pin and missed his putt for a par 5.

"That kind of bothered me," he said later. He was one over with a 37 out.

At the 10th, he was permitted a free drop when his ball became caked in mud and he got his par 4 there and also at the 11th. But at the short 12th, where the green is beyond Rae's Creek, Nicklaus hit a No. 7 iron for a tee shot and caught the far trap. Since the ball was in casual water in the sand, he again was allowed to drop in a dryer place.

In the hazard, he chipped out across the green and then pitched ball to within nine feet of the pin. He holed this long putt for a bogey 4, the sec-

ond of his round.

As the challengers ahead were putting on a spurt, Nicklaus sank a birdie 4 at the par-5 13th. He reached the tilted green with a No. 2 iron second at this 475-yard hole ans was down in two putts from 60 feet.

The next crucial hole for Nicklaus was the par-5 15th, where the green is guarded by a small pond. He hit a spoon second that seemed headed for the lake beyond the 16th hole. "But the crowd or mud stopped it," Nicklaus said. He found the ball half plugged in mud and sand and was allowed a free lift once more.

He then ran the ball to the green but his putt of 4 feet hit the cup and stayed out. The par 5 there, however, didn't hurt.

The big one then came at the 16th, where he ran in a 12-footer for his deuce, after using a No. 5 iron from the tee.

He had a regulation par 4 at the 17th before the tension and final 4 came at the 18th.

"I drove purposely to the left," he said, "as I wanted to keep away from the pine trees on the right. I just wanted my par 4. My drive fell in the sand and mud and then I got my fourth free lift. It happened that the fairway was closer than the next dry spot and I was permitted to drop it there."

The club closed the gates to spectators after 10,000 automobiles had filled the parking lots. This is some sort of a record. No tourney previously had turned away potential ticket purchasers.

April 8, 1963

THE WINNER'S ROUNDS				
PAR				
Out	454	343	454—36	
In	443	545	344—36	—72
FIRST				
Out	454	343	455—37	
In	543	634	345—37	—74
SECOND				
Out	454	343	344—34	
In	442	444	334—32	—66
THIRD				
Out	464	334	554—38	
In	443	545	344—36	—74
FOURTH				
Out	454	343	464—37	
In	444	445	344—35	—72

CARDS OF OTHER LEADERS				
TONY LEMA				
Out	544	243	454—35	
In	453	445	343—35—70	—287
SAM SNEAD				
Out	444	343	355—37	
In	443	534	445—36—71	—288
JULIUS BOROS				
Out	544	444	354—37	
In	442	545	344—35—72	—288
GARY PLAYER				
Out	354	333	454—34	
In	443	444	355—36—70	—289
ARNOLD PALMER				
Out	344	343	454—34	
In	543	445	345—37—71	—291

BOROS'S 70 WINS U. S. OPEN TITLE

Cupit Shoots 73 and Palmer Gets 76 in Golf Playoff

By JOSEPH M. SHEEHAN
Special to The New York Times

BROOKLINE, Mass., June 23—Big Julius Boros, playing with the indolent ease of a club champion in a social Sunday match with nothing at stake, reclaimed golf's most cherished title today after an interval of 11 years.

The relaxed 43-year-old pro from Southern Pines, N. C., made a runaway of the 18-hole playoff for the United States Open championship. Boros shot a one-under-par 70 that gave him a three-stroke edge on 25-year-old Jacky Cupit of Corona, Calif., and six strokes on 33-year-old Arnold Palmer of Laurel Valley, Pa.

Julius Boros won the U.S. Open in 1963 at the age of 43, eleven years after his first U.S. Open victory.

These three finished the regulation 72 holes of the 63d Open yesterday tied at 293 after three days and four rounds of battling buffeting winds and the subtle cruelties of the historic course at The Country Club.

At 43, Boros was the oldest man—by a matter of 72 hours over Ted Ray, the 1920 winner—to capture an Open title. When he had finished his round, to the ringing applause of a gallery of 12,500, he admitted he felt "old" after the ordeal here. But the smile that wreathed his weatherbeaten countenance indicated that, at least at the moment, his years were a comfort, rather than a burden.

There was extra reason for that smile. The victory was worth $16,000. Cupit and Palmer earned $7,000 each.

The way the showdown match went, there was no doubt that experience, and the imperturbability that comes with it was a great asset to Boros.

There were flashes of brilliance in his play, exemplified in four birdies. But essentially, his round was steady, marred by only one really poor shot. He calmly and coolly overcame or avoided the lurking dangers of the hilly, 6,870-yard layout.

A par 4 on the difficult 440-yard third hole put Boros in the lead, and he didn't relinquish it for the rest of the way. He got his par by putting to within 18 inches of the pin from just off the front of the green. On this hole, Cupit, the early leader on two consecutive pars, took a disastrous 6 after pulling his second shot into heavy rough behind a greenside trap. Palmer, also one over par on the first, took a bogey on the hole. Boros had a bogey on the short second, missing a 4-footer after a 60-foot chip from the fringe.

Boros Makes Turn in 33

Once in front, Boros eased the pressure on himself — and put it on his rivals—by bagging birdies on the fourth and fifth holes. On the fourth, he flipped a wedge shot to six feet from the pin and sank the putt. On the fifth, he stopped a heavily cut No. 9 iron shot three feet from the hole and tapped the ball in again.

This put Boros two strokes up on Cupit, who also got a birdie at the fifth, and three ahead of Palmer. Three more pars and a birdie 4 on the 505-yard ninth hole, where his wedge third shot came to rest nine feet from the pin, brought Boros to the turn in 33, two strokes under par.

Palmer, with a birdie at the sixth, was three strokes back at 36. Cupit, who went one over par on the sixth, stood at 37.

The match broke up to all intents on the first three holes of the second nine. Hewing closely to the line, Boros got pars on all three. Palmer, who had spent a sleepless night with an intestinal disturbance that left him visibly weakened, lost his touch.

On the 10th, the stalwart Pennsylvanian, who won the 1960 Open and was the pre-tournament favorite here, drove into heavy rough on the right. He put his second shot against a grassy bank in a trap, blasted out short and wound up with a bogey 5.

Trouble on the 13th

On the 11th, Palmer took a triple-bogey 7. He pulled his drive far into the woods and took three shots to get out, into the rough at the right side of the green. After chipping 15 feet beyond the hole, he two-putted. And on the killing 12th, which he had played better than anyone else in the open, Palmer went one over par again.

Meanwhile, Cupit carded a bogey on the 11th when his second shot, out of rough, landed well to the right of the green.

This sequence of events left Boros with a five-stroke edge over Cupit and an eight-stroke advantage over Palmer.

But it wasn't all downhill going for The Moose, as his associates on the tournament circuit call Boros. By way of showing he was human, too, Julius made a horrendously bad second shot to the 13th green. His pulled iron landed in the crowd, far to the left. From a bad lie, his wedge recovery was short. Chipping from the fringe, he skidded the ball across the green and wound up with a double-bogey 6.

This shaved two strokes from his lead as Cupit and Palmer shot 4's. But Boros made no further slips. He slammed the door in the face of his rivals by playing the last five holes in one under par, getting a birdie on the 17th by sinking a 15-footer.

But although the die had been irrevocably cast, Palmer and Cupit at least made it interesting for the national television audience that viewed the last four holes.

Recovering his touch as suddenly as he had lost it, Palmer got birdies on three of the last four holes. In between, on the 17th, he took a bogey 5 after missing a 2-foot putt, possibly because at that point he no longer really cared. Cupit matched Boros's one-under-par pace for the last five holes, also getting a birdie on the 17th.

Showman that he is, Palmer engineered the most brilliant shot of the day before the eyes of the huge throng clustered about the 18th green. He landed his iron second shot a fraction of an inch from the pin, and the ball came to rest no farther than a foot and a half away.

Iron Play Aids Boros

Sharp iron play, particularly on delicate wedge flips from the heavy rough that fringed the greens, contributed to Boro's victory. Thanks to this, he took only 25 putts, several of them tap-ins. Cupit took 27 putts, Palmer 30.

The stroke analysis shows Boros hit 10 greens and missed only four fairways. The corresponding figures were nine and four for Cupit and 10 and seven for Palmer.

There have been 22 playoffs in 63 Opens—seven involving three players. The last three-way playoff was in 1953, when Ben Hogan defeated Lloyd Mangrum and George Fazio.

It was appropriate that there should be a three-way playoff here because the tournament commemmorated the 50th anniversary of the victory of Francis Ouimet, a 20-year-old American amateur, over the British professionals — Harry Vardon and Ted Ray. That triumph is

The Cards

Out—
Par
Boros
Cupit
Palmer
In—
Par
Boros
Cupit
Palmer

123

credited with having been the biggest single factor in popularizing golf in this country.

It was breezy again on the course, but the winds weren't strong or vacillating enough to affect play seriously as they had during the last three days. In fact, the breeze was appreciated, making 80-degree temperatures tenable for the army of spectators who tramped about the course.

Boros's 70 was only the sixth round under par of the tournament. Bob Gajda shot a 69 and Cupit a 70 on Thursday. Palmer and Dow Finsterwald had 69's and Paul Harney a 70 on Friday. No one could get under par in the blustery 35-mile-an-hour winds of Saturday.

The victory gave Boros not only $16,000 in official prize money but also an extra $1,500 awarded by the United States Golf Association to each playoff participant. The windfall moved Boros to second place, with $56,780, among the year's money-winners.

But the on-the-spot financial rewards of an Open victory are minor compared to the byproduct reapings. And even the pros value the prestige of winning the tournament over any money.

By collecting $7,000 as his half of the lumped second and third money awards (the play-off in the Open is for first place only), Palmer moved to the top of the 1963 money list with $63,545. Knocked down to third place with $38,690, was Jack Nicklaus, the 1962 Open champion, who failed to survive Friday's 36-hole cut of the 150-player starting field to the low 50 scorers plus ties.

This marked the second straight year that Palmer had lost in an Open playoff. He bowed to Nicklaus, 71 to 74, at the Oakmont (Pa.) Country Club in 1962.

June 24, 1963

Nicklaus Rallies With a 68 for 279 and Takes P.G.A. Title by Two Strokes

RAGAN CARDS 281 AND TWO TIE AT 282

Crampton, on a 74, Finishes 3 Shots Behind Nicklaus, Who Earns $13,000

By GORDON S. WHITE Jr.
Special to The New York Times

DALLAS, July 21—Jack Nicklaus, a young man who has achieved more in 13 months than most golfers do in a lifetime, captured the Professional Golfers Association's 45th annual championship today.

The 23-year-old Nicklaus, slamming the ball a long way on tee shots through four rounds of the 72-hole tourney, added excellent putting today and scored 34, 34—68 for 279.

This victory on the long course of the Dallas Athletic Club Country Club goes side by side with the Masters championship Nicklaus won last spring and the United States Open he won in June of 1962.

Nicklaus thus became only the fourth golfer to win the three major United States titles. The others, all illustrious pros, were Gene Sarazen, Byron Nelson and Ben Hogan. But none did it in such a short span of time. Only Sam Snead and Jack Burke had previously won the Masters and P.G.A. the same year.

In temperatures that exceeded 100 degrees each day and went to about 110 on the fairways for the final round, the husky Columbus (Ohio) slugger toured 72 holes in five strokes under par. The narrow, 7,046-yard course, made to Nicklaus's order, has a par of 36, 35—71.

Ragan Starts With Rush

The 27-year-old Dave Ragan finished as runner-up at 281. The Florida golfer started the day with four birdies on the first seven holes, but finished with 33, 36—69.

Bruce Crampton of Australia, who led after three rounds, and Dow Finsterwald ended in a tie for third at 282. Crampton shot 36, 38, 74 and Finsterwald 39, 33—72.

Dick Hart, the unheralded pro who led after the first and second rounds, dropped to a tie for 17th with 288. The Hinsdale (Ill.) pro scored a 66 on opening day that included a hole-in-one on the 216-yard 16th hole.

Nicklaus added $13,000 to his prize winnings for the year and raised his total since January to $75,140. He moved past Julius Boros, the United States Open champion, and took second place in money winnings this year. Arnold Palmer fell to a tie for 40th place here, earned $62.50 and raised his winnings for the year to $85,607.50.

Gary Player of South Africa, the defending champion, tied for eighth. Palmer, who had putting trouble all week, shot 293 and Player had 286.

Nicklaus Right at Home

This difficult course is exceptionally long. It requires long and straight drives to get to the greens via narrow fairways lined with deep rough. Once on the greens, a golfer may have to putt 80 or 100 feet. But these barriers didn't faze Nicklaus, particularly when he began stroking putts well.

He blasted tee shots as far as 350 yards in this tournament. He opened the final round with one such drive, reached the green of the 521-yard first hole in 2 and sank an 18-foot putt for an eagle 3. This hole, the only one here that the pros consider easy, yielded to eagles time and again in the P.G.A.

Nicklaus and Crampton played in the same threesome with Billy Maxwell. Crampton got a birdie 4 on the first hole but lost a stroke of the three-stroke advantage he had at the start of the round.

Nicklaus ran into trouble before his winning surge. After getting par 4's on the second and third holes, Jack had his most difficult off-green shots of the championship.

He hit a drive well down the middle against a slight wind on the 573-yard fourth hole. Then he resorted to a driver again for the fairway second shot. This was the first time he had used a driver from the fairway since turning professional late in 1961.

He hit the ball to the right of the green in rough behind trees. Then he blasted out, but over the green toward water. Luckily, the ball hit a tree and landed in rough again, and Nicklaus finished with a bogey 6.

A birdie at the par-4 eighth with a 15-foot putt brought him nearer Crampton, who led then by a stroke. Ragan was even with Nicklaus.

Nicklaus caught Crampton at the 12th. Jack got a birdie on the par-5 hole with a No. 1 iron fairway shot and two putts to Crampton's par. Ragan was even with them after his birdie.

But Crampton took bogeys on the 14th and 16th. Ragan suffered the same fate on the 13th and 17th. Nicklaus got one more birdie and won. That birdie came at the 15th, where a long drive and No. 9 iron got him on the green of the 424-yard hole. A 30-foot putt dropped in.

The galleries were beginning to talk playoff again until Ragan and Crampton faltered. Five of the seven previous tournaments this summer were decided in playoffs.

Crampton is a slim golfer and cannot match the likes of Nicklaus off the tee. On the first hole, Crampton hit a mighty shot down the fairway. Nicklaus promptly outdrove him by 40 yards.

The power of his drives is too much even for Nicklaus at times. The 16th hole, the site of Hart's opening-day ace, is a tricky par 3. Nicklaus got a par on that hole only once in the tournament.

It came this time with a No. 5 iron tee shot that Jack said "wasn't good." It was 30 feet short. He had overdriven the green three times previously with No. 3 and No. 4 iron shots.

Jack used a wood on the fairway only three times during

P.G.A. Cards

	PAR FOR THE COURSE	
Out	5 4 4 5 3 4 3 4 4	—36
In	4 4 5 3 4 4 3 4 4	—35—71
	JACK NICKLAUS	
Out	3 4 4 6 3 4 3 3 4	—34
In	5 4 4 3 4 3 3 4 4	—34—68—279
	DAVE RAGAN	
Out	4 4 3 4 3 4 2 5 4	—33
In	5 4 4 4 3 4 3 5 4	—36—69—281
	BRUCE CRAMPTON	
Out	4 4 4 5 3 4 3 5 4	—36
In	5 4 5 3 5 4 4 4 4	—38—74—282
	DOW FINSTERWALD	
Out	5 5 4 5 4 4 3 4 5	—39
In	4 4 5 3 4 3 3 4 3	—33—72—282

72 holes—today's driver off the grass on the fourth hole, a No. 3 wood there opening day and a wood on the 543-yard 12th. This is amazing because there are par-5 holes of 521, 573 and 543 yards.

The galleries weren't too big for such a tournament. Officials estimated that 13,500 were on hand for the final round, 56,000 for the four days. Many never went beyond the first tee. Even Texans couldn't take the heat.

Ragan's strong finish earned him the final berth on the Ryder Cup team that will oppose Britain Oct. 11 through 13 at Atlanta. The others on the United States team, which will be announced officially Monday, are Finsterwald, Boros, Palmer, Maxwell, Billy Casper, Gene Littler, Johnny Pott, Bob Goalby and Tony Lema.

The carefree Lema finished with 287 and earned $1,550. He donated $151 of it—by request —to Buda, Tex. A year and a half ago, Lema was arrested there for speeding and didn't settle his bill. A police officer from Buda greeted Lema here with a warrant. Lema paid up— $1 for speeding, $15 for court costs and $100 for tardiness.

July 22, 1963

Palmer, With 276, Wins 4th Masters

By LINCOLN A. WERDEN
Special to The New York Times

AUGUSTA, Ga., April 12—Arnold Palmer became today the first to win the Masters golf title four times and he made it look easy. With a final round of 70, he won by six strokes with a 72-hole aggregate of 276, only two shots over the record set by Ben Hogan in 1953.

Palmer, who started the day with a five-stroke lead, played the 6,980-yard, par-72 Augusta National Golf Club course under little pressure. He triumphed in 1958 and 1960 by a stroke. He won two years ago after a play-off with Dow Finsterwald and Gary Player.

While Palmer has long been regarded as one of the most talented United States golfers, this latest success had special significance for the 34-year-old professional from Latrobe, Pa.

The victory ended a slump in which he had gone 11 tournaments without winning. The triumph also brought him a sizable purse, $20,000. He thus increased his earnings to $506,-496.84 since joining the pro tour in 1955 and became the first golfer to exceed half a million in official United States competition.

The most spectacular challenge to Palmer came from Jack Nicklaus, who finished in a tie for second with Dave Marr.

Hitting his drives and irons for incredible distances on the incoming nine, where he had two birdies and an eagle, Nicklaus made a determined bid with a 67. It was the low round of the day and brought the 24-year-old an aggregate of 282. When he became the youngest ever to win here a year ago, Nicklaus scored 286 and Palmer finished in a tie for ninth.

Marr, a dapper 30-year-old player from Houston who lives in New Rochelle, N. Y., rolled in a 25-foot birdie 3 at the home green for a 70. Undisturbed by the huge gallery as Palmer's playing partner, Marr saw an early lead for second place momentarily wilt when Nicklaus got his game rolling on the backstretch. But the closing putt saved an incoming 37 for Marr's best finish in three Masters appearances.

Bruce Devlin, a 26-year-old former plumber from Canberra, Australia, finished with 284. He had gained the runner-up spot to Palmer last night with a 67.

"I had visions of catching him," said Devlin, who had started the fourth round with birdies at the first two holes. "I don't know if I ran out of heart or ability."

Devlin said he almost gave up golf last year after failures had left him with little more than pocket money to return home from Ardmore, Okla. However, by winning $1,105 here, he carried on and subsequently won the French open. Then on tour last winter, he won the St. Petersburg open. He was the Masters' low scorer this time among the strong foreign contingent.

Bill Casper, who had a closing 69; Jim Ferrier, Paul Harney and Gary Player of South Africa, the only foreigner to win a Masters crown, were next in the scoring, at 286. Dow Finsterwald followed at 287 with Tony Lema, Mike Souchak and Ben Hogan.

Gene Littler with a 68, Al Geiberger, Dan Sikes, Johnny Pott and Peter Butler of Birmingham, England, were in at 288. Butler headed for Troon, Scotland, to defend his British Professional Golfers Association title in the tourney starting Thursday.

Palmer's rivals had little hope of overtaking him.

Hogan smiled and said, "Someone needs a 59."

Nicklaus was more sanguine. After he had finished, he said, "I should have been four or five strokes better."

What gave the big fellow so much confidence was a series of incidents on the incoming nine. He was only three under par for 63 holes, compared with Palmer's 11 under par, but matters then developed favorably for him.

Birdie 2 at 12th

Although he went over par at the 10th, he rolled in a birdie deuce at the short 12th. Then came an exciting shot at the par-5 13th. He hit the flag with a No. 6 iron second, and the ball spun around the pin and almost fell in. He nevertheless bagged an eagle.

Although the extent of his power hitting is sometimes exaggerated, Nicklaus put together two shots that had many in the crowd of 35,000 buzzing. They came at the 520-yard 15, a par 5 where a pond protects the green.

"My drive was so long there," said Nicklaus, "that I hit a No. 7 iron second.

A No. 7 iron is used by leading players for shots of about 130 yards. The ball rolled a few feet over the green. After Nicklaus had chipped back, he sank the putt for a birdie 4. That put him six under par for the tourney, and that's the way he stayed with pars at the last three holes.

Nicklaus and Marr received $10,100 each for their second-place tie. Officials announced that the total purse had been raised to $129,800, making this the richest tourney being staged. The amount exceeded the 1963 purse of $112,500 and the $125,-000 of the Whitemarsh open last October at Philadelphia. The Whitemarsh tourney, incidentally, was one of seven Palmer won in 1963.

Palmer said he planned a two-week rest before taking up

Palmer swings his putter on the 18th green after sinking a birdie putt to win Masters golf tournament at Augusta.

Palmer leaves the 18th green with Dave Marr, who tied for second place in tourney with four-round score of 282.

his clubs again. His next major goal is the United States Open in June at the Congressional Country Club in Washington. If he's successful there—he won the title in 1960—he will try for the British Open, which he has won twice.

But there is some doubt about his making the trip abroad, he said. The one major championship he doesn't own among the 40 on the pro tour is the P.G.A. title, which will be contested July 16 to 19 at Columbus, Ohio.

Palmer three-puttted only two of 72 holes, both today. On his previous rounds of 69, 68 and 69, his putting was letter perfect.

40-Foot Putt

He dropped a 40-footer side-hill putt at the fourth for a deuce to go under regulation figures but then got a bogey 5 at the next hole, where he chipped from the edge of the green and failed to get his putt for a par.

At the seventh, the crowd roared approval when he downed a 5-footer for a birdie 3. Then he played the next two in pars, many remembered that Palmer took a 75 in the last round of the 1962 tourney that forced him into a playoff. He had 205 for 54 holes then, one lower than he had yesterday.

But history did not repeat. His caddie, Nathaniel (Iron Man) Avery, who had toted Palmer's bag on the three previous winning occasions, said: "Mr. Palmer asks me about the fairway clubs to use, but when it comes to the greens, he reads them himself."

So Palmer faulted himself for taking three putts from 20 feet for a 5 at the 10th. But he three-putted again at the 13th, usually a birdie hole for him, for a par 5. Then he broke the spell with birdies at the next two.

Going uphill at the 14th with a fine drive, Palmer knocked in a 12-foot putt for a birdie 3. At the 15th, he reached the green with a No. 3 iron second and two-putted for a birdie 4. He sank a par 3 at the short 16th.

But at the 17th, his drive went into the trees on the right. His No. 4 iron second from near the base of a pine went over the green. He chipped short and then two-putted for a 5 to cap the round. He dropped a 20-footer for a final birdie 3 after he had reached the green with a No. 8 iron. He had 33 putts on the round.

THE LEADING CARDS

ARNOLD PALMER											
Out	4	5	4	2	5	3	3	5	4—35		
In	5	4	3	5	3	4	3	5	3—35—70		
JACK NICKLAUS											
Out	4	4	4	3	5	3	5	3	3—34		
In	5	4	2	3	4	4	3	4	4—33—67		
DAVE MARR											
Out	4	4	3	3	3	4	4	4	4—33		
In	4	4	5	3	4	5	3	4	3—37—70		
BRUCE DEVLIN											
Out	3	4	4	4	5	3	4	4	5—36		
In	4	6	3	4	4	4	3	5	4—37—73		

April 13, 1964

VENTURI TRIUMPHS BY 4 STROKES WITH 278 IN OPEN

JACOBS IS SECOND

Charles Posts 283 and Palmer Ties for Fifth With 286

By LINCOLN A. WERDEN
Special to The New York Times

WASHINGTON, June 20 — A golfer who refused to quit became the United States Open champion today. Ken Venturi, close to exhaustion after a morning round of 66, came on to win at the Congressional Country Club today with a final 70 for a 72-hole total of 278.

After being attended by a physician before starting the final 18-hole round in punishing heat, Venturi revived to beat Tommy Jacobs by four strokes. Bob Charles, a New Zealand southpaw and the British Open champion, had 283. Arnold Palmer finished at 286.

With the temperature at 100 degrees at some places on the course, Venturi staggered at the 16th tee of the third round, in which he tied a nine-hole Open record of 30 to draw even with Jacobs.

"I don't know if I can make it in," he told his playing partner, Ray Floyd. He did, but once in the clubhouse it was still questionable if he could resume in the allotted intermission of 45 minutes.

He looked haggard and was ordered to lie down and rest. He took salt tablets and drank tea and was on the mark when called to play. "I'm okay", he said to his wife, Connie, at the first tee before he started out.

The rest proved a glorious comeback story for Venturi after three lean years. In 27 starts in 1963, he earned only $3,848. As receptive as was today's $17,000 first prize, it was the tournament victory rather than the money that restored completely his lost pride and confidence.

As an amateur, out of the Army ranks in 1956, he led the field in the Masters at Augusta, Ga., only to lose by shooting 80 in the final round. Then, in 1960, again thinking he had the Masters title in his grasp, he was beaten when Palmer made birdies on the last two holes.

Disheartened, he became discouraged after a pinched nerve caused partial paralysis to his side four years ago. His fine game deteriorated. His fellow pros thought he hit bottom during the 1962 tour. His last triumph was in the Milwaukee open in 1960.

Jacobs established a 54-hole record of 206 with his 70 this morning. But he soared to a 76 in his last tour of the course he had played in an amazing 64 strokes yesterday. The 207 posted by Ben Hogan in the 1948 Open at Los Angeles had been the record.

While Venturi had trailed Jacobs at the start of today's two rounds by six strokes and was back of him by two beginning the fourth round, Palmer was farther astern following his morning 75.

Three-Putting Hurts Palmer

Three-putting at three greens this morning didn't help Palmer. As the Masters champion he had set a goal to triumph here. His only Open triumph came in 1960, but his spirited determination and concentration make him a tremendous contender. He has tied for first twice since 1960.

For the crowd of 21,993 here despite the high temperatures, Palmer was still the big attraction. Thousands poured over the longest course on which the tournament has been played, expecting any minute he would make one of his renowned surges, such as the closing 65 that won in 1960. But his concluding effort was a 74, a poor contrast to his 68 that took command in the first round on Thursday.

Palmer's 286 put him in the bracket with Gay Brewer, who finished with a 68, and Bill Collins. Billy Casper, a former Open titleholder, was ahead of him at 285.

There was more of an emotional side to this Open victory than usual for Ken is an emotional fellow. "Now that I've regained by composure," he said, "I want to thank everybody. I didn't have any Arnie's Army but there were cats I had that were solid supporters. In fact, for the last few years there were Venturi Vultures."

Venturi, with his attractive wife at his side, said that he had been greatly worried that he couldn't carry on for the last round.

This was in contrast to the Venturi that sat dejected in his home in Hillsboro, Calif., last April when the Masters was in session. "We watched it on television," said Mrs. Venturi. "Kennie was certainly blue. He hadn't been invited to the Masters and that made him feel bad."

Venturi Aided by Nelson

His career has been up and down. As an amateur he had Byron Nelson as a coach, since Byron was a friend of Eddie Lowery of San Francisco, for whom Venturi worked. This is the same Lowery who as a 10-year-old was caddie for Francis Ouimet when he won the 1913 Open at Brookline. Nelson liked Venturi's style and suggested improvements for his swing.

Another of Nelson's proteges was Harvie Ward, who went on to win two National Amateur titles. Both Ward and Venturi worked for Lowery's automobile agency.

After his failure to win as an amateur at Augusta, Venturi decided to turn pro. He tied for sixth in the 1957 United States Open.

Two weeks ago, he finished in a tie for third in the $100,000 Thunderbird and last week he finished high in the money in the Buick open.

However, he came here unheralded. It wasn't certain if he could stand the rigors demanded by this tough course. He had an opening 72, two over par, and followed with a 70 yesterday that left him at 142, tied for fourth. Then came the 66 this morning that tied the nine-hole record previously held by Jimmy McHale in the 1947 Open and by Palmer when he fired 30, 35—65 in the closing round of the 1960 championship.

He Qualifies for P.G.A.

Although he failed to qualify for the Professional Golfers' Association tournament in trials held two weeks ago, as Open champion, he qualifies automatically. The championship will be held at Columbus, Ohio, July 16.

Venturi said he would like to split the winning check with the Rev. Frank Murray of the St. Vincent De Paul Society of San Francisco. "Father Murray encouraged me. He told me to keep my composure, never to become too elated or too dejected. If I had had that attitude at the Masters in 1956 I would have won." He had been ready to quit the pro tour less than a year ago.

Nearing the end of the round he told Joseph C. Dey Jr., the executive director of the United States Golf Association, that he was tiring. "You can slap a two-stroke penalty on me for slow play, but I am going to slow down a bit".

As far as his goal was concerned, the championship was almost over then. Venturi had only to hang on. This morning, Jay Hebert, following in Venturi's gallery, said: "I expected him to keel over any time".

Venturi drew even after the second hole this afternoon when he took a par 3 there as Jacobs, trapped, ended with a 5. By the fourth, Venturi went ahead by one but he lost this advantage

at the sixth, where he three-putted. Jacobs, playing the hole later, carded a par 4.

Then came the ninth, where Jacobs lost two strokes to Venturi. Jacobs drove under a tree, played a safety shot, put his fourth off the edge of the green and sank his putt for a 6. Venturi had run in a 10-footer for a birdie 4. He was out in 35, even par. Jacobs had 39, while Palmer was 35 for that distance.

Venturi began the last nine leading Jacobs by two strokes. Palmer, ever hopeful, ever threatening but this time not capable of closing the gap, trailed Venturi by four. Venturi, the wearer of a characteristic white cap, strode those last nine holes as few champions before him have done. Fighting off a threat of heat prostration, which he admitted later he feared, he gulped 12 salt tablets and washed them down with iced tea, carried by a doctor.

The birdie putt he downed at the 13th for a 3, however, was the most refreshing potion of all. Added to pars at the three previous holes, it catapulted him farther ahead.

Jacobs, playing back of him, used 16 strokes on the four-hole stretch beginning at the 10th as did Palmer. Venturi needed only 14. Although Ken

exceeded par at the 15th, he ran in pars on each of the next three.

Venturi had to recover from the trap at the home hole to do so, but he wasn't being overtaken. His putt went in for a 4 and the 35 that meant a 70. No one can yet know how much that meant to Venturi.

Venturi Near Exhaustion

The intense heat affected all the competitors. Chi Chi Rodriquez, the colorful Puerto Rican, withdrew. He complained of a recurrence of an injury to his left thumb.

Venturi appeared to be near exhaustion when he entered the clubhouse following his 66. It was a tremendous round that included an unbelievable 30, five under par, on the first nine. Toward the end he wavered a bit and said he was chilly and hot.

A physician, Dr. John Everett, examined him and took his pulse, then recommended that he rest for half an hour. Venturi's wife sent a large thermos of tea into the locker room for him. Dr. Everett said: "I think he'll be all right. He's tired and somewhat dehydrated. He hasn't taken any liquids this morning and no salt tablets."

Venturi swallowed a few salt pellets and drank iced tea for

lunch. His face was drawn and haggard, but he was determined to go on. "I haven't been in a position—(two strokes back of leading Jacobs) like this before." A collapse in 1961, when he suffered a muscle spasm in the Palm Springs Classic, was the start of an eight week lapse in tournament play. He stayed on the tour when he wanted to quit because he had a contract with manufacturers to represent them.

Jacobs, the 29-year-old Californian who tied the record round of 64 yesterday, admitted he almost fainted at the 15th tee. "There was no air there. You know, an official told me he had a thermometer that read 112 degrees on the 14th green."

Of the three low scorers, Palmer appeared to be in the best physical condition between rounds. He was jaunty in the locker room as he asked friends whether they preferred him in a blue or white shirt to wear since the tourney was to be televised.

"I have an upset stomach," he commented whe asked if the weather bothered him, "but it's because of my putting." Palmer had three three-putt greens. Then he stripped off the leather grip of his driver and rewound it. He complained that the clubs were slipping in his hands be-

NATIONAL OPEN FINALE: A view of the 18th green at the Congressional Country Club in Washington, D.C., as Ken Venturi, tournament winner, prepares to make his final putt

cause of perspiration.

While Jacobs ate beef stroganoff, cooked apples and tea, Palmer ordered hamburgers and tea for himself and caddie. "I'm ready," he said when he was told he only had 15 minutes to go before starting out in the heat again.

The rounds this morning averaged four and a half hours. There was a 45-minute intermission for lunch. The temperature was in the high 90's. "Even the marvelous Mets might not like eight hours or more in hot weather like this," said a New Yorker in the gallery. But the golfers were expected to continue.

A 2-Stroke Lead

At the 54-hole mark, Jacobs led with 206 and Venturi followed at 208. Then came Palmer with his highest round thus far, a 75, for 212. Bill Casper, following a 69, had 214. Then came Collins, Floyd and Charles, the southpaw from New Zealand, at 215. Rosburg and Finsterwald were at 216 and Pott at 217.

One of the minor mysteries of the tournament was a 77 by Nicklaus, the pre-tourney favorite and leading money winner on the tour coming into this tournament. The 24-year-old P.G.A. champion and winner of the Open two years ago took 41 for the first nine, 11 more than Venturi. He finished the round at 222, sixteen back of the 54-hole leader.

Big Jack was putting poorly and never got his long driving controlled to give him an advantage. He missed putts of seven feet at six greens on the first nine. "I wanted to explode," he said. He ate a bowl of sliced pineapple for lunch and a fruit cocktail for dessert.

Venturi's last tournament triumph came in the 1960 Milwaukee open, but he has been on the comeback trail since the Thunderbird tourney in Harrison, N. Y., when he tied for third, two weeks ago. He went over par at the last two holes when pars would have given him a 64. As it was, his four-under-par total was extraordinary considering weather conditions.

The tees were moved up a bit and the greens had to be lightly sprayed intermittently to keep them from withering. The schedule ran an hour late and the afternoon starting times were moved back accordingly.

Off 13 minutes earlier than Palmer and Jacobs, who were paired together at 9:31 A.M., Venturi began with a birdie 3 at the first where he waited for the ball to fall into the cup. He made a valiant try for another at the third but missed. Then, at the fourth and fifth, he made 3's on 15 and 20 footers, respectively. After two more pars, he clicked for a birdie 3 at the eighth by downing a 25-foot putt. He hit his third boldly to the upper level of the green at the ninth and sank a 5-footer for his fifth birdie, a 4. His 30 going out included six 3's and three 4's.

On the inward trip, he holed a

PAR FOR THE COURSE

Out	.4	3	4	4	4	4	3	4	5—35		
In	.4	4	3	4	4	5	3	4	4—35—70		

KEN VENTURI

Out	.4	4	3	4	4	5	3	4	4—35		
In	..4	4	3	3	5	5	3	4	4—35—70—278		

TOMMY JACOBS

Out	.4	5	4	5	4	4	3	4	6—39		
In	..5	3	3	5	5	6	3	4	4—37—76—282		

BOB CHARLES

Out	.4	3	3	4	4	4	2	4	4—33		
In	..5	4	3	4	4	5	2	3	5—35—68—283		

BILLY CASPER

Out	.4	3	4	5	4	4	5	4	5—38		
In	..4	4	3	3	4	4	3	3	5—33—71—285		

ARNOLD PALMER

Out	.3	3	4	5	4	5	3	3	5—35		
In	..4	4	3	5	5	5	4	5	4—39—74—286		

deuce on an 18-footer at the 12th. It wasn't until the 17th that he encountered a bogey. It was his first in 21 holes, carrying over from yesterday. He exceeded par there by three-putting for a 5. His only wayward drive came at the 18th, where he drove into the trees. He chipped close but missed a 3-foot putt for his par.

Palmer's seconds were hitting the targets during the first nine. Behind the third green, he had to stop twice before playing his shot, as the crowd milled about. He was trapped at the fourth and went over the green at the fifth. He three-putted at the sixth, but made the turn in 37 after recovering well from a bunker back of the ninth green. He three-putted at both the 11th and 12th. He was near a tree after his drive at the 14th and had to chip out to the fairway before carding a 5, but he closed with pars at the next four holes for an inward 38.

Jacobs played so steadily and with outward coolness that he went 26 holes before going over par. This streak ended at the eighth hole of the third round. He had holed a birdie putt at the fifth this morning and pitched well to the elevated seventh green from the rough for a par. At the eighth, he was bunkered close to the putting surface and could not salvage his par.

At the ninth, his second went down the slope off the fairway to the right and he put his third into the small trap to the left of the green. His recovery never came up but fell back into the sand. On his next try he was more fortunate and once on the green two-putted for a 6. This put him out in 36. At that stage he and Venturi were tied for the lead and Palmer was two strokes astern.

Coming back, Jacobs ran in a 20-footer for a birdie at the 11th. He missed his par at the 14th after driving back of a pine. He reached the green on his fourth and sank a 5-footer for the bogey 5. "That was an important putt in the round," he said later. His next birdie came at the short 16th, where he slammed a No. 4 wood from the tee to within six feet of the flagstick. When he made his par 4's at the 17th and 18th, where Venturi had taken 5's, he was able to gain a two-stroke lead.

June 21, 1964

Mickey Wright, a leader in the LPGA tour for many years, blasts her way out of a trap.

OPEN GOLF GOES TO MISS WRIGHT

She Beats Miss Jessen in Playoff for 4th U.S. Title

CHULA VISTA, Calif., July 12 (UPI)—Mickey Wright won the United States women's open golf title for the fourth time today by carding a three-under-par 70 in an 18-hole playoff with Ruth Jessen, who shot a 72 over the 6,400-yard San Diego Country Club course.

Miss Wright and Miss Jessen had tied at 290 yesterday in the 72-hole tourney.

Miss Wright went ahead to stay today with a seven-foot birdie putt on the 16th hole. She finished with four birdies and had one bogey—on the ninth hole, where she three-putted.

Miss Jessen had 17 pars and one birdie. On the back nine, she made par putts of 10, 10, and seven feet, twice after coming out of traps.

Miss Wright won $2,200 and Miss Jessen $1,320.

It was the third time the 29-year-old Miss Wright and Miss Jessen, 27, had met in extra-hole competition. Miss Wright was the winner each time.

After carding a deuce on the sixth, Miss Wright made a 10-foot birdie putt on the eighth for a 2-stroke lead. Her three-foot putt on the ninth rimmed the cup and Miss Jessen reduced the lead by a stroke.

Miss Wright then holed a short putt for another birdie on the 10th and took the two-stroke lead that she never surrendered.

July 13, 1964

Bob Nichols, Once Near Death, Wins P.G.A. Title by 3 Strokes

By LINCOLN A. WERDEN
Special to The New York Times

COLUMBUS, Ohio, July 19—Bobby Nichols, a man who believes in the impossible, won the Professional Golfers' Association championship today with a record score of 271.

The slim Kentuckian, who lay near death after an automobile accident 12 years ago, won by three strokes with a concluding three-under-par 67 at the Columbus Country Club. He posted the best 72-hole total since the tourney became a stroke-play event in 1958.

Trailing him in one of the most exciting finishes of the year were the celebrated money and title-winning stars, Arnold Palmer and Jack Nicklaus, who finished at 274. Nicklaus blazed over the 6,751-yard, par-70 course in 64 strokes and Palmer had a 69.

Path to Championship: Chip on 16th Leads to Victory Dance on 18th

Bobby Nichols coming out of sand trap during last round of Professional Golfers Association championship yesterday

After sinking final putt, Nichols exultantly throws his cap in the air. He shot a 271 for the 72 holes of play.

A tremendously enthusiastic gathering of 17,500 golf buffs, notwithstanding the 90-degree temperature, cheered as if they were witnessing the stretch run of a thoroughbred race. A good share of the cheering was for the home-town boy, Nicklaus, whose 64 equaled the best score ever compiled in this championship as he sought to save the title he won a year ago.

But it was Nichols who gained his first major title, and this was the man who once was told he might never walk again, let alone play golf. The last rites of the Roman Catholic Church were given the high school football and basketball ace in September, 1952.

Today, by coincidence, he was paired with Ben Hogan, the 51-year-old winner of four open crowns, who is credtied with one of sport's great comebacks after he was almost killed in an auto crash in 1949.

Tom Nieporte, the Long Island champion, completed the three-some today.

Never Loses the Lead

On Thursday Nichols opened with a 64 that, until Nicklaus duplicated it today, stood as the best 18-hole score in the history of the tourney. This gave him a lead that he held through all four rounds, something never before done in this event.

Nichols was ahead by three strokes then and by one after a 71, his highest score, on Friday. Then came his 69 yesterday that had most of his fans dizzy.

It baffled Nichols, too, the way he was able to maneuver the ball from all sorts of places that seemed precarious and still get pars. When he posted the 69 to lead by two strokes after 54 holes, he admitted it was phenomenal. "I can't explain it," he said. "I don't think anyone would believe it unless they saw it." Nichols, a religious person, said he believed he was destined to win today.

As he started on what was to be an effort that withstood one of the strongest closing bids of the year, he three-putted at the first green. By the time he had completed nine holes with a one-over-par 35, he, Palmer with 34, and Mason Rudolph with 32 were all even. Nicklaus, with 32 to the turn, was three back.

Rudolph Is 4th at 276

Rudolph went on to finish with 69 for 276, while Ken Venturi, the United States Open champion, and Nieporte, regarded as a "home club" pro from the Piping Rock Club, Locust Valley, L.I., shared fifth at 279.

The check of $18,000 that

Nichols received as his share of the $100,000 purse, biggest ever offered in this tourney, was only a part of his financial success.

Under terms of his contract with the Hillerich and Bradsby Co. of Louisville, he received a $10,000 bonus for winning with their equipment. Added to this was $7,500 from the United States Rubber Company for playing the Royal golf ball. And from the real estate development where he lives in Corona, Calif., came $5,000 more for advertising his residential area.

As P.G.A. champion, Nichols automatically is eligible for the $100,000 World Series of Golf on television, Sept. 12 and 13 at Akron, Ohio. The other contestants will be Palmer, the Masters champion; Tony Lema, the British Open titleholder, and Venturi, the United States Open champion.

For the last two years Nicklaus has won the $50,000 first prize there, but by failing to win here, missed his last chance to become eligible for the event this year.

World Series Is Inspiration

The fact that Nicklaus would be shut out of the series if he didn't win today was one of the factors spurring him as he made a tremendous bid that continued to the last green. Paired with Palmer in a great slugging match, Nicklaus reached the putting surface of this 578-yard, par-5 hole in two shots, but missed his putt for an eagle 3.

Palmer uncorked a tremendous second, too, but the ball got away to the left back of a tree. With a big gallery in the grandstands and hemming him in on all sides, Palmer pitched to the green and missed the pin by inches. After an emotional scene

with thousands yelling and cheering, he stroked in the putt for his birdie 4.

Nicklaus, second in the recent British Open at St. Andrews and the leading money winner this year, and Palmer, fighting to win the only major golfing crown to elude him, seldom have been in a more exciting finish.

While Nicklaus and Palmer were hammering out a score they hoped would tie or overtake the 28-year-old Kentuckian, Nichols's touch did not falter. After the eagle, he holed pars at the next four holes. At the 15th, he drove into the rough, hit a No. 4 iron with overspin and the ball rolled to within 18 feet of the cup. Nichols then sank the putt for a birdie 3. Trapped at the 16th on his second, he recovered for a par 4 by sinking a 12-footer. "Unbelievable," said the gallery-

ites. Nichols shook his head.

Yesterday, he hit the pin from 70 yards out in the rough to make an incredible 3 at the 219-yard 17th and a deuce there today virtually sealed the victory. His putt went 51 feet, according to the manner in which Nichols stepped off the distance on the green. He seemed startled as the ball fell into the cup.

There was only one hole to go now and Nichols played it safely. He was in the middle of the green with his third at this par 5 where a row of catalpa trees line the left side of the fairway. Nichols paid no heed to them or to the traps guarding the green. He two-putted, tossed his cap in glee and was the new P.G.A. champion. "Faith" he said, "is what I had today."

July 20, 1964

Nicklaus Shoots Record-Breaking 271 and Wins Masters by Nine Strokes

PALMER, PLAYER ARE NEXT AT 280

Nicklaus Breaks Hogan's Mark of 274 in Winning Second Masters Title

By LINCOLN A. WERDEN
Special to The New York Times

AUGUSTA, Ga., April 11—Jack Nicklaus won the Masters Tournament today with a record score of 271, just as a master should. The 72-hole aggregate included a final round of 69 that sent him nine strokes ahead of his nearest challengers.

Nicklaus and the other members of golf's Big Three, Gary Player and Arnold Palmer, had tied after 36 holes at the Augusta National Golf Club. But the 64 Nicklaus forged yesterday sent him ahead by five strokes over Player while Palmer was eight strokes astern.

When Nicklaus rolled in the concluding putt today, he left Player and Palmer in another deadlock. This time they occupied the runner-up spot at 280. Player, the Masters champion of 1961, went over par by a stroke for a fourth round of 73. Palmer, who won his fourth Masters a year ago, broke the par 72 of the 6,980-yard course by two with his final 70.

When it was all over, Nicklaus seemed a bit dazed. The 25-year-old from Columbus, Ohio, said: "I've never played golf like this before. But I really

Jack Nicklaus

won't know my true reactions until tomorrow morning."

Palmer, Player and the tremendous gallery of 40,000 agreed that Nicklaus's 17-under-par performance over four days was "fantastic." The scoring record that Nicklaus smashed in this 29th Masters was Ben Hogan's. The Texan won in 1953 with a 274.

Nicklaus also surpassed the seven-stroke edge by which Cary Middlecoff carried off the honors in 1955.

Conditions Are Ideal

Light airs and sunshine greeted the contestants, the temperature was in the 80's and the tempo of the putting greens was "fast." But it was what Nicklaus liked. It was his keen, consistently accurate putting, he maintained, that was the principal factor in taking the tournament he won previously in 1963. When he triumphed that year he was the youngest ever to do so.

On his amazing rounds of 67, 71, 64 and 69 this week Nicklaus needed only 123 putts. His score on the greens for each day was 32, 31, 30 and 30. "This," he conceded, "was my best putting tournament. I drove consistently, too, but I think it was my putting that was more important."

"The way this fellow plays," suggested Kel Nagle of Australia, "he should win this tournament for the next 10 years." From the field of assembled experts, who come here by special invitation, the leading foreign star, besides Player was Ramon Sota of Spain. Mason Rudolph was fourth at 283, Dan Sikes, the lawyer who decided upon a golfing career instead of the bar, was next at 285, and Sota and Gene Littler were at 286. Downing Gray, a 26-year-old golfer from Pensacola, Fla. was the leading amateur with a total of 294.

The prize money also reached record proportions. Nicklaus received $20,000, which has been the customary winner's share, but the over-all purse went to $140,075. This is $10,-275 more than it was a year ago.

Although Nicklaus is known the world over as a power hitter, on his final tour of the par-72 course he scored a 69 without once getting a birdie at a par-5 hole. This was unusual, but so was his composite card that showed he rolled in 19 birdies and went over par five times in four days.

One of these came at the fifth hole this afternoon, the only time he exceeded regulation figures today.

There are several danger points on this course, which Nicklaus says is his favorite. He sailed by them, but Bill Casper, for example, ran aground at two of them—the 11th and 12th. Casper ran into a 6 by getting into the creek at the 11th, but the 155-yard par-3 12th, which Player called "the greatest par 3 in the world", cost Casper an 8. Twice he knocked the ball into the pond guarding the green, then overplayed into a bunker.

When Nicklaus arrived at the 12th tee, he knew what had happened there to Casper. In the gallery, Jack's wife said: "I only hope he gets by this awful 12th." Jack did.

At one hole, the danger signal flew. The eighth is an uphill par 5 of 530 yards and the fairway is flanked by pines. On three previous rounds, the long-hitting Ohioan had slammed the ball long and straight and collected birdie 4's each time. But today he pulled his drive. Trying to play around the corner to the dogleg left, his No. 5-iron shot caught the branch of a tree and rolled down a slope. Once again, as he had on the third round, he fired the ball through an opening to

safety. After pitching on, he two-putted for a par 5.

Otherwise, it was mostly all smiles. Nicklaus said he had never enjoyed a round more. He seemed relaxed and he looked cool in white shirt and blue slacks. Toward the end, he doffed his floppy white golf hat to the crowds. They cheered him when he walked onto the greens. He has a deliberate manner on the putting green and yesterday, as he watched a replay on television showing him on the last green, he said: "Well, that fellow makes me nervous. I wish he'd hit the putt." But Nicklaus wasn't nervous. His only outward emotion came minutes before he started out with Rudolph as a partner. "I'd like to get going and get the round over with," he said.

Once off, he rolled in a birdie 3 at the first hole. At the second, a long No. 1 iron second stopped to the left of the green and he chipped back, taking 2 putts for a par 5. The third found him over the green but he made his par there also.

Then at the short fourth he hit a No. 6 from the tee to within 1 1/2 feet and bagged the deuce. He was now 16 under par for the tournament. The bogey came at the next and pars followed at the subsequent six holes. He played his third from a square trap left of the 13th green, recovered and two-putted for a par 5. After a 4, he sank his par 5 at the 15th after being in the right front corner. He three-putted there but he was "charging," as he described it, for an eagle. The 4-footer for a birdie hit the cup but stayed out.

At the 16th, he used a No. 5 iron from the tee, then two-putted for the par 3. His birdie 3 at the 17th came after he smashed a No. 9 to within a foot of the flag. "My caddie, Willie Peterson, didn't want me

to use it, he thought a wedge would do," said Nicklaus.

"But I said, 'All right, Willie, I won't hit it too hard.'"

He hooked his drive at the 18th and pitched his second toward a green surrounded by thousands. But the ball spun back off and he chipped his third within 16 inches of the pin, before tapping in the last par 4 for his incoming 34 and a record score.

After congratulations and speeches, Nicklaus said he was going back to his home in Columbus for two weeks. Even a Masters champion, he said, would like a rest.

Masters Scores

Jack Nicklaus	67	71	64	69—271	$20,000
Arnold Palmer	70	68	72	70—280	$10,200
Gary Player	65	73	69	73—280	$10,200
Mason Rudolph	70	75	66	72—283	$6,200
Dan Sikes	67	72	71	75—285	$5,000
Ramon Sota	71	73	70	72—286	$3,800
Gene Littler	71	74	67	74—286	$3,800
Frank Beard	68	77	72	70—287	$2,400
Tommy Bolt	69	78	69	71—287	$2,400
George Knudson	72	73	69	74—288	$1,800
Tommy Aaron	67	74	71	77—288	$1,800
Bruce Crampton	72	72	74	71—289	$1,550
Paul Harney	74	74	71	70—289	$1,550
Doug Sanders	69	72	74	74—289	$1,550
George Bayer	69	74	74	72—290	$1,300
Wes Ellis	69	76	72	73—290	$1,300
Tommy Jacobs	71	74	72	73—290	$1,300
Byron Nelson	70	74	72	74—290	$1,300
Bruce Devlin	71	76	73	70—290	$1,300
Kel Nagle	75	70	74	71—290	$1,300
Ben Hogan	71	75	74	71—291	$1,200
Tony Lema	67	73	77	74—291	$1,200
Dow Finsterwald	72	75	72	72—291	$1,200
Al Geiberger	75	72	74	71—292	$1,200
Billy Dill	72	73	75	72—292	$1,200
Bo Wininger	70	72	75	76—293	$1,075
Billy Maxwell	74	72	76	71—293	$1,075
Bernard Hunt	71	74	74	74—293	$1,075
Tomoo Ishii	74	74	70	75—293	$1,075
Tom Nieporte	73	74	73	73—293	$1,075
Doug Ford	75	74	73	72—294	$1,050
*Downing Gray	72	75	73	74—294	—
Dave Ragan	73	74	73	74—294	$1,050
Mike Souchak	74	74	72	75—294	$1,050
Billy Casper	72	72	71	80—295	$1,050
Jimmy Demaret	71	75	76	73—295	$1,050
Bobby Nichols	73	71	75	76—295	$1,050
Chen Ching-Po	71	77	77	71—296	$1,025
*Donald Allen	70	77	74	75—296	—
Bob Goalby	72	73	75	76—296	$1,025
Jack McGowan	73	73	75	77—297	$1,025
*Bill Hyndman	73	73	75	76—297	—
Johnny Pott	74	74	73	76—297	$1,025
Art Wall	71	76	77	75—299	$1,025
Bob Charles	72	74	76	77—299	$1,025
*Richard Davies	70	78	78	76—302	—
*John Hopkins	70	78	78	77—303	—
*Dean Beman	74	72	79	79—304	—

*Denotes amateur.

April 12, 1965

Player Beats Nagle by 3 Shots in Open Playoff and Gives Away His Purse

$25,000 DONATED TO GOLFING GROUP

By LINCOLN A. WERDEN
Special to The New York Times

ST. LOUIS, June 21 — Gary Player of South Africa won the United States Golf title today in a non-American playoff. With a 71, the sprightly, 29-year-old professional from Johannesburg defeated Kelvin Nagle of Sydney, Australia, by three strokes and then turned back the winner's check of $25,-000.

He gave the $25,000 to the United States Golf Association with the stipulation that $20,-000 go to the fund for the development of junior golf and $5,000 go toward cancer research. He also gave his caddy the $1,000 bonus he received for participating in today's playoff, plus $1,000 out of his own pocket.

Player became the first foreigner to capture the trophy in 45 years as he triumphed at the 7,191-yard, par-70 Bellerive Country Club course.

The extra session was made necessary when both Nagle and Player scored 282 for the regulation 72 holes of the tournament. Player had a five-stroke

advantage after eight holes today and Nagle was unable to reduce the deficit until Player went over par at each of the last two holes. The 44-year-old Australian ran in pars, but by then it was too late.

Shortly after he walked off the course, Player said he had decided to give the purse to the U.S.G.A. because his mother had died of cancer. He also said: "I am doing this because I am so indebted to this country for the privileges they have given me in golf."

In winning the Open, Player joined Gene Sarazen and Ben Hogan as the only golfers to have taken the Open, the Masters, the British Open and the Professional Golfers Association title.

Ted Ray of England, the last

foreigner to take the trophy, in 1920, played with wooden-shafted clubs. Then came the era of steel shafts. However, Player was using something newer — fiber glass. Fishermen and pole vaulters have been using it, but only Player and Bruce Devlin, among the golfers, do.

Player, the most successful foreign money-winner in this country, disclosed that his contract for the use of fiber glass clubs was worth a minimum of $50,000 annually.

Victory Worth $500,000

Henry Shakespeare, the president of the company in Kalamazoo, Mich., that bears his name and processes the clubs, said that Player had a 10-year contract with his concern.

Mark McCormack, Player's attorney and business manager, said that "by winning the Masters in 1961 Player would have a lifetime income amounting to a million dollars; by winning today, it will be worth $500,000 to Gary."

Before leaving for his home in South Africa tonight, Player didn't forget his caddie, Frank Pagel. The youngster said he would buy a motor bike with the $2,000.

Nagle and his wife, Jean, who has accompanied him on the winter tour since January,

THE CARDS

Out—				
Par	443	443	454—35	
Player	432	543	444—33	
Nagle	533	463	554—36	
In—				
Par	444	344	354—70	
Player	544	344	365 36—71	
Nagle	544	344	354—36—74	

Player wins by 3 strokes.

also left immediately after the round. They were going directly to England to prepare for the British Open, which Nagle won in 1960 by beating Arnold Palmer by a stroke. Nagle's check for second place here was $12,500.

Nagle's inability to putt well was a major factor in his setback. His iron play was so accurate that his second shots were closer to the flag than Player's for nine consecutive holes, beginning at the sixth. But by then, Player was three strokes ahead and Nagle, who would have been the oldest ever to win the Open, had he succeeded, was simply fighting back. Time and again, he failed to roll in putts for birdies.

Too Little Too Late

It wasn't until right before the finish that Nagle gained any ground and that was because of Player's errors. The South African pulled his drive and second into the rough at the long 17th and his approach at this par 5 stopped six feet from the bank of the pond. A 6 there was his third bogey.

He had four bogeys altogether at the fourth where he was bunkered on his second, at the 10th where he played short of the creek after driving into the rough and at the home hole

© VOLK

where he drove into a small grove of sycamores.

Nagle's 36 on the inward half was an improvement over the outgoing 38, but it was of little solace. It was the second Open in which Nagle had gone beyond the first two rounds. He tied for 17th in the 1961 champion-

ship and failed to make the cutoff mark both in 1963 and 1964. There were 6,790 spectators for this 23d Open playoff.

The turning point of the duel probably came at the fifth, when Nagle was shaken after hitting two spectators on consecutive shots. The tee shot at

this 465-yard, par 4 is regarded by the course designer, Robert Trent Jones, as the most difficult in any Open. Hundreds of onlookers were along the hillside on the left where there is the notorious pond next to the sixth green. Nagle wanted to stay away from the danger of the murkish water where such stars as Arnold Palmer took 6's on two rounds.

But today his drive sailed high to the left, bounded off into the rough and struck a woman in the forehead.

Nagle, visibly shaken, since the woman was lying on the ground about 20 feet from where he was to play, compounded the trouble. Trying to get the ball from the heavy grass, he knocked it left once more. It struck another woman galleryite in the leg, bounded away and stopped 20 yards off to the right of the fairway.

Nagle seemed stunned by this last incident, but finally he took a wood and knocked the ball toward the green. It fell into a bunker. When he pitched out, he two-putted for a 6.

After he finished, Nagle conceded that this was a turn of events he could never have expected. "If it wasn't for that fifth hole I think I would have done well," he said.

He had started by three-putting the first, an indication perhaps of what was to come for him on the greens. Player's par 4 there immediately gave him the lead by one stroke. They had birdies on the next, where Player dropped a 35-footer. Nagle's was about 23 feet. Both scored 3's on the short third. Player's bunker shot cost him a stroke at the fourth and Nagle trailed only by one. Then came his disastrous fifth hole, where Player's par widened the gap to four strokes.

Nagle couldn't shake off a mediocre performance on the greens, and three putts for a 5 at the seventh sent him back another stroke. Player then ran in a 25-footer for a birdie 4 at the eighth and Nagle, after a par, was now trailing by five.

June 22, 1965

Thomson Wins His Fifth British Open by Two Strokes With 7-Under-Par 285

LEMA SLIPS TO TIE FOR 5TH WITH 289

By FRED TUPPER
Special to The New York Times

SOUTHPORT, England, July 9 — Peter Thomson of Australia today won his fifth British Open after a span of seven years. In a tumultuous finish that was in doubt all the way down the

stretch, the jaunty 35-year-old with the rhythmic swing scored birdies on the last two long holes to shake off Tony Lema's challenge and win by two strokes.

Two shots behind at the start of today's final 36 holes, Thomson scored 72, 71 in morning rain and brilliant afternoon sunshine to finish with a seven-under-par 285 total. Tied for second at 287 were Christy O'Connor of Ireland and Brian Huggett of Wales. Fourth at 288 was Robert de Vicenzo of Argentina. At 289 were Bernard Hunt of England, Kel

Nagle of Australia and Tony Lema, the defending champion from San Leandro, Calif., who cracked up on the final two holes.

The American Masters champion, Jack Nicklaus, and the two-time former British Open champion, Arnold Palmer, were far off the pace with 294 and 295, respectively.

"It was my greatest win ever," said Thomson, after he had finished seven strokes under par on the 7,037-yard course. Thomson had sunk into comparative obscurity in recent years, par-

tially through trouble with hay fever.

The curlyhaired Australian took his first Open over these shimmering sand dunes at Royal Birkdale in 1954 and won again in 1955, 1956 and 1958. Only the legendary Harry Vardon has held the "old jug" more often. Vardon won six championships over an 18-year stretch around the turn of the century.

Today, Thomson was paired with Lema, who had been tied for the lead with Bruce Devlin of Australia after yesterday's sec-

Australian Makes a Habit of Winning Britain's Leading Tournament

Roberto de Vicenzo of Argentina shoots out of a sand trap near the first green in the third round of the British Open, played at the Royal Birkdale course at Southport.

Peter Thomson of Australia putts near the edge of the first green in the third round. Thomson led de Vicenzo, going into the final round, by two strokes—214 to 216.

Associated Press Cablephotos

The Australian player beams after winning the trophy for the fifth time. His score for 72 holes of play was 285.

ond round. The crowd of 18,000 tumbled and tripped behind them as the Australian slowly cut down the American's advantage.

Thomson Finds the Touch

After an indifferent start, Thomson found the touch with his putter. He putted from off the green for a 4 at the sixth, dropped an 8-footer on the seventh and a 15-footer to an enormous roar on the eighth. A great out from a bunker for a 4 at the ninth gave him 35 on the first nine, the best score among the leaders.

In those last three holes, Thomson had picked up three strokes on Lema. By lunch time he was at 214, a stroke ahead of Lema and Devlin.

Lema had his moments in the morning round. A 15-footer went down on the sixth, a 20-footer on the 14th and a 7-foot putt on the 16th. He needed two birdies on the last two holes to regain the lead, not too difficult for a man with his length off the tee, but he finished 5-5 for 75 and 215.

By now Nicklaus was out of it with a dreary 78. The course was too fast for him and he couldn't control it, he said later. Devlin seemed drawn, too, with a 40 on the first nine, but the lean Australian had

three birdies on the inward half, pitching his approaches against the flag, and was still in contention with a 75 for a 215.

Three men were bunched at 216—40-year old O'Connor, 42-year-old de Vicenzo, who had a brilliant 34 down the homestretch, and Palmer, mired in the worst putting streak of his career.

"I three-putted twice, I missed 12 more from inside 10 feet and I had 38 putts all together — ridiculously bad," Palmer said.

It was apparent soon after lunch that either Thomson or Lema would take the title.

Thomson is Relaxed

The Australian was smiling and relaxed. He had a spring in his stride and his almost effortless irons were pitching the ball onto the heart of the green. Slowly he pulled away.

Thomson gained a two-stroke lead at the fifth when Lema missed a yard putt and Peter picked up another at the eighth when he banged an 8-footer into the back of the cup for a birdie 3.

Tenaciously, Lema hung on. The handsome pro from California had come to Britain a year ago and won the Open at St. Andrew's by five strokes

Cards in British Golf

PAR FOR THE COURSE

```
Out..........544  344  344—35
In...........443  535  455—38—73
           PETER THOMSON
             Third Round
Out..........555  344  234—35
In...........543  535  444—37—72
            Fourth Round
Out..........444  444  334—34
In...........444  535  444—37—71—285
              TONY LEMA
             Third Round
Out..........554  444  345—38
In...........543  435  355—37—75
            Fourth Round
Out..........444  454  344—36
In...........443  435  456—38—74—289
            JACK NICKLAUS
             Third Round
Out..........644  445  445—40
In...........364  445  434—37—77
            Fourth Round
Out..........455  345  245—37
In...........443  435  454—36—73—294
            ARNOLD PALMER
             Third Round
Out..........455  355  344—38
In...........443  535  445—37—75
            Fourth Round
Out..........455  465  354—41
In...........444  534  365—38—79—295
```

in his first crack at it. He had led here with a 68 on the first day and was tied with Devlin for the lead at 140 this morning.

Lema was driving well and his iron play was a revelation, but he never could get the middle-distance putts that were so vital.

Lema was three strokes down when a break came suddenly at the 190-yard 12th hole. Both men were on the edge of the green, a foot apart. Lema's first putt rimmed the hole and Thom-

son three-putted. It was two down for Lema now and the Australian's touch deserted him entirely. He pushed his third putt wide on the 13th from a scant yard away. Lema was only one down, but that was as close as he got.

Meanwhile, the Irish fairies were dancing for O'Connor. In a marvelous burst on the 12th, 13th and 14th holes he went 3, 4, 2 while Thomson was scoring 3, 5, 3—and the Irishman crept within two strokes. But that was as close as he could get.

The issue was decided for Lema on the 17th. His tee shot faded to the right into the rough and he decided to gamble all out for the green with a No. 3 wood. The lie was bad and Tony hit the ball badly, pulling it high over the palings into the crowd. Lema had a 5 there, while Thomson rimmed the cup for a 3 and finished 4, 4, 4 to a minute's solid applause from the crowd massed around the clubhouse.

Huggett had failed in his shot at glory, too. His chances apparently shot with four 6's this morning, the wee Welshman had a three-under-par 70 this afternoon with 15-foot and 9-foot putts for birdies on the 15th and 16th holes.

And de Vicenzo, a great contender in these opens, will always remember the ninth hole of this afternoon's round—he four-putted.

July 10, 1965

SOUTH AFRICANS DEFY RACIAL BAN

Nonwhites Mix With Whites in Pro Golf Tournament

GERMISTON, South Africa, Jan. 6 (Reuters) — South Africa's strict laws on segregation in sports were smashed today by a racially mixed crowd of 1,500 that followed the national hero, Gary Player, during the opening round of the Professional Golfers' Association tournament here.

The Government had permitted nonwhites to attend the tournament at the Germiston Golf Club, which is eight miles from Johannesburg, but had ordered that they be kept apart from the whites.

The crowd that followed Player and his partners from the first tee included about 300 nonwhites. Police were unable to separate them.

As the tournament progressed, the crowd dispersed over the course and attempts to enforce segregation were abandoned.

The Durban-born Indian, Sew-

sunker Sewgolum, was the first nonwhite golfer to take part in the P.G.A. tourney. It has been nearly five years since he crashed the apartheid barrier in sports by competing in the South African open championship.

Sewgolum received Government permission to play in the tournament here under the usual condition that he use separate facilities from the white golfers for eating, bathing and changing.

The luxury trailer he usually uses at tournaments did not arrive in time and he used the club secretary's house instead.

Not many nonwhites were expected to attend the tournament because the P.G.A. is charging the same entrance fee for all races. Normally, nonwhites are charged half-price at sporting events because of their lower salaries.

In sports, as in public entertainment, the Government seeks complete racial segregation. It decrees that whites should play only whites in white areas before white spectators, and the same should apply to nonwhite groups in their own designated areas.

If it is wished to depart from this policy—as Sewgolum has frequently done — permission must be obtained from the Ministry of Community Development.

January 7, 1966

Nicklaus Beats Jacobs and Brewer in Playoff to Win 2d Masters Title in Row

OHIOAN TRIUMPHS BY TWO STROKES

Cards 2-Under-Par 70 After a Tie at 288—Brewer Is 8 Strokes Back

By LINCOLN A. WERDEN
Special to The New York Times

AUGUSTA, Ga., April 11— Jack Nicklaus set another golfing record today by winning the Masters title for the second year in a row. In the 18-hole playoff necessitated by a three-way tie for first place yesterday, Nicklaus scored a two-under-par 70 to beat Tommy Jacobs by two strokes and Gay Brewer by eight.

It was Big Jack's third victory over the Augusta National Golf Club course, which he says is his favorite. The 26-year-old Ohioan exceeded the achievements of the experts who have

been competing here during 30 tournament years by succeeding himself as champion.

He became the youngest ever to carry off the honors of this event, one of golf's four major tests, by winning in 1963. A year ago he broke through the ranks again with a 72-hole total of 271 that set a scoring record and enabled him to smother the closest challengers by nine strokes.

Although Nicklaus is noted for his tremendous drives, it was his proficiency on those important short strokes—putts —that assured his triumph, which was achieved just before dusk. The three players left the first tee at 2 P.M. and it wasn't until 5 hours 2 minutes later that they holed out at the home green.

A $49.17 Bonus

Nicklaus received $20,000 of the record-size purse of $152,880, and he smiled when he learned he had a bonus of $49.17 resulting from today's extra session. Jacobs and Brewer received similar dividends. They had been advised that half of today's gate receipts would be divided equally among them.

A crowd estimated at 15,000,

enthusiastic and at times boisterous despite one of the most time-consuming rounds in championship annals, had been admitted chiefly on the basis of holding series tickets. Jacobs collected $12,300 and Brewer received $8,300.

It wasn't until the second nine of the famed layout that Nicklaus was able to pull away from Jacobs. Brewer, who had tossed away a golden opportunity yesterday by taking three putts at the last green, went two over par for the first nine.

Jacobs thrilled the spectators with a birdie 3 at the first hole and he and Nicklaus were even at 35 after completing the nine.

It was over the next three holes that the balance tipped in Nicklaus's favor. This part of the course is often called "the terrible triangle," but Nicklaus escaped its wrath.

Big Jack played this string of holes in 11 strokes, or par. Jacobs needed 13 and Brewer, caught by the tantalizing water hole 12th for a 5, used 15. Nicklaus admits that this par 3 scares him. It has cost Arnold Palmer, among others, at least one victory.

The Cards

PAR FOR THE COURSE

```
Out ...........454  343  454—36
In .............443  545  344—36—72
           JACK NICKLAUS
Out ...........444  442  445—35
In .............434  544  344—35—70
           TOMMY JACOBS
Out ...........354  343  445—35
In .............544  544  344—37—72
            GAY BREWER
Out ...........464  343  554—38
In .............455  544  265—40—78
```

By this time Nicklaus held a 2-stroke margin. Jacobs had knocked his second among the trees for a bogey at the 10th while Nicklaus holed out in 4. Then, at the 11th, Big Jack had rolled in a 25-foot putt for a birdie 3.

In late afternoon the setting at the 155-yard 12th was deceptively serene. Brewer knocked his tee shot into the water and his second attempt barely reached the bank. Nicklaus and Jacobs both sent their tee shots safely beyond the water, but to the left.

The crowd hummed with anticipation as Nicklaus walked toward the hillside back of the 12th to look for his ball. Would

United Press International Telephoto

OFF TO A GOOD START: Tommy Jacobs gestures after hitting putt that was good for a birdie on the first hole. Putt gave him the lead. He lost playoff by two strokes.

Associated Press Wirephoto

THE END OF THE AFFAIR: Jack Nicklaus using putter to play onto the green at the 18th hole of yesterday's playoff. His shot came within four feet of the cup and he sank the putt to take title for the second straight year.

this be a disaster hole for him too? But when Nicklaus located the ball, it was clear of bushes and shrubs, although in heavy grass. Then he chipped about 12 feet short of the pin.

Jacobs, on the fringe of the green, sent his chip to within five feet of the target. Nicklaus two-putted for a bogey 4, but Jacobs lost another opportunity when he failed to get his shorter putt in for a par 3. Nicklaus had passed the danger zone—or so the spectators felt.

Jacobs had another chance to reduce Jack's advantage. At the 525-yard 15th Nicklaus went over the green with a No. 2 iron and chipped back to 15 feet. Jacobs, at the right side of the green in 2, putted within 18 inches on his try for an eagle but had to settle for a birdie 4. It gained no ground for him since Nicklaus held his 2-stroke lead by bagging the 15-footer for a birdie 4, too.

Shadows were streaking the greens as Jacobs, who at the age of 17, became the youngest player ever to compete in the Masters, faced the task of overtaking one of the game's greatest in only three holes. It

had been announced that the playoff would continue on a sudden-death basis if a tie existed after 18 holes.

Little likelihood of this appeared after both Jacobs and Nicklaus took par 3's at the 16th, where Brewer ran in a deuce. At the 17th, Brewer pushed his second to an adjoining fairway and took a 6, but Nicklaus rolled in a 5-foot putt for a 4 and so did Jacobs.

In 1961, Palmer took an unexpected 6 at the home hole and Gary Player went on to win, but Nicklaus did not make that mistake today. There were a few moments of apprehension, however.

He drove wide and his second was off the green to the left. He decided to use a putter to get up the slope. As the spectators grouped close, he took a practice swing and hit a piece of ice, left from a discarded soft drink cup. He asked the caddie to wipe off the putter, then took his stance and hit the ball within 4 feet of the pin. Jacobs could do no better than a 4 and Nicklaus settled the issue by sinking his putt.

Fifth Masters Playoff

This was the fifth playoff since the tourney started in 1934. The previous one went to Palmer in 1962 as Arnie won the third of his four Masters crowns. Nicklaus now joins Jimmy Demaret and Sam Snead as the others who have been able to wear the green coat, symbolic of the Masters championship, three times. The only difference is that Nicklaus didn't get another coat as they did since, as a repeat winner, he will have to wear the same one he got last year.

That shouldn't bother Nicklaus, however — he can afford all the coats he needs. He began the year as the No. 3 money winner of the modern era despite his youth. He was credited with $429,048.92 after being the leading money winner of 1965.

Nicklaus first played here as a 19-year-old amateur in 1959. His second round of 76 this year, following an opening 68, was his highest since that freshman appearance. In the third round he scored a 72 to share the 54-hole lead with Jacobs. His fourth-round 72 sent him into the three-way deadlock yesterday.

He began today's round using a driver he selected recently to replace the one that split during a series of matches in South Africa against Gary Player in February. Nicklaus's first drive went about 330 yards, but it was somewhat overshadowed when Jacobs holed a 30-foot putt for a 3 as Nicklaus and Brewer took 4's.

On the 555-yard second hole, Nicklaus's power was in evi-

dence again as he hit the flag-stick on the fly with a No. 3 wood second shot. The ball bounced back to the right edge of the green and two putts from 30 feet gave Nicklaus a birdie 4. Jacobs had a 5 and Brewer a 6.

Brewer, who has won four tour events since September, never did get his game going, but Jacobs supplied early pressure. Nicklaus answered the challenge by brilliant putting. He ran in a 9-foot putt for a par at the third, but Jacobs went ahead with a par at the short fourth, where Nicklaus was bunkered and took a 4.

Nicklaus sank a tricky putt of a yard for a 4 at the fifth, and Jacobs holed a 7-footer. At the sixth, where the green is below the tee, Nicklaus ran in a downhill putt of 18 feet for a deuce. It brought him even with Jacobs and they led Brewer by 2.

That was the way the two leaders remained until they entered "the terrible triangle." Nicklaus unleashed a 320-yard drive at the ninth but took a bogey 5 anyway, as his wedge approach landed on the green then slowly rolled off about 10 feet. From there, he chipped weakly and putted twice. Jacobs, who had driven into the trees, hit the crowd with his second on the right side of the fairway. He took two putts from 10 feet for a 5, too, and thus stayed even with Nicklaus.

April 12, 1966

It's a Three-Billion-Dollar Business

By WILLIAM BARRY FURLONG

A LTHOUGH there may be some isolated souls who still regard golf as a form of relaxation and Good Clean Fun, the fact is that the game has become a really big business. At last count there were 8,323 courses in the nation with a total area greater than the state of Rhode Island and a capital investment estimated at $3.2-billion. Some 7.7 million persons in the U.S. now play 15 rounds of golf or more a year. This represents an increase of 55 per cent over the 1961 figure, and the National Golf Foundation expects that by 1970 there will be 10 million golfers playing on 10,000 courses.

Last year, some $140-million was spent on basic golf equipment—clubs, bags and balls. If you add to this the subsidiary merchandise sold in country club pro shops—shoes, socks, golf gloves, caps, sweaters and other items in an increasingly broad and unlikely inventory—the total sales, according to one authoritative estimate, exceeded $275-million. And that is only the start.

Add to it, first, the money turned over by golfers to private clubs, daily-fee courses, par-3 layouts and municipal courses for dues and greens fees, lessons, food and liquor, plus tips to everyone from caddies to waiters, and the figure increases. Rex McMorris, one of the leading authorities on the economics of golf, estimates that nearly $1-billion was paid last year into golf club coffers. Then add the money spent by the

WILLIAM BARRY FURLONG gave up golf years ago so he could go on with his trade—writing about it and other sports.

GOOD CLEAN FUNDS—Mr. Average Golfer soon finds out that a summer's Good Clean Fun on the links can be an expensive proposition, what with equipment, accessories and fees. One expert estimates that a billion dollars was spent last year by golfers out for relaxation.

golf clubs for various services, new or expanded courses, construction and landscaping, architects' fees, salaries, and even such subtle though costly items as seed, dirt and fertilizer. A survey of 50 select country clubs showed that they spent some $29-million last year, and that represents only a fraction of total club expenditure.

JUST getting into golf is an expensive proposition. The initiation fee at a country club can run anywhere from $1,000 to $25,000 and dues range from $50 to $500 a month. Buying the regulation 14 clubs and a good golf bag involves an investment of $350. And the cost of golf balls alone mounts up: in 1964 some $43,-473,126 was spent on 73,741,428 balls.

Of course you *can* begin the game for less. Not all golfers belong to country clubs; in fact, the National Golf Foundation estimates that four of five golfers play on municipal or daily-fee courses where a round costs $1 to $5. And the beginner can seek bargains in bags and clubs; one enterprising pro in Peoria, Ill., sells a "beginner's set"—seven clubs and an inexpensive canvas bag—for $39.95.

But once he falls prey to the game, the more manic golfer will find his costs rising astronomically in a long and agonizing career. Take, for example, putters. "There are at least 500 different kinds of putters," says one golf pro—some with mallet heads, snorkel heads, blade heads or croquet heads; others with gooseneck joints, half-gooseneck joints or quarter-gooseneck joints; still others with flat grips, round grips or pistol grips; others with brass inlays, bronze inlays or marble inlays; and many more with combinations of the above.

Or take some of the more advanced exotica of golf. A golfer may find himself compulsively buying a range-finder ("Develop your game scientifically"), or an indoor computer device that measures the distance and accuracy of a drive into a net (cost: $1,795), or even insurance to protect himself against the risks of a hole-in-one ("The drinks for the entire club are on you for the rest of the day," says one golfer, "and at most clubs your best friends will cheerfully drink you into bankruptcy"). The golfer may also pay for the privilege of playing on sneeze-proof grass (for the relief of hay-fever sufferers who play golf), using "unlosable" golf balls with tiny radio transmitters in the center (for the relief of myopics who play golf), and carrying a hollow-shafted putter filled with Scotch (for the relief of alcoholics who play golf).

In addition, a breathless variety of golf-related enterprises exploit the susceptibility of the golfer. One firm offers tees with advertising pitches on the heads or stems ("Reach the high-status group!"). Saks Fifth Avenue has developed a special sales force to merchandise its line in the pro shops of country clubs. Other

firms offer international golfing tours, and one group of 50 couples from St. Paul recently spent $60,000 on air fares for a "golf-and-gourmet" junket around the Caribbean.

In fact, pro shops in general have expanded their inventory well beyond golf and its accoutrements. In a pro shop these days you're likely to find everything from $200 Chinese beaded dresses and vibrating chairs to $322 Polaroid eight-shutter sequence cameras and sunglasses with tiny transistor radios built into the ear loop. "It's getting so you have to look around to find the golf clubs," says one pro, up to his neck in blouses and slacks and "après-golf" outfits in every color from tangerine to incarnadine. This pro estimates that 70 to 80 per cent of the space in his pro shop is devoted to non-golfing items and that a majority of his business comes from the wives of members. "We'll take the trouble to service them for a $2 item—where a department store might not bother—because we know they'll be back for the big-ticket item," he says. That combination of service and spending potential has tempted many big-ticket firms into

GOLD RUSH—Nearly 8 million golfers this year will be spending the green as well as playing on it—and the country clubs and manufacturers will post the best scores.

CASH CROP—An interesting development is the number of farmers who have changed over the "back 60" from farming to fairways. One man grossed nine times more in his first golfing year than he ever did from crops.

pro shows. "Our product is something that *requires* a salesman to take a personal interest in a customer," says a consultant for a vibrating chair firm.

BUT golf has emerged as more than a highly prosperous business; it is also a highly useful business vehicle. One of its direct uses is attested to bluntly by a bartender in a Chicago hotel: "When baseball is on TV," he says, "I sell a lot of beer in here. When it's golf, I sell Scotch." It's indirect use is indicated by several corporations which have provided golf courses for their employes or the community, on the twin theories that they can thus attract and keep better talent and free the community's resources for better services. In Minneapolis, both Minneapolis-Honeywell and Minnesota Mining and Mineral built 18-hole golf courses for their employes, and in San Diego the Convair division of General Dynamics built a putting green outside of the plant cafeteria.

In a more classic sense, golf courses have long been regarded as a vital lubricant in the business process. Indeed, some businesses offer memberships in country clubs, or pay a portion of the dues, to certain executives and salesmen.

There is no one path of golfing success that leads to business success. Sometimes it helps to be a great golfer. "I came home from college one summer to help out my dad and went golfing with a prospect," says a man who was a very good college golfer and whose family was in the real estate business in Florida. "I wound up selling him $400,000 worth of orange groves." His commission came to $20,000. "You think I ever went back to college?" he asks.

On the other hand, sometimes it hurts to be a good golfer. At a course near Chicago not long ago, a salesman frowned as he made a shot that Ben Hogan might have envied. "My boss is out here and if he saw that shot I might be in trouble," he said. Why? "It's the kiss of death for a salesman to play too well. He'd think I've been spending every day on the golf course."

Even golfing-equipment salesmen feel the same pressure. The sales manager of one such sales force told me that his salesmen don't have time to play golf with the customers. "They'd never get around to all of them if they stopped to play golf," he says. "In the time it takes them to play one round with one customer, they might make five or six calls by keeping on the road."

ON high business levels, the difficulty with making a really important deal on the golf course is that nobody can withdraw gracefully to be the first to rush back and call his stockbroker. "Actually, I've found that relatively few important deals are worked out on the golf course," says one very successful man who operates on the highest levels of the business world. "You usually establish a rapport, a feeling about your partners on the golf course, then later on you decide about the deal."

The sale of a newspaper in one of the nation's larger cities got started in exactly this manner. The rapport between two allegedly competitive publishers was established first on the golf course and the deal gradually evolved out of that. "Golf helps oil the machinery," says one executive, "but it doesn't really replace the work of negotiating the deal."

On less exalted levels, the shrewder salesmen don't press for an immediate sale. An insurance salesman explains that he selects his prospects carefully, makes dates to golf with them, but pointedly refrains from trying to make a sale on the golf course. "You say, 'How's business in general?' so you can make it tax-deductible, then you go out and have fun," he says.

ONE of the most important elements of the "business" of golf, and the most difficult to calculate, is the money won and lost on bets. Many golfers are reluctant to play a round of golf unless $5 or $10 or $20 —or $5,000—rests on the outcome. A number of professional golfers like to play for big stakes, say $500 to $1,000 a round and up; they expect to make a better living this way than from prizes or lessons, largely because many a big businessman considers it a status symbol to have lost $1,000 or more to a renowned pro.

In areas where gambling is endemic anyway, golf gambling takes a bizarre turn. In Las Vegas, a dealer in one of the gambling casinos took, of all things, a wedding chapel from a local preacher who specialized in hasty, low-cost marriages, in settlement of a golf bet. Another gambler bet on a golfer to shoot a par 72 at a club near Las Vegas. The golfer played superb golf and was three under par going into the last three holes. Then his game collapsed and he shot two bogeys and a double bogey to wind up with a 73. The gambler is reported to have lost $12,000. In Miami,

EXOTICA—For a price, the golfer can have such amenities as a hollow-shafted putter and an "unlosable" ball (with radio transmitter).

certain hoodlums are said to play for as much as $1,000 a hole with key putts worth $15,000 or more.

One legendary gambler named Titanic Thompson, who made as much as $50,000 in a few weeks of golfing, once bet that he could drive a golf ball 500 yards, or roughly 60 per cent farther than Jack Nicklaus drives it on his best days. He won the bet, too. He picked the season—wintertime. He picked the tee—on a hill overlooking a lake. The ball hit the ice on the lake, skidded swiftly across it, and never— it seemed to the losers— stopped rolling.

THE special attraction of golf for gamblers is that it is one of the few enterprises of modern man in which he can bet on his own physical achievement. In football, basketball, baseball and horse-racing he must bet on other men or animals; in golf he can bet on himself — and his own delusions of grandeur. Unfortunately, this leads many an amateur golfer into difficulties, particularly when he runs up against another "amateur" who is making a living by gambling on golf.

Not long ago, the United States Golf Association stripped one golfer of his "amateur" status for "conduct detrimental to golf." The "detrimental" conduct was his eagerness—and his success— in gambling against less sophisticated—and less skilled— amateurs.

"There is no set number of dollars at which a bet becomes a violation of amateur status," said Joseph C. Dey Jr., executive director of the U.S.G.A., when he was asked about the matter. "The amount involved means nothing in itself. Ten dollars may be a lot to you or

me but what is $50,000 to a multimillionaire? Motivation and effect are what concern us. Is the activity bad for the game? Is the golfer using the game for something other than just the joy of playing?"

The answer, all too frequently, is "yes." Just how he uses it depends upon his own enterprise. Some golfer-gamblers will bet very modestly on the course, just to warm up to something considerably more wild at the gin rummy table in the clubhouse. Others will take their more innocent victims by playing with phony handicaps or, if they are becoming well-known in an area, playing under phony names. Still others will handicap themselves and dare you to beat them. The golfer penalized by the U.S.G.A. for his successful gambling once went to a course near Houston where he bet he'd beat the best combination score of a particular threesome even if he hit all 18 of his tee shots with a paper cup over the ball. He lost the bet, not because he missed the tee shots —but because the rest of his game collapsed.

ONE mark of the audacity of golfing gamblers is the fixed "Calcuttas" which became a nationwide scandal a few years ago. In a "Calcutta," the various competitors in a tournament are "auctioned off" to members of the host club. The money goes into a pool and those "owning" the golfers who finish high in the tournament are paid out of the pool. Naturally, country club members are likely to bid high for the better-known or more accomplished golfers, to bid low for the lesser-known competitors. Obviously the return on the investment is much

greater if an unknown competitor — acquired at a low "bid"—wins the tournament.

So a few cunning men made a living out of "fixing" Calcuttas. Exceptionally good golfers, playing under phony names and phony records, were entered in the tournaments, usually local affairs that attracted good bidding but not much newspaper attention. The "fix" was arranged so that a few club members in on the deal would acquire the unknown "phenoms" at a low price in the Calcutta, then split the take all around when the unknown suddenly beat everybody.

The revelation that this and other maneuvers involving gambling were common practice affected a good many honest golfers. One businessman who plays an occasional, and excellent, game of golf told me of the time he was in a foursome with two important New York bankers—whom he didn't know—and a good friend who was a former Under Secretary of Commerce.

"I hadn't played in quite a while," he said, "and so we decided, for terms of this friendly little game, that I had a 12 handicap."

On the first hole, he got a birdie—one under par. On the second hole, he also got a birdie. On the next five holes, he shot par. So coming up to the eighth green, he was two under par instead of being roughly five or six over par as he was expected to be.

"You could see the chill in the air," recalls the businessman. "These bankers didn't know me and they'd been reading about the 'ringers' in the Calcuttas." So on his approach shot to the eighth hole, he lofted a wedge shot 50 yards beyond the green. "It was the best shot I made all day."

ANOTHER business area where the value of golf has been demonstrated most dramatically is real estate. Golf has proved to be of enormous importance in upgrading the value of real estate, both by beautifying an area and by attracting homebuilders to surrounding sites.

Take the case of Prescott, Ariz. The city built a municipal golf course on land it had originally acquired at an average cost of $25 an acre. After the course was finished, the land around the course, also owned by the city, rose dramatically in value. The city eventually sold one large parcel of it to a developer for an average of $2,277 an acre. It could still look forward to the sale of more land around the course — it expected to gain $180,000 from the sale—

as well as to the addition of taxable real estate for the city's coffers. In fact, it figured that by building the golf course and making the land around it attractive to real estate developers (not to mention satisfying the recreational needs of the city) it would add $3-million to the city's tax rolls over a 10-year period.

In more densely populated areas, where there is no "fringe land" to sell off at an increased value, it is sometimes cheaper to keep a golf course rather than to take on the added expenses of city services that emerge when it is converted into a real estate development. About 10 years ago, for instance, the Glenview Country Club in Glenview, Ill., was sold to a private developer who hoped to convert it into a subdivision of 400 homes. There would not be a great increase in tax revenue to the community since the land was already carried on the tax rolls as privately owned real estate. But it would cost the community a great deal of money to put in additional schools, utilities, streets, police and fire protection, and transportation to accommodate the 400 families.

So, by an 8-to-1 margin, the citizens of Glenview passed a bond issue to buy the land back from the developer—giving him a 20 per cent profit on the turnover—and keep it as a golf course, albeit as a public course. By last year, the income from fees charged golfers—those from neighboring suburbs as well as from Glenview—enabled the community not only to maintain payments on the bonds but to build a new clubhouse.

The *ne plus ultra* of real estate development is, of course, to do both—build homes *and* a golf course on land which has gone unused. In that way the land values are raised and

the tax revenue increased to the point where the community can support the cost of the various civic services. The trick is to build the golf course first. In Reston, Va., a new development 25 miles from Washington (where some 80,-000 persons are expected to live by 1980), the first of five golf courses was finished considerably before the first home. At a Crofton (Md.) development the pro shop and six model homes were the first structures completed — after the golf course.

Of course, a golf course doesn't guarantee success in real estate. At least three golf course-real estate developments in Florida failed in the first six months of last year, and many others throughout the nation must yet prove their health. By and large, the cause of such failures is not

poor home design or placement but saturation of the market—the golf market. "If there are already enough golf courses in an area, then golf won't sell real estate," says one veteran of such deals.

The prime effort must therefore be to tailor the golf course to the area. At Pinehurst, near Denver, Colo., a real estate developer went ahead with a large development even though there were five country clubs nearby. But the other clubs had high costs and low memberships. Pinehurst simply reversed the idea, aiming at large membership and low costs. Its technique was to develop a complete recreation center, with a Z-shaped swimming pool, fashion shows, bowling, bridge, bingo, art exbibits and special children's movies. The result was that the developer was able to sell

his 500 homesites and 37 acres of high-rise apartments that were built around the 27 holes of golf.

IT should not be assumed that the golfing urge—or its business potential—is confined to urban areas. Many a farmer has increased his revenue by transforming a "back-60" acres of crop land into grassland which can be peppered here and there with sand traps. Down in Cleveland County, N. C., for instance, a farmer named Namon Hamrick, who "never cleared more than $1,000 off farming in one year in my whole life," decided to try a new crop: golf. He mortgaged his property, sold 28 head of cattle at an average of $100 apiece, got together with a golf pro and an equipment salesman to work on the landscaping of nine holes on 60 acres and started "planting grass instead of cotton."

Soon he was charging local golfers a dollar a day on weekdays and $1.50 on weekends to play on his land, and in his first year he grossed $9,000. Naturally, he wanted to expand the course to 18 holes, but he lacked sufficient capital. So he borrowed $32,500 from the Farmers Home Administration at 5 per cent interest payable over 40 years. (Some 60 such loans totaling $6.5-million were made for construction of recreation sites for 19 states in fiscal 1964, with some 6,000 acres thus taken out of farm production.)

Before Namon Hamrick was through, he not only had his 18 holes of golf but a series of phone calls from farmers all over the country who wanted to know how they, too, could cash in on the evergrowing and ever-prosperous business of golf.

PRIMING—"Golf helps oil the machinery," says an executive, "but it doesn't replace the work of negotiating the deal."

June 5, 1966

New Rules Aimed at Speeding Play Draw Widespread Approval of Golfers

Special to The New York Times

SAN FRANCISCO, June 18— The new speedup rules appear destined to remain in golf. This was the consensus of both players and officials as the third round of the United States Open got under way today.

"I think they are great," said Arnold Palmer. "I never thought they would work out so well."

"It's the way to play," agreed Bobby Nichols, the former Professional Golfers' Association

champion. "It's better for spectators and everyone. What we do here is followed everywhere."

Dave Marr, the current P.G.A. titleholder, said it was fine with him, and Ben Hogan, the 53-year-old Texan who has played the game under so many different regulations, said: "They don't bother me a bit. Whatever rules are made, I'll play under them."

All-Round Approval

Jack Nicklaus, who was in the group that was asked to

speed up the last two days, said he found no fault with the regulations. One rule specifies that the ball must be cleaned only once on the putting green, before the first putt. The other rule in effect for the first time in an Open calls for continuous putting by a contestant on the green.

Ward Foshay, president of the United States Golf Association, said he had received approval and endorsement from all sides. The P.G.A. committee here advised him that the rule will be

followed when the P.G.A. championship is held July 21 through 24 at the Firestone Country Club in Akron, Ohio.

Nicklaus explained, however, that the rules have not been adopted on the pro circuit because conditions vary so much from those in a championship such as the present one at the Olympic Country Club course.

Gallery Is a Problem

"Few tour courses are groomed as this one," said big Jack. "Often it is necessary to 'top dress' greens before a tour event, and the ball can pick up a lot of grass or dirt on some courses. That's why we are allowed to clean at will in tour tournaments."

After being warned for slow play yesterday, Nicklaus declared he had never "been so mad before on a golf course." His playing colleagues for the last two days were Tony Lema and Bruce Devlin.

Devlin, the slim Australian, said the group could have been around yesterday in four hours,

the maximum time suggested by the U.S.G.A. Instead, the trio took 4 hours 12 minutes.

Devlin said his group had had to wait at several tees so that the gallery could cross the fairway. "A featured group like ours attracts a crowd," he said. "Several times after Tony and Jack had putted out, people milled about. Was I expected to putt when the spectators were moving?

"It was also difficult to go from green to tee. I was almost

knocked down four times trying to push through the crowd to get to a tee. All this took time. I really believe we could have finished in four hours if it weren't for the gallery. As it was, we were around in 4:12. I don't think any of us liked the idea of having an official watching."

Nicklaus did not wish to continue the discussion about the "police" who, he said, followed his play for the last 12 holes yesterday, but he and Palmer

engaged in a good-humored conversation before they started out today.

"I hear you almost got arrested," said Palmer as he greeted big Jack in the locker room. "Sure tried" was Jack's smiling rejoinder.

"If you play in three hours today," added Nicklaus, "I'll play in 2½ hours."

June 19, 1966

Casper Shoots 69 and Defeats Palmer by 4 Strokes in U.S. Open Playoff

CALIFORNIAN WINS FOR SECOND TIME

Casper Again Erases Deficit on Back Nine—Defeat Is Palmer's 3d in Playoff

By LINCOLN A. WERDEN
Special to The New York Times

SAN FRANCISCO, June 20—Just as he did yesterday, Billy Casper overcame a lead by Arnold Palmer today. This time, as he outscored his celebrated rival, 69 to 73, it brought him the United States Open golf title.

"It was the sweetest victory of all," said Casper, who is known for his many allergies almost as well as for his keen putting stroke. Casper said he had a breakfast of swordfish and tomatoes, but later, on the greens of the Olympic Country Club, he adhered to a diet of birdies. He needed only one putt on eight greens and cut down on his strokes as if they were calories.

Palmer complimented his 34-year-old rival from San Diego by saying: "He's the greatest putter on the pro tour. He putted the ball in at the right time and that made the big difference."

It was the third playoff in which Palmer had been unsuccessful after he won the game's highest honor outright in 1960. Asked how this one compared with the other two, Palmer replied quickly: "It was pretty damn similar." He lost to Jack Nicklaus in 1962 and was third when Julius Boros won in 1963 against Palmer and Jacky Cupit.

Casper became the 11th to win the Open at least twice. The others were Bob Jones, Ben Hogan and Willie Anderson, each of whom won four; Walter Hagen, Cary Middlecoff, Julius Boros, Gene Sarazen, Johnny McDermott, Alex Smith and

Associated Press Wirephoto
DONATION: Casper hands his $25,000 check to his wife, Shirley, after receiving it from Ward Foshay, right, U.S.G.A. president. Caspers at left: Billy, 9, and Linda, 11.

Ralph Guldahl, each of whom won twice.

The playoff, one of the speediest on record, required only 3 hours 5 minutes to complete. A gallery of 12,059 rushed across fairways and seemed divided as to allegiance. There were constant yells of "Come on Arnie," "Let's go Arnie," but a sizable group answered with "Billy Boy, let's go."

For the second straight day Palmer appeared to have the situation in hand. He started yesterday with a 32 and everyone, including Casper, thought he would break the scoring record of 276 for the championship set in 1948 by Ben Hogan. He needed only 36 on the back nine to do so. Then he used 39 and saw his advantage vanish against Casper's rally.

Once again the charging Palmer went to the front and held a two-stroke edge after nine holes. He was out in 33 to a par 35 for Casper. "Palmer's charge," observed Casper, "means tearing down the flags on the course with his shots. When I charge, I'm getting the ball into position on the greens for a par. That's the difference between us."

Once more it was on the back nine that Palmer's attack failed. "I don't know," he said before starting, "what happened to me yesterday. I guess it was a matter of timing." After today's round, "an experience I haven't had," Palmer said there might have been some technical deficiencies in his game. "I never seemed to get myself lined up right on a couple of the holes."

Palmer led by two through the 10th. Casper had lost a stroke at the fourth and fifth and had regained one with a deuce on a 6-footer at the eighth. But after a cameraman, who was subsequently ordered off the fairway, disturbed him as he was about to putt, Casper three-putted for a bogey at the ninth.

But the California professional, winner this year of the San Diego open, holed a 30-footer for a birdie at the 11th. Palmer hit his second from the rough to the left of the green and failed to get a 4-footer down for his par 4. There Casper found himself even. Both had 4's at the 12th.

At the 191-yard 13th, Casper went ahead for the first time by running in a 40-footer. He raised his hands above his head

in jubilation. Palmer then had a bogey 5 at the next hole after driving into the rough and being below the green in 2. Casper came through with a par and increased his lead to two strokes.

Casper widened the gap to three strokes with a par 3 at the 15th. Palmer was bunkered and took a bogey while Casper ran his approach putt so close it lipped the cup.

It was the long 16th of 604 yards where Palmer lost two of the three-stroke advantage he held over Casper as they approached the wire in yesterday's fourth round. Today, Palmer soared to a 7.

He drove into the rough, in heavy grass, and his second shot traveled only 80 yards. A third, with a No. 4 wood, was well hit but left him short of the green by 50 yards. Then he

THE CARDS

Out—		
Par	543 444	434—35
Casper	543 454	325—35
Palmer	543 344	334—33
In—		
Par	444 343	544—35—70
Casper	434 243	653—34—69
Palmer	454 354	744—40—73

Peter Thomson, seen here in 1965, won four British Opens in a span of five years.

Lee Trevino, a big winner in the late 1960's and early 1970's, was the first Chicano to become a prominent golfer.

Billy Casper was "the greatest putter on the pro tour," said Arnold Palmer in 1966.

141

failed to clear the guarding bunker and the ball fell into the sand. On with his fifth, he two-putted for the 7. Casper was on easily in three, and, despite three putts for a 6, widened his lead to four strokes.

Casper three-putted from the edge of the green for a bogey 5 at the 17th and Palmer regained a stroke with a par 4.

Leading now by three, Casper smiled broadly as he came down the 18th fairway. His wife and two of his three youngsters were back of the ropes and the marshals didn't recognise them and ordered them back. Mrs. Casper was wiping away happy tears.

Palmer drove to the right and

the ball struck a policeman's leg on the first bounce. Palmer pitched over a bunker but the ball landed in the heavy grass below the green. On with his third, Palmer was applauded as he holed a 5-footer for a par 4.

Casper ended with a champion's flourish. A fine drive, a high second to the elevated green and then a 3-foot putt that went in for a birdie 3 gave him the 69 and sealed the title. Palmer had 40 on the back nine for his 73.

"I've been hoping and praying for this for a long time," said Casper. Before he had time to sign and attest his score as the new champion, his wife and children finally broke through a

cordon of officials to hug and kiss him. "We've all waited for this day," Mrs. Casper said.

Casper's winning share of the $150,000 purse was $25,000 and Palmer's was $12,500. In addition each received a bonus of $1,500 as his share for the extra session necessitated when they tied at 278 at the end of 72 holes yesterday.

Casper said 10 per cent of his earnings would go to the Church of Jesus Christ of Latter Day Saints. Casper said this was considered as a tithing among Mormons and that 10 per cent of all his golf winnings go to the church.

Last night, he said, he and his wife, Shirley, attended a Mormon fireside service and showed films

they had taken during a recent trip to Vietnam under the supervision of the United States State Department.

Casper said there was a lot more to life than golf and that his religion had helped him relax in competition.

"At no time did I give up here," he said, "even after I was seven strokes down yesterday with nine holes to play. It was like a dream. I was challenging for second place. When Palmer slipped, I slipped inside the door he left ajar."

June 21, 1966

NICKLAUS TAKES BRITISH OPEN BY STROKE WITH 282

TWO TIED AT 283

Sanders and Thomas Trail—Birdie 4 on 17th Is Decisive

By FRED TUPPER
Special to The New York Times

MUIRFIELD, Scotland, July 9—Jack Nicklaus of Columbus, Ohio, won the British Open today by one stroke from another American, Doug Sanders, and Dave Thomas of Britain with a four-round score of 70, 67, 75, 70—282. Nicklaus now has won all the major titles in golf open to professional players.

It took him five years to win this championship. He was second to Tony Lema at St. Andrews in 1964 and third to Bob Charles at Lytham St. Annes in 1963 when he faltered on the 17th hole while leading in the last round.

Nicklaus had his rocky moments today. After a superb outgoing nine of 33, he was four under par for the tourney, three under par for the day and two strokes ahead of Sanders and the third-round leader, Phil Rodgers.

Strong Boy Is Erratic

A great iron shot off the tee and a pitch and wedge put Nicklaus seven feet from the pin at the 11th hole. His putt slid by the cup by 15 inches. Incredibly he missed it coming back and took a bogey 5. One of his precious strokes was gone as well as some of his confidence.

Associated Press Cablephoto

A VICTORY HE HAS LONG WANTED TO TASTE: Jack Nicklaus after winning the British Open championship in Muirfield. It was his first victory in the British tournament.

At the short 13th he hit a No. 9 on the edge of the green. The ball hesitated on the slope, stopped and then rolled backward and sideways between two bunkers 60 feet below the cup. There was no easy way to get near the flag. Nicklaus putted the ball and it scooted 20 feet across the slippery green. He had two more putts for a bogey 4 and another stroke had vanished.

Jack's long drive on the 14th went into a bunker and the ball was wedged on the slope. He rammed it out with a No. 9 iron shot, wedged to the green and took two putts to get down for another bogey 5. By now he had lost his lead and was tied with Sanders and Thomas.

Strong Boy Settles Down

Then the 26-year-old Columbus strong boy settled down. He was determined to play the course his way, to master it by intelligence rather than overpower it. He had his pars on the 15th and 16th. Sanders and Thomas had finished in a tie with 283. Jack needed a birdie and a par for 282.

The long par 5, 528-yard 17th hole is made to order for a big hitter like Nicklaus. But he used restraint. A No. 3 iron shot rolled straight down the middle of the fairway. His No. 5 iron split the heart of the green and landed 15 feet to the left of the flag. Two careful putts and he had that vital birdie 4.

A crowd of 12,000 was massed around the 18th fairway which ribbons between knee-high rough 429 yards to the green. Nicklaus laced a No. 1 iron shot down the narrow patch and then held a No. 3 iron into the wind, 20 feet to the right of the pin as an enormous cheer rang out. He stared at that putt seemingly forever. It rolled up 10 inches away and he tapped it in for the title.

9 Strokes Disappear

Yesterday Nicklaus had lost nine strokes in the last nine holes as he had a 39 while the roly-poly Rodgers had torn the course apart with a record-breaking 30 for a third-round lead of two strokes with 210.

Nicklaus now has won the four highest ranking professional tournaments—the United States Open, the Professional Golfers' Association, the Masters and the British Open—to join Gene Sarazen, Ben Hogan and Gary Player among the golfing immortals. Nicklaus was the United States Amateur champion twice.

Dressed in red, Sanders made a wonderful bid. A magnificent wedge shot from 75 yards into the wind on the par 5, 495-yard, ninth hole dropped dead center on the green and rolled into

THE LEADING CARDS

PAR FOR THE COURSE						
Out	444	354	345—36			
In	444	344	354—35—71			
JACK NICKLAUS						
Out	344	344	335—33			
In	454	454	344—37—70—212—282			
DOUG SANDERS						
Out	543	344	443—34			
In	464	334	354—36—70—213—283			
DAVE THOMAS						
Out	344	354	245—34			
In	544	344	354—35—69—214—283			
PHIL RODGERS						
Out	543	445	354—37			
In	644	345	355—39—76—210—286			
ARNOLD PALMER						
Out	443	354	354—35			
In	754	344	345—39—74—214—288			
DAVE MARR						
Out	444	344	355—36			
In	444	354	344—70—218—288			
DICK SIKES						
Out	634	354	354—36			
In	544	354	344—36—72—218—290			
JULIUS BOROS						
Out	444	354	454—37			
In	443	354	454—35—72—220—292			
TONY LEMA						
Out	544	354	446—40			
In	445	344	254—35—75—223—296			

the cup for an eagle 3 as the crowd roared. Doug was around the turn in 34 and two under par for the tournament. The 11th cooked his goose. His drive off the tee vanished into a sea of grass. He duffed a No. 7 iron shot 30 yards and a No. 9 iron into a trap. Sanders had a 6. A No. 2 wood shot that landed 3 feet from the cup on the 14th hole meant a birdie 3, but it

was too late. He finished quietly in pars for 70.

Earlier Thomas had set British hearts tingling with a superlative round of 69 that could have been so much better. He got a birdie on the difficult first hole into the westerly wind with a drive and a No. 3 iron shot to 5 feet and made the putt.

The 15-footer for a deuce on the short seventh brought the crowd running and suddenly he was on the ninth green 4 feet from the cup with the putt for another birdie. Sadly it skidded away. Another 4-footer refused to drop on the 10th, but the big Welshman sank a tremendous putt from 75 feet for another deuce at the 13th. He messed up a No. 6 iron shot on the 17th, and a last desperate putt for a birdie on the home hole was inches short.

Rodgers, Gary Player of South Africa, and Kel Nagle and Bruce Devlin of Australia all had 286's; Arnie Palmer and Dave Marr of the United States; the defending champion, Peter Thomson, and Sebastian Miguel of Spain all had 288's; and Dick Sikes of the United States was at 290.

For a while today Palmer was his old self, swashbuckling and on the attack. He started 4-4-3-3 —one under par—with his iron shots soaring straight to the pin and the putts going down. An 8-footer on the ninth for a birdie had him at the turn in 35 with everything to go for. But his challenge died at once. A tee shot went straight into the deep rough on the 10th and it took him four strokes to get out for a wretched 7. A wiser man would have played it safe, but that is not Arnie's method.

THE LEADING SCORES

Jack Nicklaus	70	67	75	70—282	$5,860
Doug Sanders	71	70	72	70—283	$3,780
Dave Thomas	72	73	69	69—283	$3,780
Phil Rodgers	74	66	70	76—286	$1,949
Kel Nagle	72	68	76	70—286	$1,949
Bruce Devlin	73	69	74	70—286	$1,949
Gary Player	72	74	71	69—286	$1,949
Dave Marr	73	76	69	70—288	$924
Arnold Palmer	73	72	69	74—288	$924
Peter Thomson	73	75	69	71—288	$924
Sebastian Miguel	74	72	70	72—288	$924
Dick Sikes	73	72	73	72—290	$620
Christy O'Connor	73	72	74	72—291	$554
Harold Henning	71	69	75	76—291	$554
Julius Boros	73	71	76	72—292	$504
*Ronnie Shade	71	70	75	77—293	
Alex Caygill	72	71	73	77—293	$470
Jimmy Hitchcock	70	77	74	72—293	$470
Peter Butler	73	65	80	75—293	$470
R. De Vicenzo	74	72	71	76—294	$420
Douglas Sewell	76	69	74	75—294	$420
Peter Alliss	74	72	75	73—294	$420
*Denotes amateur.					

July 10, 1966

New Solid, Molded Golf Ball Patented

By STACY V. JONES
Special to The New York Times

WASHINGTON, April 14— A solid, molded golf ball is being offered as successor to the conventional kind, which has been in general use since about 1900. A patent was granted this week to James R. Bartsch, a 34-year-old chemical engineer, for the new ball, which is all in one piece and covered only by a coat of paint. It is already on the market.

Patents of the Week

By coincidence, Mr. Bartsch received his patent 68 years to the day after the basic patent was issued for the familiar three-part ball, with core, winding and cover.

The Bartsch ball, which meets United States Golf Association regulations, is protected by Patent 3,313,545, and has been developed by Princeton Chemical Research, Inc., Princeton, N. J.

It is described as being indestructible in normal play and as having a perfect center of gravity, which promotes accuracy in flight and putting.

The early patent (622,834) was granted April 11, 1899, to Coburn Haskell of Cleveland and Bertram G. Work of Akron, Ohio. It specifies a golf ball with a central-core section, rubber thread wound under high tension, and a gutta-percha shell.

There have been changes in detail, but golf balls of this type have been standard ever

since. One exception is the Executive, a two-part ball comprising a solid, molded center and a cover, which was recently announced by A. G. Spalding & Bros., Inc.

Mr. Bartsch became interested in the technology a decade ago after acquiring a company that was engaged in replacing golf-ball covers.

In the new ball, he uses an elastomer, preferably cis-butadiene rubber, cured in the presence of another compound (a monomer). The patent says the elastomer becomes cross-linked into a

three-dimensional network.

The new ball is practically cut-free. It has been made for two years by the Faultless Rubber Company in several grades, retailing from $8 to $12 a dozen.

The Bartsch patent is owned by the Princeton Chemical Patent Development Corporation, Princeton, which has granted a license to a foreign manufacturer and is negotiating others. Patents have been obtained also in Britain and Canada.

April 15, 1967

Nicklaus Shoots 65 for 275, a Record, to Win His 2d U.S. Open by 4 Shots

BIRDIE 4 AT 18TH SURPASSES MARK

**Hogan's '48 Standard Falls
—Palmer Is Runner-Up
—Fleckman at 289**

By LINCOLN A. WERDEN
Special to The New York Times

SPRINGFIELD, N. J., June 18 — Jack Nicklaus won the United States Open golf championship today in record-breaking style. With a closing five-under-par 65, he finished with a total of 275, the lowest 72-hole aggregate in 67 championships that have been played since 1895.

With a deft touch he rolled in a 22-foot birdie putt on the last green of the Baltusrol Golf Club's Lower Course to shatter Ben Hogan's mark of 276. The 54-year-old Hogan, here as a competitor, established the previous record in 1948 at the Riviera Country Club in Los Angeles.

The husky 27-year-old golfer from Columbus, Ohio, who has gained numerous international golfing honors, demonstrated again his superior strength in long hitting and the touch necessary to master the shorter strokes on the greens.

Master of the Greens

Nicklaus triumphed by four strokes as he tied the low score for the fourth round in this championship.

Behind him, at 279, was Arnold Palmer, his respected golfing rival, who was defeated by Nicklaus in the playoff in 1962 when Big Jack won his previous Open title at Oakmont, Pa.

Nicklaus's astute play on the greens — he rolled in eight birdies—enabled him to shatter all opposition. On the eve of the tourney last Wednesday, Nicklaus scored a practice round of 62, his lowest score on a United States course.

This afternoon, since he got away as scheduled at 3:08, he seemed to be steering in that direction again. He went out in 31, only one stroke over the record for nine holes in the revered championship. But then he took a bogey 5 at the 10th, before putting on a spurt in which he played the last eight holes in three under par.

Overwhelmed by it all was 23-year-old Martin Fleckman, the young amateur who proved a sensation with his opening-round 67 and by taking the 54-

THAT DOES IT! Jack Nicklaus on the 18th green at Baltusrol yesterday giving a victorious gesture as his final putt drops for a 65 to give him a record U.S. Open total.

hole lead yesterday with a 69 for 209.

No amateur since Johnny Goodman, in 1933, had been able to do that. But despite this, Fleckman was not nervous and seemed oblivious to the pressure of competing for the first time in an Open championship.

The amateur from Port Arthur, Tex., finished with an 80. He failed to get a single birdie and brought his final aggregate to 289, 14 strokes behind Nicklaus.

Experience Favored Stars

Nicklaus, along with Palmer and Billy Casper, trailed Fleckman by one stroke as the closing round got under way. But there was much in the scales of experience that favored Nicklaus, Palmer and Casper, the defending champion.

Casper failed to stay even with par. A 36 on each half of the 7,015-yard, par-70 course was the best Casper could muster in an effort to retain the crown he won from Palmer last year in a playoff.

Casper's iron shots and short putts today were not finding the mark and, along with the other contenders, he could not compete with the birdie spurt that Nicklaus unleashed. Casper finished with 282, a stroke behind Don January who was third.

Before reaching the first tee, Nicklaus said he anticipated the

customary wild yells and exuberance displayed by Palmer's army of supporters. On the course, Nicklaus paid no heed to them. Just as he often drives his fishin gboat through storms and Atlantic Ocean currents, he maneuvered with skill and assurance through the tides of the contest today. Nicklaus was calm and serene throughout.

He had one new mechanical aide. That was a putter he recently acquired from his friend Deane Beman. The putter had belonged to Fred Mueller of Washington. The head of the putter had been sprayed with white paint. Nicklaus saw Beman using it last week, borrowed it and by agreement did not return it. He used it to sink three birdies in a row, starting at the third hole and two more at the seventh and eighth, before he closed the front nine with three-under-par 31.

A Borrowed Putter

With nine holes to go, Nicklaus had his four-stroke advantage. His total then was 241, while Palmer and Beman were 245, Casper 246, January and Fleckman 247 each. Beman, who was in the clubhouse when Nicklaus finished, wound up with 73 for 284.

Asked about the putter that Jack acquired from him, Beman said: "I just couldn't use it, but

I'm glad he could." This was Beman's first Open as a professional.

Nicklaus received the winner's check of $30,000, (double his 1962 prize) in the record purse of $175,000.

Nicklaus said he had two things in mind as he went to the 18th tee with a four-stroke lead.

The sky was overcast. In the distance, there was a faint peal of thunder. But Nicklaus was concerned with how he and Palmer stood.

"I had a four-shot lead and I figured if I made 7 and Arnold 3, we would tie. All I was trying to do was to win, so I decided to use an iron from the tee and play safe. I remembered that Dick Mayer made 7 here at this same hole to lose the 1954 Open after driving into the trees on the right. I wasn't on the right. I wasn't interested in breaking Hogan's record," Nicklaus said.

Well-Selected Irons

Then Nicklaus selected a No. 1 iron for his tee shot instead of a driver at this 542-yard dogleg, where the fairway dips down from the tee, crosses a wide creek and then continues uphill to the green. The fans were somewhat puzzled. Because Nicklaus is one of the game's longest drivers they expected him "to go for it" and hit a big drive. They of course, didn't know his thoughts.

Nicklaus's tee shot landed in a bad spot from which he was given a free lift. He played short of the water with a No. 8 iron, then slammed a No. 1 iron to the green to within 22 feet of the flagstick. Down went the putt for a birdie 4 and Nicklaus no longer worried about losing the Open.

It was the last of 29 important putts and the eighth one-putt green he had in his drive to the title.

Nicklaus said there was another thought uppermost in his mind. "If I could beat Arnie, I thought I could win," the new champion said. "Anytime we play against each other, I try to win."

Nicklaus, who is 6 feet and weighs 200 pounds, is one of four golfers (Gary Player, Gene Sarazen and Hogan are the others) who have won all four of the world's major crowns, the Open, the Professional Golfers' Association title, the Masters and the British Open. Nicklaus won the British Open last year and will defend in the championship, beginning July 13 at Liverpool. However, he is not a member of the 1967 United States Ryder Cup team slated to meet the British pros at Houston in October. He did not acquire sufficient points in the system followed on the pro tour to become eligible.

In 1963 when he won the P.G.A. crown, Nicklaus was not named to the team either because he had not been a pro the required five years. He joined the pros in 1962 after two triumphs in the National Amateur.

Earlier this season he won the Crosby tourney at Pebble Beach, Calif., but since then has not played as consistently as he wished. Last night after his round, he spent almost an hour in practice, trying to improve his putting.

Although he was charged with a two-stroke penalty for slow play along with Cary Middlecoff and Al Geiberger

during the Houston Champions tourney last month, the United States Golf Association officials here said. Nicklaus was "actually running between shots."

Nicklaus has earned $558,-685.76 playing golf which puts him third on the career money-winning list back of Palmer and Casper.

Hogan, who won the Open four times, finished with a 72 for 292. He said he doubted if he would compete in another tournament this year. He also said that if he had to qualify for next year's Open, he was uncertain if he would try.

While on the practice putting green before he started with Palmer, Nicklaus got his first glimpse of how the fans feel about Palmer. They held hand-made signs reading: "Go, Arnie, Go" and "Arnie's Army."

Earlier Nicklaus explained that the noise and excitement of the gallery was all "part of what goes with playing with Palmer."

Nicklaus and Palmer have often been paired together in events on the pro circuit. They have also been teammates in international competition. They won the Canada Cup in Paris in 1963, again in Hawaii in 1964, and last October in Tokyo. Besides that the Nicklaus-Palmer combination accounted for the national P.G.A. team laurels last December in Palm Beach, Fla.

But despite the fact they are friends and have the services of the same lawyer, Palmer has often said there was nothing he enjoyed more than beating Jack at golf. Today, however, Nicklaus didn't give him the chance to have much fun at his expense.

CARDS OF THE LEADERS
PAR FOR THE COURSE
Out ...444 344 443—34
In ....443 444 355—36—70—280
JACK NICKLAUS
Out ...453 235 335—31
In ....543 334 354—34—65—275
ARNIE PALMER
Out ...444 344 453—35
In ....443 444 344—34—69—279

June 19, 1967

Millions Watch a Masters Tie, Then Goalby Wins on an Error

By LINCOLN A. WERDEN
Special to The New York Times

AUGUSTA, Ga., April 14— Bob Goalby was declared the winner of the Masters golf tournament today after millions of television viewers and 30,000 enthusiastic spectators here believed that he and Roberto de Vicenzo had finished the 72-hole championship in a tie with scores of 277.

Officials discovered that de Vicenzo had signed an incorrect scorecard. De Vicenzo, the British Open champion from

Buenos Aires, had looked at the card before signing it but did not notice that a 4 had been marked for his score at the 17th hole instead of a birdie 3 that made him 11 under par.

"His total was 66 instead of 65 officially and that is 10 under par, not 11 under par, under the rules of golf," said Homer E. Shields, the tournament director. "That doesn't leave him in a tie with Goalby, who is 11 under par."

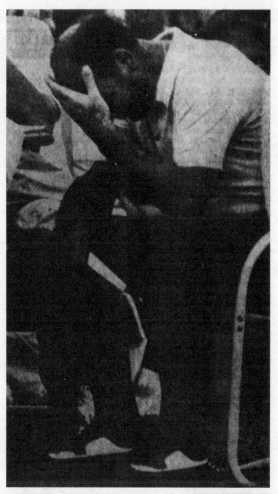

United Press International
Roberto de Vicenzo at scorer's table after he learned he had signed card with improper figure, causing loss.

The Official United States Golf Association Rule 38, Paragraph 3, specifies, "No alteration may be made on a card after the competitor has returned it to the committee. If the competitor returns a score for any hole lower than actually played, he shall be disqualified. A score higher than actually played must stand as returned."

De Vicenzo, known as "the happy fella" in the sport and celebrating his 45th birthday, was closeted at the time in a room for the telecast before he learned of his error and was asked to return to the scorer's table. According to the rules, each player has a "marker" who acts as a scorer for a competitor.

De Vicenzo's marker in this case was his pairing mate, Tommy Aaron. Aaron admitted he had incorrectly put a 4 down instead of a 3 but that when he discovered his mistake at the scorer's table alongside the 18th green of the Augusta National Golf Club, "Roberto had already left."

Aaron pointed out the mistake to one of the committeemen at the table, and when he checked

De Vicenzo's card he referred the matter to members of the rules committee.

Since a golfer and his marker are responsible for the hole-by-hole scoring and not the total, de Vicenzo did not see a 65 on the card, he said later, to remind him of his seven-under-par round.

Cheers for the Loser

The Argentine, advised of his mistake, then returned to the cottage room where the television broadcast was being conducted. En route, de Vicenzo said: "I just signed a wrong card. The other fellow put down a 4. It's my fault."

It was more than an hour later that de Vicenzo and Goalby, who had a closing 66, met newsmen. Looking drawn and tired, and with an interpreter beside him explaining some of the questions in Spanish, de Vicenzo answered questions, after receiving a rousing ovation from the reporters.

De Vicenzo declined to criticize Aaron, but said, "Tommy feels like I feel, very bad. I think the rule is hard." When someone asked what might have happened in Argentina under such conditions, de Vicenzo smiled and remarked, "We play friendly golf there."

Goalby said, "I'd be a liar if I didn't say I was happy to win. But I regret the way I had to win. I wish it could have been in a playoff tomorrow."

Clifford Roberts, the tournament chairman, had a facsimile of the official scorecard printed and distributed soon after the incident. "The legend of the Masters official scorecard," said the notice," reads, 'I have checked my score hole by hole.'"

In cases somewhat paralleling DeVicenzo's, Betsy Rawls won the women's United States open in 1957 at Mamaroneck, N. Y., after Jacqueline Pung, the apparent winner, signed a wrong card and was disqualified because the score at one hole was lower than the one she actually had.

Sanders Case Recalled

The most notable case on the pro circuit in recent years was the disqualification of Doug Sanders in the 1966 Pensacola open, but that was because he failed to attach his signature to his scorecard.

The ending today did not reflect the great golf that deVicenzo played. He began by holing out for an eagle 2 at the first hole of 400 yards and followed this with birdies at the next two holes. The overjoyed spectators, who found the easygoing Argentine to be a likable fellow, sang, "Happy Birthday, Roberto, happy birthday to you" after he holed out for the eagle 2.

Goalby had a 33, but deVicenzo needed only 31 on the front nine. Gary Player of South Africa, the 54-hole leader, began the round two strokes ahead of deVicenzo and one better than Goalby, who has been a runner-up in both the United States Open (1961) and the Professional Golfers' Association championship (1962).

Bert Yancey, with a 65 that included a 32 in, captured third

The Card and the Rule Involved

The section of Roberto de Vicenzo's card that shows a 4 on the 17th hole, where he actually scored a 3.

3. No Alteration of Scores

No alteration may be made on a card after the competitor has returned it to the Committee.

If the competitor return a score for any hole lower than actually played, he shall be disqualified.

A score higher than actually played must stand as returned.

Excerpt from the Rules of Golf: Rule 38, Paragraph 3

place at 279 and Bruce Devlin of Australia, the victim of an 8 during the second round, finished fourth at 280. Nicklaus, with a closing 67, tied Frank Beard, who stumbled into a 7 at the eighth hole, but posted a concluding 70, at 281.

Lionel Hebert, Jerry Pittman, Ray Floyd, Aaron and Player, who equaled the par of 72, were at 282. The first-round leader, Billy Casper, was at 285.

De Vicenzo captured the lead and the imagination of the crowd immediately and his gallery increased in proportions, hole after hole. It seemed he could do no wrong, for he sank a deuce at the tantalizing par-3 12th that has been an enigma to most of the field. He ran in a birdie at the 15th as the crowd hailed him and then he sank a five-footer for the birdie 3 at the 17th that should have been inscribed on his card, but wasn't.

Falters at the 18th

At the 18th, the Argentine's second shot was pulled into the crowd around the green. He chipped and two-putted for a bogey 5 that apparently gave him 277, as the scoreboards everywhere showed him then and hours later at 11 under par.

Goalby, the son of a retired truck driver in Belleville, Ill., who had never finished better than 25th in seven previous Masters, came on with a rush at three consecutive holes, the 13th through 15th.

He ran in an 8-foot birdie at the first of this trio and a 15-footer at the next. What he described as his best of the tournament came at the 520-yard 15th, when he slashed a No. 3 iron to within 8 feet of the flagstick. He downed the ensuing putt for an eagle 3 to be 12 under par.

But at the 17th he three-

putted for a bogey 5 and was 11 under par as de Vincenzo was finishing also at 11 under par. At the 18th, Goalby left himself a tricky 5-footer for his par, but he sank it for a 66. Tony Jacklin, the English professional, who finished at 288 in a tie for 22d place, commented, "Goalby has such a fine putting stroke he made that one look easy."

Goalby's share of the $172,475 purse was $20,000 and a title that has much value in fringe benefits. De Vicenzo's share was $15,000. De Vicenzo intends to remain in this country to continue on the pro circuit.

April 15, 1968

Description of Course

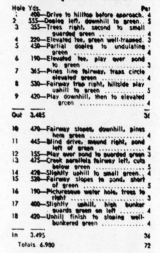

Hole	Yds.		Par
1	400	Drive to hilltop before approach.	4
2	555	Dogleg left, downhill to green.	5
3	355	Trees right, second to small guarded green.	4
4	220	Elevated tee, green well-trapped.	3
5	450	Partial dogleg to undulating green.	4
6	190	Elevated tee, play over pond to green.	3
7	365	Pines line fairway, traps circle elevated green.	4
8	530	Fairway trap right, hillside play uphill to green.	5
9	420	Play downhill, then to elevated green.	4
Out	3,485		36
10	470	Fairway slopes, downhill, pines hem green.	4
11	445	Blind drive, mound right, pond left of green.	4
12	155	Play over pond to guarded green.	3
13	475	Creek parallels fairway left, cuts below green.	4
14	420	Slightly uphill to small green.	4
15	520	Fairway slopes to pond, short of green.	5
16	190	Picturesque water hole, trees to right.	3
17	400	Slightly uphill, high bunker guards green on left.	4
18	420	Uphill finish to sloping well-bunkered green.	4
In	3,495		36
Totals	6,980		72

PAR FOR COURSE

Out	4	5	4	3	4	3	4	5	4	—	36
In	4	4	3	5	4	5	3	4	4	—36	72—72

BOB GOALBY

Out	4	5	4	3	3	2	4	4	4	—	33
In	4	4	3	4	3	3	5	4	33	—66	2·77

ROBERTO DE VICENZO

Out	2	4	3	3	4	3	4	4	4	—	31
xIn	4	4	2	5	4	2	3	4	5	—35	—66—278

xDe Vicenzo signed incorrect card. He actually had 3 on No. 17, but it was carded as 4.

Trevino Wins U.S. Open by 4 Shots With 69 for Record-Tying Total of 275

NICKLAUS FINISHES SECOND AFTER A 67

By LINCOLN A. WERDEN
Special to The New York Times

ROCHESTER, June 16—Lee Trevino, a rookie recruit on golf's professional circuit last year, won the United States Open championship today with a record-equaling total of 275.

The voluble 28-year old from Horizon City, Tex., who is of Mexican descent, scored a concluding 69 and beat Jack Nicklaus, the defending champion, by four strokes.

After receiving the victor's check of $30,000 from the $190,000 purse, Trevino conceded that he had never dreamed of being so successful. "I'm the happiest Mexican in the world right now. I never thought it would happen to me. But show me a guy who wouldn't feel great winning the United States Open."

Trevino did not continue in a serious vein for many minutes after his smashing triumph with a score that matched that of Nicklaus when he won last year at Baltusrol in Springfield, N. J.

Job on Par-3 Course

"I'll make a lot of money," predicted Trevino, who worked as a clerk on a par-3 Dallas public course before joining the Marines. "This makes me eligible for the World Series of golf and a $50,000 first prize, but it would be my luck to have them cancel that tournament. That would be like owning a pumpkin farm and they called off Halloween, wouldn't it?"

Although this was only Trevino's third bid for the big title, he outplayed an international field and rallied to overtake and pass Bert Yancey, the ex-West Pointer, who had set the pace for three successive rounds. With a 69, 68, 69 and his one-under-par performance today over the 6,962-yard Oak Hill Country Club course, Trevino became the first in 68 years of Open championships to play

LEG WORK: Lee Trevino sinking birdie on 12th hole

all four rounds under par.

Yancey and Trevino made this a head-to-head tussle until the last nine, and Yancey faded to 76 for 281 and third. Before starting, Yancey said it reminded him of a match-play event. But when the former Army golf captain required 38 to Trevino's one-over-par 36 going out, the ebullient Texan went one stroke ahead.

Palmer in Last Group

Thousands sat around the greens to catch a glimpse of the dark-haired Trevino with black hat, red shirt and socks and black slacks. But they also waited for Arnold Palmer, the golfing millionaire, who had an unusual role today. Palmer was in the last group, paired with two amateurs, Jack Lewis, a 20-year-old Wake Forest senior, and 18-year-old Jimmy Simons of Butler, Pa.

Palmer's 226 for 54 holes was responsible for his being listed at the end of today's field according to the United States Golf Association pairings.

The crowd wanted to see him, although Palmer was not pleased with his scoring and said so. He finished with a 75 for 301, only four places out of the cellar position, which went to young Simons, who had 310.

Nicklaus put together his best round, a 67, in an effort to

move closer to the top. He was in the twosome just ahead of Yancey and Trevino, who were able to watch Nicklaus and Charles Coody putting as they waited on the fairways repeatedly.

Bobby Nichols, with a 69, was fourth at 282 while Steve Spray and Don Bies had 284's. Bob Charles and Jerry Pittman were at 285 and Sam Snead, the 56-year-old campaigner, and Billy Casper, the pretournament favorite, were in the group at 286.

The first indication that Trevino might break through came at the third hole. At this par 3, Yancey hooked his shot close to a tree and holed out with a bogey 4. The Texan's 3 put them on an even basis, erasing Yancey's one-stroke advantage beginning the round.

Two holes later Trevino went one ahead as Yancey was bunkered and carded a bogey 4. But he did not hold the advantage long. Yancey drew even again with a birdie 3 at the sixth.

Yancey took a bogey 5 after being bunkered at the ninth and Trevino's 4 there gave him a one-stroke lead that he subsequently increased steadily. Trevino had a 36 out, Yancey a 38 and Nicklaus, attempting a comeback, took only 33.

As his friends yelled encouragement, Trevino added a

stroke a hole against Yancey over the next four. Two of these were pars, but he ran in a 35-footer for a deuce at the 11th and one of 22 feet for a birdie 3 at the 12th.

Only at one hole after that did Yancey outscore Trevino. That was at the 14th when he holed a 2-footer for a 3 to his rival's 4.

Yancey, however, lost ground when he three-putted at the 16th for a bogey 5 to the Texan's 4. At the final hole, Yancey was bunkered for another bogey, but Trevino, in the rough twice, salvaged a par 4 on a 4-foot putt.

The new champion, flushed with success, said he had no contracts with manufacturers of golf equipment. He is now part owner of the Horizon Hills Country Club, part of a housing development outside El Paso. "There'll be free booze there until midnight," he announced. "I'm a little nervous," he conceded later.

"I didn't telephone my wife. She knows about it by now from watching television. She'll get my check by Thursday. If I don't mail it, I'll hear about it. I expect to play in the Canadian open next week and I intend to play golf as long as I can until I'm a hundred years old."

As he came off the 13th green, he turned to Joseph C. Dey Jr., executive director of

the U.S.G.A., who was accompanying him, and remarked, "I'm trying to get a big enough lead, so I won't choke."

Others who have scored their first tournament victory in the Open where Nicklaus in 1962 and Jack Fleck in 1955.

Trevino, who used a broomstick as his first golf club and was especially adept against opponents when he played with a soft-drink bottle while they used standard clubs on the par-3 course where he was employed, had finished second in Houston and Atlanta on the tour this year.

He said his grandfather a grave-digger, was responsible for rearing him. One of his habits on the pro tour has been to skip rope in his motel room to keep in trim. "But I didn't do that this week, I just practiced hitting golf balls," he said.

CARDS OF THE LEADERS

PAR FOR THE COURSE

Out	4 4 3 5 3 4 4 4—35	
In	4 3 4 5 4 3 4 4 4—35—70	

LEE TREVINO

Out	5 4 3 5 3 4 4 4—36
In	4 2 3 5 4 3 4 4 4—33—69

JACK NICKLAUS

Out	4 4 2 4 3 4 4 4—33
In	4 3 4 5 3 3 4 4 4—34—67

BERT YANCEY

Out	5 4 4 5 4 3 4 4 5—38
In	5 3 4 6 3 3 5 4 5—38—76

June 17, 1968

Golf's No. 1 Extrovert
Lee Buck Trevino

THE 28-year-old Mexican-American who pocketed $30,000 yesterday for his triumph in the United States Open golf tournament at Rochester is an aggressive, amiable, talkative, emotional, confident ex-marine who now, presumably, considers himself a Spaniard. "You never see a rich Mexican," Lee Trevino said earlier this week. "If you have money, you're a Spaniard." In the last year, Lee Buck Trevino has epitomized the old American success story. As a $30-a-week assistant pro at the Horizon Hills Country Club near El Paso, Tex., he made his debut on the professional tour in the 1967 Open at Baltusrol in Springfield, N. J.

Man In the News

"If I hadn't won any money, I'd have whipped back home," Trevino said then after winning $6,000 for his fifth-place finish.

Since Baltusrol, the muscular, smiling Trevino has been one of the consistent moneymakers on the pro tour, although yesterday's victory was his first. His official

career earnings are now $110,899.85.

But Trevino's triumph in the Open will further pad his bank account with rich fees for endorsements, appearances and any personal promotions he may care to make.

"It means a whole bunch of money," he said when asked what the victory meant.

The son of Mexican-American peasants near Dallas, Trevino found his first golf club in a field of hay at the age of 6. He set up his own two-hole course in a pasture and proceeded to teach himself the sport.

His self-instruction is evident even today to golfing purists who flinch while watching his flat swing, which many think would be more effective in the National Baseball League than on a golf course.

"I have a lot of confidence in my game, even though I have a bad swing," Trevino said the other day in an admission rare among the golfing fraternity.

Trevino's first serious golfing was undertaken during his service with the marines on Okinawa.

"I didn't do anything but

play golf with the colonels," he said. "That's when I really learned to play. I started out as a private, but after beating the colonels a few times, I rose to sergeant."

Following his discharge, Trevino operated a pitch-and-putt course and, to pick up extra money, won bets from customers by playing the game with a large soft-drink bottle.

"I wrapped the bottle with adhesive tape and made a good hitting surface," he explained. "I got to the point where I could drive a ball 150 yards with the bottle and could hit a tree from that distance almost every time. I putted with the bottle as I would with a cue stick. I

could shoot around 56 or 58 and I could win most of my bets."

Later, Trevino got a job as assistant pro to Don Whittington at the Horizon Hills course and further shaped his game to accommodate the sand-filled winds that swept the scrubby, heat-baked fairways. Often playing with scuba - diver goggles, he learned to stroke the ball low, out of the gale-like gusts.

His wife, Claudia, has been the family financial administrator since he married her while running the pitch-and-putt course. Their family includes a daughter, Lesley, who is 3, and two dogs.

In his one year on the pro

tour, the 5-foot-10-inch, 185-pound Trevino has charmed the galleries with his talkative exuberance, his smiling, determined stride and his ever-present lucky coin to which he attributes his good fortune.

His fans are known around the circuit as "Lee's Fleas" as opposed to "Arnie's Army," the worshiping horde that follows Arnold Palmer.

Observers on the pro tour think that the colorful Trevino may eventually replace Palmer as the idol of the galleries.

If so, his fans, who shout "Ole!" at each good shot, may be in for a long, happy reign.

"My goal is to play as good as I can for as long as I can,"

he said yesterday. "I'm going to keep practicing and playing until I get about 100 years old."

And, like the late "Champagne" Tony Lema, Trevino is a free-spending happy-go-lucky winner who said, "The booze will be free all night tonight at the Horizon Hills Country Club," where several hundred members watched the Open on five television sets.

His wife's bookkeeping may also grow more complex. Speaking of the $30,000 prize, he said. "My wife will let me keep $300."

June 17, 1968

The Jones* Idea
Of a Golf Course

*That's Robert Trent Jones. He's a golf architect. He likes nightmares

By LEONARD SHECTER

"While he holds professional golfers in awe and boundless admiration, Jones delights in constructing courses that, they say, test their sanity as well as their golf." Here, the world's foremost designer of golf courses—he has laid out over 360 — surveys construction of Panther Valley at Allamuchy, N. J.

ROBERT TRENT JONES has built golf courses on every continent except Australia and Antarctica and likes to say that the sun never sets on Robert Trent Jones courses. ("Are you sure," he asks querulously, "that Antarctica is a continent?") But the important thing about Robert Trent Jones is that he is, at bottom, more golfer than golf architect, and if there is one place his enormous success is rooted it's right there.

You can tell Robert Trent Jones is a golfer because when an organization calling itself the United States Duffers Association proposed the legalization of certain popular forms of cheating—improving one's lie on the fairway, lifting balls without penalty out of divots or from footprints in sand traps—he bristled like a short, chubby porcupine and put down the proposal as being in keeping only with the license and immorality of our times. "It is also," he added stiffly, "bad for the game." As for the proposal of oldtimer Gene Sarazen that the cup be doubled in size to diminish the importance of putting, Jones sneers: "He's been saying that for 30 years. If it was a good idea it would have been adopted by now."

You can tell Robert Trent Jones is a golfer because he tells long golf jokes that are funny only to other golfers, an intense and swiftly multiplying breed that doesn't really think there is anything funny about the game. One of his stories goes like this:

A golfer died and applied for admission to heaven. The book was examined and St. Peter said that the poor fellow was indeed eligible for admission but that there was an asterisk next to his name indicating blasphemy and that this needed to be explained.

"Well, it happened this way," the supplicant said. "I was playing this tough par-four and got off the best drive of my life, 240 yards right down the middle. When I got to the ball, though, it was sitting in the deepest divot you ever saw."

"So that's when it happened," St. Peter said.

"No, that's not when it happened. I took out my three-wood and, despite the divot, swung perfectly and hit the greatest fairway shot you ever saw. Two hundred yards, straight as a string, headed precisely for the pin. Just as the ball was rolling up the apron of the green I could see it hit a pebble and kick off to the right,

LEONARD SHECTER is a contributor to magazines and a sports commentator for Westinghouse Broadcasting Company.

smack into the deepest trap in America."

"That's when it happened," St. Peter said.

"No, that's not when it happened. I said to myself, 'Well, I'll never get it out of there.' But I gave it a try. I took my sand wedge and, aiming well behind the ball, swung as hard as I could. What a blast! The whole world was sand. And when I opened my eyes, I looked up and there was the ball, a foot and a half from the cup."

Said St. Peter: "I'll be goddamned. You missed the putt."

You can tell Robert Trent Jones is a golfer because, while he holds professional golfers in awe and boundless admiration, he delights in constructing courses and holes that, they say, test their sanity as well as their golf. Sarazen, only half kidding, complains: "Jones must have a permanent crick in his neck. Every time he walks down a fairway he's looking behind him to see how he can make the hole longer."

Says Ken Harrelson of the Boston Red Sox, who regularly wins the baseball players' annual tournament and regularly plays against the pros —making friendly bets all the way: "I hate the S.O.B. There's a hole at the Dorado in Puerto Rico where he put a trap in the middle of the damn fairway. They told me I couldn't reach it, but I hit the best drive of my life—280 yards—and wound up right in that #@$%&+ trap. Cost me $30."

As a group, professional golfers refused ever again to set foot on Jones's Spyglass Hill course in Pebble Beach, Calif.—the site of the annual Bing Crosby tournament — unless Jones modified the course and made it easier. He did, making the fifth green larger and softening some of the severe contours on the others. The pros complained that the contours had made it possible to roll 30 feet past the cup on a 10-foot putt.

Before the $100,000 Greater New Orleans Open at the posh Lakewood Country Club recently, an easy 530-yard, par-five hole which had seen eight eagles (two under par) scored on it the previous year was change into a difficult 470-yard par-four. Not only was the hole now a drive and a long iron, but the hitting area of the fairway was narrow and protected by a deep sand trap. The pros threatened revolt. Said Jack Nicklaus, crown prince if not king of the professional golfing world and himself the designer of two or three courses each year: "A golf architect wouldn't have designed a hole that way." To which Robert Trent Jones, chuckling evilly, replied, "Oh, yes I would." Nicklaus insists that he would not. "Who do you build a golf course for?"

he demands. "Club members," he answers, "people who shoot between 82 and 100."

JONES, of course, contends that he understands this as well as anybody, perhaps better than most. On a recent tour of two golf courses he is building and one he is remodeling in the New York area—Panther Valley at Allamuchy, N. J.; the Fairview Country Club in Connecticut, and the Montauk Golf Club on Long Island— Jones, a small, bustling man with a comfortable paunch befitting his age (62) and wealth (uncounted), talked about his basic philosophy of building courses that will be used by both pros and weekend golfers. (Nicklaus would not discuss philosophy. He is under contract, he said, to do it elsewhere—for money.)

The Jones philosophy can be stated most succinctly this way: A hard par, an easy bogey (one stroke over par). The pros would prefer a hard birdie (one under par) and an easy par. It's a most important distinction.

"Look at it this way," Jones said, sitting in the back of his Mercury while Roger Rulewich, a young engineer on his staff, drove. "What with livelier golf balls, better clubs and better athletes playing golf, the pros have increased their average drive in the last 20 years by 20 to 25 yards. Dead level, with no wind, Jack Nicklaus will average 270, 280 yards. He plays a 440-yard par-four with a drive and an eight-iron. In the mid-twenties it would have taken the great players two wood shots. Now they're talking about an aluminum shaft that will make it possible to drive a ball 10 per cent farther. Well, if Nicklaus drove 10 per cent farther he'd be driving over 300 yards. That would make a 350-yard hole a drive and a kick.

"Don't get me wrong. I understand how the pros feel. They're playing 50 tournaments a year, and every winning purse is worth $20,000 to $30,000, with other prizes grading down from there. So one missed putt or one bad hole might make a difference of $5,000 to the player. As a result they don't like to play courses that are difficult. Out of the 50 tournaments, probably only about five — the Open, the P.G.A., the Masters, the Colonial and one or two others—are played on courses of championship caliber. Even if they have a 7,100 - yard course they're unlikely to play it that long. They probably play it at 6,500 yards. And they're not inclined to put the pins in the most difficult positions. This is because of the complete psychological shock to the player when, all of a

Three types of golf courses—Defined by an expert

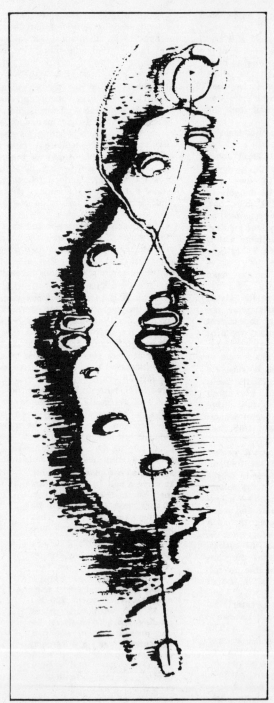

THE PENAL—Marked by numerous traps, this course, says Jones, is easily driven by the better golfer but a serious hazard to the duffer; every bad shot is severely penalized. The only safe route is the "straight and narrow," and the green is often a small target nearly surrounded by deep traps, some of them hidden from view. The golfer must hit to an "island" between traps on the fairway, then to the "island" green.

THE HEROIC—A style still used in modified form on individual holes but once much more popular. It offers a big reward for the long shot (dotted line) but promises almost certain disaster if the shot is not perfectly executed. A safer alternative (solid line) is usually available, but often at the expense of an extra stroke. To get in position for a par, the player must take his chance on the long shot.

THE STRATEGIC—Traps near the fairway force the "safe" hitter to the left (solid line), but then he must face traps near the green. The more daring golfer keeps his drive (dotted line) to the right, where the fairway is elevated. He takes less chance of catching a trap near the green and he has a better target. Though bad shots are not severely punished, the golfer must play position to score well.

sudden, he misses a shot and he realizes those thousands of dollars are flying away from him and he feels as though he's been kicked in the stomach.

"As a result, tournament directors try to alleviate these unfortunate calamities and the pro has come to accept that. So, for the most part, these tournaments are putting contests. I don't approve, but I understand."

WHAT Jones sets out to do, especially when he's called in to toughen up a course for the Open or the P.G.A., which he often is, is extract from the professional his best game. He puts it this way: "I think the best golfer should win. Any week there are probably 30 golfers who are *capable* of winning it. They just have to put all their shots together just right. Our feeling is that if the player who has put together the most shots is the best for those four rounds, the golf course should be sufficiently strong, the shot *values* sufficiently high, so that that player will win the tournament. We don't want somebody to win who's spraying his shots over in the next fairway, then knocking a wedge over a tree or two to the green and ramming in a putt for a birdie, scoring a 65 when he would have scored a 75 if the proper penalties had been exacted."

That's why Jones often lays banks of traps to the left of his fairways 230 to 270 yards out—the hitting area of most professionals. Pros have a tendency to hook, to the left. Duffers and club players have a tendency to slice, to the right.

With his penalty theory in mind, Jones developed the extra-long tee, which is now his trademark and in use by every other golf architect. (Jones first used the long tees right after the war in building Peachtree in Atlanta with golfing great Robert Tyre (Bobby) Jones, who is no relation but sufficiently famous for Robert Trent Jones to tell people to call him Trent). The tees, often 100 yards in length, can be played from in front, which turns the course into a pussycat friendly to both women and elderly club members who have lost some pazzaz. Played halfway back on the tees, the course becomes a decent test for the member with a handicap of 10 or so. When the very back tees are used and the pins are placed diabolically enough on the

green, the course can be turned into a nightmare, even for a pro. Jones rather likes nightmares.

Said Ben Hogan to Jones's wife after winning the Open at Oakland Hills, near Detroit, in 1951: "If your husband had to play this course for a living he'd be in the poorhouse." Yet four years later, Jones points out with chest-puffing pride, at a luncheon in Dallas, Hogan said to Jones: "You know, if I played more of your courses, I'd probably be the only man in history to win *five* Open championships."

The point Hogan, the winner of four Opens, was making was that he realized his kind of controlled swing could deliver the shot values Robert Trent Jones courses demand.

While Jones is most widely known for his tough courses, he is not incapable of designing easy ones. "We just built a course in California called Birnam Wood," he says. "It was meant for use by 50-year-old or 55-year-old men. It's 6,200 yards from the back tees, probably 5,200 from the front. And people say it's a fun course to play.

"I've also been experimenting with a new theory. Five par-threes [as opposed to the usual four], five par-fives [again as opposed to the usual four] and the rest par-fours. Keep them all easy. The par may be 72, but people who score 100 on other courses will score 85 to 90 on this one. It will make everybody a pro for the day."

NO matter what the pros say, everybody else seems to love Robert Trent Jones courses. Robert Trent Jones, Inc. — offices in Montclair, N. J.; Fort Lauderdale, Fla.; Palo Alto, Calif., and Leeds, England — builds 12 to 15 courses a year throughout the world. From Mauna Kea in Hawaii, where Jones had to grind up lava to act as a base for his fairways, to Sardinia, where he is building a course for the Aga Khan, to Rabat, where the King of Morocco wants to build a course to attract tourists, 360 R. T. J. golf courses stand as monuments to wealthy leisure. A golf course costs $350,000 to $650,000 to build, depending on the difficulty of the terrain (Jones is building one now in Beverly Hills which will run to a million dollars because he had to move a couple of mountains), and Jones's fee is 10 per cent of the cost plus $3,000 to $5,000 to cover a design fee and expenses.

The fact that this is a lucrative profession has attracted a lot of people to it, many of them, unfortunately, as qualified as the old-school golf architect of Scotland, who was anybody with 18 pegs and a free Sunday afternoon. ("Well, this would be a good place for the first green, MacPherson, wouldn't it?" Peg. "And we'll put the second green here." Peg.)

"Anybody with $27 can put an ad in Golf magazine and call himself a golf architect," Jones complains. "There are no standards or licenses required."

In an effort to set some standards and give themselves some standing, Jones and 34 other top golf architects have banded together to form the American Society of Golf Course Architects. Jones will heartily recommend any of them as qualified. None of them, however, attempt to operate on Jones's scale.

To conduct his widespread business, Jones has built a staff of 35 people, including civil engineers, construction engineers, landscape architects, agronomists, draftsmen and a lawyer and an accountant. He pays them well, and through the years a fierce loyalty has been built up. Only one of his employes, a landscape architect named Frank Duane, ever moved down the street to set up his own shop.

There are, Jones says, three basic types of golf course. He calls them the penal, the strategic and the heroic. "In the penal school of architecture," he says, "like Pine Valley, which was built on a sandy wasteland, you hit from the tee to an island fairway surrounded by sand. Then you hit from the island fairway to an island green. It's a penal course because you are severely penalized for any shot you miss. This is hell on high-handicap golfers.

"On the other extreme there's the strategic course, like Augusta National. This is a sort of park-like school of architecture. There is a lot of rough, the fairways are wide and you're not punished for a bad shot. On the other hand, you've got to play position to get the most out of the course.

"In the heroic school of architecture, like Merion, there are alternate routes. There is an easy shot for the weekend player. But in order to get into position for a par or birdie, you have to carry the hazard off the tee.

"We use all three philosophies and we mix them up. We're constantly striving not to get into a rut."

ROBERT TRENT JONES was born in 1906 in Ince, England, the only child of Welsh parents. His father, an engineer, came to this country when Jones was 4 and worked for the New York Central in Rochester.

At 16 and 120 pounds, Jones was a scratch, or par-shooting, golfer (he can still go around one of his own difficult courses in 80). But at a remarkably early age he developed what some people insist is golfers' disease—ulcers—and realized that, as much as he loved the game, he could never make a living playing it.

Not far from where he lived, however, Donald Ross, a well-known golf architect of the time (he built the famous course at Pinehurst, N. C.), was constructing a golf course. Jones watched the process and decided that this was what he wanted to do for a living. He set about learning his profession methodically, attacking the problem the way a golfer corrects a flaw in his swing.

He went to Cornell and proposed that he be allowed to take a conglomerate of courses that crossed the usual university boundaries. With the permission of an astonished dean of admissions, Jones attended the College of Agriculture to study agronomy, horticulture and land drainage; the College of Engineering to study surveying and engineering; the College of Architecture to study landscape architecture, and the College of Arts to study public speaking, journalism and chemistry. There is no record of his having studied salesmanship, but Jack Nicklaus says he is tops. ("He can jet into an airport," Nicklaus says, "and sell a golf course to a country-club committee by scribbling on the back of an old napkin in the cocktail lounge.") After his tour of Cornell, Jones dashed off to an art school in Rochester and studied sketching. To this day he makes lovely sketches of his greens and the traps around them. Obviously, golfdom's only Renaissance man.

Jones designed his first course in 1929 with Stanley Thompson, a Canadian architect. "It was just after the stock-market crash," he recalls, "but the Depression hadn't set in yet. Thompson and I did about three courses together, but they all went broke and we received practically no fee."

AFTER that, things got better. And pretty soon Jones was spending a good part of his life on airplanes. A large calendar on the wall of his Montclair office showed recently that he was scheduled to visit South Africa, Sardinia, Morocco and Japan in quick order. An accident in Hawaii, where he stepped out of a Jeep that was still rolling and cracked a bone in his ankle, has slowed him down temporarily, but he estimates that he flies 300,000 miles a year and spends 250 days away from Montclair. "I try to come home weekends," he says.

Home for Jones is a pleasant, rambling Tudor house in Montclair, his wife's hometown. The garage has been turned into a cluttered office and agronomist Robert Trent Jones has bare spots on his lawn. The only conspicuous luxury in the house is a basement gymnasium containing an Exercycle, a complicated machine that is capable of giving its owner a sexy back rub, and what Jones calls "my Japanese bath," a walk-down-into tub four and a half feet deep with a device that shoots a soothing stream of hot water. "It's amazing how it relaxes you before you go to sleep," Jones says.

Jones takes quiet but obvious pride in his comfortable, unpretentious home, just as he takes pride in his golf courses, which are anything but comforting or unpretentious. He will not pick the courses he's built that please him most ("Golf courses are like children. I have no favorites"), but it is clear that he has a special feeling for Spyglass Hill, where each hole is named after a character in "Treasure Island." He admits to counting it one of his most photogenic courses, but then immediately lists Mauna Kea; Broadmoor, in Colorado Springs; Incline Village, at Lake Tahoe, and Dorado Beach as being equally attractive. He modestly refuses to take credit for their beauty, although he talks constantly about the artistic value of holes, the balance of masses, how making a golf course is like painting a picture and how he sometimes puts a trap in because it looks as though it belongs there. "These courses are beautiful," he says, "because nature was very generous."

Where nature has not been generous, Robert Trent Jones uses his sketchbook. He likes to think, he says, that his business is making silk purses out of sows' ears. This is a proposition that can be challenged on several grounds. What does it profit mankind for Robert Trent Jones to take a bulldozer into 170 acres of beautiful woods and hack down enough trees to make 18 fairways and a practice tee? And what does it profit mankind to take 170 acres of land that could be made into a park to be used by thousands daily and turn them into a golf course that can be used by only 250 people a day?

To this argument Jones bobs his head, smiles his friendly smile and shrugs his tweedy shoulders. "It's true," he says. "A couple of holes on one of the courses we built were used as a ski slope in the winter. Five or six thousand a day skied there. The course will accomodate only 250 a day for golf.

"However, you can get 350 on some of the public courses we've built. No rough, wide-open greens and duplicate par-three holes to speed play. I have another idea, to light the last four or five holes of a course so that golfers can go out at five or six in the evening and still play 18 holes. That would increase play considerably, too.

"As for the value of making a golf course out of woodland—well, a lot of it is woodland that isn't any good. I think my golf courses improve on nature. In Rochester we took an area which was mostly wet and quicksand and made it into a beautiful golf course. Two papers in Rochester wrote laudatory articles about it." He nodded with satisfaction. "Anyway," he added, "I never knock down a tree unless I absolutely have to."

NOT long after saying this, Jones was inspecting one of his new fairways at Panther Valley. He pointed out a bog area that was being turned into a pretty pond and commented: "We'll have beautiful features instead of skunk cabbage." This is the kind of project with which Jones has become increasingly involved in recent years. Basically, it is a housing development designed around a golf course. Without the course, all you have is housing too far from civilization to be worth inhabiting. Panther Valley is a $60-million joint venture of Frank

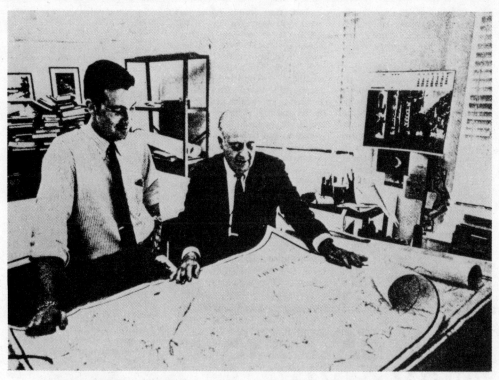

HOME COURSE—Jones going over plans with an aide in his Montclair, N. J., office —a rare sight since his work keeps him on the move around the globe 250 days a year.

The Ego Trap

Robert Trent Jones golf courses are designed for a specifically American clientele. British "links" are much more difficult; the rough is left alone to become a tangled jungle and bad shots are penalized ferociously. In addition, British courses follow natural land contours, which means that on one shot the ball will be well above the golfer's feet, on another well below. This does not make par-breaking easy.

"If we were to build a course like that," Jones says, "the next day the greens committee would decide to level the fairways. The American wants to excel. He is more apt to adapt his playing field to where his ego can be satisfied by excelling than to accept a challenge. The British golfer does not consider a bogey a failure. The American golfer does."
—L. S.

H. Taylor and Sons of East Orange, N. J., and the Travelers Insurance Company of Hartford. It's the sort of thing that Jones is doing more and more, to his own considerable profit.

When he was called upon to redesign the course at Montauk he recommended that 30 acres in the center be turned into golf villas that would not only pay for remodeling the course but turn a profit as well. He is now involved in several such golf course-real estate ventures in Europe. The spread of American culture goes on apace.

Construction costs at Panther Valley skyrocketed because of the rocky terrain. (Allamuchy, the name of the nearest town, is an Indian word for land of rock.) Much blasting had to be done at a cost of some $100,000, then heavy spring rains washed away $75,000 worth of contouring. The course will cost more than $650,000, but the developers are certain it will be worth it. (Of course they have a lot of money. They even have a set of expensive Maas Rowe electric chimes in the clubhouse which bounce "Getting to Know You" off nearby mountains. The first time a member is startled by them into missing a putt they will no doubt be retired to the

ladies' locker room.)

JONES recalls with fondness an incident while he was building a course for I.B.M. near Poughkeepsie. Thomas J. Watson, the president of the company, and his entourage accompanied Jones on a walking tour of the proposed course. Watson suggested, at one point, that a steep hill could be made into a beautiful uphill hole. "Let's walk up," Jones suggested. By the time they got to the top Watson had changed his mind.

Obviously Jones has had to learn to be a diplomat as well as a golf architect. "If you have 600 members you have 600 architects," he says. "Each one wants to adapt the course to his own personal problems. Say I'm a hooker and there's a pond to the left. I say take it out. If I'm a slicer I want to leave the pond alone but take out the trap to the right. Other golfers have favorite holes. When I'm remodeling a course certain of them will say, 'Don't you dare change that hole. I always score well on it.' It isn't until you come up with the final thing and they see what kind of golf course they have that they stop griping."

To reach the Montauk course Jones hires a pilot and

a single-engine airplane at the Westchester Airport. As the plane came in for a landing over menacing telephone wires at the tiny Montauk airport recently, Jones gleefully pointed out the dune formations along the ocean beach. "You can learn a lot about building traps looking at dunes like that," he said. There was a gleam of jealousy in his eye as he examined nature's rugged handiwork.

The Montauk course could have been constructed as a natural seaside links in the British mode, but Jones did not want it that wild. "We're taking out the heather and the gorse," he said with a laugh. He is particularly proud of the par-three 12th hole there, which, he says, will be "one of the great par-threes in the world."

It has a high tee from which the golfer can see the Atlantic Ocean, Block Island Sound and Carl Fisher's boarded-up white elephant, Montauk Manor. In front of the tee the ground breaks sharply down and then the well-trapped green rises abruptly to a level as high as the tee. It's like aiming from one frying pan to another over the fire. One could use anything from a nine-iron to a two-iron on this hole, depending on the placement of the tee markers and the di-

rection and velocity of the wind. Each position on the long tee, however, presents a different problem of getting over the traps. "I don't care what club you use," Jones said, "it's an interesting shot. It just shows you can make beautiful golf holes even if nature hasn't been good to you." As he limped around the tee, the wind tousling his sparse hair, Jones muttered, "Beautiful, just beautiful." No artist could have been more proud of his work.

While a young designer like Nicklaus insists upon having his course look as "natural" as possible, Jones doesn't mind bulldozing where he thinks nature needs some help. "A good hole has got to have trapping or something else to make it interesting," Jones says. "If you don't trap a green well you have to elevate it or plateau it or you have a listless golf hole. That's the pattern at Augusta—not many traps, but well-elevated greens. If you miss the shot to an elevated green the ball will run away from the pin; to get down in one becomes more difficult. Or on the green itself, the farther you are away from the pin, the more difficult it becomes to get down in two."

THE first step in building a golf course is to make topographic maps from terrain profiles plotted in a helicopter. Next, Jones or one of his staff walks over the ground, making preliminary sketches of the holes. ("Some builders make their mistakes with bulldozers," Jones says. "We make ours with a pencil. They can be erased.") The course is then laid out carefully on contour maps, and contractors are asked to follow the maps.

The hiring of contractors is also Jones's job. "Earth moving, drainage and watering systems are mechanical phases," he says. "Any contractor can do it. We just ask for bids. But the art work

needs training and experience. Sometimes we have to change operators several times because they are not esthetically adaptable."

One of the problems that Jones runs into with his 10 per cent fee is that it does not appear to be to his advantage to keep costs down. "That's foolish," Jones says. "If you are not ethical you won't be in business very long. But if somebody insists on a flat fee, we give them our estimate of the cost and charge a fee based on that."

IN the end, Jones has few unsatisfied customers. When he returns to a course he has built he is seldom called anything but "Mr. Jones." The look people wear when they talk to him is one of respect, if not awe.

And the Jones name is secure in golf for years to come. It is estimated that there are 10,000 golf courses and 10 million golfers in the U.S. today and that these numbers will double in the next 10 years. In other countries golf is growing even more rapidly. The world is going to need a lot of golf courses, and if Jones ever retires—a prospect he is not even considering at this point — his sons will carry on. Robert Trent Jr. is running the Palo Alto office, and Rees Lee is working in the Montclair office. At that rate, the Jones empire will last longer than Britain's. The sun may *never* set on Jones family golf courses. ∎

July 7, 1968

Gary scrambled. He had his birdie on that sixth hole and he was around the turn in 36. He lost a shot on the 10th when he found the rough and a chip slipped 12 feet past the hole. Nicklaus had missed a putt from eight feet on the eighth, but was still just a stroke behind. So was Charles.

Player Breaks It Up

They were locked in a struggle until Gary broke it up with that soaring No. 3 wood shot on the 14th. A huge crowd massed in bleachers alongside the green left out a wild yell as the ball hit the green and rolled stone dead near the flag.

'It was the first I knew," said Player. "The hole is blind, but I could tell by the noise I was awfully close."

Nicklaus had his birdie 4. On those last four holes, Nicklaus turned on the power. He hit four unbelievable shots of enormous distance and accuracy from the tee.

Player stuck it out. A great No. 6 iron out of deep grass and an eight-foot putt saved the 4 at the 15th, but a drive into the bunker and a putt that stopped on the lip from six feet out cost him a stroke on the 16th, where Charles was three strokes behind and Nicklaus two.

Nicklaus hit a drive on the 17th that nearly burst the ball. It cleared the Barry Burn and rolled to a stop 350 yards from the tee. Player was 100 yards or so behind, playing it safely. Both men had 4's, though, as Gary struck a fine pitch to the edge and rolled up to inches from 40 feet.

Nicklaus's Last Stab

Nicklaus made a last stab. The 18th is almost impossible to reach in two with an east wind blowing. He got there with a No. 1 iron on his second, which landed just off line in the trap.

Player, deep in rough, skimmed a No. 4 iron over a bunker and then hit a marvelous pitch to the heart of the green. Player had done it. He putted up to the lip for a certain par and sprinted after the ball in ecstasy.

He won the Open nine years ago at Muirfield. And he has taken them all—the Masters, the United States Open, the Professional Golfers' Association title. But this was his first big one in four years and he was hungry for it.

"It's the best he ever played," he said, "on the hardest course there is."

An eight-year-old putter he bought in Japan gets the credit.

"I threw that ping putter away," he said, "the one I borrowed from Nicklaus."

Player is going to quit the circuit for a while.

"On Monday I'll be riding a horse on my farm in South Africa thinking about all those guys with their four-footers," he said. "I haven't been home for months."

GARY PLAYER WINS BRITISH OPEN

EAGLE CLINCHES IT

Brilliant Shot Marks Player's 2-Stroke Victory on 73-289

By FRED TUPPER
Special to The New York Times

CARNOUSTIE, Scotland, July 13—Gary Player won the British Open golf championship today for the second time. With four men in the running and the championship trembling in the balance down the long homestretch, Player won it with one spectacular shot.

On the par-5, 480-yard 14th, a blind hole guarded by the dreaded "Spectacles" bunkers, the little South African rifled a No. 3 wood shot from 180 yards out to less than a yard from the cup. He tapped it in for an eagle 3 and a two-stroke lead he never lost as he finished with a 73 for a four-round total of 289.

Tied for second at 291 were Jack Nicklaus and Bob Charles of New Zealand. Billy Casper, who led the field by four shots at the halfway mark, collapsed with a 78 and finished fourth on 292.

Tied for fifth at 295 were

Neil Coles and Brian Barnes, who had 71's, and Gay Brewer, the 1967 Masters winner, who had bogeys on the last four holes after having been in the thick of the fight.

Al Balding of Canada had 296 and Arnold Palmer, the champion in 1961 and 1962, and Roberto De Vincenzo of Argentina, the defender, had 297.

The title was up for grabs this morning. Casper began with a stroke margin over Charles, who was a stroke ahead of player. Nicklaus was four strokes behind at 218. Yet none could make a par 72 today on what Player called "the toughest course in the world," the 7,252-yard, par-72 Carnoustie layout.

A knifing east wind that numbed the fingers and stung the eyes (the temperature was in the high 50's) added distance to the holes on the back nine and the knobs, narrow fairways, ragged roughs and bunkers placed in the middle of the fairways made the challenge tremendous.

For years the golf connoisseurs have talked with awe of Hogan shot 282 here, each "Hogan's Open." In 1953, Ben round better than the one before. Halfway through this one, Casper was at 140 and his second-round 68 was the same as

Hogan's last round. Billy's putting touch went awry yesterday and today his whole game disintegrated as he reached the turn in 40.

Charles Gets a Big 6

Charles was in contention until the third hole, when he got tangled in the bunkers for a 6. The pencil-slim New Zealander never got those shots back, although he and Casper were still a stroke off the pace until Player broke clear with that eagle.

Nicklaus had the best chance. He was level with par and a stroke behind Player when Gary's No. 4 iron to the fifth caught the green edge and lay buried in the deep grass, setting up a bogey 5. Jack had been playing beautifully from tee to green, but the poor putting that has plagued him all year killed his hopes today.

With a presumable birdie 4 coming up on the long sixth, Nicklaus aimed right with the intent of clearing the midway bunkers and hooking slightly to position himself for a clear shot at the green.

His aim was wrong, but the hook was there and the ball flew out of bounds to the left. Now playing three off the tee, Jack had a 6. It was disastrous. He was yards ahead of Player off the tee, the pars seemed routine, and yet he couldn't get a single birdie putt down on the par-3 and par-4 holes.

Player gets $7,200 in prize money. More important is the rich prestige the title brings. Nicklaus has finished second twice running and for the third time in all. He has won once, at Muirfield in 1966.

About 43,000 watched the tournament and takings reached $73,000, an Open record.

THE FINAL SCORES

Gary Player	74 71 71	73—289	$7,200
Bob Charles	72 72 71	76—291	$4,170
Jack Nicklaus	76 69 73	73—291	$4,170
Billy Casper	72 68 74	78—292	$2,940
Maurice Bembridge	71 75 73	74—293	$2,400

Brian Barnes	70 74 80	71—295	$1,580
Neil Coles	75 76 71	73—295	$1,580
Gay Brewer	74 73 72	76—295	$1,580
Al Balding	74 76 74	72—296	$1,140
Arnold Palmer	77 71 72	77—297	$964
Rob. De Vicenzo	77 72 74	74—297	$964
Brian Huggett	76 71 75	76—298	$770
Peter Allis	73 78 72	75—298	$770
Bobby Cole	75 76 72	75—298	$770
Tony Horton	77 74 73	74—298	$770
Kel Nagle	74 75 75	74—298	$770
Tony Jacklin	72 72 75	80—299	$699
Paddy Skerritt	72 73 77	77—299	$609
Eric Brown	76 76 74	73—299	$609
Sebastian Miguel	73 75 76	76—300	$574
*Mike Bonallack	70 77 74	79—300	
*David Webster	77 71 78	74—300	$574
Keith MacDonald	80 71 73	77—301	$443
Alex Caygill	79 76 71	75—301	$443
Peter Thomson	77 71 78	75—301	443
Dave Thomas	75 71 78	78—302	$440
Robert Shaw	75 76 73	78—302	$440

Sandy Wilson	73 81 74	74—302	$440
Malcolm Gregson	77 75 76	74—302	$440
David Huish	74 74 78	77—303	$345
Harry Bannerman	74 73 77	79—303	$345
Jaime Gallardo	78 71 78	76—303	$345
Doug Sanders	78 76 73	77—304	$324
G. Cunningham	80 70 75	80—305	$300
Jimmy Martin	81 72 74	78—305	$300
Michael Murphy	77 74 77	77—305	$300
Hubby Haulan	77 74 76	79—306	$276
Tony Grubb	79 74 75	79—307	$268
Mohamed Moussa	77 76 75	79—307	$268
Christy Green	75 77 76	79—307	$268
Barry Coxon	77 72 78	84—311	$240
Peter Mills	71 76 80	84—311	$240
Bert Yancey	78 75 74	84—311	$240
Harry Weetman	77 76 74	86—313	$240

*Denotes amateur.

July 14, 1968

The Negro Golf Tour: A Stepping Stone, for Some, to the 'Big Money'

Golfers wait their turn to putt during the United Golfers Association's national pro championships. There were 76 pros in the field.

By THOMAS ROGERS

Last Tuesday, a field of 76 professional golfers teed off on the first day of a tournament at Washington's Langston Golf Course, a tree-lined, flattish, sunbaked 6,391-yard municipal layout in the northeast section of the capital.

The golfers, all Negroes, had paid an entry fee of $30 each. They were competing for prizes totaling $3,000. First-prize money was $800.

The tournament, the professional division of the United Golfers Association's 42d national championships, was without its defending champion. Lee Elder, who had won in four of the last five years, chose instead to play in the $100,000 Philadelphia Classic, where, for a $50 entry fee, a 20th-place finish would net him more than the top spot at Langston.

Many Are Club Professionals

The absence of Elder — and the profits that he and Charlie Sifford have reaped recently on the white-dominated Professional Golfers' Association tour—served as an incentive for most of the pros at Langston.

The United Golfers' Association, founded in 1926 to provide a competitive setting for Negro golfers, is today an association of 87 Negro golf clubs. Of its 9,000 members, 317 went to Washington to compete in divisions of its national championships —men's professional, men's amateur, women's amateur, men's senior and women's senior.

Many men were club professionals and assistants, but a small group consisted of playing pros who each year enter the 30 to 40 U.G.A. events (for trifling purses) in hopes of improving their games under tournament conditions.

When they feel they are ready, they will follow Sifford and Elder (and four or five other Negroes on the P.G.A. tour) in search of the "big money."

Sifford, who won the U.G.A. pro crown six times, became last year the first Negro victor in a P.G.A. event when he won $20,000 in the Greater Hartford open.

Elder, who succeeded Sifford as the U.G.A. champion, gained national prominence earlier this month when he battled Jack Nicklaus through a five-hole sudden-death playoff in the American Golf Classic at Akron. Before a national television audience, Elder matched shots with Nicklaus before bowing on the fifth extra hole.

The success on the tour of Sifford and Elder has buoyed at least three or four U.G.A. golfers. They now plan to enter the P.G.A. qualifying school this fall and try their luck.

James Black of Charlotte, N. C., a 27-year-old long hitter who took down the U.G.A. $800 first prize with a 9-under par 279 for 72 holes, said he had the financial backing necessary to embark on the P.G.A. tour if he could qualify this fall.

Tour Tried, Found Wanting

James Walker Jr. of Los Angeles, an early favorite who tied for fourth with 286, is a 29-year-old pro who tried the tour for 14 months in 1965 and 1966 and won virtually nothing.

Pointing to three triumphs this year (which netted him $1,450), he believes he is ready.

"I've improved my game five or six shots since then and I'd like to take another crack," he said last week. "I'm

155

thinking more, not taking chances the way I used to. I'm much more confident about my iron play now.''

Another candidate is Nathaniel Starks of Atlanta, a 150-pounder who won the all-Army crown in 1965, competing against Homero Blancas and Orville Moody, present P.G.A. tour players.

Although he admits he is ''in a slump right now,'' as demonstrated by his °é° at Langston, the Atlanta pro is sure his play will pick up on the tour.

''There's more chance of improvement there,'' he said. ''The tougher competition, the

better playing conditions and the incentive of higher purses all tend to help your game.''

Black, Walker and Starks seemingly have all the shotmaking ability necessary to compete on the top level. And their lightly rewarded, but valuable, tournament experience in U.G.A. events may be a better forging ground than the collegiate and club competition white youngsters rely on when preparing for a professional career.

At Langston, attentive and silent galleries followed the more popular figures and greeted their better shots with appreciative applause.

The gathering at the 18th hole, down a roll-

ing hill near the clubhouse, was typical. Several hundred players and spectators dotted the hillside and watched the finishing strokes of each player.

All that was missing from a comparable white professional tournament were television cameras. But Black, Walker and Starks think they would have little trouble getting used to them.

Television means big money. Like their U.G.A.-trained predecessors, they're ready to make some.

August 25, 1968

Pro Golf Dispute Is Settled

NEW POLICY BOARD TO RUN TOURNEYS

3 Businessmen, 4 Players to Join 3 P.G.A. Officials on 10-Man Committee

By LINCOLN A. WERDEN

The dispute that had threatened to disrupt the ranks of professional golf ended yesterday with an amicable settlement. The 52-year-old Professional Golfers' Association and the American Professional Golfers, a group that was organized four months ago by most of the game's leading professional players, agreed to join forces under a new format.

A tournament players' division was established under the format and three prominent businessmen agreed to serve as members of a 10-man tournament policy board that would have ''complete and final authority'' over the tournament program.

J. Paul Austin of Atlanta, president of the Coca-Cola Company and a golf enthusiast, will serve as chairman of the new board. With him will be George H. Love of Pittsburgh, former chairman of the Chrysler Corporation and now chairman of the board of the Con-

solidated Coal Company, and John Murchison of Dallas, one of the Southwest's leading financial figures.

Four Players on Board

The P.G.A. is to have three representatives and the players four among the directors.

P.G.A. representatives will be Leo Fraser, its president; Warren Orlick, its secretary, and William Clarke, its treasurer. The players who are to serve as directors are expected to be named next week.

Gardner Dickinson, who made a joint announcement with Fraser of the accord that terminated two weeks of intensive negotiations, was the A.P.G. president. Jack Nicklaus, vice president; Billy Casper, treasurer, and Dan Sikes, secretary, were the other officers.

All pending litigation involving the P.G.A. and the A.P.G. has been dismissed, and it was announced further that no new litigation would be instituted ''or other punitive action taken against any sponsor, player, P.G.A. or A.P.G.''

No furthern announcement was made concerning the /éé P.G.A. championship, which had been scheduled for Dayton, Ohio. But it was understood that the tournament would be held, with the site still to be announced.

''Under this agreement,'' it was said, ''the professional tour will

continue as a P.G.A. program. The separate A.P.G. tournament schedule will be transferred to the P.G.A. and the P.G.A. will honor the commitments made by both parties.''

17 Sponsors Signed

The A.P.G. recently had announced the signing of contracts with 17 tournament sponsors.

This year's P.G.A. tour had offered a total of $5.5-million in purses.

Dickinson had been head of the P.G.A. tournament committee before it was dissolved last August when the dispute developed into a split and the formation of the A.P.G.

The players declared they wished to remain within the framework of the P.G.A. but sought to obtain the deciding vote on day-to-day conduct of the tour. When they failed to obtain that authority, they set up their own association.

The new committee will have the power to control schedules, sizes of purses and television commitments take disciplinary action and rule on all other matters pertaining to the tour. No right of interference will go to the P.G.A. or any of its officials, other than those serving on the new board.

Tourney Chief Set Up

A tournament director will be named to carry out the policy com-

mittee's regulations. He will have a wide range of power, but he will be subject to the final authority of the committee.

Fraser and Samuel E. Gates of New York, the attorney for the A.P.G., said no candidate for the post of tournament director had yet been considered. But since the 1969 program starts with the Los Angeles Open on Jan. 9, it is expected the post will be filled within a few weeks.

Fraser, Gates and the P.G.A. attorney, William D. Rogers, Secretary of State-designate, will be nonvoting advisers to the policy board. Neither side claimed victory in the settlement.

Gates said ''at long last an improved structure has been achieved.'' Fraser and Dickinson, in their statement, said they believed an improved and durable structure had been obtained.

Of the businessmen on the board, Austin is a member of the Blind Brook Golf Club, Purchase, N.Y., and the Capital City and Peachtree Golf Clubs in Atlanta. Love is president of the Laurel Valley Golf Club, Ligonier, Pa., and Murchison was one of the founders of the Preston Trail Golf Club in Dallas.

December 14, 1968

Sifford Defeats Henning in Sudden-Death Playoff to Win Los Angeles Open

EACH CARDS A 276 IN $100,000 EVENT

By LINCOLN A. WERDEN
Special to The New York Times

LOS ANGELES, Jan. 12— Charlie Sifford won the Los Angeles open tournament with a birdie 3 today that decided a sudden-death playoff with Harold

Henning of South Africa that lasted one hole.

Thousands stormed the Rancho Park municipal course to witness the closing minutes of an exciting round, and the brief extra session resulted when both professionals totaled 276 for the regulation 72 holes. Most of them knew or had heard about Sifford, the former

charlotte, N.C., caddie, a Los Angeles resident whose unusual golfing career had another full chapter here this week.

It was Sifford who became the first Negro to win on the circuit in 1957 in an unofficial 54-hole Long Beach, Calif., open. It was Sifford, whose long wait for official recognition as a tournament win-

ner came in 1967 when he carried off the Greater Hartford, Conn., open. this was the same man who waited patiently through years when only those of the Caucasian race were eligible for membership in the Professional Golfers' Association, who often found he was unwelcome as a competitor in some parts of the nation.

United Press International

AHEAD $20,000: Charlie Sifford after winning the Los Angeles open yesterday in a one-hole, sudden-death playoff with Harold Henning of South Africa. They had tied at 276.

Sifford received $20,000 as his share of the purse and had the distinction with Pete Brown, winner of the Waco Turner open in 1963 at Burneyville, Okla., to be the only two Negroes to win major pro golf tournaments.

Billy Casper, last year's winner closed with a 67 for 277 to tie Bruce Devlin of Australia. Then came Dave Hill at 278, Bert Yancey at 280 and Howell Fraser, winner of the recent national club professionals tourney, at 281. Arnold Palmer finished with 284.

Sifford Opens Well

Sifford, holding a three-stroke lead going into the last round over Henning and Dave Hill, was off to a birdie start. He rapped in a four-footer at the first green, got down in one putt for a par at the next, then rolled in a 20-footer for a deuce to be 10 under par for 57 holes. Sifford said the weather suited him because it was warm, but the temperature dropped by the time he reached the sixth hole and he put on a sweater. Sifford's game lost some keenness then for he acquired two successive bogeys at the fifth and sixth but stayed even with par, or 36 to the turn.

With nine holes left to go, Sifford led Henning and Hill by one stroke. Then for the third straight round, Sifford completed the tour of the 6,827-yard course in a par 71. He scored his eight-under-par 63 in the first round, and after that he was even with the regulation figures.

When Sifford bogeyed the 12th, however, he lost the edge to the South African and Hill. Then Henning added to the keenness of the closing minutes by bagging a birdie at the par-5 13th to forge ahead by one stroke. Sifford caught him with a 20-footer for a birdie 3 at the 16th as the crowd cheered loudly for their hometown professional. Sifford hit his second to the rim of the home green but he two-putted for the concluding par that assured a playoff at 276. Henning had 34 on each nine for 68.

The brief extra session began at the 15th hole for the convenience of television commitments Sifford knocked his second to within four feet of the flagstick but Henning's ball fell short to the right in a sandy patch. He pitched out, but Sifford, after a minute inspection of the green, stroked the ball in for the decisive birdie 3.

When asked what he thought the future would be for Negro professional golfers, Sifford said, "We have eight on the tour now. When we get the boys going to college and playing on the college golf teams, we'll have more Negro professionals. The P.G.A. can't make the boys go to school and play golf, it's up to the boys themselves."

Why did Sifford persist on becoming a professional golfer against odds? "I wanted to prove to myself that I could play and a Negro could play," he said. "I caddied and used to give a golfer the right club to hit the ball, so if I could do that, I thought I could use the right club myself."

January 13, 1969

GOLF RULE ALLOWS ADJUSTABLE CLUB

Golf clubs designed to be adjustable for weight alone are permissible under a new rules interpretation adopted jointly by the United States Golf Association and the Royal and Ancient Golf Club of St. Andrews, Scotland.

Rule 2-2a of the Rules of Golf provides in part: "The club shall not be designed to be adjustable." Heretofore this has applied to any form of adjustability. The new interpretation prohibits clubs designed to be adjustable for such things as lie or loft, but not for weight.

Thus, it will be possible to have, for example, a club with a cavity in the head to house varying numbers of lead wafers held firmly in place by some type of screw. Such a club would conform with the new interpretation if the weights are fixed immovable during play.

February 16, 1969

Elder, Negro Golf Pro, Charges Race Baiting on Tour

WASHINGTON, June 4 (AP)—Lee Elder, one of the few Negroes on the professional golf tour, says he will begin skipping tournaments next year because of racial baiting by the galleries.

The 32-year-old Dallas-born golfer said he would never again play in the Pensacola open in Florida, held the end of March.

He said he would scan several other tournaments next winter in California, Florida and Tennessee and, he said, if conditions have not improved, he will drop them from his schedule.

"Things have got better in some places on the tour," he canceled, "but there are three or four tournaments here I just can't play.

"I'm tired of being called 'nigger' or 'black boy.' It's just come to a head. I haven't said anything about this before, but I feel I've held it underneath long enough and believe it should be brought out."

"It's very difficult for a Negro to play on the tour," he said. "It's not only me, but the others fel the same pressures from galleries. It's very hard to concentrate when you hear some of the comments."

Ten Negroes are regulars on the tour, including Charlie

Sifford and his nephew, Curtis Sifford; the Browns—Pete, Cliff and Howard—who are not related, and George Johnson.

"They all get the same treatment," said Elder, who spent 10 years on the all-Negro circuit before joining the pro tour a little more than two years ago.

Elder said he was reluctant to name the tournaments where he had received the treatment, except for Pensacola, because he planned to play in them at least one more time.

June 5, 1969

FLOYD'S 202 LEADS DAYTON GOLF BY 5

Nine Persons Are Arrested as Civil Rights Group Interrupts P.G.A.

By LINCOLN A. WERDEN
Special to The New York Times

DAYTON, Ohio, Aug. 16—Gary Player received the brunt of harassment during the third round of the Professional Golfers Association championship today but finished in a three-way tie for second place, five strokes back of Ray Floyd, the leader at 202.

Civil rights protesters carried out threats made earlier in the week to disrupt play by a series of incidents, which Player and Jack Nicklaus, his pairing mate, withstood under strain.

Going to the 10th tee, a cup of ice and soft drink was thrown in Player's face after a program had been tossed on the fourth tee as he was about to drive. The principal disturbance occurred at the 10th, and reports floating back to the National Cash Register Country Club press section said that "Player had been knocked down." These proved to be erroneous.

One unidentified protester walked onto the green and said to the South African, who won the P.G.A. title in 1962, "It's not against you or your country, it's against the P.G.A. tournament."

"That was a helluva solution," said Player later, "but the one who threw the ice at me at the 10th did call me a racist."

Player was quick to suggest

at a mass post-round interview with Nicklaus, that "I think the majority of people today were so nice I don't think you should let lousy things be publicized."

Tight security measures terminated a scuffle on the 10th green, as Player and Nicklaus were lining up their putts. Big Jack had an eagle try and Player was after a birdie. A group rushed from behind the fairway ropes and Nicklaus held up his club in self-defense while someone picked up his ball and tossed it toward a bunker. Police seized the demonstrators. One demonstrator was knocked down and the green scuffed. Player subsequently holed his 10-footer for a birdie 3. But Player wasn't struck as early reports related.

An official replaced Nicklaus's ball on the putting surface and Nicklaus holed out for a birdie 4 as the excitement abated and police rushed in. According to Paul Price, chief of security, seven of the nine arrests today were made here.

Price said, "to the best of my knowledge six of the seven are

members of Mel Jackson's organization. Jackson is the leader of the Dayton branch of the Southern Christian Leadership Conference.

Ball Thrown on Green

One other incident followed at the 13th as Player was preparing to putt, a girl threw a ball on the putting surface back of him. She was subsequently taken in custody. Player then proceeded to hole the 12-foot downhill putt for a birdie deuce.

From then on, however, there were no further interruptions. A record crowd of 21,270 followed a share of these disruptions, but as Player and Nicklaus neared the end of their round, they were roundly applauded as they came to each green.

"Player will be a hero after this," said one bystander.

"He should be," commented Joseph C. Dey Jr., pro commissioner, who was out on the course in an electric cart. "Do you know what Player said to the man who threw the drink

in his face? Why he turned to him and said 'what have I done to you, sir.'"

Floyd was in the last due to start with George (Bunky) Henry, who finished with a 70 to be in the three-cornered tie for second at 207 with Player and Bert Greene. Just ahead on the course were Player and Nicklaus.

The 200-pounder rushed up the hill toward the green at the 10th when he saw the commotion. "My instinctive reaction was to go up and help, for Gary's a gutty guy and I felt I should help him. Then I saw there was nothing I could do."

Floyd completed his four-under-par 67 over the hilly 6,915-yard course with a spectacular No. 8 iron second shot from a bunker. He estimated it covered 140 yards and it stopped six inches from the flagstick. He stroked in the concluding birdie 3 for an incoming 33 and a four-under-par round.

August 17, 1969

High-Flying Pied Piper Of the Links

By LINCOLN A. WERDEN

THE one question golfers have readily answered during the last 10 years is: "Who is the most popular golfer?" The unequivocal reply always has been "Arnold Palmer."

No one has been able to equal the appeal of the Latrobe, Pa., professional. Golf has grown to become an international pastime and, through television, highly popular, a brand of sports entertainment. Palmer consequently has been exposed to an increasing audience that supplements the army of fans who trot close to him along the fairway.

There have been some attempts to analyze the so-called Palmer mystique but there is no mystery about him. Football heroes are created by long touchdown passes while baseball stars supply drama by sweeping the bases with a home run. By contrast, golf, where short putts win tournaments, is less dramatic, as it demands self control by an individual under pressure. Yet, Palmer has been able to add flair to what could be a drab contest by capturing the imagination of bystanders from Melbourne to Memphis. It is because fundamentally he is a delightful human being with an exceptional personality.

He is also a superlative competitor and an expert jet pilot and possesses the innate dignity and humanity that pleases both the heart and the mind. He takes a drink, smokes occasionally, tells a story, smiles at a miniskirt, yet demonstrates courage and compassion while being a devoted father and husband.

Although he has won 55 individual

major golf events and shared in 70 victories, he has held the admiration and affection of his fellow professional competitors. They refer to him as "The King," for they agree that the huge purses for which they now play and the multitudinous fringe benefits that accrue to them can largely be traced to the influence that Palmer has exerted in popularizing the game.

One indication of the scope of his prestige is shown whenever he pilots his plane into an airport. We flew into Albuquerque, N. M., one bright day and a voice from the tower suggested that Palmer note the new golf course off to the left of the runway. At Las Vegas, when control was advised that N-701-AP was ready to come in, the tower asked: "Is this Arnie's Air Force arriving?"

On the ground, his arrival at golf clubs is marked by a rush for autographs. His automobile is quickly surrounded and youngsters and grown-ups shove and push to get near him as he walks to the practice area of the first tee. Obligingly, he stops. Occasionally he chides them: "Please, you're stepping on my feet."

There have been days, too, in the 1960's when Palmer had to walk humbly. On the final day of the 1968 United States Open championship, he was paired ignominiously in the last group off because his scores had been too high. But he didn't quit or withdraw, as some did, and stayed on to finish, nevertheless, at the bottom of the field. Physical pain also has forced him to halt in several tournaments but he is back again as the decade comes to an end to keep the Palmer legend alive. Golf is proud of Arnie and he of the game he plays and the men in it. Put him down in the book of golf as a great guy.

December 28, 1969

Johnny Miller's record score of 63 in the 1973 U.S. Open catapulted him into a prominent position on the pro tour.

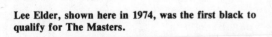

Lee Elder, shown here in 1974, was the first black to qualify for The Masters.

Jacklin Captures U.S. Open Golf Title by 7 Strokes With Final 70 for 281

United Press International

FINISHING WITH A FLOURISH: Tony Jacklin, backed by fans, after sinking a birdie putt on the 18th hole

HILL FINISHES 2D WITH CLOSING 73

Jacklin, Leader for All Four Rounds, Is First Briton to Win Since Ray in 1920

By LINCOLN A. WERDEN
Special to The New York Times

CHASKA, Minn., June 21— Tony Jacklin won the United States Open golf championship today and became the first Englishman to do so in 50 years. "I'm proud to be an Englishman," said the smiling 25-year-old British Open titleholder after sinking a 35-foot putt for a birdie that gave him a seven-stroke margin.

A fourth round of 70 at the Hazeltine National Golf Club, a 7,151-yard layout that was the subject of much criticism by United States professionals, enabled him to lead from start to finish. He compiled a 72-hole aggregate of 281, or seven under par.

The dark-haired son of a former lorry (truck) driver thus emulated Ted Ray who carried back the trophy to England in 1920. Only Walter Hagen in 1914, Jim Barnes in 1921 and Ben Hogan in 1953 besides this

likeable athlete, who once worked in a steel mill and in a lawyer's office, went on to triumph after setting the pace in each round.

Jacklin Honored by Queen

Jacklin, despite his youth, is already an English sports hero. Last year he won the British Open after an 18 year drought for English golfers. Queen Elizabeth II rewarded him with the Officer of the British Empire honor last February. "There are four categories of that honor," Jacklin said in explanation. "The Beatles," he added with a smile, "got one below my level."

Admittedly a bit nervous before starting, Jacklin said he took "emergency pills" so he could sleep last night. But today, he was wide awake as he withstood his most persistent challenger, Dave Hill, who finished second at 288 after a round of 73.

So adaptable did Jacklin prove that he weathered the 41-mile winds of opening day, the heavy course conditions that later prevailed, zephyrs and today's sunny, 70-degree temperature that made this a tourney of contrasts, and, as he said, of all seasons.

Robert Trent Jones, the architect who designed the course and who jousted with its critics, said it was Jacklin's golf background in rugged, foggy, rainy English weather that served him well here. "He got the jump on the field the first day in those high

winds," said Jones, "and he's accustomed to play in all conditions and on all types of courses."

Charles, Lunn Share Third

Bob Charles, the southpaw from New Zealand, and Bob Lunn, a former public links champion, finished at 289.

Jacklin found his boyhood hero, Arnold Palmer, down the list. While he was registering his smashing success on his third bid for the title, Palmer had a concluding 77 for 305. Gary Player of South Africa, a pre-tourney favorite, tallied 302 and Jack Nicklaus, one of four who has won all four of the world's major championships, had 304 after a 76.

The margin by which he won also was the most convincing since the hickory shaft days of the nineteen-twenties, when Jim Barnes won by nine strokes in 1921. The series of four under-par rounds equaled a performance by Lee Trevino in winning the 1968 championship at Rochester. Trevino was at 294, or 13 back of Jacklin and in a group with Billy Casper, Bruce Devlin and Larry Ziegler.

Born in Scunthorpe, he now lives in Elsham in Lincolnshire County, which he says is 175 miles northeast of London. But he has been playing since he was 9 years old and spent "hundreds of hours" putting at the course in Scunthorpe.

Putting well, he said, was vital to him and to all golfers. "If you miss two six-footers a

Cards of Leaders

	PAR FOR THE COURSE			
OUT	445	344	534	—36
IN	454	345	344	—36—72

	TONY JACKLIN			
OUT	445	334	643	—36
IN	354	345	343	—34—70—281

	DAVE HILL			
OUT	345	444	534	—36
IN	454	345	435	—37—73—288

round that's eight strokes and that's the difference of winning or placing 25th on your tour."

Jacklin lost in a playoff to Pete Brown in the Andy Williams-San Diego open last February, and he said he had been disturbed by his inaccurate putting recently. This afternoon, however, "I was tremendously tense until I holed the 25-footer at the ninth."

"I was also booked to leave on a 5:15 P.M. plane," he said, after receiving a check for $30,000, the winner's share of the $200,000 purse, "but thank the Lord I had to miss it."

He plans to return to England tomorrow and rejoin the American golf circuit in July for the National team championship at Ligonier, Pa., with Bert Yancey as his partner.

Ten others besides Jacklin have won both the British and United States Opens, but the young Englishman said he wasn't satisfied with that. "I want to be the greatest golfer in the world. No one is ever satisfied. When you are it's time to quit. If I can leave the impression that Palmer, Ben

Hogan, Gary Player or Jack Nicklaus have, I'll be very fortunate."

Jacklin's incoming nine of 34 contained some highlights. He ran in an eight-footer for a birdie 3 at the 10th, which heightened his spirits following his birdie at the ninth. Then he played easily for seven pars, "blocking out the thought of winning, not counting my chickens before they were hatched."

At the 17th, which had troubled him in previous rounds, he used a No. 4 iron from the tee at this uphill hole of 344 yards, where creek and pond guard the green. Then he knocked a No. 6 iron from the fairway to the putting surface and was safe. Two putts gave him his par 4.

It was soon settled that the cup was going to England, for Jacklin hit a No. 4 iron to the 18th green. He was quickly surrounded by exuberant fans.

Then from 35 feet Jacklin sank the putt.

A year ago, Jacklin had tied for 25th place. The previous year he failed to qualify for the tournament.

Charles had the low fourth-round score with a 67. The low amateur honors were divided between Ben Crenshaw, an 18-year-old schoolboy from Austin, Tex., and John Mahaffey Jr. of San Antonio, Tex., a member of the Houston University team at 301.

When Jacklin reached his locker in the clubhouse this morning, he found a white piece of paper with a hand-printed word "tempo" on it "That must be from my friends Tom Weiskopf or Berty Yancey. What does it mean? My old problem was swinging fast. This is a reminder to slow down my swing."

June 22, 1970

Nicklaus Wins British Open, Beating Sanders by Stroke in Playoff

LAST-HOLE BIRDIE CLINCHES VICTORY

Sanders's Late Bid Fails as Nicklaus Gets 72 for First Major Title in 3 Years

By FRED TUPPER
Special to The New York Times

ST. ANDREWS, Scotland, July 12—Jack Nicklaus won the British Open by a stroke from Doug Sanders in their 18-hole playoff today. It took an eight-foot downhill putt under almost intolerable pressure on the home hole for a birdie 3 to stave off Sanders's stirring challenge down the stretch.

Nicklaus was four strokes up with five holes to go when old Doug, now fashionably gray on top, made his heroic charge. The ball had not bounced for him earlier, and by sheer willpower he had forced putts into the holes to stay alive.

Then Sanders made his bid. He got a birdie on the 14th by wedging out of a trap to within four feet for his 4. He shaped an iron shot beautifully to the green and drilled that putt into the cup from 13 feet out as the crowd whistled him on.

Then Doug made his vital par 4 on the 16th, where Jack's putt hestiated for seconds on the lip and stayed out to give him his only bogey of the day.

Sanders Battles Back

Sanders had picked up three strokes on three holes, and the result that had seemed foregone was now trembling in the balance. It was brilliant, inspired golf as Doug tried to salvage the success that he had thrown away the day before by missing a three-footer that would have given him the championship. After four rounds the two Americans had tied at 283.

Jack Nicklaus with trophy and Doug Sanders, who just wanted to touch prize he missed

The thousands of Scots who had come out this Sunday were massed round the infamous Road Hole, with its plateau green guarded by a huge bunker on the left and a precipitous slope that runs straight down to the road on the right. The target to shoot at is a meager eight yards wide and the shot cannot be pitched on but must be run up.

Sanders curved a No. 5 iron off the slope that scooted up the bank and broke into the clear across the green ending 18 feet past the cup. With the match slipping away, Nicklaus hit a superb No. 7 iron that fled up the slope and nestled down 10 feet away from the flag. They had their par 4's, with Nicklaus still 1 up and everything at stake on the last hole.

Sanders split the middle with his drive, 275 yards out. This is what Jack had been waiting for. He pulled off his yellow sweater and decided to have a go for the green on this 359-yard hole.

He threw all of his vaunted power into that swing. The ball took off and traveled 370 yards, up to, on and across the green and bounced against the back behind it, burrowing down into the rough. It was incredible, but he had hit it too far.

Nicklaus Ends Famine

Doug rolled a No. 4 iron through The Valley of Sin in front up to five feet. Nicklaus bravely chipped out to within eight feet. Down went his putt and he hurled his putter 20 feet in the air with excitement. He had his first major title in three years, and he had his second British Open, having won at Muirfield in 1966. Sanders sank his putt for birdie, but it was too late.

The 30-year-old Nicklaus won $12,600 today and shot a par 72. More importantly, he set up a standard for his appearances in Britain that now comprise two firsts, three seconds, one third and a fifth in his last eight appearances in this country.

"I almost hit it before I was ready," said Jack, "I told myself to wait for a second and make it right."

"One of the great golf matches of all time," said William Whitelaw, captain of the Royal and Ancient, in making the presentation. "The auld gray toon" with 8,000 jammed round the clubhouse and hundreds hanging from the rooftops, loosed their cries of pleasure. In large letters on the scoreboard were "Well Done Jack"—"The Best of Tributes."

And for old Doug and his $9,000 check came waves of applause. He had set the Old Course on fire in those throbbing moments down the home holes. He had wiped out the memory of that moment yesterday when that putt of three feet had miserably gone adrift.

Good Show by Sanders

Sanders had come over to qualify and then had the championship in his grasp. And he came back again when all seemed lost. "I had the desire and the determination," he said.

Three great shots — Jack's pitch out of the rough on the fifth hole to save par, his iron to 17 and that last chip off the bank at 18—had beat him.

But Doug had fought his fight. Eighty-one thousand people, a record for the tournament, attended this 99th British Open in the birthplace of golf. "There's not a place in the world," said Nicklaus in his excitement, "that I would rather win a championship."

July 13, 1970

First Lunar Golfer Drives A Ball 'Miles and Miles'

HOUSTON, Feb. 6 (UPI)—In the true style of a weekend duffer, Capt. Alan E. Shepard Jr. — the first golfer on the moon—took a "mulligan" today.

The old pro of space loped up to the tee with his custom-made six-iron, wriggled in his moon suit and kept his head down. But his backpack shortened his swing and he missed.

With millions watching on color television, Captain Shepard took another swing—the extra chance that golf duffers call a "mulligan"—and connected solidly.

Captain Shepard said that the ball went "miles and miles and miles."

Even his pro had kept secret the fact that the astronaut had taken his "trusty club" and three special heat-resistant golf balls on the moon flight.

The first indication that golf was going to be played on the moon came when Captain Shepard said:

"Houston, you might recognize what I have in my hand is the handle for the contingency sample return. It just so happens to have a genuine 6 iron on the bottom of it. In my left hand I have a little white pellet that's familiar to millions of Americans. I'll drop it down. Unfortunately, the suit is so stiff I can't do this with two hands but I'm going to try a little sand trap shot here."

"You got more dirt than ball that time," chortled Comdr. Edgar D. Mitchell, a gallery of one, when Captain Shepard missed the first shot.

Captain Shepard's club was devised by Jack Harden, golf pro at the River Oaks Country Club near the astronaut's home in Houston.

Mr. Harden said Captain Shepard can hit a 6-iron shot 135 to 140 yards on earth. In the one-sixth gravity of the moon, he estimated that the ball would travel more than 800 yards.

The pro made the club by removing the shaft and replacing it with a 4½-inch steel shaft. It was devised so an astronaut's all-purpose 30-inch handle could be inserted in the end.

The handle is used for moonwalk chores that involve a shovel and an ax.

February 7, 1971

Britain's Golfers Take Walker Cup

By FRED TUPPER
Special to The New York Times

ST. ANDREWS, SCOTLAND, May 27 — Britain won the Walker Cup today for the first time since 1938 and for only the second time in the 50-year history of the competition.

Amid scenes of wild excitement, the men in dark blue took six of the eight singles matches on this final afternoon and won 13 to 11, from the heavily-favored American side.

The United States had led, 6½ to 5½, yesterday and 9 to 7 after the morning foursomes. It was still marginally ahead most of the afternoon and then this British team of comparative unknowns exploded in all directions.

Twenty-year-old Roddy Carr of Ireland banged in a putt of 40-feet on the 18th hole to win his match from Jim Simons, 2 up; 19-year-old Warren Humphreys dropped putts of 35 and 30 feet for successive birdies on the 14th and 15th holes and upset Steve Melnyk, a former

Associated Press

TEAMWORK: John Farquhar, rear, helping Allen Miller, United States teammate, to line up his putt on the fourth green in Walker Cup match at St. Andrews, Scotland.

pion, 2 and 1. Hugh Stuart hit an approach to the heart of the 15th green and dropped a birdie putt from a dozen feet and eventually won from Vinnie Giles, 2 and 1.

And when Bill Hyndman conceded a six-inch putt that meant the winning of the whole match to Dr. David Marsh on the 17th—most famous of all golf holes—the vast gallery of Scots roared its exultation. For it was at this cradle of golf 33 years ago that the British and Irish side had won its lone victory.

"My wonderful, wonderful team," said Michael Bonallack, the British captain. "I'd like you to remember all those players all the years before us who tried as hard as we did."

Speaking to the American team at the presentation ceremony, he said "I hope you won't feel too bad about our getting this one little go."

The United States won the

top and bottom singles. Its Amateur champion, Lanny Wadkins, beat Bonallack, 3 and 1, in the best golf of the day. He was 4 up after six holes, made the turn in a one-under-

par 35 and birdied the 17th by arrowing his long 3-iron approach dead against the pin. And Tom Kite, who finished second by a stroke to Lanny in the Amateur, fittingly birdied the 15th hole to end his match with Geoffrey Marks, 3 and 2.

In between the British side swept the scoreboard. Charlie Green won his match by a hole after Allen Miller had squared on the 17th. Miller hit his approach on the last hole to the back of the huge green and had to take three putts to get down.

George MacGregor won from Jim Gabrielsen, 1 up, when the Atlanta broker was hopelessly mired in the dreaded 17th Road hole bunker and could only cut the ball on and over the green into the shale. And Dr. Marsh beat Hyndman by a hole.

Perhaps the biggest surprise was young Carr, so lightly thought of that his selection for the team last fall was criticized. It was his decisive putt on the 18th that won the lone British foursome this morning just as his 40-footer there set the scene for victory this afternoon. His father, Joe,

an Irish golfing legend, won the British Amateur three times.

Giles, yesterday's hero, paired with Melnyk this morning and defeated Green and Marks. It was Vinnie's curling 15-footer that slid in sideways for a birdie on the 13th that meant the difference.

And the other American foursome victory came from

Miller and John Farquhar, who rolled a 70-foot putt across the first green for a birdie 3 and holed a 15-footer for another winning birdie 3 on the ninth.

THE SUMMARIES
FOURSOMES

Steve Melnyk, Jacksonville, Fla., and Marvin Giles, Richmond, defeated Charlie Green and Geoff Marks, Britain, 1 up.
Allen Miller, Pensacola, Fla., and John Farquhar, Amarillo, Tex., defeated Michael Bonallack and David Marsh, Britain, 5 and 4.

Hugh Stuart and Roddy Carr, Britain, defeated Lanny Wadkins, Richmond, and Jim Gabrielsen, Atlanta 1 up.
Bill Campbell, Huntington, W. Va., and Tom Kite, Austin, Tex., drew with Rodney Foster and Scott MacDonald, Britain.
SINGLES
Wadkins defeated Bonallack, 3 and 1.
Stuart defeated Giles, 2 and 1.
Warren Humphreys, Britain, defeated Melnyk, 2 and 1.
Green defeated Miller, 1 up.
Carr defeated Jim Simons, Butler, Pa., 2 up.
George MacGregor, Britain, defeated Gabrielsen, 1 up.
Marsh defeated Hyndman, 1 up.
Kite defeated Marks, 3 and 2.

May 28, 1971

Trevino's 68 Defeats Nicklaus by 3 Strokes in Open Playoff

Loser's Erratic Bunker Shots Rated Key

By LINCOLN A. WERDEN
Special to The New York Times

ARDMORE, Pa., June 21—Lee Trevino threw a rubber snake in jest at Jack Nicklaus on the first tee today moments before they started their playoff round. Then in earnest, the merry Texan tossed a two-under-par 68 at his noted rival to beat him by three strokes for the United States Open golf title. The two had tied yesterday after the regulation 72 holes with scores of 280.

Over the venerable Merion course, site of other historic meetings, where Bobby Jones played as a 14-year-old in the National Amateur and Ben Hogan, after a near-fatal auto crash, became the 1950 Open champion, Trevino proved the steadier performer in a match interrupted for 35 minutes by a lightning storm.

Both players huddled under umbrellas and sat on a bench at the seventh tee after Philip Strubing, the United States Golf Association president, ordered them off the course because of the cloudburst and lightning flashes.

After play resumed, Nicklaus struggled to draw even. His unusually erratic bunker play at two holes had allowed the 31-year-old El Paso professional, who rose from obscurity in 1966 to become the 1968 Open champion, to gain a two-stroke lead after three holes. "The bunker play was the turning point" commented Trevino afterward.

Bogey and Double Bogey

Nicklaus failed to recover from the sand on his first attempt at the second where he ended with a bogey 6. Then at the 183-yard third, Nicklaus again failed to extricate his ball on his first try from a trap.

The result was a double-bogey 5.

Nicklaus, the pretourney favorite, braced with a birdie 4 at the fifth just before the storm hit. But he had to wait until the par-3 ninth for his next one. There he tapped in a putt of a yard's length for a deuce. That enabled Nicklaus to be out in 37, one over par.

Trevino completed the first nine in 36, contributing a brilliant wedge to within three inches of the cup. The crowd roared approval as he nudged the ball into the cup at the eighth.

The gallery ran over the fairways repeatedly and the marshals had difficulty attempting to keep them under control. The fans did not hesitate to yell encouragement, "Come on, Jack," or "Let's go, Lee," but the noise subsided whenever the golfers got set to hit.

Weak Approach Shot

There was a groan when Nicklaus went two strokes down after a weak approach at the 10th, which just reached the edge of the green, after he had outdriven Trevino by 30 yards. Nicklaus took three from off the putting surface, for a bogey 5 to Trevino's 4.

The Nicklaus supporters received encouragement as he rolled in a 12-foot putt for a birdie 3 at the 11th, but Trevino kept his lead at two by coming back at the next hole to run in a sidehill 30-footer for a birdie 3 while Nicklaus carded a 4.

Nicklaus hit the rim of the cup with his putt at the short 13th but the ball glanced off and he took a par 3 there as did his rival. They got par 4's at the 14th, and after Trevino dropped a 15-foot birdie putt with a flourish at the 15th, Nicklaus holed a six-footer for a birdie also.

Neither gained any advantage at the 16th, where they had par 4's, but at the treacherous 17th of 224 yards, which troubled the competitors throughout the championship, Nicklaus was bunkered again. The ball fell in a tight spot in

the front corner of the hazard on the right and was partly buried. With considerable care, Nicklaus finally knocked it out to the green, some 10 feet from the cup, but two-putted for a bogey 4. When Trevino snared his par 3 there, the outcome was virtually settled. The par 4's at the home hole brought a happy Trevino to the title in another chapter of a rags-to-riches story.

"I have no ambition to win all the four major championships—the British Open, the P.G.A., the Masters and this Open," said Trevino before starting. "I just want to win tournaments, whether it's the Screen Door Open or the Canadian Bacon Open. I just want to win two or three a year to stay in the top five. My ambition is to win a million dollars. When I do that I might go south of the border."

Nicklaus was self-critical when the playoff was over and described his short iron play in the early part of the round as "sloppy." He led momentarily at the first hole, where Trevino pushed his second into a bunker, took a bogey 5 while Nicklaus seemingly was away to a flying start with a par 4 for a one-stroke lead. It was short-lived. Nicklaus took a 6

THE CARDS
PAR

Out	453 544 443	—36
In	444 344 434	—34—70

LEE TREVINO

Out	553 544 433	—36
In	443 343 434	—32—68

JACK NICKLAUS

Out	465 534 442	—37
In	534 343 444	—34—71

on the second after playing from the rear of one bunker near the green to a forward section, before getting out of the hazard. Trevino drew even with a par 5 and suddenly moved ahead with his par 3 at the third to the double bogey 5, which resulted when Nicklaus failed to dislodge the ball from the bunker on the left of the green on his first attempt.

Trevino is regarded as a "shrewd" thinker in Nicklaus's book. On the so-called thinking man's course, Marion, a 6,544-yard layout, he won $30,000 to $15,000 for Nicklaus.

Before today, Lee had earned $135,110.10 on the pro circuit, which is a far cry from his first year in big league golf when he won $600 after tying for 54th place in the 1966 Open in San Francisco.

June 22, 1971

TREVINO WINS BRITISH OPEN GOLF BY SHOT WITH 278

FINAL ROUND IS 70

Lu Finishes Second— Trevino's Title His Third in a Month

By FRED TUPPER

Special to The New York Times

SOUTHPORT, England, July 10—A horrendous 7 on the next-to-last hole today almost cost Lee Trevino the British Open that he had seemingly sewed up with a five-stroke lead halfway through the final day.

But Trevino won, it magnificently with a birdie at the end to join the thin list of golfing immortals who have taken both the United States and British Opens in the same year—Bob Jones in his Grand Slam of 1930, Gene Sarazen in 1932 and Ben Hogan in 1953.

That final birdie 4 for a 70 and a 72-hole total of 278 gave Trevino this 100th Open by a single stroke over the not so inscrutable Lu Liang Huan of Taiwan, whose toothy grins and stiff, courteous bows captured the hearts of the crowds, which for the week totaled 70,000, a record for a golf tournament in England.

Third, at 280, was Tony Jacklin, British Open champion in 1969 and United States Open winner last year, who picked up six strokes over the last nine holes on Trevino. Fourth at 281 was American-born Craig Defoy, now a 23-year-old British citizen. He was virtually unknown before the Open and holder of only a couple of titles in Zambia.

Eagle Start, Eagle Finish

Tied for fifth at 283 were Charles Coody, the Masters champion, and the great Jack Nicklaus, whose ambition this year was to take the Grand Slam. Nicklaus wound up with the Professional Golfers Association title, second in the United States Open after a playoff with Trevino and a tie for second in the Masters. He started this Open with an eagle and finished it with an eagle for a 69.

The best scores in the misty sunshine were by Billy Casper and Doug Sanders with 67's.

Trevino, who began the day leading by a stroke over Lu and Jacklin, had single putts on the first six greens and four birdies for a nine-hole total of 31.

Screaming encouragement to himself as his lead mounted, Trevino holed from 10 feet on the first, 20 feet on the third and 16 feet on the fourth for birdies. On the sixth hole, from the blind side of a ridge, he fired a three-wood into the unknown.

"It's perfect," he said. "Go far enough."

The shot carried 270 yards and landed almost far enough, a yard short of the cup. He had his fourth birdie now and at nine holes was 15 under par for the tournament.

Jacklin had faded on the first nine, Lu was 10 under and no other threats were then in sight.

Wild yells from over the sand dunes signified that Jacklin had started his charge, and Mr. Lu, as he became affectionately known, began to chip away at that lead. When Trevino finally teed up on the fateful 17th,

with his 15-under still intact, Lu was trailing by three strokes and Jacklin by four.

Trevino hit the ball full, aiming for the left hillside and expecting his reliable fade. For once the ball went straight, burying itself deep in soft sand.

"I'm not going to blow it," he said. "I tried to get a sand wedge and just hit it out of there."

The ball caught the heather on the way up and fell back in the sand. Trevino lunged again and the ball flew across the fairway into deep rough on the right. Playing four, he chipped short, 12 feet from the pin.

Down on the 18th green, Jacklin was putting from 12 feet for an eagle, unaware of the drama behind him. Jacklin missed but was now 12 under.

Lu was on a hummock beside the 17th green in two, needing a chip and a putt for his birdie 4. But the lie was poor and he cuffed it short. Trevino putted and missed, and so did Lu. A 7 for Trevino, a 5 for Lu.

It Was Some Month

The door was still just ajar, but Lu's gods deserted him. His drive down the left side of the 18th stopped on a bunker edge. Lu had to stand awkwardly below the ball to swing. Using the wood, he hooked and the ball struck a woman spectator. It caromed back into the fairway.

As he had to, Trevino went for a birdie. A 280-yard drive down the side, a six-iron to the back of the green and a roll up to 20 inches seemed safe enough.

But Lu was not through. A great iron to the heart of the green stopped 10 feet away and

in this cathedral of silence Lu sank it for his 4. Trevino didn't hesitate. He putted quick, and in.

What a month he has had! He took the United States Open in a playoff, took the Canadian open in a playoff and became a legend in his own time with his victory today.

After receiving the winner's

prize, $13,200, he typically sat down and wrote a check for £2,000 ($4,800) for a local orphanage.

"What are you going to do next?" he was asked.

"I want to win the Western open next week," he said.

July 11, 1971

Nicklaus Wins His 4th Masters Title By 3 Shots on Final 74 for 286 Total

Crampton, Weiskopf and Mitchell Tie for 2d Place

By LINCOLN A. WERDEN
Special to The New York Times

AUGUSTA, Ga., April 9— They went hunting for golf's Golden Bear today with the wrong kind of clubs. Despite some momentary lapses on the last nine, Jack Nicklaus strode to his fourth Masters victory on a winning margin of three strokes. He finished with a 74 for an aggregate of 286.

The 32-year-old professional equaled the greatest number of triumphs ever recorded in this major championship as he scored for the fourth time. Arnold Palmer, the other four time winner, finished far back today at 300.

"Nobody made a run at me, nobody was doing anything," said Nicklaus, who became one of three who led the field at the end of each round. Craig Wood did so in 1941 and Palmer in 1960.

Nicklaus, the game's leading money-winner, who earned another $25,000 on this warm, clear afternoon, received a standing ovation from the crowd as he came to the home green of the Augusta National Golf club.

Breakfast Is Cheesy

In the gathering were his wife, Barbara, and his 10-year-old son, Jack Jr. said Mrs. Nicklaus: "The only thing that went wrong for Jack today was that he had too much cheese in his cheese omelette for breakfast."

Tom Weiskopf, Bobby Mitchell and Bruce Crampton of Australia, all regulars on the pro circuit, formed the runner-up group at 289. Neither one of them, nor Nicklaus equaled par today. The slippery greens, the placements of the cups made putting a hazardous chore.

Jerry McGee, who tied for fifth at 290, said: "This is a course where you have to hit great shots, not just good ones."

Jim Jamieson, the pudgy and jovial 28-year-old golfer from

Moline, Ill., who had been second by one stroke beginning the round, took a 77 and was in the five-way tie for fifth. "I couldn't handle it," he admitted. "It was a rough day. The course was just awesome."

It was Jamieson who declared that he used a mongrel set of clubs. "They come from half a dozen manufacturers and the putter from a department store," he said. He was unable to continue his bid to overtake Nicklaus in hs first Masters through the front nine.

Nicklaus led him by five shots with nine holes to go and the other challengers also toppled over one by one. Weiskopf, an alumnus of Ohio State University as is Nicklaus, added some pressure toward the end.

Weiskopf was paired with Big Jack for this round. He had beaten Nicklaus to win the $52,000 Jackie Gleason tourney at Fort Lauderdale, Fla., last February. Today he carded birdies at the 15th and 17th holes. But the best he could do was finish with a 74, Crampton and Mitchell had 73's leaving Nicklaus as the only player with an under-par total for 72 holes.

There was added significance to this victory for Nicklaus since it gave him his 12th major championship, only one shy of the total accumulated by his idol, the late Bobby Jones, a founder of the Augusta course and its co-designer.

Nicklaus has won two United States Open titles, two British Opens, two Professional Golfers' Association championships and four Masters. No other golfer has ever done this. During his amateur days which came to an end in December 1961, he won the National Amateur Title twice.

What lies ahead? Nicklaus, unlike Jones who retired from competition at the age of 28, has no thought of quitting or "going fishing or playing too much tennis." His sights are set toward a grand slam this year, which means also winning the United States Open, the British Open and the P.G.A. tourney. "I have my sights on these, but I'm aiming at one at a time," he said.

Associated Press

Nicklaus riding away from the 18th green with his wife, Barbara, and his son, Jack Jr., after triumph in Masters.

As Nicklaus was increasing his year's earnings to $134,473 and his total to $1,527,637 Palmer and Lee Trevino did not fare well. While playing the 14th, the head of Palmer's club flew off and he took a bogey. The four-time champion, however, had his worst score in the 18 masters in which he has played with a round of 81. Trevino finished in the same bracket with him at 300 or 12 over par with a final 72.

Bruce Devlin was one of three who bettered par with a 71. That gave him 290 along with Homero Blancas, Jerry Heard, McGee and Jamieson. Gary Player and Dave Stockton also managed to break the par over the 6,980-yard course and their 71's tied them at 291.

The 1971 champion, Charlie Coody, had a 75 for 292, the same score as those of Al Geiberger, Steve Melnyk, the rookie pro, and George Archer, a former Masters champion. Bob Goalby and Billy Casper, also wearers of the green jacket in other years were at 294.

Ben Crenshaw, the National Collegiate champion from the University of Texas, was the

low amateur at 295. Paul Harney who had trailed Nicklaus by one shot as the runner-up after 36 holes, needed an 81 today for 296. Sam Snead, the 59-year-old star who was in second place after the opening 18 holes, one back of Nicklaus, took a 77 for 297.

Jamieson's rooters were saddened as their favorite took bogeys on three of the first five holes. The pressure of the competition and the slick greens appeared to affect him as he went out in 39, or three over par. Although he trailed by five he still was in second place with nine to go. Heard, Mitchell, Blancas, Weiskopf and Yancey were six back of Big Jack at that point.

"The greens were faster, maybe faster than in 1965," said Nicklaus. That year he posted the record low winning score of 271. That was his second triumph. He had won in 1963 at the age of 23, the youngest ever and he also followed with another mark in this event by winning consecutive tourneys in 1965 and 1966.

After working out some flaws

Nicklaus Wins U.S. Open by 3 Strokes

Jack Nicklaus, left, walking off the 18th green with Lee Trevino, last year's champion

in his game at the practice tee last night, Nicklaus appeared more confident today that his game would at least approximate what he wanted it to be.

Over the front nine, Nicklaus scored a 35, one under par with birdies at the two par-5 holes, the second and eighth, where his long powerful drives were important. At the 365-yard seventh, a par 4, however, he carded a bogey after his second went over the green into a bunker.

At the 10th he received a "free lift" from ground under repair in which he would have had to stand to hit his second. He had a par 4 there, but he took three putts at th 11th, 13th and 14th, two of these were for bogey 5's but that at the 13th was for a par. At the 520-yard 16th his iron shot carried over the green among the pines, he chipped back to just off the front edge, was on his fourth shot then two-putted for a bogey 6.

Of the short 16th, Nicklaus said in describing his play later, "I finally got down in two. I was about 30 feet away on my tee shot and then putted up to about three feet. My caddie, Willie (Peterson) said, "You can make it" and I said, 'say that again'," Nicklaus then holed the putt as Willie said he would for the 3.

At the 17th Nicklaus holed an important putt, too. His No 8 iron second fell into a bunker for a "fried egg" in the soft sand. He recovered, hitting about 11 feet beyond the flagstick. After carefully sighting, he rolled the ball into the cup for a par 4. At the last green, he hit a No. 3 wood from the tee and a No. 6 iron within 15 feet of the cup. With two putts he had his 4 for the 74 that gave him the championship again.

"The course was tough, I was having my troubles but so were the others. It was kind of digging away at me inside, but I had the patience to stick to my game plan. I was playing to win," he said. And he did.

April 10, 1972

Registers 74 for 290—Crampton 2d, Palmer 3d

By LINCOLN A. WERDEN
Special to The New York Times

PEBBLE BEACH, Calif., June 18 — Jack Nicklaus equaled a cherished record and took a big step toward another golfing goal as he won the United States Open championship today by three strokes.

With a final round of 74 for a 72-hole aggregate of 290 over the wind-swept terrain of the Pebble Beach Golf Links, Nicklaus captured his 13th major title, a total that only the late Bobby Jones had achieved.

When asked how he felt about this accomplishment, the 32-year-old professional, who had considered Jones his idol ever since he learned to play at his father's side in Columbut, Ohio, said, "Now that I'm there, I have a funny feeling that I've won but I feel

proud to be in the company of Jones."

President Nixon telephoned congratulations, commended Big Jack on his stunning shot that hit the flagstick at the par-3 17th hole and wished him the best of luck in the British Open and the Professional Golfers' Association championship. Last April, Nicklaus won the Masters at Augusta. With success in this tourney, he would complete his dream of a grand-slam this year with victory in the other two major events.

In Jeopardy at 10th Hole

The runner-up was Bruce Crampton of Australia, whose four-over-par 76 gave him a total of 293. He said he found the greens hard, the winds strong and hitting from the sturdy rough to small greens an "imposible" task. "Jack's got to be the greatest player in the world."

There were moments when Nicklaus seemed on the verge of jeopardy, especially when a tee shot at the 10th hole veered farfar to the right and tumbled over the cliff onto the beach.

"If it had been payable I would have hit it," he said, "but the ball was plugged in the sand." He took a penalty stroke, then hit another into a hazard and wound up with a double-bogey 6.

But as Lee Trevino, the talkative Texan and defending champion, said before starting, "Everyone will make a bogey on this course, maybe a double bogey, but then you have to keep your cool."

It's exactly what Nicklaus did.

Arnold Palmer, making a last-minute bid, came through with a 76 for 294. The 1960 champion, who lost in the playoff that gave Nicklaus his first Open crown in 1962, finished third.

Challengers Have Woes

Trevino, who was hospitalized for four days before arriving here only on the eve of the championship, struggled through with only one birdie for a 78 to tie for fourth with Homero Blancas at 295.

Some of Nicklaus's fans became apprehensive after his experience at the 10th and after

a bogey 4 at the 12th where his ball bounced over the green and down into an embankment. But his chief challengers were having more than a full measure of trouble on the 6,812-yard course, regarded as one of the most difficult sites in 72 years of Open history.

Kermit Zarley, who with Trevino and Crampton had started the last trek only a stroke back of Nicklaus, took 39 to the turn, then wrecked his chances with a triple bogey at the 14th. After being bunkered in two, his third went over the slope of the green. He finally got back in five and then three-putted. Zarley's 79 placed him sixth at 296.

The victory was worth $30,000 from the $200,000 purse and increased Nicklaus's earnings this year to $186,051, keeping him as the current leading money-winner. He also increased his career winnings to $1,569,314.73, more than any other golfer has ever earned, as he posted his 38th tournament victory.

Nicklaus recalled that it was here at Pebble that he won his second Amateur title in 1961, several months before he decided to become a professional. His dad, the late Charles Nicklaus, a druggist, thought his son might follow in his profession.

On a 5-Year Cycle

But Jack, then 21 years old, decided he would try the pro tour. In 1962, he won his first Open and repeated five years later. "It was five years apart," recalled his wife, Barbara, before today's round. "Now it's

five years since Jack last won, maybe this will be our lucky day."

Nicklaus said half the greens were "dried out and dead" because of the wind. "Every green had a different speed and you were lucky to avoid three-putting."

He did three-putt at the fourth and 18th holes.

Despite successive bogeys at the fourth and the short fifth, where he chipped from the fringe of the green and missed his par, he was out in 36.

Then came the 10th, where a gust of wind caught his backswing and he hit "the first bad drive I had all week." Two holes later his No. 3 iron tee shot bounced over the bank and he salvaged a bogey.

But at the 15th he rolled in a 13-foot putt for a birdie that left him two over par and three ahead of Crampton.

At the 17th, which cost the field 94 bogeys in the first three rounds, Nicklaus hit a tremendous No. 1 iron tee shot to the green of the 218-yard hole. The ball ran onto the green, hit the flagstick and kicked four or five inches away from being a hole-in-one. There was no doubt about a victory now, and despite three putts for a closing bogey 6 at the home green, Nicklaus had won on the course he knows and likes best.

Cesar Sanudo	72 72 78 77—299	3,500
Tom Weiskopf	73 74 73 79—299	3,500
Billy Casper	74 73 79 74—300	2,500
Don January	76 71 74 79—300	2,500
Bobby Nichols	77 74 72 77—300	2,500
Bert Yancey	75 79 70 76—300	2,500
Don Massengale	72 81 78 70—301	2,233
Orville Moody	71 77 79 74—301	2,233
Gary Player	72 74 75 80—301	2,233
*Jim Simons	75 75 79 72—301	
Lou Graham	75 73 75 79—302	1,750
*Tom Kite	75 73 79 75—302	
Al Geiberger	80 74 76 73—303	1,700
Paul Harney	79 72 75 77—303	1,440
Bobby Mitchell	74 80 73 76—303	1,440
Charles Sifford	79 74 72 78—303	1,440
Gay Brewer	77 77 72 78—304	1,428
Rod Funseth	73 73 84 74—304	1,428
Lanny Wadkins	76 68 79 81—304	1,428
Jim Wiechers	74 79 69 82—304	1,428
Miller Barber	76 74 73 80—305	1,217
Julius Boros	77 77 74 77—305	1,217
Dave Eichelberger	76 71 80 78—305	1,217
Lee Elder	75 71 79 80—305	1,217
Jerry Heard	73 74 77 81—305	1,217
Dave Hill	74 78 74 79—305	1,217
Tom Watson	74 79 76 76—305	1,217
Bud Allin	75 76 77 79—306	1,090
Larry Hinson	78 73 72 83—306	1,090
Hale Irwin	78 72 73 83—306	1,090
Barry Jaeckel	78 69 82 77—306	1,090
Ron Cerrudo	77 77 76 77—307	994
Tony Jacklin	75 78 71 83—307	994

Jerry McGee	79 72 71 85—307	994
George Rives	80 73 79 75—307	994
Mason Rudolph	71 80 86 70—307	994
Tom Shaw	71 79 80 77—307	994
Billy Ziobro	76 77 77 77—307	994
Bobby Cole	72 76 79 81—308	930
Gibby Gilbert	77 77 77 77—308	930
David Graham	77 77 79 75—308	930
Ron Letellier	75 77 74 82—308	930
John Schroeder	78 75 75 80—308	930
Mike Butler	78 73 77 81—309	890
Thomas Jenkins	73 80 75 81—309	890
Ralph Johnston	73 72 73 84—309	890
Tommy Aaron	76 76 77 81—310	835
Martin Bohen	77 76 77 80—310	835
Bob Brue	77 75 79 79—310	835
Tim Collins	79 71 81 79—310	835
Hubert Green	75 76 78 81—310	835
Bobby Greenwood	77 75 72 86—310	835
Jim Hardy	78 76 79 77—310	835
Mike Hill	75 77 75 83—310	835
Jim Colbert	74 79 76 82—311	800
Bob Murphy	79 74 83 75—311	800
George Archer	74 74 77 87—312	800
Bruce Devlin	75 78 74 85—312	800
Dick Hendrickson	80 74 79 82—315	800
Austin Straub	76 77 75 87—315	800
Dwight Nevil	76 77 81 82—316	800
*Daniel R. O'Neill	78 76 77 86—317	—

*Denotes amateur.

June 19, 1972

U.S. Open Scores

Jack Nicklaus	71 73 72 74—290	$30,000
Bruce Crampton	74 70 73 76—293	15,000
Arnold Palmer	77 68 73 76—294	10,000
Homero Blancas	74 70 76 75—295	7,500
Lee Trevino	74 72 71 78—295	7,500
Kermit Zarley	71 73 73 79—296	6,000
Johnny Miller	74 73 71 79—297	5,000
Chi Chi Rodriguez	71 75 78 75—299	3,500

Jack Nicklaus, 32, of Columbus, Ohio, is the best golfer in the world, and he means to improve.

That, in brief, is what sets him apart from the other giants of the game, and perhaps from the giants of most other games also. He first picked up a golf club when he was 10 and for the past 22 years has been laboring over his game, in the flesh by day and in the mind by night. He is certainly the most cerebral golfer since Ben Hogan, whose "Fundamentals of Modern Golf" is practically an advanced text on human anatomy and aerodynamics. And he is the coolest, the least fooled, analyst of his own game since "the immortal one" of golf, Robert Tyre Jones Jr., who, since he is now dead, is more immortal than ever.

"The golf swing for me," Nicklaus told Herbert Warren Wind, his Boswell in the best golfing biography that has appeared so far, "is a source of never-ending fascination. On the one hand, the swings of all the outstanding golfers are decidedly individual but, on the other, the champions all execute approximately the same moves at the critical stages of the swing.... There is still a lot about

It is very likely that the television audience for this joust will be larger—and more breathless—than any since the cathode ray tube turned golf into a weekend mass entertainment and Arnold Palmer into the first millionaire professional golfer. For, after Nicklaus's win in the U.S. Open three weeks ago today at Pebble Beach, on Carmel Bay, he will be on the third leg of a four-lap ambition that has never been achieved: to win in one year what are now considered the four main golf tournaments of the world—the Masters, the U.S. Open, the British Open and the American Professional Golfers' Association championship. In April in the Masters Nicklaus led the field from the first day to the last. He did the same at Pebble Beach.

Because he is acknowledged to be the best golfer to have come along since Ben Hogan, and is thought (by himself among other experts) to be in his prime, he began to tempt himself last winter with the heady vision of performing the so-called Grand Slam. The phrase is borrowed from the unique performance in 1930 of Nicklaus's boyhood idol, Bob Jones, in sweeping what a sports writer of

Nicklaus: 22 Years At Hard Labor

By ALISTAIR COOKE

the swing we don't know and probably never will. ... In any event, scarcely a day goes by when I don't find myself thinking about the golf swing."

These spells of monkish contemplation are given over to a physical act that takes approximately two seconds to perform—namely, the dispatching of a dimpled white ball 1.68 inches in diameter toward a hole in the ground 4¼ inches wide. The British, an enervated race, prefer to make the attempt on a ball only 1.62 inches in diameter. The British ball balloons less alarmingly downwind and bores more easily and accurately into the wind, but it compensates nastily for these advantages by nestling more snugly in the rough, in the sand of the bunkers, and in the lusher fringes of the putting greens. Nicklaus, at this moment, is bringing his powerful and finicky mind to bear on the problems of the British ball, since this Wednesday he will use it to tee off at Muirfield, one of the great strategical courses of Scotland, in the British Open championship.

Alistair Cooke, long time chief American correspondent of The Guardian (of England), is currently finishing a three-year television project, "America: Personal History of the United States," to be seen on NBC this fall, after which he will retire to the practice tee.

the day called "the impregnable quadrilateral."

This grandiose morsel of leftover nineteen-twenties prose described what were in those days the four main world championships. It tells us something about the social shift of golf from "a gentleman's game" to a money game that these four were then the U.S. Amateur championship, the British Amateur, the U.S. Open and the British Open. Jones's feat, done by a 28-year-old Atlanta lawyer as handsome as Apollo and as engaging as Charlie Brown, earned him a ticker-tape parade up Broadway à la Lindbergh and made him the one golfer known and adored in countries that wouldn't know a bunker from a hole in the ground. He retired, still an amateur, from all competitive golf, and it is about as sure as anything can be that his Grand Slam will never be done again.

Today, if any amateur should emerge of Jones's superlative quality, he would surely turn pro in a game which only 20 years ago rewarded the leading money-winner of the tour with $37,032 and today would guarantee him closer to $200,000. Moreover, if a second such prodigy were to remain an amateur (Jones, for most of the year, was a weekend golfer), he could not possibly hone his game to the relentless modern standard of the 100 or so pros on the tour who follow the sun from January through October, playing, on an average, about 150 days a year. The University of Houston alone scouts the country for promising lads, entices them with golf scholarships, plants them on the practice tee in the dawn of their freshman year, has them hitting 200 or 300 balls a day for four years and releases them at sunset on graduation day with the prospect of an early place on the professional tour and the bonus of a highly "relevant" degree, a Bachelor of Business Management.

It is against such an army of single-minded young warriors, dedicated from their teens to the glory of golf and one million bucks, that Jack Nicklaus is now waging his audacious, one-man war. Less than a decade ago, it was safe to wager that the Masters or the U.S. Open would be won either by Arnold Palmer, then at his peak, or by one of two or three other giants who were always pacing him, including the hulking young man from Ohio State who would soon match Palmer and eclipse him. Today, picking the winner of a given P.G.A. tournament is about as rational as lining up in one race every winning nag of the year between Belmont Park and Santa Anita and laying 100 to 1. There are at least two dozen players on the golf tour capable of winning any tournament, with the dramatic exception of the British Open whenever it is played at St. Andrews, Carnoustie or Muirfield, the three flat, ferocious, wind-driven seaside championship courses of Scotland. In the 10 times that the British Open has been played at Muirfield since 1891, only one man has won it twice (as Nicklaus now prays to do) and only once has there emerged a surprise winner—that is to say, a golfer not already established as among the two or three best players alive. For Nicklaus this week, the gods have prepared a truly Gaelic torture. Muirfield, it has been almost certainly established, was designed by Lady Macbeth.

When the golf writers began to conjure with Nicklaus's vision and approached him to name the odds on his Grand Slam, he facetiously guessed "1,000,000 to 1." When he came into the press tent at Augusta having won the Masters, the compulsive purple-prose writers pressed him again. "Well, now," he said, "I guess they're down to 1,000 to 1." Three weeks ago, two down and two to go, the touts were still at it. "You name it," sighed Nicklaus, "50 to 1, 100 to 1."

He has, by the way, developed an attitude toward the press, since the early days of his modest fame as U.S. Amateur champion, that reflects his uncalculating Midwestern assumption that everybody in sight, a President or a busboy, is his equal until proved otherwise. It is the custom at professional tournaments for the leaders of the day to retire to the press tent and go over their rounds hole by hole, club by club. It can be a dull or funny or embarrassing ceremony. There are the anxious ones who crack the snappy chestnuts known to every Sunday foursome in the land. There are fine golfers who interminably unburden their woes, usually to convey the subtle point that they ought to be leading by four strokes. A few imperious ones, presuming—often correctly—that most of the reporting pack are golfing duffers, exercise the tolerance of Aristotle discussing philosophy with a convention of high-school prize essayists.

Nicklaus's golfing intelligence (a special endowment, and one, like an actor's or banker's, quite unrelated to wisdom, horse sense or even a creditable I.Q.) used to make him brusque with neophytes. But he has matured in this as in several other traits, and is now alert to the slightest hint of golfing know-how from any reporter, no matter how green. He warms to cub reporters with candid, often long and detailed answers. Only rarely does he glare in stupefied disbelief at the reporter-statisticians who, year in year out, think of golf as a bucolic variation on roulette. Five years ago, he came dripping in from the 100-degree heat of

Baltusrol, N. J., having figured on a finishing 65, having made it, and having incidentally beaten the record four-round score for the U.S. Open. (In a practice round early in the week, he had matched the infernal heat with a scorching 62. "A freak," he called it; "it doesn't mean a thing.") "Jack," cried a palpitating reporter, "if you hadn't bunkered your approach on the second, and three-putted the tenth, and you'd made that short putt on the sixth, my God, you'd have had another 62." Nicklaus looked at the man with stony compassion. In his incongruously squeaky tenor, he snapped, "If, if, if— that's what the game is all about."

What *his* game is all about is a question now absorbing many million golfers throughout the world, not to mention the captive wives and small fry huddled around the telly who are just learning to take the old man's word that the grim-jawed blond up there scrutinizing four feet of innocent grass, and whom the gee-whiz commentators keep calling "The Golden Bear," is also the golden boy of contemporary golf.

Jack William Nicklaus (pronounced Nick-lus, not Nick-louse) is the great-grandson of an immigrant boilermaker from Alsace-Lorraine and the son of a prosperous Columbus, Ohio, pharmacist whose hobbies were Ohio State football, golf, fishing and telling his son of the miracles of St. Robert Tyre Jones Jr. Jack was born in 1940, the year of Dunkirk and the Fall of France, when the British were plowing up their golf courses and planting land mines against the anticipated Nazi invasion. (Last month, one of them exploded under an oak tree on the ninth fairway at Knole, in Kent, causing an irritated Englishman to lose his stance and his ball; he was allowed, however, to drop another, two club-lengths from the crater, without penalty.)

Nicklaus's progress through school and college makes him sound like a throwback to a De Sylva, Brown and Henderson musical of the nineteen-twenties. A Midwestern boy so albino-blond that an early golfing teammate called him "Snow White," he worked in his father's drug store after school, played basketball, baseball, football and track; never thought of going to any other college than good old Ohio State; made Phi Gamma Delta ("it was crucial to make a fraternity, for the undergraduate who didn't had no social life at all"); met a pretty blonde, Barbara Bash, Pledge Princess of the campus in her freshman year, and married her in his senior year. In the intervals of playing basketball, competing in college or national amateur golf, or fly-casting with his father, he completed a prepharmacy course and majored in insurance. "Corny?" he says; "I loved it."

He had started to toddle, and hack, around a golf course after his father injured his ankle badly, prompting the doctor to suggest that henceforth, Father Nicklaus forgo volley ball and take to gentler exercise, "the sort of movement you get when you walk on soft ground." Father turned to golf but found himself something of a lagging invalid to his regular partners so he haled in his 10-year-old son as a walking companion. The youngster got his first set

of cut-down clubs just as the Scioto golf club, to which Father Nicklaus belonged, acquired a new pro, Jack Grout, then a taut, tanned 42-year-old. Nicklaus, to this day, has had no other teacher except himself, who is probably the more exacting of the two.

So on a Friday morning in June, 1950, the golden bear cub lined up on the practice tee with 50 other youngsters. It is clear from the record that the perfectionist strain in the Nicklaus character at once took over to refine the normal, rollicking ambition of small boys to bang out a succession of rockets. The first time he played nine holes, he had a creditable 51. "My second time out, I had a 61. Then, for weeks, I got worse and worse." He supplemented the Friday morning regimental drill with private lessons from Grout. The knobbly-jointed stripling began to develop a golf swing. At the close of his tenth year, he played 18 holes in 95. The next year he shot an 81. During the third summer, he had a maddening run of eight 80's in a row, and suddenly shot a 74. At 13, he had a 69. At 16, he won the Ohio State Open.

At some points along this determined trajectory from hacking moppet to boy wonder, he admits, he occasionally flexed his ego along with his muscles. And at such times, his father deflated him with a regular recital of Bobby Jones's boyhood record: junior champion of his Atlanta club at 9, amateur champion of Georgia at 14, the South at 15, tied for fourth in the U.S. Open at 18. "Whenever I was getting too big for my britches," Nicklaus recalls, "that usually did the trick."

Three weeks ago, Nicklaus became the only golfer to tie Jones's record of winning 13 of the world's main titles.

The long trail, the making of the Nicklaus game, began on the practice tee at Scioto. What did he have to begin with? This is as good a place as any to introduce the bugaboo of "a natural golfer." According to the best players and teachers of their time—Harry Vardon, Bob Jones, Ernest Jones, Percy Boomer, Tommy Armour, Archie Compston, Ben Hogan, Henry Cotton, Bob Toski and, today, John Jacobs — there is no such thing as a natural golfer. A boy may have an aptitude for sports. He may have, according to the chosen game, the required muscle or speed or grace or stamina. Assuredly, there are born "unnatural" golfers, as there are men built like kangaroos or penguins who will never learn to dance or thread a needle. But given the best natural endowment, which in golf would be a fluid sense of timing and a habit of relaxed concentration, the gifted one has then to learn a series of coordinated movements with his feet, ankles, knees, insteps, thighs, arms, shoulders, back muscles, hands and head; a series so unnatural that he will use it nowhere else in life. The golf swing is, if anything, more unnatural than classical ballet, and the training for it is as severe as anything known to the Bolshoi. Jack Nicklaus began the grind at 10 and he is still working at it, even though he is the Nureyev of the links.

If there was any luck in the time and place of his initiation, it was in having Jack Grout newly arrived at Scioto. Grout was a teacher with some firm convictions, one of which, however, was that every golfer is an individual. This runs counter to the insistence of many young pros —and most of the textbooks — that every pupil must be broken in to the mold of a favorite dogma. For instance, 998 golfers in 1,000 use the Vardon grip, which has the little finger of the right hand resting on top of the cleft between the first and second fingers of the left.

The 999th manages, don't ask me why, with a baseball grip, the two hands completely separated. Nicklaus was the 1,000th oddity who was more comfortable interlocking or hooking the little finger of the right hand securely around the forefinger of the left. Nicklaus, indeed, the big bear of the broad beam and the 27-inch thighs, has small hands so surprisingly weak in their grip that he swears he has often asked his wife, a girl svelte to the point of fragility, to unscrew pickle jars for him. Grout let him stay with this eccentricity, and he uses it today.

But Grout's tolerance of idiosyncrasy had severe limits. He insisted from the start on two fundamentals. Since they apply to every golfer, young and old, they may help us all, if only we can absorb them well enough to let them pass over into what Ben Hogan memorably called "the muscle memory." Nicklaus avows that his game is rooted in these two fundamentals.

The first is that "the head must be kept still" throughout the swing. Nicklaus figures it took him at least two years to master this simplicity, sometimes under the duress of having Grout's assistant hold on to the hair of Snow White's head to make him, in J. H. Taylor's fine phrase, "play beneath himself." Anyone who has ever had his head gripped while trying to repeat a serviceable swing will have quickly learned the painful truth that we are all "natural" jumping jacks. I once had an easy-going friend, a cheerful hacker who refused to take any lessons on the down-to-earth assertion that "I simply try to be a pendulum." Unfortunately, the human body is constructed, with marvelous ingenuity, not to be a pendulum.

Much of the difficulty of teaching, and learning, golf has to do with the rich ambiguities of the simplest English words. Taking the club "back" is not the same as taking it "behind." "Pushing" the club back is a whole stage of development beyond "lifting" it. To take an example that prolonged one habit of dufferdom for more than 20 years, and mentally aggravated Nicklaus's trouble with his head, there is the routine injunction very popular in the nineteen-twenties to "keep your eye on the ball." It was a phrase deplored even then by Bob Jones, and it drove the irrascible Tommy Armour to swear that it was "the most abysmal advice ever given by the ignorant to the stupid." The point these dissenters wished to make was that it is possible to lurch and sway all over the place, maybe even to lie down, while still keeping your eye on the ball. To keep watching the ball as it leaves the club, instead of the spot it lay on, is always fatal. The famous phrase was later seen to mean no more, but no less, than to "keep the head still." Golf arguments, even between the best pros, often revolve not around a difference of insight but around an image which means one thing to one man and something else to another.

The second fundamental, which Nicklaus maintains gave his game its early solidity, was Grout's insistence that "the key to balance is rolling the ankles inwards," the left toward the right on the backswing, the right in to the left on the downswing. Here again, the picture in the mind has been painted many ways. Some talk of keeping the left heel down while "bracing the right leg." Jones hit off a sharp poetic image when he said that golf is played "between the knees." Nicklaus more recently said, "If you go over beyond your right instep on the backswing, if you relax the pressure there, you are dead." And George Heron, the little 80-year-old Scot who, as a boy, made clubs for Vardon, is still telling his pupils down in St. Augustine, Fla., "A knock-kneed man is going to be a better golfer than a bow-legged one."

Well, on these two fundamentals alone, Nicklaus calculates he spent four or five years, in the meantime working through the range of clubs for hours on end on the practice tee. He says that today "whenever anything goes wrong," he goes out and hits a thousand balls "flat-footed," neither lifting his heels nor moving his ankles, as a drastic way of restoring his sense of balance. He was known, fairly recently, to feel he had played a short cut - shot poorly, so, after the day's play, he chipped 400 balls in three hours.

There was a third fundamental taught to the young Nicklaus which decidedly does not apply to golfers of all ages and which, in Grout's day, was condemned for golfers of any age. The general practice was to force youngsters to resist the urge to go for distance and to teach them precision first. Grout felt that a boy should begin at once to stretch and develop the back muscles that would let him take the club as high, and as far behind, as a straight left arm would allow. The longer the arc of the club on the backswing, and the more acute the angle between the club shaft and the left arm as the hands come down and go ahead of the ball: this, not the blacksmith's mighty muscle, is the secret of distance. Nicklaus achieves it with a vast arc at the top of the backswing, his left shoulder bulging beneath and almost beyond the set of his chin, while his left arm and hands are poking into the stratosphere. I have walked along with him even on practice rounds when only a lynx could follow the trajectory from the club head through the sky.

It is a sight whose result produces flattering gasps from the crowd around the tees. It has nothing to do with Hercules and everything to do with centrifugal force. Nonetheless, it is an act which most of us over 40 had better not try to emulate, unless an ambulance is on call.

There are about a half-dozen other fundamentals. And the later refinements, which can convert an average golfer into a good one, and then a good one into a great one, can be counted by the hundreds, and by Ben Hogan into infinity. Nicklaus has wrestled with most of them, though he still believes he is only an average player of short pitch shots. The prob-

lem of mentally selecting which subtleties are applicable to any given golf situation is what explains that fixed stare and riveted jaw as he plods down the fairways, oblivious of everything but the tactical cunning of the next shot.

So you put together years of daily practice, the putting and chipping and "fading" and "drawing" and "punching" and "cutting" of a million or two golf balls; the gift of total concentration; the sure knowledge that the only opponents that matter are the golf course and yourself. You still do not get Nicklaus. These disciplines have been practiced and earned by any 12 golfers you choose to call the best living dozen.

The overriding supremacy of Nicklaus is due to what you might call calculated gall, or generalship under pressure. When Jones retired from the neurological nightmare of championship golf, he explained: "There are two kinds of golf, and they are the worlds apart. There is the game of golf, and there is tournament golf."

Every fine player cracks at some point in the three to four hours of his chosen form of tension. Nicklaus appeared to collapse on the 10th at Pebble Beach with a double bogey worthy of an average club player. He promptly forgot it. So it comes down in the end to the extraordinary self-discipline of his judgment, at the tensest times, of when to draw rein and when to cut loose. Palmer remained a thing of beauty and a boy forever because he "went for" impossible retrieves all of us fantasize on our pillows at night. Not Nicklaus.

Standing in 1966 on the 17th tee at Muirfield, where he expects to stand four times again this week, he faced a par-five, 528-yard hole rising for 200 yards and then disappearing as it turns to the left. It takes Nicklaus four crisp and explicit pages of his and Wind's book, "The Greatest Game of All: My Life in Golf," to explain exactly how he played the hole differently each day. Briefly, on Wednesday, he drove off

THE IMMORTAL ONE—Bobby Jones blasting out of a trap at Winged Foot Golf Club in Mamaroneck in 1929 the year before he won what was then called "the impregnable quadrilateral," the two major amateur and two major professional tournaments.

against an east wind with a three-wood. The next two days, with a west wind blowing right to left, he took a one-iron. On the last day, approaching the 17th, he had to have a birdie and a par to win, a challenge that nobody but Nicklaus relishes. The wind was a little stronger behind him. He decided on a three-iron and landed 290 yards away, precisely two feet short of the rough. "That meant I was 238 yards from the center of the green." (Nicklaus paces everything out before the tournament, keeps a yardage chart and makes notes on odd trees, church spires, bushes, hillocks, swales, visible landmarks. And when he says 238 yards, he does not mean 235.) If he had been playing the bigger American ball with no wind, he would have instinctively reached for a one-iron. But he paused and thought hard, always the most awesome sight in modern golf, and he decided to allow "one

club less for the small ball, one and a half clubs less for the following wind, one club less for the run on the ball, and a half club for the extra distance you get when the adrenalin is flowing." So he took — for a 238 yard approach shot that had to land on the fairway short of a bunker and bounce over it onto the green — a five-iron! (The average good player uses a five-iron for, say, 150 yards.) He stopped 16 feet from the flag, decided not to be a hero but to lag it close and tap it in for his birdie. The par on the 18th was, for Nicklaus, almost a yawn.

All of this, I am alarmed to realize, makes him come out a hero about as granitic and lovable as a Viking invader. In spite of the journalistic tradition of tying up such Titans in pink ribbons at the end of the piece, a practice which would not in the least endear me to Nicklaus, something should be said about the noticeable ease with which

he matured out of his 20's. He was not always "The Golden Bear" to the crowds. In the days of Palmer's supremacy, he padded along behind Arnie and his howling "army" stolid, unloved and, often, applauded only when he barely missed a splendid putt. He bore these outrages with great grace, and occasional clenched teeth. He has only lately gained the affection, as well as the awe, of the following crowd. In a country which overrates the sporting swinger and the fairway comedian, he has refused, under considerable outside pressure, to improvise a public image. For his health's sake, and for his much improved appearance, he took off 20 pounds and is unlikely ever again to be jeered at, by some other idol's army, as "the Kraut" or "Fatso." In a passing bow to the nineteen-seventies, he sprouted sideburns and acquired an extra tumble or two of Byronic locks.

Otherwise, he is simply a

mature and relaxed version of what he always was: a Midwestern boy of remarkable candor, quick wits, a pleasant touch of self-deprecating humor, and an unflagging devotion to the traditions and courtesies of golf. All that is formidable about him is what has put him where he is: The unwavering industry to improve his game. His refusal to know that he knows. His iron self-discipline. And the really terrifying self-confidence, which rarely nowadays sharpens into cockiness, of a golfer who is uncomfortable only when he is leading a tournament. He is probably the only great golfer alive—or dead—who could honestly have meant what he said to an English friend who casually asked him what was his idea of the most rousing prospect in golf: "Three holes to go, and you need two pars and a birdie to win." ■

July 9, 1972

TREVINO KEEPS BRITISH OPEN CHAMPIONSHIP ON 278

By FRED TUPPER
Special to The New York Times

MUIRFIELD, Scotland, July 15—Lee Trevino won the British Open, with 278, for the second year in a row today and he won it by a shot from Jack Nicklaus.

For the second day running Trevino clinched his lead by chipping in from off the green. Yesterday he knocked in a chip from the rough back of the 18th green to lead at six under par by a stroke over Tony Jacklin. Today, when it looked as if his lead had gone blithering, he chipped in from 15 feet off the 17th to save his par by playing the hole without touching fairway or green. It meant the championship as Jacklin three-putted there.

Nicklaus gave it a wonderful try with his five-under-par 66. For three rounds he had played uninspired par golf and was in sixth place. He sat in the press tent then shaking his head. "I made some swings I'm not familiar with," he said. "If I got

in a few putts, I could shoot a 65 tomorrow."

Nicklaus Challenges

For 11 holes he was six under par in a superb exhibition of shotmaking. The flair and the finesse were back, the long crackling tee shots, the high irons floating into the pin. And a few putts were going down, too. Nicklaus was on his way, picking up the thousands behind him in their determination to bring him home, to cheer him to the third leg of that fabled grand slam.

He got his first birdie at the second hole, a 349-yard par 4. He drove to the apron short of the green, pitched to six feet and got the putt down. On the third hole, he wafted an iron over the blind bunker to six feet and rolled the putt in. He was 10 feet away on the short third and his putt for a deuce slid off. A huge wood to the par-5 fifth and two putts brought his third birdie. He was hole high in two on the

Associated Press
Lee Trevino watching his putt on the ninth hole

seventh green and another birdie putt from 12 feet slid off, and then on the ninth Nicklaus stroked a chip to three feet and forced the putt in. He was four under par now and tied for the lead as Trevino and Jacklin had slipped behind him.

Was it possible? On this flawless summer day with a slight breeze from the East and Nicklaus in this mood, the course was ripe for the taking. He powered a tremendous drive on the 10th and now, sure of his touch, he hit his approach to four feet and the birdie 3 was automatic. He led by a stroke.

The 11th is a blind shot over a high plateau. Nicklaus brushed the blond hair across his forehead and swung. "You don't see it; you just hear it," said a spectator in awe. His iron soared to the heart of the green. He was bending over his four-foot putt when a roar came winging on the wind and Nicklaus backed off. Trevino and

then Jacklin had eagled the ninth hole. Trevino was six under par again, Jacklin five. Nicklaus hit the putt in and he was six under.

The thought of a 65 seemed modest now. Nicklaus had only to par his way in to make it. The old purposeful stride was there for all to see. He was confident and alert.

Nicklaus hit an iron to 12 feet on the 12th and the putt was just wide. He was hole high again on the short 13th and the putt ran over the hole. His iron carried to the back of the 14th and the 20-foot putt stopped short. Would they never go down? His putt on the 15th was just six feet away, and the ball right-angled out of the cup. Four birdie holes there for the grabbing, perfectly set up and tantalizingly close, and yet he couldn't do it. And he was running out of holes.

Nicklaus had his first poor shot of the entire round on the short 16th, left in the light rough. He took his time, wedged beautifully to five feet and once more the putt jumped out of the cup. He was back to five up now and Trevino and Jacklin were six up. It was time

for a desperate measure.

Nicklaus pulled out his driver to have a go on the long 17th and hit it into deep rough. He got out of there and fired an iron into that huge cavern of a green. He needed a 20-footer for the birdie and he was just wide. Nicklaus had his par on the 18th to enormous cheers.

He had picked up five shots over the afternoon. It might have been just enough. But then Trevino pulled out his dimpled old "Helen Hicks" sand wedge and put the ball right into the 17th hole for his second British Open title.

Trevino had a 71. Jacklin was third at 280, followed by Doug Sanders at 281, Brian Barnes of Britain at 283, Gary Player at 285, Guy Hunt, the little Briton who partnered Nicklaus, at 286, with Welshman David Vaughan, Tom Weiskopf and Arnold Palmer, the last man to win successive British Opens (1961-62).

"I felt I needed 65 to do it," Nicklaus said. "I had it, but I let it get away. Today I felt I could control my iron game and a 279 would win an Open 19 times out of 20. Today it didn't. But I lost to the best guy around and that's Lee."

Trevino said he won with his chipping. Four times he chipped into the hole from off the green —on the second hole of the second day, on the 16th and 18th yesterday and on the 17th this afternoon. Up to that stage, he had floundered all along the hole. He had pulled the ball into the rough, then landed in a bunker, hit it out in the rough and hooked a 3 wood into the stiff bent grass on the back of the green. The chip did it. He had his par 5 as Jacklin sadly three-putted from 15 feet, the second only 2½ feet away.

This Muirfield Open pulled in 84,000, breaking the record set at St. Andrews in 1970 when Nicklaus won. And he won here in 1966. But now he's been second four times.

CARDS OF OPEN LEADERS

	PAR FOR THE COURSE	
OUT	444 354 345	36
IN	444 344 354	35—71
	LEE TREVINO	
OUT	534 364 443	36
IN	534 344 354	35—71
	JACK NICKLAUS	
OUT	433 344 344	32
IN	334 344 454	34—66
	TONY JACKLIN	
OUT	544 355 343	36
IN	443 344 365	36—72
	DOUG SANDERS	
OUT	544 353 254	35
IN	444 344 354	35—70

July 16, 1972

Nicklaus and Palmer Join Hogan, Jones and Hagen in Golf's 'Top 5' Poll

Jack Nicklaus

Arnold Palmer

Associated Press
Ben Hogan

Bobby Jones

The New York Times
Walter Hagen

Jack Nicklaus and Arnold Palmer have been voted among the five greatest golfers in a national poll of golf writers.

Ben Hogan, Bobby Jones and Walter Hagen also were named in selections of the Golf Writers Association of America.

The five will be honored Feb. 19 at the annual awards dinner of the Metropolitan Golf Writers at the Americana Hotel here. Hagen and Jones will be lauded posthumously.

Strong support for a "top five" position also went to Gary Player, Lee Trevino, Gene Sarazen and Sam Snead.

Jones was an overwhelming selection. The Georgian won the Grand Slam, which included the Open and Ama-

teur titles of both the United States and Great Britain, in 1930.

Jones never played golf for money but the colorful Hagen did. He rose from the caddy ranks in Rochester, N.Y., to rule the pros in the 1920s while Jones commanded the amateurs.

Jones died in 1971, two years after Hagen.

For many years, these men ranked 1, 2 in major golf championships. Jones had 13, Hagen 11. However, the 32-year-old Nicklaus is now tied with Jones.

Nicklaus, who won a record $320,000 on the 1972 tour, became the first man to win the Big Four pro tournaments twice. His Double Slam includes the United States and British Opens, the Masters and Pro-

fessional Golf Association championship.

In 11 years, Nicklaus has won over $1.5-million.

Palmer became golf's idol in 1960 and is second to Nicklaus in career earnings. Arnie has won all the Big Four but one—the P.G.A.—and has four Masters titles.

Hogan, now retired in Texas, was the dramatic star of the 1950s. He was at the top of his game when he was critically injured in a 1949 car-bus collision. The Texas Hawk, rated as one of the purest clubswingers ever, came back from the mishap to win the third of his United States Open crowns, two Masters and one British Open titles.

January 7, 1973

Miller's Record 63 For 279 Total Wins U.S. Open Golf Title

By LINCOLN A. WERDEN
Special to The New York Times

OAKMONT, Pa., June 17 — While his peers fell back, Johnny Miller took over today for the new generation in golf with a record closing round of 63 that brought him the United States Open championship by a one-stroke margin.

A dramatic eight-under-par spurt over the par 71 Oakmont Country Club course enabled the blond-haired 26-year-old Californian to win with a 72-hole aggregate of 279, or five under par. Miller had started the round six strokes behind the leaders—Julius Boros, Jerry Heard, Arnold Palmer and John Schlee.

"I was super nervous," said Miller, who as a 19-year-old was the low-scoring amateur in the 1966 Open in San Francisco where he was born.

"I kept saying to myself, don't shank." This was an error he committed in the 1972 Bing Crosby tourney at Pebble Beach, Calif. The mistake came with two holes left to play in that tournament. Miller finally tied Jack Nicklaus for first but lost in the playoff.

Miller described himself today as "Joe Feast or Famine—: I get everything or nothing," after finishing his round.

On this warm afternoon Miller not only outscored the popular 43-year-old Palmer; Nicklaus, the defender, Boros the 53-year-old campaigner, and others but he smashed the championship record of 64. The mark was first set in 1950 by Lee Mackey and equaled in 1964 by Tommy Jacobs and again in 1966 by Reeves McBee at the Olympic Club in San Francisco where Johnny Miller played in his first Open.

Palmer was still a winner with the fans at Oakmont.

"I won't be a big shot in my mind if I win today," Miller said before the outcome was determined. "I don't know much about Open history, but how many Open 63's have there been?" he asked with a sly grin.

While thousands continuously yelled "Come on, Arnie" in their hopes for a comeback victory by their hero, Palmer could do no better than a 72 to tie for fourth with Nicklaus and Lee Trevino, two former Open champions at 282.

Palmer's pairing mate, Schlee, from Dallas, captured the runner-up spot at 280 after a 70. Four years ago Schlee was so frustrated by his play he was ready to quit the pro ranks.

He finished one stroke ahead of Tom Weiskopf of Columbus, Ohio, who pulled ahead of his older competitors and carded a 70 for 281.

"Being paired with Palmer is like a two-shot penalty," declared the 33-year-old Schlee, whose only tour victory was scored last February in the Hawaiian open. "With people yelling all the time for Arnie it was tough and noisy."

At the first hole, however, he knocked his drive so close to the out-of-bounds fence and into shrubbery that he had an unplayable lie and suffered a one-stroke penalty and in the final accounting it proved crucial to his chances.

Miller had an unimpressive 76 yesterday and he explained that it was because he had forgotten his scorecard with his notes on distances and clubs to use for shots at each hole. He had planned to carry it in his hip pocket but instead he left the card in another pair of trousers. "This upset me and I went five over par after six holes," he said.

But it was his keen putting this afternoon that carried him to the championship and produced the record score. He needed only 29 putts today in carding nine birdies, four on the first four holes.

The victory brought him the championship trophy and a $35,000 first prize of the $225,000 purse. He seemed happy but not overawed. His previous successes on the circuit have been in the 1971 Southern open and the 1972 Heritage Classic at Hilton Head, S.C.

Associated Press
Johnny Miller during his record-breaking round

CARDS OF OPEN LEADERS				
PAR FOR THE COURSE				
OUT	444	543	435—36	
IN	445	344	344—35	—71—284
JOHNNY MILLER				
OUT	333	443	444—32	
IN	434	243	341—31	—63—279
JOHN SCHLEE				
OUT	644	352	444—36	
IN	444	444	244—34	—70—280
TOM WEISKOPF				
OUT	434	543	434—34	
IN	545	354	244—36	—70—281
JACK NICKLAUS				
OUT	434	543	444—35	
IN	445	344	234—33	—68—282
ARNOLD PALMER				
OUT	444	444	434—35	
IN	446	454	343—37	—72—282
LEE TREVINO				
OUT	534	443	434—34	
IN	445	344	354—36	—70—282

For a while it seemed that the winner might emerge from among Weiskopf, Palmer or Boros. They shared the lead with nine holes to play over the 6,921-yard course. Weiskopf had one of the strangest experience anyone has ever had in a major championship.

The Ohioan carded a birdie 4 at the ninth hole to be out in 34 after an unbelievable second shot caromed off a vendor selling periscopes on the right side of the ninth green. The ball bounded into a snack bar, skimmed by three people who were sitting on the counter and stopped on shelf next to three loaves of bread.

While spectators enjoyed the predicament and offered suggestions that Weiskopf should be refreshed by a hot dog, officials went into action. At the back of the shelf was a protective awning shielding the view of the ball from curious spectators. Because of the obstruction it was decided that Weiskopf should be given two-club lengths relief from the edge of the snack bar.

This would put him in casual water and therefore he received further relief by being permitted to drop without penalty in a dry spot in rough grass. He pitched to the green about 20 yards away and the ball ended five feet from the flag stick. Then Weiskopf sank the putt for an incredible birdie 4. The crowd applauded as he smiled broadly at the conclusion of his unusual adventure.

For Palmer, hoping to win here after losing to Nicklaus in the 1962 playoff, there were no humorous incidents. Neither were there any for Nicklaus and Gary Palmer of South Africa, the leader for the first two rounds, and Boros.

Player, with a 73, finished 12th at 287 while Boros, with his 73, was at 283 with Jerry Heard and Lanny Wadkins. Wadkins, the 23-year-old Virginian, posted a 65 which was the course record set by Gene Borek two days ago until Miller's round today. Heard closed with a 73 that included two bogeys on an incoming nine of 37.

Nicklaus put together his best round of the tournament, a 68, but he relinquished the title. He had hoped to achieve his goal of winning a fourth Open championship. Weiskopf had two bogeys and a birdie on his incoming nine of 36.

The easy swinging Boros, a champion of bygone years—1952 and 1963—did even worse. He couldn't get a birdie after the fourth and accumulated three bogeys on the backstretch for a 38.

Miller reeled off four birdies in a row to start his record round of 63. He explained his feelings later: "I said to myself I'm now one under par for the tournament." His 54-hole total was 216 while Palmer, Boros, Schlee and Heard started the round at 212, tied for first place.

Although he had a 76 yesterday which caused him to be "way down," the young Californian who now lives at Napa adjoining the Silverado Golf Club, still trailed the leaders — Palmer, Weiskopf and Boros — by three strokes at the end of nine holes today.

He needed only 15 putts on the front half of the course and 29 in all. But he took three of them at the eighth green for a bogey 4. At the ninth hole, his No. 2 iron second shot cleared the guarding bunkers and hit the putting surface. He took two putts for a birdie 4 from 40 feet and had a 32 for the outgoing nine.

Miller, who had a 61 for the low round on the pro circuit three years ago in the Phoenix open, posted three more birdies in succession from the 11th through the 13th on the second nine.

He knocked in a putt of 14 feet at the 11th and then, according to him, "the turning point came at the 12th." He drove into the rough at the left of the fairway but knocked his second out into smooth territory. Then he hit a No. 4 iron to within 15 feet of the flag stick. He rolled in the putt for a birdie 4.

He used a No. 4 iron from the tee at the 185-yard 13th hole and hit the green. He sank a 5-footer for a deuce. His last birdie came two holes later. Miller's No. 4 iron second shot at the 15th stopped 12 feet below the hole and he stroked in his putt for a 3.

Pars at the next three greens concluded the lowest individual round in 70 years of the championship.

June 18, 1973

THE SCORES

Tom Weiskopf, U.S.	68 67 71 70—276	$14.300
Neil Coles, England	71 72 70 66—279	9.425
Johnny Miller, U.S.	70 68 69 72—279	9.425
Jack Nicklaus, U.S.	69 79 76 65—280	7.150
Bert Yancey, U.S.	69 69 73 70—281	6.370
Peter Butler, Britain	71 72 74 69—286	5.590
Bob Charles, New Zealand	73 71 73 71—288	4.460
C. O'Connor, Ireland	73 68 74 73—288	4.460
L. Wadkins, U.S.	71 73 70 74—288	4.460
B. Barnes, Britain	76 67 70 76—289	3.500
Gay Brewer, U.S.	76 71 72 70—289	3.500
Harold Henning, South Africa	73 73 73 70—289	3.500
Lee Trevino, U.S.	73 73 73 70—289	3.500
T. Jacklin, England	75 73 72 70—290	2.470
D. McCland, Britain	76 71 69 74—290	2.470
Arnold Palmer, U.S.	72 76 70 72—290	2.470
G. Player, So. Africa	76 69 76 69—290	2.470
H. Bain, Ir. S. Afr.	75 74 69 74—292	1.060
Hugh Boyle, Britain	75 69 73—292	1.060
Bruce Crampton, Australia	71 76 73 72—292	1.060
B. Devlin, Australia	73 78 71 71—292	1.060
B. Gallacher, Britain	73 69 75 75—292	1.040
David Good, Britain	75 74 73 70—292	1.060
Dave Hill, U.S.	75 74 74 69—292	1.060
P. Oosterhuis, Brit.	80 71 69 72—292	1.040
E. Polland, Ireland	74 74 73 72—292	1.060
P. Wilcox, Britain	71 76 72 73—292	1.060
Chi-Chi Rodriguez, Puerto Rico	73 73 73 75—293	635
Doug Sanders, U.S.	79 72 72 70—293	635
R. De Vicenzo, Arg.	72 75 74 72—293	635
C. De Foy, Britain	76 75 70 73—294	550
T. Horton, Britain	75 70 73 76—294	550
G. Marsh, Australia	74 71 78 71—294	550
E. Murray, Britain	79 71 73 71—294	550
Peter Thompson, Australia	76 75 70 73—294	550
Robert Wynn, Britain	74 71 76 73—294	550
V. Baker, So. Africa	72 74 75 74—295	500
B. Dassu, Italy	75 75 73 73—296	515
a D. Edwards, U.S.	75 75 71 75—296	
P. Elson, Britain	75 75 72 74—296	515
Donald Gammon, Rhodesia	74 70 76 74—296	515
D. Hayes, So. Africa	74 73 75 74—296	515
Kel Nagle, Australia	74 76 63 73—296	515
Guy Wolstenholme, Australia	77 72 75 72—296	515
Harry Bannerman, Scotland	73 75 75 73—297	375
M. J. Moir, Britain	76 75 70 76—297	375
D. Webster, Britain	73 76 72 76—297	375
L. Fourie, So. Africa	76 73 74 75—298	345
B. Hunt, Britain	76 74 74 74—298	345
P. A. Iiss, England	76 71 76 76—299	325
D. Jagger, Britain	76 74 74 75—299	325
J. McTear, Britain	76 74 71 78—299	325
R. Shade, Britain	75 73 76 75—299	325
P. Townsend, Eng.	79 73 71 77—300	325
David Huish, Britain	74 73 76 78—301	325
R. Lambert, Britain	78 74 72 77—301	325
Will Murray, Britain	78 71 74 78—301	325
David Dunk, Britain	73 74 74 82—303	325
G. Mueller, Sweden	76 70 78 81—305	325

aDenotes amateur

Weiskopf's 276 Wins Open by Three Shots

Coles and Miller Tied for 2d— Nicklaus 4th

By FRED TUPPER

Special to The New York Times

TROON, Scotland, July 14—Tom Weiskopf won the 102d British Open today by three strokes from Johnny Miller and Neil Coles of Britain. His two-under-par 70, put together in belts of heavy rain, gave him a four-round total of 276 to tie the Open record set by Arnold Palmer on this course 11 years ago.

"I will never consider myself a great player until I win a major championship," said Weiskopf, a 30-year-old golfer from Columbus, Ohio, who has won three tournaments on the American circuit this year.

Spectacular challenges by Jack Nicklaus and Coles came too late to worry Weiskopf. A year ago at Muirfield, with a round to play, Nicklaus correctly forecast he needed a 65 to win and got a 66. Today, he was nine strokes behind at the start and he still said he was determined to have a go.

"As long as the holes last," he said, "somebody could fall on his face." Nicklaus shot a course-record 65 and tied the British Open mark made by half a dozen players. He wound up

Associated Press

Tom Weiskopf with wife, Jeanne, after winning at Troon

with 280, four strokes back in fourth place.

The 30-year-old Coles, meanwhile, charged home with a 66 to tie Miller at 279.

Miller Misses 2-Footers

Miller, who made history four weeks ago by finishing with a 63 to win the United States Open, never really threatened today although he started only one shot back of Weiskopf. He missed two-foot putts at the 15th and 16th and finished with a 72.

"There are no excuses," said the 26-year-old Miller. "The turning point came on the 15th. I was still in with a chance and had a two-footer for a birdie. Then there were screams and yells for a Coles putt, and I backed away. I missed, and then another one on the next. When you get in the rough it was like hitting out of a pail of water. What a course."

Bert Yancey was five under par with 281, and the only other man to break par was Peter Butler of Britain with 286. Butler shares that record 65 round with Nicklaus, made

as Jack won at Muirfield in 1966.

In retrospect, Weiskopf proved his right to this championship under fire yesterday when he could have panicked. In other years, he has lost his temper and exploded. He had led by three strokes at the start of the third round, but was 2 down to Miller going to the 13th. He boomed a 5 iron to two feet under enormous pressure for the birdie that counted most and scraped out with a stroke lead at the day's end.

But it wasn't until the 17th today that he knew he had it. "I'll never be as excited again," said the 6-foot-3-inch 182-pounder. "It was so tough — a course I'm not sure I know yet how to play."

The rewards are enormous in prestige. Weiskopf's winner's stake is $14,300, which is less than he got for winning the Colonial National, the Kemper and Philadelphia tournaments and only $1,300 more than he got for finishing third in the United States Open.

What Weiskopf did today was keep his cool. An 18-foot putt gave him a birdie 3 on the third. A 9 iron from the right rough and a 25-footer sweetly sunk meant another bird on the sixth and he got his third birdie

175

on the 11th because "I hit one of my better shots ever."

A 1 iron from a downhill lie wound up 35 feet from the pin and two putts gave him his 4 on this par-5 hole. A bogey on the 13th, when his 7 iron flew out over the green, was meaningless in the end.

Buckeye Banter

"He has more natural talent and more shots than anybody in the game today," said Nicklaus, who went to Ohio State University with Weiskopf.

Big Jack came to the home hole to the roar of tremendous applause following one of the great rounds in British history. That 65 could have been anything. To get it he had an eagle-3 on the 11th where he took 10 in 1962.

He also had six birdies and one bogey. He sunk putts ranging up to 35 feet from all over; he pitched in on the 13th hole from a sidehill lie 40 feet away, and he got a 10-footer down for a birdie on the 18th to show his appreciation of the crowd's reception.

He also had a 20-footer curl out at the third and another 20-footer hit the lip at the 15th.

He came within a whisker of holing out from a bunker on the 16th. A 62 still would not have done it, but on this day Nicklaus was what most experts

consider him—the world's finest golfer.

Coles, long-time Ryder Cup player, has won nearly everything in these isles and this year has taken the Spanish open. His 66 was a revelation and his mettle showed at the end when he arched a 5 iron to six feet and got that putt down to beat Nicklaus and tie Miller. Like Weiskopf, he never three-putted over the 72 holes.

Coles a Revelation

Yancey had a good Open. For a time, he pressed seriously with a string of three birdies on five, six and seven, and he will never forget how a 14-inch putt on eight somehow curled around the back of the hole and stayed out.

There were appreciative cheers, too, for Palmer. He had a par 72 today for 290 and would have been among the few under-pars but for a wretched 7 on the hole where Gene Sarazen made his hole-in-one on the first day. And Lee Trevino lost the title he won in 1971 and 1972, finishing with a 68 for 289.

Just one amateur survived the cut to the final 60 as 22-year - old Danny Edwards of Oklahoma State University finished with a 296.

July 15, 1973

Nicklaus gained $45,000 as his winner's share of the $225,000 purse. It was his fifth victory of the year and his season earnings are now $245,424. For his pro career he is almost at the $2-million mark, a level that seemed unapproachable to the young man who left the amateur ranks in Dec. 1961. Big Jack now has earned $1,949,130.59, the most of anyone who has ever played golf.

Crampton finished with a 70 as he ran in a birdie putt on he last green for a 281. Rudolph, of Clarksville, Tenn., tied for third with 23-year-old Lanny Wadkins and J. C. Snead, nephew of the illustrious Sam, at 282. Rudolph took 38 on the back half for a 73 on a course whose fairways were wet from last night's rain. Wadkins had an incoming 32 for a 69 and J. C. Snead also posted a 69.

Sam Snead wasn't far off his nephew's pace. The 61-year-old campaigner registered his fourth consecutive par 71 to be in the 284 bracket with Kermit Zarley and Hale Irwin.

Iverson, a 27-year-old Wisconsin professional in his first major tournament, shared the first and second-round lead. But he needed 38 on the last half for a 74 and finished tied with Dan Sikes and Tom Weiskopf, the pre-tournament co-favorite with Nicklaus, at 283. Gary Player of South Africa, the defending champion, had 78 for 294.

Weiskopf, the British and Canadian Open champion, had a final 71 notable for its contrasts. He began by missing a three-foot putt for a par, hit a spectator with his drive and took a double-bogey 6 at the

fifth, and was out in 38. Then he reeled off three birdies in a row, added another at the 15th, but three-putted for a bogey 6 at the 16th. After that, he took a bogey at the 17th and when the round was over, said: "If you don't win, that's all that counts. The money doesn't mean anything to me if I finish fourth, fifth or worse."

Crampton, who was second to Nicklaus in the 1972 United States Open, retained his place as No. 1 on the money list. His check today of $25,700 brought his year's total to $246,477.

"I'm absolutely delighted," said Nicklaus, who had a junior pharmacist license and planned to work in his father's Columbus drugstore until he began winning golf tournaments. "I fouled up so many chances to win a major tournament previously this year. I didn't play sensational golf, but just good solid golf. These greens were difficult to get the ball close to the hole. No one seemed able to do it."

Nicklaus said his best shot of the tournament was his second today at the 13th hole, a 465-yard par 4. He drove into the right rough, then cut his second shot with a No. 4 iron around a tree to reach the green, 215 yards away. The ball stopped 30 feet from the flag and he two-putted for his par. At the 15th, he ran in a 22-foot birdie putt.

"But at the 18th I three-putted for a bogey 5. I knew then the tournament was over but I didn't three-putt purposely," he said. "I only three-puttd twice in the tournament and that was good on these greens."

August 13, 1973

Nicklaus Captures P.G.A. by 4 Shots; 14th Major Title

By LINCOLN A. WERDEN
Special to The New York Times

CLEVELAND, Aug. 12—As a boyhood golfer Jack Nicklaus set his goal to be the best in the world. That meant equaling the record of his idol, the late Bobby Jones, who won 13 major championships. Today, the 33-year-old Ohioan exceeded Jones by winning the Professional Golfers' Association championship for his 14th major title.

A four-stroke victory over Bruce Crampton of Australia gave Nicklaus his third P.G.A. crown to cap a string of successes that began in 1959, when he won the first of two national amateur championships. Over the years, his triumphs included three United States Opens, two British Opens and four Masters titles. Jones, one of the heroes of sport's golden age in the 1920's, retired in 1930 after winning the "Grand Slam"—the United States

and British Opens and the United States and British amateurs.

A huge segment of a gallery of 20,000 at the Canterbury Country Club followed Nicklaus, who had been unable to win any of the year's three previous big titles—the Masters, the United States Open and the British Open. As Nicklaus put together a final two-under-par 69 for his winning total of 277, there were yells of "Come on Jack." He responded with a wave of his hand and proceeded to achieve his lifetime ambition.

One by one his challengers—Crampton, Mason Rudolph and Don Iverson—gradually fell back. Crampton, the leading money winner on the tour this season, and Rudolph, a veteran of 15 years on the tour, trailed by two strokes after nine holes.

But neither could equal the steadiness of Nicklaus's game on the back half of the 6,852-yard course. A string of eight pars followed two birdies on the front nine and then Nicklaus holed a birdie putt at the 15th to be eight under par for the tournament.

However, a bogey at the last hole cost him a record for the largest victory margin in this tournament. He did equal the record of four

Nicklaus Becomes A $2-Million Golfer

By LINCOLN A. WERDEN
Special to The New York Times

LAKE BUENA VISTA, Fla., Dec. 1—Jack Nicklaus, the Golden Bear, became a $2-million golfer today. With a $30,000 reward for winning the Walt Disney World classic, Big Jack brought his career earnings to $2,012,068. He is the first in the game to reach the $2-million category.

His triumph today by one stroke over Mason Rudolph, was his seventh on the tour this year, his 51st since he

left the amateur ranks and the third in a row in this competition.

"Some year I'm going to have a super round," Nicklaus remarked. Then he quickly added: "I didn't mean it that way but my attitude is good, my game is good and I want to shoot for all four of the major championships and win them in one year. That's what I mean."

Although spectators believed they were witnessing

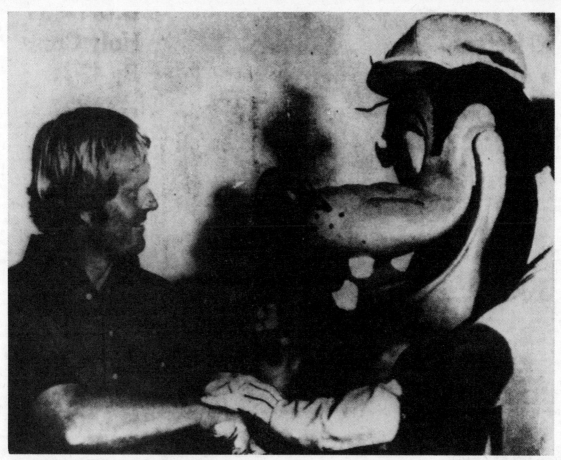

United Press International

Jack Nicklaus shaking hands with Goofy after winning the Walt Disney World classic yesterday

a performance correlated to the magic kingdom of Disney World, which adjoins the golf course, they were not entirely deceived. Nicklaus rolled in a 35-foot putt for an eagle 3 as he went out in 32 to take the lead from John Mahaffey, the young Texan, and finished with a 67 for 275.

While Disney characters cavorted and encircled him, Nicklaus smiled and said he was pleased to be the leading money-winner for the third year in succession. He earned $308,362 while competing in 18 events this season.

What also appeared to bring the long-hitting campaigner added satisfaction was that he was in the winner's circle this afternoon with an aggregate of 13 under par after he had finished the first round tied for 22d place.

Second was Mason Rudolph, the 39-year-old professional from Clarksville, Tenn. Rudolph had a chance for a tie with a birdie at the 18th hole, but he two-putted for a par 4 and closed with a 68 for 276.

Mahaffey, leader after the second and third rounds, finished in third place at 277 after a one-under-par 71.

John Schlee, the Hawaiian open champion who was runner-up in this year's United States open, finished at 278 with Lou Graham and Hubert Green. Green holed a birdie at the 18th for a 69. Nate Starks of St. Petersburg, Fla., the 33-year-old black professional who recently regained his player's card, had a concluding 72 for 280 while Miller Barber posted a 72 for 281.

Nicklaus, who won in 1971 with a total of 273, was 21 under par for 267 a year ago when he won by nine strokes. Among other golfers who have won three tournaments in a row are Arnold Palmer, who did so in the Phoenix and Texas opens several years ago; Ralph Guldahl in the Western open, Gene Littler in the Tournament of Champions and the late Willie Anderson, who won the United States Open 1903 through 1905.

Walter Hagen, however, captured the Professional Golfers' Association title four times, from 1924 through

THE LEADING SCORES

Jack Nicklaus	70	71	67	67—275	$30,000
Mason Rudolph	71	70	67	68—276	$17,100
John Mahaffey	69	68	69	71—277	$10,650
John Schlee	70	71	67	70—278	$6,200
Lou Graham	69	70	70	69—278	$6,200
Hubert Green	72	74	63	69—278	$6,200
Miller Barber	74	68	67	70—279	$4,800
Rod Curl	69	71	69	71—280	$4,425
Nate Starks	69	70	69	73—281	$3,900
Homero Blancas	73	73	67	68—281	$3,900
David Graham	72	68	70	72—282	$3,300
Gilbert Morgan	69	70	69	74—282	$3,300
Mike Reasor	71	72	71	69—283	$2,550
Lon Hinkle	71	74	70	68—283	$2,550
Julius Boros	71	73	68	71—283	$2,550
Sam Snead	69	74	69	71—283	$2,550
Jim Dent	72	73	66	72—283	$2,550
Roy Pace	72	70	71	71—284	$1,575
Lee Elder	72	72	72	68—284	$1,575
Jim Colbert	75	68	71	70—284	$1,575
Bob Menne	72	72	69	71—284	$1,575
Labron Harris	73	71	71	69—284	$1,575
Steve Melnyk	71	72	70	71—284	$1,575
Ma McLendon	72	72	69	71—284	$1,575
DeWitt Weaver	72	73	68	71—284	$1,575
Gibby Gilbert	73	73	68	70—284	$1,575
Dwight Nevil	69	70	74	72—285	$1,065
Bob Payne	69	71	72	73—285	$1,065
Butch Baird	71	71	76	67—285	$1,065
Herb Hooper	62	70	72	71—285	$1,065
Ken Still	72	73	70	70—285	$1,065

1927. The only other golfer close to the $2-million mark is Palmer, whose earnings total $1,633,651.39.

When asked if he was impressed by the $2-million figure, Nicklaus said: "It would be a bigger enjoyment if I could keep the $2-million, but you don't see much of that. I hate to think of what Ben Hogan, Sam Snead or Byron Nelson would have won if they played today."

Nicklaus and four others had trailed the 25-year-old Mahaffey, by two shots after

54 holes. Playing in the group ahead of Mahaffey, Nicklaus holed a birdie at the second green to go 9 under par. Minutes later Mahaffey also sank his 3 there to go 11 under.

But a big swing came at the 514-yard par-5 fourth hole when Nicklaus ran in his putt for an eagle 3. When Mahaffey by two shots after they were all even. A bogey at the fifth cost Mahaffey the lead.

December 2, 1973

Gary Player Captures 2d Masters by Two Strokes

By JOHN S. RADOSTA
Special to The New York Times

AUGUSTA, Ga., April 14—Gary Player, a solid little pro from South Africa, finished today what he started yesterday, catching Dave Stockton and then beating him in the homestretch with a 70 to win the 38th Masters, one of golf's four grand slam tournaments. His score was 278 and his margin two strokes.

Player first won the Masters in 1961, and he remains the only foreigner ever to wear the green jacket symbolic of that championship. In this case, the jacket is size 40 with lengthened sleeves.

The ups and downs of today's closing round resembled a stock-market ticker on an active day as the lead changed hands or was shared, and as challengers rose within a stroke of the top. Throughout the final round, there were men bunched in ties for second and third places.

But Player clinched the championship with a wizard-like 9-iron shot on the 17th hole that put him eight inches from the hole for a birdie 3. He then parred the 18th and finished with his 278, 10 strokes under par and two ahead of Stockton and Tom Weiskopf.

Jack Nicklaus, a four-time Masters champion, started the day four shots under par and worked his way into contention at eight under with an eagle on the 13th and what could be called an amphibious birdie on 15, where he waded into a pond and blasted the ball within four inches of the cup.

But the Golden Bear undid himself with bogeys caused by three putts at 14 and a poor bunker shot at 16. Nevertheless, his final-round 69 was one of the better scores of the day.

Nicklaus finished in a tie at 281 with Jim Colbert, the first-day leader, who had his usual round of yo-yo scoring, and with Hale Irwin, the former football player at Colorado, who got off to a faltering start and began his catch-up a bit too late.

Colbert's closing round of 73 included five bogeys, two birdies and an eagle—how's that for being erratic? He made the eagle on the 18th,

Associated Press
Gary Player being helped on with the Masters green coat by Tommy Aaron, the tournament winner last year.

where he holed out a 142-yard approach shot with an 8-iron.

Bobby Nichols also made a run, twice moving within a shot of the lead, but he finished weakly for 282, in a tie with Phil Rodgers.

An English pro named Maurice Bembridge also gave it a shot with a brilliant 64 —he called one of his putts a "Houdini shot"—to finish in a tie with Hubert Green at 283. Bembridge's round tied the course record set by Lloyd Mangrum in 1940 and tied by Nicklaus in 1965.

Arnold Palmer, the only other four-time Masters champion, delighted his fans with a last-round 67 to finish at 284 — with Bruce Crampton, Jerry Heard and Dave Hill.

The day started with 10 players bunched within five strokes of one another, and it was close all the way. Stockton, the leader by a shot, started at nine under par and played even par for the first eight holes.

Player, who scored a 66 yesterday to move within a shot of Stockton, caught Stockton with a birdie 2 on the sixth hole, where he put

a 7-iron 12 feet from the pin and made the putt. That tied them at nine under par.

The turnaround came on the ninth with a swing of two strokes. Stockton three-putted for the first time for a bogey 5, while Player was dropping a six-foot putt for a birdie 3. Now it was Player 10 under and Stockton eight under.

After nine holes, Weiskopf entered the picture, too, at nine under with birdies on Nos. 4, 7 and 8.

Player bogeyed the 10th hole after being trapped and missing a four-footer, and he bogeyed 12, where his 5-iron missed the green. Stockton bogeyed No. 11, and after the 12th it was Player 8 under and Stockton 7 under. Both shot birdies on 13 and pars on 14, 15 and 16.

Weiskopf, meanwhile, was

CARDS OF THE LEADERS		
PAR FOR THE COURSE		
OUT	454 343 454—36	
IN	443 545 344—36—72—288	
GARY PLAYER		
OUT	454 342 453—34	
IN	544 445 334—36—70—278	
DAVE STOCKTON		
OUT	454 343 455—37	
IN	453 445 344—36—73—280	
TOM WEISKOPF		
OUT	454 243 344—33	
IN	553 444 444—37—70—280	

fighting his jinx, the back nine, and not succeeding. He bogeyed 10 and 11, recovered two strokes at 13 and 15 and bogeyed 16. He approached the final two holes desperately needing birdies, but at each green he was 20 feet away and he lipped both birdie putts.

Player, who owns two British Open crowns, two Professional Golfers' Association championships and a United States Open title, won $35,-000. That put him in the career million-dollar club with Nicklaus, Palmer, Crampton, Lee Trevino and Billy Casper on the P.G.A. tour.

On the 13th, a par 4, he got home with a 3-wood and 4-iron, his approach shot landing 33 feet left of the pin. As he sank the putt for an eagle, he did a little jig, something like Ted Irvine of the New York Rangers when he scores a goal, and he trotted to the cup to retrieve the ball.

"At that point it was a tournament," Big Jack said afterward, for he was eight under par.

After the three-putt bogey on 14, he came to the water-hole 15th, a par 5. His approach hit a third of the way up the far bank and trickled back to the edge of the pond.

This hole had one of the largest galleries of the Masters, and the crowd couldn't wait to see what Nicklaus would do. When he reached the ball, he hesitated only a second, then took off his right shoe and sock.

Then Nicklaus rolled up his right pants leg and put the shoe back on—for traction. He stepped into the water with the right foot, holding his left foot on the bank. Twice he climbed out and returned for better footing.

The ball lay in mud a couple of inches from the water, in front of it was a sharp rise. It had to be lofted —quickly. Nicklaus took aim with a sand wedge for what must be one of the most theatrical shots he has ever made. Wham! Splash! A mass of mud went up and so did the ball to a birdie tap-in.

For his part, Player said he had never felt more confident in his 18 Masters tournaments, even though he had been "putting like a dub."

Yes, there was pressure.

"The older you get," said Player, who is 37, "the more you feel it." Player said he was a bit of a "Bible cruncher," and that he carried on his scorecard something Billy Graham, the evangelist, had told him:

"I can do anything when Jesus Christ strengtheneth me."

At one point, Player was reminded of a Masters tradition—one does not take his jacket from the Augusta National Golf Club.

"Well, nobody ever told me that in 1961" said Player. "And if they want it back, they'll travel a hell of a way to my house to get it."

. April 15, 1974

Globetrotting Golf Champion
Gary Jim Player

By DAVE ANDERSON
Special to The New York Times

AUGUSTA, Ga., April 14—Walking up the 17th fairway at the Augusta National Golf Club today, Gary Player turned to his caddie, Eddie McCoy. "In all the years I've played here," the 37-year-old South African golfer said, "I've been on this green only about six times. But when I won the Masters in 1961, this is where I won the tournament and this year it's going to win it for us again."

Man in the News

Player spun a 9-iron shot to within eight inches of the cup for a birdie 3 that provided him with a two-stroke victory.

"As soon as I hit that 9-iron," Player said later, "I told Eddie, 'we're not even going to have to putt,' and we didn't."

That confidence is typical of Gary Jim Player, the winner of seven major golf championships—two Masters, two British Opens, two Professional Golfers' Association tournaments and one United States Open.

"My life is full of little ambitions," he said, "and now I've won more major titles than anybody outside of American players."

In the hours of Easter morning before he teed off today, he hid Easter eggs for his children in the garden of the nearby home where he and his family have been house guests this week.

"Easter is very important in our family," he said. "My wife and I have five of our six children with us here."

They arrived in the United

Associated Press
"My life is full of little ambitions."

States last week for the Greater Greensboro open after a 15-hour flight from Johannesburg.

"It's expensive," he said, laughing. "I won $3,200 at Greensboro and I broke exactly even. I can't afford to take my family everywhere. Thank goodness most of them go to school."

Player is a globetrotter. He will compete in the Spanish open on Thursday, go to Japan the following week for another tournament, then return to Johannesburg for a week's rest.

"The week after that, I'll be back in the United States for the Colonial Invitation in Texas," he said. "That's one reason why I think I appreciate winning the Masters so much. The more dedicated you are, the more sacrifices you make, the more you appreciate winning a major championship. No golfer has ever practiced more than I have, no golfer has ever traveled more than I have."

One known as a physical culturist, he has been unable to exercise as much since he underwent bladder surgery early last year.

"It was a very serious operation," he recalled. "I had a blockage from my kidney to my bladder. I couldn't pass water for nine days. And do you get mean when you can't pass water? After the operation, I couldn't play golf for four months."

He returned to the United States tour last summer and won the Southern open. His victory in the Masters today was his 17th on the tour.

"You can never be considered a champion," he says, "unless you can win in America because this is where the best players are."

Only 5 feet 8 inches and 150 pounds, Player is one of the smallest golfers, but he considers himself a superior athlete.

"Some people think that golfers aren't athletes but I'm an athlete," he has said. "Give me a year to concentrate on tennis and I would be a world class player. I could play with Rod Laver or any of the tennis pros."

His pride in his strength has been another factor in his success over a span of 15 years. In a practice round once for the World Series of golf, he was consistently being outdriven by Jack Nicklaus, Lee Trevino and Gay Brewer.

"It was very embarrassing," he said later. "I kept looking for a high compression ball so I could get more distance."

Although he was born, reared and resides in South Africa, with its apartheid [separation of races] policy, he has continually struggled for equality for black golfers there. He invited Lee Elder, the American black touring pro, there for a series of exhibition matches. When he holed out today for his Masters victory, he used a "soul shake" in shaking hands with his black caddie.

"That," he explained simply, "is the way the blacks shake hands in South Africa, too."

April 15, 1974

Player's 282 Takes British Open By 4 Shots for His 3d Victory

By FRED TUPPER
Special to The New York Times

LYTHAM ST. ANNES, England, July 13 — Gary Player won the British Open golf championship today for the third time. He led from start to finish, stifled every challenge and came coasting home with a one-under par 70 for a total of 282 and a four-stroke margin—the biggest since Tony Lema took the 1964 Open at St. Andrews by five shots over Jack Nicklaus.

Peter Oosterhuis was second on 286, a notable feat for the young Briton; Nicklaus finished third with 287 and Hubert Green of Birmingham, Ala., fourth with 288, and the rest of the field tailed off out of touch.

The astonishing South African continues to make golfing history. Over a 15-year span he has taken this title, at Murfield, in 1959 and Carnoustie in 1968. At 37 he has captured eight major titles, with two P.G.A. championships, one United States Open and two Masters, the second this year at Augusta in what he thought his best chance to take the so-far untakeable Grand Slam. But he failed in the United States Open which he led for two rounds.

"It was agony to be in front all the way — the days seemed endless," said Player of the tourney just concluded. Gary was tied on 69 with John Morgan the first day; led by 5 strokes on 137 halfway through; was pulled back to 3 as Oosterhuis and Nicklaus charged yesterday, then he slammed the door on the first two holes this afternoon.

He started 2, 3 for birdie, birdie, those irons setting up the short putts. Then he bogeyed twice, being so deeply buried in a trap at the fourth hole that he had to hit out sideways, and bunkered again on the par-3 fifth.

Just ahead was Nicklaus, the man most to fear. Four behind at tee-off, Jack dropped two strokes on the first two holes and another on the fourth.

Then Player struck again. Two marvelous strokes on the 551-yard sixth and in popped an eagle putt from 5 feet. A delicate chip over the bunker hit the hole on the seventh and rimmed out for a birdie. Gary was round the turn in 32, the challengers dropping away behind him, even though Nicklaus had a birdie on the long sixth.

Oosterhuis, Nicklaus and Green all had 34's going out, and Jack thought he still had a chance. Not a single one-putt green had he until the 11th when a 10-footer rolled in for a birdie 4. He had a six-foot putt for another birdie on the 13th but that slid away, and a tremendous drive on the 4th bounced deep into a mound. A bogey 5 went down on the card as Player's birdie 3 on the 13th flashed on the boards.

"That was it," said Jack. "The strokes dropped away."

There was a great cry as Nicklaus bailed out of a bunker on the home hole and got a 20-footer down for a birdie 3. But it was all too late.

At the 14th, Player led by 7 strokes. Some of them disappeared. He hooked a drive on the 15th, lost a ball for a while in some bushes on the 17th and ran so far through the green on the 18th that he had to left-hand out of a flower bed before the final putt went down.

Oosterhuis, Nicklaus and Green carded par 71's. Jack had been third here in 1963, third he was again. A four-year American reign in the British Open had ended. Nicklaus had won it in 1970, Lee Trevino, the 1971 and 1972 winner, had a 301, and last year's winner, Tom Weiskopf, finished with 293 today.

"History was made here today," said Gary later. "The first player to win a British Open with the big ball. Let the amateurs play with the small one."

The little man had made his comeback. He had undergone major surgery 18 months ago. Today he recorded his 99th tournament victory; the Professional Golfers Association tourney in America, he hopes, will complete the century.

"Would you accept an invitation to the P.G.A.?" Oosterhuis was asked by an official of the Tanglewood Golf Club in Winston-Salem, N.C., where it is to be held, Aug. 8 through 11.

"Indeed I would," said Peter. "Tell them to hurry up."

British Open Scores

Gary Player	69	68	75	70—282	$13,200
Peter Oosterhuis	71	71	73	71—286	9,620
Jack Nicklaus	74	72	70	71—287	7,620
Hubert Green	71	74	72	71—288	6,620
Liang Huen Lu	72	72	75	73—292	5,250
Danny Edwards	70	73	76	73—292	5,250
Tom Weiskopf	72	72	74	75—293	3,645
Bobby Cole	70	72	76	75—293	3,645
Donald Swaiens	77	73	74	69—293	3,645
Johnny Miller	72	75	73	74—294	3,600
David Graham	76	74	76	69—295	3,500
John Garner	75	78	73	69—295	3,500
Alan Tapie	73	77	73	73—296	2,400
Al Geiber	76	70	76	74—296	2,400
Neil Coles	72	75	75	74—296	2,400
Peter Townsend	79	76	72	69—296	2,400
John Morgan	72	75	73	76—296	2,400
Peter Dawson	74	74	73	76—297	1,320
Tony Jacklin	74	73	75	75—297	1,320
Gene Littler	77	74	70	74—297	1,370
DeWitt Weaver	73	80	74	70—297	1,320
Lanny Watkins	78	71	75	74—298	760
Ronnie Shade	78	75	73	72—299	760
Bernard Gallacher	76	72	76	75—299	770
Angel Gallardo	74	77	75	73—299	720
Hale Irwin	76	73	79	71—299	720
Dave Jagger	80	71	76	73—300	612
Ben Crenshaw	74	80	76	70—300	612
Douglas McClelland	75	79	73	73—300	612
David Chillas	72	78	77	74—301	524
Lee Trevino	79	70	78	74—301	524
Peter Butler	75	77	77	72—301	524
Tommy Horton	78	76	76	71—301	524
Oscar Cerda	80	74	77	70—301	524
Hugh Jackson	78	76	73	74—301	524
Gay Brewer	77	79	73	73—302	460
Vincente Fernandez	78	73	78	73—302	488
Bruce Devlin	81	74	73	75—303	456
Guy Hunt	78	73	72	80—303	456
John Cook	76	79	75	73—303	456
Bernard Hunt	76	79	75	73—303	456
Derek Small	73	75	77	79—304	420
Christy O'Connor Jr.	78	76	77	78—304	420
Noel Hunt	73	73	79	80—305	366
Maurice Bembridge	76	77	73	79—305	366
John Mahaffey	78	77	75	75—305	366
Brian Barnes	74	79	78	74—305	366
Graham Marsh	79	75	77	74—305	366
John O'Leary	71	79	78	77—305	366
Stuart Levermore	77	77	76	76—306	374
R. berto de Vincenzo	80	74	77	76—307	304
Maurice Gregson	79	76	76	74—307	304
Brian Waites	78	75	74	81—307	304
Mike Sieur	77	74	80	77—308	300
Norman Wood	74	78	78	78—308	300
Ian Stanley	77	79	75	78—309	300
Christy O'Connor	80	73	77	78—309	300
John Panton	77	75	77	80—309	300
Bob Shearer	77	79	73	81—310	300
John Fourie	79	73	77	81—310	300

July 14, 1974

Miller Takes Hope Golf By 3 Shots on 68-339

Victory Third on '75 Tour— Murphy 2d

By JOHN S. RADOSTA
Special to The New York Times

PALM SPRINGS, Calif., Feb. 9—It was never in doubt. Johnny Miller, the 27-year-old superman of the pro golf tour, easily won the Bob Hope Desert Classic today by a margin of three strokes.

Miller shot a four-under-par 68 to finish at 339 strokes, 21 under par for this 90-hole, five-day event. That was one shot short of the record that Arnold Palmer set in the first Hope tournament in 1960.

Bob Murphy, the roly-poly former baseball player from the University of Florida, put on a driving finish to try and catch Miller. Murphy shot a six-under-par 66 to finish at 342, or 18 under par.

Miller's good friend, Jerry Heard, who was in second place going into the final round, finished third at 343.

This was the third tournament Miller has won in the four tournaments he has played this season—or six of the last nine, counting the end of last season.

Miller won the first two events on this year's schedule, at Phoenix and Tucson, where he was 25- and 24-under par, respectively. Then he tied for sixth in the Bing Crosby National Pro-Am.

Last year was the year Miller I as the tall blond won the first three events on the schedule and then won another five later in the season.

This begins to look like the year Miller II, and since Miller is only 27 there are likely to be many more Roman numerals ahead. This may be troubling news for Jack Nicklaus, who did not compete in this event.

Miller's share of the $160,000 purse today was $32,000, plus $512.50 he picked up in petty cash for the pro-Am segment in the first four days of the Hope Classic.

Thus far his earnings this season total $108,343. There is another way of looking at it. Miller's full-time caddie,

Johnny Miller as he missed a chance for a birdie on the 18th green yesterday in Palm Springs, Calif.

Andy Martinez, is paid about 10 per cent of Miller's purses. So the caddie's $10,000-or-so is more than many players have won this season.

Nobody believes this, but Miller acknowledged for the second straight day that he was troubled by the mechanics of his swing—"nothing you might notice, but it's there."

"I don't have it where I had it at Phoenix and Tucson," he said. "I was sure of myself there. Here I've just been hoping for the best. My alignment is a little messed up, a bit off."

That's what the man said,

but that's not how the man shot five rounds over the four par - 72 country club courses over which this tournament was played. He had only one bad round among the five, a 72 at Tamarisk on the third day, when he temporarily relinquished the lead to Don Bies. His complete rounds were 64, 69, 72, 66, 68.

Today's 68 was not earth-shattering, but it was all he needed to win. Miller entered the final round with a three-shot lead and, as he said last night, "there aren't many guys who can spot me three shots and beat me."

For a moment Miller gave his opponents something to shoot at when he three-putted the second green from 45 feet for a bogey. That put him at 16 under par for the tournament, just after Heard had birdied the first and second holes to go 16 under.

But then Miller birdied the sixth with a 10-foot putt ("that got me going again") and an eight-foot putt on No. 8. Miller was bunkered on the 11th but he saved his par by blasting out to 1½ feet and making the putt. Then he reeled off three pars on 13, 14 and 16, and by then no one had a chance.

Most of the day's action was the contest for second place. Murphy, recently recovered from surgery on his left thumb, was proud of finishing second despite a terrible first-day 74.

"It's discouraging to shoot 66 in a losing effort," he said of today's round, "but I feel real strong, and I'm going to be tough this week at San Diego."

Like most golfers, Murphy had to relive a few of the bad moments. He said he missed five short putts today, including two that dipped in and out of the hole. "And the fact is," Murphy added, "Johnny was making putts like that."

Today's victory was Miller's 14th since he joined the tour in 1969. That still is some distance behind Nicklaus's 53, but inevitably Miller's performance invites comparison

—and hope for some kind of shoot-out with Nicklaus.

"Maybe I'm No. 1," Said Miller, "but I don't really know. Jack is stronger, and he has more experience. If he lived up to his potential, he could beat me, but he's not been playing up to his potential. It's like he has 200-horsepower and he's only using 150."

"But I've been playing up to my potential, which happens to be better than Jack's been doing."

Miller often speaks of re-adjusting his goals. What are this year's?

First, I want to win one or more of the majors," he said, referring to the United States and British Opens, the Masters and the Professional Golfers Association championship. "Then I want to be the leading money-winner again." Last year he won $353,021 in domestic tournaments alone, not counting events he won abroad.

"And I want to pick up enough points to make the Ryder Cup team."

THE LEADING SCORES

Johnny Miller	64 69 72 66 68—339	$32,000
Bob Murphy	74 67 67 68 66—342	$18,240
Jerry Heard	68 70 66 68 69—343	$11,360
Tom Shaw	70 66 69 71 69—345	$7,520
John Mahaffey	70 67 69 69 71—346	$6,160
Pat Fitzsimons	73 73 67 67 66—346	$6,160
Billy Casper	75 68 66 68 70—347	$4,920
Mac McLendon	68 68 71 74 66—347	$4,920
Miller Barber	68 69 69 70 72—348	$4,160
Don Bies	71 67 66 72 72—348	$4,160
Dave Hill	70 68 71 70 70—349	$3,520
Bruce Crampton	68 69 73 74 65—349	$3,520
Curtis Sifford	72 70 71 68 69—250	$3,040
Wally Armstrong	73 71 70 72 65—351	$2,720
Dave Stockton	73 69 69 71 69—351	$2,720
Tom Jenkins	66 71 71 75 68—351	$2,720
Jim Marshall	72 68 69 72 71—352	$2,240
Mike Reasor	69 72 67 71 73—352	$2,240
Bobby Wadkins	73 69 67 73 70—352	$2,240
Bill Rogers	69 68 75 69 72—353	$1,638
Bob Stanton	72 67 73 68 73—353	$1,638
Dwight Nevil	69 69 73 69 73—353	$1,638
Joe Inman	74 71 72 66 70—353	$1,638
Arnold Palmer	68 72 71 72 70—353	$1,638
Alan Tapie	68 71 69 73 73—354	$1,184
Ray Floyd	74 70 68 71 71 —354	$1,184
Jerry McGee	70 71 69 73 74—354	$1,184
John Schlee	76 72 65 71 70—354	$1,184
J. C. Snead	70 73 72 69 70—354	$1,184
Tommy Aaron	69 70 74 72 69—354	$1,184
Orville Moody	72 71 70 71 70—354	$1,184
Hubert Green	73 70 71 71 70—355	$926
Rod Curl	73 69 69 70 74—355	$926
John Schroeder	75 69 70 69 72—355	$926
George Knudson	69 72 69 72 73—355	$926
Jim Colbert	74 73 73 66 70—356	$721
George Cadle	71 73 69 70 73—356	$721
Chuck Courtney	71 70 71 72 72—356	$721
Peter Oosterhuis	72 72 72 68 72—356	$721
Kermit Zarley	75 74 67 71 69—356	$721
Dave Glenz	71 75 69 68 73—356	$721
Larry Ziegler	76 70 69 69 72—356	$721
Gary Groh	72 69 71 72 73—357	$576
Roger Maltbie	70 73 69 72 73—357	$576
Terry Dill	75 68 70 75 71—359	$528

February 10, 1975

Lee Elder Prepares for His First Masters Tourney

By LEE ELDER

The one thing on my mind this past year is the fact of me being at Augusta, something I've wanted quite some time. I think I made it clear, when I first

came on the tour, that I would be happy to qualify for the Masters. But I wanted to qualify on my own merit, I didn't want anyone giving me a special invitation.

People have asked me if the Masters would be very important to me if it hadn't been built up by the press. I don't think so. Really, the press has made the Masters what it is. I would have to say the Masters is more important now because of the racial problem of not having a black player before.

I would like to see another black player qualify for the Masters. I've said that publicly. I think then the attention would turn pretty much to him. I wouldn't have everybody running out and addressing me solely.

It's been 51 weeks now, a telling situation, so many people to talk with, to be interviewed. It's seemed more like three years. But it's been fun at times. Now I think it's not as much fun as it was from the beginning, simply because the Masters is getting so close, and the pressure is beginning to tell pretty much.

These pressures I've been speaking about. The first is that a lot of people who cannot get tickets to the tournament are a big problem to Rose [Mrs. Elder] and me. There are people that are affiliated with me in some capacity, such as the Lee Elder Scholarship Program and Lee Elder Enterprises, people who are business associates, relatives, friends, my attorney—people of that nature, people who have been close to me all my life.

Another pressure has been the dramatic effect on my golf game. It's been bad this season simply because I've not had the time to practice the way

---

One reason the 1975 Masters is of special interest is that when it begins on Thursday the field will include a black player for the first time since the tournament's inception in 1934. He is Lee Elder, who has been on the P.G.A. tour since 1968. Elder qualified by winning the Monsanto open on April 21, 1974 at Pensacola, Fla. Because that tournament ended 51 weeks before the 1975 Masters, Elder has had the longest wait, among the newly eligible players, to tee up. Here he describes how he feels about those 51 weeks and about his appearance in the Masters.

I've wanted to practice.

Before I qualified for the Masters I used to spend a lot of time practicing and playing. I'd get to the tournament site on Monday and perhaps go out and chip and hit balls. But now on Mondays I've always been asked to be some place, something of this sort, and it's been hard for me to get there even on Tuesday. Sometimes it's not until Wednesday morning.

It was only a few weeks ago I began hitting the ball a lot more solid, and I've constantly been getting better. I think that's because I'm beginning to concentrate a little more now, with less interruption. All the distractions are pretty much behind me now.

I'm not nervous, I'm totally relaxed. I know there will be added pressure at Augusta because I've never competed there before. I don't know what type of crowds they have, but I've heard the crowds there are great.

Augusta is the type of golf course I feel I can play well on. I don't see anything really too difficult about it, with the exception of some pins that can be put in some awfully tricky places in the tournament.

Tom Weiskopf was telling me those pins will be in some places that you never dreamed you would ever see, especially on Sunday, the last day. And he said there were a few holes you could have played easily the first two or three rounds, a case of wishing you could make bogey if you put it on the opposite side of where you should be.

There's no doubt Augusta calls for high-arc shots. That's the reason I've got new irons, so I could hit the ball much higher than I've been hitting it. I've been a low-iron player, and I've thought that not just this tournament, but more and more courses are going now to elevated-type greens.

I've got a very good caddy for the Masters—Harry Brown, who caddied eight years there for Roberto de Vicenzo. These guys at Augusta are experts.

Harry's been there quite a number of years. He knows the terrain very well, he knows the safest approach to the green.

Weiskopf and his caddy have told me how Tom goes around Augusta. The thing about Augusta is that you play defensive all the time. There's just no way to play offensive, unless it's perhaps on one or two of the par-5's that you can reach in two. But the majority of the play is defensive.

I have lots of respect for the Amen Corner, the 10th, 11th and 12th holes. Just looking at 11 and 12, I can see how a man could put three or four balls in the water.

Some holes call for a draw on the ball. My game is left-to-right, unfortunately. I won't try to change my game. I can hit a draw—I just don't like it, but I will work quite a bit on drawing the ball.

On the 10th a draw is a must if you want to get there in two. On the par-5 13th you definitely have to hit a draw to get on the green in two.

Everywhere I've gone the reception has been favorable, people wishing me well. They were fantastic at Jacksonville, they bent over backwards, I guess because of the fact I was playing in a tournament so close to Augusta. Almost every restaurant extended me the courtesy of an invitation.

A lot of people in the Jacksonville gallery were asking me if I would wear green at Augusta. I told them no, just on Sunday because I think my green wardrobe would go nice with the Masters' green jacket.

Hubie Green—he and I are very close —were kidding each other about wearing green. We have a little thing going about wearing green on Sundays because, as he says, "green draws green." We're talking about the money aspect. It doesn't always work out that way, but we like to think it does.

April 6, 1975

40-Foot Birdie Putt at 16 Helps Nicklaus Win His 5th Masters

Weiskopf and Miller 2d After Misses on 18th

By JOHN S. RADOSTA
Special to The New York Times

AUGUSTA, Ga., April 13 —Jack Nicklaus, who likes to live dangerously and has a sense of show business, set up one of the most exciting finishes today in the history of the Masters golf tournament.

It came down to the last two putts on the last green, and when the delirious shouting was over, Nicklaus has fended a thrilling charge by two of the best players in the game, Johnny Miller and Tom Weiskopf—and he beat them each by a shot. And the shot he beat them with was a 40-foot putt that broke two ways before dropping for a birdie on the 16th green.

Nicklaus, widely accepted as the greatest golfer in history, became the first man to win the symbolic green jacket a fifth time. To get there he shot a final round of 68 for a 72-hole total of 276. Only two other scores have been better—Nicklous's record 271 in 1965 and Ben Hogan's 274 in 1953.

But what a finish! Miller, in a drive that he himself calls "berserk," shot a six-under-par 66 to finish at 277. Weiskopf shot a 70 for his 277.

Irwin Shoots a 64

Miller's 66, with yesterday's 65, set a record of 131 for the final 36 holes, two shots better than the record Nicklaus set in 1965. With Friday's 71, Miller set a record 202 for the final 54 holes, breaking by two the record held by Nicklaus and Hogan.

And speaking of records, there was Hale Irwin, who had been playing disappointingly all week, who shot a 64 to tie the course record shared by Nicklaus, Maurice Bembridge and Lloyd Mangrum.

No finish could have been more theatrical. The lead had swung between Nicklaus and Weiskopf three times. Twice they shared the lead. At no time was Miller in front, but with birdies at the 15th and

17th holes, he came to within one shot of the lead.

So there was Nicklaus on the 18th green — on in two, with a 10-foot putt that had to break left about 18 inches. Nicklaus misguaged the amount of break, and the ball slid past the hole. A tap-in for par-4, and Nicklaus was in, 12 under par for the tournament.

"I wanted to end the tournament right there," Nicklaus said, "but I just couldn't get that putt in. I figured a break of about a foot, and it broke at least a foot and a half."

As Nicklaus watched from the scorer's tent near the 18th green, Weiskopf and Miller marched up the hill, each 11 under. Miller hit a 9-iron 20 feet from the hole; Weiskopf's shot was about 8 feet away,

Miller knew it was a hard putt. He missed. There was no way Weiskopf could understand how he missed. Even watching a replay on television, he was convinced his ball would go in — but it didn't.

Any time Jack Nicklaus wins a Masters, the question comes up: Can he win the other components of the grand slam — the United States and British Opens and the championship of the Professional golfers' Association — all in one year?

He was asked today if he felt like facing the question. "Absolutely," he replied with a happy smile.

Nicklaus has accomplished the grand slam, although not in one year. He has won a record 15 "major" tournaments, including three United States Opens, two British Opens, three P.G.A. championships and two United States Amateur titles. His previous Masters victories came in 1963, 1965, 1966 and 1972.

Weiskopf had a heartbreaking day. This was the fourth time he had tied for second place in the Masters.

"I can't say now how I feel," he said. "How do you describe pain?"

"Nobody in golf has a better swing than I have," the lanky Ohioan continued. "Shouldn't I be disappointed? I never played any hole all week without confidence. I never doubted I was going to win.

"My next goal is the U.S. Open, that's what's on my mind."

Miller was close to defiant. He won eight tournaments last year and has won three this year, but is constantly reminded that he has won only one major, the United States Open.

He said he was deter-

mined to play well to show them he was there."

"I'm no Jack Nicklaus, but I'm not bad either," he said. "I've won one U.S. Open, placed second twice in the Masters and been second in the British Open.

"I'm not upset. I'm funny this way. I don't get down on myself when I don't win. I gave it my best, and 66 and 65 are not too shabby."

The competition between Weiskopf and Nicklaus was not unlike a motor race in which one development or another forces changes in the lead.

Nicklaus had led at the 36-hole stage, but he shot a poor 73 yesterday while Weiskopf was scoring a 66. When the final round began today, Weiskopf was leading at nine under par and Nicklaus was eight under.

Nicklaus had trouble at the start today. He opened with a poor drive, and that cost him a bogey on the first hole. In the twosome behind, Weiskopf parred the first hole. Nicklaus birdied the par-5 second by blasting out of a bunker to three feet from the hole to return to eight under. Then he birdied the third to go nine under and the sixth to go 10 under. But Weiskopf was not leafing back there. He had birdies at Nos. 3 and 6, and after six holes he still had a one-shot lead. Nicklaus finally tied Weiskopf at the ninth by holing a 15-foot birdie putt. They were both 11 under.

Weiskopf lost the lead with a bogey on 11, where he went into the water. No. 14 became a swing hole. Nicklaus missed the green and picked up a bogey to slip to 10 under; Weiskopf's birdie there put him 11 under and he had a one-shot lead again.

Both birdied the par-5 15th. The par-3 16th then became the next and last swing hole — Nicklaus's birdie put him 12 under and Weiskopf three-

putted for a bogey to go 11 under. That was how they finished.

Nicklaus's putt on 16 was a masterpiece. He knew from the instant it left his putter it was good, and when his caddie jumped up and down, that confirmed it.

The caddie's jumping was nothing compared with Nicklaus's reaction. He held his club in the air and jogged around the green as though he were doing a war dance.

Later Miller was asked if he had seen that putt from the 16th tee. "See it?" Miller replied. "I had to walk through the bear prints."

Miller was, as the golfers say, shooting out the lights. He started the day at four strokes behind Weiskopf and three behind Nicklaus. Miller shot five birdies and one bogey on the front nine to make the turn at 32, only two shots over the record 30 he scored yesterday. He gave ground by three-putting 11, but returned to nine under par with a bird at 13 and went 10 under with another bird on 15.

He closed in on Weiskopf and Nicklaus with a birdie putt of 20 feet on the 17th. The putt was so sure, so true, so pure, that he raised his hand in an exuberant wave even before the ball reached the hole. He had it made, and he knew it.

If either Miller or Weiskopf had sunk the birdie putt on 18, there would have been an

18-hole playoff tomorrow. The last playoff here was in 1970, when Bill Casper defeated Gene Littler.

"I've dreamed of a finish like this since I was a kid," said Miller. "You can't imagine how exciting that last putt was on 18 unless you were in my shoes, trying it."

Said Weiskopf, "The Masters is one of the greatest spectacles in sport, and I will win it some day. Adversity is part of this game, and the guy who beats adversity is the champion, and should be."

Said Nicklaus, "I don't think there's ever been a more exciting day. Any one of the three of us could have won. All that action on 18 — my putt and theirs — that's the fun of this game."

The others were not quite inclined to consider it fun.

But there they were, the three leading money-winners on the tour this year, the rich getting richer. Nicklaus's $40,000 purse increased his season's winings to $149,242. Miller's $21,250 kept him in the lead, at $149,476. Weiskopf's $21,250 raised his winnings to $112,488.

Hale Irwin was the unsung hero of the day. Because he was at 218 after 54 holes, two over par, he was an early starter, and did not have much of a gallery.

But as the red numbers were added to the leader boards, spectactors abandoned their stations to find him on the course. It was a flawless round, 32, 32—64, with four birdies on each nine and no bogeys. Most of the birdies were scored on giant-size putts, 25 and 30 feet.

But all it got Irwin, a former United States Open champion, was a tie for fourth place in what turned out to be a three-man race. His total of 282 was six shots behind Nicklaus's and the same as Bobby Nichols's. Nichols had a 69 today.

Billy Casper, a former winner, was sixth with a 283 after a 70.

April 14, 1975

MASTERS LEADERS

Jack Nicklaus	68	67	73	68	276	-12
Johnny Miller	75	71	65	66	277	-11
Tom Weiskopf	69	72	66	70	277	-11
Hale Irwin	73	74	71	64	282	-6
Bobby Nichols	67	74	72	69	282	-6
Billy Casper	70	70	73	70	283	-5
Dave Hill	75	71	70	68	284	-4
Hubert Green	74	71	70	70	285	-3
Tom Watson	70	70	72	73	285	-3

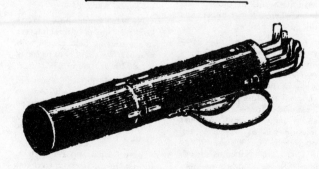

183

Nicklaus 2-Shot Victor in P.G.A. With 276

CARDS OF THE LEADERS
PAR FOR THE COURSE
Out ....454 454 344—35
In ....443 443 544—35—70—280
JACK NICKLAUS
Out ....545 434 344—36
In ....433 442 544—35—71—276
BRUCE CRAMPTON
Out ....444 454 345—35
In ....442 434 344—34—69—278
TOM WEISKOPF
Out ....344 344 335—35
In ....343 443 545—53—68—279

By JOHN S. RADOSTA

Special to the New York Times

AKRON, Ohio, Aug. 10— Jack Nicklaus won the Professional Golfers' Association Championship today for the fourth time, but it wasn't as ho-hum as all that. It was not until the closing holes that the issue was settled, with Bruce Crampton trying gallantly to catch up, only to be thwarted by putts that lipped out or missed by inches.

The tournament on the Firestone Contry Club was won—and lost—on the 15th hole, a par 3, when there was only a two-stroke gap, with Nicklaus at five under par for the tournament and Crampton three under. It could have been one of those swing holes where a leader bogeys and the pursuer birdies.

It finished the other way around: Crampton took a bogey on three putts, the second only two feet long, and Nicklaus came along in the final threesome and chopped a 20-foot putt for birdie. That made a four-shot difference, and from then on Crampton's mission was to protect second place from Tom Weiskopf.

This was Nicklaus's 16th major championship, the only kind that really interests him. He has won five Masters (the fifth only last April), three United States Opens, two British Opens, four P.G.A.'s and two United States Amateurs. He holds three more major titles than the great Bobby Jones.

All day long the pressure was on the Australian-born Crampton because he started four strokes behind Nicklaus. All Nicklaus had to do was avoid blowing it, as he did in this year's United States Open.

As it turned out, Nicklaus shot 71 on this final round, one over par, and Crampton shot 69. Nicklaus finished the 72 holes in 276, four under par for this brutal golf course of 7,180 yards. Crampton's total was 278.

Nicklaus, Crampton and Weiskopf were the only three players in the starting field of 138 who beat par. Weiskopf shot 68 today for a 72-hole total of 279.

Andy North, a 25-year-old third-year tour pro who has not yet won a tour event, placed fourth at 281. He shot a 65 today despite a double bogey on the sixth.

Billy Casper and Hale Irwin, former United States Open champions, tied for fifth at 283.

Nicklaus's victory today was worth $45,000 of a $225,000 purse. The prize raised his season's winnings to $248,599 and his career winnings to $2,492,223. The victory also was Nicklaus's fourth of this season. So much for Johnny Miller.

Eddie Dougherty, a brash kid from Linwood, Pa., who began playing golf only six years ago, hung in there for three days. Today, he was paired with Nicklaus and Irwin and for the first time he played badly. As the players say, the "wheels fell off" and he shot 77 for a 72-hole total of 288.

Nicklaus, Irwin and Dougherty formed the last pairing of the day, with Crampton, Weiskopf and Bob Murphy in the threesome immediately ahead. Nicklaus started the final round at five under par and Crampton at one under.

Nicklaus's start was inauspicious, a bogey on the first hole, where he missed the green. He offset that with a birdie 4 on the 500-yard second by pitching in a wedge shot to 12 feet and making the putt. Nicklaus bogeyed again on the third, where a "perfect" wedge shot caught the limbs of a tree.

This was hardly a way to win a P.G.A., but Nicklaus made up for it with birdies on the 11th, where he sank a 9-foot putt, and on the 15th, where he dropped the 20-footer.

He would like to have finished in style, but he took a meaningless double bogey on 18, where he drove into the trees and had to pitch out.

Crampton, meanwhile, got the jump on Nicklaus. His first three holes went par-birdie-par, and by the end of the third hole he was standing two under par to Nicklaus's four. They stayed that way until the ninth, where Crampton missed the green and bogeyed. The standing: Nicklaus, minus 4, Crampton, minus 1.

Nicklaus birdied the 11th and led by four but Crampton birdied 12 and 14 to reduce the gap to two shots. Then came the big hole at 15, where the Crampton bogey and the Nicklaus birdie made it Nicklaus, minus 6, Crampton, minus 2. The Nicklaus double-bogey on 18 made no difference.

This year's Masters and P.G.A. constitute one-half of the "grand slam" that Nicklaus has spent years pursuing. The other two events are the United States and British Opens, and no one has ever won them all in one season.

"I've never had a better chance than I did this year," said Nicklaus after today's victory. "The United States Open I had in my hand and I gave it away. The British Open was almost given to me."

He came equally close in 1972, but in retrospect he doesn't regret the outcome.

"Had I won," he reflected, "I might have got out of golf. But I'm enjoying the game too much, and I don't ever want to leave it.

"I want to win as many more majors as I can.

"Walter Hagen won five P.G.A.'s, and I'd like to tie that record. I'd like to win another two British Opens and..."

While he was saying this, Hale Irwin stood in an opening of the press tent, listening. When he heard what more Nicklaus wanted to do, Irwin shook his head in despair and walked away. As they all say, Nicklaus is a tough man to beat.

Crampton took his loss graciously and with a feeling of I've been here before. This is the fourth time he has finished second to Nicklaus in a major tournament, the second in a P.G.A.

"Next year, I guess, I'll be in a familiar role—the defending runner-up," he said.

"I'm proud to finish second to Jack any time. I'm also proud of

what I've done here. I beat 136 other players. It's something my family and I will look back to, and be proud of, for years to come."

This championship was the P.G.A.'s 57th. Nicklaus had previously won it in 1963, 1971 and 1973.

Three former P.G.A. champions, Bobby Nichols, Al Geiberger and Gary Player, finished at 291, which was 11 over par and in the petty-cash range. Another former champion, Julius Boros, scored 292. The defending champion, Lee Trevino, disappeared into the mob with 297 with a

check for $428.

Arnold Palmer, who has never been able to win a P.G.A., finished at 291, and midway in the afternoon his jet plane could be seen buzzing the course as he flew to his home in Latrobe, Pa.

August 11, 1975

Grande Dame of Golf Clubs

By NAN ROBERTSON

THE turn off Route 22 comes hard by Swingle's Colonial Diner and a strip of fast-food joints in Springfield. A few blocks north, beyond Mountain Avenue, the Baltusrol Golf Club beckons, a vision growing lusher every spring.

There are big, rolling greens built high and slick, but true and cunningly trapped; magnificent stands of beech, oak and evergreens, and lakes and streams sparkling in little dales. It is enough to make any golfer's mouth water.

The clubhouse, a stately pile of red brick with timbered gables, stands on a knoll at the foot of Baltusrol Mountain, lording it over two 18-hole courses. Together, those 470 acres have been trod by all the great names of golf in 11 United States Golf Association championships, and in 1980 the club will be host again for the United States Open.

Baltusrol is old, famous and unshatterably dignified. It was a wrench when, several years ago, it finally succumbed to women in slacks, golf carts on the links and even Muzak (muted) in the dining room. But ties and jackets are still de rigeur after dark and nobody, man or woman, wears shorts at Baltusrol.

The atmosphere is so genteel that, at lunchtime on a recent Saturday, you could hear the grandfather clock tick in the dark-paneled entry hall. At the counter across the way, two motherly receptionists, Betty Franco and Marion Colleary, dispense 17 brands of cigars, from 85-cent Macanudos to 15-cent La Coronas.

When Carl Jehlen, a very particular person, came to the club as manager 23 years ago, the officers were the

board chairmen of Worthington, Standard Oil, Johns-Manville and J.P. Morgan. "But the age moved on," Mr. Jehlen says, and today they represent F.W. Woolworth, Crum & Foster, Peat, Marwick, Mitchell and Manufacturers Hanover Trust.

Academe is little heard from, and the arts not at all; this is a place where big businessmen, bankers, doctors and lawyers relax.

"It has always been an older membership," Mr. Jehlen said. "A young man with a growing family seeks membership in a country club for his wife and children, too. Here, it is golf and golf only—no pool, no tennis, no paddle-tennis.

"We did try bowling on the green once, and that failed."

The man who founded Baltusrol, and was its moving spirit until his death in 1922, also founded New York's Social Register. He was Louis Keller, who owned the land, built the original golf course in 1895 (just seven years after golf was introduced in the United States) and brought his friends rolling up to the club's doorstep on his own personal railroad out of Jersey City.

The annual dues then were $10 a year. Today, there is a $1,800 initiation fee, a $1,500 "certificate" to be refunded when a member leaves and yearly dues of $1,200.

Golf memberships are limited to 500 persons, all male and over 21, and social memberships are held to 275. Wives of members may belong, but not women as individuals. There are no blacks, and Mr. Jehlen does not know if there are any Jewish members.

"But I wouldn't be a bit surprised," he said.

In August 1968, Richard M. Nixon, then the Republican Presidential nominee and

a Baltusrol member, resigned after a controversy over the lack of blacks and Jews made newspaper headlines. The New Jersey chapter of the American Civil Liberties Union charged discrimination, but the club denied it.

Baltusrol abhors controversy, but both murder and adultery are woven into its history—comfortably distant, of course.

The place takes its name from Baltus Roll, a farmer who owned the undulating terrain and lived atop the mountain. On the stormy night of Feb. 22, 1831—Washington's birthday—Mr. Roll was dragged from his bed and beaten to death by two thieves searching for the $1,000 that the victim was said to have hidden in his house.

One of the fleeing suspects killed himself; the other, acquitted of this crime on a legal technicality, died in jail after being convicted of other felonies.

The boys in the locker room also like to tell newcomers about the scandal that followed the night the first clubhouse burned down—Saturday, March 27, 1909. A Baltusrol member, disporting himself in New Jersey with a woman not his wife, returned to his New York brownstone the following day to say that he had been delayed and had spent the night at Baltusrol. His spouse handed him the Sunday morning newspaper describing the destruction of the clubhouse by fire.

Nobody knows what happened to the adulterer, but a new clubhouse, forming the main part of the present building, was begun in almost indecent haste.

The social hijinks within the structure are still on the sedate side. About the wildest night the members can look forward to in 1976 will be the Calypso dinner-dance in August, preceded by the

"Battle of Springfield" Bicentennial bash in the spring and the "Gay Nineties" party next fall.

The main events always have taken place on the links themselves. In its 81 years, Baltusrol has never deviated from the object stated in its original constitution: "The playing, cultivation and advancement of the royal and ancient game of golf."

The club was only six years old when it was the scene of the United States Women's Amateur championship in 1901. Since that time, Women's and Men's Amateurs and United States Opens have been played there frequently.

As the caliber of the game increased, the Baltusrol membership, seeking tougher challenges, hired A. W. Tillinghast, a renowned golf-course architect. In 1920, he designed and directed the building of the club's two 18-hole, par 72 courses, the Lower and Upper. They are essentially the same today.

The Lower Course is the more famous of the 7,000-yard layouts, but both, a nonmember said, are "not only extraordinarily beautiful, but a bitch." A Baltusrol member, Frederick H. Cook, described the two courses this way:

"The Upper has more woods, sharper slopes and trickier greens. The Lower is somewhat deceiving at first glance. It appears to offer plenty of room to the player, but the number and placement of hazards and the carry required on approaches make it fully deserving of its reputation as a severe test of golf for the average player and the expert alike."

Sports Illustrated picked the Lower's short fourth for its "Best 18 Golf Holes in America" and the legendary Bobby Jones called its 17th and 18th two of the finest finishing holes in the world.

The man who beat Jones,

185

Baltusrol—one of golf's historic courses—has been the scene of many U.S. Opens.

the greatest golfer of his day, in winning the United States Open at Chicago in 1928 was Johnny Farrell. For 38 years, from 1934 until his retirement, Mr. Farrell was the beloved professional at Baltusrol.

An upstairs room in the clubhouse is named in his honor, and it includes tributes from Gene Sarazen, Ben Hogan, Walter Hagen, Byron Nelson, Arnold Palmer, Billy Casper, Jack Nicklaus, Patty Berg, Sam Snead, Julius Boros, Bob Hope, Richard Nixon, Edward, Duke of Windsor — and Bobby

Jones, apologizing for the tormented handwriting from his crippled hand.

To Johnny Farrell and many others, two of the most thrilling U.S.G.A. events ever staged at Baltusrol occurred in 1954 and 1961.

The 1954 United States Open there was won by Ed Furgol, handicapped by a withered left arm. Stymied in the woods bordering the 18th hole of the Lower course, he played the "wrong," but not forbidden, fairway on the Upper to clinch the title.

That Open also ushered

in a new era in spectator golf: first time on national television and the first use of roped fairways to control the gallery.

In the 1961 United States Women's Open, Mickey Wright knocked them dead, coming back with a 69, after shooting an 80, and going on to win the title.

Herbert Warren Wind, the golf essayist, said of Miss Wright's classic final performance on that July Saturday:

"It is seriously to be doubted if Joyce Wethered or Babe Didrikson or any woman golfer has ever

played a stretch of 36 holes with the power, accuracy and over-all command."

Mr. Wind, like many visitors to Baltusrol on an ideal day, had a sense of another, more elegant, more leisurely time. It was, he said, like the Fourth of Julys of his youth.

"A soft breeze filtering through thick-leafed trees, bees humming, people walking slowly under old straw hats, friendliness in the air, salmon and green peas on the table." ∎

March 14, 1976

Miller's 66 for a 279 Captures British Open

By JOHN S. RADOSTA
Special to The New York Times

SOUTHPORT, England, July 10—Johnny Miller made up a three-stroke deficit today and, with a final-round 66, blitzed his way into the British Open championship, winning by six strokes. His 72-hole aggregate was 279, nine under par for the Royal Birkdale Golf Club, a seaside links course that suggests a moonscape.

The runners-up, at 285, were Severiano Ballesteros, the 19-year-old Spanish professional who gave this Open some unaccustomed excitement by leading the first three days, falling behind, and then fighting back, and Jack Nicklaus, a two-time winner whose last round 69 was gallant but late.

Nicklaus took second place on the 17th hole of the closing round today, and Ballesteros tied him with a birdie on the 18th. Ray Floyd, the winner of this year's Masters, who had been tied for second until the 17th, finished fourth at 286.

The leading Briton was Mark James, a rookie pro who set a course record of 66, tied later in the day by Miller. His 72-hole total was 288, even par, where he was tied with Tom Kite, and Hubert Green of the United States and Christy O'Connor Jr. of Ireland.

Once Miller took the lead after the sixth hole, there

United Press International

Johnny Miller throwing his ball into the gallery after he won the British Open at Southport, England.

was no way anyone could catch him—he just took off.

"I'm a heck of a front-runner," said Miller, a Mormon whose strongest word is "heck." "If you put me in

the lead, I play 'way over my head."

And that's the way he played, with a closing round of five birdies, one eagle and only one bogey-six under par.

This was Miller's second victory in the "grand slam" of professional golf, his first being the United States Open of 1973, when he posted a record 63 in the final round to win.

It gratified him enormously because he has long been fed up with talk about "the majors." He believes that it is more important to win many tournaments, the way his hero, Sam Snead, has done.

"I want to win a lot of tournaments," Miller said, "and as long as I do that, the majors are bound to come with them.

He also quoted Lee Trevino as saying, "there's a big difference between winning two majors and one major," meaning it separates true champions from lesser or lucky ones.

Collapse and Recovery

Aside from Miller's thrilling performance, the big event of the day was the collapse and flashing recovery by Ballesteros. The young Spaniard, who hopes to join the American pro tour in a few years, went into the final day with a two-stroke lead over Miller, and the lead grew to three strokes when he sank a 25-foot putt for par on the first hole while Miller was taking his only bogey.

But Ballesteros undid himself with atrociously wild driving—he hit only three fairways. What distinguishes him from many other players is his superb talent for scrambling, reminiscent of Ben Crenshaw of the United States. That scrambling carried him through a mad up-and-down round that started at five under par, soared to two over par and returned to three under par. His 74, two over par, consisted of four birdies, one eagle, three bogeys, a double bogey, a triple bogey and only eight pars.

This was the first really good English summer day of

the tournament, and 18,000 spectators turned out for the finale, perching themselves on the dunes, mounds and sandhills sculptured by centuries of rain, wind and tide. There are few places in the United States with genuine "links" courses such as Birkdale and the other seaside courses in Britain.

Miller came into the final round confident that, with the experience of a 29-year-old player, he could outthink the 19-year-old Ballesteros, who was paired with him in the final twosome.

"But when I bogeyed No. 1 and he knocked in that 25-foot putt," said Miller, "I figured, hey this kid's going to be real tough."

Miller's Plan

Miller's plan was to play par or better, and in the long run he was right. He played conservatively most of the time while the inexperienced Ballesteros, in Miller's phrase, "defied the percentages."

After the discouraging bogey on the first hole, Miller birdied the second at the same time Ballesteros was taking a bogey, a swing of two shots. Now Ballesteros was four under par and Miller was three under, as he had started.

The lead changed hands at the sixth, where Ballesteros took a double bogey after

Scores in British Open Golf

Johnny Miller, U.S.	72	68	73	66—279
Severiano Ballesteros, Sp.	69	69	73	74—285
Jack Nicklaus, U.S.	74	72	69—285	
Ray Floyd, U.S.	76	67	73	70—286
Christy O'Connor, Ireland	69	73	75	71—288
Tom Kite, U.S.	70	74	73	71—288
Tommy Horton, Britain	74	69	72	73—288
Mark James, Britain	76	72	74	66—288
Hubert Green, U.S.	72	70	78	68—288
V. Fernandez, Argentina	79	71	69	70—289
George Burns, U.S.	75	69	75	70—289
Norio Suzuki, Japan	69	75	75	70—289
Peter Butler, Britain	74	72	73	70—289
Brian Barnes, Britain	70	73	75	72—290
Eamonn Darcy, Ireland	78	71	71	71—291
John Fourie, South Africa	71	74	75	71—291
G.B.Wolstenholme, Austrl.	76	72	71	73—292
Graham Marsh, Australia	71	73	72	76—292
Jack Newton Jr., Australia	70	74	76	72—292
Tom Weiskopf, U.S.	73	72	76	71—292
David Graham, Australia	77	70	75	71—293
Steward Ginn, Australia	78	72	72	71—293
Alan Tapie, U.S.	74	72	75	72—293
Chi-San Hsu, Taiwan	81	69	71	72—293
Simon Hobday, Rhodesia	79	71	75	68—293
Robert Shearer, Australia	76	73	75	69—293
David Huish, Britain	73	74	72	74—293
Neil Coles, Britain	74	77	70	73—294
N. A. Faldo, Britain	78	71	76	69—294
Doug Sanders, U.S.	77	73	73	71—294
Gary Player, South Africa	72	72	79	71—294
Gene Littler, U.S.	75	74	73	74—296
Guy Hunt, Britain	76	68	76	76—296
Paddy McGuirk, Ireland	76	70	77	73—296
Hale Irwin, U.S.	74	72	77	73—296
Roberto de Vicenzo, Arg.	77	71	76	72—296
Martin Foster, Britain	74	71	77	75—297
V. B Hood, Britain	76	74	73	74—297
Ian Mosey, Britain	73	74	75	75—297
David Jagger, Britain	73	74	76	74—297
Peter Oosterhuis, Britain	74	75	77	72—298
Tony Jacklin, Britain	73	77	76	72—298
Barry Burgess, Australia	75	76	74	73—298
Peter Dawson, Britain	60	72	73	73—298
Malcolm Gresson, Britain	73	75	76	74—298
W. Humphries, Australia	73	77	73	75—299
S.W.R. Adwick, Britain	78	71	74	76—299
Peter Berry, Britain	80	72	71	76—299
Doug McClelland, Britain	74	73	77	75—299
Bill Garrett, U. S.	74	74	78	73—299
Carl Higgins, U. S.	75	77	73	74—299
Bob Murphy, U. S.	75	77	74	77—299
Dale Hayes, South Africa	77	71	74	77—299
Arnold Palmer, U. S.	75	72	76	77—300
Arnold O'Connor, Ireland	76	76	74	74—300
A. Oosthuizen, S. Africa	75	73	78	74—300
John Hammond, Britain	74	72	73	73—300
David Talbot, Britain	74	74	74	78—300
Danny Edwards, U. S.	74	72	79	76—301
Robert Wynn, Britain	79	70	75	77—301
B. Gallacher, Britain	73	72	76	79—301
C.A. Caygill, France	80	71	75	75—301
Peter Tupling, Ireland	75	71	77	79—302
Liam Higgins, Britain	77	74	75	76—302
W.R. Lockie, Britain	78	74	74	76—302

driving into an unplayable lie in the rough. That put the Spaniard at two under, while Miller was holding at three under.

The lanky Californian birdied No. 8 with a five-foot putt and picked up a second birdie on No. 12 and an eagle 3 on the 13th, where he chipped in from 100 feet.

Miller, "charged with adrenaline," ended with a flourish as the thousands of spectators gathered around the 17th and 18th holes. On the par-5 17th his No. 3 iron was a bit short. He chipped up to three feet and dropped the putt. On the par-5 18th he hit a 4-iron 15 feet from the hole, and the putt broke inches away from an eagle.

Not Even Perfect

While British broadcasting announcers were cautiously using phrases like "almost conclusive" and "almost the final blow"—this when Miller had a six-shot lead with two holes to go—Miller said, "I knew I could shank the rest of the way in and still win."

The 66 was not even a perfect round, from Miller's viewpoint. "I missed four putts that were makable," he reported.

Miller and Ballesteros had played together only once before, yesterday, and today they again were paired. They hit it off perfectly, and in the final holes Miller was urging Ballesteros on. "Go, go," he called out to the Spaniards' shots. They evidently struck up a friendship.

"I know Sevvy is disappointed," Miller said, "but from my own experience I know this will be good for his career. I know because coming in second in the Masters in 1971 was the best thing that ever happened to me.

"If Sevvy had won, there would have been all kinds of pressures and demands he couldn't meet. The best thing for his career happened today, to finish strong. This will be a plus for him, not a minus."

Miller came to England convinced he had "paid his dues" to the British Open, with ties for second place in 1973 and third in 1975.

"This Open," he said, "is my best major. I'm hitting the ball lower and lower now, and I'm learning to be patient."

July 11, 1976

Stockton Wins P.G.A. Title by Stroke

January and Floyd Trail With 282's

By GORDON S. WHITE Jr.
Special to The New York Times

BETHESDA, Md., Aug. 16—Although the weather cleared today for the final round of the 58th Professional Golfers' Association championship, the tournament picture remained cloudy until Dave Stockton dropped a 12-foot putt on the 18th green to win by a stroke.

Stockton knew the ball was going into the cup the moment he stroked it, and the 34-year-old Californian began waving his arms before the ball plunked into the cup at the 7,054-yard Congressional Country Club course. Stockton also won the 1970 P.G.A.

He was one of six golfers who threatened to win today during a tense final round that had been postponed a day because of severe thunderstorms that forced an end to yesterday's action. Oddly, Stockton had wanted to continue play when the decision was made yesterday to postpone the entire fourth round. He had played three holes before the round was wiped out.

Stockton, who won the 1970 title by surviving a late rush by Arnold Palmer at Dayton, Ohio, finished with a par score of 34, 36-70 today for a 72-hole total of 281, one over par.

Don January, the 46-year-old comeback attraction, and Ray Floyd, who won the Masters earlier this year, were at 282.

Next came Jerry Pate, the rookie winner of the United States Open and the Canadian open; John Schlee, who has never won a major tourney; Jack Nicklaus, four-time winner of the P.G.A., and David Graham, who makes Nicklaus's golf clubs. Each finished at 283.

On a day of trial and failure for most of the contenders, Stockton, Nicklaus, Graham and January each took a shot at the $45,000 top prize. So did Charles Coody, who started the day two strokes up on the field, and Gil Morgan, the optometrist who led after two rounds. Coody and Morgan finished in a five-way tie for eighth at 284.

Floyd was the clubhouse leader until Stockton sank his winning putt and January birdied the final hole to tie the Masters champion.

Stockton said afterward, "When that last putt was four or five feet from the hole, I knew it was going in. It was a hell of a feeling."

But the 6-foot Stockton didn't know exactly where he stood when he teed off on the final hole with a No. 3 wood. He thought he was two strokes in front of the field and didn't learn the real tightness of his struggle until he was about to hit a 2-iron approach shot of 235 yards to the last green.

This shot was short of the green and his subsequent chip shot drew a groan from the gallery as his ball stopped a dozen feet short of the cup. But a minute or two later he was the winner.

Stockton became a serious factor in bright sunshine and moderate temperatures at the long 10th hole, where January double-bogeyed by hitting an approach shot into a lateral water hazard. January had replaced Nicklaus as a contender after Nicklaus had replaced Morgan, who had passed Coody in earlier action. For two holes, Graham and January had the best scores.

Stockton had the lowest score above par for the entire trip on the back nine, although January matched him at 13 and 14. But the Texan fell off with two straight bogeys before his birdie finale.

Pin placements today were costly for Nicklaus and

length was a struggle for Stockton, who was not only short on his approach at 18 but also was short at 10, where he took charge. But he got down in two from the fringe of 10 and took it from there.

The top prize of $45,000 raised Stockton's 1976 earnings to $89,262 and his 12-year tour career earnings to $903,746. Floyd and January earned $20,000 apiece, and Floyd became the 17th man on the tour to go over $100,-00 this year. He has $118,746 for 1976.

Milestone for Hill

Dave Hill collected $2,064 for his 288 score and became the 11th pro golfer to exceed $1 million in career earnings. Hill has $1,000,660 for his 18-year career.

Other $1 million winners are Nicklaus, Palmer, Billy Casper, Tom Weiskopf, Gary Player, Bruce Crampton, Miller Barber, Gene Littler, Lee Trevino and Johnny Miller.

Nicklaus began slipping at the sixth hole, just when he appeared to be taking command and seemed a good bet to win the P.G.A. for the fifth time. He got on the skids by taking what appeared to be an unnecessarily risky shot directly at the No. 6 pin.

This hole, which plays a par 5 for Congressional members, was a 456-yard par 4 for this tourney. And it had one of the most difficult pin placements on the course today. The hole was behind a right bunker and within 20 yards of a small pond to the

CARDS OF THE LEADERS

Par out	434	444	345—35
Stockton out	435	444	235—34
Floyd out	534	543	345—36
January out	434	444	335—34
Par in	443	445	344—35—70—280
Stockton in	433	555	344—36—70—281
Floyd in	543	454	244—35—71—282
January in	643	445	453—38—72—282

right of the green.

Instead of going for the middle of the green, Nicklaus went for the pin. The ball carried over the trap, but landed to the right of the pin and kicked into the water hazard. A poor chip from the deep fringe grass and two putts gave Nicklaus a double-bogey 6. He went on to bogey the eighth, 10th, 12th and 14th holes.

It all happened shortly before Palmer, who has never won a P.G.A. title, fin-

ished with a two-over-par 72 for 287. Arnie had thrilled his Army with a 68 on Saturday.

Gary Player, the 1962 and 1972 P.G.A. champion, went out in par 35 to stay at one over par for the tourney. Then, as suddenly as Nicklaus, the South African fell away with four consecutive bogeys.

Weiskopf, the first-round leader with a 65, was the only man to go against the final day's trend and string enough birdies to make a charge. He birdied 15, 16 and 17, but it was too late as he wound up with 284 after shooting 74, 73, 72 in his last three rounds.

August 17, 1976.

Renee Powell Survives Pressures To Make Good on Pro Golf Tour

By CANDACE MAYERON
Special to The New York Times

CALABASAS, Calif., Sept. 22—It's tough to be a good golfer. It's also tough to be Renee Powell, a 30-year-old professional golfer. Miss Powell is black. In fact, Miss Powell is the only black among the 140 touring pros of the Ladies Professional Golf Association.

Miss Powell is a good golfer, so good that she is one of the 90 who qualified for this week's Carlton Grand Prix, starting tomorrow at the Calabasas Park Country Club, about 40 miles outside Los Angeles. Sponsored by the American Tobacco Company, the event boasts a total purse of $245,000, making it the richest purse in L.P.G.A. history, and with the biggest first prize —$35,000. Miss Powell is likely to make the cut of 60, which will put her in the money regardless of her finish. Her prize earnings this year rank her in the top 60, and her scoring average of "75 point something" puts her higher —in the top 40.

Kept Out of State Amateur Events

Maybe being black actually helped Miss Powell become so good. Growing up in a predominantly white section of Canton, Ohio, she had seen her share of racial discrimination. During her amateur days in the 1960's (in the tournaments she was allowed in), she had to combat not only the course and the weather, but also the animosity she felt from some of those in charge. The combined pressures forced her to concentrate that much harder. Now, in the more enlightened 70's, she no longer feels prejudice, but she has not lost the habit of honing her concentration, and as a result her mental toughness is one of the strengths of her game.

Although Miss Powell was good enough to captain the women's golf teams at both Ohio University and Ohio State, she was never permitted to run by the state's amateur championships run by

the Ohio state amateur association. Finally, in 1967, she turned pro. She had been working toward that day ("My father's proudest moment") since she was 3, and she felt she was ready.

At a trim 5 feet 5 inches and "a fluctuating 120 pounds," she looks at the world with almond eyes, and she relates stories of racial prejudice with detachment and understanding. She is even so objective as to offer an explanation for the times that caused the pettiness: "I think the associations and clubs were a bit stuffy. They just had never run into the problem before. It's not that they were malicious, they were just ignorant."

A Loner on the Tour

Miss Powell's childhood was better than most. There was a lot of love in the household, and a lot of golf outside. Her father was a good enough player to be extended a special invitation to join the white-only club. He declined. Instead he built his own nine-hole course, where all blacks would be welcome. It was there Miss Powell learned her power game, coached by her father, who was reliving through her the competition he had been denied in the "sunny days of his youth" as Powell calls them.

She was not the first black professional; Althea Gibson had turned pro three years earlier and was still on tour. But Miss Gibson was older, and had already made a name for herself in tennis. Her presence did not make things any smoother for Miss Powell. "We were friendly, sure," says Miss Powell, "but she did not take me under her wing or anything. I suppose she had her friends and I had mine."

In her second year as a professional she received life-threatening letters. "I became very paranoid," she says, and the memory obviously still bothers her. "I thought someone was going to jump out from behind a tree or something.

Renee Powell . . . only black among the 140 touring pros of the Ladies Professional Golf Association.

I thought about getting a gun but I never did. Nothing ever happened, other than some obscene phone calls. That's the only time I ever ran into anything as a professional golfer."

She is a loner on the tour, with no really close friend after nine years. The totally individual sport of golf suits her, if you will, to a tee. But she is not of gloomy countenance.

Engaged to be married, she says: "I don't look at life as everything being foggy and dusk. I see everything as sunny now." The light of her life is Christopher Lewis, a British accountant-documentary producer, and "he gives me confidence, he's brought out what was in me before but was stagnant." She is so comfortable with him that it no longer bothers her for him

to kiss her in public.

She would like to see more black women join the tour, so long as they are qualified, as she is emphatically opposed to reverse discrimination "in a field where talent is involved." Sponsored by Greyhound, she has been going to ghetto schools and talking to children. "I'm not the kind of person who can go out and agitate, it would be so out of character for me, but in my own way I can demonstrate what can be done. I know, that in a sense, a lot of people still think of me as a pioneer.

"I just think of myself as a golfer, and as a female."

September 23, 1976.

privacy, their walking galleries consisting, apparently, solely of loyal friends and relatives.

And what a distance between the leaders and the field! The closest man was Hubert Green, winner of the United States Open three weeks ago, 11 shots behind Watson.

American players won the first eight positions. The leading Briton—or first in class as they say in motor racing—was Tommy Horton, a prominent British pro, tied with three Yanks for ninth.

Watson's 72-hole aggregate was 268, eight strokes below the record 276 set by Arnold Palmer in 1962 and matched by Tom Weiskopf in 1973. Nicklaus scored 269 after precisely matching Watson the first three days on 68, 70 and 65.

Green had an aggregate of 279. Lee Trevino, like Watson and Nicklaus a two-time winner of this Open, was fourth at 280. George Burns and Ben Crenshaw tied for fifth after Crenshaw, starting today in third place, destroyed his chances with a 75.

Arnold Palmer, another two-time winner, ran seventh at 282, his best finish here in 10 years, and Ray Floyd, the 1976 Masters champion, scored 283 for eighth.

Nicklaus a King in Golf

There are many who consider Jack Nicklaus, now 37, the greatest golfer of all time. Certainly for the last decade, since he deposed Arnold Palmer, he has been the king of the game.

Now there is no question that Tom Watson, just 27, has the best chance to succeed Nicklaus. For the record, though, Watson said today he still regarded Nicklaus as the greatest.

Watson meets Nicklaus with respect but no fear, and he relishes the battle. Nicklaus has always said of this young man that his great strength lies in his temperament and iron will. Nicklaus had to yield to it in the final round of this year's Masters, and yielded again today.

Despite his history of choking in final rounds, Watson has developed cool nerves and confidence in himself. With the help of Byron Nelson, he also has honed a swing that he says will stand up under pressure.

To make the final round a better contest, there was a brisk breeze blow-

Watson, on 65—268, Wins British Open; Nicklaus 2d at 269

By JOHN S. RADOSTA
Special to The New York Times

TURNBERRY, Scotland, July 9—In an epic head-to-head match even more gripping than yesterday's tie at 65, Tom Watson came from three strokes behind today to beat Jack Nicklaus by one shot for the British Open golf championship. Watson shot 65 on seven birdies and two bogeys while Nicklaus carded 66 on four birdies and no bogeys.

This wasn't just golf, it was theater. Watson pulled up even at the 15th with a monster 60-foot putt, and the outcome appeared to be settled on the par-5 17th, where Nicklaus took two putts from four feet for a par while Watson went ahead with an easy birdie.

On the 18th, Nicklaus pushed his drive to what looked like a hopeless position beside a stand of gorse. Watson, on the fairway and away, confidently lofted a soft No. 8-iron shot to two feet from the flagstick. Nicklaus blasted from the rough to the green, 32 feet short. Now it looked like a two-shot loss.

It Wasn't Enough

But not yet: Still unbeaten, Nicklaus gallantly and incredibly rolled in that 32-foot putt for birdie 3. But it was futile. Watson admitted he was nervous over his 2-foot putt, but he knocked it in for a matching birdie—and his second British Open in three years and second major title this season.

Nicklaus put his hands on Watson's shoulders and said something like, "You know, I'm tired of giving it my best shot and finding it's not enough." The same thing had happened in April, when Watson beat Nicklaus for the

Masters, his first major victory of the season.

What an extraordinary year this has been for the 27-year-old Missourian whose trademark is his freckled Tom Sawyer look. He has won four tournaments on the American circuit, two of them in succession, and he is leading the money list at $269,115. Today's purse to the winner was 10,000 pounds, about $17,000.

Nicklaus, who won the British Open in 1966 and 1970, has now finished second six times, a record.

The final two rounds of the 106th British Open, played on the par-70 Ailsa Course of this golf resort, was nothing more than a two-man match. The other 62 players remaining from the 36-hole and 54-hole cuts played in relative

Scores of British Open Golf

T. Watson, U.S. 68 70 65 65—268—$17,000		J. O'Leary, Irlnd. 74 73 68 74—289	762
J. Nicklaus, U.S. 68 70 65 66—269	13,000	N. Suzuki, Japan 71 71 69 75—289	762
H. Green, U.S. . .72 66 74 67—279	10,200	K. Brown, Britain 74 73 71 72—290	645
L. Trevino, U.S. . .68 70 72 70—280	8,500	E. Darcy, Ireland 71 71 74 71—290	645
G. Burns, U.S. . .70 70 72 69—281	7,215	B. Barnes, Brtn. . 79 69 65 71—291	604
B. Crenshaw,U.S. 71 69 66 75—281	7,215	B. Dassu, Italy . .72 74 72 73—291	604
A. Palmer, U.S. . .73 73 67 69—282	6,376	M. N. Hseih, Tn. 72 73 73 73—291	604
R. Floyd, U.S. . .70 73 68 72—283	5,950	J. Morgan, Brtn. .72 71 71 77—291	604
M. Hayes, U.S. . .78 63 72 73—284	4,887	M. Pinero, Spain 74 75 71 71—291	604
T. Horton, Brtn. .70 74 65 75—284	4,887	N. Coles, Britain 74 74 71 73—292	528
J. Miller, U.S. . . .69 74 67 74—284	4,887	D. Vaughan, Btn. 71 74 73 74—292	528
J. Schroeder,U.S. 66 74 73 71—284	4,887	B. Charles, N.Z. .73 72 70 78—293	487
H. Clark, Brtn. . .72 68 72 74—286	3,740	J. Gonzalez, U.S. 78 72 71 72—293	487
P. Thomson, Ast. 74 72 67 73—286	3,740	T. Jacklin, Brtn. .72 70 74 77—293	487
S. Ballesteros,Sp. 69 71 73 74—287	2,280	S. Ginn, Astrl. . .75 72 72 75—294	463
P. Butler, Brtn. . .71 68 75 73—287	2,280	H. Irwin, U.S. . . .70 71 73 80—294	463
B. Cole, S.A. . . .72 71 71 73—287	2,280	V. Fernandez, Ar. 75 73 73 74—295	437
G. Hunt, Brtn. . . .73 71 71 72—287	2,280	B. Huggett, Brtn. 72 77 72 74—295	437
G. Marsh, Astrl. .73 69 71 74—287	2,280	M. King, Britain .73 75 72 75—295	437
J. Pate, U.S. . . . .74 70 70 73—287	2,280	R. de Vicenzo,Ar. 76 71 70 78—295	437
B. Shearer, Astrl. 72 69 72 74—287	2,280	R. Davis, Astrl. . 77 70 70 79—296	425
P. Dawson, Brtn. 74 68 73 73—288	1,160	J. C. Farmer,Btn. 72 71 72 78—296	425
J. Fourie, S.A. . .74 69 70 75—288	1,160	C.O'Connor.Jr.,Br. 75 73 71 77—296	425
G. Player, S.A. . .71 74 74 69—288	1,160	M. Bembridge,Br. 76 69 75 77—297	425
T. Weiskopf, U.S. 74 71 71 72—288	1,160	V.Tshabalala,S.A. 71 73 72 81—297	425
G. Burrows, U.S. 69 72 68 80—289	762	Chi San Hsu, Tw. 70 70 77 81—298	425
M. Foster, Brtn. .67 74 75 73—289	762	G. Jacobson,U.S. 71 73 70 81—298	425
A. Gallardo, Sp. .78 65 72 74—289	762	David Jones, Irl. 73 74 73 78—298	425
D. Ingram, Brtn. .73 74 70 72—289	762	Ian Mosey, Brtn. 75 73 73 77—298	425
R. Maltbie, U.S. .71 66 72 80—289	762	V. Baker, S.A. . .77 70 73 79—299	425
R.Massengale,U.S.73 71 74 71—289	762	Nick Faldo, Brtn. 71 76 74 78—299	425

ing for the first time this week.

Nicklaus and Watson spoke little during the round and often walked separately. They appeared tense, but much of the grimness was attributable to concentration against the distractions of a sometimes unruly gallery of 18,000.

They do a lot of legal betting here, and the spectators made it clear which horse they were cheering.

The pair started the round at seven under par. As early as the second hole something big happened—a two-shot swing. Nicklaus sank a 10-foot putt for birdie 3 and Watson took a bogey after being short with his approach and chip.

That made it Nicklaus eight under par and Watson six under. Then Nicklaus sank a 30-foot putt for a birdie 2 on the fourth. Nicklaus nine under, Watson six under.

It began to look like a rout, but not to Watson, who never doubted himself. He birdied the fifth, seventh and eighth holes to catch up even at nine under, but a bogey on nine put Watson back to eight under while Nicklaus held at nine.

Again Nicklaus took a two-shot lead on the 12th with a 22-foot birdie putt. Watson never flinched. He birdied 13 to get within one shot of Jack, and then he tied it up at 15.

This is a par 3 of 209 yards. Watson hit a 4-iron onto the hardpan left of the green. An instant after a television announcer said, "He'll do well to get down in two." Watson rapped it smartly and the ball hit the flagstick and dropped in.

Now they were tied at 10 under par. Watson went ahead on the 17th, a par 5 of 500 yards that has been playing like a par 4 all week. Watson hit the back of the green in two and Nicklaus was short and wide to the right. A super-delicate chip from the light rough put Nicklaus four feet from the cup.

This was the same place where Nicklaus had missed a 4-foot putt for eagle yesterday. And today he missed a 4-footer for birdie. Watson got down in two putts for birdie and now was ahead, 11 under par to Nicklaus's 10.

Then came those matched birdies on 18. You don't fool around in championship golf. You have to expect the impossible.

Watson saw the spectacular shot from the rough beside the gorse, and he had to expect Nicklaus would sink

United Press International

Tom Watson after sinking a birdie on the 18th hole and winning the British Open, one stroke ahead of Jack Nicklaus, at Turnberry, Scotland.

his 32-foot putt. And his caddie added, "I expect him to, sir." You have to count on putts like that, so Watson was not upset.

"Tom played better than I did," Nicklaus said afterward, "and he did not allow himself any mistakes."

Watson praised Nicklaus as a "true champion. He was not driving well for two days, but he still gave it every effort. It takes a lot of guts to make one part of your game compensate for another."

July 10, 1977

L.P.G.A. and P.G.A. Agree They Disagree

By MARGARET ROACH

The Professional Golfer's Association voted last week to allow women into its apprentice program, a move that was reported to be in response to a request from the Ladies Professional Golf Association that the two groups develop a closer working relationship. "The action by the P.G.A. executive committee," said Donald E. Padgett, president of the P.G.A., "was a significant and progressive move that will benefit our association, the Ladies Professional Golf Association and the entire spectrum of golf."

But according to Chip Campbell of the L.P.G.A., member women who are

Women in Sports

pros at clubs had sought recognition from, not membership in, the men's association.

Apprentices in the P.G.A. program work to amass the 36 credits necessary for Class A status. A college education, for example, counts for 8 credits. One regulation is that apprentices work under a P.G.A. Class A pro during his development period.

"The problem we are facing," Campbell, the L.P.G.A. director of public relations, explains "is that more clubs have women as head pros, and they are having trouble getting good staff. Why would a man be an assistant if the time didn't count toward his head-pro status?"

There currently are 55 female head

pros at clubs in the United States, many of whom, according to Campbell, would like to hire a top male apprentice to balance her club's teaching unit.

Campbell says a proposal from the L.P.G.A. teaching division went to the P.G.A. early last summer. "We wanted recognition for our members who were head club pros," Campbell said. "The P.G.A.'s move didn't respond to that at all. We had made it very clear that our women were not seeking membership in the P.G.A. We were asking for a professional courtesy."

"Our officers," says Earl Collings, P.G.A. director of communications, "appreciated the women's request and wanted to see it come about. But when the executive committee got into analyzing it, they found it inequitable for an apprentice working for a non-member man not to be given credit and then set a rule that allowed an apprentice working for a non-member woman to get credit.

"The committee considered that, one, the P.G.A. constitution had never said 'man' or 'woman,' and two, the nature of today is equality and the logical thing was to make the membership open," Collings continued.

The move left the nation's 55 women

head pros where they were when the L.P.G.A. proposal went to the P.G.A. in June. For these women (and the number is likely to increase if it follows the pattern of the last few years) the prospect of becoming a P.G.A. apprentice to solve their problem is not a practical one. According to Campbell, the process would take two or three years.

The possibility that the P.G.A. will allow women to enter its apprenticeship program seems unlikely to lead to mixed competition on the professional golf tour. P.G.A. Class A mem-

bers are primarily club teaching pros, and are not touring professionals.

The head of the L.P.G.A. teaching division has already written to the P.G.A., reiterating the women's situation and requests. Collings of the P.G.A. says this arrangement "is the only avenue possible in response to the problem." The L.P.G.A., and particularly its members who are teaching professionals, hopes otherwise.

December 11, 1977

Player Captures Masters by Shot On Final 64-277

By JOHN S. RADOSTA

Special to The New York Times

AUGUSTA, Ga., April 9 — Gary Player, a world-traveling golf professional who has been a fixture on the American tour for 22 years, won the 42d Masters today in one of the tightest, most crowded finishes in recent years—one stroke ahead of Hubert Green, Rod Funseth and last year's winner. Tom Watson.

Player started the final round today seven shots behind Green and shot a record-tying 64 for 277, eight under par for the Augusta National Golf Club, to pass Green and eight other players with a 72-hole total of 277. He shot seven birdies on his last 10 holes.

Player, a supremely self-confident athlete, was the only man here who thought he had a chance to win at the start of today's play. He said:

"I knew when I teed it up. I've won many times from seven shots back."

They All Missed

After he finished his round Player stood along the 18th green to see how his pursuers would finish. He was well advised to linger there because all three of the runners-up had a chance to tie him with their final putts on the final hole. They all missed—Green from 2½ feet, Watson from 12 and Funseth from 24, just inches short.

Player said he was "choking" as he watched Green address the birdie putt that would have forced a tie and a sudden-death playoff, and "how many of you can smile while choking?"

"I'm glad we didn't have a playoff," he said. "I'm scared of sudden-death playoffs because I've lost 17 of them."

This was the third time Player had won the Masters, the previous victories being in 1961 and 1974. Player, who is obsessed with physical fitness, is at 42 years of age the oldest golfer to win the Masters. He also is the only foreigner to win it and the emblematic green jacket that goes with the victory. Wally Armstrong, an earnest jour-

neyman in his sixth year on the tour, and Bill Kratzert, a third-year pro, threatened the leaders for a while and finished in a tie at 280. Armstrong shot 68 on his final round and Kratzert 69.

Jack Nicklaus, the only man who has won the Masters five times, finally got something going today on the back nine with a string of four birdies. Nicklaus, the heavy favorite when the tournament began Thursday, finished at 67-281 after being plagued for three days by bad putting.

For Player this was his 19th victory on the PGA Tour and 112th worldwide. Today's $45,000 purse brought his winnings on the United States tour alone to $1,379,107. Player joined Sam Snead and Jimmy Demaret as winners of three Masters. He also has won three British Opens and two Professional Golfers' Association championships.

When the final round began Player's name scarcely was considered in speculation about winners. He stood at 72, 72, 69—213, three under par and seven shots behind Green, the leader. He also had a relatively unflattering starting position—his pairing with Severiano Ballesteros of Spain was six groups ahead of the final group, Green and Funseth.

He was off and running with a birdie 4 on the second hole after dropping his 3-wood second shot into a sand trap. Player, who is one of the tour's best at sand shots, blasted out to a foot from the hole and sank the putt. On the par-3 fourth he sank a big 30-foot putt, and that birdie positioned him at five under par.

There was a mishap with a bogey on the seventh, where he came out of a bunker to five feet and then missed the putt.

The setback was only momentary. When Player reached the ninth hole he started his phenomenal run of birdies—seven in the next 10 holes. He sank birdie putts of 25 feet on the 10th and 15 feet on the 12th. On the two par-5's, Nos. 13 and 15, he got home in two and down in two

putts. A 14-foot birdie putt at the 16th put him at 10 under par, and then he iced the cake with a thrilling birdie on 18, where he hit a 6-iron to 15 feet and made the putt.

He needed that birdie because through the final hours of the tournament the leader boards showed ties for first place among, at various times, Green, Funseth, Watson and Player. For a couple of moments there was a four-way tie.

Out of Character

Player usually is the epitome of dignity on the golf course, and he rarely indulges in histrionics. But he stepped out of character at the edge of the 11th green when a magnificent chip shot headed for a birdie hit the rim of the cup and rolled out. Player dropped to the ground, lay on his back and kicked his legs in the air.

"Afterward I thought it was unbecoming to do such a thing at the Masters, but I did it without knowing I was doing it," Player said. "I was very tense at the time."

"I've been runner-up here three times," Player said this evening, "and I know how Green, Watson and Funseth feel."

Green, the 1977 United States Open

Masters Scores

Gary Player	72	72	69	64—277	$45,000
Tom Watson	73	68	68	69—278	21,677
Hubert Green	72	69	65	72—278	21,677
Rod Funseth	73	66	70	69—278	21,677
Wally Armstrong	72	70	70	68—280	11,750
Billy Kratzert	70	74	67	69—280	11,750
Jack Nicklaus	72	73	69	67—281	10,000
Hale Irwin	73	67	71	71—282	8,500
Joe Inman	69	73	72	69—283	6,750
David Graham	75	69	67	72—283	6,750
Jerry McGee	71	73	71	69—284	4,417
Don January	72	70	72	70—284	4,417
Tom Weiskopf	72	71	70	71—284	4,417
Peter Oosterhuis	74	70	70	71—285	3,300
Lee Trevino	70	69	72	74—285	3,300
Ray Floyd	76	71	71	68—286	2,950
*Lindy Miller	74	71	70	71—286	
Lanny Wadkins	74	70	73	70—287	2,550
Gil Morgan	73	73	70	71—287	2,550
Tom Kite	71	74	71	71—287	2,550
Jerry Pate	72	71	73	71—287	2,550
Ed Sneed	74	70	70	73—287	2,550
S. Ballesteros	74	71	68	74—287	2,550
Andy Bean	76	68	73	71—288	2,200
Leonard Thompson	72	69	75	72—288	2,200
Miller Barber	75	67	73	73—288	2,200
Gene Littler	72	68	70	78—288	2,200
Bobby Cole	77	70	70	72—289	2,000
Mac McLendon	72	72	72	74—290	1,975
Bill Rogers	76	70	68	76—290	1,975
Gay Brewer	73	71	69	77—290	1,975
Jim Colbert	74	73	75	69—291	1,950
Johnny Miller	73	73	72	70—291	1,950
Terry Diehl	74	72	74	71—291	1,950
Andy North	73	76	72	70—291	1,950
Tommy Aaron	74	71	68	73	71—248	1,925
Mike Hill	73	75	74	71—293	1,900
Tom Purtzer	78	69	74	72—293	1,900
Ben Crenshaw	75	70	74	74—293	1,900
Arnold Palmer	73	69	74	77—293	1,900
Lyn Lott	72	76	71	75—284	1,875
Al Geiberger	75	73	75	72—295	1,850
Lee Elder	73	75	74	73—295	1,850
John Schlee	68	75	77	75—295	1,850
Dave Hill	72	76	74	74—296	1,825
*Vance Heafner	72	74	74	75—296	
*Gary Hallberg	73	73	78	73—297	
Jay Haas	74	73	74	76—297	1,800
*Richard Siderowf	77	72	78	71—298	
Bob Wynn	74	70	78	77—299	1,750
Steve Melnyk	71	78	75	76—300	1,725
Bob Goalby	73	75	78	75—301	1,700
*Peter McEvoy	73	75	77	77—302	
*Amateur.					

champion and winner of two tournaments this season, started his round at 10 under par and shot a steady par-72, never getting better than 11 under par or worse than nine under. He was naturally disappointed.

"If I could have shot two under, it would have been history," Green said.

Green was lucky to get out of the pond on the 11th hole with a bogey-5, and he saved par on the 12th with a superb chip from a bank on the right.

'A Bad Putt'

He came to the 18th needing a birdie to tie Player, and he almost did it. He hit his approach shot to 2½ feet, and the massed gallery was sure he would sink it. He addressed the ball and then backed away when he was distracted by the sound of a radio

broadcaster's voice. Then he returned to the putt—and missed. Green refused to blame the broadcaster: "It's nobody's fault but my own," he said. "It was definitely a bad putt."

Watson, who had been trailing all week, played a fine round. Starting at seven under par, he recovered the putting stroke he had missed all week. Watson was at eight under par after 11 holes and then shot an eagle-3 on the 13th to reach 10 under. A bogey on 14 and birdies on 15 and 16 brought him to the 18th tee at 11 under, and he needed a par to tie Player. Unhappily, his second shot flew 80 feet wide, and from there he needed three shots to get down.

"I'll be disappointed tonight and tomorrow," said Watson, "but by Tues-

day I'll be ready to go on to other things."

The Cinderella of this golf tournament was Funseth, a low-key, easy-going Californian who, at 45, is considering retiring after 18 years on the tour.

He was tied for the lead after 36 holes, just as he was a year ago. In 1977 he faltered in the last two rounds, but this time he hung tough and shot 69, 70 on the closing days.

"In the last four major tournaments I've played, I've had a chance to win going into the last nine holes," Funseth said. "I'm not disappointed here. I played well and finished second. I didn't throw anything away."

April 10, 1978

Miss Lopez Takes Her 4th Straight

Nancy Lopez chipping from the rough to the second green in Mason, Ohio.

The New York Times

Special to The New York Times

MASON, Ohio, June 11 — Nancy Lopez left all of the other members of the Ladies' Professional Golf Association chasing rainbows again today

when she picked up her biggest pot of gold so far, winning the 24th L.P.G.A. Championship and the $22,500 first prize in her fourth straight victory.

The amazing 24-year-old rookie, never really threatened since she opened the final round five shots ahead of the field, shot a two-under-par 36, 34—70 for a 72-hole total of 275, a tournament record. Mary Mills shot the previous low of 278 to win in 1964.

By shooting 13 under par for four rounds on the 6,312-yard Kings Island course, Miss Lopez finished six strokes in front of Amy Alcott, who had 71 today for 281 and picked up the second prize of $14,650. Judy Rankin finished third at 283, followed by JoAnne Carner at 284.

Miss Lopez, continuing to be in a class by herself, gained her sixth triumph and first national title since turning professional last summer. Once again she played steady golf, utilizing her ability as the most accurate woman off the tees, the best putter, and one of the half-dozen longest hitters on the tour. She also continued to display a vivacious charm that has made her a big draw in the L.P.G.A.

Ray Volpe, commissioner of the tour, would not say what most persons feel —that Miss Lopez is the best gallery attraction the L.P.G.A. has ever had— but did say, "Nancy is certainly one of the best things that has happened to the L.P.G.A."

Miss Alcott, a Californian who is only 11 months older than Miss Lopez, praised the winner. "She's one hell of a competitor and I've never seen anyone who accepts what she does with such humility," the second-place finisher said.

Miss Lopez became the second rookie to win the L.P.G.A. championship (Sandra Post won the title in 1968) and established or came close to breaking the following records:

¶ Six victories this year are the most by a man or woman rookie professional golfer. The most rookie victories by a woman in the past was one triumph and most by a man was two. The L.P.G.A. record for victories in one year is 13, set by Mickey Wright in 1963.

¶ Tied the L.P.G.A. record of four straight victories, held by Miss Wright (1962, 1963), Kathy Whitworth (1969), and Shirley Englehorn (1970). The men's record for consecutive triumphs is 11, set by Byron Nelson in 1945.

¶ Increased her rookie earnings since joining the L.P.G.A. on July 29, 1977, to $142,086, which is $95,123 more than the previous L.P.G.A. rookie-earnings record. She is $11,016 short of Jerry Pate's PGA Tour rookie-earnings record of $153,102, set in 1976. There are seven L.P.G.A. events left before Miss Lopez's rookie status ends.

¶ Increased her 1978 earnings to $118,948 and became the first woman to earn $100,000 this early in a season. Judy Rankin surpassed $100,000 on July 12, 1976.

¶ Miss Lopez is $31,786 short of the L.P.G.A. calendar-year earnings record of $150,734, set by Mrs. Rankin in 1976. There are 19 official-money tournaments remaining in 1978.

Following her triumph, Miss Lopez said, "Now that I have won four in a row I'd like to break the record and win five in a row."

Pars First Nine Holes

She displayed her calm, concentrated approach to the game right at the start today when she missed the second green with her approach and made an unimpressive chip shot to the pin. She then drained a right-to-left 16-foot putt for par. She saved par on the seventh with a similarly-breaking 10-foot putt after a weak chip, and parred the first nine holes to make it virtually impossible to catch her.

When Miss Lopez dropped her final putt, most in the record crowd of over 20,000 cheered her wildly, with many giving the now familiar call of "Nan-Cee." She ran to her father, Domingo, and gave him a big hug.

Domingo Lopez said, "She loves to play for the people."

GORDON S. WHITE Jr.

June 12, 1978

North Wins U.S. Open by Shot on 74 for 285

By GORDON S. WHITE, Jr.

Special to The New York Times

Denver, June 18—Andrew Stewart North, a 28-year-old native of Wisconsin, blasted out of a sand bunker at the final hole of the 78th United States Open golf championship today and then sank the following four-foot putt to win by a stroke in one of the most exciting stretch finishes in the tournament's history.

The 6-foot-4-inch North, who overcame a childhood bone disease to play golf, managed to hang onto a lead that was comfortable at one point today and then began slipping away fast as he went down the last six holes at the Cherry Hills Country Club. When he putted out for a bogey 5 at the 18th after a couple of poor shots on the difficult finishing hole, he had a three-over-par 74 for the final round that gave him a 72-hole total of one-over-par 285.

That was just enough to beat Jesse Carlyle Snead, better known as J. C., and Dave Stockton, two-time winner of the Professional Golfers Association championship, who had left the course in a tie at two-over-par 286 moments before North's nervous finish.

North's victory was worth $45,000. His only previous victory during six years on the PGA Tour was a triumph in last year's Westchester Classic.

Hale Irwin, the 1974 champion who led after the first round Thursday, and Tom Weiskopf, who had the best final-round score today with 68, were tied for fourth place at 288. Then came a six-way tie for the sixth spot that included Gary Player, Jack Nicklaus and Johnny Miller, all former Open champions; they finished with 289's.

Player, who started the day a stroke back of North, and Nicklaus, five shots off at the start of the round, never threatened. Player had a final round 77 and Nicklaus a 73.

Many golfers had predicted this tournament would be finally settled at the 72d hole, which Player said was the most difficult finishing hole he had seen in a United States Open.

And that is just what happened when

each of the three golfers battling for the title came to the 18th today. They all drove the ball poorly and two of them took bogey 5's. One, with the help of some luck, parred out.

Snead and Stockton, playing together today, stepped to the 18th tee with North in front of Stockton by a stroke and leading Snead by 2. Stockton teed off first and hit his ball into the deep right rough that left him about 260 yards from the green placed high on a windy hill.

Snead, using a one iron, topped his drive and sent it right at the huge lake in front of the tee. But luck was with the nephew of Sam Snead as J.C.'s ball bounced off the lake like a stone skim-

Open Leaders

Andy North	285	$45,000
Dave Stockton	286	$19,750
J. C. Snead	286	$19,750
Hale Irwin	288	$13,000
Tom Weiskopf	288	$13,000
Tom Watson	289	$ 7,548
Andy Bean	289	$ 7,548
Jack Nicklaus	289	$ 7,548
Bill Kratzert	289	$ 7,548
Gary Player	289	$ 7,548
Johnny Miller	289	$ 7,548

ming over water and landed in the fairway.

Snead got to the green on his second shot, a 240-yard approach up hill. But he was still 30 feet from the cup. Stockton had to hit short off the green and then wedge it home. Snead and Stockton both needed two putts.

That left it up to North, who suffered from a bone desease during his early teens when he was a football and basketball player in high school. Following 18 months in bed and walking on crutches, North was told by his doctor never to play football again. He turned to golf and eventually went to the University of Florida on a golf scholarship. He was graduated in 1972 and joined the PGA Tour the next year.

Snead and Stockton sat while North and his partner, Player, battled up the 480-yard 18th. North's tee shot with a 3 wood went about where Stockton's did—into the deep right rough. He played short on his second, but pulled the shot a bit into the left rough on the hill.

All he needed then was to get up on the green, which was 50 yards away, and take two putts to win. But he babied the sand wedge out of the rough and dumped the shot into the left bunker.

"I played it too cute," North said.

Nerves seemed to be showing. North, however, smiled as he walked into the sand to do what he had to do to win—get the ball on the green and down the hole. He blasted the ball out of a bad lie in the sand and it went right for the hole, stopping four feet short.

Then North took quite a while to stroke the most important putt of his career. He stepped back after addressing the ball. He said later that it was not because of nerves but because of the wind.

"It was just a straight uphill putt and I didn't want to get thrown off balance from a gust of wind," the new Open champion said.

North denied choking or having nerves on his way down the stretch. But the big fellow certainly had his problems on the last five holes of the back nine. He was leading the field by five shots after five holes and was in front by four shots after getting a birdie at the 13th.

Troubles began happening to North when his tee shot at 14 went into the left rough behind a tree. North hit his second shot and was in rough again but nearer the green. He had to take a bogey and fell four shots in front of Stockton.

Then North hit a 5 iron tee short

Andy North dropping the putt that clinched the U.S. Open championship

at the par-3 15th into the right bunker. When he tried to put the ball too close to the pin on his explosion shot, he left the ball in the bunker and ended up with a double bogey 5.

North's lead was down to one shot over Stockton because the former P.G.A. champion birdied 15 with a 25-foot putt.

If it wasn't nerves at the 16th tee for North then it was just a strange stroke by a top professional golfer. He topped the tee shot with a 3 wood and the ball barely made it out to the

fairway, 100 yards from the teeing ground.

North then hit a 3 iron into a greenside trap but indicated what was to come at 18 when he blasted out five feet from the cup and made a big save for par by dropping the putt.

North played steady at 17, hitting a good drive, a good placement just short of the water and a pitch back of the pin followed by two putts. He then walked over the narrow bridge to play No. 18 and his victory.

June 19, 1978

GOLF is a sport in which a player uses a long-shafted club to propel a small, hard ball around a large area of land, or *course,* having a number of widely spaced holes. The object is to put the ball into the holes in order, using the least possible number of shots (*strokes*). Each player is entirely responsible for his own success or failure and may not interfere with the play of an opponent. Golf is played by men and women of all ages. The game may be played by two or more individual opponents or by opposing teams.

The Scots are credited with originating the modern game of golf. Its popularity in Scotland in the mid-15th century was such that King James II prevailed on Parliament to deemphasize the game so that people would devote more attention to archery, a sport important to the defense of the country.

Golf's appeal is universal. There are golf courses below sea level and at elevations of more than 14,000 feet, on deserts and in forests, within the Arctic Circle and inside equatorial jungles. Of about 20 million persons throughout the world who play golf, half are Americans. In the early 1970's the United States alone had more than 10,000 golf courses.

The rules of golf are determined jointly by the Royal and Ancient Golf Club (R. & A.) of St. Andrews, Scotland, established in 1754, and the United States Golf Association (USGA), formed in 1894. The former organization rules the game throughout most of the world, the latter in the United States.

The first national golf championship was held in Scotland in 1860. At first the annual affair was limited to professionals, but in 1865 the championship was declared "open to all the world," and it became known as the British Open. The British Women's Amateur championship started in 1883, the British Men's Amateur in 1885, and the Canadian Amateur in 1895. The Canadian Open was first held in 1904.

The U.S. Open for men and the men's and women's Amateur were inaugurated by the USGA in 1895. The Open Championship for women was first held in 1946; it has been sponsored by the USGA since 1953.

In matters pertaining strictly to professional play, the Professional Golfers Association of America (PGA), founded in 1916, is the controlling group. Since its inception the PGA has conducted annual tournaments to determine the U.S. men's professional champion. A PGA competition for women began in 1955. The PGA Hall of Fame, established in 1940, honors outstanding men and women professionals and amateurs.

The Masters Tournament originated in 1934 at the Augusta (Ga.) National Golf Club. Its prize money and the prestige that accompanies a victory in this tournament make the Masters one of the major competitive events in the sport.

Golf's popularity among college and high school students exploded after World War II. Formerly most of the major professional players began their careers as caddies; today they come chiefly from colleges. The national championship among college students is sponsored by the National Collegiate Athletic Association; it was first held in 1902.

HOW GOLF IS PLAYED

The Course. A golf course covers from 50 to 300 acres of ground, preferably on rolling terrain. It is a large grassed area, with obstacles (tall grass, trees, and bushes), called *the rough,* and hazards (sand and water) throughout. The course is divided into a series of holes, each representing a unit of competition in itself. Some courses have nine holes, but most have 18. A game, or round, of golf embraces 18 holes.

Each hole on the course has a teeing ground, or starting place; a green, or section that contains the target (a hole in the ground called a *cup*); a fairway from the teeing ground to the cup; and the rough and hazards, natural and prepared obstacles in or near the route to the green. The distance from a given teeing ground, commonly called a *tee*, to a given cup may range from 100 yards to more than 600 yards. Tees and greens are numbered, and holes must be played in sequence—that is, from the first tee to the first green, the second tee to the second green, and so on, until the round is completed on the eighteenth green.

The par for each hole is determined primarily by its length. Par is the number of strokes a good player can be expected to use to play a hole. USGA standards for computing par are as follows:

	Men's par	Women's par
Par 3	up to 250 yards	up to 210 yards
Par 4	251 to 470 yards	211 to 400 yards
Par 5	471 and over	401 to 575 yards
Par 6		576 yards and over

These yardages are not inflexible, because allowance is made for the configuration of the ground, any especially difficult or unusual conditions, and the severity of the hazards.

The total of pars for all the holes determines the overall par for the course. Few courses have an overall par greater than 72. That total usually comprises four par-3 holes, four par 5's, and ten par 4's. In playing a par-4 hole, a skillful player might hit the ball 225 to 250 yards down the fairway, reach the green on a second shot, and then take two strokes (putts) to get the ball into the cup. Playing a hole in one stroke less than par is referred to as a *birdie;* two strokes less, an *eagle.* Playing a hole in one stroke above par is referred to as a *bogey.*

The ground from which play for each hole begins is often somewhat elevated. The starting point is between two markers placed 5 yards or so apart. The player places his ball on a small wooden or plastic peg (also called a *tee*) behind an imaginary line between the two markers. Most teeing grounds have three sets of markers: one at the back of the teeing ground, another about in the middle, and the third toward the front. The back markers are known as "championship" tees; a player who takes his first stroke from a tee placed between these markers plays the full length of the course. (Some championship courses exceed 7,000 yards in total length; but the average course varies between 6,300 and 6,700.) The middle markers, which may make the course 300 yards or so shorter, are used by the average male golfer. The front markers are used by women.

The fairway extends in front of the teeing ground. This long stretch of turf is closely cropped to afford a fair *lie,* or position, for playing the ball. The fairway designates the preferred way of reaching the green, and golf shots are the easiest to play off this stretch. Considerably more difficult to play are shots from the rough, the area bordering the fairway. But the least desirable places for golf shots are the hazards. These include artificially built barriers, such as sand traps (bunkers) and streams and ponds.

The green is an area of finely tended turf over which the ball can roll unobstructed. On the green is the cup into which the ball must drop in order to complete the score for the hole. The cup is 4¼ inches in diameter and at least 4 inches deep. A flagstick, or pin, centered in the cup displays the number of the green; it is removed when the golfer tries a putt for the cup.

Equipment. Essential equipment for playing golf are balls and clubs. Regulation golf balls, to be approved by the USGA, must not be greater than 1.62 ounces in weight or less than 1.68 inches in diameter. In countries administered by the R. & A., the ball may be 1.62 inches in diameter. The ball consists of rubber bands wound under high pressure around a hard, synthetic core, baked and dimpled in a synthetic gum and painted white.

Golf clubs, basically, are of two types: woods and irons, including utility irons, such as wedges; in addition, there are putters. The woods have a rounded wooden head and a long shaft made of steel or aluminum; these are used for long shots. Irons have thinner, metal heads and shorter shafts, also of metal, and are used for shorter shots and more controlled flights of the ball. Club lengths generally range from 35 to 43 inches, depending on their type and the height of the player using them. The head must be longer than it is wide, and the shaft must enter the heel of the club head, except for the shaft of the putter, which may enter halfway between the heel and the toe.

The use of wood clubs or irons depends on the nature of the shot to be made. Wood shots are swept off the turf and are used primarily for distance; iron shots are clipped and are used primarily for accuracy. The angle formed by the club face in relation to the ground determines the predictable range in height and distance that a well-struck ball will attain. The sharper the angle, the more loft. The putter has almost no loft; it is a vertical-faced club with a short shaft and usually a metal head. This club, which merely causes the ball to roll, is almost always used on the green, or sometimes just off it.

Woods are formally numbered 1 through 5, although higher numbers are sometimes used. The No. 1 wood, called a *driver,* has a large head and a deep, almost vertical face. The length averages between 42 and 43 inches for men and 41 and 42 inches for women; the weight, 13 to 14 ounces and 12 to 13 ounces, respectively. Designed to supply maximum distance, the driver is used off the tees of the longer holes—par 4's and par 5's. The face of the No. 2 wood, or *brassie,* is slightly smaller and shallower than the face of the driver and has more loft. The brassie is used mostly for long shots from good fairway lies. In decreasing order of achievable distance are the

other clubs, each having increasingly greater loft on their faces. They are mainly used off the fairway, the choice of club dictated by the yardage needed to reach the green.

The irons are numbered 1 through 9, again in the order of increasing loft and, consequently, decreasing distance. Numbers 1, 2, and 3 are called *long irons.* The No. 1 iron is designed to carry a ball about 200 yards; there is little loft to the club face, and the resultant shot is long and low. Numbers 2 and 3 have slightly more loft and are used for fairway shots. Numbers 4, 5, and 6, called *middle irons,* produce a fairly high trajectory. After hitting the ground, the ball then rolls forward a short distance. These irons are effective for distances of about 150 yards. Numbers 7, 8, and 9, the *short irons,* impart greater backspin to the ball and are used for short distances, difficult lies, or tough grass. No. 9 has considerable loft and is best for shots of about 100 yards. With No. 9 the ball rises at approximately 45° and stops quickly on hitting the ground. Other irons—the *utility irons*—include the *sand wedge,* used for recovering from sand, and the *pitching wedge,* used for shots of less than 100 yards. Both of these clubs have backward slants of about 45° to the faces. Wedges are especially good for short pitch shots (which loft the ball and give it backspin) from the edge of a rough or from a bunker.

The legal limit on the number of different clubs a golfer may use in a round of golf is 14. A golfer's set of clubs usually consists of three or four woods, eight irons, a wedge, and a putter.

Methods of Competing and Scoring. There are a number of ways to compete in golf. The popularity of the game is derived largely from its system of handicapping—that is, of equalizing scores of players of varying golfing abilities.

A golf handicap is determined by subtracting par for a course from the number of strokes a golfer has averaged in playing the course over a period of time; say, his best 10 scores in his last 20 rounds. For example, on a par-72 course, a player who has thus averaged 90 over this course would have a handicap of 18 strokes. The better the golfer, the smaller the handicap. Players who generally go around a course in par are considered to play at *scratch*—their handicap is zero. Thus, in a handicap tournament, a scratch golfer with an average of 70 who draws an opponent with an average of 78, concedes 8 strokes to his opponent. After the round, the opponent deducts 8 strokes from his actual (gross) score and posts the result. So if the 8-handicap player's score is 77 and the scratch player's actual score remains 70, the former defeats the latter with a net of 69.

The two basic forms of competition are stroke play and match play. In *stroke play,* the winner is determined by the lowest total score that is recorded for the complete round. In a tournament, each golfer competes against every other player simultaneously. This form is almost always used by professionals, who usually play 72 holes, or four full rounds, in a single tournament.

In *match play,* participants reckon their scores hole by hole, the victor being the one winning the most holes in a particular round. If, while play is in progress, one golfer has won two more holes than his opponent, the former is said to be "2 up." If a golfer has lost three holes, won only one, and played evenly on the others, he is said to be "2 down." A match is decided when a player is more holes up than the number remaining to be played. For example, if one player is 3 holes up after both have completed the 16th hole, the match is over and he wins 3 and 2 (to play).

When three play, one golfer may play his ball against two opponents who play one ball between them; or each may play his own ball, with each competing against one another. With four golfers, the match may be between two pairs of players, each pair alternating strokes on the same ball; or two golfers may record the score of their better ball against the better ball of an opposing pair. Sometimes players play for two points on each hole: one point for the low individual score and one point for the low total compiled by a team of two.

In competition, golfers play in rotation, and the honor, or

privilege, of shooting first from the tee is determined by a mutually agreeable method on the first hole. On subsequent holes the honor passes to the player or pair who last made the lower score on a preceding hole. After everyone has shot in turn from the tee, the player whose ball lies farthest from the cup shoots first.

Basic Rules. A fundamental rule in golf is that once the ball has been teed up at the start of a hole, it may not be touched, except with the player's club, until it has been holed. Otherwise the player is penalized, with one or more strokes being added to his total. There are, however, a few exceptions to this rule, and these vary in different course situations. On the green a player may usually pick up his ball to clean it before the first putt. He may also lift it temporarily, at the request of his opponent, if it creates a *stymie* (lies in the direct line of an opponent's putt). If the ball lies in casual water, such as rainwater, on the green, the player may remove it from the water and place it immediately nearby but not closer to the hole. If he finds his ball in casual water anywhere else on the course, he may lift it and drop it beside the water. (When a ball is dropped, the player must face the flagstick and let the ball fall directly behind him over his shoulder. He plays it from the spot where it comes to rest.)

A golfer is penalized one or more strokes, for a variety of misplays. He is charged with a stroke if he swings at the ball with the intention of hitting it and misses. If he tops the ball, and it rolls off the tee, this counts as a stroke, and the ball must be played where it lies. If, in addressing the ball, the player moves it a fraction, it counts as a stroke, and the ball must be played as it lies. If a player cannot find his ball, he must play a new ball from the place where he made the last shot, adding a penalty stroke to his score for the hole. If the lost ball was driven from the tee, he must tee up the new ball; otherwise, it has to be dropped at the original spot.

Rules are complicated by the fact that they vary according to whether a round is being played at match or stroke. In match play, for example, a golfer must take a penalty stroke if his caddie or any part of his equipment accidentally touches the ball. He is not penalized for this in stroke play. In either case, the ball must be returned to the spot from which it was moved.

There is no penalty in match play if a player's ball moves an opponent's ball; the opponent may play the ball as it lies or return it to the spot from which it was moved. In stroke play, the ball moved must be returned to its original place, and if both balls are on the green, the player whose ball struck the other's ball must take a two-stroke penalty.

No player may repair the green in the line of a putt (the line from the ball to the cup), except to remove a loose impediment, such as a leaf or stick, repair a ballmark, or place the club in front of the ball in addressing it. Otherwise, improving the line of a putt costs him the hole in match play or two strokes in stroke play.

In match play, a player may concede his opponent's putt at any time. In stroke play, every participant must hole out on every hole; no putt is ever conceded.

Golf is usually played on the honor system; each player counts and records his own strokes and notes his misplays and violations of rules. In major tournaments, officials are required.

Hitting a golf ball effectively, although a difficult art, can be achieved with relative ease if one masters the fundamentals of form. These are described below (for a right-handed player).

The Grip. The most basic physical attribute of a sound golf swing is the grip, or the position of the hands on the club. The overlapping grip is the most widely used. To take this grip, the golfer first grasps the club with the left hand, with the shaft laid diagonally across the palm of the hand and with the point of the "V" formed by the thumb and forefinger pointing somewhere between the head and the right shoulder. He then places his right hand below the left on the shaft, the two hands unified for both power and control by allowing the little finger of the right hand to overlap the index finger of the left. The

"V" formed between the right thumb and its forefinger should point in the same direction as the "V" of the left hand. This overlapping grip may be used for all shots except putting. With the putter, the best grip is the reverse overlap. The position of the forefinger of the left hand is taken from the shaft and run diagonally down the outside of the fingers of the right hand. The club should be held firmly but lightly in both hands.

The Address. Next to the grip, the most essential element of the golf swing is the address, or the position in which a golfer places his body as he stands to the ball. With the grip assumed, the player places his club flush to the ground (it should never rest on its heel or on its toe), spreads his feet apart about the width of his shoulders, and flexes his knees. He keeps the left side of his body at right angles to the target (the green or the fairway) and keeps his weight distributed equally between both feet.

The position of the ball in relation to the feet varies. Actually, the ball is almost always played a little left of center. It should be more to the left, however, if the distance to the target is great; in such a situation the feet should be spread apart more to permit greater power in the drive. Thus, with the longer clubs (particularly the woods), the ball should be closer to the left foot than to the right; the golfer is farthest from the ball because the club shaft is longer. With the shorter clubs, the No. 9 iron for example, the ball should be close to the center of the stance.

The Stance. When the toes of both feet form a line parallel to the intended line of flight, the player's stance is said to be "square." This is the standard stance for all shots hit with full power. The player has a "closed" stance if the right foot is slightly withdrawn (pulled back) from the intended line of flight (used for the driver and fairway woods). A closed stance enhances a hook, which is a shot curving to the left. With the left foot withdrawn from the intended line of flight, the stance is "open" (used for the short irons). This position enhances a slice, which is a shot that swerves to the right. Whatever the stance—square, closed, or open—the right foot should always be aimed at 90° from the intended line of flight, the left at approximately 45° from the direction the ball is to go.

The Swing. The golf swing, an exacting technique, involves a backswing, downswing, and follow-through. To execute the backswing, the player takes his club away from the ball in a sweeping motion backward and upward by the hands and arms while keeping his head stationary. He maintains his balance by pivoting, or twisting the body, around the axis of his head position. Ideally, the upper torso should turn twice as much as the lower torso until the backswing is completed. This point is reached when the shaft of the club is parallel to the ground, or nearly so, and the hands are behind the head and above the right ear. At this point of the swing the shoulders have completed a 90° turn and the hips a 45° turn. The right leg, with flexed knee, now supports most of the weight of the body; the left knee tucks in toward the right to accommodate the turning of the hips. Thus the left heel is raised slightly off the ground, with the rest of the body's weight being supported by the ball of the left foot.

Without any conscious movement of hands and arms the player initiates the downswing by pivoting his left hip back to and past the intended line of flight. He snaps his left heel smartly back into its original position on the ground. At this point the shaft of the club is again parallel to the ground. With the hips having turned a full 90°, the shoulders should be parallel to the intended line of flight. The weight of the body is almost entirely thrown to the left side.

As the club head moves into the ball, the left arm carries the club on through the ball in a wide, sweeping motion. The hands continue upward to a point above the left shoulder, with the right arm remaining reasonably straight. At no stage throughout the entire swing should the head move unduly, either back and forth or up and down. A stationary head position is the single most important factor in hitting the golf ball with consistency. The movement of the upswing makes the head lift naturally on the follow-through, so that the head finally faces the line of flight with the eyes on the flight. This is the basic swing for all full shots (tee shots, fairway wood shots, and long iron shots).

Any differences in the dynamics or mechanics of the swing are taken care of by the nature of the club being used. For example, a driver, with its longer shaft and slight loft, requires longer arc throughout the swing than the No. 9 iron. But the rhythm of the shot remains the same.

Pitch and Chip Shots. Pitches and chips are golf shots in miniature. They both put the ball from the fairway or the rough to the green, with accuracy the prime motive.

A pitch is a lofted shot with backspin on the ball, played anywhere from 100 to 10 yards from the green. Power is of no concern, so little body pivot is required. The shot is played from a slightly open stance and with a shortened grip (down from the top of the shaft). The backswing, and consequently the follow-through, are thus reduced to about two thirds the normal arc. The best clubs to use for a pitch are those with a great deal of loft, such as the No. 9 iron or wedge.

With the chip the stance is open and the body movement is almost imperceptible. The most effective club is the No. 4 or No. 5 iron, designed to lift the ball just barely onto the putting surface. The short loft and overspin on the ball allows for a short run to the cup.

Sand Shots. The shot from sand is primarily a recovery shot. The immediate purpose is to extricate the ball; the secondary purpose is to lay the ball close to the flagstick. The sand wedge should be used with an open stance. The club may not touch the sand before the shot (no club may be grounded in a hazard); hence the player must address the shot with the clubhead slightly off the sand. The object, however, is to hit the sand an inch or two behind the ball. Because the stance is less firm on sand than on turf, the player maintains his balance by restricting the backswing. On the other hand, he never restricts the follow-through, because it is club-head momentum that does all the work.

Putting. Putting is highly individualistic. In developing a style of putting, two things are paramount: the player must keep the blade of the putter close to the ground throughout the stroke so that the ball rolls rather than skips toward the hole, and he must keep the trunk of his body motionless. The putting stroke resembles as closely as possible the pendulum swing of a clock.

Ace. A hole scored in one stroke; a hole-in-one.

Address. The position, or stance, a player takes in preparing to strike the ball.

Approach. A stroke or shot to the putting green; also, the section of the fairway near the green.

Apron. The last yard or so of fairway around the green.

Away. Farthest from the hole.

Best Ball. A match in which one player competes against the best score of two or more players.

Birdie. A score of one stroke under par on a hole.

Blind. An approach position from which a player cannot see the green.

Bogey. In the United States, a score of one stroke over par for a single hole. In Britain, the score that a better-than-average player would be expected to make for a given hole.

Borrow. In putting, to play to one side or the other of the direct line from the ball to the hole to compensate for roll or slant on the green.

Caddie. One who carries a golfer's clubs during play.

Carry. The distance traveled by a ball from where it is hit to where it first strikes the ground.

Chip. A short approach shot in which the ball flies close to the ground and then runs (rolls). It is called *pitch and run* when executed from a long distance off the green.

Concede. To grant that an opponent has won a hole before play has been completed; also, to grant that an opponent will hole out in one more stroke.

Course. The entire area within which play is permitted. See also *Links*.

Dead Ball. A ball so near the hole that putting it into the cup is a certainty.

Default. To concede a match to an opponent without playing it.

Divot. A piece of turf uprooted by a club during a stroke. Etiquette requires that it be replaced and pressed down.

Dormie. In match play, a lead of as many holes as remain to be played.

Down. The number of holes or strokes a player is behind an opponent. See also *Up*.

Draw. A slight controlled hook in the flight of the ball. See also *Hook*.

Dub. An unskillful player; also, to hit the ball poorly.

Eagle. A score that is two strokes under par on a hole.

Face. The part of the club that strikes the ball; also, the slope of a bunker (an embankment constituting a hazard).

Fade. A slight controlled slice in the flight of the ball. See also *Slice*.

Fore!. A cry of warning by a player to anyone along the flight path of his ball.

Forecaddie. A caddie stationed in advance of the players to indicate the position of the balls on the course.

Four-Ball Match. A match in which two teammates play their better ball against the better ball of two opponents.

Foursome. A group of four players; also, a match between two teams with two players each in which each team plays one ball.

Halved Hole. A hole played in the same number of strokes by each side.

Handicap. The number of strokes a player receives to equalize playing ability. It is often based on the lowest 10 of the player's last 15 scores.

Hole Out. To make the final stroke in playing the ball into the cup.

Honor. The privilege of driving off the teeing ground first, awarded to the player or pair who last made the lower score on a preceding hole and on the first hole by toss of a coin. The honor may not be declined.

Hook. For a righthanded golfer, a stroke that causes the ball to rotate counterclockwise and curve to the left of line from player to objective. A lefthanded player's hook would curve to the right. See also *Slice*.

Lie. The position of a ball on the turf; also, the angle formed by the clubhead and its shaft.

Links. A seaside golf course, usually. The most famous one is the Old Course in St. Andrews, Scotland.

Loft. To elevate the ball; also, a backward slant on the face of a club.

Nassau. A system of scoring under which one point is awarded for winning the first 9 holes, another for the second 9, and a third for the overall 18.

Net. The score after the handicap strokes have been deducted.

Open. A tournament in which both professionals and amateurs are eligible to compete.

Par. The number of strokes officially required to play a hole, assigned on the basis of ideal playing; also, the number of strokes required to play the entire course in ideal play.

Penalty. A stroke or strokes added to the score because of a rule infraction.

Pin. The pole to which the flag is attached, usually found in the cup of each hole.

Pitch. An approach shot in which the ball is lofted in a high arc.

Pitch and Run. See *Chip*.

Pull. To hit the ball so that it makes a wide and pronounced hook.

Putt. A short stroke in which the ball rolls along the ground. It is usually made on the green.

Run. The distance a ball rolls after it lands.

Slice. For a righthanded player, a stroke that gives the ball a clockwise spin so that it swerves to the right of the line from player to objective. A lefthanded player's slice swerves to the left. See also *Hook*.

Square. A match that is even.

Stroke. Any forward motion of the club for the purpose of hitting the ball.

Stroke Hole. A hole on which a handicap stroke is given.

Stymie. The situation caused when an opponent's ball lies in direct line between a player's ball and the cup.

Three-Ball Match. A match in which three players compete against one another, each playing his own ball.

Threesome. A group of three players; also, a match in which one player competes against two others, the two playing alternate strokes with the same ball.

Top. To hit the ball above its center.

Up. The number of holes or strokes a player is ahead of an opponent. See also *Down*.

Bibliography

Gibson, Nevin H., *A Pictorial History of Golf*, rev. ed. (Barnes, A.S., 1974).

Graffis, Herb B., *The PGA* (Crowell 1975).

Jones, Robert T., *Bobby Jones on Golf* (Doubleday 1966).

Nicklaus, Jack, *Golf My Way* (Pocket Books 1977).

Palmer, Arnold, *My Game and Yours* (Simon & Schuster 1965).

Price, Charles, *The World of Golf* (Random House 1962).

Steel, Donald, and others, *Encyclopedia of Golf* (Viking 1975).

U.S. Golf Association, *Golf Rules in Pictures* (Grosset 1977).

United States Open

Year	Winner
1896	James Foulis
1897	Joe Lloyd
1898	Fred Herd
1899	Willie Smith
1900	Harry Vardon
1901	Willie Anderson
1902	L. Auchterlonie
1903	Willie Anderson
1904	Willie Anderson
1905	Willie Anderson
1906	Alex Smith
1907	Alex Ross
1908	Fred McLeod
1909	George Sargent
1910	Alex Smith
1911	John McDermott
1912	John McDermott
1913	Francis Ouimet
1914	Walter Hagen
1915	Jerome Travers
1916	Chick Evans
1917-18	(Not played)
1919	Walter Hagen
1920	Edward Ray
1921	Jim Barnes
1922	Gene Sarazen
1923	Bob Jones
1924	Cyril Walker
1925	Willie MacFarlane
1926	Bob Jones
1927	Tommy Armour
1928	John Farrell
1929	Bob Jones
1930	Bob Jones
1931	Wm. Burke
1932	Gene Sarazen
1933	John Goodman
1934	Olin Dutra
1935	Sam Parks Jr.
1936	Tony Manero
1937	Ralph Guldahl
1938	Ralph Guldhal
1939	Byron Nelson
1940	Lawson Little
1941	Craig Wood
1942-45	(Not played)
1946	Lloyd Mangrum
1947	L. Worsham
1948	Ben Hogan
1949	Cary Middlecoff
1950	Ben Hogan
1951	Ben Hogan
1952	Julius Boros
1953	Ben Hogan
1954	Ed Furgol
1955	Jack Fleck
1956	Cary Middlecoff
1957	Dick Mayer
1958	Tommy Bolt
1959	Billy Casper
1960	Arnold Palmer
1961	Gene Littler
1962	Jack Nicklaus
1963	Julius Boros
1964	Ken Venturi
1965	Gary Player
1966	Billy Casper
1967	Jack Nicklaus
1968	Lee Trevino
1969	Orville Moody
1970	Tony Jacklin
1971	Lee Trevino
1972	Jack Nicklaus
1973	Johnny Miller
1974	Hale Irwin
1975	Lou Graham
1976	Jerry Pate
1977	Hubert Green
1978	Andy North
1979	Hale Irwin

British Open Golf Champions

Year	Winner
1908	James Braid
1909	J.H. Taylor
1910	James Braid
1911	Harry Vardon
1912	Ted Ray
1913	J.H. Taylor
1914	Harry Vardon
1915-19	(Not played)
1920	George Duncan
1921	Jock Hutchison
1922	Walter Hagen
1923	Arthur Havers
1924	Walter Hagen
1925	Jim Barnes
1926	Bob Jones
1927	Bob Jones
1928	Walter Hagen
1929	Walter Hagen
1930	Bob Jones
1931	Tommy Armour
1932	Gene Sarazen
1933	Denny Shute
1934	Henry Cotton
1935	Alf Perry
1936	Alf Padgham
1937	T.H. Cotton
1938	R.A. Whitcombe
1939	Richard Burton
1940-45	(Not played)
1946	Sam Snead
1947	Fred Daly
1948	Henry Cotton
1949	Bobby Locke
1950	Bobby Locke
1951	Max Faulkner
1952	Bobby Locke
1953	Ben Hogan
1954	Peter Thomson
1955	Peter Thomson
1956	Peter Thomson
1957	Bobby Locke
1958	Peter Thomson
1959	Gary Player
1960	Ken Nagle
1961	Arnold Palmer
1962	Arnold Palmer
1963	Bob Charles
1964	Tony Lema
1965	Peter Thomson
1966	Jack Nicklaus
1967	Roberto de Vicenzo
1968	Gary Player
1969	Tony Jacklin
1970	Jack Nicklaus
1971	Lee Trevino
1972	Lee Trevino
1973	Tom Weiskopf
1974	Gary Player
1975	Tom Watson
1976	Johnny Miller
1977	Tom Watson
1978	Jack Nicklaus

Masters Golf Tournament Champions

Year	Winner
1934	Horton Smith
1935	Gene Sarazen
1936	Horton Smith
1937	Byron Nelson
1938	Henry Picard
1939	Ralph Guldahl
1940	Jimmy Demaret
1941	Craig Wood
1942	Byron Nelson
1943-1945	(Not played)
1946	Herman Keiser
1947	Jimmy Demaret
1948	Claude Harmon
1949	Sam Snead
1950	Jimmy Demaret
1951	Ben Hogan
1952	Sam Snead
1953	Ben Hogan
1954	Sam Snead
1955	Cary Middlecoff
1956	Jack Burke
1957	Dough Ford
1958	Arnold Palmer
1959	Art Wall Jr.
1960	Arnold Palmer
1961	Gary Player
1962	Arnold Palmer
1963	Jack Nicklaus
1964	Arnold Palmer
1965	Jack Nicklaus
1966	Jack Nicklaus
1967	Gay Brewer Jr.
1968	Bob Goalby
1969	George Archer
1970	Billy Casper
1971	Charles Coody
1972	Jack Nicklaus
1973	Tommy Aaron
1974	Gary Player
1975	Jack Nicklaus
1976	Ray Floyd
1977	Tom Watson
1978	Gary Player
1979	Fuzzy Zoeller

Professional Golfer's Association Championships

Year	Winner
1919	Jim Barnes
1920	Jock Hutchison
1921	Walter Hagen
1922	Gene Sarazen
1923	Gene Sarazen
1924	Walter Hagen
1925	Walter Hagen
1926	Walter Hagen
1927	Walter Hagen
1928	Leo Diegel
1929	Leo Diegel
1930	Tommy Armour
1931	Tom Creavy
1932	Olin Dutra
1933	Gene Sarazen
1934	Paul Runyan
1935	Johnny Revolta
1936	Denny Shute
1937	Denny Shute
1938	Paul Runyan
1939	Henry Picard
1940	Byron Nelson
1941	Victor Ghezzi
1942	Sam Snead
1944	Bob Hamilton
1945	Byron Nelson
1946	Ben Hogan
1947	Jim Ferrier
1948	Ben Hogan
1949	Sam Snead
1950	Chandler Harper
1951	Sam Snead
1952	James Turnesa
1953	Walter Burkemo
1954	Melvin Harbert
1955	Dough Ford
1956	Jack Burke
1957	Lionel Hebert
1958	Dow Finsterwald
1959	Bob Rosburg
1960	Jay Hebert
1961	Jerry Barber
1962	Gary Player
1963	Jack Nicklaus
1964	Bob Nichols
1965	Dave Marr
1966	Al Geiberger
1967	Don January
1968	Julius Boros
1969	Ray Floyd
1970	Dave Stockton
1971	Jack Nicklaus
1972	Gary Player
1973	Jack Nicklaus
1974	Lee Trevino
1975	Jack Nicklaus
1976	Dave Stockton
1977	Lanny Wadkins
1978	John Mahaffey

U.S. Women's Open Golf Championship

Year	Winner
1948	"Babe" Zaharias
1949	Louise Suggs
1950	"Babe" Zaharias
1951	Betsy Rawls
1952	Louise Suggs
1953	Betsy Rawls
1954	"Babe" Zaharias
1955	Fay Crocker
1956	Mrs. K. Cornelius
1957	Betsy Rawls
1958	Mickey Wright
1959	Mickey Wright
1960	Betsy Rawls
1961	Mickey Wright
1962	Marie Lindstrom
1963	Mary Mills
1964	Mickey Wright
1965	Carol Mann
1966	Sandra Spuzich
1967	Catherine Lacoste
1968	Susie Maxwell Berning
1969	Donna Caponi
1970	Donna Caponi
1971	JoAnne Carner
1972	Susie Maxwell Berning
1973	Susie Maxwell Berning
1974	Sandra Haynie
1975	Sandra Palmer
1976	JoAnne Carner
1977	Hollis Stacy
1978	Hollis Stacy